//241

WORK, STUDY, TRAVEL ABROAD

WORK, STUDY, TRAVEL ABROAD

THE WHOLE WORLD HANDBOOK

ELEVENTH EDITION
1992–1993

EDITED BY DEL FRANZ
AND LÁZARO HERNÁNDEZ

Assistant Editors
FRASER BROWN, NICOLE ELLISON,
MAX TERRY, PRISCILLA TOVEY

Council on International
Educational Exchange

ST. MARTIN'S PRESS
NEW YORK

WORK, STUDY, TRAVEL ABROAD 1992–93, Eleventh Edition. Copyright © 1992 by the Council on International Educational Exchange. All rights reserved. Printed in the United States of America. No part of this book may be used or reproduced in any manner whatsoever without written permission except in the case of brief quotations embodied in critical articles or reviews. For information, address St. Martin's Press, 175 Fifth Avenue, New York, N.Y. 10010.

LC# 84-646778

10　9　8　7　6　5　4　3　2　1

IMPORTANT NOTE

All information cited in this book, including prices, is subject to change. To the best of its ability, CIEE has verified the accuracy of the information at the time *Work, Study, Travel Abroad* went to press. However, at press time, international air fares for peak summer travel in 1992 had not yet been announced. Most of the fares listed throughout this edition are those which were valid for the summer of 1991. For information on all of the above services get a free copy of the latest edition of CIEE's *Student Travel Catalog* or check with any Council Travel office.

CONTENTS

PREFACE   ix
ACKNOWLEDGMENTS   xi
ABOUT CIEE   xiii
COUNCIL TRAVEL OFFICES   xix
CIEE ADMINISTRATIVE OFFICES   xxiii

CHAPTER ONE   GOING ABROAD   1

CHAPTER TWO   THE ESSENTIALS   4

CHAPTER THREE   WORKING ABROAD   16

CHAPTER FOUR   STUDYING ABROAD   32

CHAPTER FIVE   MAKING YOUR TRAVEL PLANS   44

CHAPTER SIX   EUROPE   57

- Austria   72
- Belgium   79
- Bulgaria   82
- Cyprus   84
- Czechoslovakia   87
- Denmark   91
- Finland   97
- France   101
- Germany   119
- Greece   132
- Hungary   136
- Iceland   140
- Ireland   143
- Italy   149
- Luxembourg   159
- Malta   161
- The Netherlands   163
- Norway   168
- Poland   172
- Portugal   176
- Spain   179
- Sweden   190
- Switzerland   194
- United Kingdom of Great Britain and Northern Ireland   199
- The U.S.S.R.   221
- Yugoslavia   230

CHAPTER SEVEN THE MIDDLE EAST AND NORTH AFRICA 235

Algeria   240
Egypt   241
Israel   245
Morocco   252
Tunisia   256
Turkey   258

CHAPTER EIGHT AFRICA SOUTH OF THE SAHARA 263

Cameroon   270
Côte d'Ivoire (Ivory Coast)   272
Ghana   274
Kenya   277
Nigeria   281
Senegal   284
Sierra Leone   286
South Africa   288
Tanzania   292
Togo   294
Zambia   296
Zimbabwe   297

CHAPTER NINE SOUTH ASIA 301

India   305
Nepal   311

CHAPTER TEN EAST ASIA 315

China   319
Hong Kong   328
Japan   332
South Korea   346
Taiwan (Republic of China)   349

CHAPTER ELEVEN SOUTHEAST ASIA 355

Indonesia   358
Malaysia   362
The Philippines   365
Singapore   369
Thailand   371
Vietnam   375

CHAPTER TWELVE AUSTRALIA AND THE SOUTH PACIFIC 379

Australia   382
Fiji   390
New Zealand   392

CHAPTER THIRTEEN CANADA 399

CONTENTS

CHAPTER FOURTEEN THE CARIBBEAN 407

Bahamas 411
Dominican Republic 413
Jamaica 416

CHAPTER FIFTEEN MEXICO AND CENTRAL AMERICA 421

Belize 425
Costa Rica 427
Guatemala 431
Honduras 433
Mexico 435

CHAPTER SIXTEEN SOUTH AMERICA 447

Argentina 450
Bolivia 455
Brazil 458
Chile 464
Colombia 468
Ecuador 472
Peru 476
Uruguay 479
Venezuela 481

APPENDIX I MEMBERS OF THE COUNCIL ON INTERNATIONAL EDUCATIONAL EXCHANGE 484

APPENDIX II HIGH SCHOOL PROGRAMS 496

INDEX 499

PREFACE

The 1992–93 edition of *Work, Study, Travel Abroad: The Whole World Handbook* marks the eleventh edition of the book. The Council on International Educational Exchange has been updating and revising this book every other year since the first edition was prepared in 1972. While this new edition generally follows the format developed for the tenth edition, the number of countries covered has increased. This edition also includes brief descriptions of over 1,200 study, work, and travel programs abroad, hundreds more than appeared in the 1990–91 edition. In addition, you'll find expanded recommendations of books to read and movies to see before going to specific countries.

Two years of effort have gone into producing the eleventh edition of this book. Hundreds of people—including professors and advisers on college campuses, students recently returned from abroad, and CIEE personnel from Hong Kong to Bonn—have been involved in this project. We've researched the latest on international travel, updated program offerings, reviewed books and movies, created maps, put together fact sheets, and collected useful suggestions from people who have been overseas. We hope you'll be able to use some of the information we've gathered to make your trip more rewarding. We also hope that when you return from your trip abroad, you too will be part of the effort to revise and update the 1994–95 edition.

WE WANT TO HEAR FROM YOU

Can you tell us anything you found out during your travels that will help make the next edition of *Work, Study, Travel Abroad: The Whole World Handbook* more informative? Do you want to write a country introduction, suggest some reading material, or make some suggestions that we can quote in the next edition? Persons we quote will receive a free copy of the next edition of this book. Send correspondence to the Editor, *Work, Study, Travel Abroad*, CIEE, 205 East 42nd Street, New York, NY 10017.

ACKNOWLEDGMENTS

So many people in so many countries have been involved in the two-year effort to rewrite and update this edition that any attempt to name all the individuals who contributed would be futile. Thanks especially to the many CIEE staff members around the world who updated program information and offered suggestions and advice. Gratitude also needs to be expressed to the people at Council Travel, including Larry Feldman, Maria Giordano, Jolanta Badura, Kerry McCormack, Loren Sosna, and Walter Clune, who provided travel information and verified fares.

Also vital to the compilation of this book have been the CIEE representatives at the colleges, universities, and other organizations that are members of CIEE. These people provided information about programs abroad, suggested books to read and films to see, and helped establish contact with students across the U.S. who recently returned from work, study, and travel experiences abroad. A collective thank you to all of them.

The literature and film sections owe their usefulness to the information provided by a variety of persons familiar with certain countries or regions. Special thanks to Tamara Cohen, Kurt Gammerschlag, Carina Klein, Andrew Shaw, Priscilla Tovey, and Michael Woolf.

Finally, we would like to thank all the readers who have sent in comments and information. Receiving reactions and contributions from users of the book is especially helpful and encouraging. We hope that readers will continue to provide the feedback necessary for a useful book serving the needs of young people going abroad for study, work, or travel experience.

Del Franz
Director, Information and Student Services

Lázaro Hernández
Associate Editor

ABOUT CIEE

The Council on International Educational Exchange (CIEE) is a private, nonprofit membership organization with offices in the U.S., Europe, and Asia. In its 45 years of service to the educational community, CIEE has emerged as one of the foremost organizations promoting international education and student travel.

CIEE was founded in 1947 to help reestablish student exchange after the Second World War. In its early years, CIEE chartered ocean liners for transatlantic student sailings, arranged group air travel, and organized orientation programs to prepare students and teachers for educational experiences abroad. Over the years, CIEE's mandate has broadened dramatically as the interests of its ever-increasing number of members have spread beyond Europe to Africa, Asia, and Latin America. Today, CIEE assumes a number of important responsibilities that include developing and administering programs of international educational exchange throughout the world, coordinating work-abroad programs and international workcamps, and facilitating inexpensive international travel for students, teachers, and other budget travelers.

This section will give you an idea of what CIEE does and how it can help you. For more information on any of the following services, contact the appropriate department at CIEE in New York. Be as specific as possible about your request.

University Study Programs

Among CIEE's most widely recognized educational services are the academic programs that it administers in Argentina, Australia, Brazil, Chile, China, Costa Rica, Czechoslovakia, the Dominican Republic, France, Germany, Hungary, Indonesia, Japan, Poland, Spain, Thailand, the U.S.S.R., and Vietnam. These programs are administered by CIEE's University Programs Department on behalf of sponsoring colleges and universities that participate in policy and curriculum formation, assure academic credibility and quality control, and serve the particular academic field for which the program has been developed. Included among these programs are the following:

Argentina
- Advanced Social-Science Program at the Facultad Latino Americano de Ciencias Sociales in Buenos Aires

Australia
- Cooperative Studies Program at Murdoch University, Perth

Brazil
- Interuniversity Study Program at the University of São Paulo

Chile
- Cooperative Latin American Studies Program at the Pontificia Universidad Católica de Santiago and the Universidad de Chile

China
- China Cooperative Language and Study Programs at Peking, Nanjing, and Fudan University

Costa Rica
- Tropical Biology Program at the Monteverde Institute

Czechoslovakia
- Cooperative East/Central European Studies Program at Charles University, Prague

Dominican Republic
- Spanish Language & Caribbean Area Studies Program at the Pontificia Universidad Católica Madre y Maestra, Santiago

France
- A Language & Culture Program at the University of Paris IV
- Undergraduate Program at the University of Haute Bretagne, Brittany
- Paris Internship & Study Program at the University of Paris IX
- Critical Studies Program at the University of Paris III, France

Germany
- Cooperative Summer Program for Engineering Students at the University of Technology, Aachen

Hungary
- Cooperative East/Central European Studies Program at the Budapest University of Economics

Indonesia
- Cooperative Southeast Asian Studies Program at the Institut Keguruan Dan Ilmu Pendidikan, Malang

Japan
- Cooperative Japanese Business & Society Program in Tokyo

Poland
- Cooperative East/Central European Studies Programs at the Central School of Planning & Statistics, Warsaw

Spain
- Language & Area Studies Program at the University of Alicante
  Liberal Arts, Language & Society, and Business & Society Programs in Seville

Thailand
- Cooperative Southeast Asian Studies Programs at Khon Kaen University Thailand, and Hanoi University (Vietnam)

U.S.S.R.
- Cooperative Russian Language Program at Leningrad State University and the Leningrad Gornyi Institute
- Moscow Summer Business Program at the Plekhanov Institute of National Economy
- Cooperative Russian Language & Area Studies Program at Tver State University
- Cooperative Russian Language Program for Science Students at Novosibirsk State University
- Russian for Research Program at Leningrad State University

Work Abroad

CIEE's Work Exchanges Department operates a series of work-abroad programs that allow U.S. students to obtain temporary employment in Britain, Canada, Costa Rica, Czechoslovakia, France, Germany, Ireland, Jamaica, New Zealand, and Spain. These programs enable students to avoid the red tape and bureaucratic difficulties that usually accompany the process of getting permission to work in a foreign country. Along with the necessary employment authorization, work-abroad participants receive general information on the country, tips on employment, and helpful hints on housing and travel. In each country the program is offered in cooperation with a national student organization or CIEE office that provides an orientation on the country's culture and society, advises on seeking jobs and accommodations, and serves as a sponsor during the participant's stay.

International Voluntary Service

CIEE's Voluntary Service Department operates an international workcamp program for young people interested in short-term voluntary service overseas. Volunteers are placed with organizations conducting projects in Algeria, Belgium, Bulgaria, Canada, Czechoslovakia, Denmark, France, Germany, Ghana, Hungary, Morocco, the Netherlands, Poland, Portugal, Spain, Tunisia, Turkey, the U.S.S.R., the United Kingdom, and Yugoslavia. Some examples of the types of projects available are taking part in a nature conservation project; restoring a historical site; working with children or the elderly; and constructing low-income housing. Workcamps bring young people from many countries together to become involved in a local community. CIEE also operates workcamps at various locations around the U.S.

High School Programs

CIEE administers School Partners Abroad, which matches U.S. junior and senior high schools with counterpart schools in Europe, Asia, and Latin America. The program involves participating schools in an array of year-round curriculum-related activites, the centerpiece of which is an annual reciprocal exchange of students and teachers. During the short-term exchange, visiting students and teachers participate fully in the life of the host school, attending regular classes, joining in extracurricular activities, and living with local families.

Also available to U.S. high school students is Youth in China, a unique summer study program in Xi'an, China. The program combines travel with a period of residence and language study at a Chinese secondary school. American participants live with Chinese roommates and participate in a full academic program.

Adult/Professional Programs

Continuing education is another area of extensive CIEE activity. The Professional and Secondary Programs Department designs and administers a wide array of short-term seminars and in-service training programs for groups of international professionals, including secondary-school teachers and administrators, university faculty, business managers, and other "adult learners." As an additional service, CIEE is able to custom-design international education programs on behalf of CIEE-member or cooperating institutions.

The Professional and Secondary Programs Department also offers the International Faculty Development Seminar series for faculty and administrators at two- and four-year institutions of higher education. These overseas seminars and professional interchange opportunities are designed to assist institutions with internationalizing home-campus curricula.

Student Services

Through its Information and Student Services Department, CIEE sponsors the International Student Identity Card in the United States. Over 160,000 cards are issued each year by CIEE's New York headquarters, its 34 Council Travel offices, and more than 450 issuing offices at colleges and universities. Cardholders receive travel-related discounts, basic accident/medical insurance coverage while traveling abroad, and access to a 24-hour toll-free emergency hotline. Also sponsored by CIEE are the Youth International Identity Card for those under 26, and the International Teacher Identity Card for full-time faculty—both of which provide benefits similar to the International Student Identity Card.

The department also administers the International Student Identity Card Fund. Supported by the sale of the International Student Identity Card in the United States, the fund offers travel grants to U.S. high school and undergraduate students participating in study or service programs in the Third World countries of Africa, Asia, and Latin America.

In its role as the "information clearinghouse" of CIEE, the department answers more than a quarter of a million inquiries on work, study, and travel abroad each year. To keep campus advisers and others in the field of international education informed, CIEE publishes a free monthly newsletter called *Campus Update*.

Publications

Probably the most widely circulated publication in the student travel field is the *Student Travel Catalog*—a free, 76-page guide that is read by hundreds of thousands of people each year. The *Catalog* contains all kinds of useful information for anyone considering a trip abroad. It includes forms to order publications and apply for CIEE programs.

In addition to *Work, Study, Travel Abroad: The Whole World Handbook*, CIEE publishes:

- *The Teenager's Guide to Study, Travel, and Adventure Abroad*, compiled by CIEE and published by St. Martin's Press, an award-winning compendium of short- and long-term overseas opportunities for youth 12 to 18 years of age; updated every other year.
- *Volunteer! The Comprehensive Guide to Voluntary Service in the U.S. and Abroad*, published jointly by CIEE and the Commission on Voluntary Service and Action (CVSA), a guide to hundreds of short-, medium-, and long-term opportunities for voluntary service in every corner of the world; updated every other year.
- *Where to Stay USA*, a state-by-state listing of more than 1,700 places to spend the night for under $30, with special city sections and general travel advice for anyone touring the United States; updated every other year by CIEE and published by Prentice-Hall.

Educators, administrators, and researchers in the field of international education can request a free publications catalog describing the books, pamphlets, studies, reports, and occasional papers produced by CIEE.

Travel Services

Council Travel operates a network of 34 retail travel offices across the country that provide travel assistance to students, teachers, and other budget travelers planning individual or group trips to any part of the world. Here are some samples of what they offer:

- low-cost flights between the U.S. and Europe, Asia, the South Pacific, Africa, the Middle East, Latin America, and the Caribbean on scheduled and charter carriers; many of these fares are available only to students or young people and are offered only through Council Travel offices

- rail passes, including Eurail, BritRail, and French Rail passes
- the International Student Identity Card, International Youth Identity Card, and International Teacher Identity Card
- car rental plans in Europe
- language courses in 17 European cities and in Japan
- travel insurance, guidebooks, and travel gear

In addition to services for individuals, Council Travel provides educational institutions with a complete range of travel services designed to simplify travel planning for groups. The Group Services department can arrange anything from transportation and accommodations to lectures, study programs, special events, sightseeing, and meals.

Charter Flights

Council Charter, a subsidiary of CIEE, offers budget flights between the U.S. and Europe on scheduled and charter carriers that are open to students and nonstudents alike. Cities served vary slightly each year; in 1991 flights were available to Amsterdam, Brussels, London, Lyons, Madrid, Milan, Málaga, Nice, Paris, and Rome. Council Charter allows you to fly to one city and return from another, and offers a low-cost cancellation waiver which allows you to cancel your flight as late as three hours before your departure with no penalty.

CIEE Membership

At present, over 225 educational institutions and organizations in the United States and abroad are members of CIEE. As members, they may take advantage of CIEE's information and publication services; become involved in CIEE's advocacy, evaluation, and consultation activities; and participate in conferences and services organized by CIEE. Membership allows educational institutions and organizations to play a central role in the operation and development of exchanges at a national and international level. See Appendix I for a list of CIEE members.

Council on International Educational Exchange
205 East 42nd Street
New York, NY 10017

COUNCIL TRAVEL OFFICES

ARIZONA

Tempe

120 East University Drive, Suite E
Tempe, AZ 85281
(602) 966-3544

CALIFORNIA

Berkeley

2486 Channing Way
Berkeley, CA 94704
(415) 848-8604

La Jolla

UCSD Price Center
9500 Gilman Drive
La Jolla, CA 92093-0076
(619) 452-0630

Long Beach

1818 Palo Verde Avenue, Suite E
Long Beach, CA 90815
(213) 598-3338
(714) 527-7950

Los Angeles

1093 Broxton Avenue, Suite 220
Los Angeles, CA 90024
(213) 208-3551

San Diego/Pacific Beach

953 Garnet Avenue
San Diego, CA 92109
(619) 270-6401

San Francisco

312 Sutter Street, Suite 407
San Francisco, CA 94108
(415) 421-3473

919 Irving Street, Suite 102
San Francisco, CA 94122
(415) 566-6222

Sherman Oaks

14515 Ventura Boulevard
Suite 250
Sherman Oaks, CA 91403
(818) 905-5777

COLORADO

Boulder

1138 13th Street
Boulder, CO 80302
(303) 447-8101

CONNECTICUT

New Haven

Yale Co-op East
77 Broadway
New Haven, CT 06520
(203) 562-5335

DISTRICT OF COLUMBIA

Washington, DC

3300 M Street NW, 2nd floor
Washington, DC 20007
(202) 337-6464

GEORGIA

Atlanta

12 Park Place South
Atlanta, GA 30303
(404) 577-1678

ILLINOIS

Chicago

1153 North Dearborn Street
Chicago, IL 60610
(312) 951-0585

Evanston

831 Foster Street
Evanston, IL 60201
(708) 475-5070

LOUISIANA

New Orleans

Joseph A. Danna Center
Loyola University
6363 St. Charles Avenue
New Orleans, LA 70118
(504) 866-1767

MASSACHUSETTS

Amherst

79 South Pleasant Street
(2nd floor, rear)
Amherst, MA 01002
(413) 256-1261

Boston

729 Boylston Street, Suite 201
Boston, MA 02116
(617) 266-1926

156 Ell Center
Northeastern University
Boston, MA 02115
(617) 424-6665

Cambridge

1384 Massachusetts Avenue,
Suite 206
Cambridge, MA 02138
(617) 497-1497

Stratton Student Center
MIT W20-024
84 Massachusetts Avenue
Cambridge, MA 02139
(617) 225-2555

MICHIGAN

Ann Arbor

1220 South University, #208
Ann Arbor, MI 48104
(313) 998-0200

MINNESOTA

Minneapolis

1501 University Avenue SE,
Room 300
Minneapolis, MN 55414
(612) 379-2323

NEW YORK

New York

205 East 42nd Street
New York, NY 10017
(212) 661-1450

New York Student Center
356 West 34th Street
New York, NY 10001
(212) 564-0142

35 West 8th Street
New York, NY 10011
(212) 254-2525

NORTH CAROLINA

Durham

703 Ninth Street, Suite B2
Durham, NC 27705
(919) 286-4664

OREGON

Portland

715 SW Morrison, Suite 600
Portland, OR 97205
(503) 228-1900

PENNSYLVANIA

Philadelphia

3606 A. Chestnut St.
Philadelphia, PA 19104
(215) 382-0343

RHODE ISLAND

Providence

171 Angell Street, Suite 212
Providence, RI 02906
(401) 331-5810

TEXAS

Austin

2000 Guadalupe Street
Austin, TX 78705
(512) 472-4931

Dallas

6923 Snider Plaza
Suite B
Dallas, TX 75205
(214) 363-9941

WASHINGTON

Seattle

1314 Northeast 43rd Street,
Suite 210
Seattle, WA 98105
(206) 632-2448

219 Broadway Avenue East
The Alley Building, Suite 17
Seattle, WA 98102
(206) 329-4567

WISCONSIN

Milwaukee

2615 North Hackett Avenue
Milwaukee, WI 53211
(414) 332-4740

FRANCE

Aix-en-Provence

12, rue Victor Leydet
13100 Aix-en-Provence
(33-42) 38.58.82

Lyons

36, quai Gailleton
69002 Lyons
(33-78) 37.09.56

Montpellier

20, rue de l'Université
34000 Montpelier
(33-67) 60.89.29

Nice

37bis, rue d'Angleterre
06000 Nice
(33-1) 93.82.32.83

Paris

31, rue St. Augustin
75002 Paris
(33-1) 42.66.20.87

51, rue Dauphine
75006 Paris
(33-1) 43.25.09.86

16, rue de Vaugirard
75006 Paris
(33-1) 46.34.02.90

49, rue Pierre Charron
75008 Paris
(33-1) 43.59.23.69

GERMANY

Düsseldorf

Graf-Adolf-Strasse 18
4000 Düsseldorf 1
(49-211) 32.90.88

JAPAN

Tokyo

Sanno Grand Building, Room 102
14-2 Nagata-cho 2-chome
Chiyoda-ku, Tokyo 100
(81-3) 3581-7581

UNITED KINGDOM

London

28A Poland Street
London W1V 3DB
England
(44-71) 437-7767

CIEE ADMINISTRATIVE CENTERS

USA
CIEE International Administrative Center
205 East 42nd Street
New York, NY 10017
(212) 661-1414

FRANCE
CIEE European Administrative Center
49, rue Pierre Charron
75008 Paris
(33-1) 43-59-23-69

CIEE
Centre Franco-American Odeon
1, Place de l'Odeon
75006 Paris
(33-1) (1) 46-34-16-10

GERMANY
CIEE
Thomas-Mann-Strasse 33
5300 Bonn 1
(49-228) 659746

CIEE
Unter den Linden 36
Suite 544-546
0-1086 Berlin
(372) 203-40287

HONG KONG
CIEE Southeast Asia Office
Arts Centre, 12/f
2 Harbour Road
Wanchai
(852) 824-1925

JAPAN
CIEE Japan Administrative Center
Sanno Grand Building, Room 205
14-2 Nagata-cho 2-chome
Chiyoda-ku, Tokyo 100
(81-3) 3 581-7581

CIEE Western Japan Regional Liaison Office
Kyoto International Community House
2-1 Torii-cho, Awataguchi
Sakyo-ku, Kyoto-shi 606
(81-75) 752-1130

SPAIN
CIEE
Carranza 7, 3-3
28004 Madrid
(34-1) 593-18-86

UNITED KINGDOM
CIEE
33 Seymour Place
London W1H 6AT
(44-71) 706-3008

ITALY
CIEE
Via della Longara 233
00165 Rome
(39-6) 683-21-09

CHAPTER ONE
GOING ABROAD

"Travel is fatal to prejudice, bigotry and narrow-mindedness, all foes to real understanding. Likewise tolerance, or broad, wholesome, charitable views of men and things cannot be acquired by vegetating in our little corner of the earth all one's lifetime."
—Mark Twain

This book is *not* a traditional travel guide. In it you won't find the best night spots in Helsinki, where to stay in Madagascar, or what to see in Kyoto. Most bookstores are packed with travel guides that provide this information for virtually any country or region you may want to visit.

This book is something different. It's for the international traveler who wants to be more than just a tourist; it's for those who want to go beyond just seeing the sights to really get to know and understand another country and culture. In this book you'll find information that will help you to experience another country as an insider, such as a student, worker, volunteer, or intern. Want to know about study-abroad programs, study-travel tours, or summer language programs? What about voluntary service, international workcamps, summer jobs, or internships in other countries? All of these are included, as well as information about cheap flights, railpasses, passports and visas, student identity cards, and so on.

Most readers of this book will be college students who want to consider all the options open to them before making a decision. But *Work, Study, Travel Abroad* is for anyone thinking about international travel, whether they are going abroad for the first time or simply want their next trip abroad to be the best possible.

Why Travel Abroad?

CIEE's worldwide staff represents a vast spectrum of political and personal beliefs, but we all agree on one thing—the need to encourage all types of international educational exchange. Americans must learn more about the rest of the world, not simply to help our nation compete in international markets or maintain its role as a world leader, but also in order to understand global issues and battle global problems. Whether you're concerned with human rights, the environment, poverty and hunger, or questions of war and peace in a nuclear age, you'll need to understand the world beyond our national borders. Even issues that used to be considered only of local or national importance—like the unemployment rate, the price of gasoline, and use of chlorofluorocarbons in refrigerators—are ones that now require understanding of the transnational systems of which our own economy, political system, and natural environment are only one part. Firsthand experience abroad is probably the best way to increase one's knowledge of the world we share with so many other nations and peoples.

Experiencing life firsthand in another country or culture will not only broaden your understanding of the world around you; it also will give you a new perspective on the things most familiar to you. A professor once asked his students what their concept of color would be if they had spent their whole lives in a room where everything was red. The students quickly realized that they would have no concept of green or blue. But only after giving it some thought did they realize they would also have no idea of what red was, never having had the opportunity to experience what not-red might be. Most people who experience a foreign culture find that at least as important as the knowledge they gain about a different part of the world is the chance to see their own country and culture from a new, broader perspective.

Fortunately, we need not spend a lot of effort extolling the benefits of going abroad, since most people find that it's not only an enriching educational experience, but also great fun. But don't expect everything to be wonderful all the time. If you really try to get the most out of your experience abroad, you'll undoubtedly find that coping with a new culture and possibly a new language is not always easy. To keep problems to a minimum and to get the most out of your time abroad, you'll have to do some careful planning. And that's exactly why we've written this book.

Where to Go and What to Do

Everyone thinking of going abroad faces two basic questions: Where to go and what to do? Should you see the treasures of Europe or be more adventuresome and explore Asia, Africa, or Latin America? Should you work, study, travel, or do a little of all three? This book will help you explore the possibilities. And once you've made up your mind, it will help you make the necessary preparations.

Before you decide where to go, be sure to consider all your options. While most Americans going abroad still travel to Europe, an increasing number are opting for study, work, voluntary service, or educational travel experiences in the Third World countries of Africa, Asia, and Latin America. Why not seriously consider helping to build an irrigation system in Latin America or studying Chinese business and society in Beijing? What about traveling the Nile by felucca or seeing for yourself the effects of deforestation in the Brazilian rain forest? Because the Third World provides such vivid social, economic, and cultural contrasts with our own way of life, you'll find a radically different perspective from which to examine your beliefs, values, and assumptions. And, with over three-quarters of the world's population living there, an understanding of the nations of the Third World is valuable preparation for living and working in an increasingly interdependent world. Consider what two students said about their experiences:

"My four months in Africa proved intellectually, physically, and emotionally challenging. I discovered the intricacies of a very foreign culture, learned the commonalities that exist between African and American lifestyles, and marveled at uniquely African tradition, culture, morals, and beliefs. . . . I gained a sense of my priorities in life and set new goals for my career path. It is important to realize, however, that much of what I gained from my African experience came from frustration, loneliness, and a whole lot of soul searching. It wasn't all positive. But it was perhaps the greatest learning experience I could ever have imagined."

"Most significantly, my studies in Mexico made me a more sensitive person. As an architecture student, I was humanized and humbled to think of design in more universal terms—the simple Mayan hut is an enduring form that will persist long after the demise of the suburban shopping mall. And Mexican cities, no matter how congested, are much more civilized and humane than our sleek, modern ones. There, public squares every few blocks are a fact of life and not something you have to persuade planning boards and cities to implement."

Wherever you decide to go or whatever you decide to do, we have a couple of suggestions before you plunge in. Be open and flexible, but be realistic about yourself and your trip. Consider all the options, talking to family, friends, foreign students, academic advisers, or anyone you know who's been abroad. In the end, however, the decision is yours.

To help you decide what to do abroad, you'll find general information about working, studying, and traveling in Chapters Three, Four, and Five. But don't leave the country without looking at Chapter Two, which provides the practical information you need to know about passports and visas, student identity cards and discounts, insurance, and so on. Each of the remaining chapters focuses on a specific world region—eleven in all.

These chapters will give you information on specific countries and the work, study, and travel opportunities available in each of them.

For Further Reading

Here are some books and periodicals that can help prepare you for the cultural transition and adjustments of foreign travel.

- *Intercultural Communication: A Reader*, edited by Larry A. Samovar and Richard E. Porter, includes articles and studies about verbal and nonverbal cross-cultural communication by Edward T. Hall and other experts in the field (fifth edition published by Wadsworth Press in 1988). It's in many libraries, but if you can't find it, you can order it from Intercultural Press, PO Box 700, Yarmouth, Maine 04096 for $19.95 plus $2 postage for the first copy and 50¢ per each additional copy.
- *On Being Foreign: Culture Shock in Short Fiction*, edited by Tom J. Lewis and Robert E. Jungman, is an anthology of short selections from well-known writers around the world, including Herman Hesse, Jorge Luis Borges, Paul Theroux, Albert Camus, and more. Selections focus on different aspects and phases of adapting to life in a foreign culture. The book is available in paperback for $14.95 plus $2 for postage (50¢ each additional copy) from Intercultural Press (see address above).
- *Survival Kit for Overseas Living*, by L. Robert Kohls, discusses the things to consider, including culture shock, once you've made the decision to live abroad. Available from Intercultural Press (see address above) for $7.95 plus $2 postage (50¢ postage each additional copy).
- *Transitions Abroad* is a bimonthly magazine geared to economy travel, overseas study programs, work opportunities, and educational travel. Each issue focuses on a specific subject area or country. *Transitions Abroad* emphasizes practical, usable information in timely and informative articles and first-hand reports. The July issue includes the "Educational Travel Directory," a compilation of the best and most current information sources—by country and subject—on work, study, travel, and living abroad. Submissions from readers (feature stories, short "information pieces," and photographs) are encouraged: write for guidelines (Transitions Abroad Magazine, 18 Hulst Road, PO Box 344, Amherst, MA 01004). Subscription prices are $18 for six issues or $34 for twelve issues, but sample copies are available for $3.50 from Transitions Abroad, Department TRA, PO Box 3000, Denville, NJ 07834.
- *The Teenager's Guide to Study, Travel, and Adventure Abroad*, written specifically with high-school students in mind, contains sections to help students find out if they're ready for travel abroad, make the necessary preparations, and then get the most from the experience. From cycling in China to mosaic-making in Italy, more than 200 programs are described, including language programs, summer camps, homestays, study-tour programs, and workcamps. Also included are interviews with teenagers who have participated in some of the programs listed. Prepared by CIEE and published by St. Martin's Press, the 1991–92 edition (320 pages) costs $11.95 and is available at bookstores or from CIEE's publications department (add $1.50 for book-rate postage or $3 for first-class postage).

CHAPTER TWO
THE ESSENTIALS

"Leaving the U.S. isn't as easy as grabbing a backpack and buying a plane ticket. There are a lot of details that you'll have to deal with—like visas, passports, immunizations, and traveler's checks. Be sure to take care of all the nitty-gritty details before you go; it'll make a big difference in how well your trip goes."
—Nicki Sodoski, Bridgeport, Connecticut

Before you leave, no matter where you are heading, there are certain official documents to be obtained and arrangements to be made. As soon as you decide to leave the U.S., you should start getting the formalities out of the way.

Passports

U.S. citizens need a passport to enter just about every foreign country and to return to the United States. Exceptions include short-term travel between the United States and Mexico and Canada. For travel to many Caribbean countries a birth certificate or voter registration card is acceptable proof of U.S. citizenship. However, even when it's not specifically required, a valid U.S. passport is the best travel documentation available.

Passports for U.S. citizens 18 years or over are valid for 10 years and cost $35 plus a $7 execution fee (see below for details). For anyone under 18, they are valid for 5 years and cost $20, plus the $7 execution fee. Between March and August the demand is heaviest and the process will take longer than at other times of the year. Apply several months before departure, and if you're going to need visas, allow yourself even more time.

If it is your first passport application, you must apply in person at (1) a U.S. post office authorized to accept passport applications; (2) a federal or state court; or (3) one of the passport agencies located in Boston, Chicago, Honolulu, Houston, Los Angeles, Miami, New Orleans, New York, Philadelphia, San Francisco, Seattle, Stamford, or Washington, DC.

To apply, you'll need to bring proof of U.S. citizenship. This can be a certified copy of a birth certificate, naturalization certificate, or consular report of birth abroad. (Note: your birth certificate must show that the birth record was filed shortly after birth and must be certified with the registrar's signature and raised, impressed, embossed, or multicolored seal.) You'll also need two recent, identical photographs two inches square (most vending machine photos are *not* acceptable) and proof of identity, such as a valid driver's license (not a Social Security or credit card). Finally, you must complete the form DSP-11, "Passport Application."

You may apply by mail and avoid the $7 execution fee if (1) you have had a passport within twelve years of the new application; (2) you are able to submit your most recent passport with the application; and (3) your previous passport was not issued before your eighteenth birthday. In addition to sending your previous passport and two new passport-size photographs, you must complete form DSP-82 "Application for Passport by Mail." It generally takes four to six weeks to process a passport, or even longer during the peak travel season.

Your passport should be kept with you at all times while traveling. American passports are coveted by those who wish to work or live in the U.S. but can't due to visa restrictions. On the international black market, U.S. passports can can sell for about $1,000. One good way to assure that *your* face remains in your passport is to carry it in a pouch that is tied at the neck or worn around the waist like a belt. This pouch can hold travelers checks, too, and should always be kept inside your clothing. All Council Travel offices (see pages xix–xxi) carry passport holders and pouches.

Loss, theft, or destruction of a valid passport is a serious matter and should be reported immediately to local police and to the nearest U.S. embassy or consulate. (If the loss occurs in the U.S., notify Passport Services, Department of State, 1425 K Street NW, Washington, DC 20520.) If you lose your passport in another country, you will need to get a replacement at a U.S. embassy or consulate. This process will be much easier if you have with you two extra passport photos and a photocopy of your original showing the number and date and place of issuance. In case your passport is stolen or lost, you also should have with you—but in a separate place from your passport—both proof of citizenship (an expired passport or copy of your birth certificate) and proof of identity (a driver's license or other photo ID).

You should also be aware that a number of countries will not permit visitors to enter and will not place visas in passports which have a remaining validity of less than six months. If you return to the U.S. with an expired passport, you are subject to a passport waiver fee of $80.

Non-U.S. citizens without a valid passport from another country who have permanent residency in the U.S. can apply for a U.S. travel permit. This permit functions much like a passport and can be obtained from the Immigration and Naturalization Service in the state where the applicant resides. Note, however, that the requirements for obtaining visas are usually different from those that apply to U.S. citizens. The information on visa requirements provided throughout this book is applicable only to U.S. citizens. Non-U.S. citizens—whether traveling with a travel permit or a valid passport from another country—will have to consult the embassy or consulate of the country they want to visit to obtain the appropriate visa requirements.

Visas

Depending on the country you visit and the length and purpose of your stay, you may also need a visa. A visa is an endorsement or stamp placed in your passport by a foreign government permitting you to visit that country for a specified purpose and a limited time, e.g., a three-month tourist visa. To study in a particular country, you may need a special student visa. In most cases, you'll have to obtain visas before you leave the U.S. Apply directly to the embassies or nearest consulates of the countries you plan to visit or check with a travel agent. The Passport Services of the Department of State *cannot* help you get a visa.

In this book, you'll find visa requirements as of summer 1991 described briefly in the individual country sections. Another source of information is the booklet, *Foreign Entry Requirements*, which lists the entry requirements for U.S. citizens traveling to most foreign countries and tells where and how to apply for visas. Single copies are available for 50¢ from the Consumer Information Center, Box 438T, Pueblo, CO 81009. Although this publication is updated annually, changes can occur without notice at any time. For the latest information, check with the embassies or the nearest consulates of the countries you plan to visit.

Since the visa is usually stamped directly onto one of the blank pages in your passport, you'll need to fill in a form and give your passport to an official of each foreign embassy or consulate. You may need one or more photos. (Have extras made when you're having passport pictures taken.) You'll have to pay for most visas. The whole process can take several weeks, so if you have more than one to get, start well in advance of your trip. Also, bear in mind that some countries require evidence that you have enough money for your trip and/or ongoing or return transportation tickets.

Some countries (Mexico, for example) allow U.S. citizens to enter and stay without a passport or visa but require a tourist card. If a country you plan to visit requires a tourist card, you can get one at the airport just before you depart the U.S. or at the border crossing when you enter the country. Some tourist cards require a fee.

Customs

When you come back to the U.S., you'll have to go through customs. The U.S. government prohibits Americans from bringing back certain articles and imposes import fees or duties on other items. Everything that you'll need to know about customs regulations for your return to the U.S. can be found in *Know Before You Go*, a pamphlet available free from U.S. Customs Services, Box 7407, Washington, DC 20044. To order by phone, call (202) 566-8195.

Health

Rather than go into specifics here about something as important as your health, we'll refer you to experts and a few good books on the subject. But before we do, we want to emphasize that the two greatest threats to travelers' health today are diseases against which you *cannot* be inoculated. One is diarrhea and the other is malaria. A few travel agents or tourist bureaus don't tell travelers of the malaria risk in their country for fear that they'll go elsewhere. Most types of malaria can be prevented, but you must begin taking antimalarial drugs *before* you arrive in the infected area and must continue taking them after you leave.

Some countries require international certificates of vaccination against yellow fever and for cholera. Because smallpox has been virtually eradicated, vaccinations for that disease are rarely required. Check your health care records to ensure measles, mumps, rubella, polio, diptheria, tetanus, and pertussis (whooping cough) immunizations are up to date. The Centers for Disease Control has a hotline for determining whether any special vaccinations are needed to visit a country, or to learn of any dangerous outbreaks of disease occurring in that country. The hotline number is (404) 332-4559.

One organization that has been working energetically to alert travelers about the risks of malaria and other health problems worldwide is the International Association of Medical Assistance to Travellers (IAMAT). IAMAT is a nonprofit organization with centers in 450 cities in 120 countries. Its members receive a pocket-size directory listing IAMAT centers abroad, a world immunization chart (which we particularly recommend), and various publications and maps that alert travelers to existing health problems throughout the world. Contact IAMAT at 417 Center Street, Lewiston, NY 14092. Membership in this organization is free but donations are appreciated.

As always, when traveling you should be aware of the risk of contracting AIDS (Acquired Immunodeficiency Syndrome). Don't let exaggerated or distorted information alter your travel plans, but *do* be aware of the risks and *do* prepare ahead. Be aware that some countries may require HIV (human immunodeficiency virus) antibody tests before they'll grant a visa for an extended period of time; tourists staying for thirty days or less are usually exempt. You might want to be tested before you depart; do so only at a center that offers pre- and post-test counseling and allow two weeks for the testing process. While traveling, remember: The best way to deal with AIDS is through knowledge, foresight, and action—not ignorance and fear.

The Centers for Disease Control has issued the following advisory: "AIDS has been reported from more than 130 nations, but adequate surveillance systems are lacking in many countries. Because HIV and AIDS are globally distributed, the risk to international travelers is determined less by their geographic destination than by their individual behavior. HIV infection is preventable. There is no documented evidence of HIV transmission through casual contact; air, food, or water routes; contact with inanimate objects; or through mosquitos or other arthropod (insect) vectors. HIV is transmitted through sexual intercourse, blood or blood components, and perinatally (at birth) from an infected mother. Travelers are at increased risk if they have sexual intercourse (homosexual or heterosexual) with an infected person; use or allow the use of contaminated, unsterilized syringes or needles for any injections, e.g., illicit drugs, tattooing, acupuncture, or medical/dental procedures; or use infected blood, blood components, or clotting factor concentrates.''

There are several things that you can do to avoid contracting the HIV virus. First and foremost, bring condoms and/or dental dams with you. You may not have access to these items in certain parts of the world, and conditions, manufacturing, and storage of condoms in other countries may be questionable. More importantly, use them—even if you are aware of the HIV status of your partner. Remember, testing HIV negative does not necessarily mean that a person has not been in contact with the virus. If you do need a blood transfusion, try to ensure that screened blood is used. If you are concerned about needing a blood transfusion while abroad, contact others in your academic program or traveling group; you can arrange with those that have your blood type to be blood donors if necessary. For more information, write CIEE (205 East 42nd Street, New York, NY 10017) for a free copy of Council Travel's *AIDS and International Travel*. Other resources for information are the U.S. Department of Health and Human Services AIDS Hotline (1-800-342-AIDS) and the World Health Organization in Washington, DC (201-861-3200).

The following books are recommended reading for overall health issues. You won't need to consult all of them, but do try to look through at least one. Getting sick while you travel is miserable.

- *How to Stay Well While Traveling in the Tropics*, by Douglas T. Keshishian, (Dennis-Landman Publishers, 1150 18th Street, Santa Monica, CA 90403) a 36-page book concentrating on health problems in the tropical areas of Asia, Africa, and South America. The information is compiled from medical texts, specialists on tropical medicine, and the personal experiences of the author. It costs $2.95 plus 65¢ postage and handling.
- *The Pocket Doctor* is a pocket-size publication written especially for travelers. You can order it from Mountaineers Books, 1011 S.W. Klickitat Way, Suite 107, Seattle, WA 98134 for $3.95 plus $2 for postage and handling.
- *Health Information for International Travel*, published by the Centers for Disease Control is available for $5 from the Superintendent of Documents, U.S. Government Printing Office, Washington, DC 20402, or call (202) 783-3238.
- *Staying Healthy in Asia, Africa, and Latin America*, by Dirk Schroeder, is basic enough for the short-term traveler yet complete enough for someone living or traveling off the beaten path. Order it from Volunteers in Asia, Box 4543, Stanford, CA 94309, for $7.95 plus $1.50 postage for the first copy (50¢ each additional copy).
- *The International Travel HealthGuide* ($12.95), by Stuart Rose, M.D., is updated annually. It's a little large for stuffing in your backpack, but has country by country immunization, health, and safety listings. It also has chapters on AIDS, travel and pregnancy, and traveling with disabilities. Look for it in good bookstores or contact the publisher, Travel Medicine, Inc., 351 Pleasant Street, Suite 312, Northampton, MA 01060.

Some general advice: Make sure you're in good general health before setting out. Go to the dentist before you leave on your trip, and have an extra pair of eyeglasses or contact lenses made up (or at least have your doctor write out your prescription). If you take along any prescription drugs, pack them in clearly marked bottles, and have the prescription with you in case a customs officer asks for it.

Safety

Leaving the U.S. is not dangerous in and of itself; in fact, travelers will encounter few countries where the crime rate—especially the frequency of violent crime—equals that of the United States. But it is important to remember one thing: while traveling, you *will* be recognized as a foreigner. To some, this means you will be a novelty. To others, a rube. This means that you must be aware and thoughtful at all times because you can no longer rely on your instinctive knowledge of what may be considered unsafe, insulting, or provocative. This doesn't mean that you should not explore or stray off the tourist-beaten path. It does mean that you should be aware of your passport and money at all times and take along a good guidebook that will give you a rough idea of the situations you will be getting yourself into. Try to determine areas to avoid alone or at night and try to avoid arriving in strange cities late at night unless you have a confirmed place to stay and a secure means of getting there. You can't control everything that happens to you—at home or abroad—but you can sway the odds.

"Don't feel afraid or embarrassed to walk away from an uncomfortable situation. Whether you're on a train or in a restaurant, just change your seat if you feel threatened."
—Brenda Ellison, Los Angeles, California

Women should be especially aware of situations in which they might be harassed, robbed, or molested. When traveling, there is not only the usual burden of sexism to deal with but also the fact that, as a recognizable Westerner, you will be treated according to stereotypes of Western women (thought in some parts of the world to be promiscuous, immodest, and wealthy). *Women Travel: Adventures, Advice, and Experience*, one in the *Real Guide* series published by Prentice Hall Travel, is recommended. For each country, the book lists suggested styles of dress, valuable contacts, and advice for women travelers. For example, one woman stuffed a pillow in her dress to avoid harassment: Pregnant women are usually left alone in South American countries.

If you're planning a trip to a spot where a political problem has existed for a while or just flared up, a reliable source of information is the Citizens Emergency Center (CEC) operated by the State Department in Washington, DC. This center will inform you of any State Department travel advisories that warn travelers of danger and recommend taking special precautions, or in more extreme cases, postponing travel to certain countries or regions. Recorded travel advisories can be obtained anytime from a push button phone by calling (202) 647-5225. If you're using a dial phone, call between 8:00 A.M. and 10:00 P.M. EST, Monday through Friday, or between 9 A.M. to 3 P.M. on Saturday.

Insurance

Check to see whether your medical and accident insurance policies are valid when you are traveling outside the United States. You should never underestimate the importance of being insured when traveling abroad. If you purchase an International Student Identity Card (see the following section of this chapter), you will automatically receive basic accident/sickness insurance for travel outside the U.S., valid from the time of purchase until the card's expiration date. Also included is a toll-free emergency hotline number for travelers needing legal, financial, or medical assistance.

You should also investigate the various plans for baggage and flight insurance. Baggage or personal effects insurance covers damage to or loss of your personal belongings while traveling. Flight insurance covers the cost of your fare if you are unable to take a flight you have already paid for. One insurance package, Trip-Safe, provides a variety of options which may be purchased in any combination for any period from one month to one year. You can find details in the *Student Travel Catalog*, which is available free from CIEE, 205 East 42nd Street, New York, NY 10017 (include $1 for postage and handling). Insurance can also be obtained at any Council Travel office.

International Student Identity Card

More than a million students worldwide purchase the International Student Identity Card each year. If you are a junior high, senior high, college, university, or vocational student planning to travel outside the U.S., you should investigate the benefits this card provides.

Holders of the International Student Identity Card get student discounts on transportation and accommodations, and reduced admissions to museums, theaters, cultural events, and other attractions. Best known of the discounts are student/youth fares on regular international flights connecting cities in the United States, Africa, Asia, Europe, Latin America, and the South Pacific. Cardholders can save up to 50 percent over commercial fares on the same routes. Information on worldwide student and youth fares is available from any Council Travel office (see pages xix–xxi). A listing of specific discounts in 65 countries is contained in the "International Student Travel Guide," a booklet distributed to all purchasers of the International Student Identity Card. Even in countries that do not have their own national student travel bureaus, the International Student Identity Card is often recognized as proof of student status and can be helpful in securing whatever student discounts are around. The best thing to do, no matter where you are, is to show your card first and ask if there are any discounts available, whether it's for a ferry ticket, an entrance fee for a museum, or a stay in a hotel.

Besides the student discounts, the International Student Identity Card provides basic medical and accident insurance. Every student who buys the card in the U.S. receives coverage while they're abroad for as long as their card is valid. Also available to cardholders is a toll-free hotline for travelers in need of assistance in a legal, medical, or financial emergency. CIEE's *Student Travel Catalog* has all the details.

The International Student Identity Card is the creation of the International Student Travel Confederation (ISTC), made up of the student travel organizations in 74 countries around the world. If imitation is the sincerest form of flattery, the card has had more than its share. Forgeries and imitations of the International Student Identity Card have appeared and will probably continue to appear from time to time, both in the U.S. and abroad. The hologram, registered by the International Student Travel Confederation, distinguishes the authentic card from forgeries or imitations.

To obtain the International Student Identity Card, submit a passport-size photo and proof of student status at a junior or senior high school, college, university, or vocational school in a program leading to a degree or diploma. To get the 1992 card—valid from September 1, 1991 to December 31, 1992—you must be a student in the fall of 1991 or the spring or summer of 1992. College students can prove student status with a letter from the registrar or dean stamped with a school seal, a clear photocopy of a transcript or grade report, or a bursar's receipt. High school students can prove student status with a photocopy of a report card or a letter from a principal or guidance counselor on school stationery. You must be at least 12 years of age, but there is no maximum age limit (age restrictions may apply on some discounts).

In the United States, the International Student Identity Card is sponsored by the Council on International Educational Exchange, the U.S. member of the ISTC. Available in 1992 for $14, it may be obtained from CIEE, any Council Travel office, or one of 479 authorized issuing offices at colleges and universities across the country. The *Student Travel Catalog* contains a form that can be used to apply for the card by mail.

For details on the International Student Identity Card Fund, which provides travel grants to students studying or doing voluntary service in the Third World, see page 39.

International Teacher Identity Card

In the last several years the International Student Travel Confederation, creator of the International Student Identity Card, has worked to open its low-cost educational travel network to elementary, secondary, vocational, and college faculty. The International Teacher Identity Card provides teachers with some of the same benefits that students holding the International Student Identity Card enjoy, including the insurance and traveler's assistance service. Teachers can also get some of the same discounts on international flights that students get by booking with travel services that honor the card, such as Council Travel. Cardholders can also take advantage of a 10-percent discount on teacher refresher courses at any Eurocentre location (see page 42). The 1992 International

Teacher Identity Card, which has the sponsorship of the International Association of Universities, costs $15. Contact CIEE or any Council Travel office.

International Youth Card

Anyone below age 26 is eligible for the International Youth Card, sponsored by the Federation of International Youth Travel Organizations. This card allows all young people to take advantage of many of the same discounts students get, including the discount on many international flights. Cardholders receive a free booklet, "Discounts for Cardholders," that lists youth discounts in 40 countries. International Youth Cards issued through CIEE also carry the same insurance and traveler's assistance benefits as the student and teacher cards described above. For more information on the International Youth Card, contact CIEE or any Council Travel office (see pages xix–xxi).

"I didn't think that I was eligible for any discounts abroad since I was no longer a student. It was a nice surprise to find that I could still get a youth ID."
—Joshua Vance, Tucson, Arizona

Mail

If you want to receive mail while you are abroad but do not have a mailing address, you can have mail sent to you in care of *Poste Restante* (General Delivery) at the central post office in the cities you'll be visiting. Simply go to the post office and pick up any mail that has arrived for you; usually, you'll have to pay a small charge for each item received.

If you have American Express traveler's checks or an American Express card, you can have your letters (but not packages) sent to an overseas American Express office. *Traveler's Companion*, a brochure published by American Express, includes a list of offices abroad as well as other helpful information. It can be picked up at any American Express office.

Important Note: Many organizations abroad request that you enclose international postal reply coupons when writing for information. International postal reply coupons cost 95¢ each and can be purchased at a U.S. post office. The organization receiving the coupon can exchange it for stamps for a response sent by surface mail. For most countries, you'll need to enclose two international postal reply coupons to ensure an airmail response.

Money

Without a doubt, the best way to carry your money abroad is in traveler's checks, which can be replaced if lost or stolen. Most traveler's checks cost one percent of the total dollar amount you're buying (for example, $5 for $500 in traveler's checks). Traveler's checks in U.S. dollars are widely accepted around the world. However, it is also possible to purchase traveler's checks in other major currencies such as British pounds or German marks. If the dollar is falling in value relative to other major currencies, your money will go farther if it is denominated in marks, pounds, or yen. While it is hard to predict the course of the international currency market, you can insulate yourself from its fluctuations by purchasing traveler's checks in the currency of the country where you will be staying.

The most common traveler's checks are American Express, Citicorp, Thomas Cook, and Visa. In deciding what kind of traveler's checks you should buy, try to determine how widely the check is recognized and the number of offices the issuing agency has abroad (in case your checks are lost or stolen). Remember that you won't have to go to an overseas office of the issuing agency if you just want to convert your checks to local currency. Most banks will cash them readily; in fact, in most European countries you'll get a better exchange rate with traveler's checks than with cash. Try to avoid changing your money in hotels or restaurants where the rate of exchange is usually less favorable.

In many countries, especially those of the Third World, currency is often available in exchange shops (*bureaux de change* or *cambios*), where the rate of exchange is much better than that in a bank. Be sure to investigate all options for the best rate of exchange, especially if you're going to be changing large amounts of money. But be wary of currency exchange with money changers on the street; in most countries this type of transaction is illegal.

Conversion tables listing rates of exchange for dollars in different currencies are found in most guidebooks. Daily currency rates are quoted in many newspapers including the *New York Times* and the *Wall Street Journal*.

You'll be able to buy foreign currency in an air, ship, or train terminal when you arrive, but rates are often better once you're in town. It's a good idea, however, to have some local currency with you when you first arrive in a country, especially if it's late at night.

If you run short of money, traveler's checks or cash can be cabled to you from the U.S. in care of a bank or an agency, such as American Express or Thomas Cook. If your bank has a foreign branch, you can have money transferred to you there. It is best to do this in major cities and to make arrangements as far in advance of imminent destitution as possible. You can get more information on wiring money abroad from the agencies that issue your traveler's checks or from a Western Union office.

Your own credit card or ATM (Automatic Teller Machine) card may allow you access to ATMs overseas. Check with the financial institution that issues the card to find out if it participates in an ATM network with overseas members.

A Word of Warning: Many countries restrict the entry of persons who can't demonstrate that they have a return plane ticket and/or a certain amount of money for each day they plan to spend in the country. These regulations are designed to keep out people whose lack of money may make them wards of the state. Usually, however, these regulations are enforced (or not enforced) quite erratically, based most often on the person's age and appearance. Check with the consulate of the country you plan to visit to see what kind of proof of solvency you will be expected to show.

"It's a good idea not to get too much of any unstable currency because it can't be exchanged at a rate anywhere near the original exchange. In countries plagued by hyperinflation where the currency loses value daily, you should keep your money in dollars until it is absolutely necessary to change some."
—Nadine Jones, Baton Rouge, Louisiana

Becoming Informed

In order to get the most out of your experience abroad, you'll need to do some reading on the countries you'll be visiting. Guidebooks, novels, movies, histories, and social, economic, and political studies are some of the items that you might want to take a look at before going. Investigate your library, ask professors what they recommend, and check to see what your local bookstore has in stock. We especially recommend that you look at some books and movies from the country you will be visiting. For many of the countries covered in this book, you'll find we've suggested films and works of literature that provide insight into the country's culture. In addition, described below are some reading suggestions appropriate for persons going anywhere—from Canada to Madagascar.

"Read about the history, economy, and politics of the country. Study a map to learn about its location, terrain, and climate. Request as much information as you can get about trains, hotel accommodations, et cetera. You'll understand things better once you get there."
—C. D. Nichols, Fort Worth, Texas

No matter where you go, you'll be asked questions about U.S. foreign policy, especially matters that directly affect the countries you visit. The best thing to do is prepare yourself a little in advance by reading newspapers like the *New York Times*, the *Washington Post*, and the *Christian Science Monitor*, which, although not always objective or without bias, are known for their coverage of international affairs. Especially valuable are the publications of the Foreign Policy Association, a nonprofit, nonpartisan organization dedicated to informing Americans of the complexities of foreign-policy issues. One of the best ways to quickly inform yourself about foreign policy topics is to read *Great Decisions*, which describes the pros and cons of alternative courses of action on eight different foreign policy issues each year. *Great Decisions* (the 1991 edition is $10 plus $2 postage and handling) and other publications on foreign-policy topics are available from the Foreign Policy Association, 729 Seventh Avenue, New York, NY 10019.

For a quick and easy introduction to the culture of the country you're going to, we recommend *Culturgrams*. These are country-by-country profiles of the customs, manners, and lifestyles you'll encounter in 102 countries. (The four-page briefings also discuss typical greetings and attitudes, religion, politics, and so on.) Published by Brigham Young University's David M. Kennedy Center of International Studies, the guides are available for $1 each (50¢ each if you buy more than five) or $40 for the entire set of 102. Order them from the Center's Publication Services, 280 HRCB, Brigham Young University, Provo, UT 84602, or by phone: (801) 378-6528.

Also useful in getting to understand the country you're going to is the *Transcultural Study Guide*, prepared by Volunteers in Asia, an organization that emphasizes increased understanding between cultures. Believing that the questions asked to a large extent determine the answers and conclusions that follow, the guide suggests questions for looking at another culture from a humanitarian perspective. To order, write to Volunteers in Asia, Box 4543, Stanford, CA 94309 ($4.95 plus $1.50 postage).

"Read, read, read! Read as many books, pamphlets, guides, et cetera, as you can before going on your trip. It is so much easier to understand places that you visit if you know some kind of background about them. Plus, it helps to alleviate any fears you may have about your trip and helps you form realistic expectations."
—Kathy A. Flotz, Calumet City, Illinois

Packing

On their first trip abroad, everybody seems to take more than what they need. A good way to avoid this is to pack everything you want to bring and then walk around the block with it. Then bear in mind that most hotels and youth hostels are going to be a healthy jaunt, or at least a crowded bus ride, from the train station. Remember, clothes can be washed and laid out to dry overnight for use the next day. (Quick-drying fabrics like cotton and Lycra will prove to be invaluable.) Keep in mind that you will probably want to purchase some clothing and/or souvenirs. Fashion is not a necessity when you're traveling; being comfortable and able to enjoy your surroundings is.

A backpack is probably your best bet if you're going to be touring. Be sure to get a good one that won't fall apart on the plane trip over. Also, bring a canvas bag or daypack for wallet, camera, maps, passport—stuff you'll want with you during the day and shouldn't leave with your backpack at the hotel or stored in a locker at the train station. Be sure to take a passport-holder that you can wear around your neck or a sturdy, inconspicuous money-belt. It may be a good idea to get a backpack or suitcase that you can lock. At night you'll also want to lock it *to* something immovable: the luggage rack of a train, for example.

Bring good, comfortable walking shoes and a pair of plastic thongs for scary showers. A pocketknife is sure to come in handy, as will a small flashlight, but most basic toiletry items can be purchased outside of the U.S. This is especially true if you are traveling to Europe or to large cities elsewhere. Plan ahead if you wear glasses or contact lenses, and bring any special medication you might need along with a signed note from your doctor explaining what it is (handy in emergencies or when dealing with suspicious border guards). Keep in mind that it is easier to pack light and buy any necessities you may have forgotten than to prepare for any emergency and end up carrying a splint across half of Africa. *You really do not need that much stuff*, and it will only make your life miserable to have to drag it around.

Be sure to take clothes that are sturdy, climate-friendly, and easy to care for. Plan to dress comfortably but be sensitive to local customs; for example, in many countries shorts should only be worn when involved in sports. Bring a pair of long pants or a long skirt or you won't be let into many places of worship; it's no fun to have to wait outside. Remember too that without an electrical converter and an adapter plug, your U.S. electrical appliances will be worthless in most other countries. For suggestions on what to pack, check guidebooks for the region you are going to or ask someone who has recently been there.

"Pack all the equipment you plan on bringing, and then go for a long hike with it. This will help you make choices on what to bring and what to leave at home, but at least bring rain gear."
—Don Groeneveld, Muskegon Heights, Michigan

Drugs

Over 2,860 American citizens were arrested abroad in 1990. More than 1,180 of those arrested were held on charges of using or possessing drugs. The notion that drug laws (and their enforcement) in other countries are more lenient than in the U.S. is simply not true. While there may be a few countries that seem to have a more liberal attitude toward drugs, in most countries prosecution of offenders for both the possession and sale of drugs and narcotics can be more severe than in the United States. Many travelers assume that, as American citizens, they are immune from prosecution under foreign laws. The truth is that Americans suspected of drug violations can face severe penalties, even the death penalty, in some foreign countries. It is not uncommon to spend months or even years in pretrial detention, only to be sentenced to a lengthy stay without parole. Many countries do not permit bail in drug-trafficking cases.

You should be aware of the serious consequences that can result from the possession or sale of drugs, including marijuana, in many parts of the world. In some countries, local laws make no distinction between soft and hard drugs in arresting, detaining, and sentencing Americans. You've certainly heard some of the horror stories of young people jailed in foreign countries. Americans have been jailed abroad for possessing as little as one-tenth of an ounce (three grams) of marijuana.

Once an American leaves U.S. soil, U.S. laws and constitutional rights no longer apply. U.S. consular officers can visit jailed Americans to see that they are being fairly and humanely treated, but cannot get them out of jail or intervene in a foreign country's legal system on their behalf. Should you get into some legal difficulty, the U.S. consulate can provide you with a list of local attorneys and contact your family at home for you —but it can't get you out of trouble or even furnish money for your legal fees.

Be particularly wary of persons who ask you to carry a package or drive a car across a border. Also, if you are required for medical reasons to take any drug that may be subject to abuse statutes, be sure to have your prescription bottle and a copy of your prescription with you. Remember too that the U.S. Bureau of Customs will inspect your baggage upon your return to the United States, and that it is tightening its enforcement procedures.

For people who want more information, the brochure entitled "Travel Warning on Drugs Abroad" (available free from the Bureau of Consular Affairs, Public Affairs Staff, Room 5801, Department of State, Washington, DC 20520) has all the hard, cold facts.

For Persons with Disabilities

In the last decade there has been growing participation in the world of international travel and exchange by persons with disabilities. This is partly the result of laws passed by the federal government which reflect a national commitment to end discrimination on the basis of handicaps and to bring persons with disabilities into the mainstream of American life. But it is primarily the result of a growing number of people with disabilities insisting upon their right to face the challenges and enjoy the benefits of international travel and exchange.

An organization that is active in the advocacy of the disabled traveler is Mobility International. The organization, with its main office in London, was founded in 1973; the U.S. branch was opened in 1981. Working both with persons with disabilities as well as with the organizers and administrators of international educational exchange programs, Mobility International USA (MIUSA) has helped persons with disabilities participate more fully in the world community. Besides publishing a quarterly newsletter called "Over the Rainbow," MIUSA has put together two books, written and edited by Cindy Lewis and Susan Svgall, that are highly recommended. The first, a new and expanded version of an earlier booklet, is entitled *A World of Options for the 90s: A Guide to International Educational Exchange, Community Service and Travel for Persons with Disabilities* ($14 for members, $16 for nonmembers). The book contains more than 300 pages of programs for volunteer, study, and host-family living, especially for persons with disabilities. It also contains useful information on travel, accommodations, and publications. Participants provide firsthand accounts of what can be learned from international exchange. The second publication, entitled *A New Manual for Integrating Persons with Disabilities into International Educational Exchange Programs*, is mainly targeted to the staff and volunteers of service and exchange organizations. It costs $16 for MIUSA members, $18 for nonmembers. *You Want to Go Where? A Guide to China*, by Evelyn Anderton and Susan Sygall, is an invaluable resource written for "travellers with disabilities and anyone interested in disability issues." MIUSA has also produced two videocassettes about its work: "Mi Casa Es Su Casa" (in Spanish or English) describes a Costa Rica Exchange, and "Looking Back, Looking Forward," also available with captions for the hearing-impaired, features interviews with participants in various MIUSA exchanges.

In addition, MIUSA sponsors month-long international exchanges for persons with and without disabilities; recent programs have been offered in Germany, the People's Republic of China, Costa Rica, and England. Upcoming exchanges are planned for the Soviet Union, China, and Mexico; also ahead is an international disability leadership program to be held in Oregon. For more information write to Mobility International USA, PO Box 3551, Eugene, OR 97403, or call (503) 343-1284 (voice or TDD).

Another useful source of information is the Information Center for Individuals with Disabilities, which publishes a fact sheet listing basic information about tour operators, travel agents, and travel resources for the disabled. The fact sheet is $5, prepaid, and can be ordered from the Information Center, Fort Point Place, 27-43 Wormwood Street, Boston, MA 02210-1606.

Itinerary: The Magazine for Travelers with Physical Disabilities ($10 for six issues) is another publication of interest to those who want to travel in the U.S. or abroad. To subscribe, contact Whole Person Tours, PO Box 2012, Bayonne, NJ 07002-2012.

"Going abroad—whether you are handicapped or not—requires planning, patience, flexibility, and a sense of humor. If you're handicapped, you'll need to possess these qualities in even greater quantities. You might be surprised by some people's reactions, but remember that you may be the first handicapped traveler they've ever seen. You'll probably have to ask for help more often than you are used to, but that's a great way to meet people and make friends."

—Carina Klein, New York, New York

For Further Reading

The U.S. Department of State has several pamphlets that can help you make the necessary preparations. A good source of basic information, including such subjects as how to judge a travel program, information on charter flights, and where to get help when you are in trouble abroad, is "Your Trip Abroad." Another Department of State pamphlet, "A Safe Trip Abroad," reminds travelers of some common-sense precautions and also gives tips on protecting against the possibility of terrorism. Finally, "Tips for Americans Residing Abroad" introduces the reader to such topics as tax considerations and voting procedures while abroad. These can be ordered for $1 each from the U.S. Government Printing Office, Washington, DC 20402, or by phone: (202) 783-3238.

CHAPTER THREE
WORKING ABROAD

"Working there I really learned a lot about the culture, the people, and the language . . . but more than anything else, I learned a lot about me."
—Jeff Peters, Seattle, Washington

Have you ever considered picking grapes in southern France? A business or marketing internship in Japan? What about volunteering to work in a clinic in Kenya or teaching school in Bolivia? Each year, CIEE receives about 50,000 inquiries on the subject of working overseas. Getting a job abroad can help finance the trip, furnish valuable job experience, and provide a good way of really understanding a country and its people.

Finding a job abroad is not easy, but it is most certainly possible. To deal with the wide range of options available, we've divided this chapter into four general sections: Short-Term Jobs, Voluntary Service, Teaching Abroad, and Long-Term Employment.

SHORT-TERM EMPLOYMENT

Summer Jobs

"I wanted to live in Europe for an extended period and couldn't afford it otherwise. When posed with the option of waitressing in London or Lansing, Michigan, the choice was obvious."
—Jenny Dailey, DeWitt, Michigan

The choice, however, is seldom that simple. For most countries, you will be required to have a work permit before you can obtain work. Some countries will not grant a permit until you have a promise of a job from an employer, and some employers say they cannot hire you without a work permit. This can be frustrating, to say the least, and many students never get beyond this catch-22 situation.

Fortunately, there is an easy way to avoid these difficulties. For over 20 years, CIEE has been operating a unique work program that eliminates the red tape and enables students to get work permits in Canada, Czechoslovakia, France, Germany, Britain, Ireland, Spain, New Zealand, Costa Rica, and Jamaica. In 1990, more than 6,000 American students took advantage of the program. As a participant in the CIEE Work Abroad Program, you receive the necessary authorization to work in the country you have chosen to visit, along with a program handbook containing general information on the country, tips on employment, a list of possible employers to contact, and helpful hints on housing and travel. In each country, the program is offered in cooperation with an overseas national student organization whose staff is available to advise you on hunting for a job, as well as a place to live, and will provide you with an informal, cultural orientation upon arrival. For most countries in this program, work authorization is for summer jobs only. But in France, Ireland, and the United Kingdom, work authorization for short-term employment can be arranged any time of the year. For details on the program, write the Work Exchanges Department at CIEE, 205 East 42nd Street, New York, NY 10017.

Working a short-term unskilled job in another country probably will earn you enough to cover food, lodging, and day-to-day living expenses. You should not expect to earn enough to pay for your air transportation, but if you are lucky you may save enough to cover some of your travel costs after you leave your job. Whatever job you find probably will not be glamorous, although two students participating in the program found themselves serving the Queen during Prince Andrew's royal wedding reception in 1986. Remember that, in the final analysis, employers only want someone who will do the job well and are not interested in any romantic notions you may have about working in a foreign country.

"Working abroad made me feel like a 'real' German for a while. Travel doesn't give you the flavor of living inside the society, experiencing its daily routine, social habits, and etiquette. It was satisfying to improve my language abilities and feel I really lived there—to know where to shop, where to go, and be stopped and asked for directions. But only working can also become dreary; if possible, do some traveling!"
—Indra Reinbergs, Attleboro, Massashusetts

"The whole experience [working in Wales] really helped me to learn not only about other people and their ideas, feelings, and the way they live, but also about myself. Not that everything was always wonderful and without problems. Far from it. But my overall feeling is that I wouldn't have given up the experience for anything. In many ways it was just as much, if not more of an education, than the one I received at school."
—Russell Lehrer, Suffern, New York

CIEE's Work Abroad Program is open only to U.S. students. Canadians who wish to go on a working holiday abroad should contact Travel CUTS/Canadian Federation of Students—Services (187 College Street, Toronto, Ontario M5T 1P7). This member organization of CIEE operates SWAP (Student Work Abroad Programme), which sends students to a number of overseas destinations.

Another possibility for summer employment abroad is working as a group leader with one of a number of U.S. organizations that offer international programs. A couple of examples follow:

- American Youth Hostels seeks group leaders for a number of hiking, bicycling, and train tours abroad. Contact AYH, PO Box 37613, Washington, DC 20013-7613. Candidates must successfully complete an AYH leadership training course, which is offered at five locations in the U.S.
- The Experiment in International Living, an organization that sends small groups of U.S. high school and college students abroad, has summer leader and semester academic director positions available around the world. You must have experience in cross-cultural living and working with American teenagers or college students. Language proficiency is required for some countries.

One of the best sources for more information is the *Directory of Overseas Summer Jobs*, which lists 50,000 jobs worldwide from Australia to Yugoslavia. Listings include names and addresses of employers, length of employment, rates of pay, how and when to apply, duties, and qualifications sought. Published by Vacation Work (Oxford, United Kingdom), this book is revised annually. It is available from Peterson's Guides, PO Box 2123 Princeton, NJ 08543, for $14.95 plus $4.75 shipping and handling.

Another useful publication is *Work Your Way Around the World*, which contains good advice for anyone planning a long working trip. Although at times the advice verges on the bizarre, overall it's very practical and comprehensive. The book, written by Susan Griffith and published by Vacation Work is also available in the U.S. through Peterson's Guides for $16.95 plus $4.75 shipping and handling (see address above).

Finally, *Working Holidays*, which is updated annually, contains approximately 300 pages of information on paid and voluntary work opportunities worldwide. Published in the United Kingdom, it's available from the Institute for International Education, 809 United Nations Plaza, New York, NY 10017, for $19.95 plus $3 shipping and handling.

Internship and Trainee Programs

Although finding internships or trainee programs abroad may require some research, they have become quite popular. Interns not only get the opportunity to learn the skills required for a specific profession, but also the chance to develop the cross-cultural understanding and communication skills that have become vital in the global environment in which many professionals and business executives now function.

Internships may be paid or unpaid positions—more often the latter—in a company, an organization, or an educational institution. The motivating factor is the applicant's overall desire to train, update, or strengthen a particular skill or field of study. Some assignments may include tedious or clerical tasks in addition to the more meaningful project work. Remember, too, that an overseas internship will no doubt require some economic initiative on your part, since few positions are salaried and most likely you will have to spend some money getting there.

Begin planning your internship experience abroad as far in advance as possible. You'll find internship/traineeship opportunities described under the "Work" heading of the individual country sections later in this book. Also check under the "Study" heading for internship options that may be part of the study-abroad programs offered by U.S. colleges and universities. You should also be aware of three organizations that arrange traineeships around the world for students possessing certain skills:

- AIESEC—U.S. The International Association of Students in Economics and Commerce (known by its French initials, AIESEC) is a worldwide association of students that offers opportunities for college/university students to gain practical management and leadership skills with a global perspective. Opportunities include organizing and participating in international conferences and working abroad through a reciprocal internship exchange program in a variety of business-related fields. Internships are offered in 70 member countries lasting 6 weeks to 18 months. Living expenses are covered by the hosting firm. The programs are restricted to full-time students active in local AIESEC chapters at 65 U.S. colleges and universities. The program is open to freshmen, sophomores, juniors, seniors, and graduate students at the U.S. colleges and universities that are AIESEC members. To find out if your institution has an AIESEC chapter, check with the career placement or study abroad office on your campus. For more information, contact AIESEC—U.S., 841 Broadway, Suite 608, New York, NY 10003; (212) 979-7400.
- IAESTE Trainee Program. The International Association for the Exchange of Students for Technical Experience (IAESTE) provides on-the-job training for students in engineering, architecture, mathematics, computer sciences, and the natural and physical sciences in 50 countries around the world. Juniors, seniors, and graduate students enrolled in an accredited college or university are eligible to apply. Each trainee is paid a maintenance allowance to cover living expenses while training. Fluency in the language is required for some countries. The application deadline for summer placements is December 10; for long-term placements of 3 to 12 months, a minimum of four months processing time is required. For more information, contact IAESTE Trainee Program, c/o Association for International Practical Training, 10 Corporate Center, 10400 Little Patuxent Parkway, Columbia, MD 21044-3510; (301) 997-2200.
- Overseas Development Network (ODN). ODN's Internships for Social Justice Program places interns with a variety of grassroots development organizations in Latin America, Zimbabwe, India, and the Philippines. These community-based organizations are dedicated to such issues as education and literacy, environmental and agricultural concerns, youth employment, and women's empowerment, among others. Interns serve for six months and are responsible for their own expenses. For further information contact the Overseas Development Network, 333 Valencia Street, Suite 330, San Francisco, CA 94103.
- People to People International. In collaboration with the University of Missouri—

Kansas City, People to People sponsors summer internship programs in England, Ireland, and Holland. Prospective interns are required to fill out a questionnaire and specify the desired field of placement. People to People will arrange an internship based upon the applicant's background and interests. Though the program is available for six academic credits from the University of Missouri, check with your academic adviser to confirm whether or not the credits will be accepted by your institution. Noncredit participation is also available. For further information, contact People to People International, 501 East Armour Boulevard, Kansas City, MO 64109; (816) 531-4701.

- YMCA Intern Abroad. The YMCA Intern Abroad program, conducted by the YMCA of Metropolitan Washington, offers an opportunity to work with YMCA staff members in project countries. Participants live in local YMCAs or with YMCA host families; assignments last from six to ten weeks and range from teaching English or sports to working in camps or with development projects. Internships have been conducted in Australia, Austria, the Bahamas, Bangladesh, Brazil, Chile, Colombia, Costa Rica, Egypt, England, France, The Gambia, Gaza, India, Ireland, Kenya, Sri Lanka, Switzerland, Tanzania, Thailand, Trinidad, Uruguay, Venezuela, Zambia, and Zimbabwe. Contact Washington DC Metro YMCA, 1625 Massachusetts Avenue NW, Suite 700, Washington, DC 20036, for further information.

Before taking off, be certain to plan your project carefully with a study-abroad or academic adviser. Talk to someone who has completed an internship abroad—if possible, one in your field of study. Keep an open mind even if the feedback you get is not all positive—some individuals require a more structured program.

The most helpful resource book on internships is the *Directory of International Internships*, which is put together by various offices at Michigan State University. Listed are descriptions of international internships offered by educational institutions, government agencies, and private organizations. It is available for $20 and can be ordered from the Office of Overseas Study, 108 International Center, Michigan State University, East Lansing, MI 48824; (517) 353-8920.

Another helpful book, *Internships*, is revised annually and focuses mostly on internships available within the U.S. but includes a chapter on positions overseas. You can check in your library or career-placement office for a copy or order it from the publisher, Peterson's Guides, PO Box 2123, Princeton, NJ 08543. The 1991 edition costs $27.95 plus $5.75 postage.

Now somewhat out of date is *The International Directory for Youth Internships*, which lists more than 400 intern positions within the United Nations system. Other nongovernmental organizations sponsoring internships programs are also listed. The most recent edition was published in 1984 and is available for $5.75 plus $2.80 shipping and handling from Apex Press, 777 United Nations Plaza, Suite 9A, New York, NY 10017.

Au Pairs, Nannies, and Mother's Helpers

If you enjoy working with children, you may want to consider becoming an au pair, nanny, or mother's helper overseas. As largely live-in jobs, these positions will provide you with firsthand exposure to family life in another culture.

Au pair positions are primarily geared toward young, single people who are interested in learning the language and culture of a foreign country. Working about 30 hours per week, six days per week, an au pair cares for children but usually has less responsibility than a nanny. Nannies usually have sole responsibility for the children around-the-clock, with one or two days off per week. Certification or substantial experience working with children is required. Mother's helpers usually work with the mother; sometimes they will have complete charge of the children. Household tasks such as cooking or cleaning may also be required. The helper usually works eight hours per day and babysits a few nights a week.

The Experiment in International Living sponsors an "Au Pair/Homestay Abroad" program which places young people between the ages of 18 and 26 in Belgium, France, Germany, Great Britain, Italy, the Netherlands, Norway, and Spain. Basic language competence in the country of employment is required. Full room and board are provided along with a weekly stipend. Contact Au Pair/Homestay Abroad, 1015 15th Street NW, Suite 750, Washington, DC 20005; (202) 408-5380.

For further information consult *The Au Pair and Nanny's Guide to Working Abroad*, by Susan Griffith and Sharon Legg. This book discusses the pros and cons of working as an au pair, nanny, or mother's helper and provides suggestions on preparing for and coping with the experience. Also included is a discussion of working regulations in different countries and a listing of agencies that provide placement services. This guide is available for £5.95 plus £1.50 for surface mail shipping, from Vacation Work, 9 Park End Street, Oxford OX1 1HJ, England. Checks should be payable in British pounds and made out to Vacation Work.

Farm Camps

Have you ever been enticed by the notion of working on a farm? Farm camps bring together an international group of students during the summer to help with labor-intensive farm work, usually picking grapes or strawberries. Workers get paid by the amount of fruit they pick but must pay for their own room and board. Wages are not lucrative, but depending on how long and how fast you work, it is possible to earn some extra money. For specific information, see the sections on France and the United Kingdom in Chapter Six.

VOLUNTARY SERVICE

Workcamps

"I think we surprised ourselves at what a difference we made, and we all respected each other's contributions after three weeks of working, cooking, arguing, laughing, and encouraging each other."
—R. Mashek, Germany

"The work provides a loose structure and a continuity which holds people to a place and to one another long enough for bonds to form. You spend enough time with people to see through the differences to underlying similarities, and through the similarities to underlying differences. The greatest works of a culture are its people."
—Don Hudson, Auburn, Alabama

If you want to do something a bit unusual but very rewarding, you might consider joining a workcamp. Workcamps bring together groups of people from various parts of the world to work (usually manual labor) on projects as varied as building a school in Africa to restoring a castle in France. The focus is on projects that meet community needs such as health care, education, environmental conservation, construction of low-cost housing, or restoration of historical sites.

There are hundreds of workcamps all over the world open to Americans. For a directory of organizations conducting such camps, consult the book *Volunteer! The Comprehensive Guide to Voluntary Service in the U.S. and Abroad* (see page 25). Usually there are no special requirements for participants other than a willingness to work. Most participants are young, and often time is set aside for cultural activities, group discussions, and field trips.

CIEE recruits several hundred volunteers for placement each year with workcamp organizations in Algeria, Belgium, Bulgaria, Canada, Czechoslovakia, Denmark, France, Germany, Ghana, Hungary, Morocco, the Netherlands, Poland, Portugal, Spain, Tunisia,

Turkey, the U.S.S.R., Wales, and Yugoslavia, as well as in its own workcamps in the U.S. The camps are located in a wide variety of settings, from small villages to big cities, from national parks and forests to archaeological digs, and from farmhouses to historic monuments and castles. They usually last two, three, or four weeks. No salary is paid, but room and board are provided. Write CIEE's Voluntary Service Department for further information on current workcamps. Canadians can apply for similar opportunities through the Canadian Bureau for International Education (see below).

Another organization involved in international workcamps is Volunteers for Peace (VFP), a nonprofit membership organization that has been coordinating workcamps in 34 countries in Western and Eastern Europe, the U.S.S.R., Africa, Asia, and the Americas since 1981. Most volunteers participate for two to three weeks during the summer; those who register by May have the best selection. Volunteers must be at least 16 years old and pay a fee of $100. A membership fee of $10 entitles you to a copy of the annual *International Workcamp Directory*. For more information and a free newsletter, write or call VFP, PO Box 202, Belmont, VT 05730; (802) 259-2759.

The World Council of Churches sponsors short-term workcamp projects during the summer in several countries of Africa, Asia, and the Middle East. Locations vary from year to year. Some workcamps require a knowledge of French; for others, English is sufficient. Most involve the construction of schools or other community buildings or rural development work. Local people often work alongside the volunteers on the project. Volunteers must be 18 to 30 years old, pay their own travel expenses, and contribute $3 per day toward their living expenses. For further information on what workcamps are planned in a particular year, write to Ecumenical Youth Action, World Council of Churches, 150 rue de Ferney, PO Box 2100, 1211 Geneva 2, Switzerland.

In addition, the Fourth World Movement sponsors work/information camps that are committed to the rights of the poor in Belgium, Canada, France, Great Britain, the Netherlands, and Switzerland. Participants work for ten days during the summer on projects which may involve construction, gardening, sewing, typing, and library or research activities. Volunteers are housed in cabins or tents and are responsible for their own meals, the cost of preparing the camp, and health insurance. For more information, contact the Fourth World Movement, 7600 Willow Hill Drive, Landover, MD 20785; (301) 336-9489.

For Canadian citizens, the Canadian Bureau for International Education (CBIE) offers a program of international workcamps in most European countries that is similar to those described for CIEE. Canadians should contact CBIE, 85 Albert Street, Suite 1400, Ottawa, Ontario K1P 6A4, Canada.

Also be sure to check the work sections in the country-by-country descriptions later in this book. The workcamp programs of CIEE-member organizations and institutions are described under the countries in which they are located.

Other Short-Term Voluntary Service

Workcamps, which involve an international group of volunteers working together on a project for two or three weeks, are only one type of short-term voluntary service experience. Some other volunteer opportunities for persons who are interested in spending part of their summer or academic year as a volunteer are described below:

- The American Friends Service Committee offers short-term voluntary-service opportunities in Mexico and Cuba. Projects last about seven weeks and involve working in construction, recreation, education, and other fields. Volunteers must be 18 to 26 years of age and able to speak Spanish. There is a participation fee of $700 plus transportation costs for Mexico and a fee of $250 plus transportation costs for Cuba. Contact the American Friends Service Committee, 1501 Cherry Street, Philadelphia, PA 19102; (215) 241-7295.
- Amigos de las Americas conducts summer programs that provide community health

services in a variety of Latin American countries. Volunteers need no experience in health care but must be proficient in Spanish; the minimum age is 16. Programs last from four to six weeks. For further information contact Amigos de las Americas, 5618 Star Lane, Houston, TX 77057.

Archaeological Digs and Field-Research Projects

Participating in a scientific-research project or an archaeological dig can be especially appealing. Working as part of an international team, volunteers find themselves in an exotic setting where the excitement of making some new discovery is always a possibility. Field-research projects and archaeological digs offer the opportunity to be an active rather than passive learner and to expand in some small way what is known about the world in which we live. Possibilities include helping to excavate a Bronze Age city in Israel, studying sea lions off the coast of Mexico, or scuba diving to explore a long-submerged French settlement in the Caribbean. While some organizations require volunteers to make a rather large "contribution" to the project they will be involved in, it is still possible to find inexpensive opportunities where you can trade your hard work in the sun for room and board.

Some archaeological excavations accept inexperienced volunteers while others insist on volunteers who have some training or experience. The best source of information on archaeological fieldwork is the Archaeological Institute of America (AIA). Each January, AIA publishes *Archaeological Fieldwork Opportunities Bulletin*, which includes a listing of opportunities for volunteers at excavations, field schools, and educational programs in several countries, including the U.S. Good health is always required for participants in archaeological fieldwork, as well as adaptability to unusual foods or other local conditions. The *Bulletin* costs $10.50 for AIA members and $12.50 for nonmembers. The Institute is also the publisher of *Archaeology* magazine, which twice yearly presents the "Travel Guide," a special feature listing excavations in progress, as well as archaeological sites that welcome visitors as observers or active members of the field crew. Contact the Archaeological Institute of America, 675 Commonwealth Avenue, Boston, MA 02215.

The University of California sponsors a University Research Expeditions Program (UREP) to support research in the natural and social sciences and provide educational opportunities for students, teachers, and the general public. Expeditions take place all over the world and activities range from excavating archaeological remains to surveying wildlife and collecting marine specimens. Expeditions last from two to three weeks and no experience is necessary. Participants are expected to make tax-deductible contributions to cover program costs and pay for their own transportation. Programs range anywhere from a low of $800 to a high of about $1500. Scholarships are available for undergraduates and grants are available for teachers; academic credit can be arranged. For more information contact UREP, University of California, Berkeley, CA 94720; (415) 642-6586.

The Foundation for Field Research is a nonprofit organization that supports scientific projects by recruiting volunteers willing to donate their labor and pay a fee to participate. Projects in the disciplines of archaeology, botany, geology, mammology, ornithology, paleontology, and primatology are conducted all over the world and vary in length from two days to one month; the contribution can range from $125 to $1,900. The Foundation also publishes *Explorer News*, a free newspaper describing the projects volunteers can join. Contact the Foundation for Field Research, PO Box 2010, Alpine, CA 91903; (619) 445-9264.

Another nonprofit organization, Earthwatch, recruits volunteers 16 and over for field research expeditions in 50 countries and 25 states in the U.S. Projects include working with Australian scientists studying the kangaroo, helping with archaeological excavations in France and England, or gathering data on volcanos in Costa Rica. Expeditions are directed by university professors and volunteers participate for two to three weeks. Membership in Earthwatch costs $25 per year, which includes six issues of *Earthwatch Magazine*. Though no special skills are required to participate, volunteers must be members of Earthwatch and pay a tax-deductible fee to cover the cost of room and board, equipment, and ground transportation; this fee ranges from $790 to $2,500, depending on the project. For further information, contact Earthwatch, 680 Mount Auburn Street, Box 403N, Watertown, MA 02272; (617) 926-8200.

Long-Term Voluntary Service

Many people prefer a longer term of voluntary service abroad than is available through a workcamp or field-research project. Fortunately, the options in the field of voluntary service are unlimited, with programs all over the world involving individuals in all sorts of opportunities lasting anywhere from a few weeks to several years. All share the same underlying goal—to involve participants in cooperative projects that respond to human needs and enrich people's lives. Volunteers in such programs are motivated by a sense of commitment, as well as by the rewards of personal and professional growth that derive from this type of work. A sample of such organizations is listed below; a more complete listing is available in the CIEE's book *Volunteer! The Comprehensive Guide to Voluntary Service in the U.S. and Abroad.* Be sure to check the country sections later on in this book for voluntary-service programs specific to a particular country.

- Brethren Volunteer Service is a Christian service program dedicated to advocating justice and peace, as well as serving basic human needs in the U.S. and 18 countries overseas. Volunteers, who must be at least 18 years old, provide a variety of community services, including education, health care, office work, construction, et cetera. Contact Brethren Volunteer Service, 1451 Dundee Avenue, Elgin, IL 60120, for further information.
- The Episcopal Church's Volunteers for Mission acts as a clearinghouse, matching volunteers with projects in the U.S. and abroad. Assignments last from six months to two years and include, teaching, health care, social work, technology, agriculture, et cetera. For further information, contact Volunteers for Mission, Episcopal Church Center, 815 Second Avenue, New York, NY 10017.
- International Christian Youth Exchange (ICYE) offers persons ages 18 to 24 voluntary service opportunities in the fields of health care, education, environment, construction, et cetera. The one-year program has homestay and academic credit options; scholarships are also available. Service opportunities are offered in Australia, Austria, Belgium, Brazil, Bolivia, China, Colombia, Costa Rica, Denmark, Finland, France, West Germany, Ghana, Honduras, Iceland, Italy, Japan, Kenya, South Korea, Liberia, Mexico, New Zealand, Nigeria, Norway, Poland, Sierra Leone, Spain, Sweden, Switzerland, and the United Kingdom. For more information, contact International Christian Youth Exchange, 134 West 26th Street, New York, NY 10001.
- The International Liaison of Lay Volunteers in Mission is the official center for the U.S. Catholic Church's promotion, referral, and recruitment of lay mission volunteers. While it does not have its own voluntary service programs, it does serve as a clearinghouse for others. *The Response*, its free annual publication provides information on over 144 organizations with openings for volunteers in the U.S. and abroad. Write to the International Liaison of Lay Volunteers in Mission, 4121 Harewood Road NE, Washington, DC 20017, or call (800) 543-5046 for further information.
- International Voluntary Services (IVS) is an independent, nonprofit organization that provides skilled and experienced volunteer technicians for projects serving the needs of low-income people in the Third World. The organization recruits internationally for technicians with relevant overseas experience to work with locally based groups in agriculture, health care, business cooperatives, community development, and water resources. IVS volunteers serve a minimum of two years and receive an "allowance package" to cover the costs of food, housing, and local travel; benefits include life and health insurance, an education allowance for families with school-age children, and round-trip transportation to the country of assignment. Contact International Vol-

untary Services, Recruitment, 1424 16th Street NW, #204, Washington, DC 20036.
- The Mennonite Central Committee (MCC) offers overseas programs that enable volunteers with skills in agriculture, rural development, public-health education, water development, and appropriate technology to serve in about 50 countries in Asia, Africa, Latin and North America. In most cases a college degree is essential, along with a desire to do Christian service work. A three-year commitment is required for overseas placements; a two-year commitment is required for service in North America. MCC also offers the Youth Discovery Team Program which combines service work with the study of language and culture and the exploration of faith. Three-month to one-year terms are available. For further information on any of MCC's programs, contact MCC, 21 South 12th Street, Akron, PA 17501; (717) 859-1151.
- The Presbyterian Church's Mission Volunteers/International program offers overseas voluntary service opportunities for periods usually ranging from one to two years. Requirements include a B.A./B.S. degree and membership in the church. The *Mission Service Opportunities* bulletin, published through the MV office, lists information about positions available. Contact the Mission Volunteers/International, Recruitment Office, Presbyterian Church (USA), 100 Witherspoon Street, Louisville, KY 40202-1396.
- The YMCA World Service Worker program provides participants with a two-year internship position working with YMCAs in Africa, Asia, and Latin America. Typical assignments are in community development, youth programs, physical education, recreation, camping, and teaching English as a foreign language. Transportation, health and life insurance, retirement, room and board, and a stipend are provided. Applicants must be college graduates with relevant experience and skills, and must be sponsored by a local U.S. YMCA. For more information, contact Overseas Personnel Programs, YMCA of the USA, 101 North Wacker Drive, Chicago, IL 60606; (312) 977-0031. Note: At press time this program was under review and may not be continued.

For volunteer teaching opportunities see the "Teaching Positions" section later in this chapter.

Service-Learning

You may also want to consider an interesting, relatively new opportunity which combines the concept of voluntary service with academic credit. In the words of Howard Berry, founder of an organization called The Partnership for Service-Learning, "Service-learning is a powerful union of two traditional goals, academic study and service to the world. Through service-learning programs for a semester, a summer, or a year, college students or recent graduates may continue formal learning and, at the same time, have the experience of working with others to address human needs."

The Partnership offers programs in England, Ecuador, Jamaica, the Philippines, France, India, Mexico, and South Dakota (with Native Americans). Projects in the fields of health care, education, and community development are available during the academic year, the January interim, and the summer. Students spend from 15 to 25 hours per week in a service capacity while taking a full academic load at the university affiliated with the program. There is an administrative fee covering academic instruction, service placement and supervision, orientation, room, basic board, field trips; air fare is extra. Financial aid and loans usually may be applied to program costs. For more information, contact Partnership for Service-Learning, 815 Second Avenue, Suite 315, New York, NY 10017; (212) 986-0989. Most colleges and universities grant academic credit for participation in the programs of the Partnership for Service-Learning; check with your own institution before applying.

Publications on Voluntary Service

CIEE publishes *Volunteer! The Comprehensive Guide to Voluntary Service in the U.S. and Abroad*, a guide to short-, medium-, and long-term service programs worldwide. Copublished with the Commission on Voluntary Service and Action (CVSA), the book lists over 170 organizations that place participants on voluntary service assignments. Opportunities may last a week, a month, six months, or up to a year or two and range from positions for highly skilled professionals to assignments for people with nothing more than a sincere desire to help. *Volunteer*! costs $8.95 (plus $3.00 for first-class or $1.50 for book-rate postage) and can be ordered directly from CIEE, 205 East 42nd Street, New York, NY 10017.

Another publication on the subject, written primarily for a British audience, is the *International Directory of Voluntary Work*, by David Woodworth. Published by Vacation Work, in England, this book is available from Peterson's Guides, P.O. Box 2123 Princeton, NJ 08543, for $13.95 (paperback) plus $4.75 shipping and handling.

If you're interested in short-term voluntary service, you may want to consult *Volunteer Vacations*, by Bill McMillon. Revised and expanded in 1989, this book includes opportunities in the U.S. and overseas. Available from Chicago Review Press, Inc., 814 North Franklin Street, Chicago, Illinois 60610, for $11.95 plus $3 shipping and handling.

TEACHING ABROAD

Teaching is perhaps the most common way that Americans have found to support themselves during extended stays overseas. Teaching opportunities range from informally teaching English as a private tutor to working as an intern, aide, or regular teacher in a public school abroad; from volunteering to teach in a Third World country to working as a regular faculty member in an "American" school abroad. Other long-term employment possibilities are discussed later in this chapter.

Teaching English

Most American college graduates possess a skill that's in demand throughout the world: They know how to speak English. Today, for mostly economic reasons, English is being used as an international language more than ever before, and more and more people are being encouraged to learn it. New English-language schools are popping up all over Europe and Asia. Private companies conduct in-house language classes for their staff. And families look for tutors for their children. Most Americans, as native speakers, can easily find work teaching English overseas.

If you want to stay in a foreign city for an extended amount of time, teaching English privately to individual students or groups is a good way to support yourself and meet people as well. Of course, this is true only if you are staying in an area where people can afford the luxury of private lessons. Some countries, such as Japan, maintain a very high demand for teachers. Opportunities in individual countries will be mentioned later in the appropriate chapters, but in general the best way to contact would-be students is to post notices on university bulletin boards and in English language bookstores.

Your university's career development office may have information on overseas companies or language institutes in need of recent college graduates to fill teaching positions. You can also look through the want ads in foreign English language newspapers. Arranging employment before you go gives you the security of a legal work permit. The other route, finding work after arrival, may leave you little option but to teach privately without legal authorization. In fact, however, teaching privately is often more profitable than teaching for an institute or business. On the other hand, it is less secure. Schools and companies maintain different standards for their teachers. Many do not require certification in Teaching of English as a Foreign Language (TOEFL), but most prefer some teaching experience. It's a good idea anyway to gain some experience before you leap into teaching, even if you're planning only to teach informal conversation. Consider volunteer work in your university community before you go abroad.

If you have a degree in Teaching of English as a Second or Other Language (TESOL), your chances of finding well-paying overseas positions are enhanced. Every two months an organization called Teachers of English to Speakers of Other Languages publishes the *TESOL Placement Bulletin*, a list of opportunities for people trained in the field. Most of these jobs require a master's degree and experience in teaching English as a second language. To receive the *Bulletin*, TESOL members should send $12 and nonmembers should send $20 ($18 or $24, respectively, if you want it sent outside the U.S.) to TESOL, 1600 Cameron Street, Suite 300, Alexandria, VA 22314-2751; for more information, call (703) 836-0774.

Through its English Teaching Fellow Program, the U.S. Information Agency (USIA), a federal agency which promotes understanding of the United States overseas, provides job placement abroad for U.S. citizens with master's degrees in TESOL. Teaching Fellows generally serve as full-time teachers of English as a foreign language but may be assigned to materials development, teacher training, or supervisory activities. Most are placed in Latin America and assigned to binational centers—local, independent associations that promote mutual understanding between the people of the U.S. and the people of the host country. Teaching Fellows may be placed in other institutions such as national universities and teacher-training institutes. Contracts are for twelve months with a possibility of one renewal. Salaries vary from one country to another but are sufficient to live modestly on the local economy. Round-trip transportation is provided from the Fellow's U.S. residence; no allowances are provided for dependents. USIA publishes announcements and processes applications for the English Teaching Fellow Program; however, a Fellow is an employee of the binational center or similar local institution rather than of the U.S. government. For further information, contact USIA, English Teaching Fellow Program (E/CE), Room 304, 301 4th Street SW, Washington, DC 20547.

Other Teaching Positions Abroad

If you like the idea of getting teaching experience abroad by doing volunteer work, AFS Intercultural Programs sponsors programs in Chile, Thailand, and the U.S.S.R. While living with a host family, volunteers give presentations on American culture, and assist with the teaching of English. Programs in Chile and Thailand take place during July and August for seven weeks; in the U.S.S.R. from October to December for ten weeks. For further information, contact AFS Intercultural Programs, 313 East 43rd Street, New York, NY 10017; 1-800-AFS-INFO.

WorldTeach, a program of Harvard University's social-service organization, the Phillips Brooks House, has placed over 400 volunteer teachers in Africa, Latin America, Central Europe, and Asia. In 1991–92, volunteer opportunities were available in China, Costa Rica, Namibia, Poland, and Thailand. Most volunteers teach English as a Second Language, but science and math teachers are greatly needed in Namibia. No special language skills or teaching experience are necessary. A bachelor's degree from an accredited college or university and a one-year commitment are required for all programs but the Shanghai Summer Teaching Program, open to undergraduate and graduate students. For further information, contact WorldTeach, Harvard Institute for International Development, One Eliot Street, Cambridge, MA 02138-5705; (617) 495-5527.

If you are a recent college/university graduate interested in teaching but lacking experience, you may want to contact the International School's Internship Program (ISIP). ISIP arranges internships worldwide for graduates who lack teaching degrees. Opportunities are available for ten months on the elementary, junior high, and senior high school levels. Interns receive a cost-of-living stipend and health insurance. Round-trip air fare is paid by the sponsoring institution. For further information, contact the International School Internship Program, PO Box 103, West Bridgewater, MA 02379; (508) 580-1880.

Another teaching program that has employed many American teachers abroad is operated by the Department of Defense. This program maintains approximately 270 elementary, junior high, and senior high schools, along with a community college, in 19 countries for children of U.S. military and civilian personnel overseas. It is responsible for staffing these schools with teachers, counselors, librarians, nurses, psychologists, and social workers. Some of the elementary schools are small, and teachers are required to teach more than one grade; some junior high schools require that you teach two or more subjects. Assignments are for one or two years. The Department of Defense is emphatic that applicants must "agree to accept an assignment to any location throughout the world where a vacancy exists and where their services are needed." For information on openings, write for the latest copy of *Overseas Employment Opportunities for Educators*, to the Department of Defense, Office of Dependents' Schools, Recruitment and Assignment Section, 2461 Eisenhower Avenue, Alexandria, VA 22331-1100.

Teachers interested in positions abroad might find a job opening through the International Schools Services (ISS), a private organization that recruits and recommends personnel for American and international schools abroad. At present, ISS serves over 200 schools in Africa, Europe, Asia, Latin America, and the Middle East. Applicants must have a bachelor's degree and have at least two years of current experience either at the elementary or secondary level. There is a $50 registration fee and an additional fee if the candidate is placed. For information on registration procedures, contact ISS, 15 Roszell Road, PO Box 5910, Princeton, NJ 08543. ISS also publishes a directory of American schools abroad, the *Directory of Overseas Schools* ($29.95). It is distributed by Peterson's Guides, PO Box 2123, Princeton, NJ 08543.

Teacher Exchanges

The U.S. Information Agency also operates a teacher-exchange program open to elementary- and secondary-school teachers, college instructors, and professors. Participating countries include Argentina, Belgium, Bulgaria, Canada, Chile, Colombia, Cyprus, Czechoslovakia, Denmark, Egypt, Finland, France, Germany, Hungary, Iceland, Italy, Luxembourg, Mexico, the Netherlands, Norway, the Philippines, Poland, Portugal, Senegal, South Africa, Switzerland, Turkey, the United Kingdom, and the U.S.S.R. Most assignments are for a full academic year. Applicants must be U.S. citizens and have at least a bachelor's degree, three years full-time teaching experience and, often, facility in the language of the host country. In addition, the applicant's school must be willing to accept a teacher from abroad to fill the applicant's position. *Opportunities Abroad for Educators* gives details of the opportunities available under this program for qualified U.S. teachers. Also included in the booklet is information about short-term seminars abroad for teachers. Copies are available from the Fulbright Teacher Exchange Branch, E/ASX, USIA, 301 4th Street SW, Washington, DC 20547. Applications for these positions should be completed by October 15 of the year preceding the assignment.

Teacher exchanges can also be arranged with the help of the nonprofit Faculty Exchange Center (FEC), which was established in 1973 to help college professors and teachers at all levels to exchange positions and/or houses with colleagues at home or abroad. The FEC acts as a clearingahouse, issuing a catalog with the names of instructors, their qualifications, where they want to teach, and whether they're willing to exchange their homes. A house-exchange supplement, which includes geographical preferences and descriptions of the homes to be exchanged, is also available. To be listed in these catalogs, the cost is $25 for one and $35 for both. To register and receive a current directory, send your fee to FEC, 952 Virginia Avenue, Lancaster, PA 17603.

Publications on Teaching Abroad

A good book on the subject of teaching abroad is *Educators' Passport to International Jobs*, written by Rebecca Anthony and Gerald Roe and published by Peterson's Guides. According to the authors, it "can take you from your first tentative daydreams about foreign teaching through a step-by-step process of finding information, learning and applying effective job-seeking skills and strategies, preparing to live abroad and finally returning to stateside employment." The book contains some specific contacts for jobs, but for the most part, concentrates on telling the reader how to prepare a resume, evaluate a job offer, and so on. Available for $4.95 (plus shipping and handling) from Peterson's Guides, PO Box 2123, Princeton, NJ 08543.

Another directory that's useful for those seeking teaching positions abroad is *Schools Abroad of Interest to Americans*. Now in its seventh edition, the book is actually meant to describe over 700 elementary and secondary schools in 125 countries for parents who wish to send their children to a school abroad. The book is available from the publisher, Porter Sargent Publishers, 11 Beacon Street, Boston, MA 02108 ($30 plus $1.75 for postage and handling).

Divided into country-by-country sections, *Teaching English Abroad*, by Susan Griffith, provides an introduction to the range of opportunities available overseas, including training requirements, how to start the job search, and a listing of specific schools which have openings for teaching English as a Second Language. Published by Vacation Work, this book is available from Peterson's Guides, PO Box 2123, Princeton, NJ 08543, for $13.95 plus $4.75 shipping and handling.

Another reference for overseas employment is *The International Educator*, a newspaper dedicated to international education for the elementary-and secondary-level educator. Included are numerous job openings in American and international schools worldwide. A yearly subscription (5 issues) is $25. Contact The International Educator, PO Box 103, West Bridgewater, MA 02379.

LONG-TERM EMPLOYMENT

Finding a long-term job outside the U.S. is not easy. It can be done, and has been done, but it takes a great deal of patience and perseverance. Most governments are extremely strict about the employment of foreigners in their country. In most countries, before a work permit is issued, the employer must convince his or her government that the job being given to a foreign citizen can be done only by that person and that there isn't a local worker who can do the job. What this means is that your chances of getting a job overseas are related directly to the skills you've acquired before you apply. If you're a doctor, nurse, or teacher, you may be needed. If you've had a liberal arts education with little specialization, you have problems.

There are plenty of horror stories about people who have paid substantial fees to employment agencies that lure people with promises of foreign positions and then do absolutely nothing for them. Very often these organizations go unpunished since they word their advertisements cleverly and are careful not to promise anything at all in writing. Your best bet, whether you decide to use an employment agency or not, is to become informed using some of the directories and other resource materials listed in this chapter.

"Personal connections are all-important when looking for work in a foreign environment. Try to build up a list of people you can contact. A letter of introduction can work wonders. Ask your college professors if they have friends abroad who would be willing to meet you."

—Jack Maxson, Albuquerque, New Mexico

Jobs with the U.S. Government

The U.S. Department of State, the U.S. Department of Commerce, the U.S. Department of Agriculture, the U.S. Information Agency, and the Agency for International Development all hire personnel for positions abroad. Overseas assignments are made primarily to the 230 diplomatic and consular posts abroad.

Foreign service officers manage overseas posts and perform political, economic, consular, administrative, and cultural functions. They are selected through a rigorous written and oral examination process. Interested applicants for entry-level foreign service positions in the Department of State, the United States Information Agency, and the Department of Commerce's Foreign Commercial Service should write to the Recruitment Division, Department of State, PO Box 9317, Rosslyn Station, Arlington, VA 22209.

Other departments of the U.S. government also offer positions overseas. Anyone interested in positions abroad with the Department of Agriculture should write to the Department of Agriculture, 14th & Independence Avenue SW, Washington, DC 20520. Those interested in positions overseas with the Agency for International Development (AID) should write to the Agency for International Development, Office of Recruitment, Room 242, SA-1, Washington, DC 20523-0114. Most successful candidates for AID have graduate degrees and several years of relevant work experience.

The Peace Corps is another government agency that offers positions abroad, and although remuneration is not great, a living allowance is provided. Both generalists and specialists are in demand, including health-care workers, civil engineers, industrial arts teachers, architects, accountants, agriculturalists, urban planners, and forestry experts. The Peace Corps requires that participants have either a four-year degree from a college or university, or five years of experience in the field of placement. Volunteers serve for two years with an additional 7 to 14 weeks of training, including intensive language, cultural, and technical studies. The living allowance corresponds to what the volunteer's counterpart in the host country would earn. In addition, a readjustment allowance of $200 per month is payable upon completion of service. Applications for Peace Corps positions are available from Peace Corps, Public Response Unit, 1990 K Street NW, Washington, DC 20526, or by calling (202) 606-3000.

Jobs with International Organizations

There are many nongovernmental organizations that are active worldwide and that hire U.S. citizens for posts abroad. Included are organizations like the American Red Cross and CARE. Their needs and requirements are as varied as the organizations themselves. The best way to investigate employment possibilities in this category is to find out what organizations of this type exist. Check your library for a copy of the most recent edition of the three-volume *Encyclopedia of Associations*, published by Gale Research Company. This reference work contains one of the most complete and best annotated listings of organizations in the United States; check especially the "Public Affairs" and "Foreign Interest" listings.

Designed for current or recent students, the *ODN Development Opportunities Catalog* lists opportunities with U.S.-based international development organizations. The Overseas Development Network (ODN) is a nonprofit national student organization which, in its own words, "joins students and communities in addressing the fundamental issues of global poverty and injustice." The 1991 catalog was available for $10 ($7 for students; $15 for institutions) plus $2.50 for postage. For information about the 1992 catalog, write the Overseas Development Network, 333 Valencia Street, Suite 330, San Francisco, CA 94103.

Another source of information on long- or short-term employment opportunities with international development organizations is the *Job Opportunities Bulletin*, published by TransCentury, a consulting group based in Washington, DC that recruits highly qualified people to work in the Third World on various development projects. A year's subscription to the *Bulletin* (six issues) is $25 in the U.S. and $40 overseas. For information, write to TransCentury, 1724 Kalorama Road NW, Washington, DC 20009.

Jobs in International Business

U.S. companies seldom hire people for overseas positions unless the person has already had considerable experience living and working in that country. If an overseas job is not filled by a person with this type of experience, it is almost always filled by someone who has been working for the company for a number of years in the U.S. Generally, a company will take very few risks on untried personnel in overseas positions. If you'd like to work for a bank or some other international business operation, you might have to resign yourself first to serving a few years on U.S. soil. Be sure, though, that your employer knows that you'd eventually like to go abroad.

If you want to apply for business positions abroad, a useful publication is the three-volume *Directory of American Firms Operating in Foreign Countries*. It describes some 3,000 U.S. corporations with more than 22,500 subsidiaries and affiliates in 122 countries. The *Directory* is published by World Trade Academy Press Inc., 50 East 42nd Street, Suite 509, New York, NY 10017, and is available in most college as well as many public libraries. Many foreign embassies also put out lists of the U.S. companies that have branches in their country.

Jobs in the Health Professions

People with health-related skills are probably the most in demand throughout the world. The American Nurses Association, a member of the International Council of Nurses, can provide limited information to registered nurses interested in professional visits or work abroad. For information, contact Careers, American Nurses Association, 2420 Pershing Road, Kansas City, MO 64108.

The American Medical Student Association (AMSA) sponsors an international partnership program in community-based medical education, linking select medical schools in the U.S. with those in Mexico, Central America, and the Caribbean. For further information contact the AMSA Foundation, 1890 Preston White Drive, Reston, VA 22091.

A useful publication for dental personnel is *Suggestions for U.S. Dentists Seeking Employment Abroad*, available free from the American Dental Association, Office of International Affairs, 211 East Chicago Avenue, Chicago, IL 60611. *Overseas Demand for Dental Personnel and Materials: Directory of Programs*, is available from the same office. This publications is free to members of the ADA; for nonmembers the charge is $10.

Publications on Long-Term Employment

You may want to begin by reading *International Careers: An Insider's Guide* (1987), by David Win. In this guide, the author provides advice on how to build an international career and transfer your skills into the international employment market. Included are descriptions of the public and private sectors, U.S. and foreign governments, and international trade and businesses. Available for $10.95 (plus $2 postage) from Williamson Publishing Co., PO Box 185, Charlotte, VT 05445.

The *International Employment Hotline* is a monthly newsletter providing current jobs and advice for "career" international job seekers. Published since 1980, a year's subscription is $36; contact International Employment Hotline, PO Box 3030, Oakton, VA 22124.

A useful booklet that realistically covers all of the possibilities for long-term employment is *Employment Abroad: Facts and Fallacies*. The major considerations involved in seeking employment overseas are discussed. It's available for $7.50 from U.S. Chamber of Commerce, International Division, 1615 H Street NW, Washington, DC 20062.

The *Guide to Careers in World Affairs*, published by the Foreign Policy Association, is a paperback that presents more than 250 listings of some of the best sources of international employment in business, government, and nonprofit organizations. Published in 1987, it is available for $10.95 from the Foreign Policy Association, 729 Seventh Avenue, New York, NY 10019. At press time a new edition was being compiled. Contact the Foreign Policy Association for publication date (tentative date: fall, 1991).

Another source of information on the subject is *International Jobs: Where They Are, How to Get Them* (1989), by Eric Kocher, published by Addison-Wesley, Route 128, Reading, MA 01867 ($12.95). Aimed at college students, this book begins by offering a strategy for job-hunting abroad and then gives a listing of international businesses and organizations that might have openings. The second part is all quite general; don't take the title too literally.

The Overseas List: Opportunities for Living and Working in Developing Countries (1985), by David M. Beckmann, Timothy J. Mitchell, and Linda L. Powers is for those looking for a job in the Third World. Written especially for Christians who are interested in service work, this book includes information on teaching, journalism, commerce, and government employment. It describes opportunities for salaried work and volunteering in Asia, Africa, or Latin America. Though the book is slightly dated, the organizations described are still worth contacting. Published by Augsburg Fortress, 426 South Fifth Street, Box 1209, Minneapolis, MN 55440, this book is available for $13.95 plus postage and handling.

The *Directory of Work and Study in Developing Countries* (1990), by David Leppard, is divided into three parts: work, voluntary work, and study. Described are nonprofit organizations, employment agencies, government offices, educational institutions, and business firms that provide opportunities for work, study, or voluntary service in the Third World. It's available from the publisher, Vacation Work, 9 Park End Street, Oxford OX1 1HJ, United Kingdom, for £7.95, plus £1.50 for surface mail shipping to the U.S. Checks should be made out in British pounds and payable to Vacation Work.

CHAPTER FOUR
STUDYING ABROAD

> "*Responsibility and awareness confront you head on. You develop new qualities, refine some, and get rid of others. And through it all, you become much more globally aware and culturally sensitive.*"
> —Stacey M. Coito, Turlock, California

There was a time not all that long ago when study abroad was the exclusive privilege of the rich. Now, for many reasons, study abroad has become a possibility for all—and the opportunities are boundless. The number of American students studying abroad continues to grow; figures gathered from colleges and universities across the U.S. indicate that more than 60,000 U.S. undergraduate students study abroad each year. Why do they choose to pursue part of their education overseas? A survey commissioned by CIEE in the mid-1980s indicates that nearly one-fifth of the participants in study programs abroad sponsored by U.S. institutions said career goals influenced their decision; many felt an overseas experience would add a new dimension to their schooling, improve foreign-language skills, and help them to become more independent. Of Americans preparing for a second trip abroad, the survey found that as a result of their first international experience "an overwhelming number became more interested in international events, saw an improvement in academic performance, and became more self-confident."

The experience of living and studying abroad is one that enhances understanding, helping people see beyond their own world views to empathize with and really comprehend other cultures. In fact, it was the belief that international understanding would promote peace and stability that brought about the formation of CIEE shortly after the end of the Second World War. Today, in addition to the goal of achieving international peace and understanding, less lofty concerns about the United States' international competitiveness in the global arena of business and finance prompt leaders in business, government, and education to emphasize the need for enhanced foreign-language training and improved international education.

Like everything else, studying abroad means different things to different people. To one student it may mean a three-week course in French culture on the Riviera during July, while for another it may mean a year of research on a doctoral thesis in the stacks of a German library. First, you'll have to decide what kind of study experience you want. Your choice will depend on things like your field of interest, your capabilities (particularly language skills), the amount of time available to you, and the amount of money you can afford to spend. You should also ask yourself: Am I independent and outgoing? Serious and academic? How organized and academically focused am I? How hesitant am I about going out on my own?

Be certain to talk with your academic adviser or with your school's study-abroad adviser early in your planning. Your adviser will help you decide what kind of study-abroad experience you want, evaluate program possibilities, and arrange for credit transfers and the continuation of any financial-aid packages you might be receiving. If you don't have a study-abroad or academic adviser, make an effort to speak with your school's admissions officer, registrar, or dean of students for help and assistance. Other good sources of practical information are foreign students or students who have returned from study abroad.

Also, think ahead to the time of your return to your home, friends, and school. There's a phenomenon in foreign travel that some have termed "culture shock." The process of preparing for a trip and then leaving behind the customs and values familiar to you, as well as family and friends, can be very difficult. In addition, while overseas, you may find that you change your outlook about many important things. This may include changing goals—both personal and educational. Depending on the length and type of experience you have had, you may find readjustment to your old life somewhat trying.

"Study abroad provides more than just immediate learning opportunities. After you return to your home, you will begin to examine systems, practices, cultural norms, and many other concepts you previously took for granted. You will begin to make comparisons between these practices and those you experienced during your travel abroad. You will learn just as much about your own country as you did about the country you visited."
—Marilyn Helms, Chattanooga, Tennessee

STUDY-ABROAD OPTIONS

Once you have set your personal and academic goals, you need to look at all the different types of programs available to you. Should you enroll directly in a university abroad or should you participate in the study-abroad program of a U.S. institution? Do you want to be integrated into classes with regular students at the university or in classes specially designed for foreigners? Below are discussed the basic program models for study abroad and the advantages and disadvantages of each.

Enrollment in a Foreign University

Direct enrollment in a foreign university can be an exacting venture, and is best suited to the independent and highly motivated individuals who already have experience living abroad and are fluent in the language of the country where they plan to study. Others will probably need the support system of a program sponsored by a U.S. institution (see the following section).

Students considering enrolling directly in a university overseas should be well aware that university systems and teaching methods in other countries are very different from those in the United States. For one thing, students entering a university in Europe are, generally speaking, at about the same educational level as juniors in a U.S. college or university. This generally makes it impossible for a U.S. freshman or sophomore to enroll in a university abroad except in a special program of some kind.

Because of the differences between higher education systems from country to country, credit is not easily transferred from a foreign university to a U.S. university. Students who want to transfer credit earned at an institution abroad to a university in the United States should try to make an arrangement with the U.S. institution *before* going abroad. In general, this is a somewhat risky business; many American students return to the States to find that their home institution will not give them full credit for courses taken at a foreign university.

"The biggest hassle I encountered was registration at my university. There is no method to the madness and even French students haven't quite figured it out. Just relax—the bureaucracy is slow. That's normal. Try to stay calm and realize that things will eventually work out."
—Charlotte Gerstner, Metairie, Louisiana

Besides the problems of adapting to another educational system and transferring credit, there is also the problem of language. Study-abroad advisers at U.S. institutions report that a number of students without proficiency in a foreign language ask about the possibilities of direct enrollment at universities where the language of instruction is not English. According to one adviser: "The fact of the matter is that most Americans do not have sufficient foreign-language skills to qualify for enrollment as a regular student at foreign universities in non-English-speaking countries. Many Americans grossly underestimate the time it takes to acquire the proficiency in a foreign language necessary to follow a formal lecture, take notes, participate in class discussions and then compete on tests on an equal footing with those students who are native speakers of the language."

Special Courses for International Students at Foreign Universities

Instead of enrolling in regular university courses, you may find it easier to enroll in some of the special courses many universities abroad offer foreigners, which usually include language classes and courses in the history and culture of the country. Some of these courses are taught during the academic year but most are given during the summer when foreign universities usually suspend their regular classes. Your classmates will be students from around the world, but not local students. For these courses you won't be expected to be completely fluent in the language and already knowledgeable about the country's history, literature, and culture. However, as indirect enrollment in regular university classes, credit for these courses is granted by the foreign university and may not be readily accepted by a U.S. university. Students who want to transfer credit to a university in the United States should try to make arrangements before going abroad.

The two best sources to consult for this kind of program are *Vacation Study Abroad* and *Academic Year Abroad*, both published by the Institute of International Education (see "For More Information" near the end of this chapter). Also be sure to talk with the study-abroad adviser at your school.

Study-Abroad Programs of U.S. Colleges and Universities

Due to the challenges of direct enrollment in a foreign university, most Americans studying abroad choose a program sponsored by a U.S. institution instead. American colleges and universities sponsor hundreds of these programs. In fact, you should first check to see whether your own school sponsors an overseas program or is a member of a consortium (an association of colleges and universities) that sponsors such a program. Going abroad with your own university will ease the problems of transferring academic credit and maintaining any scholarships or loans you might have.

It's possible, though, that your college may not sponsor the type of program that you are looking for. If this is the case, don't be discouraged. Of the hundreds of colleges and universities that sponsor overseas-study programs, most accept students from other campuses. In fact, there are so many programs to choose from that selecting a course from the listings in *Work, Study, Travel Abroad* or one of the other books described later in this chapter can be a formidable task. Of course, you'll eliminate many of them after taking into consideration such things as language requirements, cost, academic focus, and whether or not your own school will grant academic credit for them. In making your selection, be sure to consult the office on your own campus that advises students on foreign study or administers your school's foreign-study programs. People in this office may be personally familiar with some of the programs you are considering and might also be able to direct you to students on campus who were participants at an earlier time.

Programs sponsored by American institutions grant academic credit that is usually quite easy to transfer to your home college or university, but there may still be problems. To be absolutely sure, have your courses approved for credit by your college or university before you commit yourself to a program.

The study-abroad programs of U.S. colleges and universities encompass a wide range of program types. In many programs you can enroll in the regular courses of a university abroad. Others place students in the courses for foreigners offered by a college or university abroad. Often special courses are designed by the U.S. institution that are taught by a regular member of the school's faculty. Most of the study-abroad programs of U.S. colleges and universities involve a mix of options that can be adjusted to the individual's needs and language abilities.

Study-Abroad Programs of Other U.S. Organizations

In addition to colleges and universities, there are a number of other U.S. organizations that also offer study-abroad programs. One option you may want to consider is enrolling in a study-abroad program offered not by an individual college or university but by a consortium of colleges and universities. Examples of organizations that offer study-abroad programs on behalf of their member colleges and universities are the Great Lakes College Association, the Associated Colleges of the Midwest, and the Council on International Educational Exchange. In a program sponsored by a consortium of colleges and universities, one or more of the participating colleges grant academic credit. As with any study-abroad program, be sure to check on the transfer of credit at your school before you sign up. However, programs sponsored by consortia of colleges and universities are really no different from those sponsored by an individual college and university; the same advantages and disadvantages apply (see previous section). In the country and regional sections later in this book, you'll find listed all the study programs of CIEE-member institutions, both individual schools and consortia of colleges and universities.

There are a handful of other U.S. organizations that offer study-abroad programs similar to those offered by U.S. colleges and universities. If you are considering a study-abroad program offered by an organization other than a college or university (or consortium of colleges and universities), make sure you ascertain whether the organization is a nonprofit educational institution or a profit-making company. If you are considering a program offered by a for-profit organization, it is especially important to look into credit transfer in advance; most U.S. colleges and universities transfer credits only from other nonprofit educational institutions. All study programs listed in this book are offered by nonprofit educational institutions.

American Colleges Abroad

Another possibility for U.S. students is to study at one of the "American" colleges and universities that have been established abroad. Two of the better-known institutions of this type are the American University in Cairo and Sophia University in Japan. Organized like U.S. institutions, these universities generally host an international student body and offer a varied curriculum. You can enroll for a term or a year and transfer credits to your home institution, or you can enroll in a regular degree program offered by the school. Since most of these American colleges abroad are accredited by the same institutions that accredit colleges and universities in the United States, you shouldn't have much trouble transferring credit. However, be sure to check on credit transfer before you leave.

Some of these U.S-style institutions abroad have a student body made up largely of Americans. Others, however, designed to give local students the option of obtaining an American-style education in their own country, are composed mainly of nationals of the country where they are located. More information on these schools is available in two publications of the Institute of International Education: *Vacation Study Abroad* and *Academic Year Abroad* (see "For More Information" near the end of this chapter).

SELECTING A PROGRAM

Once you have decided to study abroad, many factors will enter into your decision of which specific program is best for you. Two of the most important factors, the type of program and the length of program, are discussed in this section.

Type of Program

One of the first things you will have to consider is what types of courses are provided? Does the program provide American-style courses or does it utilize the regular courses of a foreign university? Some programs, at one extreme, export U.S. professors to teach the same courses they would teach at home (in English, of course); others enroll their students in the large lecture classes typical of foreign universities. In between are a range of compromises: American-style courses taught by foreign professors (some in English, some in the language of the visiting professor); special courses set up by the foreign university for all of their foreign students (occasionally in English); or regular courses with tutorial assistance provided by students from the university. Some programs offer several of these options. Decide what's best for you. Students with language competence and good academic skills may profit most by enrollment in the regular courses of a foreign university where they will meet students of the host country and experience its university system firsthand. Students with more limited language skills or academic backgrounds may be wise to seek a program offering special classes for Americans or other foreigners.

Also of major importance is the question of how much the living arrangements provided as part of the program will involve you in the social life of the students of the host country. In this area, too, U.S.-sponsored programs provide a range of possibilities. Some programs arrange for all U.S. students to live together in a hotel or dormitory; others house participants in university dormitories with students from the host country. Still others provide housing in rented rooms or in private homes. Students living with foreign families may face particular difficulties in adapting to a different family setting, but in general they will acquire a better understanding of the host country and its language.

Of course, there are some personal considerations to take into account as well. How do you feel about the size of the institution? Would you prefer studying in a major city or in a more rural setting? And last (but certainly not least), what should you expect to spend in the way of daily living expenses?

Each section devoted to a specific country later in this book contains listings, by subject area, of study programs for undergraduate and graduate students. These programs are sponsored by member colleges, universities, and organizations of the Council on International Educational Exchange. Addresses for the institutions offering these programs appear in Appendix I.

"Develop a plan or focus for your studies, but don't let it restrict you. Have certain goals to guide you or you'll be overcome by all the possibilities and opportunities. An abstract of your goals or a series of questions you want answered by your studies is a good start."

—Dee Redwine, Plano, Texas

"Live with a family that has children. You'll learn more of the language and there's no better way to understand a culture than to see how children are brought up. Best of all, you'll never be bored."

—Gary Lemons, Albuquerque, New Mexico

Length of Program

How long will you be studying abroad? A summer, a semester, or a full academic year? Or maybe a month during the winter-term break?

There are a number of factors students should consider in deciding how long to study abroad: timely fulfillment of graduation requirements; pertinence of courses to a particular field of study; degree of strain placed upon personal financial resources; and personal maturity and independence. It is generally assumed that the traditional year abroad (usually at the junior-year level) is the most beneficial. A growing number of students are participating in more than one study-abroad program during their college career, often going for a summer or other short-term experience initially, and later for a semester or year abroad. It should be pointed out, however, that many programs do not accept college freshmen.

A semester or academic year of study abroad will give you enough time to become involved in the student life of the country. It can also give you enough time to get miserably homesick. After all, being away from home and friends for six months or a year and having to cope with the pressure of another academic system doesn't appeal to everyone. On the other hand, periods of homesickness or alienation are often inevitable phases in the process of expanding one's cultural awareness. Most students abroad feel that this experience makes them stronger and passes away in time.

"Don't depend on your work or school program to do everything for you. Strike out on your own and do something."
—Dee Redwine, Plano, Texas

If you can't, or don't want to, interrupt your regular course of studies and go abroad for a semester or year, a summer program might be best for you. An extraordinary variety of opportunities is available. You can study journalism in London, botany in Brazil, or archaeology in Israel. Taking a summer course might also be a good way to find out whether you would like to study abroad for a longer period of time.

More and more colleges and universities have switched to calendars that have an "interim" period between terms. During the interim, usually in January between the fall and spring semesters, students can select one of a variety of programs, many of which involve an off-campus experience. An example of an interim program might be an architecture tour in which participants spend a week attending classes in London and the rest of the time in an organized "tour" studying important works of architecture in several countries of Europe. Classes are usually taught by professors from the sponsoring school. Students can join such programs arranged either by their own or another school.

In the country sections of this book, we've arranged the listings into two broad groups: (1) semester and academic-year programs and (2) summer programs. You'll find interim programs—although they are short-term in character—listed in the "Semester and Academic Year" section, since they take place at various times during the school year.

Evaluating a Program

Once you've decided to join a study-abroad program, you'll soon discover how many there are to choose from. Chances are that at first they will all sound good to you—and probably most of them are. But there are some that will not suit your purposes and some that are just not worth the money. Unfortunately, there have been incidents in which students have enrolled in programs only to find, on the eve of their trip, that the organization has disbanded and there is no program. The U.S. Information Agency often receives complaints from people who have found themselves taking courses of limited academic value as well as complaints from students who have discovered, too late, that they had paid fees far exceeding the value of the services received. Often, if the right questions had been asked *before* the student committed his or her time and money, the disappointments would have been avoided.

Lily von Klemperer, one of the pioneers in the field of study abroad, wrote a useful guide entitled "How to Read Study Abroad Literature." We have borrowed most of what follows in this section on evaluating a program from this now-classic article.

Spend Your Summer in Sunny Spain!

(1) Live in a Medieval Castle or with a Local Family
(2) Learn Spanish at a Renowned Academic Institution
(3) Outstanding Faculty

(4) International Student Body
(5) Academic Credit Available
(6) Limited Enrollment—All Ages Eligible
(7) All-Inclusive Charge
(8) Write to the Director of Admissions, PO Box 000, Cambridge, MA

Above is the text of an imaginary advertisement. How does this program sound? Let's take this mock advertisement line by line and see what it really does and does not say.

First, the emphasis seems to be on spending the summer in sunny Spain. Not an unappealing idea, of course, but if your objective is to learn the language, how will that be accomplished? How serious does the program sound if it uses as its "hook" a travel brochure's view of Spain?

Line 1: A medieval castle sounds great, but how close is it to the place where you will study or to town? Are there places to eat nearby? It may be a castle, but how has it been converted? Will you sleep in a dorm with six other students? And what about the host family? Is it going to turn out, in fact, to be someone who simply wants to make some extra money by having an American boarder?

Line 2: Just what is this famous university? Why isn't it named? Foreign universities *do not* have regular classes during the summer, so what is probably referred to here is a special course for foreigners—not a regular university class. Whenever the ad or brochure uses the words "recognized" or "accredited" to describe a learning institution, find out exactly who does the recognizing or accrediting, and what are the criteria used.

Line 3: This reference to outstanding faculty needs to be explained carefully in any brochure. Their names, titles, and affiliation should be given. This phrase is much too vague.

Line 4: Get specifics on this. The students who are categorized as "international" may actually be sons and daughters of U.S. parents working abroad. Find out how many countries are really represented.

Line 5: This vague reference to credit is of little use, since the transfer of credit is such an individual matter. Whether or not you can get credit where you want it is something that only you can determine. You should, however, ask the sponsor to give you a list of institutions that have granted credit for the program in the past. This will be excellent ammunition if you need to approach your own guidance counselor or academic dean to request credit.

Line 6: How selective is this organization? What are the standards for limited enrollment? Are there, indeed, standards? And if all ages are eligible, how will you like being together with people much younger or older than you? If some are working for credit and others aren't, will that affect the seriousness of the work?

Line 7: "Inclusive charge" is much too vague. This is where the small print comes in. Find out exactly what is included and get an estimate of the total expenses, whether or not they are included.

Line 8: The actual name of a responsible person would be better here. When the backup brochure arrives, it should list (besides the director of faculty) a board of advisers, trustees, and so on. Don't let the Cambridge address mislead you into assuming that the program is affiliated with Harvard. Remember that anyone can get a post-office box anywhere.

We obviously aren't able to give you an absolute qualitative framework for evaluating a program. In the final analysis, you have to decide what's best for the goals you have identified for yourself. We do suggest that you judge whether the costs of any particular program seem fair and representative of the course offerings and objectives. If you have questions, ask a study-abroad adviser if he or she has heard about the program.

SCHOLARSHIPS, LOANS, AND FELLOWSHIPS

You may be surprised to learn that study abroad (transportation included) is not necessarily more expensive than study in the United States. In fact, studying in many Third World countries, where the U.S. dollar generally has more purchasing power than it does at home, may even be cheaper than studying at your own institution.

Your school may be willing to apply your regular scholarship or loans to the cost of study abroad. Check with your academic dean or financial-aid office. And if cost factors are important to you, remember that your tuition costs may be lower if you apply for programs available through public universities in the state of which you are a resident.

The U.S. Department of Education's Office of Student Financial Assistance administers five financial-aid programs for students who are enrolled at least half-time in a regular program of study at a school that participates in the programs. The programs are the Pell Grant, the Supplemental Educational Opportunity Grant, the College Work-Study Program, the Perkins Loans, and the Guaranteed Student Loan Program. A student attending a foreign school may receive aid from one of these programs in most cases if that school is affiliated with an eligible institution located in the United States. Students attending school abroad may receive guaranteed student loans if they are attending an eligible foreign institution. To find out if a particular school is eligible, contact that school's financial-aid office.

A good source of information on how to apply all types of scholarship, loan, and grant programs to overseas study is *Financial Aid for Study Abroad*, edited by Stephen Cooper, William W. Cressey, and Nancy K. Stubbs. While not a listing of individual scholarships and grants, the book provides general information and discusses the application of financial resources provided through major government and private programs to study abroad. It's available for $6.95 from NAFSA—Association of International Educators, 1860 19th Street NW, Washington, DC 20009; (202) 462-4811.

CIEE's International Student Identity Card Fund, financed with revenues from the sale of the International Student Identity Card, provides travel grants to high-school and college students planning a study or service experience in a Third World country. Applicants must be sponsored by a nonprofit organization or educational institution. Applicants must be students at a CIEE-member institution or planning to participate in a program sponsored by a CIEE-member institution. Awards are made twice a year. Application deadlines are October 31 and March 31. For information, contact CIEE, Information and Student Services Department, 205 East 42nd Street, New York, NY 10017.

While there are only a limited number of scholarships set aside for undergraduates who wish to study abroad, a greater number of grants are available to graduate students. *Fulbright and Other Grants for Graduate Study Abroad*, a free brochure put out each year in May by the Institute of International Education (IIE), describes fellowships and scholarships administered by that organization. This 96-page booklet includes grants offered by foreign governments, universities, corporate and private donors, as well as U.S. government grants for graduate study funded under the Fulbright-Hays Act. Application deadlines for these awards are not until the following October; the period for which these grants apply begins in the next academic year. Write to U.S. Student Programs, Institute of International Education, 809 United Nations Plaza, New York, NY 10017, or call (212) 984-5330.

In New York City, a good place to do research on all kinds of foundation grants is the information library at The Foundation Center, open to the public for free. The library, at 79 Fifth Avenue, is open 10 A.M. to 5 P.M., Monday through Friday (Wednesday until 8 P.M.). The next best thing to being there, however, is to look through the Center's directory, *Foundation Grants to Individuals*, a listing of grants, updated in 1991. This book is available for $40 (plus $3 shipping and handling) from The Foundation Center, 79 Fifth Avenue, New York, NY 10003-3050; (212) 620-4230. Another excellent source of information on fellowships and scholarships is the Information Center of the Institute of International Education (see page 40).

A number of directories—usually available in college and university libraries—provide information on specific scholarships, grants, and fellowships available for study abroad. However, most of the scholarships and grants in the directories listed below are available only at the graduate level:

- A comprehensive information source on the subject is *Financial Resources for International Study*, which lists hundreds of grants, fellowships, and awards available to U.S. nationals for study and research abroad at all academic levels. Compiled in 1989 by IIE, this directory is available for $36.95 (plus $5.75 shipping and handling) from the publisher, Peterson's Guides, PO Box 2123, Princeton, NJ 08543.
- *The Grants Register 1991–93* offers a detailed compendium of graduate-level awards offered for study, research, and training for nationals of all countries. Compiled by Ronald Tunner and published by St. Martin's Press, it costs $85.
- *The International Scholarship Book*, edited by Daniel Cassidy and recently updated by Prentice-Hall in 1990, provides a comprehensive list of scholarships, grants, and internships available in the public and private sector for study in dozens of countries. The author states that $6.6 billion in funds from corporations is unclaimed, "not because people were unqualified, but because no one knew where to look." The cost of the book is $22.95.
- *Study Abroad* is an international directory of fellowships, scholarships, and awards that can be applied to study and travel opportunities in over 100 countries. The 1992–93 edition, produced by UNESCO, is available from UNIPUB, 4611-F Assembley Drive, Lanham, MD 20706-4391. It costs $24 (order # U7154).
- *Fellowships, Scholarships, and Related Opportunities in International Education* is published by the Center for International Education, 201 Anaconda Court, University of Tennessee, Knoxville, TN 37996-0620. The cost of the most recent edition (1989) is $10 including postage; make checks payable to the University of Tennessee.
- The seventh edition (1989) of the *Fellowship Guide for Western Europe* is available from the Council for European Studies, Box 44 Schermerhorn Hall, Columbia University, New York, NY 10027. The cost is $8 (make checks payable to Columbia University).

A special note for veterans: Many university-sponsored study-abroad programs are open to veterans, in-service students, or eligible dependents. The Department of Veterans Affairs (VA) awards educational assistance for the pursuit of an approved program leading to a degree at an institution of higher learning. Additional information may be obtained at VA regional offices located in each state, or from the Director, Education Services (22), Department of Veterans Affairs, 810 Vermont Avenue NW, Washington, DC 20420.

FOR FURTHER INFORMATION

There are several places to go for additional information on study abroad. Start on your campus with the study abroad adviser or international programs office. Also of assistance might be the placement office, the dean's office, or the library. One of the best and most often overlooked sources of study information on any given country is that country's embassy or consular offices in the U.S. Most of these offices will provide, at no charge, lists of the specific courses available to you and instructions on how to go about enrolling in them. Addresses of representatives of foreign governments and the titles of useful information packets are included in the individual country chapters later in this book.

If you are in or near New York City, you may want to stop at the Information Center of the Institute of International Education (IIE), 809 United Nations Plaza, open Monday through Friday (except major holidays) from 10 A.M. to 4 P.M. Volunteers will assist you in utilizing the extensive resources of the Center, which include books, brochures, and audiovisual materials.

Publications on Study Abroad

The most comprehensive guide to study programs outside the U.S. open to Americans is *Academic Year Abroad*. Updated annually, this book by IIE lists, country by country, nearly 1,900 semester and academic-year study programs abroad for undergraduates and graduates. Full of necessary information on each program, this directory also offers guidelines for choosing a program, and with five indexes is very easy to use. The cost is $31.95 (plus $3 shipping and handling). Write to IIE Books, 809 United Nations Plaza, New York, NY 10017.

The companion volume to the book above is *Vacation Study Abroad*, also published annually by IIE. It includes information on 1,400 programs abroad that are open to U.S. students. Most take place during the summer but short-term programs at other times of the year, including the January interim and spring break, are also included. The cost is $26.95 (plus $3 shipping and handling). Order from IIE Books at the above address. Most international centers and study-abroad offices at U.S. universities also have copies of these two books.

For information on study-abroad opportunities offered through Canadian universities and colleges, look for Athabasca University's *Educational Travel Planner*. This 250-page directory also gives information on volunteer and socially responsible travel opportunities, language and cooking schools, and retreat centers throughout Canada and the U.S. It is available for $13.95 from Marketing and Communications, Athabasca University, Athabasca, Alberta T0G 2R0, Canada.

For students planning to study at a foreign university—either through direct enrollment or by participating in a program sponsored by a U.S. institution—there are several reference works that might be useful. Since these are quite expensive, you'll probably want to check a library for a copy rather than purchasing your own. The *World Education Encyclopedia* (1988, Facts on File, $195), by George Kurian, provides descriptions of the educational system of every country in the world, from Afghanistan to Zaire. *The World of Learning* (London: Europa Publications, $290), updated annually, gives details of more than 26,000 academic institutions all over the world. Another useful source is *Higher Education in the European Community: A Directory of Higher Education Institutions*, produced by the European Community Information Service (2100 M Street NW, Washington, DC 20037). It can be ordered from UNIPUB for $24.95 (plus $2.50 shipping and handling) at 4611-F Assembly Drive, Lanham, MD 20706; (800) 274-4888. The American Association of Collegiate Registrars and Admissions Officers (AACRAO), in cooperation with NAFSA, publishes the World Education Series, a series of profiles of foreign education systems. Although designed for U.S. admissions officers evaluating foreign academic credentials, these publications are also of use to the prospective student. For ordering information or catalogs, write AACRAO, One Dupont Circle, Suite 330, Washington, DC 20036-1171, for a complete list of titles.

In addition to these, a number of publications on study abroad tailored to specific disciplines such as medicine and business can be of great help to students planning to study abroad:

- **For medical students:** *The World Directory of Medical Schools*, compiled by the World Health Organization (WHO) and updated in 1991, costs $31.50 (plus $3 for postage and handling) and is available prepaid from WHO Publications Centre—USA, 49 Sheridan Avenue, Albany, NY 12210; (518) 436-9686. You may be able to find a copy of the now out-of-print *Barron's Guide to Foreign Medical Schools*, by Carla Fine, in your public library or study abroad office. *Note*: Some agencies promising to place U.S. students in foreign medical schools charge high fees for their service; the Association of American Medical Colleges warns that these agencies usually charge fees for information that is available without cost from other sources.
- **For business students:** *Barron's Guide to Graduate Business Schools* (1988), by

Eugene Miller, lists many foreign as well as domestic institutions. It is available for $12.95 from Barron's Educational Series.
- **For engineering students:** The *World Directory of Engineering Schools* lists 1,350 institutions in 115 countries as well as the programs offered at each one. It can be ordered from Geographics, Box 133, Easton, CT 06612, for $25.

High School Programs

Although the focus of this book is on work, study, and travel opportunities for college students, there is also a rapidly expanding number of programs abroad for high school and junior high school students. Too numerous to be listed here, these programs are described in *The Teenager's Guide to Study, Travel, and Adventure Abroad* (see page 3). Also check Appendix II of this book for a listing of the programs abroad for high school students that are sponsored by CIEE-member institutions.

It has become fairly common for students to take off the year between high school and college to do something "different" for a while before settling down to more school routine. For those who want to spend this interim year in another country, there are many alternatives. Some of the study-abroad programs listed in the country sections of this book are open to graduating high school seniors; the *Teenager's Guide* contains a more complete listing of such opportunities. If you feel you want to take a break from studying, there are many other options open to you as well; for example, check the sections on international workcamps, voluntary service, service learning, and field research projects in Chapter Two of this book. You'll find more options of this type in the *Teenager's Guide*.

"Working and studying abroad during high school opened my eyes to the idea that there could be something else besides the expectations I knew growing up. Going abroad earlier than the traditional time contributed towards answering some fundamental questions I had about myself. I realized better what those questions were."
—Steve Johnson, Tulsa, Oklahoma

Programs for Adults

The number of educational programs abroad designed specifically for adults is growing by leaps and bounds. At CIEE we receive brochures almost daily describing programs abroad sponsored by museums, alumni organizations, and the continuing-education divisions of foreign universities. While the focus of this book is on work, study, and travel opportunities for college students, many of the programs described here are also open to adults not currently attending any type of school. To find these, check through the eligibility requirements for the study and travel programs listed in the country sections later in this book. For some ideas for learning vacations, you might also look at Chapter Five as well as the various sections on workcamps, field-research projects, and voluntary service in Chapter Two.

Traditionally, one of the most popular ways of taking a learning vacation has been to enroll in a language center in a foreign country and to spend a few weeks immersed in the study of the language. These language centers exist everywhere. Some are quite well known, like the Instituto Allende in San Miguel de Allende, Mexico. Eurocentres, a nonprofit organization based in Switzerland, operates 28 language centers in nine countries around the world. French is offered at various locations in France and Switzerland; German in Cologne and Lucerne; Italian in Florence; Spanish in Barcelona and Madrid; and Japanese in Kanazawa, Japan. Holiday courses last from two to six weeks, and intensive courses up to three months. Students can live with host families or in hotel/pension facilities. More information and application information on Eurocentres is available from Council Travel offices across the country (see listing on page xix) or from

Eurocentres' new United States location at 101 N. Union Street, Alexandria, VA 22314; (703) 684-1494/1495.

For people age 60 or older seeking a learning vacation, there's the popular Elderhostel program, which "combines the best traditions of education and hosteling." Elderhostel is based on the belief that retirement doesn't have to mean withdrawal but, on the contrary, can be an opportunity to enjoy new experiences. Besides an extensive network of Elderhostels in the U.S., where participants spend a week on a college campus studying different topics and enjoying activities in the local setting, the organization sponsors programs in Australia, Bermuda, Canada, France, Germany, Great Britain, Holland, India, Ireland, Israel, Italy, Mexico, Scandinavia, and Spain. International programs usually last two to four weeks, involving one-week stays at each of several colleges or universities. For example, in a typical Elderhostel in Australia, participants spend a week at Dunmore Lang College studying the city of Sydney, a week on Heron Island focusing on the Great Barrier Reef, and a week at the Gippsland Institute in rural Victoria studying the relationship between humans and the environment. For details on Elderhostel offerings, write to Elderhostel, 75 Federal Street, Boston, MA 02110.

One of the best sources of information on unusual educational opportunities for adults is *Learning Vacations*, published by Peterson's Guides, which focuses on short-term "take-your-mind-along" vacations that include a learning experience of some sort—seminars, music tours, art and folk festivals, archaeological digs, and so on. Although most of these programs are in the U.S., there are some in other countries as well. The 1989 edition is available for $11.95 (plus $4 shipping and handling) from Peterson's Guides, PO Box 2123, Princeton, NJ 08543.

"My experience abroad of studying and traveling allowed me the opportunity to grow so much as an individual. Day after day there were challenges to be met, and day after day I grew—both through successes and failures"
—Kevin Anderle, Wheaton, Illinois

CHAPTER FIVE
MAKING YOUR TRAVEL PLANS

"International travel broadens the mind, warms the heart, sharpens the senses, and exercises the legs. It will also test your wits and challenge your adaptability. Knowing the language makes the whole experience twice as rewarding."
—Chris Allert, Minneapolis, Minnesota

By now you're ready to see the world, be it as a student, volunteer, or tourist. Whether you plan to trek the Himalayas or simply find your way to a school in London, you need to know a little about your travel options in order to make the best decision about how to get to where you're going. And once you're there, you'll probably have to make some plans for getting around. Good research and planning can help you make the most of the time you have and can make a big difference in keeping your costs low.

If you live near a Council Travel office, your research will be a bit easier. Council Travel offices are full-service travel agencies that specialize in providing services for students and other budget-minded travelers. There are 34 of them in the United States, as well as a number in Europe and Asia (see pages xix–xxi). Many are located near university campuses. All are staffed by trained personnel who can answer your questions about student discount fares, rail passes, and other ways to save money while traveling. CIEE's other travel subsidiary, Council Charter, is discussed later in this chapter.

Whether or not you live near a Council Travel office, your research should begin with a copy of the 72-page *Student Travel Catalog*, published every year by the Council on International Educational Exchange. It's available free of charge at Council Travel offices and at many study-abroad offices and international centers at colleges and universities. You can also get a copy by writing the Council in New York and enclosing $1 for postage. Its pages are filled with information on travel basics, as well as air fares, car-rental options, and rail-pass plans. Looking at it before going to a travel agency or making your own travel plans will help you make sure you are getting what you want at a reasonable price. Remember: Research is really the only way to make your overseas experience an economical one.

"Researching your country before visiting can make all the difference in the world. Trekking by the 'seat of one's pants' usually results in disaster."
—Dale Moyer, Chicago, Illinois

GETTING THERE

Finding the Best Air Fare

Over the last several years, the airline industry has seen a number of changes—not uncommon in an industry that's always in a state of flux. In general terms, international air fares remain highly competitive and prices for tickets to some international destinations are actually falling. In addition, because of low air fares, more and more travelers are heading to non-European destinations such as Asia, the South Pacific, and South America. Before you begin researching fares, you'll need to make a few decisions about your trip. You should have a rough idea of your general itinerary, your travel budget, how many stopovers you plan to make, what time of year you plan to travel, and the length of time you plan on staying. Give some thought to when you plan to travel. There are "low" and "high" season cut-off dates that apply to fares; length of stay is another factor in fare determination. Also remember that many bargain airfares are limited in availability and must be purchased far ahead of your departure date.

Be aware, too, that although some advertised fares may be lower than others, there are usually certain restrictions attached that you'll learn about only by reading the fine print. In some situations you may even be better off buying a more expensive ticket, particularly if you wish to make stopovers or need the flexibility to change travel dates. More expensive fares may allow you a number of "free" stopovers, resulting in an airfare that's better suited to your particular itinerary. As you do your research, keep in mind that inexpensive fares abound; they just require a certain amount of investigation, flexibility, and a good deal of creative planning. Let this be your guiding principle when it comes to airfares: Usually, the more conditions attached to a certain fare, the cheaper it's going to be.

If you're a student, you'll find as you plan your travels that your International Student Identity Card is worth many times what you paid for it (see page 8). This card entitles you to travel on a student-fare basis to almost any destination in the world at savings of up to 50 percent off regular economy-class fares. Even if you're not a student but are still under 26, you are eligible for most of the discounts if you get an International Youth Card. Educators, too, are eligible for some discounts on air fares at Council Travel offices if they have a valid International Teacher Identity Card. See the section "Student/Youth Airfares" on page 47.

With all that in mind, it's not possible at press time for us to tell you exactly what international fares will be when you want to travel. What we can do, though, is advise you on how to go about getting the latest consumer information on the best fares available. For starters Council Travel publishes "Airfare Updates," fact sheets which provide the latest information on nearly every type of international air fare; you can get these at a Council Travel office or have them automatically mailed to you as they are published by completing the appropriate form in the *Student Travel Catalog*. A book that uncovers a treasure trove of money-saving ideas, many that even a seasoned traveler wouldn't have imagined, is *Beat the High Cost of Travel*, by Tom Brosnahan (Prentice-Hall, Frommer Books: $6.95). Also check the Sunday travel sections of large metropolitan newspapers such as the *New York Times*, the *Chicago Tribune*, the *Los Angeles Times*, and the *Washington Post*. Usually, these are full of ads for competitive airfares and contain the latest travel information in columns or feature articles.

Consolidator Tickets and Charter Flights

Charter flights were once a popular airfare alternative, but in the last couple of years the number of charter flights has drastically diminished. Instead, consolidator flights have become more popular among those looking for an inexpensive way to fly. In many ways the two options offer similar advantages; however, they differ in terms of how they operate. A charter flight is one in which a tour operator charters a plane to fly a specific route on certain dates. Unlike the early days of charter travel, anyone can now take a charter, regardless of age or student status. Consolidators work on a smaller scale; when airlines can't fill seats, they sell them to a consolidator at a big discount. In turn, the consolidator offers them at about 20 to 50 percent below normal prices to travel agents, other consolidators, or directly to the public through newspaper ads. Usually the tickets are nonrefundable and cannot be changed, and if the flight is delayed you may not receive free meals or other compensation. This isn't true for all charter and consolidator companies, though: If you book with Council Charter, for example, tickets are at least partially refundable as long as you cancel before your scheduled departure from the United States. Council Charter return flights can be changed in Europe for a fee of $75. If you shop around early enough, using a consolidator or charter flight could result in substantial savings.

When making any travel arrangements be sure to ask for the policy in writing. Before purchasing your ticket, read the contract—operators are by law required to supply you with one when you book a charter. Know your rights and responsibilities beforehand to avoid headaches later. Some companies, Council Charter included, put your payment into an escrow account until departure, which protects you should the airline or consolidator go under. In layperson's terms, this means that the company opens an account and places all the money it receives for a specific flight into it. By law, this money cannot be touched until the flight takes off. Therefore, you are protected from paying for a flight that never departs.

There are a lot of pros and cons to consider in deciding whether or not you want to take a consolidated or charter flight. Keep in mind that consolidator flights are merely discounted seats on regularly scheduled airlines and flights. Here are some facts you should be aware of in making a decision:

- Generally, charters depart only from major cities; however, some operators offer low-cost "add-on" fares for connecting flights to other cities. Consolidated tickets on U.S. carriers will often be available from all cities served by the airline.
- Some charters are available year-round, but others only operate seasonally. Consolidators operate year-round.
- Many operators, including Council Charter, offer a "mix-and-match" option, allowing you to pick and choose from among several arrival and departure cities.
- Charter and consolidator fares are usually lower than the lowest fares available on regular airlines.
- Delays: every airline is occasionally beset by the vagaries of schedule, weather, or aircraft changes. Most can't be predicted; the best advice is to allow some leeway for schedule changes in your itinerary.
- Fuel surcharges and ticket price increases sometimes occur after you have booked a flight; ask the operator about their likelihood. With most consolidated tickets, once you pay for and are issued a ticket you are protected against increases.

If you decide to book a consolidated or charter flight, here are some tips on avoiding an unpleasant experience:

- Read the fine print of ads—"OW" fares, for example, are often one way but based on a round-trip purchase.
- Get the ticket as soon as possible, possibly by overnight mail; you'll have time to correct any scheduling errors. Also, make sure there are no alterations (flight times or dates covered with revalidation stickers).
- Pay by credit card, if at all possible. This way, you can cancel payment if problems aren't corrected.
- Try to book with a company that places your money in an escrow account.

Some consolidators are reluctant to or refuse to name their airlines. This is because airline companies sometimes feel that this information, if released to the general public, could undermine their fare structure. Use your judgment to determine if you are comfortable with this; the country to which you are flying and the political climate at the time you book your tickets should be the main factors to consider. Most consolidators will simply promise "a major scheduled carrier." If you are uncomfortable with this, book with a company, like Council Charter, that has access to and will release all travel information.

Taking everything into consideration, consolidators tickets and charter flights are good options for people looking for an inexpensive way to get to where they're going. Getting beyond the popular European destinations, however, may require further exploration.

You may want to combine a charter flight with a regular flight offering a student/youth fare to your final destination, for example. Allow plenty of time for the unexpected when combining two such flights: a delay that causes you to miss your connection may not only be inconvenient but also quite expensive.

Council Charter, which offers discounted seats on regularly scheduled flights, has more than 40 years of experience in the budget-travel field. Two features that make its service unique are the mix-and-match plan, which lets you fly into one city and return from another, and the trip cancellation waiver. The latter, an optional waiver, is available for a modest fee at the time of booking and guarantees a full refund of all money paid if the cancellation notice is received anytime up to your scheduled check-in time. Although the actual cities served vary slightly from year to year, Council Charter's destinations generally include Amsterdam, Brussels, London, Lyon, Madrid, Malaga, Nice, Paris, Rome, and other European cities. Many of the destinations are offered on a year-round basis. Council Charter also offers special low-cost, add-on fares from a variety of U.S. cities including Chicago, Cleveland, Denver, Las Vegas, Los Angeles, Minneapolis, Portland, Salt Lake City, San Diego, San Francisco, Seattle, and Spokane. You'll find fares for Council Charter flights across the Atlantic listed in the "Getting There" section of the chapter on Europe. For more information contact a Council Travel office or call Council Charter's toll-free number: (800) 800-8222.

Student and Youth Airfares

For those who are eligible, student/youth fares can save as much as 50 percent over the regular economy fare on a scheduled flight. Besides the low cost, student/youth fares have the advantage of having few of the restrictions that apply to most budget airfares. Student/youth fares are valid on regularly scheduled flights of a number of major international airlines. In order to qualify for most student/youth airfares, you must have either the International Student Identity Card (see page 8) or the International Youth Identity Card (see page 10).

Council Travel offices can issue these cards and book your flight; students not living in the vicinity of one of these offices often book their flight with Council Travel by phone after obtaining an International Student Identity Card at their school. In fact, since a number of these student and youth fares are the result of contracts directly between CIEE and the airline, many student/youth fares are available *only* from Council Travel and other specially authorized travel agents. Student/youth fares are generally not sold directly by the airline, and airline ticketing offices will not have information about them. If you are dealing with a travel agency, make sure that it has access to student/youth flights.

Since student/youth flights are generally the lowest fares to most parts of the world, it is these fares that you'll find quoted as examples in the "Getting There" sections throughout this book. Some international airlines also allow teachers with the International Teacher Identity Card (see page 9) to take advantage of the same low fares for students and young people. However, although students any age are eligible for the International Student Identity Card, a number of airlines have placed age restrictions on student fares.

Other Budget Airfares

If you aren't eligible for a student or youth fare, there are several other options you probably will want to check out. In contrast to charter, consolidator, and student/youth tickets, the options discussed in this section can generally be obtained directly from the airline. If you use a travel agent, however, select one who is interested in selling budget travel. Many agents simply aren't interested in scrolling through their computer databases on your behalf in return for the small commission a budget fare earns them. Similarly, those agents who don't normally devote a good deal of time to reading and studying bargain fares won't be of much help to you.

Below you'll find listed a variety of budget fares available for scheduled flights in

1991. Remember that in the highly competitive airline industry, fares, restrictions, and special promotions change frequently and without notice.

- **Advance Purchase Excursion (APEX) Fares:** In some ways the airline industry's answer to charters, APEX fares are between 30 and 40 percent lower than regular economy class. Since low fares seem to go hand in hand with restrictions, however, be aware that there are minimum- and maximum-stay requirements, cancellation and change penalties, and stopover restrictions. You must also purchase your ticket anytime from 7 to 30 days in advance. "Super" APEX fares are somewhat cheaper than regular APEX but are in effect on a limited number of routes.
- **Special Bargain or Promotional Fares:** Bargain fares pop up sporadically; usually, they are part of a "quick sale" strategy that airlines use to fill seats during slow periods. One drawback is that they usually require the traveler to act immediately rather than meticulously plan an itinerary ahead of time. However, if you have the luxury of flexibility, promotional and bargain fares can be a dream come true.
- **Economy Fares:** The term "economy," when applied to an airline fare, is a contradiction in terms for anyone but the wealthy. As it is used today, "economy" usually indicates an unrestricted, full-fare ticket for economy-class seating. Usually, you'll be able to find a cheaper fare, but if you are making reservations at the last minute or if you intend to make a number of stopovers en route, an economy fare may be your best—or only—option.
- **"Last Minute" Youth Fares:** Almost every major carrier has replaced its old "standby" fares with what we call "last minute" youth fares. These are available usually to passengers 12 to 24 years of age on a one-way or round-trip basis. The catch is you can only book your seat within three days of your departure. What can be an attractive fare in low season is much harder to obtain during the high season. If your travel plans are flexible, this may be just your ticket—but if you've a schedule to keep, a serious delay could be a major problem for you.
- **Around the World Passes:** Most major carriers sell "Around the World" passes, which are good for a specified period of unlimited travel (usually one year) on the airline and a limited group of partner airlines. These can be an economical alternative, but only if you really intend to be a "world" traveler (the average price was about $2,700 in 1991). Regulations vary slightly depending on the airline, but most require a 14-day advance purchase, allow a limited number of stops, and require that you travel in one continuous direction. There are no student discounts for these passes, but around-the-world itineraries for students and young people can also be custom designed using a combination of various student and discount fares linked together. This option is almost always cheaper than purchasing a pass. Again, be sure to consult with a travel agent familiar with student fares, such as Council Travel Services.

In addition, there are many special low-cost excursion fares on commercial routes connecting cities outside the United States. Many of these can only be sold in the country where the flight originates and cannot be advertised in the U.S. Check with the airlines wherever you are to see if such fares exist on the route you intend to travel. Certain cities have emerged as excellent places to look for inexpensive air travel. London, Bangkok, and Singapore, for instance, are famous as starting points for inexpensive scheduled and unscheduled flights to other parts of the world. It's possible to do some wheeling and dealing in these three cities and thus end up with real airfare bargains. But don't forget that it almost always takes time and effort, and that the expenditure of both may not be worth the savings.

Flying as an International Air Courier

International courier companies use regularly scheduled flights on major airlines to ship items like film, documents, blueprints, advertising material, and canceled checks. Since the packages accompanying the courier are considered personal baggage, they are cleared through customs immediately, thereby considerably reducing the time that would otherwise be required for shipment. Persons wishing to fly as a courier can schedule a flight weeks in advance or at the last minute, although last-minute choices as to flight, return date, and destination are limited. Flights as a courier are available from major international airports in the U.S. including New York, San Francisco, Los Angeles, and Chicago. Usually, you pay a registration fee to a courier service which entitles you to fly at about ⅓ to ½ of a standard fare. Some examples of round-trip fares: New York–Tel Aviv for $400, New York–London for $323, and New York–Paris for $259. However, couriers are allowed only carry-on luggage and must be *very* flexible regarding dates. For further information you can contact one of several agencies that screen and select couriers. In New York, one such agency is Now Voyager; (212) 431-1616. Another is World Courier; (800) 221-6600.

An invaluable resource for anyone interested in traveling as a courier is a recently updated book entitled *The Insider's Guide to Air Courier Bargains*, by Kelly Monaghan. This budget-minded book lists all the information you need to become a courier, from what to wear to how to fly for free. The index lists courier services from around the globe, including flight patterns, sample fares, even the names of friendly agents at each company. You might not find it in your local bookstore, but it can be ordered from Inwood Training Publications, Box 438T, New York, NY 10034 for $14.95, plus $2 postage and handling.

Getting There by Ship

Although there are still many passenger ships sailing the high seas, most of these are pre-packaged tours geared for the vacationer rather than the budget traveler. If you want to sip piña coladas on the deck while sailing in a big circle, you'll probably find a ship that's going your way. Be prepared to pay, however. You can still find an ocean liner that will take you across the Atlantic or the Pacific, but transoceanic sailings are infrequent so you'll have to do a little research to find a ship crossing the Atlantic or Pacific that is leaving around the same time you plan to go. Rates for one-way passage will vary according to ship, departure date, ports of call, and cabin location but are generally much more expensive than air travel.

Travel by freighter is not much cheaper. Although there are still lots of freighters operating all over the world, not many have room for passengers. Polish Ocean Lines, (514) 849-6111, operates freight ships with six cabins for passengers; one way passage to Europe was $1,010 in 1991. Another company, the Gdynia America Line, 39 Broadway, 14th floor, New York, NY 10006, (212) 952-1280, operates passenger-carrying freighters between the United States and Europe. There are more choices on routes from the West Coast to Asia, from New York to Africa, and from New York or Miami to South America. Accommodations on freighters vary from modest to luxurious. Staterooms on many current American flag cargo vessels are equal and even superior to rooms on cruise liners, which cost considerably more. Not everyone will be happy on a freighter, however. There is no entertainment except that provided by the 6 to 12 passengers and the officers. Also, it's more expensive than you might think: this method of travel averages around $100 per day per person. But if you enjoy the sea, good food (you usually dine with the officers), restful days and peaceful nights, exotic ports, and have plenty of time, then freighter travel can be just what you have been looking for. Freighter schedules are changed to meet the demands of cargo; therefore to enjoy a freighter cruise you must have a very flexible schedule.

TravLtips Cruise and Freighter Travel Association (PO Box 188, Flushing, NY 11358, 800-872-8584) publishes the *Freighter Bulletin* ($15 per year), a compilation of the personal travel experiences of the Association's members. Another useful reference is *Ford's Freighter Travel Guide and Waterways of the World* (19448 Londeluis Street,

Northridge, CA 91324). Published twice a year, it lists freighter cruises, describes ships, gives fares, and so on. The cost is $8.95 for a single copy, $15 for a year's subscription.

Another option might be working your way overseas. But according to the National Maritime Union: "Unless they have very special skills or seniority, nobody can pick up a job on a U.S. ship to earn money during a summer vacation. There are no opportunities for working your way just for transportation on an American flag ship. 'Workaways,' as they are called, are prohibited by union policy and company rules." While you may not be able to work on a freighter, a job on a cruise ship is a possibility. A book entitled *Guide to Cruise Ship Jobs* (1991), by George Reilly, describes the different departments on a ship, positions within each department, qualifications needed, and the best way to apply. Copies are $4.95 plus $1 postage and are available from the publisher, Pilot Books, 103 Cooper Street, Babylon, NY 11702.

TRAVELING AROUND

Getting the Most Out of Your Trip

Since you're already well into the fifth chapter of this book, you're obviously not like the character in Anne Tyler's *The Accidental Tourist*, who, when forced to travel, wanted to know things such as: "What restaurants in Tokyo offered Sweet 'n' Low? Did Amsterdam have a McDonald's? Did Mexico City have a Taco Bell? Did any place in Rome serve Chef Boyardee ravioli?" Forget the Holiday Inn slogan, "No surprises"; much of the excitement of an overseas trip is due precisely to the fact that it's different and full of surprises. In fact, if there's any advice that we feel is vital to pass along, it's "keep an open mind" and "expect the unexpected." Trite though these phrases may be, everyone coming back from a good experience abroad gives this advice in one way or another.

"For any traveler abroad, an open mind is a necessity. This helps to avoid culture shock and any prejudgmental feelings which may prohibit understanding and enjoyment of the new culture."
—Marcie A. Alexander, Barrington, Illinois

"Be open and be flexible. Try to meet as many people as you can and try your best to speak the language because that's the only way to learn it."
—Chris Ann D'Alessandro, Dallas, Texas

If you're going to a Third World country, you have to be especially ready to adjust to new ways of doing things. Relax and don't worry if train and bus schedules seem to have little to do with reality. Try to see beyond the "poverty" you'll encounter to understand and appreciate other aspects of the culture. You may well in fact discover that you "wouldn't want to live there." But then, no one is asking you to. Instead, enjoy your stay in the country for the positive things it does have to offer.

"Forget the lack of progress and respect the traditions instead. Let go of being an American and sit back and watch the people operate in their own world. It's easier to be an observer than a critic."
—Heidi Kolk, Fulton, Illinois

Deciding How You Want to Get Around

Because there are so many options for traveling around once you've arrived at your destination, you'll have to make some choices. Do you want to travel by yourself or with a group of people? Do you want to see as much as possible or stay in one place and really get to know it? How do you want to travel—by foot, bus, train, car, boat, or bike?

One of the questions you should ask yourself is if you would feel safer, less isolated, and more at home with a group. Certainly, there is safety in numbers, and a tour means you'll always have somebody to talk to—traveling can be lonely sometimes. And if you take an organized tour, you won't have to worry about planning the logistics of your trip and arranging transportation, accommodations, and meals. But there are disadvantages to traveling in a group, too. A lot of the adventure is planned out of your trip, and since you have to go along with the group, your individual needs may not always be served. And if you really want to meet the people of the country and learn another language, the worst thing you can do is travel with other Americans. Remember, too, that most organized tours are usually more expensive than traveling on your own; tours always have an administrative fee built into them.

In the following sections, we'll discuss some of the options you have as to modes of travel. More specific information on getting around can be found in the following chapters on particular regions.

- **By Train:** In many countries, travel by train is the least expensive, safest, and most convenient way to get around. On a train you can eat, sleep, see the countryside, and meet interesting people. And the train leaves you in the center of the city without having to worry about traffic or parking. Train systems are well developed in the countries of Western and Eastern Europe, as well as in Japan, Canada, and some Third World countries such as Argentina, Thailand, China, and India. Even in nations without extensive rail networks, like most Latin American nations, the train—usually slower and cheaper than the bus—can be one of the most comfortable and interesting ways to travel.

    Most countries with extensive rail systems offer foreigners special rail passes that are good for unlimited travel over a certain period of time. You'll find information on these in the country and region sections of this book. A good source of further information is the *Eurail Guide—How to Travel Europe and All the World by Train*, which covers train travel in 141 countries around the world. The 816-page 22nd edition is available for $14.95 in bookstores. To order by mail, send $17 to Eurail Guide Annual, 27540 Pacific Coast Highway, Malibu, CA 90265. To get revved up to travel by rail, read Paul Theroux's *The Patagonian Express, Riding the Iron Rooster*, and *The Great Railway Bazaar*.

- **By Bus:** Buses are the world's most common form of public transportation. While intercity bus service in Europe is relatively limited, buses are the only means of public transportation in some Third World countries. Buses go everywhere—and relatively cheaply—although the level of comfort varies greatly depending on the bus, the road, the mood of the driver, the weather, and the number of passengers. Bus passes that provide unlimited mileage over a national system are available in a few countries and regions; you'll find more information about these in appropriate sections of the remaining chapters in this book.

- **By Car:** The independence and flexibility that a car offers when you're traveling cannot be matched. On the other hand, being in your own car will not put you in contact (and we mean contact) with local people the way public transportation will. And a car that is useful in getting to out-of-the-way places can become a major headache in a traffic-choked city where you don't know your way around.

    You can use your own car to get to and around Canada and Mexico, but traveling by car in most foreign countries means renting one. Fortunately, car rentals are available all over the world. In fact, companies such as Hertz, Avis, and Budget have offices worldwide, and you can get car-rental information just about anywhere by calling their toll-free numbers. Often, however, local agencies will offer cheaper rates. Finally, Council Travel offers economical car-rental plans in both Europe and the South Pacific.

    Most English-speaking countries allow American citizens 18 years of age and over to drive with a valid U.S. driver's license. And your ordinary U.S. license is all you need in a number of other countries where American tourists are common, including Belgium, France, Israel, Mexico, Spain, Portugal, and most of the Caribbean. Be sure to check specific regulations and insurance requirements before setting off. Driving in most other countries will require an International Driving Permit. This document provides an official translation of the information on your regular license, which you must also carry with you. The permit, established by a 1949 United Nations treaty, must be obtained in the country where your regular license is issued. In the United States, the International Driving Permit can be obtained at a local office of the American Automobile Association (AAA). If you apply in person, a permit will be issued while you wait; however, it will take at least two weeks if you apply through the mail. You'll have to complete an application form and provide two passport-size photos and a fee of $10. The International Driving Permit is valid for one year unless your regular license expires earlier. Some South American countries do not honor International Driving Permits and instead require an Inter-American Driving Permit, which can also be obtained through AAA.

- **By Boat:** A wide range of options awaits those who want to travel by water. A barge gliding through the canals of France, a hydrofoil speeding to a Mediterranean island from the mainland, a luxury cruise boat on the Nile, a hovercraft skimming across the English Channel, or a steamer on a 2,000 mile journey on the Amazon are a few of the possibilities. Because it is relatively slow, boat service usually focuses on routes where road and rail transportation is not possible. Unlimited passes similar to those available for rail transportation are not available, but youth or student fares can sometimes be obtained upon presentation of the International Student Identity Card or International Youth Card.
- **By Bicycle:** Bicycling allows you to escape the confinement of the motor vehicle's steel shell and enjoy the countryside at a more leisurely pace. Taking your own bicycle on the plane is usually no problem and can be done at little or no extra charge; or you can rent or buy a bicycle abroad.

There are two ways to go if you decide to see a foreign country by bike: on your own or with an organized bicycle tour. On a tour, a group of 20 or so participants and two to three leaders bike a prescribed route, followed by a van carrying luggage and anyone who is just plain tuckered out. Sometimes the use of a bicycle is included in the price of the tour. Check the listings of travel programs in the remaining chapters of this book for the bicycle tours abroad offered by American Youth Hostels and Council Travel. Other organizations that offer bicycling programs abroad include Backroads Bicycle Touring (1516 5th Street, Suite Q452, Berkeley, CA 94710-1740, (800) 245-3874); Breaking Away Bicycle Tours (1142 Manhattan Avenue, Suite 253, Manhattan Beach, CA 90266); EUROPEDS (883 Sinex Avenue, Pacific Grove, CA 93950), and the International Bicycle Fund (4887 Columbia Drive South, Seattle, WA 98108-1919).

Budget Accommodations

If you know where to look, low-cost accommodations can be found in all parts of the world. In fact, staying in major cities abroad is often cheaper than staying in U.S. cities. Of course, the options vary in type as well as in quality. In some countries, you can stay in Western-style hotels with all the amenities for the same cost as the average American roadside motel. In other countries, you might have to settle for a shared room with a shower down the hall for the same amount of money.

Pensions, or private boardinghouses, are generally your best bets. Most small pensions are family-run. Some are geared to tourists staying only a few days, while others cater to longer-term guests. Finding a good pension in an unfamiliar city can be an exhausting process, requiring lots of legwork. Most guidebooks include a list of pensions and low-cost hotels; but often you'll find their prices have doubled. It is a good idea to talk to as many other travelers as you can to gather information. Another valuable resource is the local tourist-information center; the staff will usually point you to several places in your price range, and some will even call ahead for you.

There's a worldwide network of accommodations operated by YMCAs and YWCAs. As in the U.S., international Ys usually offer a range of activities and events as well as recreational and exercise facilities. Some are single-sex but many welcome both men and women. Their prices vary, however, from cheap to somewhat expensive. One of the most convenient services offered by Ys is their central computerized reservation system, which allows you to book accommodations in many countries around the world. For more information, or for a *Y's Way* travel brochure, write to The Y's Way, 356 West 34th Street, New York, NY 10001.

The International Youth Hostel Federation oversees over 5,000 youth hostels around the world where you can spend the night for approximately $10. Accommodations are dormitory style, with a number of people sharing rooms: you are provided with a bed-mattress and blankets. A sleeping sack (a sheet sewn up on three sides) is usually required, although some of the larger hostels rent sheets. Different regulations exist for youth hostels in each country, and although they vary, there are certain similarities from country to country. Hostelers usually are expected to share in the cleanup, to abstain from drinking and/or using drugs in the hostel (and smoking in some areas), to stay no more than three days, and to be in the hostel by 10 P.M. Some hostels embrace the lockout system, which saves them from having to employ help during the day but can translate into major hardships for hostelers. During the lockout period, usually from 10 A.M. to 5 P.M., no one is allowed back into the hostel: not for a nap, not for a forgotten bathing suit, not even for a quick peek at a beloved *Whole World Handbook*.

In order to stay in many hostels around the world you must have a membership card issued by American Youth Hostels (AYH), the U.S. member of the International Youth Hostel Federation. Some hostels will admit you without a card, but cardholders usually get priority so it is recommended that you get one before you leave. The cost of the AYH membership varies according to age: $10 if you are under 18; $25 if you are over 18 but under 55; and $15 for persons 55 or over. AYH also offers a family membership for $35, which includes all children under the age of 18 (16 in Europe). Cards are valid for 12 months from the date of purchase. You'll find a listing of hostels by country and information on hostel rules in the annual *International Youth Hostel Handbook*, which is available from AYH in two volumes: Volume I covers Europe and the Mediterranean, Volume II covers Asia, Australia, Africa, and the Americas ($10.95 each plus $3 postage per book). For the AYH membership card, the handbooks, and for general information on hosteling, write to American Youth Hostels, PO Box 37613, Washington, DC 20013-7613, or call (800) 673-2733.

Cutting Costs

Perhaps the question we hear most often is "How much will it cost?" Up to this point, we've tried to give you information on low-cost travel options; in this section you'll find additional tips for people who want to keep the cost of traveling as low as possible. In general, we recommend that you be frugal—but not at the expense of skipping the things you should do to make your trip enjoyable. Also, try to avoid the mistake of overspending during the first few days of the trip, which is easier than you'd think due to the unfamiliar surroundings and the feeling that the foreign currency is "play money."

If you're traveling with a friend, you can save money in hotels and pensions where two in a room can mean considerable savings. Purchasing food in the local markets is another money-saving technique. Should trains be your chosen mode of travel, a Eurail or comparable train pass is security in itself. You won't need to worry about money for train tickets, and many young travelers short on cash for lodging have found themselves jumping on a midnight train to another city. If your funds are running low, you can head for a less expensive destination. Finally, be sure to take advantage of the many youth and student discounts that may be available (see page 8 for information about the International Student Identity Card).

We strongly suggest that you set aside an emergency money supply—a stash not to be used under any circumstances unless you absolutely have to. Hide it in a place that is safe and dry, as well as a secret from fellow travelers. Also keep with it a list of emergency addresses, phone numbers, medical information in case of an accident, and a photocopy of your passport.

If you are going to join an academic program or tour, you will have a pretty good idea of what the whole trip will cost ahead of time and will probably pay for most of it before you leave. Costs vary from program to program. Before you leave on a prearranged program, be sure that you understand just what you are expected to pay for and what is going to be paid for you.

Organized Tours

If you're convinced that an organized tour is the way to go, prepare for it by having realistic expectations. There are different types of tours, from a standard three-week tour of the European capitals to a 23-day grasslands horseback trip in Inner Mongolia. Some are sponsored by nonprofit organizations or universities, others by private agencies and tour operators. Many are designed to give participants the opportunity to see major cultural attractions through a sightseeing program led by a guide. Others are organized around a particular interest shared by members of the group, such as kayaking, wine tasting, or art appreciation. Check the travel programs offered by CIEE-member institutions and organizations listed in the chapters that follow. You will also find a wide selection of tours listed in newspapers and travel magazines.

Whatever your choice, make sure it's run by a reliable operator or an institution with proven experience. If possible you should talk to a previous participant. Licensed tour operators should belong to a professional organization with clearly defined operating standards. If you want to avoid the risk of losing your entire vacation budget, try to check them out before putting your money down.

Among the tours worth checking into are those offered by student travel bureaus around the world. These student travel bureaus—many of which are nonprofit or run by the government—organize a number of interesting tours in their individual countries geared especially to students and youths. Here are some examples of those recently offered:

- horseback riding in Raculka (Poland)
- a Hong Kong harbor tour on a Chinese junk
- an eight-day bicycle tour of the Netherlands
- diving to explore the undersea world of the Gulf of Eilat (Israel)
- a sightseeing tour of Budapest (Hungary) and excursion to the Danube Bend

Holders of the International Student Identity Card receive a discount on most tours offered by student travel bureaus. You'll find the addresses for these student travel bureaus listed in the appropriate country sections later in this book. CIEE itself organizes student/youth tours to the U.S.S.R., China, and Thailand through its travel subsidiary, Council Travel (see the tour descriptions in the appropriate country sections).

Meeting the People

If you want to spend a short time with a family while you travel, there are organizations in many countries—often, government tourist offices—that will arrange an afternoon or evening visit for you. These organizations are listed throughout this book by country or geographic area.

One possibility is SERVAS, an organization that sponsors a worldwide program of person-to-person contacts for travelers in 100 countries, with the ultimate aim of helping to build world peace, goodwill, and understanding. Here's how SERVAS works: You apply and are interviewed; if accepted, you receive a personal briefing, written instructions, a list of SERVAS families in the area that you are going to visit, and an introductory letter. Using this introductory letter, you can arrange by letter to stay with families who are listed. The average stay with SERVAS hosts is two nights. One CIEE staff member took advantage of SERVAS's program and came back from Italy and France raving about the wonderful families he had met and excited about the possibility of returning this kind of hospitality to others visiting the U.S. For more information write to the U.S. SERVAS Committee, 11 John Street, Room 407, New York, NY 10038. If you use its services, SERVAS asks for a travel membership fee of $60 ($15 of this is refunded when you return its list).

Another program with a "meet the people" philosophy behind it is the Friendship Force, a nonprofit, private organization that organizes exchange visits between the U.S. and other countries. It works like this: A group of citizens from an American city flies to a city in another country, where they stay in private homes for one to two weeks. At a later date, a contingent of people from the community visited travels to the U.S. for a similar experience. For information, write to Friendship Force, 575 South Tower, One CNN Center, Atlanta, GA 30303.

If you'd like a complete listing, with appropriate addresses, of meet-the-people programs in 35 countries, you can order the *International Meet-the-People Directory* ($6) compiled by the International Visitors Information Service, 733 15th Street NW, Suite 300, Washington, DC 20005.

Resources for the Traveler

If you plan to do any traveling at all, you will need a good guidebook that provides listings of hostels, cheap restaurants, and other practical information. For most countries and regions, there are a number of these on the market, each tailored to a different financial bracket and set of interests. Look them over carefully before buying one.

One series actually written by college students—and therefore tailored to the student budget—is *Let's Go*. Written by Harvard Student Agencies and published by St. Martin's Press, these books are often spotted clutched in the hands of many a low-budget traveler trekking through Europe. A secret to getting around the bulkiness problem is to tear out the sections you need and ditch the rest along the way. They are available in bookstores and Council Travel offices or by mail order from CIEE (see prices and ordering information in the *Student Travel Catalog*).

"The 'Let's Go' series is invaluable to the young adult, low-budget traveler. They point out the cheaper spots, but the downside is that EVERYONE carries them—let them guide you, but if you pick up a hint from a local or a fellow traveler, go with it."
—Jennifer Lynch, Haworth, New Jersey

The *Let's Go* series focuses on Europe; for more exotic destinations, check out the guidebooks published by Lonely Planet Publications. Lonely Planet's *Travel Survival Kit*s cover specific countries in Africa, Asia, and Latin America as well as many of the islands in between. Their *On a Shoestring* guides cover wide regions such as Africa or Eastern Europe. If you can't find these books in your local bookstore, you can order them directly from Lonely Planet Publications, Embarcadero West, 112 Linden Street, Oakland, CA 94607, or by calling (800) 229-0122. The Moon handbooks also focus on nontraditional destinations and provide historical and cultural background as well as tips on where to stay, what to eat, and so on. Moon Publications, Inc. is located at 722 Wall Street, Chico, CA 95928. Call (916) 345-5473 for more information or to place orders by phone. Finally, a very good guidebook series covering both European and nontraditional destinations is *The Real Guide*s (New York: Prentice-Hall Travel Books). *The Real Guide*s also provide interesting literature, music, and language sections for each country.

The drawback of every guidebook is that it is consulted by thousands of travelers other than yourself. Many of the places in *Let's Go* will be swarming with other readers—a definite drawback when there's only one youth hostel in town or the "authentic" Italian bistro is suddenly full of hungry North Americans demanding a slice.

If you want a larger selection of travel books than what's available in your local bookstore, there are a number of travel bookstores that publish mail-order catalogs. Some of those that will send a free catalog are Hippocrene Books (171 Madison Avenue, New York, NY 10016); Forsyth Travel Library (PO Box 2975, 9154 West 57th Street, Shawnee Mission, KS 66201); and Wide World Bookshop (401 NE 45th Street, Seattle, WA 98105). For $2, Traveller's Bookstore (22 West 52nd Street, New York, NY 11019) will put you on their mailing list—forever.

Later in this book, you'll find listings for guidebooks and other materials relating to specific countries or areas of the world. For now, however, here are a few books that encompass the four corners of the globe.

- *1991 Adventure Holidays*, by David Stephens, covers all sorts of adventure travel, from scuba diving in the Red Sea, to mountain climbing in Wales, to camel caravanning in the Sahara. It's available in the U.S. for $12.95; write to Peterson's Guides, PO Box 2123, Princeton, NJ 08543, or call (800) 338-3282.
- The *Directory of Low-Cost Vacations with a Difference* was put together by a former chairman of the board for SERVAS (see page 54). A healthy portion of its brief organizational descriptions pertain to homestays; other listings include bed-and-breakfasts, vacation work programs, and home exchanges. It is available for $5.95 from Pilot Books, 103 Cooper Street, Babylon, NY 11702.
- The *Educational Travel Planner* provides 250 pages of alternative travel ideas. Published every February, this guidebook describes study tours, language schools, volunteer opportunities, retreat centers, and cooking schools around the world. It's available for $11.95 from Marketing and Communications, Athabasca University, Athabasca, AB TOG 2RO, Canada.

There are a growing number of magazines that cater to the travelers of the world. One worth investigating—although it may not be on your local newsstands—is *Great Expeditions*, which features firsthand information from travelers, free classified ads, and an information exchange. Article topics in recent years have included "Biking Baja California," "Fly Cheap as an Onboard Courier," and "Streetsmarts for South America." Five issues cost $18, or you can request a free sample copy from Great Expeditions, Box 8000-411, Sumas, WA 98295-8000.

If you are planning to do a lot of traveling, a subscription to the newsletter *Travel Unlimited* might be a good investment. The idea behind this monthly update of domestic and worldwide courier services and general low-budget travel information is that it *is* possible to buck the system big airline companies have created with fare and travel restrictions and costly tickets. The newsletter can be ordered by contacting Travel Unlimited, PO Box 1058, Allston, MA 02134 ($25 for 12 monthly issues).

CHAPTER SIX
EUROPE

Travelers to Europe in the coming years will have the chance to witness historic change in the making. In Eastern Europe, the liberalizing events which followed the dismantling of the Berlin Wall and the breakup of the Soviet bloc have opened up a new era of social freedom and economic reform. In Western Europe, preparations are underway for the much-heralded economic unification of the 12-nation European Community, a breaking-down of trade barriers that doubtless will be accompanied by an increase in movement from country to country. These two halves of the continent, which we have been trained to regard as opposites, now seem headed toward a common cooperative future.

On the other hand, the temptation to regard Europe as a single entity had better be avoided. While the multitude of nation-states with which we are familiar is a relatively modern phenomenon, the peoples of Europe have always comprised, by the influence of their geography, many distinct populations not easily lumped together. This is nowhere so apparent as in the ethnic tensions that have flared up in such far-apart nations as Belgium, Spain, and Yugoslavia, not to mention the Soviet Union. Even on the economic front, unity will not be easily achieved, as demonstrated by the difficulties of transforming eastern Germany's economy and creating a central European bank.

Only by traveling to Europe—albeit with some preparation beforehand—can the American student begin to understand the extent and quality of changes taking place today. Europe has long been the most popular destination for American travelers. Today there are more opportunities for work, study, and travel in more countries than ever before. However, to reap the maximum benefits from your experience abroad, we suggest that you concentrate on a particular region or even a single country. Rushing from city to city may be an exhilarating experience, but chances are you'll emerge from such a whirlwind tour with only a blur of images.

Central and Eastern Europe

The rapid social transformation recently undergone by many central and east European countries has attracted hosts of curious travelers to their borders. While these changes have made the countries of central and eastern Europe most interesting to visit, however, they also make the conditions of travel itself somewhat uncertain.

Even the official tourist boards of most former Soviet-bloc countries are sometimes confused as to visa requirements for foreign nationals. The most accurate sources of information are consular offices in the U.S., but you should always keep your ears open for new information while traveling. Check with travelers who've been in the eastern part of the continent; cities like Vienna are full of travelers heading to and coming from this region.

Also, be aware that in most of the countries that once formed the Soviet bloc, you will encounter an active black-market money exchange. In most of these countries the official exchange rate is set by the government and you will probably find more attractive rates on the street. However, unauthorized currency exchange is always illegal, although in some eastern European countries it is done quite openly. It is best not to take risks! Until a few years ago, most countries in the Soviet bloc had mandatory daily foreign-currency exchange requirements; fortunately for the budget traveler, these are no longer in effect anywhere in the region.

ATLANTIC OCEAN
UNITED KINGDOM
IRELAND
NORWAY
SWEDEN
FINLAND
DENMARK
NETHERLANDS
BELGIUM
LUXEMBOURG
BALTIC SEA
USSR
POLAND
GERMANY
FRANCE
CZECHOSLAVAKIA
AUSTRIA
SWITZERLAND
HUNGARY
ROMANIA
PORTUGAL
SPAIN
YUGOSLAVIA
ITALY
BULGARIA
MEDITERRANEAN SEA
ALBANIA
GREECE
MALTA

GETTING THERE

In the previous chapter, we gave basic information on international travel. If you want to know what your options for international travel to Europe are—and the advantages and disadvantages of each—be sure to read Chapter Five. We will repeat here that most prices quoted throughout the book are for comparison purposes only, owing to the constantly changing nature of air fares. Fares quoted here were those available in 1991. For more up-to-date information, write for a free copy of Council Travel's regularly updated "Airfare Update" fact sheet; you can get these at a Council Travel office, or use the order form in your *Student Travel Catalog*.

When making travel plans, you'll need to decide not only your destination but also the time you want to go. Air fares are generally determined by the "high" and "low" travel seasons. For example, transatlantic flights are most expensive during the period between June 1 and August 31. If you want to go for the summer, you should consider an earlier May departure or, if possible, a later return. Planning at least one leg of your trip at an off-peak time may save you money. Know too that fares go up during the weeks before and after major holidays, such as Christmas. However, if you don't mind traveling on the date of the holiday itself, when most people stay at home, you might be able to find a rare bargain.

Of course, cheap air fares aren't the only standard upon which to base your decision. You should research the country you plan to visit to get a rough idea of what it will be like when you get there. How's the weather? Will there be any public holidays during your stay? What are the chances of bumping into another American every third step? These are some of the questions you might want to ask. But whatever dates you choose, plan early: at least seven or eight weeks ahead of departure if you want to get the lowest fares available.

"When I took everything into consideration—weather, crowds, cultural events—I decided that Paris in September would be much more desirable than it would be in August (when the Parisians themselves are on vacation and shops are closed). And by flying there in the off-season, I saved a lot of money."

—Tammy Landt, Manchester, New Hampshire

Consolidator and Charter Flights

Consolidator and charter fares continue to be some of the best bargains in air travel to Europe. CIEE's subsidiary, Council Charter, offered flights to Brussels, London, Madrid, Málaga, Milan, Nice, Paris, and Rome in 1991. Any Council Travel office (see listings on pages xix–xxi) can help you make connections from a starting point in the U.S. to the flight's city of departure. Sample *round-trip* fares for the 1991 peak travel season were as follows:

From New York:	
Amsterdam	$538
Brussels	$619
London	$598
Madrid	$738
Málaga	$718
Milan	$778
Nice	$698
Paris	$538
Rome	$778

From Boston:	
Brussels	$618
Paris	$598

Student/Youth Fares

Students and young people are often able to find special discount fares on regular scheduled airlines. Although regulations vary depending on the carrier, generally you must be under the age of 26 or, if a student, under the age of 31. In most cases, you will need proof of your student status, such as an International Student Identity Card (see page 8) or an International Youth Card (see page 10). Here are some examples of *round-trip* youth and student fares available through Council Travel in 1991:

	Off-peak Season	Peak Season
New York–London	$350	$570
New York–Paris	$480	$598
Boston–Brussels	$398	$598
Boston–London	$378	$498
Chicago–Amsterdam	$470	$618
Dallas–Frankfurt	$650	$798
Seattle–London	$590	$690
New York–Warsaw	$635	$635
New York–Leningrad	$858	$858
Chicago–Warsaw	$695	$695

Other Discount Fares

If you watch the Sunday travel sections of your newspaper, you're likely to find real bargains in the off season. Other good resources are the weekly papers of major cities, such as the *Village Voice* or *L.A. Weekly*. Small travel agencies list discount ticket prices in these papers every week. While you can usually find great deals through these agencies, realize that once you put your money down, you can't expect a refund. Budget-minded travelers to Europe should also keep in mind Icelandair and Virgin Atlantic, two smaller airlines known for their affordable transatlantic fares. Remember, too, that by making arrangements in advance, you can make use of APEX or Super APEX fares, both of which require advance purchase and a stay of at least seven days but less than one year. For more information, see Chapter Five.

Getting There by Ship

There was a time when people could cross the Atlantic on student ships. Between 1947 and 1969, more than 150,000 students made the trip on liners chartered by CIEE specifically for student travel. Today travel by air is both cheaper and faster. To give you some idea of what a transatlantic voyage might cost you, round-trip summer fares (air passage on return) on Cunard's *Queen Elizabeth II*, with sailings from New York to Southampton, cost upwards of $2,000. Passage on freighters is somewhat lower-priced, but still very expensive. See Chapter Five for more information.

TRAVELING AROUND EUROPE

If you're a student or under 26, and you have an International Student Identity Card or an International Youth Card, you can benefit from a number of travel discounts offered by student travel bureaus in each country. Refer to Chapter Two for basic information on how to obtain a card.

By Train

Train travel in Europe is an unexpected pleasure for North Americans, who will have the chance to experience a way of travel quite different from that available in the United

States. In Europe, you'll find an international group of fellow travelers on the trains, many of them eager to talk and swap stories and share their bread and wine. Add to that the unsurpassed vistas of country and seaside—like the Mediterranean's waves breaking along the shore on the ride from Rome to Nice—and you get an idea of what's in store for you.

"My friend and I tried to schedule a lot of overnight train trips so that we could sleep on the train. For long hauls, night trains saved a lot of wasted travel time during the day which we wanted for sightseeing. This also avoided the inconvenience of arriving in a strange city too late to find a hostel or change money. Plus, we saved the cost of accommodation for one night! That's why the extra expense of the first-class Eurail vs. the Youthpass was worth it to us—the first-class compartments were usually empty and we were able to sleep. However, trying to spend more than two or three nights in a row on the train is very exhausting. If you're a light sleeper or can't function unless you get a good eight hours of slumber, overnight trains aren't worth the grief."
—Tyrone Rogers, Dallas, Texas

Rail Europe's Eurail pass offers a number of special discount rail-pass options providing unlimited train travel over specified periods of time. All Eurailpasses are valid for travel in 17 European countries: Austria, Belgium, Denmark, Finland, France, Germany, Greece, Hungary, Ireland, Italy, Luxembourg, The Netherlands, Norway, Portugal, Spain, Sweden, and Switzerland. These passes are also valid on many lake and river steamers, ferry boats, and buses. It's a good idea, however, to compare the cost of any one discount plan to the combined individual ticket prices for your journey before laying out your money. You can do this by consulting the *Eurailtariff Manual*, which lists prices for individual European point-to-point train trips, at a travel agency. The general rule of thumb is that you'll save money buying a Eurail pass if your plans call for visiting more than three countries, making frequent stops along the way. If you concentrate on only one or two countries, you should look into the appropriate national rail passes; you'll find information on these in the individual country sections later in this chapter. All of the Eurail passes mentioned below must be purchased in the U.S. You can get them from Rail Europe (800-345-1990), the U.S. offices of the various national railroads, or from any Council Travel office.

- **Eurail Youthpass.** If you are under 26, you can purchase the Eurail Youthpass, which entitles you to unlimited *second-class* travel. In 1991, a two-month pass cost $560; a one-month pass cost $425. There are supplementary fees for seat reservations, sleeping cars, and special express trains.
- **Youth Flexipass.** This pass, also restricted to *second class*, allows you to choose a number of travel days within a three-month period. Considering that most people don't travel every day of their trip, the Youth Flexipass is probably a more economical alternative to the Youthpass. Fifteen days of travel within three months costs $340; 30 days will run you $540.
- **Eurailpass.** The Eurailpass, which has no age cap, entitles you to unlimited *first-class* travel. Since some trains get very crowded on certain routes during vacations and summer, first class may be the way to go for comfort-conscious students. In 1991, a pass valid for 15 days cost $390; for 21 days, $498; for one month, $616; for two months, $840; and for three months, $1,042. Sleeping compartments and meals are not included in the price, but you won't have to pay extra to travel on the European luxury trains.
- **Eurail Saverpass.** If you plan to travel with some companions, the Eurail Saverpass is good for 15 days of unlimited, first-class travel for $298 per person in 1991. Three people must travel together sharing the same itinerary to be eligible for this pass during the peak travel season; between October 1 and March 31, only two people are required to travel together.

- **Eurail Flexipass.** Following the same principle as the Youth Flexipass, the Flexipass allows a number of travel days within a fixed time frame. Costs in 1991 were $230 for 5 days in 15; $378 for 9 days in 21; and $498 for 14 days in one month.

While the Eurail pass covers a lot of territory, it is not accepted in the United Kingdom or in most of eastern Europe. Those planning to travel widely in the U.K. should look into the BritRail passes described later in this chapter. For travel in eastern Europe, however, Rail Europe has devised the new **European East Pass**, valid in Austria, Czechoslovakia, Hungary, and Poland. Prices for the European East Pass in 1991 were $160 for 5 days of travel in 15, and $259 for 10 days of travel in one month.

As noted above, buying individual tickets—rather than a rail pass—may be cheaper. A number of travel agencies in Europe offer the under-26 population what are commonly known as "BIJ" tickets *(Billets Internationals de Jeunesse)*. Two agencies that sell them are Eurotrain and Transalpino.

- **Eurotrain.** If you're under 26, you may be able to save up to 50 percent off second-class rail fares on routes connecting nearly 500 cities throughout Europe. Information and bookings are available from student travel bureaus in Europe.
- **Transalpino.** Transalpino is a commercial agency that also offers discount point-to-point tickets for people under 26. There are branches and agents in many major European cities. For information check with the student travel bureaus abroad.

If you are going to be living in Europe for a while before traveling, you may be eligible for the **Inter-Rail Pass**. This pass allows *European* youth a one-month rail plan similar to the Eurail Youthpass offered to North Americans. But if you are under 26 and can prove that you have at least two months' residence in a European country, you too are eligible. Inter-Rail holders will receive a 50-percent discount on train fares in the country of purchase and unlimited free travel in all other countries subscribing to the plan. The pass is available at many European train stations and at student travel bureaus in Europe.

There are a number of good guidebooks geared especially to train travel in Western Europe. The *Eurail Guide*, by Kathryn Turpin and Marvin Saltzman, highlights 796 one-day excursions from 157 European base cities and includes information on schedules for intercity train travel (see page 51 for ordering information). Another book on the Eurailpass and how to use it is *Baxter's Eurailpass Travel Guide*, by Robert Baxter, available from Rail-Europe, PO Box 3255, Alexandria, VA 22302 for $9.95. *Cook's European Timetable* has train schedules for all of Europe and the Mediterranean and will save you the hassle of waiting in endless lines trying to get complicated information from harassed ticket officers behind glass partitions—a chore unless you're incredibly multilingual, extremely patient, and good at reading lips. You can find *Cook's* in most European bookstores.

How to Camp Europe by Train (1988–1989 edition), by Lenore Baken, describes how to combine train travel with stays in any of the thousands of campgrounds throughout Europe. The book is available for $12.95 plus $2 postage from Ariel Publications, 14417 SE 19th Place, Bellevue, WA 98007. *Europe by Train*, by Katie Wood and George McDonald, covers budget train travel in Europe and includes helpful information on transportation to and from rail stations. Published by Harper & Row, the 1988 edition is available in bookstores for $12.95.

By Air

While traveling on a European train can be a delightful experience, the charm quickly dwindles as the number of uninterrupted days and nights of train travel increases. Trans-European train trips are best broken down into shorter segments with stops along the way. If you have only a few far-flung destinations on your itinerary you should investigate air travel options. Not only will this save you valuable time, but intra-European student/youth airfares are usually comparable to the price of a long-distance train ticket.

There are a number of student flights as well as special student/youth fares on scheduled flights connecting the major European cities. In many cases, savings can be more than 50 percent off the regular economy fares. As with transatlantic student discounts, regulations vary depending on the airline, but generally you must be a student under the age of 31 or a young person under the age of 26 and have either an International Student Identity Card (see page 8) or an International Youth Card (see page 10). Student/youth fares on most of these flights can be booked at a Council Travel office. Here are some sample *round-trip* fares within Europe from 1991:

Paris–London	$138
Paris–Copenhagen	$258
Rome–Madrid	$278
Nice–Barcelona	$158
Amsterdam–Madrid	$180
Copenhagen–Rome	$300
London–Moscow	$530
London–Budapest	$378
Frankfurt–Warsaw	$330
Frankfurt–Moscow	$480

By Bus

Bus travel is not as popular as train travel in Europe, primarily because the various national railway systems are so good. As a result, buses are usually used for tour groups rather than for regular international transportation. They are fairly cheap, however, and there is one bus plan that will save you money if you have a Eurailpass or Youthpass. It's administered by Europabus, the motorcoach division of the European railroads, and has 70,000 miles of scheduled lines throughout Europe. Holders of the Eurailpass and Eurail Youthpass are entitled to substantial reductions on most European lines. For information and reservations, contact a travel agent or the ticket offices of the European railroads. You can also check with the student travel bureaus (see addresses in the individual country sections later in this chapter).

By Ship

Boats continue to serve as vital transportation links between many European countries. You'll find boats of all types connecting Britain and Ireland to the Continent. In northern waters, a number of ferry routes link the Scandinavian countries to Britain, Germany, Poland, and the U.S.S.R. But it is probably in the Mediterranean region that ferries and passenger boats are most numerous. Ships connect the mainland to numerous islands including Sicily, Sardinia, Corsica, and Crete. They also provide an economical way to get from Europe to North Africa and Israel. Especially popular with tourists are the boats to the resort isles of the Mediterranean such as Mallorca, Ibiza, Capri, Mykonos, and Corfu. If you're interested in exploring the southern Mediterranean coast and nearby islands, check out *Undiscovered Islands of the Mediterranean*, by Linda Lancione Moyer and Burl Wiles, available for $14.95 (plus $2.75 postage and handling) from John Muir Publications, PO Box 613, Santa Fe, NM 87504.

Several national student travel bureaus offer special student rates on Channel, Baltic, and Mediterranean sailings. For example, an International Student Identity Card will give you a discount on ferries between Finland and Sweden, Norway and Denmark, Italy and Greece, and Britain and various countries on the Continent. Information and bookings can be made at any of the student travel bureaus in Europe. Your Eurailpass also entitles you to discounts on many boats and ferries.

By Car

If you have a fairly loose itinerary, try ride-sharing. In most countries, it's quite easy to find drivers looking for riders, both for company and the sharing of expenses. Sharing a ride costs you less than taking the train and it's also a great way to meet people. Your driver will probably be familiar with your destination and may even extend an offer of hospitality or an evening out. Of course, ride sharing carries with it some of the same hazards as hitchhiking, but it is generally a more business-like arrangement.

University student-center bulletin boards are especially good sources for finding rideshares. Students frequently seek riders for weekend trips. And driving with an American is as much as a diversion for them as it is for you.

Another alternative is to register with a ride-share agency, which for a small fee puts you in touch with drivers. These agencies go by various names; in Germany, for example, they are known as *mitfahrcentrales*. Drivers who register with agencies have certain contractual obligations, such as gasoline-cost limits, which protect the rider. If you have your own car and want to list with such an agency, the service should cost you nothing.

The pros and cons of driving your own vehicle abroad were discussed in Chapter Five. If the idea appeals to you, there are numerous options for purchasing, leasing, and renting cars in Europe. If you plan to travel with friends and cover a lot of territory in Europe, renting a car may actually be cheaper than travel by rail or bus. But remember that gasoline prices are much higher in Europe than in the United States—usually around $6 a gallon. Western European roads are generally in good condition and the network of superhighways is extensive, especially in Germany, where the idea originated.

Car-rental arrangements should be made well before you leave the U.S., since cars (as well as campers, vans, and trailers) are scarce during the peak summer season. In fact, reserving a car before you leave for Europe will often make you eligible for a cheaper rate. Arrangements can be made through most travel agencies or through an international car rental company like Hertz or Avis. Council Travel offices can arrange leases or rentals with a selection of companies (like Renault and Kemwel) that offer cars with unlimited mileage at budget rates as low as $20 a day. If you plan to drive through Europe for two or three months, it will actually cost you less to lease a car or to purchase one from a company that will guarantee to repurchase it at the end of your trip. Council Travel offices' Renault Plan can give you these options.

Be sure to ask about minimum-age requirements; most rental companies require that drivers be at least 25 years of age. However, Auto Europe (PO Box 1097, Camden, ME 04843) requires a minimum age of only 21; call (800) 223-5555.

You may need an International Driving Permit (see page 52). Even if the permit is not always required, it's helpful to have it along when traveling in a non-English-speaking country where your regular license might not be understood.

When making car-rental arrangements, be sure to check whether insurance coverage is included in the cost. Most companies take care of this for you; they'll also provide you with the International Insurance Certificate or ''green card,'' required for all European countries. If you buy or lease a car, you can obtain insurance coverage and the green card through the dealer.

By Bicycle

Traveling by bicycle allows you to slow down, enjoy the pleasures of the countryside close-up, and get away from the tourist trail. Bicycling is also a very safe way to travel in Europe, as most major highways are paralleled by separate bicycle lanes.

Most international airlines permit bicycles in the luggage compartment. You do, however, have to take the pedals off, turn the handlebars sideways, and pack it into a special bag. Costs vary with the destination and the carrier, so make sure to ask. If you want to avoid the hassle, you can always buy or rent top-quality bicycles in Europe. In fact, many train stations have bike rental facilities, and most rail lines will let you carry your bike as baggage.

In most countries, bicycling is very popular indeed, especially in regions where the terrain is relatively flat, as in Denmark, Holland, and France's Loire Valley. If you're thinking of biking through Europe, the following books might be helpful. *Europe by Bike: 18 Tours Geared for Discovery*, written by Karen and Terry Whitehill during 11,000 miles of bicycling, gives detailed information on several touring routes ranging from 100 to 806 miles in length. It's available for $10.95 (plus $2 shipping and handling) from Mountaineers Books, 1011 S.W. Klickitat Way, Suite 107, Seattle, WA 98134. *Biking Through Europe*, available in bookstores for $13.95 (or from Williamson Publishing, PO Box 185 Charlotte, VT 05445), describes 17 bicycle tours taken by the authors, Dennis and Tina Jaffe. Also, don't forget to check with government tourist offices; each will have information on biking in its respective county, and in most cases can put you in touch with national bicycle clubs or similar organizations.

Hiking

For those who want to escape the cities, railways, and highways to enjoy the peaceful beauty of the countryside, mountain trails and cross-country paths can be found throughout Europe. In the Swiss Alps, for example, you'll find, in addition to the well-maintained and scenic mountain trails, a network of comfortable trailside chalets that accept phone reservations in advance. For an introduction to the wide range of trails that await you, read *100 Hikes in the Alps*, which describes alpine routes in Austria, France, Germany, Switzerland, and Yugoslavia. It can be ordered for $10.95 (plus $2 shipping and handling) from Mountaineers Books, 1011 S.W. Klickitat Way, Suite 107, Seattle, WA 98134. Mountaineers also publishes a number of more specific regional hiking guides. If you have a particular country in mind, call the government tourist office and ask for information on hiking clubs and parks services.

Hitchhiking

Hitchhiking, or "autostop," as it is frequently called on the Continent, is a popular way for European students to get around. Some people say it's risky and that they will never do it, while others argue that it's both the cheapest and the most interesting way of getting around. For anyone who is going to hitchhike in Europe, here are a few pointers:

- Look legitimate; dress in a way that will make car drivers feel they can trust you.
- Find out the local conditions for hitchhiking—your best source is the people who are doing it.
- Carry a sign that states clearly the direction in which you are headed and your destination.
- Women: Don't hitchhike alone. The best team is a man and a woman.
- Travel light—you should be able to jump in and out of a car quickly and not burden the driver with having to find room for your luggage.

"Hitching definitely has its pros and cons, but I enjoyed most of my rides. If you use smaller roads, as opposed to motorways and autobahns, you'll meet people who don't see travelers as often and are usually pretty excited to talk to you. Always carry some food and water with you each day you are hitchhiking, because you never know how long you might be waiting in the middle of nowhere."
—Mark Spitzer, Fullerton, California

Organized Tours

On the other hand, if you prefer the security and companionship offered by an organized tour, there's a wealth of options for you in Europe. In fact, a number of CIEE's member institutions and organizations offer organized, escorted tours by bus, bike, or foot in Europe.

American Youth Hostels organizes biking and hiking tours through several European countries. For example, AYH's new "United Germany" tour is a 16-day cycling trip from Berlin to Frankfurt. For those who prefer mountains, AYH's "Alpine Hike" tour will take you by foot through the Swiss Alps.

Moorehead State University, in Minnesota, offers two summer study tours. Its "Europe Summer" tour is a four-week program focusing on comparative education with visits to several major cities, such as London, Paris, Rome, and Heidelberg. Its "Soviet Study Tour," a two-week program, will take you to Moscow, Leningrad, and Kiev.

Ohio University's School of Journalism (614-593-2590) sponsors a three-week winter "Communications Capitals" tour which studies news media in New York, London, Paris. The Office of Continuing Education (614-593-1776) has two summer tours: "Exploring Greece," which includes Athens, Livadia, Delphi, and Sparta; and "Norway Tour," going to Oslo, Bergen, and other sites.

Finally, Western Michigan University offers "The Grand Tour," a one-month summer study tour (even-numbered years only) that takes in the art and architecture of Europe's major cities.

Consult Appendix I for the addresses of these institutions, so you can contact them for further information. For information on a host of other tour packages, contact Council Travel.

Student Travel Bureaus

In nearly every European country you'll find a student travel organization that is affiliated with the International Student Travel Confederation (ISTC). In the individual country sections that follow, we've included the addresses of the headquarters of these organizations. In addition, most have a network of branches around the country, usually in university cities and towns. As ISTC members, these offices issue the International Student Identity Card and arrange discounted tickets for student travel. Many also provide information on travel and accommodations, arrange tours, conduct language courses, and more. If you're going to be spending some time traveling in a country, be sure to make use of the information, discounts, and services offered by that country's student travel bureau.

Finding a Place to Stay

For decades, young Americans traveling in Europe have been greeted by a wide variety of inexpensive lodgings. Today, these bargains are harder to find. While the budget traveler can still go a long way on the dollar in many countries in eastern Europe and the Iberian Peninsula, prices in northern Europe are generally quite high. And, of course, the price for food and accommodations increases during the height of the tourist season.

Still, if you use your head (and your feet), you can find affordable youth hostels, pensions, and budget hotels anywhere you go. You'll find many listed in booklets put out by tourist offices and in the guidebooks mentioned later in this chapter. But beware—once they get into a guidebook, many of these places raise their rates. However, besides the regular budget hotels in Europe, there's a network of student hostels and youth hostels (see page 53) whose prices remain consistently affordable. If you need advice, next to talking to other travelers your best bet is to head for the nearest student travel bureau (see above). And, in most European cities of any size, you will find a general tourist office—usually in or near the railroad station, airport, or another central location—which also lists accommodations and will often call and book your stay for you, saving you the legwork.

If, however, you decide to stay in one city for an extended period of time (say, one year), you'll find that the price of renting a room becomes considerably less expensive. Often, if you arrive a few weeks before the school year begins, you'll be able to share an apartment with local students. Check out the local university bulletin boards for apartment-share notices.

"Youth or student hostels are a good place to get travel information—like good hostels in other countries, train routes . . . sometimes even news from home! If you're traveling alone, chances are that you will meet someone who is going in roughly the same direction. There's an international camaraderie among students, travelers, and young people out there that is well worth plugging into."
—Gillian Gottlieb, Seattle, Washington

The accommodations situation in Eastern Europe deserves special mention. Because the hotel industry in former Soviet-bloc countries is relatively underdeveloped, a fortunate alternative to the usual paid lodgings has cropped up in recent years: rented rooms in private homes and apartments. Eager to meet Westerners and to earn a little extra income as well, many families in Czechoslovakia, Hungary, and Poland enthusiastically open their doors to foreign travelers. Rooms are homey and comfortable, helpings of local food are generous, and your host will be happy to make conversation. To find a room in a private home, go to a tourist information center or ask a fellow traveler. These accommodations are less expensive than hotels.

Camping

There are campgrounds located all over Europe—on the outskirts of large cities, along major highways, and in resort areas at beaches, lakes, and mountains. Many are accessible by foot or by public transport, although having a car is usually more convenient. Most are well equipped with hot and cold running water, stoves, electrical outlets, laundry facilities, and a small store. Each person using the campsite has to pay a small fee per night plus a nominal charge for a car or motorcycle.

If you are going to camp in Europe, you might want to get an International Camping Carnet, a membership card issued by the National Campers and Hikers Association, 4804 Transit Road, Building 2, Depew, NY 14043. Some campgrounds require this card, but you can usually purchase it on the spot. At some campgrounds it can get you a small discount off the regular price, but unless you're planning to camp for an extended period of time, don't expect to save much money. The card costs $23 and includes membership in the National Campers and Hikers Association, which can also put you in touch with hikers' groups and supply you with information on camping.

You don't necessarily need a campground to camp. Most Scandinavian countries permit you to camp for one night anywhere in the countryside except on fenced land. And in the other countries of Western Europe, camping for a night in the open countryside is generally acceptable as long as you are discreet and ask permission before setting up camp on a farmer's land. Not only will you save money, you'll also avoid the crowds found at most European campgrounds during July and August.

Suggestions for Further Reading

Let's Go: Europe, updated each year by Harvard Student Agencies (1991 edition, $15.95), is probably the most popular guidebook for students going to Europe. It includes basic information on getting around, seeing the sights, and finding inexpensive places to sleep and eat. Published by St. Martin's Press, it's available in bookstores, from Council Travel offices, and by mail from CIEE (if ordering by mail, please add $1.50 for book-rate postage or $3 for first-class). Besides *Let's Go: Europe*, Harvard Student Agencies produces a number of more specific regional guides listed later in the appropriate country sections.

While the *Let's Go* guides are full of down-to-earth travel information, readers might turn to other guidebooks for greater cultural detail. Among the better guidebook series for comprehensive information about the artistic and historical sights of Europe are Prentice-Hall's *Real Guides*. These guides, which focus on particular countries and even single cities, are most impressive for weaving historical narrative and social observation with tips on places of current interest, all in a budget-travel framework.

The *Blue Guides*, published in the U.S. by W. W. Norton & Co., are renowned for their thorough, factual descriptions of most European countries. While they don't suggest hotels or restaurants, they give ample information on places of interest, and include helpful sections on language and the local cuisine.

If you plan to do a lot of driving, you'll find Michelin's European roadmaps and guidebook series of good use. *Michelin Green Guides* are especially good for road directions to various sights.

Guidebooks, however, should not be strictly adhered to. Don't expect things to be exactly the same as they are described in a book. Remember, even the most up-to-date guides will have been compiled the previous year.

The best preparation you can make for your trip, after narrowing down your itinerary, is to read as much about the region as you can. Chances are you know something of the history of the country or countries you plan to visit. But you can always learn more. Aside from literature and history, a faithful daily reading of a good newspaper should give you some idea of what's going on now.

STUDYING IN EUROPE

The options for study in Europe are virtually unlimited. In the individual country sections that follow, you'll find descriptions of the academic programs in Europe offered by CIEE-member institutions. In this section, we've listed only those study programs that take place in more than one country of the region. Consult Appendix I for the addresses of the sponsoring institutions.

Semester and Academic Year

Economics

Northeastern University. "Europe 2000." London and Antwerp. Fall and spring quarter. Study of European Economic Community. Juniors and seniors with 3.0 GPA. Apply by April 15.

General Studies

Associated Colleges of the Midwest. "Arts of London and Florence." Eight weeks in each city. Spring semester. Sophomores, juniors, and seniors with 2.75 GPA. Apply by October 15.

Eastern Michigan University. "European Cultural History Tour—Fall Semester." Travel-study program visiting 45 cities in Western Europe, the Soviet Union, and the Mediterranean. History, art, literature, and political science taught in an interdisciplinary context. Freshmen to seniors. Apply by June 1.

The Experiment in International Living/School for International Training.
"College Semester Abroad—Berlin: Germany Between East and West." Berlin, Erfurt, Weimar, and Dresden, Germany; and Prague, Czechoslovakia. Fall or spring semester. Interdisciplinary seminars, field-study methods seminar, homestays, educational travel, and independent-study project. Sophomores to seniors with 2.5 GPA. Apply by May 15 for fall and October 15 for spring.
"College Semester Abroad—Eastern European Studies." Budapest, Hungary; Cracow and Warsaw, Poland; Vienna, Austria. Interdisciplinary seminars, field-study methods seminar, homestays, educational travel, and independent-study project. Fall and spring semester. Sophomores to seniors with 2.5 GPA. Apply by May 15 for fall and October 15 for spring.

Friends World College. "European Studies." London, with trip to continental Europe. Academic year or semester. European culture, history, politics, and individualized program combining independent study with fieldwork or internships. Sophomores, juniors, seniors. Apply by May 15 for fall and November 15 for spring.

Moorhead State University. "European Humanities Tour" eight-week spring-quarter humanities program beginning in Oxford with tour through Paris, Florence, Rome, Venice, and Berlin. Freshmen to seniors. Apply by December 1.

Northeastern University. "Ireland: North and South." A bicultural experience, including social studies at Dublin's Institute of Public Administration and the Queen's University, Belfast, with internships in the Irish Parliament. Fall and winter quarter. Juniors and seniors with 3.0 GPA. Apply by April 15.

University of Pittsburgh. "Semester at Sea." Fall or spring semester. Students, based aboard the S.S. *Universe*, attend classes on board and travel to various countries in Europe, the Middle East, Africa, and Asia. Sophomores, juniors, and seniors with 2.75 GPA. Contact: Semester at Sea, Eighth floor, William Pitt Union, University of Pittsburgh, Pittsburgh, PA 15260; (412) 648-7490.

German Language and Culture

Macalester College. "Associated Colleges of the Twin Cities German Program." Spring semester. Intensive German language in Germany during January and February; culture and literature study in Vienna, March through May. Sophomores, juniors, and seniors with two years of college German. Apply by October 15.

Urban Studies

Great Lakes Colleges Association. "GLCA European Academic Term." Yugoslavia, Poland, Germany, and United Kingdom. Fall quarter. Offered with Great Lakes Colleges Association. Juniors and seniors. Apply by March 15.

Women's Studies

Antioch University. "Women's Studies in Europe." The Netherlands, Germany, and United Kingdom. Fall quarter. Juniors and seniors. Apply by March 15.

Summer

Art

Brigham Young University. "Europe for the Artist." Greece, Italy, Switzerland, France, and England. Drawing, watercolor painting, and readings. All students. Apply by February 1.

Miami University/University of Minnesota. "European Design Workshop." London, Paris, Luxembourg, Florence, and Venice. Interior design and architecture. Sophomores to seniors. Apply by April 2.

University of North Texas. "UNT Summer Art in Europe: Watercolor Painting & Drawing." France, Italy, England, Switzerland. Studio and fieldwork, with emphasis on landscape. Freshmen to graduate students and nonstudents. Apply by February 1.

Art History

Syracuse University. "The Journey of Vincent Van Gogh." Amsterdam, Paris, Nice, Arles. Freshman to seniors. Apply by March 15.

Business

University System of Georgia/University of Georgia. "International Business Perspectives—London and Tours." Undergraduate and graduate students with 2.5 GPA and one course in basic finance and business law. Apply by April 1.

Western Michigan University. "Business in Europe." Leicester, London, and Brussels. Juniors to graduate students and adults. Business or economics majors. Apply by May 15.

Chemistry

Southern Illinois University at Carbondale. "The History of Chemistry." Belgium, France, Germany, Great Britain, Netherlands, Italy, Switzerland, and Czechoslovakia. Visits to science museums and laboratories of historical importance. Juniors to graduate students and teachers. Apply March 1.

West Georgia College. "International Banking and Finance in Paris and London." Juniors to graduate students with 2.5 GPA and one course in corporate finance and banking. Apply by April 1.

Communications

Michigan State University. "Telecommunications in Europe." Paris, Geneva, Brittany, and Brussels. Juniors to graduate students. Apply by April 20.

Drama

University System of Georgia/University of Georgia.
"Drama in Italy and England." Parma and London. Freshman to graduate students with 2.8 GPA. Apply by April 1.

Environmental Design

University of Colorado. "Comparative European Environments." England, Switzerland, Italy, Greece. Urban policy and planning in several countries. Juniors and seniors with 3.0 GPA and background in environmental design or related field. Apply by end of January.

Michigan State University. "Interior Design in Europe." London and Milan. Study interior design and architecture from the 16th century to present. Contemporary design will be offered in Italy as an option. Juniors, seniors, and graduate students. Apply by April 20.

General Studies

Eastern Michigan University. "European Cultural History Tour—Summer." An intensive travel-study program visiting 35 cities in Western Europe, Eastern Europe, and the Mediterranean. Freshmen to seniors. Apply by April 1.

State University of New York at Oneonta. "Cultures and Cities of Europe." London, Paris, and Berlin. Participants visit two or more European cities to study on-site their key geographic and cultural aspects. Freshmen to graduate students; noncredit and nontraditional students are welcome to participate. Rolling admissions.

History

Eastern Michigan University.
"European Travel Study." Munich and other European cities. High school graduates, college students, and adults. Apply by May 15.
"Discover Russia and Poland." Warsaw and Cracow, Poland; Moscow, Leningrad, and other cities in the Soviet Union. Freshmen to seniors. Apply by March 1.

Syracuse University.
"The Medieval Pilgrimage Routes from Southern France to Santiago de Compostela: Romanesque Art in the Making." Sophomores to graduate students and professionals. Apply by March 15.
"Revolution in Eastern Europe." Vienna, Budapest, Prague, and Belgrade. Political science and European studies. Apply by March 15.

University of Connecticut. "The History of Jews in East Europe from the Origin of the Community to 1945." Warsaw, Bialystok, Cracow, Prague, and Amsterdam. Freshmen to graduate students with 2.5 GPA.

University System of Georgia/Dalton College. "Western Civilization in London and Paris." College students with 2.5 GPA. Apply by March 15.

International Studies

Boston University. "Summer Program in the Soviet Union and Eastern Europe." Moscow, Leningrad, Minsk, Warsaw, Crakow, Bratislava, Prague, Budapest, Helsinki. Field course in economic geography. Topics include development, modernization, ecology, and ethnic relations. Sophomores to graduate students and professionals. Apply by April 1.

University System of Georgia/Georgia Southern University. "Changes in Eastern Europe." Berlin, Poland, and Czechoslovakia. Undergraduate students with a 2.5 GPA and graduate students with a GPA of 3.0. Apply by April 1.

Wittenberg University. "Global Issues and World Churches." Geneva and Rome. Germany and Hungary in alternate years. Sophomores to seniors. For early decision apply January 6; deadline is March 1.

Journalism

University System of Georgia/University of Georgia.
"Journalism in Italy and England." Parma and London. Freshmen to graduate students with 2.8 GPA. Apply by April 1.

Management

Michigan State University. "International Management in Europe: Sweden, Denmark, France, Switzerland, and Germany." Juniors, seniors, and graduate students. Apply by April 20.

Social Science

Michigan State University. "Social Science in Scandinavia." Helsinki, Leningrad, and Stockholm. Freshmen to graduate students. Apply by April 20.

AUSTRIA

"There are no kangaroos in Austria," declares a popular T-shirt, indicative of the confusion foreigners sometimes have regarding this historic country in the heart of Europe. Its neighbors include Czechoslovakia, Germany, Hungary, Italy, Liechtenstein, Switzerland, and Yugoslavia. Due to its geographic position and its traditional political neutrality, this small, landlocked nation often serves as a crossroads between East and West and is the site of one of three United Nations complexes.

From Innsbruck in the west, the Alps stretch east to Austria's capital and most populous city, Vienna. Small towns dot the Alps, their architecture closely Bavarian and the country pristine. Remote inhabitants of the alpine region still wear lederhosen, 19th-century leather garb, and still dance to ancient refrains, including waltzes. Salzburg, a small city in the heart of the Alps, overflows each summer with tourists eager to see the picturesque medieval city where Mozart was born and the *Sound of Music* was filmed. In the East lies Vienna, spreading from the Alpine foothills to the Danube and across the plain towards Hungary.

In general, the standard of living is very high. Most families can afford cars and electronics imported from Germany and Japan. Austria produces most of its food and manufactures many products exported to its Central and Eastern European neighbors. Due to economic agreements that Austria has with the Common Market, it has access to a free-trade area that includes most West European countries.

It was an Austrian monarch's assassination—Archduke Franz Ferdinand—in Sarajevo in 1914 by a Serbian nationalist that precipitated World War I. The monarch was a Hapsburg from a dynasty that for hundreds of years ruled a large central European empire including all or part of what is now Germany, Italy, Hungary, Yugoslavia, Romania, Czechoslovakia, Poland—and Austria.

The country still contains a diverse mix of peoples. Descendants of Bavarians and Swiss reside in the west; descendants of Turks, Slavs, and Hungarian Magyars in the east. The various groups are fiercely protective of their ethnicity. Austrians of all backgrounds resent being thought of as German; their country ruled much of Europe more than 500 years before Germany arose as a nation-state. German is Austria's language, but it is distinct in many ways from its northwestern neighbor's tongue, particularly in a lilting dialect often unfathomable to northern German speakers.

—*Peter Stadtfeld, Ypsilanti, Michigan*

Official name: Republic of Austria. **Size:** 32,374 square miles (about the size of Maine). **Population:** 7,595,000. **Population density:** 233 inhabitants per square mile. **Capital and largest city:** Vienna (pop. 1,500,000). **Language:** German. **Religion:** Roman Catholic. **Per capita income:** US$12,521. **Currency:** Schilling. **Literacy rate:** 99%. **Average daily high/low*:** Vienna: January, 34°/26°; July, 59°/75°. **Average number of days with precipitation:** Vienna: January, 8; July, 9.

TRAVEL

Americans will need a passport to travel to Austria; however, a visa is not required for a stay of up to three months. Persons planning a stay longer than three months should check with the Austrian Embassy, 2343 Massachusetts Avenue NW, Washington, DC 20008, for information on specific requirements.

Getting Around

A good deal for anyone who wants to travel by rail is the new Rabbit Card, valid for four days of travel within 10 days of purchase. For travelers from 6 to 26 years of age, first class costs $78 and second class $53. Outside of Austria, Rabbit Card vouchers may be purchased from German Rail in the U.S. and at all major railway stations in Germany, The Netherlands, Switzerland, Italy, and other surrounding countries. It may be obtained at all Austrian rail stations. For those over 26, Rabbit Cards cost $87 second class and $124 first class.

You might also consider the "Network Pass," which offers one month's unlimited travel on all Austrian Federal Railways systems, including trains, some boats, buses, and cable cars for AS 3,100 (US$255) second class and AS 4,650 (US$382) first class, available at all Austrian rail stations or from the central rail offices in Frankfurt, Munich, or Zurich. One-year Network Passes are also available. Eurail passes are valid for train travel throughout Austria, as well for steamboat service on the Danube River and discounts on Lake Constance boats (see page 51). The "European East Pass" is valid in Austria, Czechoslovakia, Hungary, and Poland. It is available in first class only at a cost of $160 for rail travel on any 5 days within a 15-day period, or at a cost of $259 for rail travel on any 10 days within a one-month period.

Many Austrian railway stations rent bikes from April through October. Rental fees are AS 80 (US$7) per day, with a 50-percent reduction if you submit a railway ticket to the station where you intend to rent. Pick up a list of participating train stations from any Austrian Federal Railways office. During nonpeak periods, bikes are permitted as free hand baggage on Austrain trains.

Austrian Federal Railways also offers rental car services at 52 stations in several cities. Reservations (at least three hours in advance) can be made Monday through Friday from 8 A.M. to 6 P.M. by travelers 21 years of age or older.

For those who want to see the Alps as the Austrians do, a trip walking from one mountain hut to the next is an energetic option. Huts are open from early July until mid-September, and vary from extremely basic to ones equipped with hot showers. To help plan your itinerary, *Walking Austria's Alps, Hut-to-Hut*, describes 82 routes through

---

*All temperatures are Fahrenheit.

craggy peaks and flower-filled meadows for both novices and experienced hikers. The book is available for $10.95 (plus $2 shipping and handling) from Mountaineers Books, 1011 SW Klickitat Way, Suite 107, Seattle, WA 98134.

"Walk! The climate is wonderful and the people are warm and friendly and willing to share Austria with you."
— Paula K. Morris, Deerfield, Illinois

Especially for Students and Young People

Students going to Austria should be aware of two student travel organizations, both issuers of the International Student Identity Card:

- OKISTA provides an accommodation service, daily sightseeing tours, weekend excursions to Budapest and Prague, and student discount tickets for flights and trains. The organization also sponsors language courses, an international youth center, and a sports vacation program during the summer for young people ages 16 to 30. Available from the organization are various brochures including "Skiing in Austria." OKISTA branches are located in Graz, Innsbruck, Linz, Salzburg, Klagenfurt, and Bregenz. For further information, contact OKISTA, Turkenstrasse 4, A-1090 Vienna.
- Buro fur Studentenreisen (BfSt) offers a student accommodation service, student discount tickets for flights and trains, and language courses. You can write them at Schreyvogelgasse 3, A-1010 Vienna.

Holders of the International Student Identity Card in Austria are entitled to reduced or free entrance to many museums, palaces, and historical buildings in Vienna and Salzburg and up to 50-percent discounts on admission to some concerts and theaters. The International Youth Card is good for discounts on many hotels in Vienna, many museums all over the country, and selected tours and recreational facilities.

For Further Reading

A number of publications, including the *Austria Vacation Kit*, are available from the Austrian National Tourist Office, 500 Fifth Avenue, New York, NY 10110. From the same source you can get a copy of "Youth Scene," a brochure written by the staff of a Viennese magazine called *Falter* that's full of information on Austria's cities including meeting places, cultural events, restaurants, and accommodations. The tourist office also distributes listings of moderately priced hotels and pensions, information about camping, hiking, and skiing, and special brochures with information on Salzburg and Vienna for young people. Up-to-date information on Austria can be found in "Austrian Information," the monthly bulletin of the Austrian Press and Information Service of the Austrian Consulate General, 31 East 69th Street, New York, NY 10021.

Let's Go: Germany, Austria, and Switzerland, a recent addition to the Let's Go family, is tailored to the student budget. It's available for $14.95 in most bookstores and at Council Travel offices. The best cultural guide to Austria is the *Blue Guide: Austria* ($18.95). For information on places to stay and eat, primarily in the medium price range, try Frommer's *Guide to Austria and Hungary '91–'92* ($14.95).

"Salzburg is one of the great centers of European musical life and there are orchestras, bands, and choirs everywhere. Bring your musical instrument with you and join a choir or band, because it's a great way to meet the people. Be sure to attend a concert or recital while in Austria."
— Jesus Martinez, Miami, Florida

WORK

Getting a Job

According to the Austrian Consulate General, government regulations regarding employment in Austria have been tightened. Foreigners wishing to work in the country must be in possession of a valid work permit, which is issued by the local State Employment Office upon application by the prospective employer. Visas are only issued to holders of valid work permits. Further information is included in *Employment of Foreigners in Austria*, which is available from the Austrian Consulate General, Austrian Press and Information Service (address above).

A fact sheet, "Teaching in Austria," is available from the Austrian Cultural Institute (11 East 52nd Street, New York, NY 10022). The Institute also has a list of addresses of boards of education for the various Austrian provinces and suggests that teaching positions often exist in the smaller cities of these provinces. They add that "a very good command of the German language is absolutely necessary for anyone to be appointed as a teacher at an Austrian public school."

Internships/Traineeships

Programs offered by members of the Council on International Educational Exchange are described below. Consult Appendix I for the addresses of the organizations sponsoring these programs. In addition to the those listed here, Moorhead State University sponsors a program open only to its own students.

AIESEC-US. Reciprocal internship program for students in economics, business, finance, marketing, accounting, and computer science. See page 18 for further information.

Association for International Practical Training.
"IAESTE Trainee Program." On-the-job training for undergraduate and graduate students in technical fields such as engineering, computer science, agriculture, architecture, and mathematics. See page 18 for more information.
"Hotel & Culinary Exchanges Program." On-the-job training for young people beginning a career in the hotel and food-service industries. Participants must have graduated, or be currently enrolled in a university or vocational school and possess at least six months of training or experience in the chosen field. Training usually runs from 6 to 18 months.

Voluntary Service

One possibility for persons interested in voluntary-service work in Austria is the Year Abroad Program sponsored by the International Christian Youth Exchange. Open to persons 18 to 24 years of age, it offers long-term voluntary-service opportunities in the fields of health care, education, the environment, construction, et cetera. See page 23 for more information.

STUDY

The Austrian Cultural Institute (11 East 52nd Street, New York, NY 10022) distributes several free publications on study opportunities at Austrian universities, including *Information for Foreign Students Intending to Study at an Austrian Institute of Higher Learning* and *American Educational Programs in Austria*, a listing of U.S. colleges and universities that sponsor their own programs in Austria open to students from other schools.

Described below are the academic programs of CIEE-member institutions. Consult Appendix I for the addresses where you can write for more information. In addition to the programs listed here, Illinois State University, the University of California, the University of Connecticut, the University of the Pacific, and the University of Utah offer programs open only to their own students.

Semester and Academic Year

Business

Northern Illinois University. "International Business Internship in Salzburg." Spring semester. Internship plus two courses in economics, business, marketing, or finance. Housing with Austrian families. Sophomores, juniors, and seniors with 2.7 GPA. Apply by November 1.

European Studies

American Heritage Association. "Midwest Consortium for Study Abroad—Vienna." Fall or spring semester. Sophomores to seniors. No language requirement. Apply by June 15 for fall and November 1 for spring.

American University. "Vienna Semester." Fall or spring semester. Politics and foreign policy of Austria, Germany, and Switzerland. Internships with international organizations and Austrian agencies. Second-semester sophomores, juniors, and seniors with 2.75 GPA. Apply six months prior to start of program.

Beaver College.
"Study in Austria: Modern European Studies." Vienna. Academic year, fall or spring semester. Offered in cooperation with the Austro-American Institute of Education. Co-curricular escorted field-study trips to Paris and Berlin. Juniors and seniors with 3.0 GPA. Apply by April 20 for academic year and fall and October 15 for spring.
"Study in Austria: Southeast European Studies." Vienna. Spring semester. Offered in cooperation with the Austro-American Institute of Education. Co-curricular escorted field-study trips to Bulgaria, Hungary, Romania, and Yugoslavia. Juniors and seniors with 3.0 GPA. Apply by October 15.
"Study in Austria: Soviet and East European Studies." Vienna. Fall semester. Offered in cooperation with the Austro-American Institute of Education. Co-curricular escorted field-study trips to Czechoslovakia, Poland, and USSR. Juniors and seniors with 3.0 GPA. Apply by April 20.

Northern Illinois University. "European Studies in Salzburg." Semester or academic year. Internships in business available spring semester. Housing with Austrian families. Sophomores, juniors, and seniors with 2.7 GPA. Apply by June 1 for fall and November 1 for spring.

State University of New York at Fredonia. Vienna. Spring semester. Austrian and Central European history, economics, and culture. Juniors and seniors. Some German preferred but not required.

General Studies

Alma College. "Program of Studies in Austria." Vienna. Extensive excursions, homestays available, and instruction in English. Sophomores, juniors, and seniors with 2.5 GPA. Apply by June 15 for fall and October 15 for winter.

Brigham Young University. "BYU Study Abroad." Vienna. July–December and January–June. Sophomores, juniors, and seniors. Some German required. Apply by February 1 for fall and October 1 for spring.

International Student Exchange Program. Direct reciprocal exchange between U.S. universities and the Karl Franzens University in Graz. Academic year. Full curriculum options. Open only to students at ISEP-member institutions.

St. Lawrence University. "Vienna Fall Semester Program." Fall semester. Sophomores, juniors, and seniors with 2.8 GPA. No language prerequisite. Apply by Feb 20.

State University of New York at Binghamton. Graz. Academic year or fall semester. Study at Karl Franzens University. Juniors and seniors with four semesters of college German.

University of Arkansas. "Austrian Exchange Program." Graz. Study at Karl Franzens University. Open only to students at member-schools of the Arkansas Consortium for International Education. Juniors and seniors. Four semesters of college German required. Rolling admissions.

University of Maine. "New England Study Abroad Program." Salzburg. Academic year or spring semester. Sophomores to graduate students with four semesters of German. Apply by April 15 for academic year and November 15 for spring.

University of Notre Dame. "International Study Program in Innsbruck." Academic year. Focus on German language and Austrian history and philosophy. Priority is given to students at Notre Dame and St. Mary's College. Sophomores and juniors with one year of college German; 2.5 GPA with 3.0 GPA in German. Apply by December 1.

Wilmington College. "Semester Abroad with Midwest Consortium for Study Abroad." Vienna. Fall or spring semester. Courses in music, art and architecture, history and civilization, economics, and German language. Housing with families. Includes tours in Austria and surrounding countries. Sophomores to seniors. Apply by November 15.

German Language

Adventist Colleges Abroad. Bogenhofen. Academic year or semester. Open only to Adventist Colleges-Abroad consortium institutions. Freshman to seniors with 3.0 GPA in German and 2.5 overall GPA. Apply 60 days before beginning of academic term.

Beaver College. "Study in Austria: January Term in Intensive German Language Study." Vienna. Offered in cooperation with the Austro-American Institute of Education. Beginning and intermediate language levels. Sophomores, juniors, and seniors. Apply by November 15.

Central University of Iowa. "Central College in Germany and Austria." Vienna. Semester or academic year. Sophomores, juniors, and seniors with intermediate-level German, 2.5 GPA (3.0 in German). Apply by October 15 for spring and March 15 for fall.

Ohio University. Salzburg. "Spring Quarter in Austria." Freshman to seniors with two quarters of German. Apply by January. Contact Department of Modern Languages, (614) 593-2765.

University of Minnesota. "German and Austrian Studies in Graz." Winter and/or spring quarter. Freshman to graduate students and adults with three semesters of German and 2.5 GPA. Apply by October 15 for fall; December 15 for spring.

Photography

Northern Illinois University. "Photography Program in Salzburg." Academic year only; requests for one-semester option considered on an individual basis. Housing with Austrian families. Two years of photography required. Apply by June 1.

Summer

Austrian Studies

American Heritage Association. "American Heritage Cultural Summer Program." Vienna. No language requirement. Must be 18. Apply by April 15.

General Studies

Hope College. "Vienna Summer School." Austrian history, music, art, economics, German language and literature. Freshmen to seniors. Apply by February 25.

North Carolina State University. Vienna. Study arts or German language. Sophomores to seniors with two semesters of German. Apply by March 1.

Southern Methodist University. "SMU-in-Austria." Salzburg. Liberal-arts studies focused upon Austria and Central Europe. Sophomores, juniors, and seniors. Apply by March 15.

German Language

Eastern Michigan University. "Intensive German Language Program." Vienna. Beginning, intermediate, and advanced German language. Freshmen to graduate students.

Indiana University. "Summer Language Study in Graz." Intermediate German. Freshmen to seniors with three semesters of German. Apply by February 1.

University of Arkansas at Little Rock. "Summer in Austria." Graz. Freshmen to seniors with intermediate-level German. Apply by February 28.

EXPLORING AUSTRIAN CULTURE

Readings

There is an Austrian tendency towards dark introspection which stretches back to the moody decadence of the last days of the Austro-Hungarian Empire at the turn of the century. Austrian literature tends to turn inward on deep personal problems, which perhaps reflects both a preoccupation with the shadow of a glorious past and a search for identity now. Peter Handke, one of the best-known Austrian writers today, is preoccupied with these kinds of ideas and has written many books that have been translated into English. *The Goalie's Anxiety at the Penalty Kick* (1972) is the story of a former soccer player who is a pathological killer. Handke's latest collection of musings is titled *The Weight of the World: A Journal*.

Ingeborg Bachmann, another modern writer, wrote *Three Paths to a Lake* (1989) and many short stories, some of which are collected in *The Thirtieth Year*. She explores different ways of interpreting life in an idiosyncratic stream-of-consciousness style. A more bitterly humorous approach is taken by Thomas Bernhard, a novelist and playwright who wrote about his country in a cynical, pessimistic way that brought him many admirers but at least an equal number of enemies in his home country. *The Chalk Factory* is a novel about a misanthropic man who kills his wife in order to write a study about hearing. *The Ignoramus and the Madman* is a play about alienated individuals who have lost the ability to be spontaneous. In *Heldenplatz* (1988), a play written just before his death, Bernhard risked a head-on collision with his countrymen, once again bringing up their Nazi past and connecting this with the moral state of the country now—after the storms of the Waldheim affair.

BELGIUM

Although Belgium has existed as an independent state since 1830, there is no Belgian language and there are no real Belgians. Two cultures—the Flemish and the Walloons—coexist within the state's borders. About 55 percent of the people speak Flemish, or Dutch, while the remainder are French-speaking Walloons. Today, as the historic forces that have unified Belgium (such as a common religion and king) have weakened, linguistic battles and other disputes between these two groups have become more pronounced. While an international soccer championship can sometimes unify the two groups to do justice to the national motto, *L'union fait la force* (Union makes strength), Belgium is evolving into two separate semi-autonomous regions within a federal system.

The Flemish region (known as Flanders) encompasses the flat lowlands of the northern part of the country. In the late Middle Ages the area produced some of the wealthiest trading cities in the world. Visitors to the cities of Antwerp, Ghent, and Bruges will find the inhabitants intensely proud of their rich heritage of art and architecture from the "Golden Century."

Farther south, in the French-speaking area known as Walloonia, the countryside becomes progressively more hilly and scenic. Here travelers enjoy hiking and biking, exploring quaint villages and castles, and visiting caves and spas (in fact, the Belgian town of Spa gave its name to the whole concept).

In the center of the country lies the booming "Eurocity" of Brussels. Although the capital of Belgium, Brussels is now more important as headquarters for NATO, headquarters for the European Community, and European headquarters for a growing number of multinational corporations. New high-rise buildings surround the city but the Grand Place, the town's medieval center, retains its charm. South of Brussels is Waterloo, site of Napoleon's crushing defeat in 1815.

In this small bilingual and bicultural country tucked between France, Germany, Luxembourg, and the Netherlands, people are used to dealing with cultural and linguistic differences. Most people speak more than one language and many, especially the young, speak some English.

Although split by ethnic rivalry, Belgium has consistently been a leading supporter of greater European unity. Such a stand is not surprising. The country's modern industrial economy is dependent on international trade and the nation's very existence depends on friendly relations between its much more powerful neighbors. In fact, greater European unity might prove to be the final denouement of the country's ethnic rivalry as well as an end to the international conflicts between Belgium's neighbors that have, twice in this century, made the small nation a world battlefield.

—*Vera van Brande, New York, New York*

Official name: Kingdom of Belgium. **Size:** 11,799 square miles (slightly larger than Maryland). **Population:** 9,941,000. **Population density:** 840 inhabitants per square mile. **Capital and largest city:** Brussels (pop. 1,000,009). **Language:** Flemish, French. **Religion:** Roman Catholic. **Per capita income:** US$10,890. **Currency:** Belgian franc. **Literacy rate:** 98%. **Average daily high/low*:** Brussels: January, 42°/31°; July, 73°/54°. **Average number of days with precipitation:** Brussels: January, 12; July, 11.

TRAVEL

A passport is required for Americans visiting Belgium. A visa is not required for business or tourist stays of up to 90 days. For longer stays, a temporary residence permit is required. For residence authorization, check with the Belgian Embassy, 3330 Garfield Street NW, Washington, DC 20008.

Getting Around

Most travelers to Belgium will also want to visit neighboring countries. Eurail passes, of course, are a good option for multicountry trail travel. Those planning to spend most of their time in Belgium, the Netherlands, and Luxembourg would do well to inquire about the "Benelux Tourrail Pass," which allows 5 days of travel throughout the three countries during a 17-day period. Youths under 26 pay $65 for second class and $97 for first class. The "Benelux Tourrail" can be purchased from the Netherlands Board of Tourism at 355 Lexington Avenue, 21st Floor, New York, NY 10017; (212) 370-7367.

For travel exclusively within Belgium, the Belgian Tourrail "B" Pass allows unlimited travel on any 5 days within a 17-day period. Youths under 26 receive special discounts; BF1,300 ($37) second class. The "16-Day Pass" is good for 16 days' consecutive travel year-round and costs BF3,050 ($86) second class. The "Half-Rate Card," costs BF500 ($14) for one month and gives the holder a 50-percent reduction on first- or second-class rail tickets bought in Belgium for travel within the country. These passes can be bought only in Belgium. For further information on rail passes, contact Belgian National Railroads, 745 Fifth Avenue, New York, NY 10501; (212) 758-8130.

Another way to explore Belgium is by bike, as most major roads are accompanied by bike paths. Bicycles can be rented year-round at most train stations, can be taken on Belgian trains at no extra charge, and can be returned at any station.

In Brussels, the Tourist Information Office, rue du Marché aux Herbes, 61 (or, in Flemish, Grasmarkt 61), can help find accommodations throughout Belgium to suit your budget.

Especially for Students and Young People

One good source of information on student travel in Belgium is the office of ACOTRA (rue de la Madeleine, 51, B-1000 Brussels). Another source of information is Connections, which has offices in Brussels (13 rue Marché au Charbon, Kolenmarktstraat, 1000 Brussels) as well as in Ghent, Liège, Antwerp, and Leuven. In Belgium, holders of the International Student Identity Card receive reduced train and plane fares to international destinations and a discount on tours offered by ACOTRA. Available free at Connections offices is a handbook describing discounts available to cardholders. The International Youth Card is good for discounts on specific hotels, mainly around Brussels, as well as many museums throughout the country. It also offers reduced airfares to and from Brussels,

---

*All temperatures are Fahrenheit.

which are available through ACOTRA and its associates around the world. In the city of Liège, holders of the card receive free entry into all city museums.

For Further Information

You can get maps and information on camping, budget hotels, and more from the Belgian Tourist Office, 745 Fifth Avenue, New York, NY 10151. Also available from the tourist office is "Windrose," a listing of accommodations with host families in Belgium. In Belgium, be sure to pick up a copy of the English-language weekly *Bulletin*, which lists cultural events as well as job opportunities.

WORK

It is necessary to obtain a work permit for employment in Belgium. The permit is issued by the appropriate Belgian authorities upon application by the prospective employer in Belgium. If you are planning to stay for more than 90 days, it is necessary to obtain a temporary residency permit as well. For further information contact the Belgian Embassy, 3330 Garfield Street NW, Washington, DC 20008.

Internships/Traineeships

Programs offered by members of the Council on International Educational Exchange are described below. Consult Appendix I for the addresses where you can write for more information. In addition to those listed below, Moorhead State University sponsors an internship program open only to its own students.

AIESEC-US. Reciprocal internship program for students in economics, business, finance, marketing, accounting, and computer science. See page 18 for more information.

Association for International Practical Training. "IAESTE Trainee Program." On-the-job training for undergraduate and graduate students in technical fields such as engineering, computer science, agriculture, architecture, and mathematics. See page 18 for more information.

Voluntary Service

CIEE places volunteers in Belgian workcamps organized by Compagnons Batisseurs (Rue Notre-Dame de Grâces, 63, B-5400 Marché-en-Famenne). At these workcamps, groups of volunteers from around the world work on a variety of construction projects. Applicants must be 18 years of age or older. Applications of U.S. residents are processed by CIEE. For more information contact CIEE's Voluntary Service Department.

For persons interested in longer-term voluntary-service work, the Year Abroad Program sponsored by the International Christian Youth Exchange offers persons ages 18 to 24 voluntary-service opportunities in the fields of health care, education, the environment, construction, and others. See page 23 for more information.

In addition, the Fourth World Movement sponsors work/information camps in Belgium. For more information see page 21.

STUDY

For those who want to study in Belgium, the Embassy of Belgium (3330 Garfield Street NW, Washington, DC 20008) offers two free publications: *University Studies in Flanders (Belgium)* and *The French-Speaking Community in Belgium and its Universities*.

For predoctorate graduate students wishing to pursue independent study and research in Belgium, the Belgian American Educational Foundation offers a $10,500 fellowship for a ten-month period. Candidates must speak and read either German, French, or Dutch. The application deadline is December 31. For details write to the Belgian American Educational Foundation, 195 Church Street, New Haven, CT 06510.

Described below are the academic programs sponsored by CIEE-member institutions. Consult Appendix I for the addresses of the colleges and universities listed in this section.

Semester and Academic Year

General Studies

International Student Exchange Program. Direct reciprocal exchange between U.S. universities and the Katholieke Universiteit te Leuven and Université Catholique de Louvain. Academic year. Full curriculum options. Open only to students at ISEP-member institutions.

Northern Illinois University. "Academic Internships in Brussels." Fall or spring semester. Students take two courses plus internship. Wide range of internships available for own students; more limited selection for others. Sophomores, juniors, and seniors with 3.0 GPA and two years of French. Apply by April 4 for fall and November 1 for spring.

International Relations

American University. "Brussels Semester." Fall or spring semester. U.S.–Western European relations. Internships with multinational organizations. Second-semester sophomores, juniors, and seniors with 2.75 GPA. Apply six months prior to start of program.

Summer

International Relations

Michigan State University. "International Relations in Brussels." For students with an interest in political science, international studies, and international relations. Sophomores, juniors, and seniors. Apply by April 20.

University of Pennsylvania. "Penn-in-Leuven." Antwerp, Brussels, and Leuven. International relations and international business. Apply by April 1.

BULGARIA

Bulgaria is one of the least visited of the countries formerly known as the Soviet bloc. The Bulgaria of today, however, can no longer be considered an intimidating place to visit. The adventurous traveler who makes the trip will encounter people with a fresh interest in visitors and a fascinating country that has been largely spared the crush of Western tourism.

A common alphabet and real gratitude for being freed from Ottoman Turks in the late 1800s are but two of the ties that contribute to the closeness which Bulgaria truly seems to feel for the Soviet Union, and more specifically for Russia. Perhaps because of this, the spirit of change that swept eastern Europe in the late 1980s was felt differently in Bulgaria than it was in Hungary or Poland, for example. Bulgarians, like the other peoples of eastern Europe, are searching for new directions and the country's economy and society are engaged in a difficult, fascinating period of transition.

The capital city of Sofia, with its historic ruins, university centers, and nearby modern alpine skiing facilities on Mount Vitosha, frequently hosts international sports competitions and conferences. The ancient city wall and ruins just off the main city square, the lively market area with its live chickens and varied aromas, and the structures and monuments of several cultures are all linked by an inexpensive public transportation system.

Visitors to the area near Varna on the Black Sea coast will find a different Bulgaria—one designed to attract the tourist through various vacation packages. Soviet citizens mingle with Western tourists, often from the United Kingdom, who fly in to enjoy an inexpensive seacoast holiday; here the visitor is more apt to find English or German understood.

Travel away from Sofia and Varna reveals another perspective on the country. Monasteries in the remote mountains have survived hundreds of years and remain in remarkable condition, relics of the various cultures that Bulgaria has seen throughout the centuries. There is a real sense of history in Bulgaria and the preparation time spent in reading a little about the country's past—and learning a few phrases of the language—will be richly rewarded with warmth, smiles, and helpfulness.

Bulgarian students and business people alike are intensely interested in the world of ideas and you can easily find yourself debating the merits of von Mises or Piaget over a tiny cup of the strong, dark, local coffee. It's always useful to understand some of the local body language: the thumb is used to indicate one (such as in ordering coffee) and the "yes/no" head nods are reversed from the United States custom. As always, there is no substitute for a healthy sense of humor and a willingness to accept things as they are.

—*Bill Peirce, Forestdale, Massachusetts*

Official name: People's Republic of Bulgaria. **Area:** 44,365 square miles (about the size of Ohio). **Population:** 8,978,000. **Population density:** 203 inhabitants per square mile. **Capital and largest city:** Sofia (pop. 1,119,000). **Language:** Bulgarian, Turkish. **Religion:** Atheism (85% of people have Orthodox background). **Per capita income:** US$7,510. **Currency:** Lev. **Literacy rate:** 98%. **Average daily high/low*:** Sofia: January, 35°/22°; July, 82°/57°. **Average number of days with precipitation:** Sofia: January, 6; July, 7.

TRAVEL

U.S. citizens will need a passport and a visa to travel in Bulgaria. Tourist visas cost about $15 and must be applied for in advance. The maximum stay is 30 days. For more information, contact the Bulgarian Embassy at 1621 22nd Street NW, Washington, DC 20008.

Getting Around

Bulgaria's rail network is extensive, making train travel the most convenient way to get around. Trains are also inexpensive, and holders of the International Student Identity Card receive a 25-percent discount on domestic and international travel. Bulgaria's trains do, however, have a reputation for being quite crowded, and lines to purchase tickets

---

*All temperatures are Fahrenheit.

may be quite long. It is therefore suggested that tickets be purchased well in advance, if possible. To do this, one must find the central ticketing offices in each city; in the stations themselves, tickets go on sale two hours before departure. Trains do not run along the Black Sea coast, but buses do.

A good way to beat the crowds is to hop on a Balkan Air shuttle flight. Though perhaps twice as expensive as train service, domestic flights are still affordable.

Especially for Students and Young People

ORBITA is Bulgaria's student travel office and issuer of the International Student Identity Card. Its main office is at 45A Stambolijski Boulevard, 1000 Sofia, with branches in many cities throughout the country. Besides serving as an information source, ORBITA runs a chain of student hostels, for which Westerners must make advance reservations. ORBITA also sponsors several tours and offers sports and cultural activities at the Georgi Dimitrov International Youth Centre in the Black Sea town of Primorsko. Holders of the International Student Identity Card receive discounts on all of ORBITA's services.

For Further Information

For more detailed information on traveling in Bulgaria, read *Eastern Europe on a Shoestring*. The recently updated second edition is available for $21.95 (plus $1.50 book-rate postage; $3 for first-class) from Lonely Planet Publications, Embarcadero West, 112 Linden Street, Oakland, CA 94607.

WORK

It's virtually impossible for Americans to obtain regular employment in Bulgaria. However, internship and voluntary-service opportunities are described below.

Internships/Traineeships

Following is a program sponsored by a member of the Council on International Educational Exchange.

AIESEC-US. Reciprocal internship program for students in economics, business, finance, marketing, accounting, and computer science. See page 18 for more information.

Voluntary Service

CIEE places young people in voluntary-service workcamps in Bulgaria organized by ARGO (11 Stambolijski, 1041 Sofia). At these workcamps, small groups of volunteers from various countries work on a range of community-service projects. Volunteers must be at least 18 years old; room and board are provided by the camp. The applications of U.S. residents are processed by CIEE. For more information, contact the Voluntary Service Department at CIEE.

CYPRUS

The Mediterranean island nation of Cyprus was the site of early Phoenician and Greek colonies. Because of its strategic position in the eastern Mediterranean, it has fallen prey to numerous other conquerors over the centuries. The British seized the island from the Turks in the First World War and held it until 1960, when it was granted independence.

Turkish-Greek animosity on the island is rampant. In fact, the majority of the population regard themselves as either Greeks or Turks, rather than Cypriot nationals. To make matters worse, violence between Greek and Turkish Cypriots has been provoked by the interference of Greece and Turkey in the island's affairs. In 1974, Turkish troops invaded Cyprus in defense of the Turkish minority, and Turkey still controls about a third of the island. Greek Cypriots—most of whom support self-determination for the island (that is, union with Greece)—have fled to the southern and western parts of the country. Turkish Cypriots, however, have set up a government in the area they control and proclaimed their independence. While the international community still recognizes Cyprus as a single independent state, in fact the island is split into two belligerent states, divided by linguistic, religious, and ethnic differences.

Tourists are prohibited from crossing the militarized border ("Green Line") between the Greek and Turkish sections of the island. Most tourists visit the Greek section, which is linked by plane to Western Europe and the Middle East and by ferry to Greece, Israel, and Lebanon. Good beaches, a warm sunny climate, and inexpensive food and accommodations have made the Greek section popular with tourists in spite of the continuing conflict between Greeks and Turks.

—*Michael La Pierre, New York, New York*

Official name: Republic of Cyprus. **Area:** 3,572 square miles (one and a half times the size of Delaware). **Population:** 708,000. **Population density:** 194 inhabitants per square mile. **Capital and largest city:** Nicosia (pop. 124,300). **Language:** Greek, Turkish (both official), English. **Religion:** Greek Orthodox, Islam. **Per capita income:** U.S. $5,210. **Currency:** Cypriot pound. **Literacy rate:** 99%. **Average daily high/low*:** Nicosia: January, 58°/42°; July, 97°/69°. **Average number of days with precipitation:** Nicosia: January, 10; July, less than 1.

TRAVEL

U.S. citizens will need a passport to travel to Cyprus; however, a visa is not required. Check with the Embassy of the Republic of Cyprus (2211 R Street NW, Washington, DC 20008) for specific requirements.

Getting Around

The routes between the major towns and cities are served by buses and shared taxis. The taxis follow regular routes, departing when they are full and picking up and dropping off passengers along the way. Hitchhiking is relatively easy, and on secondary routes it can be the only alternative. Car rentals can also be arranged. Remember that driving is on the left side of the road.

For Further Information

Let's Go: Greece and Turkey contains a chapter on Cyprus with helpful information for the budget traveler. It's available for $14.95 in most bookstores and at Council Travel offices. General tourist information is available from the Cyprus Tourist Office, 13 East 40th Street, New York, NY 10016.

---

*All temperatures are Fahrenheit.

WORK

In order to work in Cyprus you need to obtain a work permit; positions are granted only to foreigners who possess a needed skill that can't be filled by a Cypriot national. It is difficult to get a permit while in the country unless you have a prearranged position with a company in the private sector. For more information contact the Consulate of Cyprus, 13 East 40th Street, New York, NY 10016.

Internships/Traineeships

The following program is sponsored by a member of the Council on International Educational Exchange.

Association for International Practical Training. "IAESTE Trainee Program." On-the-job training for undergraduate and graduate students in technical fields such as engineering, computer science, agriculture, architecture, and mathematics. See page 18 for more information.

STUDY

Described below are the educational programs offered by CIEE-member institutions. Consult Appendix I for the addresses of the colleges and universities listed in this section.

Semester and Academic Year

Business

State University of New York/Empire State College. "Semester Program in Cyprus." Nicosia. Semester or academic year. Business and technology in the Eastern Mediterranean. Sophomores to graduate students and adults. Apply by November 30 for spring and June 15 for all.

General Studies

International Student Exchange Program. Direct reciprocal exchange between U.S. universities and Frederick Polytechnic University. Semester. Full curriculum options. Open only to students at ISEP-member institutions.

Summer

Archaeology

Boston University. "Archaeological Field School at Kalavasos-Kopetra." Intensive study of the history and monuments of Cyprus. Students enroll in two courses (eight credits): Greek archaeology and archaeological field methods. Sophomores to seniors with 3.0 GPA in major. Apply by April 1.

CZECHOSLOVAKIA

Czechoslovakia's Gothic and baroque buildings stand amidst rows of stark gray apartment blocks. From Prague, the city of a hundred spires, to Bratislava, the home of a hundred decaying towers, the country's colorful political history has left its mark. Signs of the most recent political upheaval are visible everywhere. Timid smiles stand in contrast to the weary faces that prevailed before the revolution in 1989. Now is certainly an exciting time to visit Czechoslovakia.

But these are also challenging times. The country is experiencing a dramatic rise in inflation which is not being matched by wages. Czechoslovakians therefore find the cost of living exorbitant and increasing daily—the cost of a subway ticket more than quadrupled in just one month. In contrast, Western tourists find the cost of living very cheap, and with the visa requirement removed, visitors from wealthier neighboring countries have begun to take advantage of bargain holidays and weekend breaks. Some come simply to buy large quantities of exquisite crystal.

On the weekends there is a mass exodus from the cities to the country. The scenery, lakes, mountains, wildlife, and a legacy of Victorian elegance in spa towns such as Karlsbad and Marienbad, are strong reasons for leaving the bleak and depressing housing areas. Trains tend to be slower than the buses, but the metro in Prague is so clean and efficient that it puts most other subway systems to shame.

With its fairy-tale castle gazing down on the Vltava River flowing under the baroque statues on Charles Bridge, Prague has been called the most beautiful city in Europe. Steeped in history with Viennese-style squares, palaces, formal gardens, and street musicians, as well as a church where Mozart played and a library where Kafka worked (now the U.S. embassy), Prague was fortunate in emerging from both World Wars virtually unscathed.

The nation's numerous castles, which once guarded tiny principalities, are perhaps testament to the conflict and division that have characterized the area for centuries. Roughly divided into three regions—Bohemia, Moravia, and Slovakia—Czechoslovakia is now experiencing internal problems due to the rise of nationalism. In fact, the term "Czechoslovakia" was born in 1918, along with the country, when two nationalities—the Czechs and the Slovaks—were placed by the Treaty of Versailles in a new state that occupied territory that had long been part of the Austro-Hungarian Empire. These two peoples, each with their own language and traditions, continue to live in uneasy coexistence within the modern state; furthermore, the Slovaks have recently started an independence movement. President Vaclav Havel, a political activist and author, has expressed his frustration over the problems of keeping the country from dividing so soon after achieving its freedom from the Kremlin.

The people are difficult to meet and get to know. After 40 years of oppression they are still very suspicious, but once the initial barriers are broken they can become good friends. More often than not, they will invite you to drink with them. They will be offended if you try to pay, however, so on this basis visitors should be considerate and try not to order too much.

Waiting in long queues has made patience another marked quality of the people, for self-service is still rare and many items are still unavailable in the larger city shops. Visitors may find this frustrating, but after a couple of weeks, they will find a hitherto unrealized joy at finding fresh bananas or salad dressing at the local supermarket.

—*Sarah J.B. Eykyn, London, United Kingdom*

Official name: Czech and Slovak Federative Republic. **Area:** 49,365 square miles (about the size of New York State). **Population:** 15,695,000. **Population density:** 317 inhabitants per square mile. **Capital and largest city:** Prague (pop. 1,200,000). **Language:** Czech, Slovak. **Religion:** Roman Catholic. **Per capita income:** US$10,130. **Currency:**

Koruna. **Literacy rate:** 99%. **Average daily high/low*:** Prague: January, 34°/24°; July, 74°/58°. **Average number of days with precipitation:** Prague: January, 12; July, 14.

TRAVEL

Holders of American passports no longer need a visa to enter Czechoslovakia, provided they stay for fewer than 30 days. If you wish to stay longer, you must get a visa, which will allow you to stay for up to 180 days. Contact the Embassy of the Czech and Slovak Federal Republic, 3900 Linnean Avenue NW, Washington, DC 20008 for details. The minimum obligatory currency exchange has also been abolished.

Getting Around

Travel by rail in Czechoslovakia is inexpensive. Interrail passes are now valid in the country, but Eurail passes aren't, at least as of early 1991. The recently introduced "European East Pass," which can be used for travel in Czechoslovakia, Austria, Hungary, and Poland, can be purchased through Council Travel or through Rail Europe (800-345-1990). It's only available for first-class travel; any 5 days within a 15-day period is $160, any 10 days within one month is $259. Buses are faster than trains but charge slightly more. Bicycles can be brought across the border, but renting them in Czechoslovakia is difficult.

Especially for Students and Young People

CKM is Czechoslovakia's student/youth travel bureau and issuer of the International Student Identity Card. Its main office is located at 9 Zitna Ulice, 121 05 Prague 1, and it also has an office in Bratislava.

Students with the International Student Identity Card get a 25-percent discount on rail tickets to other Eastern European countries and a 50-percent discount on admission to most museums, galleries, and theaters. Cardholders will also get a discount in the student/youth hotels and dormitories operated in nine cities by CKM.

Meeting the People

Cedok, the Czechoslovakian government's travel bureau (Overseas Department, Na Prikope #18, 11135 Prague 1), will organize group visits to schools, factories, and cooperative farms; it can also arrange for you to meet people with interests similar to your own. You must write either to the Prague office directly or to Cedok in New York (10 East 40th Street, New York, NY 10016) and explain what type of visits you would like arranged and your exact date of arrival. There is a small fee for its services.

For Further Information

Cedok (10 East 40th Street, New York, NY 10016) can provide general tourist information for people considering a visit to the country. The brochure "Czechoslovakia, Eastern and Western Europe" offers information for individual tourists, including hotel and tour information. Frommer's *Eastern Europe & Yugoslavia on $25 a Day* includes chapters on Prague, Bohemia and Moravia, and Slovakia and the Tatras, and has a good introductory section on Czechoslovakia in general. Also good is *Eastern Europe on a Shoe-*

---

*All temperatures are Fahrenheit.

string, available for $21.95 (plus $1.50 book-rate postage; $3 for first-class) from Lonely Planet Publications, Embarcadero West, 112 Linden Street, Oakland, CA 94607.

WORK

Getting a Job

It is difficult for Americans to obtain the necessary permits for regular paid employment in Czechoslovakia; you can contact the Czechoslovakian Embassy (3900 Linnean Avenue NW, Washington, DC 20008) for the complicated regulations on the subject.

However, if you are a student, CIEE can provide you with authorization to work in Czechoslovakia for two months during the summer, from the end of June to the end of August. This pilot program, conducted in cooperation with CKM, places students in jobs in the tourist industry, agricultural cooperatives, workcamp administration, CKM offices, or other opportunities as available. CKM will place students according to background, interests, and job availability. Room, board, some pocket money, and an orientation are provided. A tourist visa is necessary. To qualify, you must be a U.S. citizen, at least 18 years of age, and a matriculating, degree-seeking student. German language facility is strongly recommended. The cost of the program is $150. For further information and an application, contact CIEE's Work Exchanges Department, 205 East 42nd Street, New York, NY 10017.

Internships/Traineeships

Two programs offered by members of the Council on International Educational Exchange are listed below.

AIESEC-US. Reciprocal internship program for students in economics, business, finance, marketing, accounting, and computer science. See page 18 for more information.

Association for International Practical Training. "IAESTE Trainee Program." On-the-job training for undergraduate and graduate students in technical fields such as engineering, computer science, agriculture, architecture, and mathematics. See page 18 for more information.

Voluntary Service

CIEE places young people in voluntary-service work camps in Czechoslovakia organized by the Czechoslovak student/youth travel bureau, CKM (Zitna 12, 12105 Prague). At these workcamps, groups of international volunteers get involved in various agricultural or conservation projects. Czechoslovak workcamps, which last two weeks, are scheduled during the summer vacation (July through September). Volunteers must be in good health, between the ages of 18 and 35, and able to do hard physical labor. In return for their service, they receive room and board. The applications of U.S. residents are processed by CIEE. For more information, contact the Voluntary Service Department at CIEE.

STUDY

Study programs offered by CIEE-member institutions are listed below. Consult Appendix I for the addresses of these colleges and universities.

Semester and Academic Year

General Studies

American University. "Prague Semester." Fall. Intensive Czech language introduction, history, culture, and society. General studies or focus on film and media. Internships available. No language prerequisite. Juniors and seniors with 2.75 GPA. Apply six months before start of program.

Council on International Educational Exchange. "Cooperative East and Central European Studies Program." Charles University, Prague. Czech area studies. Fall and/or spring semester. Undergraduates with 2.75 GPA and six semester-hours in economics, history, or social sciences. Courses taught in English. Apply by April 10 for fall and November 1 for spring. Contact University Programs Department.

Summer

American Heritage Association. "American Heritage Cultural Summer Program." Prague. Czechoslovakian culture and its history. No language requirement. Apply by April 15.

New York University. "NYU in Prague." Fall and summer. Trips to Poland, Austria, and Hungary. Freshmen to seniors. Apply by April 15 for summer. Contact: NYU in Prague, FAS Summer Programs, 6 Washington Square North, New York, NY 10003; (212) 998-8170.

EXPLORING CZECHOSLOVAK CULTURE

Readings

Czech and Slovak literatures are two distinct literatures in two different languages. At the same time, the literature of the country is divided into two distinct periods as a result of the impact of the 1948 communist takeover. The most famous Czech book dating from the pre-1948 era is probably Jaroslav Hasek's *Good Soldier Schwejk* (1921), which presents the absurdities of war and its bureaucratic machinery from the point of view of a common soldier who manages to survive its horrors through imagination and cunning. Among other well-known authors of the pre-takeover period is Karel Capek, whose collection of short stories *Money and Other Stories* (1930) and novel *War with the Newts* (1937) are available in translation. The acute sense of black humor in these early books also runs through modern Czech works, especially Bohumil Hrabel's stories and novels, such as *Closely Watched Trains* (1981). Its subject is, typically, the tragicomedic lives of everyday people, while the plays of Vaclav Havel, especially *The Memorandum* (1981), take a bleak look at modern man's inability to communicate, in the tradition of Beckett and Pinter. While only a few Czech books have found their way into English translation, none of the modern Slovak writers whose works concentrate mainly on rural life and the transition from village to modern city life have been translated into English. To read Slovak authors such as Razus, Fabry, Urban, or Buncak, one will have to turn to German or French translations.

Since 1968, many emigrant and dissident Czechoslovakian writers have received attention in the West. Not surprisingly, their books—including Josef Skvorecky's *The Engineer of Human Souls* (1984), which contrasts communist Czechoslovakia with an emigrant community in Toronto—are marked by bitterness. Milan Kundera is probably the best known of this group; and probably the best known of his works are *The Joke*

(1969), a satire on Czechoslovakian politics, and *The Unbearable Lightness of Being* (1975), in which he attempts to overcome the failure of the Prague uprising in 1968 with a somewhat desperate philosophy of acceptance.

Films

"For us, film is the most important of the arts!" V. I. Lenin's statement is often evoked when speaking about Eastern European filmmaking, and indeed much of the history of Czechoslovakian film is deeply intertwined with politics and the socialist agenda. The Czech "New Wave" flourished during the sixties with directors like Milos Forman—who later went on to direct Hollywood features—and Vojtech Jasny, but was violently halted by the Soviet occupation of Czechoslovakia in January 1968. Most of the films recommended here are products of the Czech New Wave, but current Czechoslovakian cinema is beginning to emerge once again as a powerful force.

Closely Watched Trains is one of the best-known Czechoslovakian films; it won an Academy Award for Best Foreign Picture in 1966. Directed by Jiri Menzel, it is the story of a young man working in a small-town railroad station and his attempts to get sexually initiated. Two great films by Jan Nemac are *Diamonds of the Night* (1964), the story of two boys who escape from a Nazi transport train, and *A Report on the Party and the Guests* (1966); the latter was supposedly "banned forever" in Czechoslovakia. In the U.S., Milos Forman is probably the best-known Czech director. His film, *Loves of a Blonde* is a funny, touching film about a young girl in a small Czech village. Another Forman masterpiece is his 1968 film, *Fireman's Ball*. The plot of this comedy revolves around the annual firemen's ball, where *everything* goes wrong: someone steals the headcheese and the prize for the beauty contest, and in the ensuing deliberations the house next door burns down. Forty thousand firefighters quit their jobs in protest when this film was released! Other good Czechoslovakian films include Jan Kadar's *Shop on Main Street* and Vojtech Jasny's *All My Good Countrymen*. Milan Kundera's well-crafted novel, *The Unbearable Lightness of Being*, was adapted to film by Philip Kaufman; the story revolves around the politics and loves of a young Czech doctor in the 1960s.

DENMARK

Small is beautiful, so say the Danes. Denmark, a constitutional monarchy, is the smallest and most densely populated of the Scandinavian countries. Although there have been periods—such as the Viking era and in the 17th and 18th century—when Denmark was a major European power, the smallness of the country and its virtual lack of natural resources has generally been a steady guarantee against dreams of grandeur. Hitler walked over Denmark in 1944 and called it his "little canary." But Danish resistance to this insult, which included heroic efforts to save virtually all the Danish Jews headed for his extermination camps, express a Danish spirit and spunk which remains gigantic to this day.

Denmark serves as a geographic, cultural, and commercial bridge between the Continent and the rest of Scandinavia. Composed of a substantial part of the Jutland peninsula and 500 islands, Denmark is neatly surrounded by the sea and has a temperate, windy, rainy climate. There are no mountains or rivers but a changing scenery of fields, hills, forests, lakes, and small bucolic streams. Good beaches can be found almost everywhere on the coastline, which is about 450 miles long. Across its span of islands and inlets, sounds and seascapes, this tiny country sustains the illusion of space and quietude. It has a culture keenly devoted to design and beauty—urban blight is unknown and few billboards mar the countryside. The red-roofed houses and carefully tended farms shelter one of the most courteous and sophisticated peoples in Europe.

Denmark became a full-fledged member of the North Atlantic Treaty Organization in 1949, and national consensus opened its borders to the European Economic Community in 1972. But with a current national deficit in the billions due to high unemployment and ever-higher taxes to pay the huge costs of maintaining one of the most humane and generous social welfare systems in the world, there are good, objective reasons for the Danes to be pessimistic about their long-term economic future. Yet, as so often happened in the past, pragmatism, solidarity, and optimism prevail. With built-in cultural defenses and perspectives, Danes remain cheerful and relaxed—much more like Victor Borge than Hamlet!

Denmark is delicious pastries, great coffee, world-class design in home furnishings and urban architecture, people on bicycles, old manor houses, Tivoli (the original and some say still the best amusement park in the world), Legoland, Carlsberg and Tuborg beers, and multilayered sandwiches, which are an aesthetic and gustatory delight. But it is also much more, both for the gregarious and charming Danes who live there, and for visitors fortunate enough to become short-term guests. Indeed, in a recent American survey of 124 nations, Denmark ranked first in the world for "Quality of Life."

For most travelers, Copenhagen is the gateway to Scandinavia. The airlines use it as a base from which flights go on to Stockholm, Oslo, and Helsinki. By car or train, you have to pass through the city unless you embark on a series of long ferry journeys. Fortunately, the Danes honor this responsibility with gusto. You will always be made to feel welcome in this lovely city. Nearly every Dane speaks English readily and capably. Copenhagen resembles Paris with its cellar galleries and miniscule shops, its faded yet durable charm, its winding streets and walkways. Twenty years ago, Copenhagen seemed exciting and risqué; today, most of the world's capitals have accelerated beyond it. But its charm and appeal are unmistakable.

Yet not to visit the pastoral beauties of the rest of Denmark is to miss much. Danes who live elsewhere describe it as "the *real* Denmark." Driving or taking the train to these places is easy and convenient. Modern ferries, bridges, and good roads connect all corners of the country. The island of Funen, for example, contains some of the most lush and breathtaking countryside in the entire Nordic region. Verdant farmland also fills Jutland, the huge peninsula jutting north from Germany, where you will also find a profusion of firm, sandy bathing beaches and dunes in recreational areas on each coast. Although the land is almost totally flat, most of the landscape is enhanced by gently undulating fields bright in summer with the charlock, or wild mustard, unique to this part of the world. It is rare to find someone who has spent time in Denmark not recommending it enthusiastically to others.

—*William W. Hoffa, Amherst, Massachusetts*

Official name: Kingdom of Denmark. **Size:** 16,633 square miles (about half the size of Maine). **Population:** 5,134,000. **Population density:** 305 inhabitants per square mile. **Capital and largest city:** Copenhagen (pop. 619,000). **Language:** Danish. **Religion:** Lutheran. **Per capita income:** US$19,750. **Currency:** Krone. **Literacy rate:** 99%. **Average daily high/low*:** Copenhagen, January, 36°/29°; July, 75°/55°. **Average number of days with precipitation:** Copenhagen: January, 9; July, 9.

TRAVEL

Americans must have a passport to visit Denmark. However, a visa is not required for stays of up to 90 days—a period that begins when entering the Scandinavian area (Denmark, Norway, and Sweden). For specific visa requirements, check with the Royal Danish Embassy, 3200 Whitehaven Street NW, Washington, DC 20008.

---

*All temperatures are Fahrenheit.

Getting Around

If you arrive in Copenhagen and don't know where you're going to stay, go straight to the information desk in the Central Station or to USE IT at Radhusstraede 13, DK-1466, Copenhagen K. USE IT distributes an excellent newspaper called *Playtime*—"an alternative introduction and guide to Copenhagen especially for low-budget tourists." USE IT also distributes a number of free brochures, provides a mail drop and free luggage storage for travelers, and puts hitchhikers in touch with people driving their way. The bulletin boards at USE IT are full of information and when the office is closed, there's a notice board outside.

Travelers flying SAS round-trip to the Scandinavian countries of Denmark, Sweden, or Norway are eligible for SAS's Visit Scandinavia fare. The special fare allows the purchase of up to six discounted flight coupons for travel within the three countries. The coupons, which cost from $80 for one flight to $420 for six, must be purchased in the U.S. before departure and must be used within three months of arrival in Scandinavia. Normally valid in summer only, the 1991 ticket has been extended until December 31. It can be used on any of the three Scandinavian airlines: Danair, Linjeflyg, and SAS (excluding flights to the Faroe Islands and Greenland).

Danish State Railways (DSB) and other private companies have created a dense network of train services with many interconnecting links to Norway and Sweden. The most important routes are spanned by high-speed IC3 trains. Trains also cross the Great Belt (the body of water separating mainland Jutland from the islands) by ferry. For these ferry-going trains, reservations are required (at additional cost).

DSB offers discount fares for groups of three or more traveling together. They also have an Inexpensive Day system which grants a 20-percent discount on second-class travel beyond 100 kilometers on Tuesdays, Wednesdays, Thursdays, and Saturdays. Ten-Ride passes (at a 20-percent discount) are also available for specific distances.

Eurail passes of all types are valid in Denmark. Eurailpass holders can take advantage of free service on most state-run ferry lines (including the line from Helsingor to Helsingborg, Sweden). Those planning to travel extensively in Scandinavia should consider the following options:

- The ScanRail Pass is valid for travel on the state railway systems of Denmark, Finland, Norway, and Sweden on a certain number of days within a fixed period of time. For example, one may travel on any 14 days within one month for $499 first class and $349 second class. ScanRail also allows free passage on a number of ferry lines. For information and reservations, contact Council Travel or Rail Europe (800-345-1990).
- The Nordturist Ticket allows for 21 days of free travel on the state railway systems of the above-mentioned countries, including certain ferries. It's also good for a 50-percent discount on the Hirtshals-Hjørring private railway as well as other ferry lines and bus routes. This pass can only be bought in Scandinavia. The cost for youths ages 12 to 25 traveling second class is approximately $200.

Bicycles can be rented at major train stations and tourist offices for approximately $6 a day or $31 a week. Bikes can also be checked on trains as checked baggage for a small fee. For information on bicycle rental, pick up DSB's brochure *Take the Train—Rent a Bike*. Serious cyclists should contact the Dansk Cyklist Forbund (Danish Cyclist Federation) at Kjeld Langes Gade 14, 1367 Copenhagen K.

Especially for Students and Young People

Denmark's student travel agency and the organization that issues the International Student Identity Card, DIS Travel (Skindergade 28, DK-1159 Copenhagen K), provides a number of useful services for the student traveler, including bookings and information on transportation, accommodations, and tours. Branch offices are located in Aarhus, Esbjerg, and Odense. Another helpful service is the Youth Information Centre (Raadhusstraede 13, DK-1466 Copenhagen K), a good place to look for inexpensive accommodations.

Many museums in Denmark offer discounts to holders of the International Student Identity Card. Cardholders can receive discounts on bus, plane, and train travel to European destinations and discounts on ferries to Norway and the United Kingdom. The International Youth Card is good for many discounts in Copenhagen, including free entry to some museums and art galleries and percentage discounts on hotels.

Meet the People

Friends Overseas is an American-Scandinavian people-to-people program which helps put travelers in touch with Scandinavians who share similar interests. The service is offered to families and groups as well as single travelers. For further information, send a stamped, self-addressed, business-size envelope to Friends Overseas, 68-04 Dartmouth Street, Forest Hills, NY 11375.

For Further Information

A number of publications geared to the student or budget traveler can be obtained from the Danish Tourist Board, 655 Third Avenue, New York, NY 10017, including publications on camping, hiking, and youth hostels, as well as maps and a calendar of events. One of the best general guidebooks to Denmark and the entire Scandinavian region is *The Real Guide: Scandinavia*, available in bookstores for $14.95.

"Although it may seem absurd to generalize about an entire nation of people, an account of Denmark is criminally incomplete without mention of how kind and hospitable the Danes are. And the customs which are unique to them make the Danes even more fun to be around. The Danes are quick to invite participation in all of their activities. It would be silly not to accept."
—Jeffrey Seth Jacobson, Hartford, Connecticut

WORK

At present, work permits for foreign guest workers are not being granted, with the exception of those foreigners possessing special training or skills not readily available in Denmark. In such cases, the employer applies for the work permit. Contact the Royal Danish Embassy (3200 Whitehaven Street NW, Washington, DC 20008) for further information. The American Scandinavian Foundation (Exchange Division, 725 Park Avenue, New York, NY 10021) can also assist Americans under the age of 30 with obtaining the requisite permit.

Internships/Traineeships

Programs offered by members of the Council on International Educational Exchange are listed below.

AIESEC-US. Reciprocal internship program for students in economics, business, finance, marketing, accounting, and computer science. See page 18 for more information.

Association for International Practical Training. "IAESTE Trainee Program." On-the-job training for undergraduate and graduate students in technical fields such as engineering, computer science, agriculture, architecture, and mathematics. See page 18 for more information.

In addition, the American Scandinavian Foundation sponsors a program that provides summer training assignments for full-time students majoring in engineering, computer science, horticulture, agriculture, forestry, and chemistry, among others. The deadline for application is December 15. Note, however: No traineeships are available in teaching, social work, or medically related fields. Contact the American Scandinavian Foundation, Exchange Division, 725 Park Avenue, New York, NY 10021.

Voluntary Service

CIEE places young people in Danish voluntary-service workcamps organized by Mellemfolkeligt Samvirke (Borgergade 10–14, DK-1300 Copenhagen). These workcamps, which bring together small groups of international volunteers, involve projects such as protecting the environmental or shipping clothing and tools to the Third World. Volunteers must be 18 years or over. The applications of U.S. residents are processed by CIEE. Contact the Voluntary Service Department at the CIEE's New York office for details.

For persons interested in longer-term voluntary-service work, the Year Abroad Program sponsored by the International Christian Youth Exchange offers persons ages 18 to 24 voluntary-service opportunities in the fields of health care, education, the environment, construction, et cetera. See page 23 for more information.

STUDY

There are several sources of information on study programs for foreigners in Denmark. The Exchange Division of the American Scandinavian Foundation (725 Park Avenue, New York, NY 10021) publishes *Study in Scandinavia*, which includes a listing of English-language programs offered in Denmark during the academic year and summer. In addition, a useful pamphlet titled *Studying in Denmark* can be obtained from the Royal Danish Embassy (address above) or from any Danish consulate.

The Danish Cultural Institute (Kultorvet 2, DK-1175 Copenhagen K) is a nonprofit institution receiving an annual grant from the Danish Ministry of Culture. Its aim is to disseminate information about Denmark and improve cultural relations and international understanding. Among its activities are short-term courses and study tours on sociocultural subjects, such as education for children and adults, libraries, social care, architecture, design, and so on. For details, contact the Institute.

Academic programs sponsored by CIEE-member institutions are described below. Consult Appendix I for the addresses of the colleges and universities listed in this section. In addition to the programs below, California State University, New York University, Ohio State University, the University of California, and the University of Kansas offer programs open only to their own students.

Semester and Academic Year

General Studies

Scandinavian Seminar. "College Year in Denmark." Individual placement in Danish folk colleges throughout Denmark. Danish language and cultural immersion, with emphasis on liberal arts. Undergraduate credit granted through University of Massachusetts—Amherst. Sophomores to graduate students and adults. Apply by April 1.

State University of New York. International Study Program at the University of Copenhagen. Academic year or semester. Juniors and seniors with 3.0 GPA; residents of New York State only. Apply by October 15 for spring and April 1 for full year and fall.

State University of New York/Empire State College. "Semester Program in Denmark." Elsinore and Thy. Semester or academic year. Sophomores to graduate students and adults. Apply by June 15 for fall and November 30 for spring.

Denmark's International Study (DIS) Program at the University of Copenhagen. Semester or academic year. Architecture and design, Danish language, international business, and liberal arts. Courses conducted in English, but Danish language instruction is available. Juniors and seniors with 3.0 GPA. Apply through the more than 60 cooperating U.S. colleges and universities; contact the study-abroad office or international center at your school for further information.

University of Wisconsin—Madison. Copenhagen. Academic year or fall semester. Open to juniors, seniors, and graduate students with four college semesters of Danish and 3.0 GPA. Apply by February 15.

Social Sciences

Scandinavian Seminar. "Semester Program on Nordic and Global Issues." Helsingor (fall or spring) and/or other locations. Focus on global issues from a Nordic perspective. Coursework in English. Field trips. Undergraduate credit through University of Massachusetts—Amherst. Sophomores to graduate students and adults. Apply by April 1 or October 1.

Summer

Architecture

Denmark's International Study (DIS) Program at the University of Copenhagen. Architecture and design. Also humanities and political science. Courses conducted in English. Juniors and seniors with 3.0 GPA. Apply through one of the more than 60 cooperating U.S. colleges and universities, including the University of Oregon.

Communications

New York University. "Media Ecology: Studies in Communication." Copenhagen, Denmark. Graduate students. Apply by April 15. Contact: School of Education, Health, Nursing and Arts Professions, 32 Washington Place, 3rd floor, New York, NY 10003; (212) 998-5030.

General Studies

University of Oregon. International Summer Program at the University of Copenhagen. See listing under Denmark's International Study (DIS) Program.

Theater Arts

University of Pennsylvania. "Penn-in-Holstebro." Study of methods of director Eugenio Barba. Apply by March 1.

EXPLORING DANISH CULTURE

Readings

It is somewhat ironic that Denmark's best known writers are Hans Christian Andersen and Sören Kierkegaard; both provide a glimpse of the Danish collective unconscious. For a less schizophrenic introduction to Danish culture, however, turn to the novels. Although Isak Dinesen (Karen Blixen) is usually associated with her autobiographical *Out Of Africa* (1938), her well-crafted *Winter's Tales* (1985) has a strong Danish context and is well respected for its subtle irony, unusual sensitivity, and ambiguous characterization. H. C. Branner, Jacob Paludan (*Birds around the Light*) and Hans Kirk (*The Fishermen*) are other Danish writers worth hunting down.

In 1958, Klaus Rifbjerg published *Chronic Innocence* and, to some, has been the dominant Danish novelist since. The 1970s witnessed a surge of women authors, some consciously pursuing a feminist agenda, others seeking to portray life as experienced by Danish women. *No Man's Land*, edited by Annegret Heitmann, is a recent anthology of the country's modern women writers containing a powerful Danish perspective. For a glimpse into life in the poorer quarters of Copenhagen try *Early Spring* (1985), by Tove Ditlevsen, an autobiographical account of growing up in the working-class Vesterbro district of Copenhagen during the 1930s.

Films

Gabriel Axel's *Babette's Feast*, which was awarded best foreign-language film of 1987 by the Academy of Motion Picture Arts and Sciences, is a poignant, beautiful film about an exiled French woman who serves as cook/housekeeper for a couple of devout, elderly Danish sisters. When she wins the lottery, she spends the money preparing a sumptuous Gallic feast for the women and their friends to show her appreciation. Axel's latest film, *Christian* (1990), is an awkwardly directed tale about a young Danish criminal who finds love and happiness among warmhearted Arabs in Northern Africa. Another recent Danish film, *Pelle the Conquerer* (1988), is the story of a Swedish father who travels to Denmark in search of a new wife for his son Pelle. This film, directed by Billie August, also won an Academy Award for best foreign-language film.

FINLAND

For more than seven centuries, the Finns—who had come eons before with their distinctive language from beyond the Ural Mountains in Asia—were ruled by their powerful neighbors to the west, the Swedes. Hence, while Finns come from a different racial and linguistic stock, Finnish culture is now irretrievably Scandinavian. When Sweden ended up on the losing side in the Napoleonic wars in 1808, Finland became a Grand Duchy of the Russian empire. During the next century, Finnish nationalism led to the unification of its ancient language and culture. During this time the *Kalevala*, the great Finnish folk epic, was written, and the basis of modern nationhood was formed.

Taking advantage of the Bolshevik Revolution, Finland declared its independence in 1917. A brief and bitter civil war raged over just how the new state should develop. The national unity that emerged remains strong to this day. It inspired Finns to defend their independence against both Germany and the Soviet Union during World War II, and to remain vigorously neutral in the ensuing Cold War struggles between the East and West. With the recent easing of these tensions and the emergence of democratic and national aspirations both within the U.S.S.R. and in Central/Eastern Europe, the example of the democratic republic of Finland has become a much-envied symbol of consensus politics and economic stability held together by a vigorous and deeply cherished nationalism.

Finland is noted worldwide for wood and paper products; the design of glass, ceramics, furniture, and textiles; and industrial production ranging from icebreakers to dental equipment. It is also a world leader in architecture, urban planning, and medical technology. While roughly one-quarter of Finnish trade is with the Soviet Union and eastern Europe, the remaining 75 percent is with the European Community and North America. With low unemployment and a steady growth in GNP over the past decade, Finland enjoys a healthy balance of payments and relatively low public debt. Finnish living standards are nearly as high as those of Sweden, Norway, and Denmark; the tax burden is lighter; and industry is competitive and innovative.

Comparable in size and climate to New England, but considerably less crowded, Finland has a population of five million inhabitants. Separated from the rest of Scandinavia by two deep inlets of the Baltic Sea, it is a land of deep, brooding forests, shimmering lonely lakes, rocky pastures and wet lowlands, and granite coasts. Since the end of World War II, Finns have abandoned rural living and built modern towns and cities throughout the country. Native Swedish-speaking Finns now constitute about 6 percent of the population; both English and Swedish are commonly known languages.

The Finns are reserved but friendly people who are extremely proud of their country's scenic majesty and rustic heritage. They are equally proud of their native crafts, their world-class athletes, their musicians, and their architects. While most Finns now make their living in urban or suburban settings, they nurture their souls at every chance in lakeside cabins, with their adjoining sauna houses. Jogging, fishing, hiking, and berry-gathering in the summer and cross-country skiing in the winter are just some of the many outdoor recreational activities enjoyed by Finns and visitors to Finland. Helsinki, the Jewel of the Baltic, is a thoroughly modern city which blends Finnish, Scandinavian, and Northern European qualities.

—*William W. Hoffa, Amherst, Massachusetts*

Official name: Republic of Finland. **Size:** 130,119 square miles (about the size of Montana). **Population:** 4,977,000. **Population density:** 38 inhabitants per square mile. **Capital and largest city:** Helsinki (pop. 487,000). **Language:** Finnish, Swedish. **Religion:** Lutheran. **Per capita income:** US$11,900. **Currency:** Markkaa. **Literacy rate:** 99%. **Average daily high/low*:** Helsinki: January, 27°/17°; July, 71°/57°. **Average number of days with precipitation:** Helsinki: January, 11; July, 8.

TRAVEL

Americans will need a passport to visit Finland. However, a visa is not required for a stay of up to three months. Persons planning a longer stay should check with the Embassy of Finland, 3216 New Mexico Avenue NW, Washington, DC 20016.

Getting Around

If you want to cover a lot of territory in a short time, check with Finnair about their Youth Holiday Ticket, which allows 15 days of unlimited economy travel by plane throughout Finland for $250. The equivalent adult Holiday Ticket costs $300.

Finnish railway fares are among the least expensive in western Europe. Discounts of 20 percent are offered to groups of three or more traveling together, and discounts of 25 to 50 percent to groups of ten or more. Groups of five or more students can pay one-way fares for round-trip tickets.

Eurail passes of all types are valid for travel in Finland. Another option is the Finn-

---

*All temperatures are Fahrenheit.

railpass, which entitles the holder to unlimited travel on all passenger trains throughout the country. A second-class pass costs $128 for 8 days, $198 for 15 days, and $250 for 22 days. More expensive first-class passes are also available. Tickets may be purchased at railway stations in Finland or, before departure, from Holiday Tours of America in New York (800-677-6454) and Scantours in California (800-223-SCAN). Those planning to travel extensively in Scandinavia should investigate these other options:

- The ScanRail Pass is valid for travel on the state railway systems of Denmark, Finland, Norway, and Sweden on a certain number of days within a fixed period of time. For example, you can travel on any 14 days within one month for $499 first class and $349 second class. ScanRail also allows free passage on a number of ferry lines. For information and reservations, contact Council Travel or Rail Europe (800-345-1990).
- The Nordturist Ticket allows for 21 days of free travel on the state railway systems of the above-mentioned countries, including certain ferries. It's also good for a 50-percent discount on the Hirtshals-Hjørring private railway as well as other ferry lines and bus routes. This pass can be bought only in Scandinavia. The cost for youths ages 12 to 25 traveling second class is approximately $200.

A good option for those who prefer the more leisurely bus routes, The Coach Holiday Ticket, for about $76, entitles the bearer to up to 625 miles of travel within a two-week period. This ticket can be purchased at bus stations and travel agencies throughout Finland.

Finland boasts a good number of budget accommodations, especially in the summer, when student dormitories are used as hotels. Also, camping season starts in late May or early June; there are 360 campsites throughout Finland to choose from. More information is available in the *Budget Accommodation* brochure distributed by the Finnish Tourist Board, 655 Third Avenue, New York, NY 10017.

Especially for Students and Young People

FSTS Travela is Finland's student/youth travel bureau and issuer of the International Student Identity Card. You can obtain information on travel and get student and youth discounts on tickets to, from, and within Finland. The organization also offers a selection of tours in Finland and to the Soviet Union. It's headquartered at Mannerheimintie 5C, 00100 Helsinki, and has branch offices in Jyväskylä, Oulu, Tampere, and Turku.

A number of discounts are available to students traveling with the International Student Identity Card in Finland. There are discounts of 25 to 50 percent on some domestic airfares, discounts of up to 40 percent on international train fares (from Sweden), and discounts of up to 50 percent on ferries to Sweden. The International Youth Card is good for general 10-percent discounts on some hotels, special rates for many theaters and concerts, and substantial discounts on lake cruises.

Meet the People

Friends Overseas is an American-Scandinavian people-to-people program that helps put travelers in touch with Scandinavians who share similar interests. The service is offered to families and groups as well as single travelers. For further information, send a stamped, self-addressed, business-size envelope to Friends Overseas, 68-04 Dartmouth Street, Forest Hills, NY 11375.

For Further Information

A number of publications geared to the student or budget traveler can be obtained from the Finnish Tourist Board (655 Third Avenue, New York, NY 10017). These include publications on camping, hiking, and youth hostels as well as maps and a calendar of events. One of the best general guidebooks to Finland and the entire Scandinavian region is *The Real Guide: Scandinavia.*

WORK

According to embassy personnel it is very difficult for U.S. citizens to work in Finland. An offer of employment is required before you apply for a work permit. Contact the Embassy of Finland (3216 New Mexico Avenue NW, Washington, DC 20016) for details. The American Scandinavian Foundation, Exchange Division, 725 Park Avenue, New York, NY 10021, can also assist Americans under the age of 30 with obtaining the requisite permit.

Anyone interested in living as an au pair in a Finnish family should contact the Ministry of Labor, International Trainee Exchanges, PO Box 30, SF-00101, Helsinki. The Ministry's Finnish Family Program is for young people who are native speakers of English, German, or French and want to learn about Finnish culture by living with a family. Besides teaching English, you are expected to take part in the family life—domestic or farm work, child care, gardening, and so on. The summer program lasts for a maximum of three months, a minimum of one. During the winter the minimum stay is six months. Participants in the summer program should be 17 to 22, while those in the winter program should be 18 to 25.

Internships/Traineeships

Programs sponsored by members of the Council on International Educational Exchange are listed below.

AIESEC-US. Reciprocal internship program for students in economics, business, finance, marketing, accounting, and computer science. See page 18 for more information.

Association for International Practical Training.
"IAESTE Trainee Program." On-the-job training for undergraduate and graduate students in technical fields such as engineering, computer science, agriculture, architecture, and mathematics. See page 18 for more information.
"Hotel & Culinary Exchanges Program." On-the-job training for young people beginning a career in the hotel and food-service industries. Participants must have graduated, or be currently enrolled in a university or vocational school and possess at least six months of training or experience in the chosen field. Training usually runs 6 to 18 months.

In addition, the American Scandinavian Foundation sponsors a program that provides summer training assignments for full-time students majoring in engineering, computer science, horticulture, agriculture, forestry, business, and chemistry, among others. The deadline for application is December 15. Note, however: Traineeships are not available in teaching, social work, or medically related fields. Contact the American Scandinavian Foundation, Exchange Division, 725 Park Avenue, New York, NY 10021.

Finland's Ministry of Labor also sponsors internship opportunities. Students ages 18 to 30 with at least one year of study in their field may apply for openings in tourism service, forestry, agriculture, horticulture, and a limited number in commerce, from May to October. In addition, graduates under 30 years of age may apply for six-month openings in commerce, catering, agronomy, horticulture, and language teaching. Deadline for application is March 31. Your campus placement office or international-program office may have applications; if not, contact the Ministry of Labor, International Trainee Exchanges, PO Box 30, SF-00101 Helsinki.

Voluntary Service

One opportunity for voluntary service in Finland is the Year Abroad Program of the International Christian Youth Exchange. It offers persons ages 17 to 24 voluntary-service opportunities in health, education, environment, construction, and other fields. See page 23 for more information.

STUDY

To acquaint yourself with Finland's educational system, read *An Introduction to Higher Education in Finland*, distributed by the cultural information officer at the Finnish Embassy. This guide also lists a number of valuable addresses, including those of foreign student advisors at major Finnish universities.

The Exchange Division of the American Scandinavian Foundation (725 Park Avenue, New York, NY 10021) publishes *Study in Scandinavia*, which includes a listing of English-language programs offered in Finland during the academic year and summer. Also available from the Consulate General of Finland (380 Madison Avenue, New York, NY 10017) are publications on adult-education options in Finland and opportunities for Finnish-language study.

Academic programs offered by CIEE-member institutions are described below. Consult Appendix I for the addresses of the colleges and universities listed in this section.

Semester and Academic Year

General Studies

International Student Exchange Program. Direct reciprocal exchange between U.S. universities and institutions in Helsinki, Espoo, Joensuu, Turku, Oulu, and Tampere. Semester or academic year. Full curriculum options. Open only to students at ISEP-member institutions.

Scandinavian Seminar. "College Year in Finland." Individual placement in Finnish folk colleges throughout Finland. Finnish language and cultural immersion with emphasis on liberal arts. Undergraduate credit granted through University of Massachusetts—Amherst. Sophomores to graduate students and adults. Apply by April 1.

Social Sciences

Scandinavian Seminar. "Semester Program on Nordic and Global Issues." Fall and spring in Hauho and/or other locations. Focus on global issues from a Nordic perspective. Coursework in English. Field trips. Undergraduate credit through University of Massachusetts—Amherst. Sophomores to graduate students and adults. Apply by April 1 or October 1.

FRANCE

Some say it was the French who first defined the term civilization. France has nurtured and subsidized the arts, and the results are visible in its cathedrals, palaces, art, literature, architecture, high fashion, gastronomy, and viniculture. Even Julius Caesar lauded the wines. France provides a sumptuous feast for the senses and the mind.

Still, while it is the lure of a 2,000-year-old heritage that attracts millions of tourists each year, the French would rather be praised for their present accomplishments. France is a technologically advanced nation and the fourth leading exporter in the world. Entirely dependent on others for its petroleum—gasoline is costly—it has made the development of hydroelectric and nuclear energy a high priority. A modernized rail system links Paris to the other major French cities, but cycling, backpacking, and hitchhiking are all popular alternatives. France competes with, sometimes envies, and often emulates the U.S., which lessens but does not totally eliminate the cultural shock for most Americans.

The French are prompt to declare that "Paris is not France." While that is indisputable, Paris is the nation's capital, France's largest city by far, and has been the hub of its highly centralized government for over 900 years. Paris remains the stellar French attraction for most foreign visitors: a cosmopolitan city in which the well-preserved or carefully restored past vies for attention with the ultramodern present. It is best explored on foot. Tourists flock to its major landmarks and throng its bustling boulevards but the charm of the *quartiers*, of its meandering streets, of its picturesque surprises, and serene parks are reserved for the adventurous stroller. The North African neighborhoods and Vietnamese restaurants that dot Paris are both a symbol of the country's diversity and a reminder of the country's past. If time is a concern, public transportation such as the metro and the RER suburban railway line is both first-rate and affordable. The city languishes during the summer doldrums after Bastille Day; theaters and concert halls close as Parisians head south to the sea, west to the ocean, and east to the mountains for the six-week peak vacation period that follows.

Hexagonal in shape and relatively small in size, France is nevertheless noted for its diversity. Despite systematic efforts to homogenize its culture and its language, strongly ingrained regional traditions endure: Alsace, Brittany, and Corsica are just the more striking examples of the cultural ferment that underlies the country's seeming uniformity. Politically, it is a pluralistic society. Those who know France are prone to conclude that it has a population of 50 million individualists. The wonder is that it has only 366 varieties of cheese.

On the whole, the French are formal and reserved but gracious. Their word *hôte* means both guest and host, and this implies that there must be a reciprocity of conduct. Off the beaten paths, some knowledge of the language is a necessity. The effort made to speak French is a courtesy that is always appreciated and that is volubly rewarded. And while friendships develop gradually, the French have always been hospitable to students; study opportunities for a full year, a semester, or a summer abound.

—*Alfred F. Massari, Oneonta, New York*

Official name: French Republic. **Size:** 220,668 square miles (about the size of Texas). **Population:** 56,184,000. **Population density:** 252 inhabitants per square mile. **Capital and largest city:** Paris (pop. 2,188,918). **Language:** French. **Religion:** Roman Catholic. **Per capita income:** US$13,046. **Currency:** Franc. **Literacy rate:** 99%. **Average daily high/low*:** Bordeaux: January, 48°/35°; July, 80°/58°. Nice: January, 56°/40°; July, 81°/66°. Paris: January, 42°/32°; July, 76°/55°. **Average number of days with precipitation:** Bordeaux: January, 16; July, 11. Nice: January, 8; July, 2. Paris: January, 15; July, 12.

TRAVEL

Americans going to France will need a passport, but a visa is no longer required for stays of up to three months. Students planning a stay of over three months should see the special information under the "Study" heading later in this chapter. More information

---

*All temperatures are Fahrenheit.

on French visa requirements is available from a French consulate or from the French Embassy, 4101 Reservoir Road NW, Washington, DC 20007.

Getting Around

In addition to the Eurailpass, there are several other discount packages for rail travel throughout France:

- The France FlexiPass, available in first and second class, allows unlimited travel for any 4 days over a 15-day period (second class is $119, first class is $179), or any 9 days over a one-month period (second class is $209, first class is $309). In addition, the package includes a free transfer by rail from Orly or Roissy-Charles de Gaulle airports to Paris and back, and a free one-day second-class Metropass valid on the Paris subway and bus systems within the Paris city limits. The pass can be purchased through Council Travel, travel agents or Rail Europe (800-345-1990). If you're between the ages of 12 and 25, check with SNCF, the French rail company, for other rail discounts.
- The Rail 'n' Fly package combines the FlexiPass with the services of Air Inter, the French domestic airline. With this option, you can fly from one region to another and then take the train locally. Option One (4 days rail and one day of air travel within a 15-day period) costs $249 for first class, $189 for second; Option Two (9 days of rail travel and one day of air within a one-month period) costs $379 for first class and $279 for second. You can also buy one additional air-travel day for $75. If you want to make local automobile excursions, the Rail 'n' Drive package allows you to take the train and then pick up a car at your destination. The rates are lower than usual, but they are still fairly expensive.
- Another option, the BritFrance Railpass, offers unlimited travel over the entire French and British rail network, including a round trip on the Hovercraft between Dover, England, and Boulogne or Calais, France. Any 5 days in a 15-day period cost $229 for second class or $309 for first class. Any 15 days in one month will cost $349 for second class, $459 for first. The Youth Railpass is $189 for the 5/15 days option, $279 for the 15 days/one month option.
- Bicycles are permitted free of charge on most French trains; you'll know that's the case if there's a bike symbol on the timetable for that particular train. Passengers take their bikes to a special car and load and unload the bikes themselves. It is also possible to rent bicycles at many train stations. Full-day rentals will set you back around $11.

If you're in Paris and interested in ride sharing to any destination in Europe, call Allostop (47-70-02-01). Located at 84, Passage Brady, 75010 Paris, this organization matches persons looking for rides with drivers looking for someone to share gas costs. You pay an annual membership fee of 150 francs for unlimited ride referrals for a one-year period, or pay 30 (about US$5) francs per referral for short trips and 60 (about US$10) francs for long trips. In addition, there is a charge of 16 centimes per kilometer for members and nonmembers alike.

Especially for Students and Young People

CIEE/Council Travel operates travel offices in Paris, Nice, and Aix-en-Provence. You'll find offices are located at:

- 31, rue St. Augustin, 75002 Paris
- 16, rue de Vaugirard, 75006 Paris
- 51, rue Dauphine, 75006 Paris
- 37bis, rue d'Angleterre, 06000 Nice
- 12, rue Victor Leydet, 13100 Aix-en-Provence

These offices specialize in providing information and making arrangements for students and other budget travelers. They also issue the International Student Identity Card, book discount train and plane tickets for students, buy tickets for transatlantic charter flights, and more.

Another organization that issues the International Student Identity Card is OTU, 39 Avenue Georges Bernanos, 75004 Paris. They have some 25 offices located all over France. Furthermore, the Paris Discount List, with over 200 shops and restaurants, is available at the OTU office in Paris.

A youth-oriented organization in France that provides useful services is Accueil des Jeunes en France (in Paris, 119 rue St-Martin, 4th floor). This youth welcome service offers low-cost guaranteed accommodation in and near Paris (approximately $10 to $14 per person per night, bed and breakfast) in youth centers, student residences, or tourist hotels. It has four travel offices in Paris, including one at the Gare du Nord.

Students are a privileged class in France and are entitled to discounts in many museums, theaters, cinemas, restaurants, and other places. International Student Identity Cardholders under 27 and youth under 25 may obtain discounts of from 40 to 50 percent on flights within France on the domestic airline Air Inter—except on "red," or commuter, flights. Discounts are also available to students under 27 and youth under 22 on international flights from France. Be sure to show your International Student Identity Card everywhere. It entitles you to discounts on international bus lines, on domestic and international trains (up to 40 percent on off-peak travel) and on boats to Great Britain, Ireland, and Greece. The International Student Identity Card also allows you to eat in *restaurants universitaires* (student restaurants) and to obtain discounts on admission to films, theaters, and museums. In Paris, check the prices at any metro station for the *carte orange*, a money-saving subway pass. The International Youth Card is good for a great many discounts throughout France on hotels as well as on restaurants, museums and exhibitions, recreational facilities, and certain tours, cruises, and excursions traveling through France and neighboring countries.

Meet the People

There are many reputable organizations that make hospitality arrangements for students to meet with a family for an afternoon or to live with a French family as a paying guest. General information on homestays is available from French Cultural Services, 972 Fifth Avenue, New York, NY 10021.

"Americans tend to view the French as being unfriendly, impossible-to-get-to-know people. In some ways this is very true—don't expect them to approach you with open arms, unless they want to practice their English. But once you get to know them, you'll realize how warm and generous they are."
—Sherry Cohen, Huntington, New Jersey

For Further Information

For a comprehensive listing of low-cost accommodations, plus suggestions on what to do and see throughout France, get a copy of *Let's Go: France*. It's available for $14.95 in most bookstores and at Council Travel offices.

The Real Guide: France ($12.95) is substantially larger and more detailed. In the same series, *The Real Guide: Paris* ($9.95) takes you through France's capital city neighborhood by neighborhood.

You'll find an array of other travel guidebooks about France at bookstores. Especially well known are the Michelin Green Guides, invaluable for their historical and background information on the sights of France. There are English-language guides available for Paris ($10.95) and various regions of France.

General travel information is available from the French Government Tourist Office

(610 Fifth Avenue, New York, NY 10020). A useful book for anyone planning on spending some time in France is *Cultural Misunderstandings: The French-American Experience*, by Raymonde Carroll. The book contains revealing vignettes and commentary that bring to light fundamental differences in French and American presumptions about life, friendship, raising children, as well as everyday activities such as using the telephone and asking for information. It's available in paperback for $10.95 plus $2 for postage from Intercultural Press, PO Box 700, Yarmouth, ME 04096.

"Prepare yourself mentally and emotionally for the French mentality. For it is impossible to separate the museums, the monuments, the shops, the countryside, from the people. They have a different way of doing things and they are very proud of it. Extensive traveling in France made me realize that Paris alone does not represent French culture."
—Shanda Gibson, Milpitas, California

WORK

Getting a Job

"As a travel agent arranging for pet travel to such exotic places as Izmir, Palerme, and La Nouvelle Orleans, I gained new understanding of the depth of poodle-Parisian relationships. And I had the opportunity to work closely with Dominique, Madeleine, and Frederic, and to explain to client Monsieur Foisy that he cannot see all of the United States by car in five days. My work experience was unforgettable."
—Samuel Engel, Philadelphia, Pennsylvania

In recent years a variety of new, quite stringent rules have gone into effect regarding working in France. In general, nonstudents will find it virtually impossible to find a job in France. With unemployment currently running at unacceptably high levels, the government is anxious to discourage immigration.

For students seeking employment, there are some specific regulations that must be followed. The best source of information on the subject is the French Cultural Services division of the French Embassy (972 Fifth Avenue, New York, NY 10021) which puts out a helpful information sheet, *Employment in France for Students*. Foreign students who come to France during the summer must do so under the aegis of an organization approved by the government. However, if you have questions regarding the work visa, contact the French Consulate, 954 Fifth Avenue, New York, NY 10021.

"Many French still adhere strictly to traditional sex roles, not merely shutting women out of traditionally male, high-power work, but shutting men out of traditionally female, service-oriented work. Many times, I arrived for a job interview with a business that had specifically requested American students from CIEE, only to be told, 'Mais non, merci. Nous recherchons une femme.' Even after protesting that I could wash dishes, seat customers, answer telephones, etcetera, as well as my female colleagues, I usually received a curt, 'Bah, tant pis.' Sexism is rampant in the scut sector of the French employment marketplace."
—Samuel Engel, Philadelphia, Pennsylvania

CIEE can provide you with work authorization, which allows you to seek employment in France for up to three months any time during the year. To qualify, you must be at least 18 years of age, a full-time college or university student with two years of college French, and be a U.S. citizen or permanent resident. The cost of the program is $125. Past participants have taught English in Paris, worked in the vineyards of Bordeaux, and served as lifeguards on the Côte d'Azur. For details and an application form, contact

CIEE's Work Abroad Department, 205 East 42nd Street, New York, NY 10017. Additional assistance is available from CIEE's Paris offices on arrival.

Persons seeking a job in France might be interested in *Emplois d'été en France*, a do-it-yourself guide to job-hunting, updated annually. Written in French, it can be ordered from CIEE for $12.95 plus $1 postage.

Au Pair

Au pair work, open to young women and men (although men are harder to place), requires that participants help their French "mother" by taking care of the children and helping with light household chores for an average of five hours a day. In return, an au pair receives room, board, and pocket money. French law requires that au pairs be between the ages of 18 and 30 and that they take courses at a school or university while employed. Although some organizations placing au pairs have summer positions available, most prefer stays of at least six months.

Three organizations in France have earned solid reputations for au pair placements. These are listed in *Au Pair Work in France*, compiled by the French Cultural Services division of the French Embassy (address above). You can write to the organizations directly for information on their particular programs: L'Accueil Familial des Jeunes Étrangers, 23 rue du Cherche-Midi, 75006 Paris; Relations Internationales, 20 rue de l'Éxposition, 75007 Paris; and Séjours Internationaux Linguistiques et Culturels, 32, Rempart de l'Est, 16002 Angoulême, Cedex.

"For an insider's view of France and the French, get to know a French family. Becoming involved in family interactions is a wonderful way to experience the national personality—values, customs, lifestyle. I strongly recommend the au pair system because of this."

—Kris Santiago, Brooklyn, New York

"Working as an au pair in France provided me with a wonderful opportunity to improve my language skills while gaining firsthand experience of French family life. Through working with French children and their parents on a daily basis, I experienced true cultural immersion. Living with a family exposed me to one of the roots of French society—I became an integral part of their daily life. Though it was difficult and lonely at times, it was an incredibly enriching experience."

—Cynthia Banks, Providence, Rhode Island

Farm Work

It is possible that you will be able to find work at grape harvest time without having to prearrange it. But if you prefer to do things ahead of time, you may contact Maison des Jeunes et de la Culture (25 rue Marat, Boîte Postale 26, 11200 Lézignan, Corbières), which sets up workcamps during the grape harvest in the Languedoc section of France. The harvest lasts from 15 to 20 days beginning sometime in late September. Students over 16 years of age are eligible. All inquiries must be accompanied by an international postal reply coupon.

Teaching

The French Government Teaching Assistantships in English offer candidates the opportunity to teach English conversation in French secondary schools for an academic year. Most assignments are to provincial centers. "Strong preference in the competition is given to unmarried candidates under 30 years of age who plan careers in the teaching of French." Contact the Institute of International Education, U.S. Student Program Division, 809 United Nations Plaza, New York, NY 10017. Ask for their booklet, *Fulbright and*

Other Grants for Graduate Study Abroad (1992–93), which describes the awards available.

Internships/Traineeships

Opportunities for internships in France include the following programs offered by CIEE-member institutions and organizations. In addition, Southwest Texas State University and Moorhead State University have internships open only to their own students. See Appendix I for the appropriate addresses where you can write for more information.

AIESEC-US. Reciprocal internship program for students in economics, business, finance, marketing, accounting, and computer sciences. See page 18 for further information.

Association for International Practical Training.
"IAESTE Trainee Program." On-the-job training for undergraduate and graduate students in technical fields such as engineering, computer science, agriculture, architecture, and mathematics. See page 18 for more information.
"Hotel & Culinary Exchanges Program." On-the-job training for young people beginning a career in the hotel and food-service industries. Participants must have graduated from a university or vocational school and possess at least six months of training or experience in the chosen field. Training usually runs from 6 to 18 months.

Boston University. "Paris Internship Program." Fall, spring; half-semesters in fall or spring. Sophomores through seniors; post-Baccalaureate students. 3.0 GPA in major and adviser's approval. Four semesters of college-level French with a grade of B or better. Intensive study of French followed by eight-week internship in areas such as arts administration, public relations, tourism, entertainment, and economic research.

Council on International Educational Exchange. "Paris Internship and Study Program." Juniors, seniors, graduates; two and a half years of French, and French course in semester immediately preceding program; 3.0 GPA in French and 2.75 overall. Apply by April 1 for fall and October 1 for spring. Contact the University Programs Department.

University of Louisville. "Work Exchange Program in Montpellier." Summer. Sophomores to graduates. Minimum GPA of 2.75 and completion of one full academic year required. Apply by April 30. For more information, contact the International Center, Brodschi Hall, University of Louisville, Louisville, KY 40292.

Voluntary Service

The Council on International Educational Exchange places young people in French voluntary service workcamps arranged by the following organizations:

- Concordia (38, rue du Faubourg St. Denis, 75010 Paris) sponsors two- to three-week workcamps during the spring and summer. Projects take place all over France and generally involve construction, restoration work, conservation, or social work.
- Études et Chantiers (33, rue Campagne Première, 75014 Paris) accepts volunteers for workcamps throughout France. Projects include restoring old houses and public buildings, creating playgrounds, maintaining riverbanks, and protecting sand dunes.
- Jeunesse et Reconstruction (10, rue de Trevisse, 75009 Paris) specializes in two- to four-week workcamps that involve volunteers in a variety of construction, conservation, and ecology projects.
- Compagnons Batisseurs (5, rue des Immeubles Industriels, 75011 Paris) organizes workcamps mainly in Brittany that involve construction and renovation work.

Volunteers must be 18 years of age or older and speak French. The applications of U.S. residents are handled by CIEE. For more information, contact the Voluntary Service Department at the CIEE.

A four-week study tour in France that includes a short workcamp experience is offered by the International Christian Youth Exchange. Persons ages 18 to 35 are eligible. Application for the summer program should be made by May 1. Contact the Short-Term Programs Department at ICYE (see Appendix I for address). The Fourth World Movement also sponsors workcamps in France. For more information see page 21.

In addition, there are a couple of French organizations that conduct workcamps for persons interested in volunteering to help restore historic buildings and monuments in various parts of France.

- R.E.M.P. ART (1, rue des Guillemites, 75004 Paris) organizes workcamps that last anywhere from a weekend to a month or longer. An application fee is charged and volunteers pay a daily fee (which varies according to location) to cover food and lodging expenses. Generally participants must be at least 18 years old.
- **Club du Vieux Manoir** (10, rue de la Cossonnerie, 75001 Paris) sponsors workcamps during spring vacation and from July 2 to September 30; a few operate year round. During the summer, volunteers are required to stay at least 15 days, beginning on either the 2nd or 16th of the month. Camping facilities are provided at a cost of approximately $8 per day. Anyone over 15 years of age is eligible.

For persons interested in longer-term voluntary service work, the Year Abroad Program sponsored by the International Christian Youth Exchange offers persons ages 18 to 24 voluntary service opportunities in the fields of health care, education, environment, construction, et cetera. See page 23 for more information.

STUDY

A U.S. citizen who wishes to study at the undergraduate level in France for longer than 90 days must apply for a student visa at the French Consulate having jurisdiction over his or her place of residence. Consulates are located in Boston, Chicago, Houston, Los Angeles, Miami, New Orleans, New York, San Francisco, and Washington, D.C. Contact the French Consulate General (934 Fifth Avenue, New York, NY 10021) for further information. Be sure to allow plenty of time, since applications received by mail take at least two weeks to be processed.

The Studies Office of French Cultural Services (972 Fifth Avenue, New York, NY 10021; (212) 439-1400) is an excellent source of information if you plan to study on your own in France. For a list of French language courses, ask for *Cours de français pour étudiants étrangers*, which is published in French but includes an English insert. Other publications include *Studies in France*, which explains the basics of the French educational system. General information on fellowships and assistantships for graduates is also available. The New York office of French Cultural services is open weekdays from 2 to 5 P.M. and serves the states of New York, New Jersey, Connecticut, and Pennsylvania. Students from beyond this area must consult one of the eight regional offices.

For graduate students in French and French-language teachers, the American Council on the Teaching of Foreign Languages (ACTFL) offers scholarships for advanced French study in Paris, Nancy, and Besançon. For applications and information, contact ACTFL, 6 Executive Plaza, Upper Level, Yonkers, NY, 10701.

Educational programs offered by CIEE-member institutions are described below. Consult Appendix I for the addresses of the colleges and universities listed in this section. In addition to the programs below, the American Graduate School of International Management, California State University, College of Charleston, Cornell University, Illinois

State University, Lewis and Clark College, New York University, Pennsylvania State University, Stanford University, the University of California, the University of Rhode Island, the University of South Carolina, the University of Utah, and Valparaiso University offer programs open to their own students only.

Semester and Academic Year

Business

Experiment in International Living/School for International Training. "College Semester Abroad—International Business." Toulouse. Fall or spring semester. Intensive language, international business, and French institutions seminar with internship and homestay. Sophomores to seniors with 2.5 GPA and two years of college French. Apply by May 15 for fall and October 15 for spring.

University of Connecticut. "International Business Program." Grenoble. Spring semester. Open to students enrolled in the New England Consortium of Business Schools. Apply by Oct. 1

University of Hartford. "Paris MBA." Academic year. Three months in Hartford; eight months in Paris. Graduate students.

Critical Studies

Council on International Educational Exchange.
"Critical Studies Program at the University of Paris III." Semester or academic year. Juniors, seniors, and graduate students. Two years of college French required for academic year and fall semester; three years required for spring semester; 3.0 GPA in French and overall. Apply March 1 and October 15. Contact University Programs Department.

French Language and Civilization

Adventist Colleges Abroad. Collonges-sous-Salève. Open only to students at Adventist Colleges Abroad consortium institutions. Academic year or quarter. Freshman to seniors with 3.0 GPA in French and 2.5 overall GPA. Apply 60 days before beginning of academic term.

Boston University. Grenoble. Intensive French language study or direct enrollment at University of Grenoble. Homestay. Academic year and semester. Sophomores to seniors with 3.0 GPA in major and one semester of French (five semesters of French for direct enrollment at University of Grenoble). Apply by March 15 for academic year or fall semester; October 15 for spring.

Central University of Iowa. "Central College Paris Program." Academic year or semester. Sophomores, juniors, and seniors with intermediate French and 2.5 GPA (3.0 in French). Introductory program also available. Apply by March 15 for fall and October 15 for spring.

Experiment in International Living/School for International Training. "College Semester Abroad." Tours. Intensive language, life and culture seminar, homestay, and excursions. Option for full academic year. Sophomores to seniors with 2.5 GPA. Apply by May 15 for fall and by October 15 for spring.

Macalester College. "PAAT (Paris, Aix, Avignon, and Toulon) French Program." Spring semester. January orientation in Paris prior to study in Aix, Avignon, or Toulon. Sophomores, juniors, and seniors with two years of college French. Apply by September 15.

Michigan State University. "French Language, Literature, and Culture in Paris." Spring quarter. Sophomores, juniors, and seniors with two years of college French. Apply by February 3.

Middlebury College. Paris. Sophomores to graduate students. Fluency in French required. Rolling admissions.

Northern Illinois University. "French Studies in the South of France." Aix-en-Provence or Avignon. Semester or academic year. Courses offered in cooperation with the Institute for American Universities. No language prerequisite for Aix-en-Provence; two years of college French required for Avignon. Housing with French families. Sophomores, juniors, and seniors with 2.5 GPA.

Scripps College. "Scripps Program in Paris." Academic year, semester, or summer through University of Paris. Sophomores to seniors with B minus average. Four semesters of college French required for year or semester program; no prerequisite for summer. Apply by March 1 for fall or year; October 15 for spring.

State University of New York at Binghamton. "Mediterranean Studies Program." Aix-en-Provence. Spring semester. Literature and language. Juniors and seniors with five semesters of college French. Apply by October 15.

State University of New York at Brockport.
"Multi-Level French Language Immersion Program." Tours. Spring semester. Homestay. Juniors and seniors with one year of college-level French and 2.5 GPA. Apply by November 1.
"Paris Social Science Program." Exploration of contemporary French society. Fall or spring semester. Juniors and seniors with one year of college French and 2.5 GPA. Apply by February 15 for fall and November 1 for spring.

State University of New York at Buffalo. Université de Grenoble III. Fall or spring semester, or academic year. Language and culture. Juniors and seniors with four semesters of college French and 3.0 GPA. Apply by April 1. Contact International Education Services, 409 Capen Hall, Buffalo, NY 14260; (716) 636-2258.

State University of New York at Oswego. Paris. Semester or academic year. Study at Université de Paris—Sorbonne and the Institut Catholique de Paris; Juniors and seniors with two years of college French. Apply by April 1 for fall and November 1 for spring.

State University of New York at Stony Brook. Avignon. Semester or academic year. Juniors and seniors with five semesters of college French. Apply by April 1 for fall and October 15 for spring.

Stetson University. Dijon. Semester or academic year. Sophomores, juniors, and seniors with two years of French and 2.5 GPA (3.0 in major). Apply by March 1 for fall and October 15 for spring.

University of Kansas. "Paris Orientation Program." Mid- to late September. Intensive language review appropriate for students enrolling directly in French universities. Sophomores to seniors with four semesters of college French and 3.0 GPA. Apply by July 1.

University of LaVerne. "Semester/Year Abroad in Nancy or Strasbourg, France." See listing under Brethren Colleges abroad.

University of Massachusetts—Amherst. "French Studies in Rouen." Academic year. Sophomores, juniors, and seniors with one year of college French. Apply by March 1.

University of Minnesota. "French in Montpellier." Fall, winter, or spring quarter. Freshmen to graduate students with one year of college French and 2.5 GPA. Apply May 15 for fall, October 15 for winter, and December 15 for spring.

University of North Carolina—Chapel Hill. "UNC Year at Montpellier." Academic year. Sophomores to graduate students with 2.7 GPA and two years of pre-college French plus three semesters of college French. Apply by March 1.

University of Notre Dame. "International Study Program in Angers," Academic year (October 15–June 1) with four-week preliminary session in September. Sophomores and juniors with two years of French. Apply by December 1.

University System of Georgia/Columbus College.
"Quarter/Year Study in France." Tours. Undergraduate and graduate students with three quarters of college French; 2.5 overall GPA and 3.0 in French. Apply six weeks prior to beginning of quarter.

General Studies

Alma College. "Program of Studies in France." Paris. Academic year or semester. Study at Alliance Française. Culture and language, literature, history, and current events. All instruction in French. Homestays and excursions. Sophomores, juniors, and seniors with 2.5 GPA. Apply by June 15 for fall and October 15 for winter.

American Heritage Association. "Northwest Interinstitutional Council on Study Abroad—Avignon." Fall, spring, and/or winter quarters. Sophomores, juniors, and seniors with two semesters of French and 2.5 GPA. Apply by June 15, November 1, and January 15.

Beloit College. "French Seminar." Rennes. Spring semester. Sophomores to graduate students with a minimum of intermediate French and 2.5 GPA. Apply by November 1.

Brethren Colleges Abroad.
University of Strasbourg. Intensive language, excursions, and study tour to south or central college, optional week in village. Semester or academic year. Juniors and seniors with two years of college French and 3.0 GPA. Rolling admissions cut off by April 15 for fall and year; November 1 for spring.
University of Nancy. Full range of academic programs available. Emphasis on language. Homestays, excursions, and English teaching work can be arranged. Intermediate French required. Juniors and seniors with 3.0 GPA. Apply by April 15 for fall and year; November 1 for spring.

Brown University. "Brown in France." Lyons, Nice, Paris. Fall, spring, and academic year. Juniors and seniors with two years of college French. Apply by February 28 for fall in Lyons, Nice, and Paris; November 15 for Paris in the spring.

Central Washington University. "Northwest Interinstitutional Council on Study Abroad—Avignon." See listing under American Heritage Association.

Council on International Educational Exchange.
"Academic Year Program." Rennes-Paris. Fall semester in Rennes, spring semester in Paris. Sophomores to seniors with two years of college French. 3.0 GPA required. Apply by February 15. Contact University Programs Department.
"Paris Internship & Study Program." Fall or spring semester. Sophomores to seniors with 2.75 GPA (3.0 GPA in French), previous study in a French-speaking country, or intermediate-high rating in oral proficiency interview required. Apply by February 1 for fall and October 1 for spring. Contact University Programs Department.
"Undergraduate Program at the University of Haute-Bretagne." Rennes. Fall or spring semester. Sophomores, juniors, and seniors with two years of college French. 3.0 GPA required. Apply by February 15 for fall and October 15 for spring. Contact University Programs Department.

Davidson College. "Davidson College Junior Year Abroad in Montpellier." Integrated program at University of Montpellier III. Academic year. Two years of French and 2.75 GPA required. Apply by February 1.

Experiment in International Living/School for International Training. "College Semester Abroad." Toulouse. Fall or spring semester. Intensive language, interdisciplinary seminars on French life and culture, field-study methods seminar, homestay, educational travel, and independent-study project. Sophomores to seniors with 2.5 GPA and two years of college French. Apply by May 31 for fall and October 31 for spring.

Guilford College. "Semester in Paris." Spring. Sophomores, juniors, and seniors with three semesters of college French. Apply by September 30.

Hollins College. "Hollins Abroad Paris Program." Semester or academic year. Juniors and seniors with 2.0 GPA and intermediate college French. Apply by April 1 for fall and September 30 for spring.

Indiana University. "Overseas Study in Strasbourg." Academic year. Limited to students at Indiana and Purdue. Juniors and seniors with two years of French and 3.0 GPA. Apply by first week of November.

International Student Exchange Program. Direct reciprocal exchange between U.S. universities and institutions in Aix-en-Provence, Angers, Besançon, Caen, Chambéry, Grenoble, Lyons, Montpellier, Nantes, Nice, Rennes, Saint-Étienne, Le Havre, and Lille. Academic year. Full curriculum options. Open only to students at ISEP-member institutions.

Kalamazoo College. Caen, Clermont-Ferrand, or Strasbourg. Fall and winter quarter (September 15–February 15.) Juniors and seniors with 20 quarter-hours of French (15 for Strasbourg) and 3.0 GPA. Students are required to spend the summer prior to going abroad at Kalamazoo. Apply by May 1.

Lake Erie College. Caen. Semester or academic year. Juniors and seniors with intermediate French and 2.5 GPA. Apply by June 1 for fall and October 1 for spring.

Marquette University. "Strasbourg Program." Spring. Instruction in French. Sophomores to seniors with four semesters of college French with a B average. Apply by November 1.

New York University. "NYU in France." Paris. Semester or academic year. Juniors, seniors, and graduate students with at least three semesters of college French and 3.0

GPA. Apply May 1 for fall and October 1 for spring. Contact: NYU in France, 19 University Place, Room 631, New York NY 10003; (212) 998-8722.

Northern Arizona University. Université Paul Valéry in Montpellier. Academic year. Sophomores to seniors with two years of college French and 2.5 GPA. Apply by April 1.

Portland State University. "Northwest Interinstitutional Council on Study Abroad." See listing under American Heritage Association.

Purdue University. "Strasbourg Program." Academic year. Priority is given to Purdue and Indiana students. Juniors and seniors with two and a half years of college French. Apply by first Friday in November.

Rosary College. "Rosary in Strasbourg." Semester or academic year. Internships also available. Juniors and seniors with two years of college French. Apply by February 1.

Rutgers University. "Junior Year in France." Study in Tours, with six weeks in Paris. Academic year. Juniors with two years of college French and courses in French literature. Apply by March 1.

St. Lawrence University. "France Year Program." Academic year in Rouen, with one-month orientation in Paris. Sophomores to seniors with 2.8 GPA and intermediate college French. Apply by February 20.

Skidmore College. "Junior Year Abroad." Paris. Semester or academic year. Internship available. Juniors and seniors with 3.0 GPA; intermediate proficiency in French required for single semester, third-year level for academic year. Apply by October 15 for spring and February 15 for fall.

Southern Methodist University. "SMU-in-Paris." Semester or academic year. Liberal-arts studies focused on French experience. Sophomores, juniors, and seniors with one year of college French. Apply by October 15 for spring and by March 15 for fall.

State University of New York at Stony Brook. Paris. Academic year or fall semester. Juniors and seniors with two years of college French and 3.0 GPA required. Apply by April 1.

Syracuse University. "Syracuse University in Strasbourg." Fall or spring semester. Sophomores, juniors, and seniors with 3.0 GPA. Apply by March 15 for fall and October 15 for spring.

Tufts University. "Tufts in Paris." Juniors with two years of college French and 3.0 GPA. Apply by February 1.

University of Colorado at Boulder. "Study Abroad in Bordeaux." Academic year. Juniors and seniors with two years of college French and 2.75 GPA. Apply by March 1.

University of Connecticut. "Study Abroad Program in France." Rouen and Paris. Academic year. Sophomores to seniors with two years of college French. Apply by February 15.

University of Kansas. "Exchange at the University of Franche-Comté." Besançon and Paris. Academic year or spring semester. Sophomores with four semesters of college French and 3.0 GPA. Apply by March 15; October 1 for spring.

University of Maryland. "Maryland-in-Nice." Academic year or spring semester. Sophomores, juniors, and seniors with 12 semester-hours of college French and 2.5 GPA. Apply by March 15 for academic year and October 15 for spring.

University of North Carolina—Chapel Hill. "UNC Program to Lyons." Academic year. Juniors and seniors. 3.0 GPA and fluency in French required. Apply by February 15.

University of Oregon.
"Northwest Interinstitutional Council on Study Abroad—Avignon." See listing under American Heritage Association.
"OSSHE—Lyons Universities Exchange Program." Academic year. Juniors, seniors, and graduate students with three years of college French and 3.0 GPA. Preference is given to Oregon State System of Higher Education (OSSHE) students. Apply by January 2.
"OSSHE—Poitiers Exchange Program." Academic year. Juniors, seniors, and graduate students with two years of college French and 2.75 GPA. Preference given to Oregon State System of Higher Education (OSSHE) students. Apply by February 15.

University of Wisconsin—Madison. Aix-en-Provence. Academic year. Juniors to graduate students with five semesters of college French and 3.0 GPA. Apply by November 15.

Wesleyan University. "Wesleyan Program in Paris." Semester or academic year. Sophomores, juniors, and seniors with five semesters of college French and 3.0 GPA in French. Apply by March 10 for fall and October 10 for spring.

Western Washington University. "Northwest Interinstitutional Council on Study Abroad—Avignon." See listing under American Heritage Association.

Marketing

University of New Hampshire. "Spring Semester in Grenoble." Study international marketing at the Université de Grenoble II. Juniors and seniors at state universities in New England. Contact Whittemore School of Business and Economics, McConnell Hall, University of New Hampshire, Durham, NH 03824; (603) 862-3885.

Teacher Education

State University of New York at Cortland. "Cortland International Programs—Versailles." Academic year at École Normale de Versailles. Elementary teaching methods and curriculum. Juniors, seniors, and graduate students with advanced French courses. Apply by February 15.

Summer

Art

Boston University. "Museum Studies Abroad: Theories and Practices of Collecting Art." Monte Carlo, Monaco. Course on art in society complemented by guest lecturers and field trips to galleries, foundations, museums, and private collections. Sophomores to graduate students with good academic standing and background in art. Apply by mid-March.

State University of New York at Albany. Poitiers. Video production. Graduate students with adequate French. Apply by April 15.

University of Kansas. "Art and Design in Peyresq." Tour through Belgium and France before stay in shepherd village. Undergraduates with 3.0 GPA. Apply by February 1.

Art History

Miami University. "Gothic Architecture: A Survey of Metz Cathedral." Juniors and up. Apply by mid-April.

University of Louisville. "Art History and French Language in Paris." Freshmen to graduate students with background in French. Apply by April 30.

University of Pennsylvania. "Penn-in-Cannes." Perspective on film: survey of international cinema. Apply by February 1.

Business

Ohio State University. "International Program in Business." Nantes. European civilization, business, and the financial environment of the EEC. Business majors with 2.75 GPA. Apply by April 1.

Monterey Institute of International Studies. "French Business and Culture." Rouen. Upper division program on the campus of the Institut de Formation Internationale. Homestay with French families. Program followed by optional internship with a French firm. Limited enrollment for students outside the Monterey Institute. Apply by March 15.

Syracuse University. "International Business and Human Resources. Strasbourg with field trips to Germany, Switzerland, Czechoslovakia, and Hungary. Juniors, seniors, and graduate students. No language requirement. Apply by March 15.

University of Pennsylvania. "Penn-in-Compiegne." Language study, economics, and internship. Apply by March 1.

Engineering

Ohio State University. "International Engineering at Centrale Paris." Summer. Mechanical and aerospace engineering. Juniors and seniors with 3.0 GPA. Apply by March 1.

Foreign Language Education

New York University. "Foreign Language Education." Graduate students. Apply by April 15. Contact: School of Education, Health, Nursing and Arts Professions, 32 Washington Place, Third floor, New York, NY 10003; (212) 998-5030.

French Language and Culture

American Heritage Association. "American Heritage Cultural Summer Program." Avignon. French culture and history. No language requirement. Apply by April 15.

Boston University. "Summer Program in Paris." Choice of courses in French language, literature, cinema, and art. Dormitory housing. Sophomores to seniors with 3.0 GPA in major. Apply by April 1.

Council on International Educational Exchange.
Co-sponsored with University of Wisconsin-Madison. "France Today: Language and Culture." Paris. Sophomores to graduate students with 2.5 GPA. No language requirement. Apply by April 1. Contact University Programs Department.

Experiment in International Living/School for International Training.
"Summer Academic Study Abroad." Tours. Intensive language, life, culture seminar, excursions, and homestays. Freshmen to seniors. Apply by March 15.

Illinois State University. "ISU Summer Program at University of Grenoble." Eight weeks. Freshmen to seniors with one year of college French. Apply by March 1.

Indiana University. Dijon. "Language Study in France." Freshmen to seniors with one year of college French and 2.8 GPA. Apply by mid-February.

Marquette University. "Summer Study Program in France." Limoges. Undergraduates with one year of college French or two years of high-school French. Apply by April 25. Contact: Director, Department of Foreign Languages, Lalumiere Language Hall, Marquette University, Milwaukee, WI 53233.

Mary Baldwin College. "May Term in Paris." Classes conducted in French. Undergraduates with intermediate French. Apply by December 1.

Miami University. "French in Dijon." Sophomores to graduate students with 3.4 GPA and 100-level French. Apply by April 15.

Michigan State University. "French Language, Literature, and Culture in Tours." Sophomores, juniors, and seniors with two years of college French. Apply by April 20.

New York University. "Foreign Language Education in Paris." Seniors and graduate students with knowledge of French. Apply by April 15.

Rutgers.
"Cours d'été à Tours." Freshmen to seniors with one year of college French. Apply by January 15.
"Summer Institute in Art History in Paris." Sophomores with 2.7 GPA. Apply by March 1.

Southern Methodist University. Tours. "SMU-in-Tours." Sophomores, juniors, and seniors. Apply by March 15.

State University of New York at Oswego. Paris and St. Malo. Freshman to seniors with intermediate-level French. Apply by April 1.

State University of New York at Stony Brook. Avignon. Juniors and seniors with 3.0 GPA and one year of French. Apply by April 1.

University of Alabama. "Academic Summer Program in France." Aix-en-Provence. Freshmen to graduate students with two semesters of college French. Apply by April 1.

University of Arkansas at Little Rock. "Summer in France." Strasbourg. Freshmen to seniors with intermediate French. Apply by February 28.

University of Kansas. "French Language and Culture in Paris, Picardy, Brittany, and Toraine." Undergraduates and advanced high school students with two semesters of college French. Apply by February 1.

University of Pennsylvania. "Penn-in-Tours." French language, literature, art, and civilization. Apply by February 15.

University System of Georgia/West Georgia College.
Montpellier. Freshmen to seniors with 2.5 GPA. Beginners may participate. Includes two weeks in Paris. Apply by March 15.

University System of Georgia/Georgia College.
Tours. Undergraduates and graduate students with three quarters of college-level French or equivalent and 3.0 GPA in French and 2.5 overall GPA. Apply by April 1.

University of Wisconsin. "France Today: Language and Culture." Paris. See CIEE program this section.

Western Michigan University. "Summer Study in France." Lyons and/or Paris. Sophomores to graduate students with three semesters of French. Apply by April 15.

General Studies

Alma College. "Program of Studies in France." Paris. Study at Alliance Française. French language. Special course in Art and Architecture. Sophomores, juniors, and seniors with 2.5 GPA. Apply by March 15.

Louisiana State University. "LSU in Paris." French language and culture, history and art, political science. Sophomores to seniors with 2.5 GPA; graduate students with 3.0 GPA. Apply by April 1.

New York University. "NYU in France." Paris. High school graduates, freshmen to graduate students with 2.5 GPA. Apply by April 1. Contact: NYU in France, 19 University Place, Rm 631, New York, NY 10003; (212) 998-8722.

Skidmore College. Paris. High-school graduates and all undergraduate levels. No prior knowledge of French required. Field trips within Paris area and French provinces. Homestays and student hostel accommodations. Apply by April 1.

Syracuse University. "Summer in Strasbourg: A Taste of France." Field trips to Germany and Czechoslovakia. Apply by March 15.

Law

University of Iowa. "International and Comparative Law." Study program in Arcachon, France, followed by law-clerk options in Paris, London, Madrid, and Frankfurt. Students at accredited law schools and practicing attorneys. Apply by March 1. Contact: Dean, College of Law.

Human Rights

Faith Evangelical Lutheran Seminary. "International Seminar in Theology and Law." International Institute of Human Rights in Strasbourg. Four-week study session integrating Bible, jurisprudence, and human rights. Undergraduates, graduates, lawyers, pastors, teachers, or anyone interested in human rights. No language prerequisites. Apply by May 1.

EXPLORING FRENCH CULTURE

Readings

Some classics of French literature continue to provide a useful introduction to today's country. Although a lot has changed since the days of Balzac and Flaubert, reading the works of such seminal influences can only add to your knowledge of French culture. Honoré de Balzac chronicled 19th-century France; his book *Père Goriot* (1835) deals with the decline of the French aristocracy and the rise of the bourgeoisie. From the same time period is Gustave Flaubert's *Madame Bovary* (1857), about a woman who is unable to adapt to the provincial life she is forced to lead. *Germinal* (1885), by another French master of the pen, Émile Zola, depicts the miseries of urban life in the 1860s. The novels of the Nobel laureate François Mauriac deal with the challenge of reconciling traditional values with the realities of the modern world. Mauriac's *Thérèse* (1927) is the story of a woman who tries to murder her husband and spends the rest of her life dealing with the consequences.

The 1930s saw the emergence of existentialism in France. Jean-Paul Sartre's *Nausea* (1938) is about a man who is disgusted with life and has no friends or family—a typical specimen of existential bliss. *The Age of Reason*, the first volume in Sartre's trilogy *The Roads to Freedom*, is set in the streets and cafes of 1938 Paris. Another existential landmark is *The Plague* (1947) by Albert Camus, which chronicles the story of a town hit by an epidemic, often seen as an allegory for France under the German occupation.

During the 1940s and 1950s the "new novel" emerged. New novelists saw themselves as inventors rather than transcribers of reality. They often portrayed characters without names, such as Nathalie Sarraute's *Portrait of a Man Unknown* (1948). And their stories were often timeless, such as Alain Robbe-Grillet's *The Erasers* (1953), which takes place within 24 hours, but not in any particular time in history. In *Zazie dans le metro* (1959), Raymond Queneau writes about a girl living in the suburbs whose long-time dream is to ride the metros of Paris. Claude Simon, who won the Nobel Prize in 1985, experiments with stream-of-conciousness; *The Flanders Road* (1960), his most widely read book, deals with the capitulation of France with Germany in 1940.

Paris provides a tantalizing setting for many French writers. *Life: A User's Manual* (1978) is a fragmented depiction of life in a Paris apartment building and revolves around one wealthy resident's obsession with jigsaw puzzles. The episodes of this book are like pieces that the reader must put together. Georges Simenon's Maigret series has given new life to the detective novel. Many of his books are set in Paris, including *The Glass Cage* (1973) and *The Girl with a Squint* (1978). Christiane Rochefort's *Josyanne and the Welfare* is about a young girl coming of age in the projects of Paris.

Marguerite Duras's novel *The Lover* (1984) chronicles the end of France's colonial era. Set in Indochina, it is the story of a teenage girl and her wealthy Chinese lover. Colette is one of France's best-known women writers; *The Collected Stories of Colette* includes 100 stories written between 1908 and 1945. For contemporary French fiction, read the works of Michel Butor (*Boomerang*, 1978), Philippe Sollers (*Paradise*, 1978), and the detective novels of Sebastien Japrisot (*The Lady in the Car with Glasses and a Gun*).

Films

Since the invention of the film projector in France by August and Louis Lumière in 1885, French films have been among the world's best known. This is especially true of the productions made during the 1920s and 1930s, a stylistically mixed period that saw such "classical directors" as Jean Renoir with his lyrical, witty treatments of contemporary issues in films such as *Grand Illusion*, *A Day in the Country*, *The Human Beast*, and *Boudu Saved from Drowning*, as well as the more surrealistic films of the avant-garde directors such as Jean Cocteau and René Clair. Films of this period often address issues of mechanization, modernity, class differences, internationalism, and modern warfare.

The French *nouvelle vague*, or "New Wave," has been an internationally influential film movement for the past 30 years. Early New Wave directors such as Jean-Luc Godard, François Truffaut, Alain Resnais, Eric Rohmer, and Agnes Varda have gone on to produce enormously varied works dealing with themes as different as adolescent coming of age, religious mores and repression, Maoist political philosophy, objectification of women, and the rationalization of sexual conquest. The principal characteristics linking their work, however, have been a desire to experiment with the language and conventions of cinema as well as an adventurous manipulation of the ways to view a subject. Easily found titles include *Breathless* (Godard), *The 400 Blows* and *Shoot the Piano Player* (Truffaut), *Hiroshima Mon Amour* and *Last Year at Marienbad* (Resnais), and *Cleo from 9 to 5* (Varda).

More recent French film releases include productions by the original New Wave directors such as Louis Malle (*Au Revoir les Enfants*) and Agnes Varda (*Vagabond*). In addition, a number of younger French directors such as Claude Berri (*Jean de Florette* and *Manon of the Spring*) and Jean-Jacques Beineix (*Diva* and *Betty Blue*) have established themselves as ones to watch in the 1990s.

GERMANY

October 3, 1990, marked the reunification of a country divided for 45 years into two entities: one with a communist government and centrally planned economy, the other with a democratic government and capitalist economy. The destruction of the Berlin Wall was an emotionally charged symbol of the reunification of the German people and the German land. Germany, like its eastern and central European neighbors, is in the process of resituating itself within the political reordering of Europe.

Wonderful as the long-awaited reunification seemed at first, it has left a huge number of problems in its wake, especially in the social and economic spheres. Most poignant is the closing down of more than 50 percent of formerly GDR industry and the attendant steep rise in unemployment figures in the five new eastern German states. The western states, meanwhile, are struggling to absorb thousands of new citizens and incorporate another economic entity into their own infrastructure. Experts reckon that it will take about a decade before the split will be overcome—economically, politically, and socially.

Fragmentation is not a new phenomenon to the Germans, though. Germany's location in the heart of Europe has made it a crossroads of cultures and has produced a variety of German peoples rather than a completely uniform nationality. German history shows the efforts of these different people to accommodate and adapt themselves to their geographical circumstances, struggling to achieve a common cultural identity, and create a single political entity.

In fact, diversity may be the foremost characteristic of Germany. The nation encompasses a varied landscape that extends from the flat grasslands of the northern coast to the picturesque valleys of the Elbe and the Rhine, to the Black Forest and the Bavarian alps in the south, or the Erzgebirge in the east. Linguistically, Germany is divided into the Low-German dialects of the north and the High-German dialects of the south. In terms of culture, language, and mentality you will find great differences between Friesians, Westphalians, Berliners, Swabians, Saxons, and Bavarians—to name just a few of the German regional groups.

As a result of World War II and the division of Germany and its capital city, Berlin ceased to be the nation's predominant urban center. One consequence was that the traditional regional centers of Germany regained their importance. On the north coast are the seaports of Hamburg and Bremen, both rich in the traditions of the medieval Hanseatic merchant league. In western Germany are Cologne, famous for its medieval city and cathedral; and Frankfurt, Germany's railway, communications, and banking center. In the south there's Stuttgart—the heart of the thriving high-tech state of Baden-Wurttemberg—and Munich, home of the Hofbrauhaus and capital of Bavaria. In the east are Leipzig and Dresden, the capital of Saxony, with its rich collection of museums and architectural gems.

In spite of the reunification problems, Germany remains one of the leading exporting nations of the world, enjoys a booming economy, and maintains a stable currency. However, the unemployment rate in the western states has hovered around 6 to 8 percent for most of the last decade, and estimates for the next few years run around 30 percent for the new eastern states. Though an extensive welfare network provides a safety net for those out of work, there is no denying the considerable frustration and unrest among the young, who face the increasing possibility of joblessness after graduation.

Except during summer vacation, Germans travel infrequently. Come July, however, millions of Germans depart for the beaches of Italy, Greece, and Spain. This exodus makes room for the foreign tourists who flock to Heidelberg, Neuschwanstein, and other romantic spots made famous in tourist brochures. Berlin, once again the capital of Germany, is a popular destination, both because of its historic importance and its reputation as having a nightlife among the liveliest in Germany. The opening of the eastern parts has added a phenomenal amount of internal east-west traffic about which the foreign traveler should be warned.

Tourists will find getting around Germany fairly easy. Efficient public rail and bus services exist at least in the western states, and hitchhiking is common among students (but not permitted on the autobahns). In addition, ride-sharing agencies can be found in any large city. And if you lose your way, you'll soon find people willing to try their English on you. The language, people, culture, and history may be difficult to make sense of initially; however, a little effort to get tuned in will prove to be extremely rewarding.

— *Kurt Gamerschlag, Bonn, Germany*

Official name: Federal Republic of Germany. **Size:** 137,594 square miles (about the size of Montana). **Population:** 77,555,000. **Population density:** 563 inhabitants per square mile. **Capital:** Bonn (pop. 292,600). **Largest city:** Berlin (pop. 3,000,000). **Language:** German. **Religions:** Protestant and Roman Catholic. **Per capita income:** US$17,670. **Currency:** Deutsche Mark. **Literacy rate:** 99%. **Average daily high/low*:** Berlin: January, 35°/26°; July, 74°/55°. Munich: January, 33°/23°; July, 72°/54°. **Average number of days with precipitation:** Berlin: January, 10; July, 10. Munich: January, 10; July, 14.

TRAVEL

U.S. citizens need a passport, but a visa is not required for stays of up to three months. For longer stays, check with the Embassy of the Federal Republic of Germany (4645 Reservoir Road NW, Washington, DC 20007) or a German consulate for specific requirements.

Getting Around

In addition to Eurail and Interrail passes, GermanRail—known in Germany as Deutsche Bahn (DB)—offers a variety of discount plans:

---

*All temperatures are Fahrenheit.

- The GermanRail Flexipass allows you unlimited travel for *any* 5, 10, or 15 days within a one-month period. Rates for a "junior" (under 26 years) coach pass are: 5 days for $90, 10 for $120, and 15 days for $150. Your GermanRail Flexipass also allows you free travel on KD German Rhine Line steamers on the Rhine, Main, and Moselle rivers, as well as on selected bus lines.
- An unlimited mileage GermanRailpass is valid for 4, 9, or 16 days of consecutive travel. Nine days at junior rates is $105, 16 days at junior rates is $135. Second-class prices are slightly higher: 4 days are $110, 9 days are $170, and 16 consecutive days of travel will run you $230.
- The Tramper Ticket is available to nonstudents under 23 and students under 27. It allows one month of unlimited train travel in second class throughout the GermanRail network. It must be purchased in Germany; the cost is DM 290 (US$108).
- The Junior Pass entitles the bearer to a 50-percent discount on regular fares on point-to-point tickets for a period of one year. Youth from 18 to 22 years of age and students under 27 are eligible. This card is available for DM 110 (US$63) at rail stations in Germany.

On trains with baggage cars, bikes can be placed aboard the train, provided the passenger has obtained a bike card from the ticket seller. Under GermanRail's Bicycle at the Station plan, passengers can rent a bicycle for about $2.75 a day (nonpassengers pay about $5.50) Bikes may be dropped off at any of nearly 300 stations participating in the program. Most operate from April to October, some operate year-round. Brochures listing rental stations can be obtained at GermanRail offices.

"There are a lot of Americans in West Germany—perhaps more than in any other European nation. It is very easy (and tempting during bouts of homesickness) to surround oneself with fellow expatriates and tourists. Anyone who gives in to the lure of familiarity is doing himself a great disservice. Most West Germans are not only fluent in English (for those unwilling or unable to try German), but also eager to introduce interested foreigners to the delights of their country."
—Crystal Mazur, Cheektowaga, New York

"The Germans are an excessively political people, especially Berliners, and are very interested in debating with foreigners on national and international policy, on the role of a government, political decisions of the past and future, and so on—be prepared to talk politics."
—Christopher Lisle, Lincoln, Nebraska

Especially for Students and Youth

The following German organizations specialize in student travel; all of them issue the International Student Identity Card.

- Council Travel Service (CTS), Graf-Adolf-Strasse 18, 4000 Dusseldorf
- Reisedienst Deutscher Studentenschaften (RDS), Niederlassung Rentzelstrasse 16, 2000 Hamburg 13
- AStA-Reisen, Pfaffenwaldring 45, 7000 Stuttgart 80
- Studenten Reise Service (SRS GmbH), Voltairestrasse 8, 1026 Berlin

Holders of the International Student Identity Card can get reduced fare tickets for plane and train both within the country and from Germany to points in Europe and beyond. They are also entitled to discounts on Berlin bus travel, on entrance fees to some museums and historical sites and to many theaters, opera houses, and concert halls. The International Youth Card is good for discounts on selected accommodations as well as many museums, concerts, and theaters.

For Further Information

The best all-around budget guide to Germany is *The Real Guide: Germany* ($13.95). *The Real Guide: Berlin* ($11.95) is an excellent introduction to Germany's most popular city. *Let's Go: Germany, Austria, and Switzerland* is a recent addition to the *Let's Go* family, with a revised section on former East Germany. It's available for $14.95 in most bookstores and at Council Travel offices.

Some sources of general cultural and tourist information on Germany are the German National Tourist Office (747 Third Avenue, New York, NY 10017) and the German Information Center (950 Third Avenue, New York, NY 10022).

WORK

Getting a Job

In almost all cases it is necessary to obtain a work permit in order to get a job in Germany. U.S. citizens may apply at the local employment office after they enter the country. Students studying in Germany may work during the between-term period without a permit.

CIEE's Work in Germany Program is administered through its offices in New York and Bonn. The program enables you to work for a period of five months, from May 1 through October 15. Participants must be U.S. citizens at least 18 years of age, and a full-time college or university student during the spring semester immediately preceding work in Germany. A minimum of two years of college German is required. Past participants have worked in all types of jobs including farming in rural areas, hotel and restaurant work in tourist centers and large cities, and office and sales help all over the country. The cost of the program is $125. For details, contact CIEE's Work Exchanges Department, 205 East 42nd Street, New York, NY 10017. Students who participate in the program receive overnight accommodations and an orientation from CIEE's Bonn office, which also provides information on living, working, and traveling in Germany.

CDS International offers both a Career Training Program and an Internship Program in the fields of business, engineering, or a technical field, as well as training in the hotel industry, or as a bilingual secretary. The Career Training Program is open to young professionals with degrees in any one of the above-mentioned areas. The program includes intensive language training, followed by a year to 18 months working in a German company. Participants should have at least one year of full-time experience in the desired field of placement; trainees are responsible for finding their own jobs. The CDS Internship Program offers U.S. college seniors and recent graduates the opportunity to receive in-depth language training followed by a five-month paid internship with a German company. Internships are arranged by CDS for students who have majored in any one of the program areas. Applicants must be U.S. citizens and have a good knowledge of German for both programs. Details are available in the U.S. from CDS International, 330 Seventh Avenue, New York, NY 10001.

Teaching

Teachers of German, as well as anyone else with a college degree and an interest in teaching German, may apply for a teaching assistantship in a German high school; participants will assist with the teaching of English, American studies, and American literature. Applicants should be under 30 years of age and unmarried. A stipend of DM 1,000 per month is provided. For more information, contact U.S. Student Programs, Institute of International Education, 809 United Nations Plaza, New York, NY 10017. Ask for their booklet, *Fulbright and Other Grants for Graduate Study Abroad*.

"Being registered at a German university means you receive a work permit allowing you to seek part-time and vacation jobs. One of the most accessible and lucrative jobs in Germany is teaching English. If you're in a major city, just drop by any of the various foreign language schools, often plagued by the problem of too many students wanting to learn American English, and an all-British faculty. If you're in a small town, or do not have a work permit, put up ads around your school offering to teach American English at a reasonable rate. This could bring you DM 15 an hour. Proficiency in German will help your search even more."

—Christopher Spahr, Lake Forest, Illinois

Internships/Traineeships

Programs sponsored by member organizations of the Council on International Educational Exchange are listed below. In addition, Southwest Texas State University and Moorhead State University sponsor internship programs in Germany that are open only to their own students.

AIESEC-US. Reciprocal internship program for students in economics, business, finance, marketing, accounting, and computer science. See page 18 for more information.

Association for International Practical Training.
"IAESTE Trainee Program." On-the-job training for undergraduate and graduate students in technical fields such as engineering, computer science, agriculture, architecture, and mathematics. See page 18 for more information.
"Hotel & Culinary Exchanges Program." On-the-job training for young people beginning a career in the hotel and food-service industries. Participants must have graduated, or be currently enrolled in a university or vocational school and possess at least six months of training or experience in the chosen field. Training usually runs 6 to 12 months. See address in Appendix I.

Carl Duisberg Sprachcolleg München, in cooperation with the Fachhochschule Nürnberg, sponsors a German language and traineeship program. Opportunities are available in economics, business, and engineering. Participants are required to complete an eight-week language course in business or technical German. Trainees are then placed in German companies for two to three months. For more information contact Carl Duisberg Sprachcolleg, Professor Horst M. Robura, Pfanderstr 6-10, D-8000 Munchen 19, Germany.

Voluntary Service

CIEE places young people in German voluntary service workcamps organized by the following organizations:

- Internationale Jugendgemeinschaftsdienste (Kaiserstrasse 43, D-5300 Bonn 1) sponsors three- to four-week workcamps from the end of June to October. Workcamps are organized around historical-preservation projects, environmental-protection projects, and urban recreation activities. Volunteers must be over 16; knowledge of German is required for some workcamps.
- Internationale Begegnung in Gemeinschaftsdiensten (Schlosserstrasse 28, D-7000 Stuttgart 1) sponsors three-week workcamps from June to September, that involve constructing hiking paths, renovation of youth centers, and forest conservation. Volunteers must be over 18.
- Vereinigung Junger Freiwilliger (VJF) (Unter den Linden 36–38, 1086 Berlin) sponsors three-week workcamps in July and August involving a range of ecological and restoration projects. Volunteers must be over 18.

The applications of U.S. residents for the workcamps of the organizations above are processed by CIEE. Contact the International Voluntary Service Department at the Council's New York office for details.

For persons interested in longer-term voluntary service work, the International Christian Youth Exchange's Year Abroad Program offers persons ages 18 to 24 voluntary service opportunities in health, education, environment, construction, and so on. See page 23 for more information.

In addition, Goshen College offers a study-service term open primarily to Goshen students; limited spaces are available to transient students.

STUDY

An excellent source of information on study and research in Germany is the Deutscher Akademischer Austauschdienst (German Academic Exchange Service), at 950 Third Avenue, 19th floor, New York, NY 10022; (212) 758-3223. DAAD (its German initials) not only distributes information but also administers academic grants and study programs both in the U.S. and in Germany. Ask for their brochure "Grants and Research Programs in German Studies."

Another source of information on study in Germany is the Consulate General of the Federal Republic of Germany (460 Park Avenue, New York, NY 10022). Its brochures include *Goethe Institute—Language Courses, Summer Courses at German Universities*, and *Academic Studies in the Federal Republic of Germany*.

Educational programs offered by CIEE-member institutions are listed below. Consult Appendix I for the addresses of these sponsoring institutions. In addition to the programs below, the American Graduate School of International Management, California State University, Goshen College, Illinois State University, Indiana University, New York University, Northern Arizona University, Ohio State University, Pennsylvania State University, Pomona College, the University of California, the University of Kansas, the University of Rhode Island, Stanford University, the University of Toledo, the University of Utah, and Valparaiso University all offer programs open only to their own students.

Semester and Academic Year

Business

State University of New York at Cortland. Study at the Fachhochschule, Münster. Juniors, seniors, and graduate students with three years of college German and 3.5 GPA in major. Apply by March 1.

General Studies

American Heritage Association. "Northwest Interinstitutional Council on Study Abroad—Cologne." Fall or spring quarters. Sophomores with one term of college German. Apply by June 1 for fall; January 15 for spring.

Beloit College. "German Seminar." Hamburg. Fall semester. Sophomores to graduates with intermediate German and 2.5 GPA. Apply by April 1.

Brethren Colleges Abroad. Marburg. Academic year and fall or spring semester. Intensive language, study tour to Berlin and Eastern Europe. Juniors and seniors with two years of college German and 3.0 GPA. Apply by April 15 for academic year and fall; November 1 for spring.

Central Washington University. "Northwest Interinstitutional Council on Study Abroad—Cologne." Spring quarter only. See listing under American Heritage Association.

Cornell University. "Cornell Abroad in Hamburg." Academic year or semester. Juniors and seniors with two years of German and a 3.0 GPA. Apply by February 15 for fall and November 1 for spring.

Davidson College. "Davidson College Junior Year Abroad in Würzburg." Integrated program at the University of Würzburg. Academic Year. Juniors of all majors with two years of German and 3.0 GPA. Apply by February 1.

Experiment in International Living/School for International Training.
"College Semester Abroad—Berlin: Germany, between East and West." Excursions to Ehrfort, Wiemar, and Dresden, Germany; and Prague, Czechoslovakia. Fall or spring semester. Intensive language, interdisciplinary seminar, field-study methods seminar, independent-study project, homestays and excursions. Sophomores, juniors, and seniors with 2.5 GPA. Apply by May 15 for fall and October 15 for spring.
"College Semester Abroad—German Language Immersion." Tübingen. Fall or spring semester. Intensive language immersion, life and culture seminar, homestays and excursions. No language prerequisite. Sophomores to seniors with 2.5 GPA. Apply by October 31 for spring; May 31 for fall.

Guilford College. "Semester in Munich." Fall semester. Sophomores, juniors, and seniors. Apply by October 31.

Heidelberg College. "American Junior Year at Heidelberg University." Academic year, and fall or spring semester. Juniors, seniors, and graduates with two years of college German and 3.0 GPA. Apply by March 15 for academic year or semester; October 15 for spring. Contact American Junior Year at Heidelberg, 310 East Market Street, Tiffin, OH 44883-2434; (419) 448-2216.

Indiana University. "Overseas Study in Hamburg." Academic year. Limited to students at Indiana, Purdue, and Ohio State. Juniors and seniors with two years of German and 3.0 GPA. Apply by first week of November.

International Student Exchange Program. Direct reciprocal exchange between U.S. universities and institutions in Braunschweig, Eichstätt, Giessen, Kassel, Marburg, and Trier. Semester or academic year. Full curriculum options. Open only to students at ISEP-member institutions.

Kalamazoo College.
"Kalamazoo College in Bonn." Study at the University of Bonn. Fall and winter quarter (September 15–February 15). Orientation at Kalamazoo the summer prior to study abroad. Juniors and seniors with 2.75 GPA and 20 quarter-hours of German. Apply by May 1.
"Kalamazoo College in Erlangen." Fall and winter quarter at the University of Erlangen. Orientation at Kalamazoo. For juniors and seniors with 15 quarter-hours of German and 3.0 GPA. Apply by May 1.
"Kalamazoo College in Hannover." Orientation at Kalamazoo. Juniors and seniors with 15 quarter-hours of German and 2.75 GPA. Apply by May 1.

Lake Erie College. Constance. Juniors and seniors with intermediate German and 2.5 GPA. Apply by June 1 and October 1.

Lewis and Clark College. "Junior Year in Munich." Academic year or semester. Sophomores to seniors with two years of German and 3.0 GPA. Apply by February 15.

Michigan State University. "Junior Year in Freiburg." See program listing under Wayne State University.

Millersville University. "Junior Year in Marburg." Philipps University. Juniors with two years of university-level German and 2.4 GPA. Apply by February 15.

Northern Arizona University. Tübingen. Juniors to graduate students with two years college-level German and 2.5 GPA. Apply by March 15.

Northern Illinois University. "Academic Internships in Bonn/Cologne." Fall and spring semesters. Students take two courses plus internship. Wide range of internships available for own students; more limited selection for others. Sophomores, juniors, and seniors with 3.0 GPA and two years of German. Apply by April 4 for fall; November 1 for spring.

Portland State University.
"Baden-Württemberg Program." Academic year. Juniors, seniors, graduates, and teachers with two years of college German. Apply by January 31.
"Northwest Interinstitutional Council on Study Abroad—Cologne." See description under American Heritage Association.

Purdue University. "Overseas Study in Hamburg." See program listing under Indiana University.

Rutgers University. "Junior year in Germany." Constance. Academic year. Juniors with two years college German, German literature, and 3.0 GPA. Apply by March 1.

Scripps College. "Scripps Program in Heidelberg." Semester or academic year through University of Heidelberg. Sophomores to seniors with four semesters of college German and B–minus average. Apply by March 1 for fall and year, October 15 for spring.

State University of New York at Albany. "Würzburg University Exchange." Academic year, fall and spring semester. Juniors, seniors, and graduates with two years of college German, 2.8 overall GPA and 3.0 in German. Apply by March 15 for academic year and fall and November 15 for spring.

State University of New York at Cortland.
Heidelberg. Fall or spring semester. Sophomores, juniors, and seniors with one semester of college German and 2.5 GPA. Apply by March 1 for fall, October 15 for spring.
Tübingen. Spring semester (March 1 to mid-July). Juniors, seniors, and graduates with two years of college German and 2.5 GPA. Apply by November 1.

State University of New York at Oswego. "Georg-August-Universität/SUNY Oswego Exchange Program." Göttingen. Academic year. Junior or senior German majors or education concentrations. Apply by April 1.

State University of New York at Stony Brook. Tübingen. Academic year. Sophomores to graduate students with two years of college German and 3.0 GPA. Apply by April 1.

Stetson University. Freiburg. Academic year or semester. Sophomores, juniors, and seniors with two years of German and 2.5 GPA (3.0 in major). Apply by March 1 for fall and academic year and October 15 for spring.

Syracuse University. "Syracuse in Germany." Marburg. Exchange program with Philipps Universität. Academic year or spring semester. Juniors and seniors with two years of college German and 3.0 GPA. Apply by March 15 for academic year, October 15 for spring semester.

Tufts University. "Tufts in Tübingen." Academic year or spring semester. Mainly juniors with two years of college German and 3.0 GPA. Apply by February 1.

University of Colorado at Boulder. "Academic Year in Regensburg." Juniors and seniors with four semesters of college German or equivalent and 2.75 GPA. Apply by March 1.

University of La Verne. Semester or year in Marburg. See listing under Brethren Colleges Abroad.

University of Massachusetts—Amherst.
"Freiburg/Baden-Württemberg Exchange." Academic year at Freiburg, Stuttgart, Konstanz, Heidelberg, and five other Baden-Württemberg universities. Juniors, seniors, and graduates with 3.0 GPA and fluency in German. Apply by March 1.

University of North Carolina—Chapel Hill.
"UNC Program to Berlin." Academic year. Juniors and seniors, fluency in German and 3.0 GPA required. Apply by February 12.
"Semester Program in Berlin." Fall. One year German required. Apply by February 12.
"UNC Program to Göttingen." Academic year. (See above for eligibility and deadline).
"UNC in Tübingen." Academic year. Sophomores, juniors, and seniors with 3.0 GPA and two years college German. Apply by March 15.

University of Oregon. "Northwest Interinstitutional Council on Study Abroad—Cologne." See listing under American Heritage Association.

University of Washington. "Northwest Interinstitutional Council on Study Abroad—Cologne." Spring quarter only. See listing under American Heritage Association.

University of Wisconsin—Madison.
Bonn. Academic year at Rheinische Friedrich Wilhelms University. Juniors and seniors with 3.0 GPA and one year of German. Open only to students at a college or university in Wisconsin or to Wisconsin residents studying outside the state. Apply by February 1.
Frankfurt. Exchange for academic year. Open to juniors, seniors, and graduate students with five semesters of German and a 3.0 GPA. Includes a monthly stipend. Apply by March 1.
Freiburg. Academic year at Albert Ludwigs University. Open to juniors and seniors with five semesters of college German and 3.0 GPA. Apply by April 1.
Frankfurt. Exchange for academic year. Open to juniors, seniors, and graduate students with five semesters of German and 3.0 GPA. Includes a monthly stipend. Apply by March 1.
Giessen. Exchange for academic year. Open to juniors, seniors, and graduate students with five semesters of German and 3.0 GPA. Includes a monthly stipend. Apply by March 1.

Wayne State University.
"Junior Year in Freiburg." Academic year at Albert Ludwigs University. Cosponsored with Michigan State University, University of Michigan, and University of Wisconsin. Program offered to juniors with four semesters of college German and 3.0 GPA. Seniors occasionally accepted on a space-available basis. Apply by April 1.
"Junior Year in Munich." Program offered to juniors with four semesters of college German and 3.0 GPA. Seniors occasionally accepted on a space-available basis. Apply by April 1.

Wesleyan University. "Wesleyan University Program in Germany." Regensburg. Spring semester. Preparatory language course plus spring semester at the University of Heidelberg, where regular classes are supplemented by program tutorials. Sophomores, juniors, and seniors with three semesters of German with a B average. Apply by November 1.

Western Washington University. "Northwest Interinstitutional Council on Study Abroad—Cologne." See listing under American Heritage Association.

German Language and Civilization

Alma College. "Program of Studies in Germany." Kassel. Courses in language, literature, culture, and current events. All instruction in German. Homestays and excursions. Academic year or semester. Sophomores, juniors, and seniors with 2.5 GPA. Apply by June 15 for fall and October 15 for winter.

Antioch University. "Antioch in Germany." Tübingen. Academic year or semester. Juniors and seniors with two years of German. Apply by January 15.

Central University of Iowa. "Central College in Germany and Austria." Prien and Murnau. Academic year or semester. Sophomores, juniors, and seniors with intermediate German and 2.5 GPA (3.0 in German). Apply by March 15 for fall and academic year, and October 15 for spring.

Hiram College. "Hamburg Quarter." Academic courses and travel in Germany. Sophomores, juniors, and seniors with one year of German and 2.5 GPA. Apply by October 1.

Kalamazoo College. "Kalamazoo College at Münster." Fall and winter quarter. Juniors and seniors with 15 quarter-hours of German and 2.5 GPA. Apply by May 1.

Lewis and Clark University. "Year of Study in Munich." Academic year. Juniors and seniors with two years of college German with a B average. Apply by February 15.

Middlebury College. Mainz. Sophomores to graduates. Fluency in German required. Rolling admissions.

Portland State University. "Spring Intensive Language Program." Tübingen. Limited to students from the Oregon State System of Higher Education. Spring quarter. Freshmen to graduate students with two quarter-terms of first-year German and 2.5 GPA. Apply by January 31.

University of Oregon.
"OSSHE—Baden-Württemberg Universities Exchange." Tübingen, Stuttgart, Konstanz, Hohenheim, Freiburg, Karlsruhle. Academic year. Preference given to juniors at schools in Oregon State System of Higher Education (OSSHE). Two years of college German with a B average. Apply by January 31.
"OSSHE—Intensive German Language Program." Tübingen. Spring semester. Sophomores to graduate students with two quarters of college German and 2.5 GPA. Preference given to Oregon State System of Higher Education (OSSHE) students. Apply by January 31.

Mechanical Engineering

Michigan State University. "Engineering in Aachen." Study at the Technical University of Aachen with opportunities to participate in research and explore German industrial activities. Spring quarter. Juniors and seniors with mechanical-engineering background. Apply by February 3.

Physical Education

State University of New York at Cortland. Study at the Deutsche Sporthochschule. Cologne. Spring. Juniors and seniors with one semester of college German and 2.5 GPA in major. Apply by October 15.

Social Work

University of Louisville. "Social Work in Munich." Exchange program with the Katholische Stiftungsfachhochschule. Spring semester. Open to graduate students and social-work professionals. Apply by January 16.

Summer

Engineering

Alma College. "Program of Studies in Germany." Kassel. Four- or eight-week program. All instruction in German. Homestays and excursions. Sophomores, juniors, and seniors with 2.5 GPA. Apply by April 15.

Council on International Educational Exchange. "Cooperative Summer Program for Engineering Students." Aachen, Germany and Maastricht, the Netherlands. Sophomores to graduate students majoring in engineering. No language prerequisite but knowledge of German is preferred. Apply by March 1. Contact University Programs Department.

German Language and Civilization

Illinois State University. "Summer Program in the Federal Republic of Germany." Bonn. Freshmen to graduates. Apply by March 17.

Marquette University. "Marquette University's Language Center in Germany." Rhineland, Berlin, and Hildesheim. Sophomores, juniors, and seniors with one year of German. Apply by February 15. Contact: Dr. E. L. Hudgins, Lalumiere Language Hall, Marquette University, Milwaukee, WI 53233.

Miami University. Intensive German in Heidelberg and Berlin. Homestay and excursions. High school graduates and up with one year of college German. Apply by February 15.

Michigan State University. "German Language Program in Mayen." Juniors and seniors with two years of college German. Apply by April 21.

State University of New York at Albany.
"Braunschweig Summer Language Program." Freshmen to graduates with one year of German. Apply by April 15.

State University of New York at Oneonta. "German and European Studies." Würzburg. Participants study (in English) about German and European history, politics, economics, and culture while living with German students at a German university. German language instruction at beginning and intermediate levels. Juniors, seniors, and holders of A.A. degrees. Rolling admissions.

University of Alabama. Weingarten, Munich, Berlin, and Switzerland. Freshmen to seniors with two semesters of college German. Apply by April 1.

University of Colorado at Boulder. "Study Abroad in Kassel." Intensive language program at all levels. Freshmen to seniors with 2.75 GPA. Apply by March 1.

University of Kansas.
"Intermediate Summer Language Institute, Eutin." Freshmen to seniors with one year of German language study. Apply by February 15.
"Advanced Summer Language Institute in Holzkirchen/Munich." Freshmen to seniors with four semesters of college German. Apply by February 1.

University of Louisville. "German Language and Culture in Mainz and Saarbrueken." Freshmen to graduate students with background in German. Apply by April 21.

University of Maryland. "Summer in Munich." Sophomores, juniors, and seniors with 12 credits college German and 3.0 GPA. Apply by March 1.

University of Pennsylvania. "Penn-in-Freiburg." For students interested in German language studies. One year of German required. Apply by April 1.

University of Utah. "Kiel German Language Program." Six weeks. Freshmen to graduate students and others. One or two quarters of college German or the equivalent is recommended. Apply by March 1.

University System of Georgia/Georgia State University. Erlangen. Freshmen to seniors with 2.5 GPA and three quarters of college German with 3.0 GPA in those courses. Apply by April 1.

EXPLORING GERMAN CULTURE

Readings

Until recently, postwar German literature has been divided into two camps: East and West. However, on both sides of the Iron Curtain, similar themes were explored and together the two bodies of work offer insight into Germany's fascinating political and historical background.

The legacy of World War II is a theme which pervaded West German writing. Thomas Mann's *Mario and the Magician* is a 40-page novella dealing with the rise of Nazi Germany. One of the pioneers of postwar German literature, Heinrich Böll, is the author of *The Bread of Those Early Years*, the story of love transforming a cynic in a post–World War II Rhineland town. Günther Grass, a prolific writer, continues to address the problems and guilt caused by the war. *The Tin Drum* is one of his finest works; along with *Cat and Mouse* and *Dog Years* it forms the well-known Danzig Trilogy. Siegfried Lenz, another critical, politically oriented writer of Grass's generation, is the author of *The German Lesson* (1986) and *Homeland Museum* (1978). Botho Strauss's novels and plays, such as *A Rumour* and *The Young Man* (1989), reflect modern German concerns with establishing identity by looking back at German history, particularly to World War II.

Peter Schneider, who lived in West Berlin, is the author of *Knife in the Head* and *The Wall Jumper* (1985), which deal with the tensions of life in this West German island in the middle of East Germany during the Cold War era. *Berlin Alexanderplatz: The Story of Franz Biberkopf*, by Alfred Doblin, is an unsettling, experimental novel set in Berlin in the twenties. A more current novel about Berlin and the symbolic division that it represented until recently is Ian Walker's *Zoo Station* (1987). Littered with ultra-hip references to underground dance clubs, Engels, and black-market Levi's jeans, Walker's rambling prose chronicles the two Berlins, "where two systems of life and thought wage war."

Franz Xavier Kroetz depicts the lower depths of Bavarian society in books like *Agnes Bernauer* and *Maria Magdalena*, the story of a single working-class woman and the problems she encounters when she discovers that she is pregnant. Gabriele Wohmann writes about women trying to find themselves in an atmosphere of modern urban angst. In *Serious Intention*, for instance, a woman's account of her life during an illness deals with problems of women in modern Germany and the conflicts between the older World War II generation and the younger generation. Walter Abish, a noteworthy modern German-American writer, recently treated the same subject with surprising insight in *How German Is It* (1980).

Like their Western counterparts, East German writers also have a strong political streak. After World War II, they had to confront not only the legacy of the war but also a new political system and way of life. In *A Model Childhood* (1980), Christa Wolf writes about her childhood in Nazi Germany and coming to terms with it in later life. *Cassandra* (1984), perhaps her most widely read book, is a very personal and searching look at the complexities of life in East Germany.

After living abroad during the war, the playwright Bertolt Brecht chose to make his home in East Berlin. His play *Mother Courage* illustrates his vision of communism, while *Stories from Mr. Keuner* is a collection of antiwar stories.

Other modern writers from the eastern sector include Ulrich Plensdorf, who used a famous work by Goethe (*The Sorrows of Young Werther*) as the basis for a novel dealing with the problems of life in East Germany in the 1970s, *The New Sorrows of Young Werther* (1978). In a similar vein, *Sleepless Days*, by Jurek Becker, describes the monotony of living in an authoritarian society. Herman Kant, whose novels were published mostly in the 1960s and 1970s (*The Assembly Hall* among them), was another critic of life in East Germany, although he believed in the principles on which the government and economy were organized.

Films

Early German filmmaking is best represented by the films made between the two world wars, pictures known for their production values and high technical quality. Many of the themes in films such as *Die Niebeulungen*, by Fritz Lang, *The Student of Prague*, by Henrik Galeen, and *The Cabinet of Dr. Caligari*, by Robert Wiene, call upon German folklore and tradition. Later films of this period delved into subjects associated with modern urban life: crime, graft, and seduction are the focus of G. W. Pabst's *The Threepenny Opera* (1931); sexual intrigue characterized Josef Von Sternberg's *The Blue Angel* (1930) and Pabst's *Pandora's Box* (1929); and the life of a pathological child murderer and mob justice was the subject of Lang's *M* (1931).

Since World War II, the American film industry has largely had control of West German film production and distribution. In the early 1960s, a loose-knit group of younger German filmmakers began to explore the funding options available for independent production and soon inaugurated what became known as the New German Cinema. The best-known of the group is R. W. Fassbinder, whose *The Marriage of Maria Braun* (1979) was an extended metaphor for postwar Germany, and who linked contemporary Germany with German history in *Berlin Alexanderplatz* (1979) and *Lili Marlene* (1980). This preoccupation with German history and tradition and Germany's peculiar relationship with the U.S. is also found in the films of Hans Jurgen Syberberg, which include *Our Hitler*, *Parsifal*, and *Ludwig the Mad Bavarian King*. Similar themes pervade Wim Wender's work: *Wings of Desire* (1988), a love story under the big top, and *The American Friend* (1977), loosely based on a psychological thriller by Patricia Highsmith.

Other German films of note include Volker Schöndorf's *The Tin Drum* (1979), the story of a boy who refuses to grow physically while the Nazis take power, and *The Lost Honor of Katherine Blum* (1975), a film based on a Heinrich Böll novel. Ulrike Ottinger's *Ticket of No Return*, an investigation into female identity, is also worth viewing. *The Nasty Girl* (1989), directed by Michael Verhoeven, is an award-winning black comedy with an misleading English translation as a title. Based on a true story, the plot revolves around a young student attempting to write an essay about the Nazis; she quickly becomes an object of scorn from townspeople with a surprising amount to conceal. The film offers a fascinating glimpse of today's Germany, moving forward but still trying to deal with its past.

GREECE

The land of ancient Greece has little in common with the country of today. The arid, hilly land that gave birth to many seminal Western philosophers is now often seen as a year-long party by youthful visitors from around the globe in search of sunny beaches and cheap beer. This superficial image does little justice to Greece's multifaceted culture. Absorbing both European and Middle-Eastern influences, Greece's seemingly effortless Mediterranean lifestyle belies the complexity of its history and the character of its people. To view Greece as little more than a global soirée is to overlook the rich culture and fascinating past of a group of islands whose contributions to Western culture have spread far beyond its water-bound boundaries. Like Plato's analogy of the Cave, Greece's tourist-forged images are merely shadows of its deeper identity.

Greece was ruled by Turkey for much of the Middle Ages, until the allied navies of Britain, France, and Russia helped Greece regain independence—keeping, however, a few fingers on the political steering wheel. The twentieth century for Greece was tragically littered with uprisings, coups, and a debilitating civil war between the Communists (who formed the core of wartime resistance against the Germans during WWII) and the western-backed right-wing "government" forces. A coup in 1967 instituted a military dictatorship that lasted until 1974. For the last decade or so, Greece has experienced relative democratic stability and economic growth, due in part to its healthy tourist economy and its EC membership.

Greece is truly a country of natural beauty. Its beaches and mountains will fulfill anyone's postcard-photo expectations; the only problem might lie in finding an alcove that hasn't already been "discovered." Culturally, Greece is an interesting mélange of influences—ancient and modern, Middle Eastern and European. Slightly embittered by the never-ending stream of tourists, the simple courtesy of learning a few words in Greek will soften even the toughest: "Please" is *Parakaló*, "Thank you" is *Efharistó*.

The treasures of its ancient civilization are often overlooked by tired travelers eager for a place to set down their bags, but should be seen at all costs. The Acropolis in Athens, the Parthenon, the isle of Lesbos, Mount Olympus: your knowledge of and curiosity about Greek history and mythology will help shape your itinerary. Museums, local artisans, archeological wonders—these things make Greece fascinating. Renting a moped and whizzing along hilly roads, passing every once in a while through the musky stench of rotting olives (a scent unlike anything else in this world); swimming through clear warm water without another being in sight; or sitting at a small café on the oceanside, munching on feta cheese and fresh bread: To be sure, the other pleasures of Greece are not to be ignored.

—*Nicole Ellison, New York, New York*

Official name: Hellenic Republic. **Size:** 51,146 square miles (about the size of Arkansas). **Population:** 10,066,000. **Population density:** 196 inhabitants per square mile. **Capital and largest city:** Athens (pop. 3,016,457). **Language:** Greek. **Religion:** Greek Orthodox. **Per capita income:** US$4,350. **Currency:** Drachma. **Literacy rate:** 95%. **Average daily**

high/low*: Athens: January, 54°/42°; July, 90°/72°. **Average number of days with precipitation:** Athens: January, 7; July, 1.

TRAVEL

A passport is required for American citizens visiting Greece. However, a visa is not required for stays of up to three months. For regulations regarding residence in Greece for over three months, contact the Greek Embassy, 2211 Massachusetts Avenue NW, Washington, DC 20008.

Getting Around

The Greek islands of the Aegean and Ionian seas are some of the most popular destinations in Europe for young people from all over the world. Attracted by beaches, warm sunny weather, historic ruins, and some of the lowest prices in Europe for food and accommodations, young people fill the ferries that shuttle between the islands.

Travel by train or ferry in Greece is generally inexpensive. Passes for unlimited rail travel (called "Tourist Railway Cards") may be purchased upon arrival: 6,000 drachmae (US$31) for ten days; 10,000 drachame (US$52) for two people for ten days; and 10,500 drachmae (US$55) for one person for one month. Eurail and Interrail passes may be used on the Greek rail network (see page 61).

Greece offers outstanding opportunities for hiking and mountaineering. *Greece on Foot: Mountain Treks, Island Trails*, by Marc S. Dubin, suggests hiking itineraries to suit almost anyone. Order it for $10.95 (plus $2 shipping and handling) from Mountaineers Books, 1011 S.W. Klickitat Way, Suite 107, Seattle, WA 98134 (800-553-4453).

Especially for Students and Young People

There are a number of students travel bureaus in Greece:

- Usit, 1 Filellinon Street, Syntagma Square, 105 57 Athens (Open summer only)
- ISYTS-International Student and Youth Travel Service, 11 Nikis Street, 2nd floor, Syntagma Square, 105 57 Athens
- CTS Student Travel Centre/Hello Travel, 86 Solonos Street, 2nd floor, Athens
- VITAL STS, 1 Filellinon Street, Syntagma Square, 105 57 Athens

All of these student travel bureaus offer student/youth discounts on ferries, international flights, and international train tickets. A variety of student tours and cruises are also available. With your International Student Identity Card you'll be entitled to discounts at museums, including the Acropolis archaeological site, the National Archaeological Museum, the Temple of Olympian Zeus, and the Theater of Dionyssos, to name a few. The ISIC is also good for discounts at a variety of cultural events throughout Greece. And there are student discounts on international flights, trains, and ferries from Greece to Italy and the rest of Europe. The International Youth Card is good for discounts on accommodations, cruises, tours and excursions, restaurants, and car rentals.

"The Greek train system, planes, and ferries do not run on schedule. They go day-by-day at different times, so it's difficult to get a set schedule. Your best bet is to go to a travel agent and get help there."
—Jeanine Hecker, Phillips, Maine

---

*All temperatures are Fahrenheit.

For Further Information

For a wealth of budget travel information, *Let's Go: Greece and Turkey* is probably the most comprehensive guidebook. It's available for $14.95 in most bookstores and at Council Travel offices. For a more detailed guide to the sights about the Greek islands, try *The Real Guide: Greece*, available in bookstores for $12.95. In addition, general information about Greece is available from the Greek National Tourist Organization, 645 Fifth Avenue, New York, NY 10022.

WORK

Job opportunities are scarce and the Greek government tries to limit employment to Greek citizens and visitors from the European Community (EC). A work permit from the Ministry of Labor, 40 Pireos Street, 10437 Athens, is mandatory and is granted for specialized work only. Foreign firms located in Greece are allowed to secure work permits for their foreign employees. For $40, you can get a list of American firms and subsidiaries operating in Greece from The American Hellenic Chamber of Commerce, 17 Valaoritou Street, 10671 Athens. They can provide advice on how to get a short- or long-term position in Greece.

"A lot of young people teach English either privately or in a school. Since there are several foreign schools in Athens, they quite regularly are looking for stand-in or permanent teachers. People might check with the American Embassy in Athens or check the Athens News."
—Paul Thompson, New Orleans, Louisiana

Internships/Traineeships

Programs offered by members of the Council on International Educational Exchange are listed below.

AIESEC-US. Reciprocal internship program for students in economics, business, finance, marketing, accounting, and computer sciences. See page 18 for more information.

Association for International Practical Training. "IAESTE Trainee Program." On-the-job training for undergraduate and graduate students in technical fields such as engineering, computer science, agriculture, architecture, and mathematics. See page 18 for more information.

In addition, the American Farm School/Summer Work Activities Program sponsors a program on the farm in Thessaloniki for eight weeks during the summer. Participants bale hay, harvest crops, milk cows, and do other various types of farm work. For more information, contact the American Farm School, 1133 Broadway at 26th Street, New York, NY 10010.

Study

Contact the Office of Press Information of the Greek Embassy for their eight-page fact sheet on "American-Sponsored or Affiliated Educational Programs and Schools in Greece." It includes elementary and secondary schools, university-level programs, and summer programs.

The study programs offered by CIEE-member institutions are listed below. Consult Appendix I for the addresses of the colleges and universities listed in this section. In addition to the programs below, Pennsylvania State University has a program open only to its own students.

Semester and Academic Year

General Studies

Brethen Colleges Abroad. University of La Verne in Athens. Full range of academic programs, excursions, and study tours. English teaching work can be arranged. No language prerequisite. Sophomores to graduate students (in business and management studies) with 2.8 GPA. Apply by April 15 for fall and year; November 1 for spring.

Experiment in International Living/School for International Training. "College Semester Abroad." Athens and Thessaloniki. Fall or spring semester. Intensive language, life, and culture seminar, field-study methods seminar, urban and village homestays, and independent-study project. Sophomores, juniors, and seniors to graduate students with 2.5 GPA. Apply by May 15 for fall and October 15 for spring.

Portland State University. "PSU in Athens." Fall and spring quarters. Liberal arts and modern Greek. Sophomores to graduate students. Apply by July 15 for fall; August 25 for spring.

University of La Verne. Athens. Academic year or semester. See listing under Brethren Colleges Abroad.

Western Washington University. "Study in Greece." Athens. Fall or spring quarter. First-year students to seniors with 2.5 GPA. Applications accepted up to 60 days prior to departure. Program cosponsored by Portland State University and Central Washington University.

Greek Studies

Beaver College. "Semester in Greece: Classical, Byzantine, and modern Greek Studies." Athens. Academic year, fall or spring semester. Co-curricular escorted field-study trips to northern Greece and the Peloponnesus. Juniors and seniors with 3.0 GPA. Apply by April 20 for academic year and fall; October 15 for spring.

Summer

General Studies

Southern Illinois University at Carbondale. "Ecstacy, Honor, and Reason: Searching for the Universal in Religion, Philosophy, and the Sciences of Ancient Greece." Greece and Turkey. Seminars on the ancient Greek experience. High-school graduates to university graduates, and adults with college background. Apply by April 1.

University of North Carolina. "UNC Summer Program to Greece." Excursions to various cities. Sophomores to graduate students.

Greek Mythology

State University of New York at Brockport. Programs include instruction at relevant sites, such as Crete, Athens, the Acropolis and Philopapas. Undergraduates and graduates.

EXPLORING GREEK CULTURE

Readings

Greek literature is divided into two very distinct categories: ancient and modern. The two bear little resemblance to one another, but Plato, Sappho, Aristotle, Sophocles, and Euripedes—some of the most influential figures in the history of Western thought—are products of an ancient civilization that one cannot help but evoke when speaking of today's Greece. Modern bards include Nikos Kazantzakis; in his novels *Zorba the Greek* (1952) and *The Last Temptation of Christ* (1971), he attempts to embody ideas from various philosophers and religions in characters that wrestle with existential questions. *The Fratricides* (1964), a novel about the Greek Civil War, and *The Greek Passion* (1971), about a Greek village that enacts a passion play, deal more explicitly with life in Greece.

After World War II, Greek prose writing was dominated by reflections on the eight years of war; Iannis Beratis recounted his experiences of 1941 in *The Broad River* (1946). Later, during the 1960s, Greece's troubled political and social situation resulted in a number of works that attempted to explore the underlying historical factors. *The Third Wedding* (1970), by Kostas Tachtsis, is representative of this trend. The female narrator in this well-known novel tells the story of her life with bitter honesty, unwittingly exposing the oppressive nature of the Greek family. For a glimpse of life in Thessaloniki (Salonika) and Athens from the 1930s to the 1980s, Yorgos Ioannous's short prose pieces are an interesting mélange of fiction and autobiography.

HUNGARY

Having embarked upon a path toward a market-driven economic system, Hungary now faces the challenge of preserving and perpetuating its 1,000 years of tradition and culture in the midst of the resultant social and economic upheaval. Exciting signs abound in Budapest of the change and growth underway. Logos of Austrian and other Western firms brighten the drab, polluted surfaces of major boulevards, squares, and buildings. Shop windows display a variety of goods that are not yet available in neighboring former Soviet-bloc nations. This new appearance of material wealth and well-being, however, is only a superficial harbinger of what may come over the next decade.

Hungarians are struggling to cope with the stress brought on by changes. As prices rise to reflect the actual value of goods, Hungarian buying power diminishes. An average family can rarely afford to shop in the stores under those colorfully lit Western logos. New social and economic freedoms also introduce positive change—rejuvenation of religious and charitable organizations and the opening of private schools. Even eating habits are now under examination, and there is a growing interest in alternative cuisines—vegetarianism, low-fat diets, and macrobiotics, to name a few.

Change and outside cultural influence are hardly new to Hungarians. Over the past centuries they have endured and survived numerous occupations and wars that resulted in either contraction or expansion of borders. Today's nation is but one third of the territory Hungary controlled at the beginning of this century as part of the Austro-Hungarian Empire. Thousands of ethnic Hungarians live outside the borders in Romania, the U.S.S.R., and Czechoslovakia; many more live as émigrés in North America. Whether invaded by Turks, bombed by Austrians, held captive by Germans, or separated from each other by artificially drawn borders, Hungarians have always held on fiercely to their traditions and culture. They have also absorbed some new traditions and even languages along the way. Magyar, a member of the Finno-Ugric language group, is spoken nearly uniformly throughout the country, save for the Paloc region where a distinct ancient dialect survives to this day. The Hungarian language, as with all aspects of the culture, currently is beginning to reflect Western influences as European and American slang slowly find their way into the language.

True to their tenacity, Hungarians will always maintain their distinctive Magyar nature and flavor. The country will also celebrate its rich cuisine, known for gulyas, palacsinta, paprikas, and fine wines. Hunting and horseback riding on the Great Plain will never go out of style. Hopefully, as the country develops a new Western-style economy, it can preserve the best of its past.

—*Elizabeth Winship, Budapest, Hungary*

Official name: Republic of Hungary. **Area:** 35,919 square miles (about the size of Indiana). **Population:** 10,546,000. **Population density:** 293 inhabitants per square mile. **Capital and largest city:** Budapest (pop. 2,115,000). **Language:** Magyar. **Religion:** Roman Catholic, Protestant. **Per capita income:** US$8,650. **Currency:** Forint. **Literacy rate:** 98%. **Average daily high/low*:** Budapest: January, 30°/20°; July, 82°/61°. **Average number of days with precipitation:** Budapest: January, 6; July, 7.

TRAVEL

As of November 1, 1990, holders of a U.S. passport can stay in Hungary for up to 90 days without a visa. If you wish to stay for more than 90 days, you must report to the local police authority in Hungary for the proper documentation. For further information, contact the Embassy of the Republic of Hungary, 3910 Shoemaker Street NW, Washington, DC 20008; (202) 362-6737. There is no mandatory daily currency exchange for visitors to Hungary.

Getting Around

Whether you're traveling by bus, train, or car, the quickest route between any two points in the country will probably be through Budapest, the hub of the nation's transportation system. Hungarian trains are inexpensive, clean, and reliable. Eurail and InterRail passes are valid (see page 61), and the recently introduced European East Pass is valid in Hungary, as well as in Czechoslovakia, Poland, and Austria. Available in first class only, rail travel on any 5 days within a 15-day period is $160, any 10 days within one month is $259. Bus service is also cheap but slower and more crowded than the train. One of the most enjoyable ways to travel (and the most expensive) is on the Danube hydrofoils between Vienna and Budapest.

Accommodations are inexpensive and easy to find. IBUSZ, the Hungarian national travel agency, with offices in city centers throughout the country, will reserve rooms in hotels or private homes. In Budapest, the main IBUSZ office is located on the Pest side of the Danube near the Hotel Continental. IBUSZ also cashes traveler's checks, provides maps, and sells tickets to various cultural events.

"Hungary receives thousands of tourists a year and is a relatively easy country to gain entry into. If you aren't staying with friends, the best way to stay is by renting

---

*All temperatures are Fahrenheit.

a room through one of the tourist agencies. Renting a room in a family's apartment is usually very cheap and will give you an idea of how a typical Hungarian family lives. Book early in the day since in the summer months Budapest fills up with tourists."
—Lisa Hidem, Minneapolis, Minnesota

Especially for Students and Young People

EXPRESS is Hungary's youth and student travel bureau and issuer of the International Student Identity Card. You'll find the main office, EXPRESS—Budapest, located at Semmelweis utca 4, Budapest 5, and it also has offices in seven other Hungarian cities. For students and young travelers, EXPRESS operates 32 hostels and hotels around the country as well as holiday activity centers on Lake Balaton. Vouchers for accommodations at EXPRESS hostels and hotels are available through Council Travel offices.

Student Cardholders can get discount standby tickets on domestic flights, a 25-percent discount on rail travel to most other countries in Eastern Europe, and reduced prices at EXPRESS hotels, hostels, and holiday centers, as well as free admission to most museums.

For Further Information

The U.S. office of IBUSZ, the Hungarian government's official travel agency (1 Parker Plaza, Suite 1104, Fort Lee, NJ 07024), can provide general tourist information on Hungary. Their catalogue includes information on tours, hotels, and car rentals. They also have maps and updated visa information. *The Real Guide: Hungary* ($12.95) is an invaluable source of information on independent travel on a budget in Hungary. Also good is *Eastern Europe on a Shoestring*, especially if you plan to travel to surrounding countries. If you can't find it in bookstores, it's available for $21.95 (plus $1.50 book-rate postage; $3 for first-class) from Lonely Planet Publications, Embarcadero West, 112 Linden Street, Oakland, CA 94607.

WORK

It is possible to work for a company in Hungary that is partially or totally foreign-owned. To get a regular paid job you will need to obtain a work permit, which is granted to foreigners who possess a staying permit from the Ministry of Interior. Contact the Embassy of the Republic of Hungary (3910 Shoemaker Street NW, Washington, DC 20008) for specific regulations on the subject. As an alternative to regular employment, you might be interested in a trainee program or participation in a workcamp.

Internships/Traineeships

Programs offered by members of the Council on International Educational Exchange are described below.

AIESEC-US. Reciprocal internship program for students in economics, business, finance, marketing, accounting, and computer sciences. See page 18 for more information.

Association for International Practical Training. "IAESTE Trainee Program." On-the-job training for undergraduate and graduate students in technical fields such as engineering, computer science, agriculture, architecture, and mathematics. See page 18 for more information.

Voluntary Service

CIEE places young people in voluntary service workcamps in Hungary organized by Demisz (Konyves K, Krt 76, 1087 Budapest). At these workcamps, groups of volunteers from different countries work on a variety of restoration and environmental projects. Volunteers must be 18 years of age or older; room and board are provided. The applications of U.S. residents are processed by CIEE. For more information contact CIEE's Voluntary Service Department.

STUDY

The following educational programs are offered by CIEE-member institutions. Consult Appendix I for the addresses where you can write for further information. In addition to the programs below, the University of California offers a program open only to students already enrolled at its various schools.

Semester and Academic Year

Eastern European Studies

American University. "Budapest Semester." Fall. Politics, economics, history, Hungarian, German, and Russian. Internships available. No language prerequisite. Second semester sophomores with 2.75 GPA. Apply six months before start of program.

Council on International Educational Exchange.
"Cooperative East & Central European Studies Program." Budapest. Fall or spring semester. Courses taught in English at the Budapest University of Economics. Undergraduates with 2.75 GPA and six semester-hours in economics, history, or social sciences. Apply by April 10 for fall and November 1 for spring. Contact University Programs Department.

Experiment in International Living/School for International Training. "College Semester Abroad." Budapest. Fall or spring semester. Intensive Hungarian language, interdisciplinary Eastern European studies and field-study methods seminars, independent-study project, excursions to Poland and Vienna, Austria, and homestays. Sophomores, juniors, and seniors with 2.5 GPA. Apply by May 15 for fall and October 15 for spring.

General Studies

Beloit College. "Hungary Exchange Program." Eotvos Kollegium in Budapest. Spring semester. Hungarian language, literature, history. No language prerequisite. Sophomores to graduate students with 2.5 GPA. Apply by December 1.

International Student Exchange Program. Direct reciprocal exchange between U.S. universities and Janus Pannonius University and the Technical University of Budapest. Summer, semester or academic year. Full curriculum options. Open only to students at ISEP-member institutions.

University of Massachusetts—Amherst. "Exchange with Janus Pannonius University." Pecs. Fall and spring semesters. Sophomores, juniors, and seniors with 3.0 GPA. Apply by March 15 for fall; October 15 for spring.

University of Oregon. "OSSHE—Hungary Exchange Program." Szeged. Academic year. Sophomores, juniors, and seniors with 2.75 GPA. Preference given to Oregon State System of Higher Education (OSSHE) students. Apply by March 1.

University of Wisconsin—Madison. Budapest. Fall semester or academic year. Sophomores to graduate students with 3.0 GPA. No language prerequisite. Apply by February 1.

Summer

Eastern European Studies

State University of New York at Albany. Cultural history and democratization. Courses taught in English. Freshmen to seniors with 2.5 GPA and one course in European history or political science. Apply by April 15.

General Studies

University of Massachusetts—Amherst. "Exchange with Janus Pannonius University." Pecs. Sophomores, juniors, and seniors with 3.0 GPA. Apply by March 15.

University of Pennsylvania. "Penn-in-Budapest." Central European–studies courses taught in English: economics, history, sociology, and political science. Apply by April 1.

ICELAND

Viewed from any angle, Iceland is a natural and cultural phenomenon and a terrific place to visit. The average lifespan of Icelandic women is the longest in the world, while that of men is the second longest. Its popular woman president Vidis Finnbogadottir was swept into office for a third term in the summer of 1988. In social legislation Iceland has followed the example of the other Nordic countries; there is universal health insurance and an old-age pension plan. The streets are safe and there is almost no violent crime. Its water is among the purest in the world, and stunning, unspoiled nature dominates everywhere. Geothermal sources yield hot water year-round for 85 percent of all local homes. Beauty, strength, longevity, political enlightenment, and no environmental pollution—what more could one ask!

Iceland has existed precariously for centuries, perched atop the mid-Atlantic geological fault line. It is often called "the land of fire and ice" because volcanic eruptions have occurred with great regularity over the centuries, and a full 11.5 percent of the island is covered with glaciers—including one called Vatnajokull that, exclusive of Antarctica and Greenland, is the largest ice cap in the world. But due to the tempering influence of the Gulf Stream, Iceland enjoys a surprisingly moderate climate, given the fact that its northern tip crosses the Artic Circle. Winters are mild, though stormy and humid, with the January temperature in Reykjavik averaging roughly the same as in Copenhagen (a lot milder than Chicago); summers are cool and can be rainy. But in June, July, and August, days, even weeks, of crisp and glorious sunshine are not uncommon. Whatever the weather, the stark and beautiful landscape of Iceland is pure, stunning, dramatic, and utterly unforgettable for most visitors.

Iceland was for centuries the furthest outpost of Scandinavian Viking culture and for centuries the most Western extension of Christianity. The quarter of a million Icelanders living today on this large mid-Atlantic island are mainly the descendants of settlers who arrived from Norway in 879 to 950 with their families, slaves, sheep, and horses. Iceland has succeeded in preserving many of the rural values of its earliest Norwegian inhabitants, as well as their language—modern Icelandic is essentially old Norse. The Icelandic

Commonwealth came under the Norwegian Crown in 1262, then was ruled by Denmark in 1814. Iceland became independent in 1918, yet recognized the king of Denmark as a titular head of state until 1944—when Iceland declared itself a republic. Its Althing, or parliament, was established in 930 and is one of the oldest national legislative assemblies in the world. Bravely and against many environmental and cultural odds, Iceland has evolved into an independent culture which is thoroughly modern, humane, vigorous, and technologically advanced.

Over the past half-century, Icelanders have increasingly gravitated to the larger cities and towns along the coast. The Greater Reykjavik area, with well over 120,000 inhabitants, now contains nearly half the nation's population. Fewer than 20 percent of Icelanders live in rural areas. Iceland is self-supporting in fish, meat, and dairy products—as well as in a few other areas. However, the economy is still so one-sided that foreign trade per capita is greater than in any other country. Fish products account for some 75 percent of all exports, while industry contributes 20 to 25 percent of the total.

Educational and cultural standards have been high from the earliest times. All young people learn both Danish and English; those going to university studies are likely to master two or three additional languages. More books per capita are published in Iceland than in any other country.

Because it has a special history, beauty, and tranquility, and because its tourist and transportation industry is modern and efficient, Iceland is rapidly becoming more popular among Europeans and Americans who spend their lives in big cities, and who seek a place with real wilderness and space for adventurous hiking, fishing, bird-watching, horse-trekking, camping, or just roaming and getting away from it all. You can wander up mountains, over sands and rivers, even catch trout, and in the evening be able to relax in a hot spring. Once you've had this invigorating experience, it's likely you'll want to return again and again.

—*William W. Hoffa, Amherst, Massachusetts*

Official name: Republic of Iceland. **Size:** 39,769 square miles (about the size of Virginia). **Population:** 251,000. **Population density:** 6 inhabitants per square mile. **Capital and largest city:** Reykjavik (pop. 93,000). **Language:** Icelandic. **Religion:** Lutheran. **Per capita income:** US$21,600. **Currency:** Kronur. **Literacy rate:** 99%. **Average daily high/low*:** Reykjavik: January, 36°/28°; July, 58°/48°. **Average number days with precipitation:** Reykjavik: January, 20; July, 16.

TRAVEL

Americans will need a passport to visit Iceland. A visa is not required for stays of up to three months. For specific requirements, check with the Embassy of Iceland, 2022 Connecticut Avenue NW, Washington, DC 20008.

Getting Around

Iceland has no railroads, but its bus network reaches even the most isolated communities. While bus transportation is the best way to see Iceland, it can be quite slow. In the winter, many roads are impassable. For twice the cost of a bus ticket, you can fly point to point within Iceland. The Iceland Airpass enables four stops within Iceland for US$165. It must be purchased in the U.S. before departure.

The Omnibus Passport is a special discount bus ticket, valid for unlimited travel on all scheduled bus routes in Iceland within specified time limits ranging from one week

---

*All temperatures are Fahrenheit.

($220) to four weeks ($410). Stopovers can be made anywhere and as often as you like. The Full Circle Passport ($190) is valid for travel on Iceland's main road (the ring road); there is no time limit, but you have to maintain a continuous direction around the island. Both Passports are valid from May 15 to the end of September. They can be purchased from airlines and travel agencies in the U.S. or in Iceland.

Hitchhiking can be fairly safe and easy but traffic is sometimes sparse. Be prepared for rain and cold weather.

Especially for Students and Young People

Icelandic Student Travel (University Student Center, v/Hringbraut, IS-101 Reykjavik) is the nation's student travel bureau. Among the discounts for holders of the International Student Identity Card is a 20-percent discount on plane tickets within Iceland. The International Youth Card offers a 10-percent discount on several guest houses in Reykjavik and a 15- to 20-percent discount on tours around Iceland. Space permitting, standby flights in Iceland allow those under 26 to fly at a 40-percent discount.

For Further Information

Iceland has lately become the subject of an increasing number of travel guidebooks. *Iceland, Greenland and the Faroe Islands: a travel survival kit* is available for $14.95 (plus $1.50 book-rate postage, $3 for first-class) from Lonely Planet Publications, Embarcadero West, 112 Linden Street, Oakland, CA 94607. *Iceland: The Visitor's Guide* is available from Traveller's Bookstore (75 Rockefeller Plaza, New York, NY 10019). One of the best general guidebooks to Iceland and the entire Scandinavian region is *The Real Guide: Scandinavia*, available for $14.95 in most bookstores. General tourist information is available from the Icelandic Tourist Board, 655 Third Avenue, Suite 1810, New York, NY 10017.

WORK

In order to work in Iceland it is necessary to obtain a work permit. The American Scandinavian Foundation (Exchange Division, 725 Park Avenue, New York, NY 10021) can assist Americans under the age of 30 with obtaining the requisite permit.

Internships/Traineeships

Two programs offered by members of the Council on International Educational Exchange are listed below:

AIESEC-US. Reciprocal internship program for students in economics, business, finance, marketing, accounting, and computer science. See page 18 for more information.

Association for International Practical Training. "IAESTE Trainee Program." On-the-job training for undergraduate and graduate students in technical fields such as engineering, computer science, agriculture, architecture, and mathematics. See page 18 for more information.

In addition, the American Scandinavian Foundation sponsors a program that provides summer training assignments for full-time students majoring in engineering, computer science, horticulture, agriculture, forestry, and chemistry, among others. The deadline for application is December 15. Note, however, that no traineeships are available in teaching, social work, or medically related fields. Contact the American Scandinavian Foundation Exchange Division, 725 Park Avenue, New York, NY 10021.

Voluntary Service

Voluntary service work can be arranged through the Year Abroad Program sponsored by the International Christian Youth Exchange. The program offers persons ages 18 to 24 voluntary-service opportunities in the fields of health care, education, the environment, construction, et cetera. See page 23 for more information.

STUDY

For general information on Iceland's educational system, contact the Ministry of Culture and Education, Solvholsgata 4, 150 Reykjavik. The Exchange Division of the American Scandinavian Foundation (725 Park Avenue, New York, NY 10021) publishes *Study in Scandinavia*, which includes a listing of English-language programs offered in Iceland during the academic year and summer.

IRELAND

Visitors to Ireland are often perplexed by the realities of a nation that has been consistently mythologized by its emigrant daughters and sons. As the steel-and-glass blandness of Shannon Airport's main terminal looms out of the dawn, images of leprechauns are quickly dispelled. This is no country of blarney-spouting peasants leaning over half-doors—modern Ireland has too much on its mind for all that, but you'll find plenty to interest you just the same.

Topographically, Ireland consists of a central plain surrounded by coastal highlands, with the exception of the east-coast stretch where the plain penetrates to the sea. The country is blessed with a profound natural beauty, most notably in its rugged western regions. But the isolation you might feel in its sparsely populated rural areas contrasts sharply with the urban bustle of its cities and towns. All of the cities are compact—even Dublin, the capital, has a central area of scarcely one square mile—and can be explored leisurely on foot.

The economy is a typical European model. Health and social services are heavily regulated by the state. Most businesses are privately owned, with the government exercising a shrinking monopoly in others. Agriculture, though on the decline, is still a vital element, and a lack of natural resources has led to a heavy dependence on foreign investment in industry. Indeed, attempts to modernize the economy over the years have tended to concentrate on marketing Ireland as an ideal manufacturing center for foreign corporations, and much has been made of its highly skilled but severely underemployed work force. With the jobless rate consistently in the 15 to 20 percent range in the past decade, there has been a tidal wave of emigration, as the nation's youth have sought out better opportunities in Britain, Australia, and the United States.

Social and economic affairs, of course, provide excellent fuel for debate. There is a keen interest in politics among the Irish, and lively conversations on the subject rage nightly in that hallowed focal point of Irish social life: the pub. Although the Irish are not nearly as drink-sodden as the stereotype suggests, there is no shortage of atmospheric bars in the land. Indeed, you will find them difficult to avoid.

Long a respected literary center, Ireland boasts an impressive theatrical heritage and a number of highly regarded theater companies. Much in evidence as well is a lively music scene, where traditional practitioners coexist with a rock and pop scene rejuvenated in recent years by the international success stories of U2, Sinéad O'Connor, and others.

Physically isolated from Europe's mainland, Ireland has a distinctly individual flavor. Although the evolution of Europe into a single economic entity is entering its final stages, the Irish do not readily regard themselves as "Europeans." After centuries of occupation and exploitation by colonial powers, with the resultant suppression of its richly textured culture, Ireland is still struggling to find its voice. Not surprisingly for a state that has been politically independent for fewer than 50 years, there are still many problems to be solved. The mood, however, is quietly optimistic.

—*Denis Murphy, New York, New York*

Official name: Republic of Ireland. **Area:** 27,137 square miles (about the size of West Virginia). **Population:** 3,557,000. **Population density:** 137 inhabitants per square mile. **Capital and largest city:** Dublin (pop. 502,000). **Language:** English, Irish Gaelic. **Religion:** Roman Catholic. **Per capita income:** US$6,200. **Currency:** Irish pound (punt). **Literacy rate:** 99%. **Average daily high/low*:** Dublin, January, 47°/35°, July, 67°/51°. **Average number of days with precipitation:** Dublin: January, 13; July, 13.

TRAVEL

U.S. citizens need a passport, but a visa is not required for tourists staying up to 90 days. Tourists may be asked to show an onward/return ticket or sufficient funds for their stay. For residence authorization, consult the Embassy of Ireland, 2234 Massachusetts Avenue NW, Washington, DC 20008.

Getting Around

Eurail and InterRail passholders receive free boat passage between France (either Le Havre or Cherbourg) and Rosslare in southeastern Ireland. Ferries also link Ireland with several ports in Wales and England, with easy connections to cities around Britain. Discounts on ferries between Ireland and ports in France and Britain are available to holders of the International Student Identity Card on Irish ferries. Within Ireland, Cardholders receive up to 10-percent discount on Aer Arann flights between Galway and the Aran Islands.

Trains connect the cities of Ireland to Dublin but the other cities are not always well connected with one another. Buses fill in the gaps in rail service. Eurailpasses are valid on trains and some buses in Ireland, and students can save 50 percent on rail and bus travel in Ireland if they have an ISIC with the Travelsave stamp (see "Especially for Students and Young People" below).

A student/Youth Rambler ticket, good for unlimited combined rail and bus travel within Ireland, is available for anyone between 14 and 26. Rambler tickets for 8 days of travel within a 15-day period cost $130; tickets for 15 days of travel in a 30-day period cost $180; and tickets good for 30 consecutive days of travel are $265. Rambler tickets may be purchased in the U.S. or in Ireland. Students who present a Travelsave stamp upon purchase in Ireland receive a 10-percent discount (see "Especially for Students and Young People" below). Contact CIE Tours International, 108 Ridgedale Avenue, Morristown, NJ 07960 (800-243-7687).

If standing in the rain doesn't deter you, hitching in Ireland, especially in rural areas, often is the best way to get around. People will generally stop, and will always be interested in tales of your travels.

One of the most popular ways to see Ireland is by bicycle. Renting a bike in Ireland is very easy, and you usually have a choice of racing, touring, or mountain bikes. The rental rate for a mountain bike is about US$40 per week.

Campgrounds are plentiful and inexpensive. A two-person tent site goes for around US$10 per night. Youth hostels are a little more expensive, but buying your hostel card

---

*All temperatures are Fahrenheit.

in Ireland is less expensive than in the U.S. Bed-and-breakfasts are another viable option, somewhat more comfortable than the former. Open vouchers, good for accomodation in approved bed-and-breakfasts, can be bought for around US$20 per night (though the prebooking fee is US$8).

"Irish people tend to be easygoing, lighthearted, and quick-witted, with a wonderful sense of humor about themselves as well as about life in general. About 94 percent of the population is Roman Catholic. Families tend to be large and closely knit. Tradition is much valued, and the Irish place less emphasis on material possessions and status than do Americans. The Irish love sports, both as participants and spectators: rugby, soccer, hurling, Gaelic football, and cycling are some of the more popular pastimes. And, of course, the Irish love to talk and to share their great pride in their beautiful country."

—Katherine Aziz, Winter Park, Florida

Especially for Students and Young People

Any information that you might need about Ireland is available at the travel offices of Usit (formerly called the Union of Students in Ireland—Travel), Ireland's student/youth travel organization. The main office is at 19 Aston Quay, Dublin 2, but Usit also has offices in Limerick, Belfast, Waterford, Cork, Galway, Jordanstown, and Coleraine. Usit offices will affix the Travelsave stamp to your ISIC card for Irish £7 (about $10); this stamp entitles you to 50 percent off train and bus tickets for travel within Ireland.

Museums in Ireland are free to everyone. Holders of the International Student Identity Card can take advantage of the Student Theatre Standby Scheme, which makes available reduced-rate theater tickets 15 minutes before the performance. Those who purchase the card in Ireland will be eligible for the Countdown plan, which offers 10-percent discounts in some 1,500 shops, restaurants, and accommodations. Check with Usit for more information.

For Further Information

For suggestions on budget accommodations in Ireland as well as what to see and how to get around, consult a copy of *Let's Go: Britain and Ireland*. It's available for $14.95 in most bookstores and at Council Travel offices. Another good book for the budget traveler is Frommer's *Ireland on $35 a Day*, available in bookstores for $13.95.

General tourist information, including a free booklet entitled *Ireland: Ancient Birthplace of Good Times*, is available from the Irish Tourist Board, 757 Third Avenue, New York, NY 10017. In addition, persons interested in visiting Northern Ireland can get information from the Northern Ireland Tourist Board, 276 Fifth Avenue, Suite 500, New York, NY 10001.

WORK

Getting a Job

To work in Ireland, you must be in the country when applying for a job. Application for a work permit should be made by the prospective employer on your behalf. As with most Western European countries, preference is given to Irish citizens, then to members of the EC. For further information, contact the Embassy of Ireland, 2234 Massachusetts Avenue NW, Washington, DC 20008.

CIEE will help you secure a work permit good for up to four months anytime of the year in Ireland. Full-time college or university students who are at least 18 years of age and permanent residents or citizens of the U.S. are eligible. Once you're in Ireland, the

Usit office in Dublin will advise you on the current job situation. There is a $125 fee which includes one night's accommodation and breakfast. Contact CIEE's Work Exchanges Department for more information.

Internships/Traineeships

Programs sponsored by members of the Council on International Educational Exchange are listed below:

AIESEC-US. Reciprocal internship program for students in economics, business, finance, marketing, accounting, and computer sciences. See page 18 for more information.

Association for International Practical Training.
"IAESTE Trainee Program." On-the-job training for undergraduate and graduate students in technical fields such as engineering, computer science, agriculture, architecture, and mathematics. See page 18 for more information.
"Hotel & Culinary Exchanges Program." On-the-job training for young people beginning a career in the hotel and food-service industries. Participants must have graduated from a university or vocational school and possess at least six months of training or experience in the chosen field. Training usually runs 6 to 18 months. Consult Appendix I for the address of the sponsoring institution.

STUDY

The Consulate General of Ireland (515 Madison Avenue, New York, NY 10022) distributes an information sheet on Irish universities and other institutions of higher education in Ireland. Usit recommends that students who are planning to study in Ireland contact the Central Applications Office, Tower House, Eglinton Street, Galway, Ireland.

The Irish Tourist Board (address above) publishes a pamphlet entitled "Study Abroad—Ireland," which lists a number of academic year and semester programs, as well as study tours, summer schools, and high-school programs.

On behalf of Usit, CIEE administers the "Encounter Ireland" program, six weeks of Irish studies for college credit. This summer course (June 26 to August 8) is run in association with Trinity College, Dublin, and covers aspects of Irish literature, history, politics, social and cultural studies, and the visual arts. It carries a maximum of six credits. Costs of the program include tuition, field trips, theater tickets, cultural activities, homestay accommodation, and transportation from New York. Students should be enrolled full-time at an accredited U.S. college or university. The application deadline is May 31. Usit also offers a number of other summer study programs.

Following are the study programs offered by CIEE-member institutions. Consult Appendix I for the addresses of the sponsoring institutions. In addition to the programs listed below, the University of California offers programs open only to its own students.

Semester and Academic Year

Business Management

Beaver College. "Business and Management Studies at the University of Limerick." Academic year, fall or spring program. Juniors and seniors with 3.0 GPA. Apply by April 20 for year and fall; October 15 for spring.

Drama

Beaver College. "Drama at Trinity College, Dublin." Academic year. Juniors and seniors with 3.0 GPA. Apply by January 1.

Education

Beaver College. "Educational Studies with Practice Teaching at Mary Immaculate College, Limerick." Academic year. Juniors and seniors with 3.0 GPA. Apply by January 20.

Engineering

Beaver College. "Engineering at the University of Limerick." Semester or academic year. Juniors and seniors with 3.0 GPA. Apply by April 20 for year and fall; October 15 for spring.

English Literature

Michigan State University. "English Literature in Dublin." Spring quarter. Irish history, literature, and culture, with field trips. Sophomores to graduate students. Apply by February 3.

General Studies

Beaver College.
"Mary Immaculate College, Limerick." Academic year, fall or spring programs. Juniors and seniors with 3.0 GPA. Apply by April 20 for year and fall; October 15 for spring.
"University College, Cork." Academic year. Juniors and seniors with 3.0 GPA. Apply by April 20.
"Trinity College, Dublin." Academic year. Juniors and seniors with 3.0 GPA. Apply by January 1.
"University College, Dublin." Academic year, fall or spring semester. Juniors and seniors with 3.0 GPA. Apply by April 20 for year and fall; October 15 for spring.
"University College, Galway." Academic year or semester. Juniors and seniors with 3.0 GPA. Apply by April 20 for year and fall; October 15 for spring.
"St. Patrick's College, Maynooth." Academic year. Juniors and seniors with 3.1 GPA. Apply by April 20.

Northeastern University. "Ireland: North and South." A bicultural experience including social studies at Dublin's Institute of Public Administration and the Queen's University, Belfast, with internships in the Irish Parliament. Fall and winter quarter. Juniors and seniors with 3.0 GPA. Apply by April 15.

Rollins College. "Rollins Fall Term in Dublin." Fall semester. Sophomores, juniors, and seniors with 2.8 GPA. Apply by April 15.

Rutgers University. University College, Dublin. Academic year. Juniors, with 3.0 GPA. Apply by February 1.

State University of New York at Stony Brook. "Stony Brook in Ireland." Limerick. Spring or fall semester. Various fields, especially business, engineering, and sciences. Juniors. Apply by April 1.

Irish Studies

State University of New York at Cortland. Cork. Fall or spring semester. Juniors and seniors with 3.5 GPA in major. Apply by March 1 for fall and November 1 for spring.

University of Iowa. "Ireland in Comparative Perspective." Belfast. Northern Ireland. Fall semester. Study of intercommunal relations, politics, ethnic and cultural conflict. Sophomores to seniors with 3.0 GPA. Apply by March 15.

Peace Studies

Experiment in International Living/School for International Training. "College Semester Abroad." Dublin and Northern Ireland. Fall or spring semester. Peace-studies seminar, field-study methods seminar, independent-study project, educational travel, and homestay. Sophomores, juniors, and seniors with 2.5 GPA. Apply by May 15 for fall and October 15 for spring.

Summer

State University of New York at Cortland. British or European Studies at the University College, Cork. Sophomores to seniors with 2.5 GPA. Apply by April 15.

EXPLORING IRISH CULTURE

Readings

The great shadow of James Joyce falls across Irish literature, sometimes obscuring other important figures. Joyce's *Ulysses* (1922) is, however, the central text of modern literature and its influence stretches far beyond the borders of Ireland. It is both a comic masterpiece and a profound exploration of the human psyche in its strengths and weaknesses. The novel is, in the end, a celebration of humanity in all its flawed complexity. Readers sometimes find the novel a difficult prospect because of the length and complexity of Joyce's technique. Other works, particularly *Dubliners* (1914) and *Portrait of the Artist as a Young Man* (1916), may offer a less daunting introduction to the Irish master.

Characteristic of much Irish literature is a great capacity for verbal wit and linguistic inventiveness. Oscar Wilde's *The Importance of Being Earnest* (1895) is rich in inversion and comic paradox. Another Irish playwright with a highly developed ear for language and the ability to exploit its comic potential is J. M. Synge. *Playboy of the Western World* (1907) is a rich comedy that precisely captures the cadence of Irish speech. Continuing in this tradition today are Hugh Leonard and Brian Friel. Leonard's *Da* describes how a son, returning to Ireland for the funeral of his father, comes to terms with their relationship. Friel's *Philadelphia, Here I Come* evokes the rural Ireland of the 1950s on the eve of an only son's emigration to the States.

Witty and poetic literature still abounds in contemporary Ireland. In *The Pornographer* (1979), John McGahern comically writes about a Dubliner whose formula porn stories begin to happen in real life. Christy Nolan writes about his life with cerebral palsy in *Under the Eye of the Clock* (1987). In his first work, *Damburst of Dreams*, he releases the poetic outpourings that had built up before he had a means to communicate.

The short story is a pervasive form in Irish literature. Frank O'Connor's stories provide funny, insightful glimpses into the lives of children in rural Ireland. *My Oedipus Complex and Other Stories* includes one of his best-loved stories, "My First Confession." Other notable collections of short stories by contemporary writers include William Trevor's *The*

Ballroom of Romance and Other Stories, Edna O'Brien's *Mother Ireland*, Mary Lavin's *The Shrine and Other Stories*, and Benedict Kiely's *The State of Ireland*.

Ireland also has a long tradition of poetry ranging from Jonathan Swift through William Butler Yeats to Seamus Heaney, whose contemporary poetry reflects some of the traumas associated with the political and religious conflict in Northern Ireland. The troubled relationship with Britain has been a recurrent theme in Irish literature, in which myth, poetry, and politics have tended to be inseparable

Films

Film in Ireland definitely has taken the back seat to Irish literature. Not surprisingly, many films set in Ireland are adaptations of books or short stories. *The Dead* (1987), John Huston's filmic adaptation of Joyce's last *Dubliners* story, is one of the most beautiful films about Ireland ever produced. It portrays Joyce's country—the Ireland of the early part of the 20th century, with all its politics and socializing. More current representations can be found in the films of Jim Sheridan: his *My Left Foot* (1989) is the critically acclaimed film about the writer Christy Brown. *The Field*, Sheridan's most recent film, depicts one man's struggle to retain the land on which he has spent his life's labor.

Other films include *The Lonely Passion of Judith Hearne* (1987), Jack Clayton's adaptation of Brian Moore's 1955 novel about the solitary life of an Irish spinster, and *Odd Man Out* (1946), a film directed by Carol Reed about a wounded Irish revolutionary on the run. Another good film that will will give you some insights into Irish family life is Matt Clark's 1988 adaptation of an autobiographical stage comedy, *Da*.

ITALY

Italy's character is attributable more to the tastes and traditions of its diverse provinces than to a strong sense of national identity. Natural barriers—both mountains and seas—and the lack of national unity from the fall of the Roman Empire until the establishment of Italy as a nation-state in 1861, have encouraged deep-rooted regional identities. This regionalism is reflected in distinctive architectural, gastronomic, and linguistic styles; a host of political parties; and 16 highly competitive soccer teams—all of which contribute to Italy's flavor and charm.

At the heart of the Italian culture is a tremendous respect for history and tradition coupled with the innovation and dynamism of an advanced and modern society. However, the antique and the avant-garde, the rustic and the cosmopolitan coexist with little sense of continuity. In the Northern provinces, fast-food restaurants, designer department stores, and Fortune 500 companies flourish amidst Etruscan ruins, Renaissance palaces, and Gothic cathedrals. One of the most productive regions in the European Community, northern Italy is almost entirely responsible for a rapidly growing GNP that has recently surpassed that of Great Britain. By contrast, the South—*il Mezzogiorno*—a testament to Italy's rural tradition of artisan craftsmanship and strict Catholic values, has been unable to sustain itself economically. Likened to a Third World country, *il Mezzogiorno* has an unemployment rate of 20 percent and a level of production one-third that of the North.

The Italian central government has been unable to reconcile these cultural and economic schisms. The fact that Italy has seen 47 different governments since the Second World War may be attributed to the lack of political concensus in a multiparty arena and seen as a symptom—or cause—of a widespread sense of disillusionment and apathy of the populace. Instead, Italy's principal political powers, the Christian Democrats, the Socialists, and the Democratic Party of the Left (formerly the Communist Party), often exert their power through other institutions such as Italy's TV stations, newspapers, and large corporations.

However, if one were to ascribe a national trait to the Italian people, it would be the innate ability to live life to its fullest. Great emphasis is given to ritual, tradition, and simple pleasures. Both young and old take their *passeggiata*, or daily evening stroll, old men congregate in the town piazzas for a *vin santo* and a discussion of the latest soccer scores, and paramount importance is placed on the preparation, presentation, and consumption of food—regarded as not merely sustenance for the body but also medicine for the soul.

The traveler to Italy may find its people stubborn and opinionated, but generally warm and receptive to foreigners, particularly Americans, as the Italian youth continues to be obsessed with American pop culture. Italians are always eager to interact and are quick to help foreigners with their language in exchange for a few lessons in English slang. Italy has always welcomed visitors, and visitors have gladly journeyed there, remembering always to toss a coin in the Roman Trevi Fountain to ensure their speedy return.

—*Christina Bennett, New York, New York*

Official name: Italian Republic. **Size:** 116,303 square miles (slightly larger than Arizona). **Population:** 57,657,000. **Population density:** 493 inhabitants per square mile. **Capital and largest city:** Rome (pop. 2,800,000). **Language:** Italian. **Religion:** Roman Catholic. **Per capita income:** US$14,383. **Currency:** Lira. **Literacy rate:** 97%. **Average daily high/low*:** Florence: January, 49°/35°; July, 89°/63°. Rome: January, 54°/39°; July, 88°/64°. **Average number of days with precipitation:** Florence: January, 9; July, 4. Rome: January, 8; July, 2.

TRAVEL

U.S. citizens will need a passport, but a visa is not required for tourist stays of up to three months. For stays over three months, a visa should be obtained before departure. Check with the Italian Embassy, 1601 Fuller Street NW, Washington, DC 20009, for specific requirements.

Getting Around

Italy has a modern railroad network, and travel on Italian trains is still relatively inexpensive. Eurail passes are valid for use on the Italian rail network. Buses are also a common means of intercity transport and, for short trips in mountainous regions, may be faster than the train, which often takes a more circuitous route. Another option is to rent a car. Although most of the pre-Fiat, intercity streets are too narrow for cars, Italian roads are generally good and the high-speed expressway, or *autostrada*, network is comprehensive and runs the length of the country.

CIT Tours (594 Broadway, New York, NY, 10012, or 6033 W. Century Blvd., Suite 980, Los Angeles, CA, 90045) offers the B.T.L.C. or "go-anywhere" ticket good for unlimited train travel within Italy. The second-class pass costs $136 for 8 days, $172 for 15 days, $198 for 21 days, and $240 for 30 days. A first-class B.T.L.C. ticket costs $206 for 8 days, $258 for 15 days, $298 for 21 days, and $360 for 30 days. Although they are available only to nonresidents of Italy, you may buy the B.T.L.C. tickets in Italy.

Another option is the I.F.R., or Italy Flexi Railcard. This pass entitles you to a set number of days of travel on the Italian State Railway within a specified period of time. The cost for second-class passes is $104 for 4 days of travel within 9 days of validity, $148 for 8 days of travel within 21 days, and $190 for 12 days of travel within 30 days. You can also get a K.L.M., or Italian Kilometric Ticket for $238 (first class) or $140

---

*All temperatures are Fahrenheit.

(second class), which is valid for 20 trips on the entire rail network—limited to 3,000 kilometers (1,875 miles) within two months—and may be used by more than one person even if not related. Contact CIT Tours or a travel agent to order.

Throughout Italy, except on some express trains, bicycles may be taken as checked baggage. You pay an extra charge based on weight and distance traveled.

"Traveling within Italy was an integral part of my understanding of a fairly recently unified nation, whose citizens still feel a foremost allegiance to their state or region—there is a tremendous diversity of cultures, dialects, and languages—from the Alto Adige to Sicily, for example."
—Elizabeth Alixandre Schijman, New York, New York

Especially for Students

Centro Turistico Studentesco e Giovanile (CTS) is Italy's main student travel bureau, with offices around Rome and in 70 other Italian cities. You can contact them at Centro Turistico Studentesco, Via Nazionale, 66, 00184 Rome.

Students will find that the International Student Identity Card entitles them to discounts on night flights within Italy; on ferries from various Italian ports to Egypt, Greece, Sardinia, Spain, and Yugoslavia; and on bus, train, and plane travel from Italy to various international destinations. In addition, cardholders can get discounts on CTS tours in Rome and reduced admission fees for the Vatican Museum and a number of other museums in Rome, as well as cinemas, theaters, and concerts. The International Youth Card is good for discounts on accommodations, vacation centers, camping sites, museums, restaurants, and recreational facilities, as well as some shopping discounts.

Meet the People

Several tourist offices in Italy can introduce you to a local Italian host for an afternoon or evening get-together. The Italian Government Travel Office distributes a list of tourist offices in Italy, but not all offices can provide this kind of service. Write ahead and find out whether the town you're going to offers this kind of hospitality service, and if they do, make your arrangements in advance of your arrival in Italy.

For Further Information

Italy—General Information for Travelers, which covers virtually everything you need to know about travel in that country, is available free from the Italian Government Travel Office (ENIT), 630 Fifth Avenue, New York, NY 10111. Also available are maps and hotel lists.

Let's Go: Italy contains a wealth of information for the student traveler on where to stay, what to see, and how to get around. It's available for $14.95 in most bookstores and at Council Travel offices. For more detailed treatment of points of interest, try *The Real Guide: Italy* ($13.95) and *The Real Guide: Venice* ($11.95). The Cadogan city guides to Venice and Rome ($14.95 each) are also quite informative.

"Read about the country, especially the art and architecture. Try to learn at least a few words in Italian. Italians are very, very, friendly, and if you show interest in them and their country they will embrace you even more."
—Nina Martinez, Takoma Park, Maryland

WORK

In Italy, laws regulating work by foreigners are very strict. The Italian Ministry for Home Affairs must first grant the prospective employee a residence permit for work purposes.

When the permit has been issued, the employer must provide a certified declaration that there are no nationals in the area who are able to perform the work in question.

American teachers interested in teaching in Italy should write for the booklet, "Schools for English-Speaking Students in Italy." It is available from the Italian Cultural Institute (686 Park Avenue, New York, NY 10021).

Internships/Traineeships

Two programs offered by members of the Council on International Educational Exchange are listed below:

AIESEC-US. Reciprocal internship program for students in economics, business, finance, marketing, accounting, and computer sciences. See page 18 for more information.

Association for International Practical Training. "IAESTE Trainee Program" On-the-job training for undergraduate and graduate students in technical fields such as engineering, computer science, agriculture, architecture, and mathematics. See page 18 for more information.

Voluntary Service

For persons interested in voluntary service work, the Year Abroad Program sponsored by the International Christian Youth Exchange offers persons ages 18 to 24 voluntary service opportunities in the fields of health care, education, the environment, construction, et cetera. See page 23 for more information.

STUDY

There are numerous schools and academies throughout Italy—particularly in Florence—that specialize in instruction of foreigners in art, language, history, and so on. *Schools for Foreigners in Italy*, a directory of Italian schools offering programs for foreign students, is available from the Italian Cultural Institute (686 Park Avenue, New York, NY 10021). *The Italian Educational System: A Brief Outline* is available from the same source.

Following are the educational programs offered by CIEE-member institutions. Consult Appendix I for the address of the colleges and universities listed in this section. In addition to those listed below, California State University, New York University, Northern Illinois University, Pennsylvania State University, Texas A&M University, the University of California, the University of Kansas, and the University of Notre Dame offer programs open only to their own students.

Semester and Academic Year

Architecture

Syracuse University. "Masters of Architecture: Second Professional Degree, Florence." Academic year. Graduate program. Apply by February 15.

Art

Syracuse University. "Renaissance Art in Florence." Three-semester program. Fall semester at Syracuse and following spring and fall in Italy. Graduate students only. Some Italian required. Apply by February 1.

Classics

Stanford University. "Intercollegiate Center for Classical Studies in Rome." Fall or spring semester. Juniors and seniors who are classical studies majors with B average. Apply by March 15 for fall and October 15 for spring.

General Studies

American Heritage Association. "Northwest Interinstitutional Council on Study Abroad—Siena." Fall, winter, and/or spring quarter. Sophomores, juniors, and seniors with 2.5 GPA. Apply by June 15 for fall, November 1 for winter, and January 15 for spring.

American University. "Rome Semester." Most courses supplemented by field trips and excursions. Orientation in Siena. Sophomores, juniors, and seniors with 2.75 GPA. Apply six months prior to start of program.

Associated Colleges of the Midwest. "ACM Florence Program." Fall semester. Courses in art history, language, and other social sciences and humanities. Sophomores, juniors, and seniors with 2.75 GPA. Some Italian recommended. Apply by March 15.

Boston University. Padua. Intensive Italian language and culture or advanced Italian and direct enrollment at the University of Padua. Academic year or semester. Homestay or dormitory housing. Sophomores to seniors with 3.0 GPA in major. Four semesters of college Italian for advanced course and direct enrollment. Apply by March 15 for year or fall; October 15 for spring.

Drake University. "Drake-ISI Italy." Florence. Semester or academic year. Courses in humanities, art, fashion design, photography and language at the Instituto di Studi Italiani. Sophomores to graduate students with 2.5 GPA. Rolling admissions.

Experiment in International Living/School for International Training. "College Semester Abroad." Siena. Fall or spring semester. Intensive language, life and culture seminar, field-study methods seminar, independent-study project, and homestays. Sophomores to seniors with 2.5 GPA. Apply by May 15 for fall and October 15 for spring.

Gonzaga University. "Gonzaga in Florence." Academic year. Juniors and seniors with 2.5 GPA. Apply by April 1.

Hiram College. Rome. Study at John Cabot University. Academic year or fall, winter, or spring quarters. Sophomores, juniors, and seniors with 2.5 GPA.

Indiana University. "Bologna Cooperative Studies Program." Academic year. Program offered by consortium of City University of New York, Indiana University, University of Minnesota, University of North Carolina, University of Pennsylvania, and University of Wisconsin. Direct enrollment in University of Bologna. Juniors and seniors with two years of Italian and 3.0 GPA. Apply by January 15.

International Student Exchange Program. Direct reciprocal exchange between U.S. universities and institutions in Milan, Pavia, Rome, and Urbino. Academic year. Full curriculum options. Open only to students at ISEP-member institutions.

Kent State University. Fall or spring semester. Fine and liberal arts, Italian language, music. Sophomores to seniors (graduate students in music) with 2.5 GPA. Rolling admissions.

Lake Erie College. Perugia. Juniors and seniors with intermediate Italian and 2.5 GPA. Programs all year long. Apply by June 1 and October 1.

Rutgers University. "Junior Year in Italy." Florence, with six weeks in Urbino. Juniors with two years college Italian, preferably with some Italian literature courses. Apply by March 1.

State University of New York at Buffalo/College at Buffalo. "Siena Semester Program." Sophomores, juniors, and seniors with one college Italian course and 2.5 GPA. Apply by April 1 for fall and October 1 for spring.

State University of New York at Stony Brook. Rome. Juniors and seniors with two years of Italian and 2.5 GPA. Apply by April 1.

Syracuse University. "Syracuse in Florence." Semester or academic year. Sophomores to graduate students with 3.0 GPA. Apply by March 15 for fall and October 15 for spring.

Trinity College. "Trinity College/Rome Campus." Fall or spring semester. All enrolled students must take Italian in Rome. Sophomores, juniors, and seniors. Apply by mid-March for fall and mid-October for spring.

University of Connecticut. "Study-Abroad Program in Florence." Academic year. Sophomores to graduate studies with one year of college Italian. Apply by April 1.

University of North Carolina—Chapel Hill. "UNC Program to Bologna." Academic year. Sophomores, juniors, and seniors with 3.0 GPA and fluency in Italian. Apply February 12.

University of Oregon. "Northwest Interinstitutional Council on Study Abroad—Siena." See description under American Heritage Association.

Portland State University. "Northwest Interinstitutional Council on Study Abroad—Siena." See description under American Heritage Association.

Western Washington University. "Northwest Interinstitutional Council on Study Abroad—Siena." See description under American Heritage Association.

University of Wisconsin—Madison.
Bologna. Academic year. Juniors to graduate students with 3.0 GPA and five semesters of college Italian. Limited to students at colleges or universities in Wisconsin and Wisconsin residents studying outside of the state. Apply by February 1.
Florence. Semester or academic year. Instruction is in English. Open to juniors and seniors studying at colleges and universities in Wisconsin and Wisconsin residents studying outside of the state. Apply by March 1.

Italian Language and Culture

Middlebury College. Florence. Sophomores to graduate students fluent in Italian. Rolling admissions.

University of Hartford. "Discovering Italy." Rome, Florence, Venice. Ten-day program in March. Freshmen to seniors. Apply by January 22.

University of Massachusetts—Amherst. "Semester in Siena." Spring semester. Sophomores to seniors with two semesters of college Italian. Apply by October 15.

University of North Carolina—Chapel Hill. "UNC Program of Siena." Semester or academic year. Sophomores to seniors. No language prerequisite. Apply by March 15 and October 15.

Summer

Archaeology

Michigan State University. "Prehistoric Archaeology in Italy." Siena. Sophomores to graduate students. Apply by April 20.

Architecture and Design

Syracuse University.
"Architecture: Summer Semester in Florence." Students with three years of architectural design in a B.A. program or two years in an M.A. program. Apply by March 15.
"Pre-Architecture in Florence." Freshmen to seniors. Apply by March 15.

University of Oregon. "Summer Study in Rome." Sophomores and above. Apply by March 1.

Art History and Studio Art

New York University.
"Studio Art in Venice." Graduate students. Apply by April 15. Contact: School of Education, Health, Nursing and Arts Professions, 32 Washington Place, Second floor, New York, NY 10003; (212) 998-5030.
"International Development: Graphic Communication." Milan. Seniors and graduate students. Apply by April 15. Contact: Graduate Admissions, 32 Washington Place, New York, NY 10003; (212) 998-5090.

Southern Methodist University. "SMU-in-Rome." Sophomores, juniors, and seniors. Apply by March 1.

State University of New York at Brockport. "Ceramics and Art History in Faenza." Instituto Statale d'Arte per la Ceramica. Juniors to graduate students with 2.5 GPA. Apply by May 1.

Syracuse University. "Visual Arts in Florence." Sophomores to graduate students, and professionals. Apply by March 15.

University of Colorado at Boulder. "Art History in Italy." Formal classroom instruction, with visits to many of the masterpieces of art and architecture. Sophomores to graduate students with 2.75 GPA and some knowledge of fine arts. Applications are accepted from the end of November until program is full.

General Studies

Brigham Young University. "BYU Study Abroad." Florence. Sophomores, juniors, and seniors with some Italian. Apply by February 1.

Drake University.
"Drake-ISI Italy." Florence. Courses in humanities, art, fashion design, photography,

and language at the Istituto di Studi Italiani. Sophomores to graduate students with 2.5 GPA. Rolling admissions.

"Drake-ISI Italy." Rome. Courses in the humanities, international business, language, and history. Sophomores to graduate students with 2.5 GPA. Rolling admissions.

Hiram College. Rome. Study at John Cabot University. Full course load plus field trips. Sophomores, juniors, and seniors with 2.5 GPA.

Louisiana State University. "LSU in Italy." Six weeks of coursework in Italian language and culture, history, and art. Excursions to various cities. Sophomores to seniors with 2.5 GPA; graduate students with 3.0 GPA. Apply by March 15.

Michigan State University. "Social Science in Rome." Politics, economics, educational, and cultural aspects of Italy. Freshmen to seniors. Apply by April 20.

Syracuse University. "Humanism and the Arts in Renaissance Italy." Florence, with excursions to other cities. Sophomores to graduate students, and professionals. Apply by March 15.

Trinity College. "Rome Campus Summer Program." Sophomores to seniors.

University of Louisville. "Art, Language, History, and Culture in Perugia." Freshmen to graduate students. Apply by April 30.

Italian History and Civilization

Mary Baldwin College. "Renaissance Studies in Italy." May term. Florence, Venice, and Rome with field trips to Milan, Padua, Mantua, and Siena. Undergraduates. Apply by December 1.

Michigan State University. "History in Rome." Italian language, Medieval and Renaissance studies. Sophomores to graduates. Apply by April 20.

University of Wisconsin—Madison. Florence. Two different six-week summer sessions: Mid-May to late June or early July to mid-August. Instruction is in English. Open to sophomores, juniors, and seniors studying at colleges and universities in Wisconsin and to Wisconsin residents studying outside of the state. Apply by March 1.

Italian Language and Culture

American Heritage Association. "American Heritage Cultural Summer Program." Siena. Italian culture and history. No language requirement. Apply by April 15.

Boston University. "Summer Program in Padua/Venice." Choice of courses in Italian language, literature, and art history. Based in Padua with excursions to Venice and throughout the Veneto. Sophomores to seniors with 3.0 GPA in major. Apply by April 1.

Indiana University. "Overseas Study in Florence." Studio art also offered. Freshmen to graduate students with 2.8 GPA. Apply by first week in February.

Michigan State University. "Italian Language, Literature, and Culture in Florence." Freshmen to graduate students with previous study of Italian. Apply by April 20.

EUROPE: ITALY

Portland State University. "A.L.P.S. in Italy—Italian Language Program." Montefalco. Culture excursions to medieval churches, ancient monuments, and museums. All students, but undergraduate credit only. One term of college Italian is recommended. Apply by May 1.

Rosary College. "Rosary in Florence." Italian language with emphasis in literature and art history. Sophomores, juniors, seniors, and others interested in Italian culture. Apply by April 1.

State University of New York at Stony Brook. "Summer in Rome." High-school seniors to college seniors. Apply by April 1.

Syracuse University. "Italian Language and Literature." Florence, with field trips to Rome and Venice. Sophomores, juniors, seniors, and professionals. Apply by March 15.

University of Kansas. Florence. Language and culture. Freshmen to graduate students with one year Italian language study. Apply by February 1.

University of Oregon. "Summer Study in Perugia, Italy." Sophomores and above. Apply by April 1.

University of Pennsylvania. "Penn/Bryn Mawr Italian Studies Summer Institute in Florence." For students interested in Italian language and culture. Apply by March 15.

University of Utah. "Siena, Italy: Italian Language Program." Four weeks. Freshmen to graduate students, and others. One or two quarters of college Italian or the equivalent is recommended. Apply by March 1.

University System of Georgia/University of Georgia.
Florence. Study at the Centro Linguistico Italiano Dante Alighieri. All students with 2.5 GPA. Apply by March 15.

Western Washington University. Siena. See listing under American Heritage Association.

Music

New York University. Graduate students. Apply by April 15. Contact: School of Education, Health, Nursing and Arts Professions, 32 Washington Place, Second floor, New York, NY 10003; (212) 998-5030.

Social and Political Philosophy

Boston University. "Summer Institute on the Transformation of Democracy." Cortona. Directed research for qualified graduates and advanced undergraduates. Apply by April 1.

Social Work

Michigan State University. "Social Work in Italy." Santa Maria. Juniors, seniors, and graduate students. Apply by April 20. Internship possible with prior arrangements.

EXPLORING ITALIAN CULTURE

Readings

Since the days of Dante and Petrarch, Italy has produced memorable, poetic literature that is both intellectually challenging as well as emotionally rewarding. Since World War II, a personal and experimental literature has been the norm in Italy—in contrast with the more socially oriented literature of the prewar years. Alberto Moravia has written a number of novels including *The Conformist* (1951), *The Women of Rome* (1947), and *Roman Tales* (1954), neorealist portrayals of Italian life in which he explores the power of sex, money, and social alienation. Italo Svevo's best known is *The Confessions of Zeno*, an experimental, comic novel about a wistful elderly man; the work is said to have been a favorite of James Joyce. Carlo Levi's *Christ Stopped at Eboli* (1945) deals explicitly with the poverty and culture of Italy's southern regions.

There are a number of contemporary Italian writers readily available in English translation. Cesare Pavese's books are about the difficulties of coming to terms with life. His work *The Moon and the Bonfire* (1968) deals with the narrator's quest for the truth about both his past and future possibilities in a village of the Piedmont; his *Selected Works* (1968) contains four novels that depict the confining and restricting nature of modern urban middle-class life. Italo Calvino's novel *Under the Jaguar Sun* (1988) is a modern retelling of Italian folktales.

Umberto Eco is another well-known contemporary Italian writer: his best-selling novel *The Name of the Rose* (1983) is an allusive, tightly plotted medieval mystery, whereas the critically acclaimed best-seller *Foucault's Pendulum* (1989) takes place in modern times. *The Leopard* (1982), by Giuseppe di Lampedusa, is one of the best-known Sicilian novels. It recounts the dramatic transition from Bourbon to Piedmontese rule and includes some well-written descriptions of the Sicilian landscape. Luigi Barzini's *The Italians* (1964) is widely regarded as the definitive portrait of the Italian character. The Italian sociologist touches upon many aspects of Italian life: its virtues, vices, and charms.

The dramatic Italian landscape lends itself well to almost any plot; many Western writers have seized upon this fact and have used Italy as a backdrop for their narratives. Classics of this nature include Joseph Heller's *Catch-22*, Ernest Hemingway's *A Farewell to Arms*, E. M. Forster's *A Room with a View*, and Thomas Mann's *Death in Venice*.

Films

Italian film is recognized throughout the world, and rightly so; directors such as Bertolucci, De Sica, and Rossellini have put Italy indelibly on the cinematic map. Despite funding problems and increasingly restrictive legislature, old masters like Antonioni and Fellini are still churning out stylized flicks, along with a host of new young directors who continue to flood the market with films unmistakably marked with television nuances. Like Italy itself, the history of Italian film is filled with the ghosts of a passionate political and social history.

The majority of Italian films prior to World War II consisted of either large, lavish spectacles with epic, classical themes, or, during the reign of Mussolini, the aptly named "white telephone" pictures. The term refers to a succession of rather dull bedroom farces with an ever-present white telephone prop—always a sure sign of affluence.

The postwar rebuilding of Italy, however, also meant the reinvigoration of the Italian film industry. Directors Roberto Rossellini (*Rome Open City*), Vittorio De Sica (*The Bicycle Thief*), and Luchino Visconti (*Ossessione*), made films that illustrated the drastic disruptions experienced by Italian society by focusing on the daily routines of the "average" Italian. This style, called neorealism, was marked by the use of nonprofessional actors, unconstructed, austere sets, and a moving, fluid camera. Well-known Italian filmmakers who started in the neorealist style include Michelangelo Antonioni and Federico Fellini. Fellini went on to direct some of the most unforgettable films of the postwar

Italian cinema, including *La Dolce Vita* (1960), *8½* (1963), and *Amarcord* (1973). Travelers going to Rome might be especially interested in Fellini's 1970s portrait of the city, *Roma*.

Other notable postwar Italian filmmakers include Lina Wertmuller—director of *Swept Away* (1974) and *Seven Beauties* (1974)—and Pier Paolo Pasolini—director of *Oedipus Rex* (1967)—both of whom explore the dynamics of sexual politics. Bernardo Bertolucci, another directorial wizard of the postwar Italian cinema, has concentrated on the darker side of Italian life, both past and present, in such films as *The Conformist* (1969) and his epic saga, *1900* (1976). *The Conformist* is an examination of fascism and the security it offers—especially to a man uncomfortable with his country, his romance, and his sexuality. Beautifully filmed and psychologically complex, this film is one of Bertolucci's best. *1900* chronicles the lives of two Italian boys—one born a peasant, the other a nobleman—and provides hours (literally) of cinematic pleasure. But perhaps the most popular Italian movies of the postwar period, if not the most critically acclaimed, have been the so-called "spaghetti Westerns" of director Sergio Leone, including *The Good, the Bad, and the Ugly* (1966), and *Once Upon a Time in the West* (1969), which should be seen for its soundtrack if nothing else.

The Italian film industry continues to produce a variety of films that are well received around the world. Giuseppe Tornatore's *Cinema Paradiso* (1990) is a recent film about a young Italian boy coming of age. The film explores his relationship with the old man who runs the local movie theatre; at the same time it chronicles his relationship to film itself and the escape from rural Italy it offers. *The Icicle Thief* (1990), a hilarious satire borrowing liberally from De Sica's masterpiece, is another recent release from Italy. Marco Risi's *Forever Mary* (1989) is the story of an idealistic teacher caught up in the problems of modern society as reflected in a prison classroom in Sicily.

LUXEMBOURG

Founded in A.D. 963, the Grand Duchy of Luxembourg is one of the oldest nations in Europe. Yet for much of its history it was a highly fortified no-man's-land between the major families and countries of Europe—who were almost constantly at war with each other until the late twentieth century. Luxembourg has been called the "Gibraltar of the North" for all of the castles and fortresses that dot its landscape. Its name comes from "Lucinburhuc," or "small fortress."

Luxembourg was a major battleground most recently during World War II; the Battle of the Bulge was fought in the Ardennes Forest, which covers the north. Luxembourg City was liberated by American troops in 1944, only to be recaptured and subsequently reliberated. American and German tanks and weapons are placed as memorials to the battles fought in Luxembourg. Do not be surprised if you round a corner and find a Sherman tank or a German 88 staring you in the face—they are part of the landscape now.

Although the Grand Duchy once comprised an area some three hundred times larger than it does today, its occupation by a succession of Burgundians, Spaniards, Austrians, French, and Germans from 1448 to 1815 led to a reduction of the country's size and importance. Its importance seems to be rising again, however, as its central location and strict bank secrecy laws have been made it an important part of the emerging European Community. Today, medieval walls and spires share the skyline with modern office complexes in Luxembourg City. Strikingly poised on two sides of the gorge formed by the Alzette river, this small city is home to a great deal of international business and the European Courts of Justice.

Most Luxembourgers speak German, French, and Luxembourgish, a Middle-High German dialect similar to Dutch and German but unintelligible to native speakers of either. Their unique language has contributed to the strong sense of identity Luxembourgers have maintained. Because of the country's small size and the stubbornly rural atmosphere outside its capital, Luxembourg provides a pocket of relative peace and tranquility for those seeking to escape the tourist crush in the cities of its much more populous neighbors.

—Marta Escovar, Austin, Texas

Official name: Grand Duchy of Luxembourg. **Size:** 998 square miles (smaller than Rhode Island). **Population:** 369,000. **Population density:** 369 inhabitants per square mile. **Capital and largest city:** Luxembourg (pop. 86,000). **Language:** Luxembourgeois, French, German. **Religion:** Roman Catholic. **Per capita income:** US$13,980. **Currency:** Luxembourg franc. **Literacy rate:** 100%. **Average daily high/low*:** Luxembourg: January, 36°/29°; July, 74°/55°. **Average number of days with precipitation:** Luxembourg: January, 14; July, 13.

TRAVEL

U.S. citizens will need a passport but not a visa for stays of up to three months. Travelers must be in possession of sufficient funds and an onward/return ticket. For specific requirements for stays beyond three months, check with the Embassy of Luxembourg, 2200 Massachusetts Avenue NW, Washington, DC 20008.

Getting Around

Most travelers to Luxembourg will also want to visit neighboring countries. Eurail passes are a good option for multicountry train travel. Those planning to spend most of their time in Luxembourg, Belgium, and the Netherlands would do well to inquire into the Benelux Tourrail Pass, which allows 5 days of travel throughout the three countries during a 17-day period. Youths under 26 pay $65 for second class and $97 first class. The Benelux Tourrail Pass can be purchased from the Netherlands Board of Tourism at 355 Lexington Avenue, 21st floor, New York, NY 10017; (212) 370-7367.

If you decide to stay awhile, the youth hostel organization, Centrale des Auberges de Jeunesse Luxembourgeoises at 18 Place d'Armes, L-1136 Luxembourg, has travel information for students and youth and will arrange accommodations or local tours.

"Appreciate the many activities and chances to get to know the Luxembourgers. It is a small country and at first glance it appears that there is not much to do. There is hiking, kayaking, ice skating, and swimming—the possibilities are endless. Great way to meet people."

—Ann Gardner, Tallmadge, Ohio

Especially for Students and Young People

Holders of the International Student Identity Card are entitled to a 50-percent discount at most museums. For further information on student discounts, contact the youth hostel association mentioned above or Voyages Sotour-Tourisme des Jeunes, 15 Place du Theatre, L-2010 Luxembourg (phone: 461514).

For Further Information

The Luxembourg Tourist Office (801 Second Avenue, New York, NY 10017) has general tourist information, including a brochure on camping in Luxembourg.

---

*All temperatures are Fahrenheit.

WORK

It is necessary to obtain a work permit through the prospective employer for work in Luxembourg. Nationals and members of the European Economic Community are given first priority.

Internships/Traineeships

A program offered by a member of the Council on International Educational Exchange is listed below.

Association for International Practical Training. "IAESTE Trainee Program." On-the-job training for undergraduate and graduate students in technical fields such as engineering, computer science, agriculture, architecture, and mathematics. See page 18 for more information.

STUDY

A program offered by a CIEE-member institution is listed below. Consult Appendix I for the address to write for more information.

Semester and Academic Year

European Studies

Miami University. John E. Dolibois European Center. Academic year or semester. European studies with French or German language. Field tours to other cities. No language prerequisite. Freshmen to juniors with 2.5 GPA. Apply by January 24.

MALTA

The small nation of Malta—comprised of the islands of Malta, Gozo, and Comino—is strategically located in the heart of the Mediterranean Sea, where a blend of Eastern mysticism and Western pragmatism shapes daily life. Phoenicians, Carthaginians, Greeks, Romans, Byzantines, Arabs, Normans, the Knights of St. John, the French, and the British have all left their mark on the islands. Today the southern-Italian influence is most obvious in the Maltese people, their food (lots of pasta), and their churches. Arabic influences are apparent in the architecture, the narrow winding streets of Valletta, and the language; Maltese is closely related to Arabic, but also includes elements of languages from the many different countries that once dominated these small islands.

The relics of colonial Britain can be seen everywhere—nearly everyone speaks English as well as Maltese. Under British control in World War II, its populace earned Britain's George Cross for refusing to surrender under a devastating Axis bombardment. The George Cross now appears on the flag of Malta, which became an independent nation in 1964 after 150 years of British rule. The abundance of British pubs and restaurants serving fish and chips around Silema and St. Julians make it a popular destination for British vacationers.

Malta is only 19 miles long by 7 miles wide, but once you escape the crowded coast, the island is relatively unspoiled. The shores of Malta provided a safe haven for many passing ships during winter storms, although it has been the scene of some famous shipwrecks—most notably St. Paul on his way to Rome.

Valletta, the capital of Malta, is an 18th-century fortress city, famous for its lacemaking and silversmithing. Its palaces, churches, museums, and the imposing St. John's Cathedral are worth visiting, as is the Grand Harbour. Valletta can be explored on foot, but the rest of the island can be reached by the green buses which depart from the city gate terminus in Floriana. Take a bus to Mdina, the ancient capital city, and get a feel of what Malta was like before the advent of the car. Cars are not allowed inside this walled medieval city, where the inhabitants still live behind huge carved wooden doors.

The neighboring islands of Comino and Gozo can be reached only by ferry. Comino is a small, dry island with only two hotels and no cars; Gozo is half the size of Malta and much greener.

The Maltese are an incredibly outgoing and friendly people. All that's needed to experience the real Malta is to leave behind the hotel complexes of Silema and St. Paul and head for the smaller towns and fishing villages.

—*Wendy Tabuteau, London, United Kingdom*

Official name: Republic of Malta. **Size:** 122 square miles (about ⅕ the size of Rhode Island). **Population:** 373,000. **Population density:** 2,934 inhabitants per square mile. **Capital:** Valletta (pop. 13,962). **Largest city:** Birkirkara (pop. 20,000). **Language:** Maltese, English (both official). Religion: Roman Catholic. **Per capita income:** US$4,750. **Currency:** Maltese pound. **Literacy rate:** 90%. **Average daily high/low*:** Valletta: January, 59°/31°; July, 84°/72°. **Average number of days with precipitation:** Valletta: January, 13; July, 1.

TRAVEL

A passport is required for U.S. citizens traveling to the island. However, a visa is not required for stays of up to three months. Check with the Embassy of Malta, 2017 Connecticut Avenue NW, Washington, DC 20008, for specific requirements.

Getting Around

Ferries link Valletta with several cities of southern Italy; smaller ferries connect Malta to the outer islands of Gozo and Comino, both of which are more rural and relaxed than the crowded, bustling main island. The buses that serve all parts of the island of Malta provide an inexpensive way of getting around. Mopeds, which can be rented at various locations around the island, are another popular means of travel.

Especially for Students and Young People

NSTS–Student and Youth Travel (220, St. Paul Street, Valletta) is Malta's student travel organization and issuer of the International Student Identity Card. NSTS provides information on travel and accommodations in Malta, offers student tours and cruises, operates a student accommodations center, and runs a water-sports facility. Students with the International Student Identity Card will receive discounts on all of these NSTS services. Other discounts for cardholders include free entrance to all government museums and discounts at a number of retail stores. NSTS organizes many social activities for visiting young people from June to September—contact them for details.

There are many inexpensive guesthouses on Malta suitable for students. Contact NSTS for further information on places to stay (NSTS requests people writing for information

---

*All temperatures are Fahrenheit.

enclose two international postal reply coupons). The International Youth Card is good for discounts on tours, excursions and cruises around the island, recreational facilities, restaurants, and accommodations.

For Further Information

Let's Go: Italy contains an informative chapter on Malta with an especially helpful guide to ferry links with Italy. It's available for $14.95 in most bookstores and at Council Travel offices.

WORK

In order to work in Malta, foreigners must secure a job offer prior to going to the country. The prospective employer then applies for the work permit on your behalf. For further information contact the Administrative Secretary, Immigration and Nationality Branch, Auberge de Castille, Valletta, Malta.

Internships/Traineeships

Two programs offered by members of the Council on International Educational Exchange are listed below.

AIESEC-US. Reciprocal internship program for students in economics, business, finance, marketing, accounting, and computer sciences. See page 18 for more information.

Association for International Practical Training. "IAESTE Trainee Program." On-the-job training for undergraduate and graduate students in technical fields such as engineering, computer science, agriculture, architecture, and mathematics. See page 18 for more information.

STUDY

A program offered by a CIEE-member institution is listed below. Consult Appendix I for the address to write for more information.

Semester and Academic Year

General Studies

International Student Exchange Program. Direct reciprocal exchange between U.S. universities and the University of Malta. Semester or academic year. Full curriculum options. Open only to students at ISEP-member institutions.

THE NETHERLANDS

The Netherlands' proximity to the North Sea, plus the fact that much of the country lies below sea level, are dominant factors in the character of the country. The Dutch have long been sailors and vigorous entrepreneurs, inspiring an outward-looking society that takes pride in welcoming and assimilating foreigners. But while the sea is a door opening outwards, it is also a source of potential catastrophe. The successful battle to keep the water at bay has brought to the society a strong sense of community, which in turn is the foundation for one of the strongest welfare states in the world. The Dutch pay very high taxes and social premiums; their expectations of government services are accordingly much higher than in most countries. The Delta Project, an elaborate system of dikes and dams designed to protect the low-lying coastline, was publicly financed. Similarly, virtually all education, including religious schools, is state sponsored. By American standards, health care, public transportation, the arts, sports, and social services are all heavily subsidized.

Discussing national or international political issues is a daily pastime for the Dutch, either among family members, with co-workers during the morning coffee break, or with friends in one of the country's pubs and bars. American visitors are encouraged to be well informed about their country's foreign policy, as the topic is likely to come up sooner or later. Such discussion will be in English, which most Dutch speak quite well. (In comparing political systems, it is helpful to know that the Dutch word *liberaal* does not translate into "liberal" in English; *liberaal* refers to laissez-faire economic policy, and the Dutch *liberalen* are considered conservatives, though many do share the American "liberal" views on issues such as abortion, gay rights, and so on.)

Current challenges facing Dutch society include the maintenance of its welfare system, which has become a heavy burden for the lackluster Dutch economy of the 1980s. Another challenge is assimilating the growing numbers of ethnic peoples into Dutch society. Since the early 1960s, the Netherlands, like many northern European countries, has become a magnet for migrant workers from the Mediterranean region. In addition, many people from former Dutch colonies like Suriname and Indonesia have emigrated to the Netherlands. And refugees from all over the world have sought and been granted political asylum there. As a result, the country known for its tolerance now has the difficult task of finding solutions for the problems this influx of newcomers has created.

—*Angelique Dietz, Northfield, Minnesota*

Official name: Kingdom of the Netherlands. **Size:** 15,770 square miles (about twice the size of New Jersey). **Population:** 14,864,000. **Population density:** 931 inhabitants per square mile. **Capital and largest city:** Amsterdam (pop. 691,100). **Language:** Dutch. **Religion:** Roman Catholic, Dutch Reformed. **Per capita income:** US$13,065. **Currency:** Guilder. **Literacy rate:** 99%. **Average daily high/low*:** Amsterdam: January, 34°/40°; July, 59°/69°. **Average number of days with precipitation:** Amsterdam: January, 19; July, 14.

TRAVEL

U.S. citizens will need a passport; however, a visa is not required for pleasure or business stays of up to 90 days. The tourist may be asked to show an onward/return ticket or sufficient funds for stay. For residence authorization, check with Embassy of the Netherlands, 4200 Linnean Avenue NW, Washington, DC 20008.

Getting Around

Holland's railway system is an efficient network providing excellent service to all parts of the country, of which Eurailpass holders may take full advantage. To use Holland's public transportation system—comprising buses, trams, and the underground—you must purchase a *strippenkaart*. The *strippenkaart* is a zone card accepted universally instead of cash (you can't use coins). It is also valid for second-class rail travel within the city

---

*All temperatures are Fahrenheit.

limits of Amsterdam, Rotterdam, The Hague, Utrecht, and Zoetermeer. *Strippenkaarts* are sold in railway stations, transportation offices, post offices, and tobacconists.

Those planning to spend most of their time in the Netherlands, Belgium, and Luxembourg would do well to inquire into the Benelux Tourrail Pass, which allows 5 days of travel throughout the three countries during a 17-day period. Youths under 26 pay $65 for second class and $97 for first class. The Benelux Tourrail Pass can be purchased in the Netherlands or, in the U.S., from the Netherlands Board of Tourism at 355 Lexington Avenue, 21st Floor, New York, NY 10017; (212) 370-7367.

There are two more rail-pass options for those who wish to remain in the Netherlands. However, because the major points of interest require only short journeys, one should think carefully before investing in either. Rail Ranger tickets allow one week of unlimited travel within the country for $70 second class and $107 first class. The Holland Railpass allows 3 days of travel in a 15-day period for $42 second class and $53 first class. Both of the above are also available in the Netherlands or, in the U.S., through the Netherlands Board of Tourism.

The flat lowlands of the country are probably best seen by bicycle. Most streets and highways have separate bike lanes. Bicycle rental agencies are plentiful and include most train stations. There is an extra charge for carrying bikes on trains which varies depending on distance, season, and day.

Especially for Students and Young People

Check with NBBS, Holland's student and youth travel bureau for travel information, and student discounts on international travel by plane or train. Their head office is in Leiden, but the most convenient office for most travelers is at 17 Dam Square in Amsterdam. NBBS has many other offices in 25 cities around the country. NBBS also offers tours of Amsterdam and an eight-day bicycle tour of the Netherlands; holders of the International Student Identity Card get discounts on various NBBS products. The International Youth Card is good for discounts on selected accommodations, tours, museums, and exhibitions.

For Further Information

The Real Guide: Amsterdam takes an in-depth look at the Netherlands' most vital city, with budget information for the surrounding country as well. It's available in bookstores for $9.95.

The Netherlands Board of Tourism (355 Lexington Avenue, New York, NY 10017) has a number of publications of general interest to the young traveler. Also available from the Netherlands Board of Tourism, the Holland Leisure Card, which costs $12 and is good for one year, provides substantial discounts on car rentals, bus and rail fares, selected hotels, and many tourist attractions. Another card, the Holland Leisure Card-Plus, costs $30 and offers free admission to 375 of Holland's museums in addition to the above discounts.

WORK

A work permit is required, but it is difficult to obtain because there are very few positions open to students. Contact the Embassy of the Netherlands (4200 Linnean Avenue NW, Washington, DC 20008) for further information. The American Scandinavian Foundation (Exchange Division, 725 Park Avenue, New York, NY 10021) can assist Americans under the age of 30 with obtaining the requisite permit.

Internships/Traineeships

Programs offered by members of the Council on International Educational Exchange are listed below.

AIESEC-US. Reciprocal internship program for students in economics, business, finance, marketing, accounting, and computer science. See page 18 for more information.

Association for International Practical Training.
"IAESTE Trainee Program." On-the-job training for undergraduate and graduate students in technical fields such as engineering, computer science, agriculture, architecture, and mathematics. See page 18 for more information.

"Hotel & Culinary Exchanges Program." On-the-job training for young people beginning a career in the hotel and food-service industries. Participants must have graduated, or be currently enrolled in a university or vocational school and possess at least six months of training or experience in the chosen field. Training usually runs 6 to 18 months. Consult Appendix I for the address where you can write for more information.

Voluntary Service

CIEE places young people in voluntary service workcamps in the Netherlands organized by SIW International Voluntary Projects (Willemstraat 7, NL-3511 RJ Utrecht). Projects include construction work, forest management, working in homes for the physically disabled, et cetera. Volunteers work in groups of 10 to 15 people for about three weeks during the summer. Room and board are provided, although no wages are paid. Applicants must be between the ages of 18 and 30. The applications of U.S. residents are processed by CIEE. For more information, contact the Voluntary Service Department at CIEE.

In addition, the Fourth World Movement sponsors workcamps in the Netherlands. For more information see page 21.

STUDY

Information on higher education, international courses and scholarships available to foreign students in the Netherlands is available from the Netherlands Organization for International Cooperation in Higher Education. Publications available include: *Basic Data on International Courses Offered in the Netherlands, Living in Holland: Practical Tips for Adjusting to Life among the Dutch, Dutch Language Courses for Foreign Students,* and *Studying at a University in Holland: Should You?* Write to NUFFIC, Information Department, Badhuisweg 251, PO Box 90734, 2509 LS The Hague, Netherlands. Information is also available through the Press and Cultural Sections of the Netherlands Consulate General in New York, San Francisco, Los Angeles, Houston, and Chicago, as well as the embassy in Washington, DC. Two other booklets, *Vademecum: A Concise Guide to Studying in the Netherlands for Foreign Students* and *Non-University Dutch-Language Courses* are both available from the Foreign Student Service, Oranje Nassaulaan 5, 1075 AH Amsterdam.

Following are the educational programs offered by CIEE-member institutions. Consult Appendix I for the addresses of colleges and universities listed in this section. In addition to the programs below, Indiana University offers a business program open only to it own students.

Semester and Academic Year

Business

Michigan State University. "Business Law." Rotterdam. Spring quarter. Juniors and seniors with previous courses in business studies. Apply by February 3.

Northern Arizona University. Haarlem Business School. Fall or spring semester. Juniors and seniors with 2.5 GPA. Apply by October 15 for spring and March 15 for fall.

University of Connecticut. "Study-Abroad Program in Maastricht." International business and economics. Fall semester. Juniors and seniors at New England land-grant universities only; others accepted on a space-available basis. Apply by February 15.

University of Oregon. "University of Oregon-Netherlands School of Business Exchange." Breukelen. Academic year. Juniors with 2.75 GPA. Preference given students at the University of Oregon. Apply by April 1.

General Studies

Central University of Iowa. "Netherlands Study Program." Leiden. Academic year or semester. Sophomores, juniors, and seniors with 2.5 GPA. Apply by March 15 for fall; October 15 for spring.

International Student Exchange Program. Direct reciprocal exchange between U.S. universities and institutions in Amsterdam, Groningen, Leiden, Nijmegen, Tilburg, and Utrecht. Semester or academic year. Full curriculum options in Dutch; special programs available in English. Open only to students at ISEP-member institutions.

Lake Erie College. Amsterdam. Semester or academic year. Juniors and seniors with 2.5 GPA. Apply by June 1 for fall and October 1 for spring.

University of Wisconsin—Madison. Utrecht. Academic year or fall semester. Open to juniors, seniors, and graduate students with 3.0 GPA. Two college semesters of Dutch recommended. Instruction is in Dutch and/or English. Apply by February 15.

Linguistics

State University of New York at Albany. "Netherlands Exchange Program." Nijmegen. Fall or spring semester. Juniors and seniors with two previous courses in linguistics. Apply by April 1 for fall and October 15 for spring.

Public Policy and Administration

Indiana University.
Rotterdam. Spring semester at Erasmus University. Juniors and seniors from Purdue and Indiana Universities with 3.0 GPA. Apply by October 1.
Leiden. Fall semester at University of Leiden. Purdue and Indiana University juniors and seniors with 3.0 GPA. Apply by February 1.

EXPLORING DUTCH CULTURE

Readings

Much of Dutch literature seems to focus upon World War II and its effects. Anne Frank's *The Diary of a Young Girl* is probably among the most revealing documentation of the plight of Amsterdam's Jews. Other books about Jewish children's experiences of the war include *Etty: An Interrupted Life*, by Etty Hillesium, and Jona Oberski's *Childhood*. A novel that deals with WW II and its emotional effects is Harry Mulisch's *The Assault*. The first novel by this prominent Dutch writer to be translated into English, it revolves around the sole young survivor of a family slaughtered in a Nazi vendetta massacre and his attempt to come to terms with it many years later. Mulisch's most recent novel, *Last Call*, is set in contemporary Amsterdam and explores the link between illusion and reality.

Another prolific Dutch writer is Janwillem Van de Wetering. His novel *The Streetbird* is a murder mystery set in the red-light district of Amsterdam. *Corpse on the Dike* and *Hard Rain* are other Holland-based offbeat detective tales by this quirky, humorous novelist. Another contemporary Dutch novelist is Jan Wolkers; his novel *Turkish Delights*, a semiautobiographical book about marital turbulence and infidelity set in Amsterdam in the 1970s, was made into a successful film by Paul Verhoeven in 1974.

NORWAY

A long Atlantic coastline, punctuated by innumerable fjords, mountainous terrain, and a climate warmed by the Gulf Stream characterize the natural conditions of Scandinavia's most westerly nation. Norway offers a landscape that resembles—and often exceeds— that of Switzerland, with its small towns nestling among peaks and beside lakes, its chalets and tumbling streams, and its superb rail network. As in Switzerland, too, the mountain landscape offers beauty and peace, encourages sports and outdoor recreation, but takes its toll in increasing the costs of commerce and communications.

For most visitors the fjords constitute Norway's claim to a unique place in the world's geography. Their mirror-still waters, the rearing height of the rocky sides, veined with waterfalls and studded with enormous boulders—all radiate a majesty and a tranquility that encroaching civilization has not yet contrived to spoil.

For most of its long history, Norway was a nation of subsistence farmers and woodsmen, fishermen, and sailors. Between approximately A.D. 700 and A.D. 1000, profiting from their superior nautical technology and extensive coastline, Norwegian Vikings exerted great power. These bold and rapacious adventurers roved the seas as far as North America, striking fear into the hearts of more-settled peoples. Their aggressive outreaching was finally muffled by the pacifying forces of Christianity in about the year 1000.

For centuries Norway was ruled by its more populous neighbors, Denmark and later Sweden. Throughout the 19th century, a wave of ardent Norwegian nationalist fervor grew, leading to independence from Sweden in 1905. A Danish prince became the first king of Norway and his son, Olav V, remained on the throne until his death in 1990, a beloved symbol of national unity and independence.

Following the example of its richer and more innovative neighbors, Sweden and Denmark, Norway also enacted an array of social-welfare legislation. Norwegians are proud of their legal and educational systems, designed to give everyone an equal chance in life. Its people have a passionate concern for individual independence, the equitable distribution of wealth, and outdoor life. Since the discovery and development of offshore oil, Norwegians have struggled to preserve their natural environment and the traditional sources of income it provides—fishing, forestry, and farming. Indeed, Norway's protection of its natural heritage, which includes a humble respect for the powers of nature, offers an ecological model for the world to follow.

In 1971, after a prolonged national debate, Norway rejected membership in the European Community, in part because its large North Sea oil fields promised new long-range economic power. Oil revenues indeed brought sudden wealth to the country during the seventies and early eighties, along with increased urbanization, industrialization, and social benefits for its four million citizens. But revenues from this source dropped sharply during the mid 1980s, resulting in subsequent inflation and deficit spending. Norway has thus become an expensive country, for both Norwegians and visitors. But for your money, you will be well looked after. Hotels and homes are clean and well ordered. "The Solid Standard" in all goods and services is something Norwegians are justly proud of.

As a traditionally rural people, Norwegians are wonderfully hospitable, even in very sophisticated and up-to-date Oslo, with its many museums, shops, restaurants, and parks. Manners are relaxed and dress is largely casual throughout the country. As an old "folk culture," Norway has more than its share of tales and legends, arts and crafts, all now in full flourish.

—William W. Hoffa, Amherst, Massachusetts

Official name: Kingdom of Norway. **Size:** 125,181 square miles (about the size of New Mexico). **Population:** 4,214,000. **Population density:** 33 inhabitants per square mile. **Capital and largest city:** Oslo (pop. 449,000). **Language:** Norwegian. **Religion:** Lutheran. **Per capita income:** US$13,900. **Currency:** Kroner. **Literacy rate:** 100%. **Average daily high/low*:** Oslo: January, 30°/20°; July, 73°/56°. **Average number of days with precipitation:** Oslo: January, 8; July, 10.

TRAVEL

A passport is required for U.S. citizens visiting Norway. However, a visa is not required for stays of up to three months, a period that begins as soon as one enters the Scandinavian region (Sweden, Denmark, and Norway). For specific requirements, check with the Royal Norwegian Embassy, 2720 34th Street NW, Washington, DC 20008.

Getting Around

Travelers flying SAS round-trip to the Scandinavian countries of Norway, Denmark, or Sweden are eligible for SAS's Visit Scandinavia fare. The special fare allows the purchase of up to six discounted flight coupons for travel within the three countries. The coupons, which cost from $80 for one flight to $420 for six, must be purchased in the U.S. before departure and must be used within three months of arrival in Scandinavia. It can be used on any of the three Scandinavian airlines: Danair, Linjeflyg, and SAS (excluding flights to the Faroe Islands and Greenland).

Another airline, Braathens SAFE, offers discounts on its flights within Norway from May 1 to September 30. Their Visit Norway tickets are valid for one month. Short journeys cost $57 and long journeys $114. Contact STC Tour Consultants at 8939 Sepulveda Boulevard, Suite 220, Los Angeles, CA 90045.

Norway has five major railroad lines, branching out from Oslo to cities such as Bergen, Trondheim, and Bodö, north of the Arctic Circle. The Bergen Line, connecting Oslo to Bergen, is one of the world's most spectacular railway routes, reaching heights of over 1300 meters.

Eurail passes of all types are valid in Norway. Those planning to travel extensively in Scandinavia should consider the following options:

- The ScanRail Pass is valid for travel on the state railway systems of Norway, Denmark, Finland, and Sweden on a certain number of days within a fixed period of time. For example, one may travel on any of 14 days within one month for $499 first class and $349 second class. ScanRail also allows free passage on a number of ferry lines. For information and reservations, contact Council Travel or Rail Europe (800-848-7245).
- The Nordturist Ticket allows for 21 days of free travel on the state railway systems of the above-mentioned countries, including certain ferries. It's also good for a 50-percent discount on the Hirtshals-Hjörring private railway as well as other ferry lines and bus routes. This pass can only be bought in Scandinavia. The cost for youths ages 12 to 25 traveling second class is approximately $200.

---

*All temperatures are Fahrenheit.

If you have the time you may also want to investigate the legendary coastal steamers that link towns along the coast from Bergen to Kirkenes, near the Soviet border.

Especially for Students and Young People

Univers Reiser (UR), the Norwegian student travel bureau, is a good source of information on travel and student discounts in Norway. Besides its Oslo office (Universitetssentret, Boks 54, Blindern, 0313 Oslo 3) it has offices in As, Bergen, Stavanger, and Tromsö. In Norway, students with the International Student Identity Card get reductions on tickets to some museums, discounts on train and plane fares from Norway to international destinations, and 25-percent discounts in certain hotels in Bergen, Oslo, Stavanger, and Tromsö. The International Youth Card is good for discounts on some accommodations and museums.

Meet the People

Friends Overseas is an American-Scandinavian people-to-people program which helps put travelers in touch with Scandinavians who share similar interests. The service is offered to families and groups as well as single travelers. For further information, send a stamped, self-addressed, business-size envelope to Friends Overseas, 68-04 Dartmouth Street, Forest Hills, NY 11375.

For Further Information

A number of publications geared to the student or budget traveler can be obtained from the Norwegian Tourist Board (655 Third Avenue, New York, NY 10017) including information on camping, hiking, youth hostels, as well as maps and a calendar of events. One of the best general guidebooks to Norway and the entire Scandinavian region is *The Real Guide: Scandinavia*, available in bookstores for $14.95.

WORK

Getting a Job

Foreigners may work in Norway during the summer for up to three months without obtaining a work permit before entering the country. According to the Arbeidsdirektoratet (Directorate of Labor), "The best opportunity for obtaining jobs occurs from May to mid-June and from mid-July to the end of September, as the influx of young Norwegians seeking summer employment is greater during the intermediate period."

To work for a period longer than three months, a work permit is necessary. And to get a work permit, a written offer of employment from the prospective employer is required. For the most part, work permits for long-term employment are issued only to a specific few: aliens with long-standing and special ties to Norway, scientists, performing artists and musicians, trainees admitted under agreement with other countries, and young people who enter Norway sponsored by any of the youth exchange programs of the Norwegian Foundation for Youth Exchange. The American Scandinavian Foundation (Exchange Division, 725 Park Avenue, New York, NY 10021) can assist Americans under the age of 30 with obtaining the requisite permit.

Farm Work

Atlantis—Norwegian Foundation for Youth Exchange (Rolf Hofmosgate 18,0655 Oslo 6) has been granted permission to organize work programs which are not affected by the general regulations for work permits. Atlantis will place young people 18 to 30 years of age as working guests or au pairs in Norwegian families. Chores may include haymaking, weeding, milking, picking fruit, feeding cattle as well as normal housework, and childcare. Free-time activities include walking tours in the mountains and forests, swimming, fishing, boating and excursions to famous Norwegian sights. Placement occurs year-round, with a minimum placement of four weeks and a maximum of 12 weeks. Applicants must be between the ages of 18 and 30. The organization can also arrange practical experience programs for students in groups. Participants receive room and board and approximately $55 per week in pocket money. The registration fee is approximately $45. Enclose two international postal reply coupons when writing for information.

Internships/Traineeships

Two programs offered by members of the Council on International Educational Exchange are described below.

AIESEC-US. Reciprocal internship program for students in economics, business, finance, marketing, accounting, and computer science. See page 18 for more information.

Association for International Practical Training. "IAESTE Trainee Program." On-the-job training for undergraduate and graduate students in technical fields such as engineering, computer science, agriculture, architecture, and mathematics. See page 18 for more information.

In addition, the American Scandinavian Foundation sponsors a program that provides summer training assignments for full-time students majoring in engineering, computer science, horticulture, agriculture, forestry, and chemistry, among others. The deadline for application is December 15. Note, however: traineeships are not available in teaching, social work, or medically related fields. Contact the American Scandinavian Foundation, Exchange Division, 725 Park Avenue, New York, NY 10021.

Voluntary Service

For persons interested in voluntary service work, the Year Abroad Program sponsored by the International Christian Youth Exchange offers persons ages 18 to 24 voluntary service opportunities in the fields of health care, education, the environment, construction, and so on. See page 23 for more information.

STUDY

The Norwegian Information Service (825 Third Avenue, 17th floor, New York, NY 10022) distributes several publications of interest, including *Foreign Students in Norway* and *Education in Norway*. It also publishes a list of grants for U.S. citizens who wish to study in Norway.

The Exchange Division of the American Scandinavian Foundation (725 Park Avenue, New York, NY 10021) publishes *Study in Scandinavia*, which includes a list of English-language programs offered in Norway during the academic year and summer.

The following study-abroad programs are offered by CIEE-member institutions. Consult Appendix I for the addresses of the colleges and universities listed in this section. In addition to the programs below, the American Graduate School of International Management, Ohio University, and the University of California system offer programs open only to their own students.

Semester and Academic Year

Environmental Sciences

Scandinavian Seminar. "Semester Program on Nordic and Global Issues." Sogndal and/or other locations. Fall and spring. Focus on global issues from a Nordic perspective. Coursework in English. Field trips. Undergraduate credit through University of Massachusetts—Amherst. Sophomores to graduate students and other adults. Apply by April 1 or October 1.

General Studies

Scandinavian Seminar. "College Year in Norway." Individual placement in Norwegian Folk Colleges throughout Norway. Norwegian language and cultural immersion with emphasis on liberal arts. Undergraduate credit granted through University of Massachusetts—Amherst. Sophomores to graduate students and other adults. Apply by April 1.

University of Oregon. "University of Oregon-University of Bergen Exchange Program." Academic year. Juniors with one year of Norwegian and summer intensive program in Norway or two years of Norwegian. Preference given to students at University of Oregon. Apply by March 1.

University of Wisconsin—Madison. Tromsö. Academic year at the University of Tromsö. Open to juniors, seniors, and graduate students with 3.0 GPA. Four college semesters of Norwegian required for undergraduates. Apply by February 15.

Social Sciences

Scandinavian Seminar. "Semester Program on Nordic and Global Issues." Vesby and/or other locations. Fall or spring semester. Focus on global issues from a Nordic perspective. Coursework in English. Field trips. Undergraduate credit through University of Massachusetts—Amherst. Sophomores to graduate students and other adults. Apply by April 1 or October 1.

POLAND

Everywhere in Poland you can see evidence of the nation's fascinating history and the profound changes shaping the future of the country. You can explore the medieval walled city of Cracow, where Copernicus taught, or visit the Gdánsk shipyards where Lech Walesa started Solidarity. You can see the most sacred icon of Catholic Poland, the Black Madonna at Czestochowa, or visit Auschwitz, a symbol of Nazi atrocities still fresh in many Poles' memories.

With the exception of the extreme south, Poland is a flat plain that stretches on into Germany to the west and the Soviet Union to the east. Its geography helps explain why the history of Poland has been one of repeated invasions: Germans, Russians, Tartars, Turks, Swedes, even Genghis Khan, all have taken advantage of Poland's lack of natural obstacles at one time or another. And yet, for a brief period in the 16th and 17th centuries, Poland rose to become a leading European power. Polish kings were even credited with saving Western Europe in 1683 by turning back the invading Turks outside the gates of Vienna. Eventually, however, Poland lost its independence—partitioned by Russia, Prussia, and Austria in 1795—and did not regain it until 1918. Twenty years later, the Nazis again made Poland an occupied territory; by the time the Second World War ended, in

1945, six million Poles had been killed and the country lay in ruins. Poland officially regained its independence after the war, but until recently remained under the influence of its "friendly" local superpower, the Soviet Union.

But Polish history is not just the history of military invasions and bitter defeats. Poles are proud of their contributions to science, literature, and the arts, and point to Copernicus, Marie Curie, Chopin, three Nobel prize–winning authors, and other notables in many fields. Two Polish generals, Pulaski and Kosciusko, played vital roles in helping Americans win their own struggle for independence.

Today, Poland seems to be a country wracked with crises. The political and economic system imposed in 1945 has failed, and the fundamental reforms currently underway won't revitalize the country overnight. In 1989 the country witnessed the swearing in of Eastern Europe's first noncommunist prime minister in 40 years, Tadeusz Mazowiecki, the editor of Solidarity's newspaper. In 1990 Lech Walesa, former leader of Solidarity, was elected president. The radical reforms that have been enacted to bring Poland toward a free-market economy have drawn protests from unions, farmers, and miners.

In spite of improved East-West relations, Poland does not receive many visitors from the United States. Few Poles speak English, and a trip there will require some initiative and preparation. However, Americans who do travel to Poland will find the people especially friendly. Perhaps it's the mixture of fascination and admiration (and a bit of jealousy) with which they look at the United States. Or perhaps it's the ethnic tie to eight million Polish-Americans. In any case, a visit to Poland is sure to be an interesting one.
—*Jan Rudomina, New York, New York*

Official name: Republic of Poland. **Area:** 120,727 square miles (about the size of New Mexico). **Population:** 38,363,000. **Population density:** 317 inhabitants per square mile. **Capital and largest city:** Warsaw (pop. 1,600,000). **Language:** Polish. **Religion:** Roman Catholic. **Per capita income:** US$2,000. **Currency:** Zloty. **Literacy rate:** 98%. **Average daily high/low*:** Warsaw: January, 32°/22°; July, 75°/58°. **Average number of days with precipitation:** Warsaw: January, 8; July, 11.

TRAVEL

U.S. citizens traveling to Poland will need a passport; however, a visa is not required for stays of up to three months. Check with the Embassy of the Republic of Poland, 2640 16th Street NW, Washington, DC 20009 for specific requirements.

Getting Around

Travel by train in Poland is inexpensive, and the rail network serves almost every town. But be forewarned: Ticket lines are long and trains are slow, crowded, and uncomfortable. It's always advisable to make reservations at least a day in advance at an office of ORBIS (the official government travel bureau) or at the railroad station where it costs less. Try to use express trains whenever possible—they make very few stops. Neither the InterRail nor Eurail passes are valid in Poland, but the European East Pass is. Good for first-class travel, passes are also good for travel in Austria, Czechoslovakia, and Hungary. Available through Council Travel, and 5 days of travel within a 15-day period is $160 and any 10 days within one month is $259. In addition, Polrail passes can be purchased at ORBIS for 8, 15, 21, or 30 days of unlimited travel by rail. These passes are fairly expensive, so you won't save money unless you plan to do a lot of traveling. International train tickets must also be purchased at ORBIS; holders of the International Student Identity Card get a 25-percent discount on most fares.

---

*All temperatures are Fahrenheit.

Buses are slow and crowded—even more so than the trains. ORBIS sells advance tickets, which are often a necessity. Fares on the nation's bus system are about the same as on the train. Faster and more comfortable travel is available on the national airline, LOT, which serves a number of Polish cities. Flights within Poland are quite expensive, but students with the International Student Identity Card can pay half-price and fly standby.

Especially for Students

ALMATUR (ul. Ordynacka 9, 00-364 Warsaw) is Poland's student/youth travel and tourism office. It has offices in Warsaw—the most complete being the ALMATUR Travel Shop, ul. Kopernika 23, 00-359 Warsaw—as well as in 16 other Polish cities. ALMATUR offices provide travel information and maps, and sells student accommodation vouchers. Student associations at every major university have a foreign travel branch which will arrange meetings between Polish and visiting students. To find the location and hours of this office, ask at the information booth of each campus. In Poland, benefits for travelers with the International Student Identity Card include a 50-percent discount on domestic standby flights, 10-percent discount on ferry routes, and a discount on the entrance fees to most museums. Cardholders get a special price on entrance to all student clubs and accommodations in International Student Hotels (ISH) from July 1 to August 30 as well. ALMATUR will also arrange student holidays in Polish resorts.

For Further Information

The Polish Travel Bureau (500 Fifth Avenue, New York, NY 10110) distributes general information about travel and tourism in Poland. Another useful source of information is the *Insider's Guide to Poland*, published by Hippocrene Books and available in many bookstores for $9.95. Also recommended is *Eastern Europe on a Shoestring*, by David Stanley. The recently updated guide is well researched, thorough, and well worth every penny. It's available for $21.95 (plus $1.50 book-rate postage, $3 for first-class) from Lonely Planet Publications, Embarcadero West, 112 Linden Street, Oakland, CA 94607. Frommer's *Eastern Europe & Yugoslavia on $25 a Day* includes a lengthy section on Poland and chapters on Warsaw, Krakow and Southern Poland, the Baltic Coast and Northeast Poland, and Western Poland. The *Hippocrene Companion Guide to Poland* is also recommended as a good introduction into the history and culture of Poland.

WORK

Foreigners are not allowed regular employment in Poland. As an alternative, you might be interested in a trainee program or a workcamp.

Internships/Traineeships

Two programs offered by members of the Council on International Educational Exchange are listed below.

AIESEC-US. Reciprocal internship program for students in economics, business, finance, marketing, accounting, and computer science. See page 18 for more information.

Association for International Practical Training. "IAESTE Trainee Program." On-the-job training for undergraduate and graduate students in technical fields such as engineering, computer science, agriculture, architecture, and mathematics. See page 18 for more information.

Voluntary Service

CIEE places young people in voluntary service workcamps in Poland organized by the Foundation for International Youth Exchange (ul. Grzybowska 79, 00-844 Warsaw). At these workcamps, groups of volunteers from various countries are involved in construction, maintenance work, gardening, or archaeological excavations. Volunteers must be at least 18 years old. Room and board are provided by the camp. The applications of U.S. residents are processed by CIEE. For more information contact the Voluntary Service Department at the CIEE.

For those interested in long-term voluntary-service work, the Year Abroad Program sponsored by International Christian Youth Exchange offers people ages 18 to 24 voluntary service opportunities in the fields of health care, education, the environment, construction, et cetera. See page 23 for more information.

Persons interested in volunteering to teach in Poland should contact WorldTeach. For more information see page 26.

STUDY

For information on scholarships, grants, and study programs administered by the Kosciuszko Foundation, write to the Kosciuszko Foundation at 15 East 65th Street, New York, NY 10021. Most of the scholarships are for graduate study only, but there is one exception: study at the summer sessions of the University of Cracow. The deadline for application is January 15.

The following are the educational programs offered by CIEE-member institutions. Consult Appendix I for the addresses of the colleges and universities listed in this section. In addition to the programs below, Stanford University offers a program open only to its own students.

Semester and Academic Year

East European Studies

Council on International Educational Exchange. "Cooperative East and Central European Studies Program." Warsaw. Fall or spring semester. Courses in English at the Warsaw School of Economics. Undergraduates with a 2.75 GPA and six semester-hours in economics, history, or social sciences. Apply by April 10 for fall; November 1 for spring. Contact University Programs Department.

General Studies

American University. "Poland Semester." Poznan. Fall or spring semester. Polish language and liberal arts courses. Second-semester sophomores, juniors, and seniors with 2.75 GPA. Apply six months prior to start of program.

State University of New York at Stony Brook. Warsaw and Wroclaw. Airfare is paid by government grant. Juniors and seniors with one year of Polish or Russian and 3.0 GPA. Apply by April 1.

Polish Language and Culture

University of Massachusetts—Amherst. Poznan. Academic year and semester. Sophomores to graduate students with 3.0 GPA. Apply by January 29 for fall and academic year and September 19 for spring.

Summer

Agriculture

Michigan State University. "Food and Agricultural Systems in Poland." Gdánsk, Warsaw, Cracow. Juniors to graduate students. Apply by April 20.

Economics and Political Science

University of Pennsylvania. "Penn-in-Warsaw." Designed to acquaint students with the political and economic system of Poland, to familarize them with Polish history and culture, and to provide insight into the conditions for doing business with socialist countries. Apply by March 1.

Polish Language and Culture

American Heritage Association. "American Heritage Cultural Summer Program." Wroclaw. No language requirement. Apply by April 15.

State University of New York at Buffalo. Summer program in Polish language and culture. Cracow. Six-week program at Jagiellonian University. Freshmen to graduate students. No language prerequisite, but preference given to those with college-level Polish language studies. Apply by April 1.

University of Connecticut. "Summer Program in Poland." Cracow. Freshmen to seniors. Apply by March 15.

University of Massachusetts—Amherst. Poznan. Sophomores to graduate students with 3.0 GPA. Apply by January 29.

PORTUGAL

Portugal is a treasure house of history. The Portuguese, proud of their rich cultural heritage, have preserved their past and delight in sharing it with visitors. Portugal was once a great seafaring kingdom that spanned the globe—Magellan and Vasco da Gama are two of the many Portuguese explorers who ventured to discover new lands and seas. Portugal now survives on manufacturing, farming, wine production, tourism, and the income sent home by a large population of Portuguese workers in the wealthier countries of Europe.

Throughout Portugal, at every turn, you may find reminders of the country's glorious past, such as royal castles, ancient monuments, and antique *azulejos* (tiles) on walls and buildings. The past of a once-powerful empire is still remembered nostalgically by the people of a country that is now one of the poorest in Europe. Consequently, many people, especially from the countryside, have sought work in other countries, chiefly France, but also in Germany, and Spain. The themes of a seafaring past and a bleak present are mournfully heard throughout the land in *fados*, a singing style that is often compared to the blues. But the nostalgia and melancholy associated with the people of Portugal have not changed their genuine hospitality and their gentleness. The country's many festivals or *festas*—both religious and secular—provide an excellent opportunity to meet the Portuguese people and share their food, wine, and folklore.

Lisbon offers the visitor a change of pace from life in larger European capitals. Its relatively small size encourages its discovery on foot. In this city, as in many others throughout Portugal, the architecture proves to be a feast for the eyes. Ceramic-tiled walls, orange tile roofs, and mosaic sidewalks add structural texture to the pastel stucco buildings.

EUROPE: PORTUGAL

Portugal was the last European power to maintain a hold on a large colonial empire in Africa. After a successful revolution overthrew Portugal's 50-year military regime in 1974 and installed the current democratic government, Portugal finally granted independence to Mozambique, Angola, and its other African colonies. Today, all its formal colonies are gone, with the exception of the tiny enclave of Macao, due to be ceded to China at the end of the century. Yet both the nation's warm people and fascinating points of interest constantly remind visitors of the nation's past greatness—and by implication, its future potential.

—Sandra L. Fontes, Providence, Rhode Island

Official name: Republic of Portugal. **Size:** 36,390 square miles (about the size of Kentucky). **Population:** 10,528,000. **Population density:** 281 inhabitants per square mile. **Capital and largest city:** Lisbon (pop. 2,000,000). **Language:** Portuguese. **Religion:** Roman Catholic. **Per capita income:** US$2,970. **Currency:** Escudo. **Literacy rate:** 83%. **Average daily high/low*:** Lisbon: January, 56°/46°; July, 79°/63°. **Average number of days with precipitation:** Lisbon: January, 9; July, 1.

TRAVEL

Americans will need a valid passport, but a visa is not required for visits of up to 60 days. Sixty-day extensions may be applied for within that time at the Servico de Estranjeiros office. If you plan a stay of more than two months, contact the Embassy of Portugal, 2125 Kalorama Road NW, Washington, DC 20008, for specific requirements.

Getting Around

Portugal is still one of the least expensive countries to visit in Europe and is well worth considering when you plan your itinerary.

Except for express trains between Lisbon and Oporto and between Lisbon and the Algarve, train travel in Portugal is slow. The Intercity buses are faster and more comfortable, although usually a little more expensive than the train.

Eurail passes are valid throughout Portugal (see page 61). Unlimited train passes called Tourist Tickets are available: 13.200 escudos (US$89) for 7 days; 21.050 (US$142) for 14 days; and 30.060 escudos (US$203) for 21 days. The Saver Pass, valid for two people, is also an option; however, two people must always travel together and no change in the original itinerary is permitted.

The Portuguese Youth Hostel Association, Pousadas de Juventude (Rua Andrade Corvo, 46, 1000 Lisbon), has hostels throughout Portugal. The organization also offers a variety of low-cost tours in mainland Portugal as well as in the Azores and Madeira. Included are tours by railroad, bus, bicycle, and foot; also available are seven-day vacation packages featuring a particular activity like archeology, canoeing, pottery, tapestry, windsurfing, or diving.

Especially for Students and Young People

Portugal has two student travel organizations:

- TAGUS-Turismo Juvenil, Praça de Londres 9B, 1000 Lisbon, with branches in Coimbra, Porto, and Albufeira
- ATEJ, Rua Joaquim Antonio de Aguiar 255, 4300 Porto

---

*All temperatures are Fahrenheit.

Both organizations provide travel information, sell discounted train, bus, and plane tickets for students, and operate sightseeing tours.

Holders of the International Student Identity Card receive a discount of up to 20 percent on buses and 50 percent on trains within Portugal as well as discounts on train travel to the rest of Europe. Cardholders also get free admission to more than 30 government museums and a number of shopping discounts (both TAGUS and ATEJ provide a list of stores offering discounts). The International Youth Card is good for discounts on a wide range of accommodations, cultural events, including museums, palaces, and theaters, plus many restaurants, shops and stores, and tours and excursions.

For Further Information

A good guide for the budget traveler is *The Real Guide: Portugal*, available in bookstores for $10.95. Cadogan Guides' *Portugal*, while not concerned exclusively with budget travel, is exceptionally well researched and generally more up to date. Useful information can also be found in *Let's Go: Spain and Portugal*, which also includes a section on Morocco. It's available for $14.95 in most bookstores and at Council Travel offices. Brochures available from the Portuguese National Tourist Office (590 Fifth Avenue, New York, NY 10036) include tourist information, camping guides, and a list of youth hostels.

WORK

For regular employment in Portugal—which is very difficult for a U.S. citizen to obtain—it is necessary to have a work permit, which is obtained by the employer. After application for the permit is approved by the Ministry of Labor, the employee must get the appropriate visa from the Portuguese Consulate (630 Fifth Avenue, Suite 655, New York, NY 10111).

Internships/Traineeships

Two programs offered by members of the Council on International Educational Exchange are listed below.

AIESEC-US. Reciprocal internship program for students in economics, business, finance, marketing, accounting, and computer sciences. See page 18 for more information.

Association for International Practical Training. "IAESTE Trainee Program." On-the-job training for undergraduate and graduate students in technical fields such as engineering, computer sciences, agriculture, architecture, and mathematics. See page 18 for more information.

Voluntary Service

CIEE places young people in voluntary service workcamps in Portugal organized by Turicoop (Rua Pascoal de Melo, 15-1 DTO, 1100 Lisbon), which sponsors two- to three-week workcamps based in small, rural towns. Volunteers, who must be 18 or over, are involved in conservation and archaeological projects. The applications of U.S. residents are processed by CIEE. For more information contact the Voluntary Service Department at the CIEE.

STUDY

The Cultural Counselor at the Embassy of Portugal (2125 Kalorama Road NW, Washington, DC 20008) distributes several fact sheets, including *Information on Study in Portugal* and *Higher Education in Portugal*, a list of universities and general information.

The following is an educational program offered by a CIEE-member institution. Consult Appendix I for the address of the university listed. The American Graduate School of International Management and University of California also have study programs in Portugal; however, these programs are open only to their own students.

Summer

Economics

University of Pennsylvania. "Penn-in-Lisbon." For students interested in economics and international relations. Apply by April 1.

EXPLORING PORTUGUESE CULTURE

Readings

For many years, Portuguese authors were limited by the controlling regime of Antonio de Oliveira Salazar, whose 40-year dictatorship ended in 1974. Much of the literature written immediately after 1974 can be seen as a reaction, direct or indirect, to the repression of this period. Jose Cardoso Pires's mystery novel *Ballad of Dogs' Beach* analyzes the fear that gripped the nation during the Salazar regime. *The Promise*, by Bernando Santereno, also deals with the repression and censorship of this period.

Women novelists have recently brought a new voice to Portuguese literature. A collage of stories, letters, and poems, *New Portuguese Letters: The Three Marias*, by Maria Isabel Barreno, Maria Teresa Horta, and Maria Velho de Costa, is a modern feminist parable based on a seventeenth-century collection of letters. This book became a cause célèbre when it was published in 1972 because its authors were put to trial by the state. *Lemon Verbena* is a novel by one of these authors, Velho de Costa, that explores the role of women in a repressive society.

A couple of other modern Portuguese writers are worthy of note. Jose Saramago came to the fore in the 1980s. His 1982 *Memorial of the Convent* is about the building of a magnificent convent and, like his other novels, combines an acute observation of reality with flights of poetic fancy. Jorge de Sena's collection of well-crafted stories, *By the Rivers of Babylon and Other Stories*, was written between 1946 and 1964; many of the pieces involve Portuguese historical figures. His 1978 novel, *Signs of Fire*, concerns the effects of the Spanish Civil War on Portugal.

SPAIN

Merely mentioning Spain conjures up familiar images, even among those who have never been there: images of spirited bullfights, crowded tapas bars, passionate flamenco dancers, sun-drenched castles, colorful Easter processions. This is the Spain, exotic and romantic, which last year alone drew some 50 million visitors to a country of 36 million people. Those who arrive in quest of Don Quixote's Spain will still find enough of it to satisfy their romantic expectations: from the Altamira cave paintings in Asturias, to the Roman aqueduct in Segovia, the Moorish Alhambra Palace in Granada, the medieval walls of Avila, and the Royal Palace in Madrid, the remains of Spain's rich and glorious past are easy to find.

However, most visitors will also be struck by the ways that many of today's images differ from those featured in the travel brochures. That tradition-bound Spain, which for centuries asserted its uniqueness by proudly declaring that "Europe ends at the Pyrenees," has in recent years transformed itself into one of Europe's most dynamic and rapidly changing countries.

Madrid, the thriving capital, has grown to a population of nearly five million. The city is renowned for the variety and energy of its night life, especially during the spring and summer when *Madrileños* young and old follow an evening at the theater or a restaurant with a stop at one of the many sidewalk cafes well into the early morning hours. Within modern, cosmopolitan Madrid can still be found the more traditional Spanish city with its bullring, Rastro flea market, Prado art museum, and old quarter around the Plaza Mayor. A word of caution: Madrid's heady plunge into modernity has transformed it into one of Europe's most expensive capitals.

The change in Spain has not been confined to Madrid. Barcelona, Madrid's long-time commercial and cultural rival on the Mediterranean coast, thrives as a center of trade and industry and the focus of a resurgent Catalan language and culture. And outside the major cities, television, improved transportation, and economic growth have spread modern consumer culture into traditionally isolated areas.

Much of Spain's ongoing transformation can be traced to the emergence of democracy in 1976 after nearly 40 years of military dictatorship under General Francisco Franco. Today Spain is a constitutional monarchy. Its king, Juan Carlos I, officially has little political authority under the terms of the 1978 constitution; however, he generally is credited with having saved the young democracy in 1981 when he energetically intervened to help put down an attempted coup by dissatisfied military officers. Now regarded as a stable Western-style democracy, Spain officially ended its many years of political isolation from Europe when it joined NATO and the European Community in 1986.

—*Michael Vande Berg, Kalamazoo, Michigan*

Official name: Kingdom of Spain. **Size:** 194,896 square miles (about ¾ the size of Texas). **Population:** 39,623,000. **Population density:** 204 inhabitants per square mile. **Capital and largest city:** Madrid (pop. 3,500,000). **Language:** Spanish, Catalan, Basque, Galician. **Religion:** Roman Catholic. **Per capita income:** US$4,490. **Currency:** Peseta. **Literacy rate:** 97%. **Average daily high/low*:** Barcelona: January, 56°/42°; July, 81°/69°. Madrid: January, 47°/33°; July, 87°/62°. **Average number of days with precipitation:** Barcelona: January, 5; July, 4. Madrid: January, 9; July, 3.

TRAVEL

A passport is required for U.S. citizens going to Spain. A visa is not required for tourists staying up to six months. You may be required to show a nontransferable return plane ticket and adequate means of support. For specific regulations, check with the Spanish Embassy, 2700 19th Street NW, Washington, DC 20009.

Getting Around

Eurail and InterRail passes are valid in Spain (see page 61). However, if you're traveling to Spain by rail, you'll have to change trains at the French border, since most of Spain's railroads are a different gauge than the rest of Europe. Spain welcomes more tourists than any other country in the world, and Spanish trains are especially crowded in summer. Persons with Eurail passes are required to make advance reservations for all long-distance trains and pay supplements on *talgo* (express) trains.

RENFE, the national rail system, sells passes good for unlimited travel in Spain. Eight

---

*All temperatures are Fahrenheit.

days of second-class travel cost about $116 and the price for 15 days is $182. First-class passes cost $159 and $259, respectively. Passes may be purchased in the U.S. but are also available in Spain. The Spain Flexipass, which is good for any 4 days within a 15-day period, costs $83 for second class, $109 for first. RENFE also offers the *Tarjeta Joven* to travelers ages 12 to 26. For 2500 pesetas (US$23) you receive a 50-percent discount on all train trips over 100 km on specially designated "blue days" (roughly three-quarters of the year). All of these passes can be purchased through Council Travel.

A number of different bus companies also provide intercity service in Spain, which cost about the same, or even more than the train. However, along the Cantabrican coast and in the southern region of Spain, buses fill in the gaps in the national rail network, providing more direct and convenient service than that available by rail.

Iberia Airlines has a "Visit Spain" fare which provides unlimited mileage air travel in Spain and to and from the Balearic Islands. The ticket costs $249 for 60 days, $299 if the Canary Islands are included. You must fly Iberia Air to Spain to be eligible for the pass, which must be purchased in the U.S. or Canada.

Passenger boats link Spain's Mediterranean ports with the famed Balearic islands of Mallorca, Menorca, and Ibiza. However, before hopping on a boat, check the airfare; in many cases, going by plane is actually cheaper. Ferries also link Mediterranean ports with Spain's enclaves on the African continent (Ceuta and Melilla) and numerous boats make the short crossing to Morocco across the Strait of Gibraltar.

Bicycling is enjoyable but difficult because rough pavement characterizes most Spanish secondary roads, and mountains crisscross the country. However, bikes may be carried on trains as baggage at no extra charge.

Spain also offers some of Europe's best hiking, with an unusual and highly varied terrain. A good guide for hikers is *Trekking in Spain*, available for $11.95 (plus $1.50 book-rate postage; $3 for first-class) from Lonely Planet Publications, Embarcadero West, 112 Linden Street, Oakland, CA 94607.

"Be sure to take advantage of the siesta. It is a great way to get refreshed and so necessary in order to properly enjoy Spanish night life."
—Nathan Kreie, Princeton, Minnesota

Especially for Students and Young People

Check with TIVE, Spain's student travel bureau, for information on travel, accommodations, and student discounts. It has offices in Madrid (José Ortega y Gasset, 71, 3rd floor, 28006 Madrid) as well as 30 other Spanish cities.

In Spain, holders of the International Student Identity Card can get reduced train and bus tickets for travel from Spain to points around Europe and reduced plane tickets to destinations all over the world. They also receive discounts on TIVE's tours in Madrid and excursions to Salamanca, Toledo, and El Escorial. Cardholders get free admission to state museums, including the Prado, with its unrivaled collections of El Greco, Velásquez, and Goya. The International Youth Card is good for discounts on a variety of accommodations, restaurants, tours, and excursions; it also provides free admission to many museums.

For Further Information

Let's Go: Spain and Portugal contains much useful information for the student traveling on a budget. It includes a section on Morocco and is available for $14.95 in most bookstores and at Council Travel offices. For more detailed information on Spain's less-visited northern regions, get *The Real Guide: Spain* ($12.95) or Cadogan Guides' *Spain* ($15.95).

The National Tourist Office of Spain (665 Fifth Avenue, New York, NY 10022) has brochures describing the various regions of Spain, maps, and publications on camping sites, pensions, and so on. Every city of Spain has its own tourist office where you can get maps, brochures, and help in finding accommodations.

WORK

Getting a Job

According to the Spanish authorities, employers may obtain a work permit for a U.S. citizen only if there are no Spanish applicants for the job. Young people may be able to find summer employment in resort areas, but the pay is very low. The best place to look for au pair jobs and other positions suitable for English speakers is the English-language newspaper, the *Iberian Sun*.

CIEE has developed a pilot program which can assist you in obtaining the necessary permit to work in Spain for up to three months from June 1 to September 1. Participants must secure a prearranged job before leaving the U.S. Though a list of potential employers is provided, CIEE encourages you to utilize any personal contacts you may have for job possibilities. To qualify, you must be at least 18 years of age, a U.S. citizen, and a full-time college or university student with two years of university-level Spanish. Overnight accommodations and an orientation in Madrid are provided. The cost of the program is $150. For further information contact the Work Exchanges Department, CIEE, 205 East 42nd Street, New York, NY 10017.

Internships/Traineeships

Programs sponsored by member organizations of the Council on International Educational Exchange are listed below. In addition, Southwest Texas State University and Moorhead State University sponsor programs open only to students enrolled in those institutions.

AIESEC-US. Reciprocal internship program for students in economics, business, finance, marketing, accounting, and computer sciences. See page 18 for more information.

Association for International Practical Training. "IAESTE Trainee Program." On-the-job training for undergraduate and graduate students in technical fields such as engineering, computer science, agriculture, architecture, and mathematics. See page 18 for more information.

Voluntary Service

CIEE places young people in voluntary service workcamps in Spain that are organized by Servicio Voluntario Internacional (Calle José Ortega y Gassett, 71, E-28006 Madrid). At these summer workcamps, groups of international volunteers work on a variety of projects involving archaeology, forestry, social work, and so on. Applicants must be between 18 and 26 years of age and have some knowledge of Spanish. The average length of service is 15 to 20 days. The applications of U.S. residents are processed by CIEE. For more information contact CIEE's Voluntary Service Department.

For persons interested in longer term voluntary-service work, the Year Abroad Program sponsored by the International Christian Youth Exchange offers persons ages 18 to 24 voluntary service opportunities in the fields of health care, education, the environment, construction, and more. See page 23 for more information.

STUDY

For information on studying in Spain, contact the Education Office of the Spanish Embassy (2700 15th Street NW, Washington, DC 20009) or a consulate in your region. They have a number of useful fact sheets, including *American Programs in Spain*, as well as a book of Spanish language programs entitled *Cursos de Lengua y Cultura para Extranjeros en España*.

Study programs offered by CIEE-member institutions are described below. Consult Appendix I for the addresses of the colleges and universities listed in this section. In addition to the programs below, the American Graduate School of International Management, California State University, Cornell University, New York University, Pennsylvania State University, the University of California, and the University of Notre Dame offer study-abroad programs open only to their own students.

Semester and Academic Year

Business Administration

Council on International Educational Exchange. "Business & Society Program." Seville. Fall or spring semester. Sophomores to graduate students (not for graduate credit) with advanced Spanish, 2.75 GPA, and previous courses in business or economics. Apply by October 15 for spring and April 1 for fall. Contact University Programs Department.

Experiment in International Living/School for International Training. "College Semester Abroad." Intensive language, international business seminar and internship, homestay, and educational travel. Sophomores to seniors with 2.5 GPA and two years of college Spanish. Apply by October 31 for spring; May 31 for fall.

General Studies

Alma College. "Program of Studies in Spain." Madrid or Segovia. Sophomores, juniors, and seniors with 2.5 GPA. Courses in language, literature, culture, and art history. All courses taught in Spanish. Homestays and excursions. No language prerequisite for Madrid. Two years of Spanish required for Segovia. Apply by June 15 for fall; October 15 for winter.

Brethren Colleges Abroad. University of Barcelona. Intensive language, study tour to central or southern Spain, plus day excursions. Semester or academic year. Juniors and seniors with two years of college Spanish and 3.0 GPA. Rollover acceptance cut off by April 15 for fall and year; November 1 for spring.

Council on International Educational Exchange.
"Language and Area Studies Program." Alicante. Fall or spring semester. Sophomores to graduate students (not for graduate credit) with one semester of college Spanish. Apply by April 1 for fall and October 15 for spring. Contact University Programs Department. "Liberal Arts Program." Seville. Semester or academic year. Sophomores to graduate students (not for graduate credit) with five semesters of college Spanish. Apply by April 1 for fall and academic year and October 15 for spring. Contact University Programs Department.

Experiment in International Living/School for International Training. "College Semester Abroad." Granada, with excursions to Madrid, Seville, and Cordoba. Spring or fall semester. Intensive language, life, and culture seminar, village stay, field-study methods seminar, independent-study project, and homestay. Sophomores to seniors with 2.5 GPA and two years of college Spanish. Apply by May 15 for fall and October 15 for spring.

Indiana University. "Overseas Study in Madrid." Academic year. Study at University of Madrid. Limited to students at Indiana, Purdue, and the University of Wisconsin. Juniors and seniors with two years of Spanish and 3.0 GPA. Apply by first week of November.

International Student Exchange Program. Direct reciprocal exchange between U.S. universities and institutions in Madrid and Santiago de Compostela. Academic year. Full curriculum options. Open only to students at ISEP-member institutions.

Lake Erie College. Salamanca. Academic year or semester. Juniors and seniors with intermediate Spanish and 2.5 GPA. Apply by June 1 or October 1.

Marquette University. "Marquette University Study Center at the University of Madrid." Semester or academic year. Sophomores, juniors, and seniors with 3.0 GPA and one college Spanish course beyond intermediate level. Apply by May 15 for fall and November 30 for spring. Contact: Director, Madrid Study Center, Marquette University, Milwaukee, WI 53233.

New York University. "NYU in Spain." Madrid. Semester or academic year. Undergraduate program and M.A. programs in Hispanic literature and Hispanic civilization. Juniors and graduate students. Intermediate Spanish and 3.0 GPA required for undergraduates. Major in Spanish required for M.A. program. Apply by May for fall and by November for spring. Contact: NYU in Spain, 19 University Place, Room 409, New York, NY 10003; (212) 998-8760.

Northern Illinois University. "Academic Internships in Madrid." Fall semester. Students take two courses plus internship. Wide range of internships available for own students; more limited selection for others. Sophomores, juniors, and seniors with 3.0 GPA. Apply by April 4.

Ohio State University. "Study in Spain: The Toledo Program." Semester or academic year. Juniors and seniors with one and a half years of Spanish. Open only to Ohio residents and students at Ohio schools. Apply by June 1 for fall and November 1 for spring.

Portland State University. "ISIS Program in Spain." Barcelona. Fall or spring semester. Courses offered by Institute for Social and International Studies. Language of instruction is English. Juniors, seniors, and graduate students with 3.0 GPA. Apply 12 weeks prior to beginning of semester.

Purdue University. "Overseas Study in Madrid." See program listing under Indiana University.

Rutgers University. "Junior Year in Spain." Valencia and Madrid. Juniors with two years of college Spanish and a B average. Apply by March 1.

St. Lawrence University. "Spain Year Program." Academic year in Madrid with orientation in Salamanca and one-month village homestay. Sophomores, juniors, and seniors with intermediate college Spanish and 2.8 GPA. Apply by February 20.

Skidmore College. "Junior Year Abroad." Semester or academic year. Juniors and seniors with intermediate proficiency for single semester, third-year level for academic year; 3.0 GPA required. Apply by October 15 for spring and February 15 for fall.

Southern Methodist University. "SMU-in-Spain." Madrid. Semester or academic year. Liberal arts studies focused on the Spanish experience; courses in international business also available. Sophomores, juniors, and seniors with one year of college Spanish. October 15 for spring and March 15 for fall.

State University of New York at Cortland. Salamanca. Semester or academic year. Sophomores to seniors with two years of college Spanish and 2.5 GPA in major. Apply by March 1.

State University of New York at Oswego. "Oswego Barcelona Program." Academic year. Estudios Hispanicos at the University of Barcelona. Sophomores to graduate students with 2.5 GPA and intermediate Spanish. Apply by April 1.

Syracuse University. "Syracuse University in Madrid." Fall or spring semester. Sophomores, juniors, and seniors with 3.0 GPA. Apply by March 15 for fall and October 15 for spring.

Tufts University. "Tufts in Madrid." Juniors with two years college Spanish and 3.0 GPA. Apply by February 1.

University of Connecticut. "Study Abroad Program at the University of Granada." Fall or spring semester. Sophomores to juniors with five semesters of college Spanish. Apply by October 15 for spring; March 15 for fall.

University of La Verne. "Semester/Year in Spain." See listing under Brethren Colleges Abroad.

University of Minnesota. "International Program in Toledo." Freshman to graduate students and adults with two years of college Spanish. Apply by July 15 for fall and December 1 for spring.

University of North Carolina—Chapel Hill. "UNC Year at Seville." Semester or academic year. Juniors and seniors with two years of college Spanish and 2.5 GPA. Apply by March 15 for fall and October 15 for spring.

University of Oregon. "Study in Seville." Winter and spring quarters. Sophomores, juniors, and seniors with two years of college Spanish and 3.0 GPA. Apply by May 1.

University of Virginia. "Hispanic Studies Program." Spring, fall, or summer. High-school graduates to graduate students with intermediate Spanish. Apply by June 15 for fall; November 1 for spring; April 15 for summer.

University of Wisconsin—Madison. Madrid. Academic year. Open to juniors and seniors at Indiana, Purdue, and the University of Wisconsin with five semesters of Spanish and 3.0 GPA. Apply by November 15.

University of Wisconsin—Platteville. "Seville Study Center." Semester or academic year. Study at Spanish-American Institute. Spanish language and literature, liberal arts, and international business. Courses taught in English and Spanish. Sophomores, juniors, and seniors with 2.5 GPA. Apply by April 30 for fall and October 20 for spring.

Social Science

American Heritage Association. ISIS at Barcelona. Fall, winter, spring, or summer quarters. Social sciences and language. Sophomores to graduate students with 3.0 GPA. No language prerequisite. Apply by July 1 for fall; November 1 for winter; February 1 for spring; May 1 for summer.

American University. "Madrid Semester." Spring semester. Spanish politics, economics, and foreign policy. Internships with multinationals. Juniors and seniors with two years of college Spanish and 2.75 GPA. Apply six months prior to start of program.

Spanish Language and Culture

Adventist Colleges Abroad. Sagunto. Open only to students at Adventist Colleges Abroad consortium institutions. Academic year or quarter. Freshman to seniors with 3.0 GPA in Spanish and 2.5 overall GPA. Apply sixty days before beginning of academic term.

Boston University. Madrid. Academic year or semester. Intensive Spanish language, literature, and civilization. Homestays. Sophomores to seniors with 3.0 GPA in major and one semester college Spanish (five semesters for advanced course). Apply by March 15 for year and fall; October 15 for spring.

Brigham Young University. "BYU Study Abroad." Madrid. Spring term. Sophomores, juniors, and seniors. Some Spanish required. Apply by February 1.

Central University of Iowa. "Central College Spanish Program." Granada. Semester or academic year. Sophomores, juniors, and seniors with intermediate-level Spanish and 2.5 GPA (3.0 in Spanish). Apply by October 15 for spring; March 15 for fall.

Council on International Educational Exchange. "Language & Society Program." Seville. Fall or spring semester. Sophomores to graduate students (not for graduate credit) with three to four semesters of college Spanish and 2.75 GPA. Apply by October 15 for spring and April 1 for fall. Contact University Programs Department.

Davidson College. "Spring Semester in Spain." Madrid. Spring semester, odd-numbered years only. Freshman, sophomores, and juniors with intermediate Spanish and 2.75 GPA. Apply by October 1.

Experiment in International Living/School for International Training. "College Semester Abroad—Language Immersion." Fall or spring semester. Intensive language immersion, Spanish life and culture, homestay, village stay, and excursions. No language prerequisite. Sophomores to seniors with 2.5 GPA. Apply by October 31 for spring; May 31 for fall.

Heidelberg College. "The Center for Cross-Cultural Study." Seville. Semester or academic year. Sophomores to graduate students with intermediate college Spanish and 3.0 GPA. Apply by May 15 for fall and November 15 for spring. Contact American Secretary, Center for Cross-Cultural Study, 219 Strong Street, Amherst, MA 01002; (413) 549-4543.

Kalamazoo College. "Kalamazoo College in Madrid." Fall and winter quarter (September 15–February 15). Juniors and seniors with 15 quarter-hours in Spanish and 3.0 GPA. Apply by May 1.

Michigan State University. "Spanish Language, Literature, and Culture in Caceres." Spring quarter. Sophomores, juniors, and seniors with two years of Spanish. Apply by February 3.

Middlebury College. Madrid. Sophomores to graduate students fluent in Spanish. Rolling admissions.

North Carolina State University. "Semester in Spain." Santander. Fall semester. Sophomores to graduate students with four semesters of Spanish and 2.5 GPA overall and in Spanish. Apply by March 15.

State University of New York at Albany. Madrid. Semester or academic year. Juniors and seniors with 2.8 GPA and more than two years of college Spanish; advanced courses in language or literature desirable. Apply by March 15; November 1 for spring.

State University of New York at Oswego. "Oswego Barcelona Program." Estudios Hispanicos at the University of Barcelona. Academic year. Sophomores to graduate students with 2.5 GPA and intermediate Spanish. Apply by April 1.

Stetson University. Madrid. Semester or academic year. Sophomores, juniors, and seniors with 2.5 GPA (3.0 in major). Apply by March 1 for fall and October 15 for spring.

University of Massachusetts—Amherst. Oviedo. Academic year and semester. Students with four semesters of college Spanish and a 2.75 GPA. Apply by April 1 for fall and academic year, November 1 for spring.

University of Toledo. "International Program of Spanish Language, Latin American and European Studies and Liberal Arts." In conjunction with the Instituto Jose Ortega y Gasset in Toledo. Language and liberal arts taught in Spanish. Includes excursions and cultural activities. High school graduates through graduate students. Apply by May 15 for summer; August 1 for fall; December 15 for spring.

University System of Georgia/Augusta College.
"Semester/Year Study in Spain." Seville. Undergraduate and graduate students with one year of Spanish and 2.5 overall GPA (3.0 in Spanish). Apply three months prior to beginning of term.

Summer

Art History

Syracuse University. "Azahar." Toledo. Art and architecture of Islam and the Reconquista. Freshmen to graduate students. Apply by March 15.

General Studies

Alma College. "Program of Studies in Spain." Madrid or Segovia. Homestays and excursions. Sophomores to seniors with 2.5 GPA. No language prerequisite for Madrid. One year of Spanish required for Segovia. Apply by March 15.

New York University. "NYU in Spain." Salamanca. Undergraduate and graduate program. Elementary Spanish required for undergraduates; major in Spanish or equivalent required for graduate students. Apply by May. Contact: NYU in Spain, 19 University Place, Room 409, New York, NY 10003; (212) 998-8760.

Portland State University. "ISIS in Spain." Barcelona. Four-week program in international studies. Courses offered by the Institute for Social and International Studies. Juniors to graduate students with 3.0 GPA. Apply by May 1.

Rollins College. Madrid. "Verano Español." High-school graduates, college students, and teachers with two years of college Spanish. Apply by March 15.

Political Science

Syracuse University. "Spanish Politics and Culture." Madrid with field trips to Toledo, San Sebastian, and Barcelona. Apply by March 15.

Spanish Language and Culture

Boston University. "Summer Program in Madrid." Choice of courses in Spanish language, literature, and culture. Internships available for advanced students. Local excursions and field trip to southern Spain. Sophomores to seniors with 3.0 GPA in major and two semesters of college Spanish. Apply by April 1.

Central Washington University. León. Four-week program. Sophomores, juniors, seniors, and teachers. One year of Spanish required. Apply by June 15.

Council on International Educational Exchange. "The Spanish Mediterranean: Language and Area Studies." Alicante. 2.5 GPA. No language requirement. Apply by March 15. Contact University Programs Department.

Experiment in International Living/School for International Training. "Summer Academic Study Abroad." Granada, with excursions to Madrid, Seville, and Cordoba. Intensive language and life and culture seminar. Freshmen to seniors. Apply by March 15.

Indiana University. "Summer Study in Salamanca." Spanish language and culture. Freshmen to seniors 3.0 GPA and five semesters of college Spanish. Apply by February 15.

Michigan State University. "Spanish Language, Literature and Culture in Denia." Sophomores, juniors, and seniors with two years of college Spanish. Apply by April 20.

Ohio State University. "Study in Spain: The Toledo Program." Juniors and seniors with one and a half years of Spanish. Open only to Ohio residents and students at Ohio schools. Apply by April 1.

Rutgers University. "Summer Study in Spain/Portugal." Salamanca, Spain and Coimbra, Portugal. Spanish language study. High school graduates to graduate students and others with intermediate Spanish. Apply by March 1.

State University of New York at Buffalo. "Programa de Estudios Hispanicos." Five-week program at the University of Salamanca. Sophomores to graduate students with one year of college Spanish. Apply by March 15. Contact International Education Services, 409 Capen Hall, Buffalo, NY 14260; (716) 636-2258.

State University of New York at Oswego. Madrid. Freshman to seniors. Apply by April 1.

University of Alabama. "Academic Summer Program in Spain." Pamplona, with tour to Madrid and other cities. Spanish language, civilization, and literature. Freshmen to graduate students with four semesters of college Spanish. Apply by April 1.

University of Arkansas at Little Rock. "Summer in Spain." Freshmen to seniors. Two semesters of Spanish required. Apply by February 28.

University of Louisville. "Spanish Language and Culture in Segovia." Freshmen to graduate students with background in Spanish. Apply by April 30.

University of Kansas. Barcelona and Madrid. Undergraduates with two semesters of college Spanish. Apply by February 15.

University of Maryland. "Summer in Madrid." Sophomores to seniors with two years of college Spanish and 3.0 GPA. Apply by March 1.

University of Massachusetts—Amherst. "Summer Program in Spain." Salamanca. Juniors to graduate students with three years of college Spanish. Apply by April 6.

University of Minnesota.
"Quincentennial Summer Program for Teachers of Spanish." Open to graduate students and teachers with intermediate Spanish proficiency as defined by ACTFL guidelines. Apply by April 15.
"International Program in Toledo." Freshman to graduate students and adults with one year of college Spanish. Apply by April 15.

University of Pennsylvania. "Penn-in-Salamanca." Provides an intensive introduction to the many facets of the Spanish language and culture. Apply by April 1.

University of Utah. "Salamanca Spanish Language Program." Four weeks of Spanish language study preceded by two weeks of travel study in Europe. Freshman to graduate students and others. One or two quarters of college Spanish or the equivalent is recommended. Apply by March 1.

University System of Georgia/West Georgia College.
Salamanca. Graduates and undergraduates with one year of college Spanish and 2.5 overall GPA (3.0 in Spanish). Apply by April 1.

EXPLORING SPANISH CULTURE

Readings

Federico García Lorca is the leading playwright of twentieth-century Spain. Lorca's dramatic works, written in verse, delve deeply into Spanish customs and traditions. *Blood Wedding* (1933) deals with love that defies village tradition and leads to an inescapably tragic end. *The House of Bernarda Alba* (1936) tells of the conflict between a domineering mother and her five daughters, who find themselves imprisoned by Spanish traditions and beliefs.

Camilo José Cela's *The Hive* was banned in Spain upon publication in 1951. It depicts the suffering post–Civil War nation and its disillusioned people. Life in Madrid is portrayed as brutal, hungry, and senseless. In *Journey to the Alcarría* (1948), Cela draws upon personal experience while writing about travels through the rural countryside. Cela was awarded the Nobel prize for literature in 1989.

More recent views of Spain are presented by a variety of contemporary authors. *The Heliotrope Wall and Other Stories* (1961), by Ana Maria Matute, is a collection of her best stories, in which the theme of a rural childhood in Spain is rendered in the style that has become known as "magical realism." In *The Countryside of Nijar* (1960), Juan Goytisolo writes two novels of travels to Andalusia, and in his *Forbidden Territory: Memoirs, 1931–1956*, a victim of the Franco regime fights his way out of a cultural and intellectual wasteland. *Marks of Identity* (1966) is Goytisolo's autobiography. *Five Hours with Mario* (1966), by Miguel Delibes, depicts the troubled marriage of a politically active novelist and his comfortably middle-class Francoist wife. In Juan Benet's *Return to Region* (1967), the mythical Region represents all that is paradoxical and mysterious about Spain. Benet depicts Spain after the war as a decaying corpse that is deteriorating slowly and painfully. Finally, Carmen Martin Gaite's *The Back Room* (1983) provides a portrait of the lives of women in Spain.

The traditions, excitement, and struggles of Spain have attracted a number of noted American and British writers. Hemingway's *The Sun Also Rises* (1926), the story of a group of expatriates in Pamplona for the annual running of the bulls, blends passion and excitement with the violence of bullfighting. George Orwell's *Homage to Catalonia* (1952) deals with the heavy and often savage fighting that took place in the northeastern corner of the country during the Spanish Civil War. James Michener's nonfiction work *Iberia* (1968) provides an insightful portrait of Spain during the Franco era.

Films

The films of pre–Civil War Spain were, for the most part, popular comedies often based on folkloric themes and romantic dramas marked by a strong Catholic influence. This trend continued after Franco's coming to power in 1936, but with a much heavier dose of official ideology as government censorship became widespread. Films celebrating nationalism, patriotism, and national heroics were the norm until filmmakers such as Juan Antonio Bardem, with *Death of a Cyclist* (1955) and *Calle Mayor* (1956), and Luís Buñuel in *Viridiana* (1961) and *Tristana* (1970), began to obliquely criticize Spanish society and government. Only since Franco's death in 1976 have filmmakers been free to delve into themes of Spanish society and government without fear of censorship.

Among the best-known contemporary filmmakers of Spain is Carlos Saura, whose films range from the *Garden of Delights* (1970), a satire of Spanish society and human venality to *Blood Wedding* (1981), a filmed version of Lorca's play told without any dialogue—only music and flamenco ballet. Saura's latest film, *Ay Carmela!*, is the story of a vaudeville act that entertained the troops during the Civil War. Another noteworthy contemporary Spanish filmmaker is Victor Erice; in *The Spirit of the Beehive* (1973) he explores a child's world of reality and imagination.

The years since Franco's death have produced a whole series of raucous, humorous investigations of changing Spanish social and sexual norms. Best known of these in the U.S. are the films of Pedro Almodóvar, *Matador* (1986), *Law of Desire* (1987), *Women on the Verge of a Nervous Breakdown* (1988), and *Tie Me Up, Tie Me Down!* (1990).

SWEDEN

Sweden, the largest, most populous, and most industrialized of the Scandinavian nations, is also a land of forests, farms, and lakes. Frequently cited as the model social-welfare state, this constitutional monarchy enjoys one of the highest standards of living in the world. It is highly regarded as a leader in urban design, economic planning, and social engineering. As a country and as an economy, Sweden functions as well as any in the world.

Because of its size, resources, and geography, and traditionally strong monarchy, Sweden has almost always been in a position of relative political and economic dominance, vis-à-vis the other Scandinavian countries. Only Denmark, for periods in the 16th and 17th centuries, has threatened this hegemony. Three hundred years ago, Sweden was regarded as warlike, and Swedish armies rampaged abroad. But the glamor of foreign exploits and a Nordic empire greatly diminished throughout the 18th century. By the beginning of the 19th century it had lost all of its Baltic possessions, including Finland. In 1905, Norway declared its independence, establishing Swedish borders where they are today. Sweden has pursued a neutral foreign policy since the early 19th century, which kept it out of both world wars. Instead, Sweden has been a major force for international peace and disarmament, working both unilaterally and within the framework of the United Nations. It frequently serves as a mediator of international conflicts.

Parliamentary democracy combined with the rise of industrialism in the late 19th century to establish "the middle way" of the modern Swedish welfare state—a combination of humane social justice, equitable wealth distribution, respect for individual liberties, and a degree of economic planning between labor and industry. Swedish efficiency, energy, and organization created major triumphs during the 1950s and 1960s. Ninety-three percent of Swedish corporations are privately owned and nearly half of its production is exported to foreign markets. Unemployment runs below two percent. Over the past decade it has become one of the world's leaders in electronics and high technology. Sweden is also known as a pioneer in "workplace democracy."

This affluent society, however, is now being somewhat shaken by the same economic crisis that has struck the rest of Western Europe. Additionally, Swedes have begun to question the degree to which the government's social policy should be involved in all aspects of life, cradle-to-grave, as well as the huge tax burden necessary to finance such involvement. One finds, especially among young Swedes, an increasing skepticism over the ability of the politicians and the social experts to solve all human problems through national policies, however well intentioned. The debate rages over how to find a new "middle way" that will balance fundamental social benefits and securities against private freedoms and responsibilities.

Sweden offers some of the best urban sophistication (especially in Stockholm, the most urbane and opulent of the Nordic capitals), plus the rural charm of an old and rustic countryside, with its villages, customs, and crafts largely intact, plus spacious tracts of some of the last true wilderness remaining in Europe. Moreover, travel from one corner to another is made possible by convenient air routes, extensive railways, modern and safe highways—or, for the recreational tourist, boating canals and biking, hiking, and skiing trails. Visitors will find a welcome everywhere, as well as the engaging informality and cheerful efficiency that are the envy of many nations.

—*William W. Hoffa, Amherst, Massachusetts*

Official name Kingdom of Sweden. **Size:** 173,731 square miles (slightly larger than California). **Population:** 8,407,000. **Population density:** 48 inhabitants per square mile. **Capital and largest city:** Stockholm (pop. 663,000). **Language:** Swedish. **Religion:** Lutheran. **Per capita income:** US$11,783. **Currency:** Krona. **Literacy rate:** 99%. **Average daily high/low*:** Stockholm, January, 30°/13°; July, 71°/57°. **Average number of days with precipitation:** January, 8; July, 9.

TRAVEL

U.S. citizens traveling to Sweden will need a passport. Visas are not required for stays of up to three months, a period that begins as soon as one enters the Scandinavian region (Sweden, Norway, and Denmark). Check with the Embassy of Sweden, 600 New Hampshire Avenue NW, Washington, DC 20037, for specific requirements.

Getting Around

Travelers flying SAS round-trip to the Scandinavian countries of Sweden, Norway, and Denmark are eligible for SAS's Visit Scandinavia fare. The special fare allows the

---

*All temperatures are Fahrenheit.

purchase of up to six discounted flight coupons for travel within the three countries. The coupons, which cost from $80 for one flight to $420 for six flights, must be purchased in the U.S. before departure and must be used within three months of arrival in Scandinavia. Normally valid in summer only, the 1991 ticket has been extended until December 31. It can be used on any of the three Scandinavian airlines: Danair, Linjeflyg, and SAS (excluding flights to the Faroe Islands and Greenland).

The Swedish rail network serves all of southern Sweden and much of the north, even crossing the Arctic Circle. However, trains are expensive. If you can, take advantage of "red departure" tickets, half-price one-way fares valid during certain hours. Eurail passes of all types are valid throughout Sweden. However, those planning to travel extensively in Scandinavia should consider the following options:

- The ScanRail Pass is valid for travel on the state railway systems of Denmark, Finland, Norway, and Sweden on a certain number of days within a fixed period of time. For example, one may travel on any 14 days within one month for $499 first class and $349 second class. ScanRail also allows free passage on a number of ferry lines. For information and reservations, contact Council Travel or Rail Europe (800-848-7245).
- The Nordturist Ticket allows for 21 days of free travel on the state railway systems of the above-mentioned countries, including certain ferries. It's also good for a 50-percent discount on the Hirtshals-Hjörring private railway as well as other ferry lines and bus routes. This pass can only be bought in Scandinavia. In 1990, for youths ages 12 to 25 traveling second class, it cost approximately $200.

Especially for Students and Young People

Check with SFS-RESOR, Sweden's student travel bureau, for information on travel and student discounts in Sweden. In addition to the main office (Kungsgatan 4, 111 43 Stockholm), it has offices in Göteburg and Lund. Holders of the International Student Identity Card get discounts on plane and train travel from Sweden to destinations around the world. The International Youth Card is good for discounts on limited accommodations, museums, and restaurants.

Meet the People

Friends Overseas is an American-Scandinavian people-to-people program that helps put travelers in touch with Scandinavians who share similar interests. The service is offered to families and groups as well as single travelers. For further information, send a stamped, self-addressed, business-size envelope to Friends Overseas, 68-04 Dartmouth Street, Forest Hills, NY 11375.

For Further Information

A number of publications geared to the student or budget traveler can be obtained from the Swedish Tourist Board (655 Third Avenue, New York, NY 10017) including information on camping, hiking, and youth hostels, as well as maps and a calendar of events. One of the best general guidebooks to Sweden and the entire region is *The Real Guide: Scandinavia*, available in bookstores for $14.95.

WORK

In order to work full-time in Sweden on a long-term basis, you will need to obtain a work permit before entering the country. To be eligible for a permit, you will have to show written proof that your job and living accommodations in Sweden have already been arranged. For more information, contact the Embassy of Sweden (600 New Hampshire Avenue NW, Washington, DC 20037) for a copy of *Employment and Residency in Sweden*. The American Scandinavian Foundation, (Exchange Division, 725 Park Avenue, New York, NY 10021) can also assist Americans under the age of 30 with obtaining the requisite permit.

Internships/Traineeships

Programs offered by members of the Council on International Educational Exchange are listed below.

AIESEC-US. Reciprocal internship program for students in economics, business, finance, marketing, accounting, and computer science. See page 18 for more information.

Association for International Practical Training. "IAESTE Trainee Program." On-the-job training for undergraduate and graduate students in technical fields such as engineering, computer science, agriculture, architecture, and mathematics. See page 18 for more information.

In addition, the American Scandinavian Foundation sponsors a program that provides summer training assignments for full-time students majoring in engineering, computer science, horticulture, agriculture, forestry, and chemistry, among others. The deadline for application is December 15. Note, however: Traineeships are not available in teaching, social work, or medically related fields. Contact the American Scandinavian Foundation, Exchange Division, 725 Park Avenue, New York, NY 10021.

STUDY

The Swedish Information Service (One Dag Hammarskjold Plaza, New York, NY 10017) distributes a number of brochures including *Studying in Sweden* and *Summer Opportunities in Sweden*. The service also provides numerous fact sheets ranging in subject from education to Swedish foreign policy and social issues. Ask for their *Fact Sheets on Sweden* order form. The Exchange Division of the American Scandinavian Foundation (725 Park Avenue, New York, NY 10021) publishes *Study in Scandinavia*, which includes a listing of English-language programs offered in Sweden during the academic year and summer.

Following are the study programs offered by CIEE-member institutions. Consult Appendix I for the addresses of the colleges and universities listed in this section. In addition to the programs below, the American Graduate School of International Management, California State University, and the University of California offer programs open only to their own students.

Semester and Academic Year

Environmental Sciences

Scandinavian Seminar. "Semester Program on Nordic and Global Issues." Trosa and/or other locations. Spring only. Focus on global issues (e.g., global resources/ecology, sustainable development) from a Nordic perspective. Coursework in English. Field trips. Undergraduate credit through the University of Massachusetts—Amherst. Sophomores to graduate students and others. Apply by October 1.

General Studies

International Student Exchange Program. Direct reciprocal exchange between U.S. universities and Växjö University. Semester or academic year. Full curriculum options. Open only to students at ISEP-member institutions.

Scandinavian Seminar. "College Year in Sweden." Individual placement in Swedish folk colleges throughout Sweden. Swedish language and cultural immersion with emphasis on liberal arts. Undergraduate credit granted through the University of Massachusetts—Amherst. Sophomores to graduate students and others. Apply by April 1.

University of Oregon. "University of Oregon—University of Linkøping Exchange." Fall semester or academic year. Juniors and seniors with two years of college Swedish and 2.75 GPA. Apply by March 1.

University of Wisconsin—Madison. Linkøping. Academic year or fall semester. Juniors to graduate students with four semesters of college Swedish and 3.0 GPA. Apply by February 15.

Summer

Marketing

Michigan State University. "Packaging in Sweden." Lund. Juniors and seniors. Apply by April 20.

EXPLORING SWEDISH CULTURE

Films

Swedish film is closely related to Swedish theater. Many filmmakers, including Ingmar Bergman, have worked regularly in the theater, and many traditional themes of Swedish theater have been explored in their movies. Bergman's films, for example, are usually stark psychological portraits of individuals grappling with issues of death, religion, sexuality, and repression. The weightiness of their intellectual content is complemented by their cinematography, which often displays an intensely spare, barren atmosphere. *Persona* (1967) is one of Bergman's best-known works. It is the story of two women, a nurse and her mentally ill patient, who begin to identify with each other—a little too closely. Other films include *Wild Strawberries* (1957) and *Fanny and Alexander* (1983).

My Life as a Dog (1987), a more recent film directed by Lässe Hälstrom, is a charming tale of a young boy learning to cope with his mother's illness, and his own propensity for getting in trouble, while staying with relatives in the idyllic Swedish countryside. The film is funny, sad, and poignant without being cloying.

SWITZERLAND

Anyone visiting Switzerland for the first time will be amazed at the cleanliness and prosperity that greets one upon arrival in Zurich, Basel, or Geneva. Over the course of the last century, the Swiss have been able to transform a poor federation of small agricultural cantons into one of the world's wealthiest and most stable countries.

Switzerland is a land of exceptional natural beauty—mountain peaks, Alpine skiing resorts, and quaint villages alternate with green well-kept meadows. But there is another Switzerland as well, the Switzerland of modern banks and investment houses connected to other world financial capitals via computers and satellite; of highly efficient rail, highway, and air networks; of cities with a healthy blend of old-world charm and high-tech convenience. Where else in the world can one walk into a 24-hour convenience center to change currencies, make account transfers, and even buy gold bullion and coins—all at the push of a button?

It is difficult to find any evidence of poverty in Switzerland. Everyone seems to work; at last count the unemployment rate was less than one percent. The major industries are tourism, watchmaking, precision instruments, banking, and agriculture. Much of the unskilled labor is provided by foreigners who are allowed to work in Switzerland for limited periods of time.

The young Swiss who have grown up in this idyllic land seem to live a charmed life. Fluent in many languages, they benefit from Switzerland's role as the crossroads of Europe. They eat French food, wear Italian clothes, drive German cars, and are fed a steady diet of American and British rock music through video programs broadcast via satellite. Unfortunately, drug abuse also seems to flourish in affluent countries like Switzerland.

There is no "Swiss" language; depending on the region of the country, the people speak French, German, or Italian as their native language. The majority speaks German—actually a dialect called Schweizerdeutsch, which is difficult for foreigners, even Germans, to understand. However, most Swiss speak more than one language, and many speak English. The Swiss living in the cantons bordering on France are the exception; many of them have adopted the French custom of not really learning any language other than French.

Divided by language and split by geography, it's rather amazing that the country of Switzerland, founded in 1291, exists at all. The world's oldest continuous democracy, Switzerland has a federal system of government much like the United States, with most of the actual decision-making power in the hands of the 23 cantons. And, despite its peace-loving image, Switzerland maintains an enormous army for a country of its size; the Swiss see military power as a necessary part of their country's policy of strict neutrality which since 1815 has kept it at peace with its more powerful and often belligerent neighbors.

—*Randy Epping, Zurich, Switzerland*

Official name: Swiss Confederation. **Size:** 15,941 square miles (about the size of Hawaii). **Population:** 6,628,000. **Population density:** 406 inhabitants per square mile. **Capital:** Bern (pop. 136,000). **Largest city:** Zurich (pop. 346,000). **Language:** German, French, Italian. **Religion:** Roman Catholic, Protestant. **Per capita income:** US$26,309. **Currency:** Swiss franc. **Literacy rate:** 99%. **Average daily high/low*:** Geneva: January, 39°/29°; July, 77°/58°. Zurich: January, 36°/26°; July, 76°/56°. **Average number of days with precipitation:** Geneva: January, 10; July, 9. Zurich: January, 11; July, 15.

TRAVEL

U.S. citizens need a passport for travel to Switzerland. A visa is not required for stays of up to three months. For specific requirements, check with the Embassy of Switzerland, 2900 Cathedral Avenue NW, Washington, DC 20008.

---

*All temperatures are Fahrenheit.

Getting Around

Switzerland has an excellent national railway network connecting government and private lines. Eurail and InterRail passes are valid only on the government railroads (see page 61). Travel by train is quite expensive in Switzerland but persons under 26 can purchase the Half-Fare Travel Card. This gives the holder a 50-percent reduction on all trips on both government and private railways in Switzerland; the card costs SFr110 (about $73) for one year. The Half-Fare Travel Card is also available for one month at a cost of SFr75 (about $50). In addition, a six-day unlimited Youthpass costs SFr150 (about $99). There is also a Swisspass which allows unlimited travel on the railway network (including private railroads), lake steamers, and postal buses. It also gives 25- to 50-percent discounts on important mountain cog and cable lines—such as Jungfrau, Matterhorn, and Pilatus. The pass can be purchased in the U.S. through Council Travel or through Rail Europe (800-345-1990). For second-class travel, the pass is available for approximately $125 for 4 days, $155 for 8 days, $180 for 15 days, and $250 for one month. Comparable first-class passes cost approximately $190, $225, $270, and $365, respectively. The Swiss Flexipass is valid for any 3 days in a 15-day period. It is available in second class for approximately $120 and in first class for $190. For further details contact the Swiss National Tourist Office (608 Fifth Avenue, New York, NY 10020).

One of the most spectacular ways to see Switzerland's natural beauty is to hike its alpine trails. Berghotels or Auberges de montagne are rustic mountain guesthouses—popular with both the Swiss and foreigners—that provide hikers with food to eat and a place to stay in scenic spots far from the nearest road or railway. For more information, get a copy of *Walking Switzerland*, by Marcia and Philip Lieberman, available for $12.95 (plus $2 shipping and handling) from Mountaineers Books, 1011 Klickitat Way, Suite 107, Seattle, WA 98134.

"In Switzerland, the way of life is slower paced, more conservative. It takes time to get used to it. Make every effort to understand the culture. The more you show your understanding, the more open the people will be."
—Robert Merino, Stockton, California

Especially for Students and Young People

SSR-Reisen is the student travel bureau and issuer of the International Student Identity Card in Switzerland. You can contact the organization at Bäckerstrasse 52, 8004 Zurich. In addition, it has 16 offices around Switzerland where you can get international plane and train tickets, book accommodations, and obtain travel information. SSR operates a student hotel in Lucerne and also offers river rafting and canoeing trips.

SSR-Reisen also distributes the *National Student Discount Directory*. Students with the International Student Identity Card can get discounts on international plane and train fares. They also receive discounts at SSR's student hotel as well as on SSR tours. The International Youth Card is good for 10- to 15-percent discounts on some accommodations and various reductions to museums.

Meet the People

"Meet the Swiss" is what the Zurich Tourist Office calls its hospitality program. You can make arrangements to meet Swiss families of similar backgrounds and interests at the tourist office, Bahnhofplatz 15, CH-8023 Zurich.

For Further Information

The Swiss National Tourist Office (608 Fifth Avenue, New York, NY 10020) can provide a wide range of useful materials, including information on rail travel, camping, and youth hostels as well as general information about Switzerland. *Let's Go: Germany, Austria, and Switzerland* is tailored to the student budget. It's available for $14.95 in most bookstores and at Council Travel offices. For detailed advice on what to see in Switzerland, get a copy of Frommer's *Guide to Switzerland* ($14.95).

WORK

Anyone who wishes to work in Switzerland must obtain a work permit in advance of arrival; application for the permit is made by the prospective Swiss employer. The possibilities for finding permanent employment in Switzerland are very limited; in general, only applications from specialists or skilled workers are considered.

Internships/Traineeships

Programs offered by members of the Council on International Educational Exchange are listed below.

AIESEC-US. Reciprocal internship program for students in economics, business, finance, marketing, accounting, and computer science. See page 18 for further information.

Association for International Practical Training.
"IAESTE Trainee Program." On-the-job training for undergraduate and graduate students in technical fields such as engineering, computer science, agriculture, architecture, and mathematics. See page 18 for more information.
"Hotel & Culinary Exchange Program." On-the-job training for young people beginning a career in the hotel and food-service industries. Participants must have graduated, or be currently enrolled in a university or vocational school and possess at least six months of training or experience in the chosen field. Training usually runs 6 to 18 months. Consult Appendix I for the address to write for more information.

Syracuse University. "Graduate Internship in International Studies." Geneva. Summer. Graduates with basic knowledge of French or German. Apply by March 1.

Voluntary Service

For persons interested in voluntary service work, the Year Abroad Program sponsored by the International Christian Youth Exchange offers persons ages 18 to 24 voluntary service opportunities in the fields of health care, education, the environment, construction, and so on. See page 23 for more information.

In addition, the Fourth World Movement sponsors workcamps in Switzerland. For more information see page 21.

STUDY

The Cultural Affairs Office at the Embassy of Switzerland (2900 Cathedral Avenue NW, Washington, DC 20008) distributes a fact sheet entitled *Educational Facilities in Switzerland with Instruction on English*, as well as a list of Swiss universities.

Following are the study programs offered by CIEE-member institutions. Consult Appendix I for the addresses of the colleges and universities listed in this section. In addition to the programs below, Pomona College offers a program open only to its own students.

Semester and Academic Year

General Studies

Cornell University. "Cornell in Switzerland." Geneva. Academic year. Juniors to graduate students with two years of French and a 3.0 GPA. Apply by February 15.

International Student Exchange Program. Direct reciprocal exchange between U.S. universities and the Université de Fribourg and Université de Lausanne. Academic year. Full curriculum options. Open only to students at ISEP-member institutions.

La Salle University. "La Salle-in-Europe." Fribourg. Academic year. Liberal arts, science, international studies; lectures in French, German, and English. Freshmen and sophomores with one year of college French or German and 2.5 GPA. Apply by April 1.

State University of New York at Cortland. Neuchâtel. Semester or academic year. Sophomores to graduate students with intermediate French and 2.5 GPA in major. Apply by March 1 for fall and February 15 for spring.

Syracuse University. Leysin. Fall or spring. Liberal arts and international business. Sophomores to seniors. Apply by March 15 for fall; October 15 for spring.

International Studies

Experiment in International Living/School for International Training. "College Semester Abroad." Geneva. Fall or spring semester. Intensive French language, academic seminar including U.N. contributors, international organizations and field-study methods seminars, independent-study project, educational travel, and homestay. Sophomores to seniors with 2.5 GPA. Apply by May 15 for fall and October 15 for spring.

Kent State University. "KSU Semester in Geneva." Fall or spring semester. International relations and the U.N., international business, and French language study. Internships available. Sophomores to seniors with 2.5 GPA. Rolling admissions.

Summer

French Language

University of Utah. "Neuchâtel French language Program." French language study for four weeks preceded by two and a half weeks of travel study in Europe. Freshmen to graduate students and others. One or two quarters of college French or the equivalent is recommended. Apply by March 1.

General Studies

State University of New York at Cortland. Neuchâtel. Sophomores to graduate students with intermediate French and 2.5 in major. Apply by April 1.

University of North Carolina—Chapel Hill. "UNC Program to Switzerland." Thun. Sophomores, juniors, and seniors. Apply by February 1.

Hotel and Restaurant Management

Michigan State University. "International Hospitality." Lausanne. European food selection, marketing, preparation, and service systems. Juniors and seniors. Apply by April 20.

University of Massachusetts—Amherst. "Summer Program in Hotel, Restaurant, and Travel Administration." Sophomores, juniors, and seniors. Some French required. Apply by January 15.

Political Science

The University of Toledo. "Summer Study in Switzerland." Lausanne, Geneva, Bern, Montreux, Zermatt, Gruyères. High school students to graduate students and nonstudents. Apply by May 1.

UNITED KINGDOM OF GREAT BRITAIN AND NORTHERN IRELAND

Britain frequently is seen through the distorting lens of stereotypes popularized by movies, novels, and songs. It is neither the fog-bound, subterranean nightmare of Dickens' imagination nor the cheery, quaint landscape of 1950s comedies, and it is certainly not the trendy playground for young people that is depicted in the pop songs of the recent past. Visitors will look in vain for the relics of the Beatles' Britain, and even the punks have become a bizarre tourist attraction rather than a representation of real social protest.

The current reality is that, for good or ill, Britain has undergone a quiet revolution in sensibility since Margaret Thatcher became Prime Minister in 1979. The country has moved closer to an American economic model with an emphasis on self-reliance and competitiveness. This has led toward a change in many of the traditional British beliefs and practices, including the commitment to the welfare state. In many ways, Britain is becoming a tougher place where the weak are no longer supported, where the dispossessed can no longer be sure of a safety net. The election of John Major as prime minister may not signal any great political change of direction, but he might represent a significant shift in British society. He is unusual in British political life in that he comes from a relatively poor background and never attended a university. Perhaps this represents a small step towards a classless society in Britain.

Recent reforms suggest that educational institutions will be encouraged to move away from state control. British political reality is turning from the paternalistic model to a more independent form, and power is moving from the center to the periphery. Certainly, the government's drive toward privatization of industry and services formerly controlled by the state seems to be part of this process. The thoughtful visitor cannot fail to see that Britain is undergoing substantial shifts in the social and political environment.

One impact of this period of change has been the revival of Britain as two nations—rich and poor, South and North. The South, with London as its center, is relatively prosperous and characterized by high incomes (and high prices). The North of England, in contrast, has suffered most from industrial decline and the resulting unemployment. The two regions are also culturally distinct. For many visitors, an exclusive focus on London has obscured the rich variety of British life and customs.

Scotland and Northern Ireland further illustrate the political, social, and cultural complexity of the United Kingdom. Economic problems in Scotland and political/religious conflict in Northern Ireland should not hide the fact that both locations are of considerable interest. Besides being rich in natural beauty, these regions have distinct cultures worth discovering. Wales also has a separate identity, with its own language and a strong nationalist movement. The United Kingdom is not a single coherent unit but several distinct cultures coexisting in a sometimes uneasy alliance.

Since 1945, Britain has moved away from the center of world affairs. Adjustment to a post-imperialist role has characterized Britain's foreign policy and has led to some ambiguity in its relationship with other countries. The country has become an uneasy member of the European Community, but the sense of "Europeanness" is provisional and the commitment to European unity is by no means unanimous. Traditional links with the English-speaking world remain strong in political and emotional terms. Britain may be part of Europe but the British do not necessarily feel that Europe is where they belong.

For the U.S. visitor, Britain is a particularly attractive destination. Although the common language allows easy entrance into the culture, British society is profoundly different from our own. For example, in comparison to the States, Britain is still a formal society where status and class continue to be important factors. In a country with a strong sense of its past, there is an inevitable nostalgia for the age when British political and economic power were preeminent. Britain has one foot in its past and another in the future, maintaining an uneasy balance between the two. It clings to the symbols of past grandeur while looking toward the high technologies of the future.

In spite of Britain's decline from its former imperial greatness, there is still cultural dynamism in the country. Postwar immigration from the West Indies and the Indian subcontinent has created a cosmopolitan society that continues to attract immigrants and visitors. A vibrant theater and innovative art scene flourish. Britain is a society of paradox: decadent and forward-looking, traditionalist and modernistic, smug and uneasy. Like most paradoxes, it is worth investigating.

—*Michael Woolf, London, United Kingdom*

Official name: United Kingdom of Great Britain and Northern Ireland. **Size:** 94,226 square miles (about the size of Wyoming). **Population:** 57,121,000. **Population density:** 601 inhabitants per square mile. **Capital:** London. **Largest city:** Greater London (pop. 6,700,000). **Language:** English, Welsh, Gaelic (Scots, Irish dialects). **Religion:** Anglican, Roman Catholic. **Per capita income:** US$13,329. **Currency:** Pound sterling. **Literacy rate:** 99%. **Average daily high/low*:** Edinburgh: January, 45°/35°; July, 63°/52°. London: January, 44°/35°; July, 73°/55°. **Average number of days with precipitation:** Edinburgh: January, 18; July, 17. London: January, 17; July, 13.

TRAVEL

U.S. citizens will need a passport. For stays of up to six months, however, a visa is not required. Nor are visas required of students enrolled in a course of study. Check for specific regulations with the British Embassy, 3100 Massachusetts Avenue NW, Washington, DC 20008.

Getting Around

"England is scenically much more beautiful than most people realize. If you are really interested in enjoying your time in England rather than taking pictures of pigeons in London, spend your time in the smaller towns, especially in the north of England. You'll find the people there much more friendly and interested in you."
—Timothy Doyle, Burnsville, Minnesota

---

*All temperatures are Fahrenheit.

If you want to travel throughout Britain by air, you may purchase a Visit UK ticket good for travel to the ten cities served by Dan Air. Valid for 60 days, passes cost $99 for the first segment and $89 for each additional segment. Visit UK tickets are available from travel agents in the U.S.; they are not sold in Britain.

Though a comprehensive railroad network covers Britain, the Eurailpass is not valid (the InterRail pass is, however). Travel by train is generally more expensive in Britain than on the Continent, but BritRail offers a number of passes and discounts. BritRail passes are valid throughout England, Scotland, and Wales, but not in Northern Ireland or Ireland.

The best value for youths ages 15 to 23, or full-time students at British schools, is the Young Person's Railcard which provides a 33-percent discount off any train ticket. Good for one year, this card can only be purchased in Britain, where it is available at BritRail Travel Centres. It costs £16 (approximately $26), and you'll need two photos and proof of your age and student status.

The BritRail Youth Pass, for those between 16 and 25, entitles you to 8 days of unlimited second-class travel for $169, 15 days for $255, 22 days for $319, and one month for $375. Persons over 25 pay $209, $319, $399, and $465, respectively, for the same options. More expensive first-class versions of the BritRail pass are also available.

Britrail also offers the Youth Flexipass, which allows second-class travel on any 4 of 8 days for $145, any 8 of 15 days for $199, or any 15 days in 2 months for $295. For those over 26 years of age, the adult Flexipass allows second-class travel on any 4 of 8 days for $179, any 8 of 15 days for $254, or any 15 days in one month for $369. More expensive first-class Flexipasses are available as well.

Those planning to cover territory in both Britain and France should look into the BritFrance Railpass, which is valid for the entire British and French rail networks, including round-trip Channel crossing via hovercraft. Youths under 26 can travel second class on any 5 of 15 days for $199 or any 10 days in one month for $299. Adult second-class fares are $249 and $375, respectively.

All BritRail passes must be purchased before entering the United Kingdom; you can get them at Council Travel offices (see pages xix–xxi), from most travel agents, and from Britrail Travel International at 1500 Broadway, New York, NY 10036.

In Scotland, regional Rail Rover tickets offer a week's travel within certain areas for £28 to £32 (about $46 to $53). They can be purchased at ScotRail locations.

"Try to see Wales. Learn a little Welsh—it will steal the Welshs' hearts. The Welsh and the English are very different. I learned especially not to call an Englishman a Welshman and vice versa."

—Teri Snyders, Ankeny, Iowa

Travel by train is not your only option; long-distance express buses, called coaches, provide service that's generally cheaper and nearly as fast as the trains. The main intercity bus network is National Express/Scottish Citylink, which covers most of Great Britain. Holders of the International Student Identity Card can obtain the Student Coach Card, which for £5 (about $8) entitles you to a 33-percent discount off National Express' regular fares. Foreign citizens of any age can buy the BritExpress Card and get a 33-percent discount on all trips made on coaches of the National Express/Scottish Citylink network in a 30-day period. The BritExpress Card can be purchased for £12 (about $20) at travel agencies outside Britain or from the National Express office at 13 Regent Street, London SW1.

In addition, you'll find a number of local buses. For example, if you'd like to travel around rural Scotland cheaply, consider going by mail bus. Run by the postal service, these buses carry passengers as well as mail and their fares are extremely reasonable. There are 130 routes—all of them to areas not serviced by regular buses. You can get route and schedule information from the central post office, 2–4 Waterloo Place at North Bridge and Princes Street.

Another option in the U.K. is hitchhiking. The fastest hitching is on the expressways or "M-roads" where you are allowed to hitch only on the entrances or exits to the gas station and restaurant-service complexes located along the road at regular intervals.

Rural areas of Britain are ideally suited to bicycling. The secondary roads are smooth and well maintained, and British drivers are more courteous than those you'll encounter on the Continent. As in most European countries, rural people are more hospitable than their urban counterparts. With pubs and lodgings readily available in the villages of the countryside, you'll be well taken care of. On most trains (except a few express trains with limited baggage space) you can take your bicycle at no extra charge. However, rules vary from route to route; be sure to ask the ticket collector which trains accept bikes and where they should be taken for loading. To acquaint yourself with England's cycle routes, get the *CTC Route Guide to Cycling in Britain and Ireland*, published by the Cyclists' Touring Club. This and other practical guides, as well as a complete selection of Ordinance Survey Landranger Maps, are available through the British Travel Bookshop, 40 West 57th Street, New York, NY 10019. Write for a free catalog.

Especially for Students and Young People

A number of student travel bureaus operate in the United Kingdom. For travel information, train, plane, and ferry tickets, and accommodations bookings, you can check with the Council Travel Office at 28A Poland Street, London W1V 3DB.

Student unions on the campuses of colleges and universities throughout Britain issue the International Student Identity Card and serve the needs of the student traveler. Many of these student unions operate bars, restaurants, and recreational facilities; the majority welcome traveling students to their facilities and all are a good source of information about accommodations, student discounts, and student life in the area. Many student unions also have an accommodations booking service and, during the summer, arrange accommodations for travelers in student residences. If you would prefer to arrange your accommodation before you leave, Council Travel can reserve rooms at British university dormitories starting at about $20 per night.

In Britain, persons with the International Student Identity Card can obtain discounts on ferry service to the Continent, on international train and plane fares, and on train and intercity bus travel within the U.K. A Theatre Standby Scheme offers discounted standby tickets at West End theaters; to find out what plays are giving discounts, look for an "S" with a circle around it in the entertainment section of the newspapers or go to the kiosk in Leicester Square. The International Youth Card offers discounts on a large variety of accommodations throughout Great Britain, as well as many theaters and concerts, and, to a lesser extent, on museums, exhibitions, and restaurants. For a substantial listing of accommodations geared to the young traveler, ask for the *Young Britain* guide from the British Tourist Authority at 40 West 57th Street, New York, NY 10019.

Meet the People

A number of agencies can make arrangements for a visitor to stay with a family as a paying guest. Stays of a week or more are preferred, but weekend visits can sometimes be arranged. There's a list of these agencies in an information booklet, "Stay with a British Family," available from the British Tourist Authority, 40 West 57th Street, New York, NY 10019.

For Further Information

There's no lack of tourist guides to the United Kingdom. For students and other young travelers, the best all-around guide is *Let's Go: Britain and Ireland*. It's available for $14.95 in most bookstores and at Council Travel offices. For more detailed information on the city of London, pick up a copy of *Let's Go: London* ($10.95). If you're looking for a specialized guide to one particular district, contact the British Travel Bookshop (40 West 57th Street, 3rd floor, New York, NY 10019) for a catalog. Those who plan to travel in Scotland should check out Cadogan Guides' *Scotland* ($14.95), an extremely thorough guide distributed by the Globe Pequot Press.

For current information on what is going on in London, buy a copy of *Time Out* magazine, a weekly that lists just about everything that is happening in the city. This is also a good place to look for classified ads about sharing flats, overland travel from London (the world center for that kind of trek), and for traveling companions.

In London, you can get all sorts of tourist information from the London Tourist Board, which has branches at Victoria Station, Harrods (fourth floor), Heathrow Airport, Selfridges (ground floor), and the Tower of London. Another useful London address is the British Travel Centre (12 Regent Street, London SW1), a booking center for accommodations, tours, and car/rail/air/motorcoach travel. The Center also has up-to-the-minute information on cultural events and entertainment, and maintains both a bookshop and a currency-exchange service.

WORK

Getting a Job

In order to obtain a work permit to work in Britain, you must have a specific job offer. First priority is always given to British nationals; for almost all types of employment, the prospective employer must obtain a permit from the Department of Employment on your behalf. The employer is responsible for sending the permit to you; you will be required to present it at the port of entry.

CIEE, in cooperation with BUNAC (British Universities North America Club), can obtain permission for U.S. students to work in Britain for a period up to six months any time during the year. In addition to work authorization, CIEE gives participants information on living and working in Britain and details on the best way to find work. Jobs are relatively easy to find upon arrival; participants work as secretaries, temps, waiters, and similar positions. You can expect to make enough money to cover your daily living expenses and usually save something toward the cost of travel once you finish your job. To be eligible, you must be a U.S. citizen at least 18 years of age, enrolled as a full-time student in an accredited U.S. college or university, and residing in the U.S. at the time of application. Upon arrival in Britain you are required to have proof of minimum funds of $500 for support until you receive your first paycheck. There is a $125 fee for the service; application forms are available from CIEE's Work-Exchanges Department.

Persons thinking about working in the U.K. might want to get a copy of the annually published *Summer Jobs in Britain* (1991 edition, $12.95), which lists names of employers and describes jobs available. Copies are available from CIEE (add $1.50 for book-rate or $3 for first-class postage) or from Peterson's Guides, PO Box 2123, Princeton, NJ 08543-9925.

For those who want to teach in Britain, send for a copy of *Teaching in Britain*, a fact sheet put out by the British Information Services (845 Third Avenue, New York, NY 10022).

"A naturally shy and introverted person, I was forced out of my shell by having to deal with finding and maintaining employment. I found myself maturing and expanding in my perception of human nature and the world. If anything, the program helped in discovering who I was, my limitations and abilities. As a "pet Yank" I was exposed to an England few tourists could ever dream of experiencing. As the weeks progressed I even began to feel myself growing 'British' in attitude and manner—I even began to enjoy tea with milk!"

—Libatique Prudiel, Simi Valley, CA

Farm Work

Tiptree International Farm Camp recruits people from all over the world to pick fruit and berries during the summer. Workers are paid according to the amount of fruit they pick, but must pay for their room and board. Positions, which are available from about the second week of June until mid-July, are open only to students 18 to 25 years old. For more information, write the Camp Organizer, International Farm Camp, Hall Road, Tiptree, Colchester, Essex CO5 OQS.

Internships/Traineeships

The programs offered by organizations and institutions that are members of the Council on International Educational Exchange are listed below. Consult Appendix I for the addresses where you can write for further information. In addition to those listed below, Moorhead State University and Southwest Texas State University have internship programs open only to their own students.

AIESEC-US. Reciprocal internship program for students in economics, business, finance, marketing, accounting, and computer sciences. See page 18 for further information.

Association for International Practical Training.
"IAESTE Trainee Program." On-the-job training for undergraduate and graduate students in technical fields such as engineering, computer science, agriculture, architecture, and mathematics. See page 18 for more information.
"Hotel & Culinary Exchanges Program." On-the-job training for young people beginning a career in the hotel and food-service industries. Participants must have graduated from a university or vocational school and possess at least six months of training or experience in the chosen field. Training usually runs 6 to 18 months.

Beaver College. "London Internship Program in Arts Administration, Business, Communications, Government, Social Services." In cooperation with City of London Polytechnic. Semester students take two courses plus the internship. Fall or spring semester or summer. Juniors and seniors with 3.0 GPA. Apply by April 20 for fall and October 15 for spring; March 1 for summer.

Boston University. "London Internship Program." Fall, spring, and summer. Sophomores to graduates; post-baccalaureate students. Twelve credits of course work plus a four-credit internship in one of the following areas: business, the arts, comparative legal studies, economics, communications, politics, and psychology, among others. 3.0 GPA and adviser's approval. Apply six weeks before program begins.

Syracuse University.
"Fashion Design Internships in London." Summer. Juniors to graduates; portfolio of five slides of work. Apply by March 15.
"Management Internships in London." Summer. Juniors to graduates; three years of college in a program that includes management courses or one year of graduate course work in management; six credits of undergraduate or three credits of graduate accounting.
"Law in London." Summer. Internship in comparative clinical legal education. Six-week program with a firm of solicitors, a barrister's chambers, or one of a variety of legal entities in the London area. Any student in good standing at an American Bar Association–approved law school who has completed one year of full or part-time legal study.

Voluntary Service

CIEE places young people in voluntary service workcamps in Wales organized by the United Nations Association (Temple of Peace, Cathays Park, Cardiff CF13AP, Wales). At these workcamps, small groups of volunteers from various countries work on a range of nature-conservation projects and recreational programs for underprivileged children. Volunteers receive room and board in return for their labor and must be at least 18 years old. The applications of U.S. residents are processed by CIEE. For more information, contact the Voluntary Service Department at the Council.

Another organization sponsoring workcamps in Britain is the Fourth World Movement. For more information see page 21.

Short-term voluntary service opportunities are also available through the 43-year-old Winant-Clayton Volunteer program. British participants (the Claytons) come to the U.S. to do social work and Americans participants (the Winants) go to Britain to do the same. Volunteers, who must be 18 or older, are usually placed in central city areas, drug-crisis centers, shelters for the homeless, and rehabilitation centers for the mentally disabled. Participants pay for transportation to and from the site; room and board are provided during the placement. The cost of the summer program is usually about $1,600, which covers air fare and personal expenses. Volunteers spend six weeks in service and three weeks traveling on their own. There is a $15 application fee; the deadline is January 31 for placement the following summer. For details, write to the Winant-Clayton Volunteers, St. Bartholomew's Church, 109 East 50th Street, New York, NY 10022.

Community Service Volunteers (CSV) matches volunteers with projects that need them in Great Britain and Northern Ireland. Participants work with those who are disabled, elderly, homeless, or in trouble. No special skills are required, but volunteers must be between the ages of 18 and 35. A personal interview is required; the volunteer is responsible for finding his or her own accommodations in Britain during the two- to four-week placement period. After being placed, CSV provides you with room, board, and pocket money. Terms of service range from four months to a full year. About two thousand volunteers participate each year—250 or so are from outside the U.K. A placement fee of 395 British pounds (about $700) is required. For more information contact Community Service Volunteers, 237 Pentonville Road, London, NI 9NJ.

The Royal Society for Mentally Handicapped Children and Adults (MENCAP) organizes holidays for people with mental handicaps all over England. Volunteers take care of the personal needs of these people and share in the cooking, cleaning, laundry, and so on. Participants are required to work from 9 to 16 days. For more information contact the Royal Society for Mentally Handicapped Children and Adults, 119 Drake Street, Rochdale, Lancashire OL16 1PZ, England.

In addition, Quaker International Social Projects sponsors short-term voluntary-service projects that include working with inner-city children, participating in holiday camps for young people or handicapped adults, doing manual work such as renovating and painting, among other things. For more information contact Quaker International Social Projects, Friends House, Euston Road, London NW1 2BJ, England.

Other types of short-term volunteer work are also available. For persons interested in volunteering for an archaeological dig, the Council for British Archaeology (112 Kennington Road, London SE11 6RE) publishes a newsletter called "British Archaeological News" (six issues a year, $18 surface mail; $28 airmail), which lists information about archaeological projects in Great Britain as well as indicating which ones will accept volunteers. For persons interested in working on a restored narrow-gauge railway, the Ffestiniog Railway Company (Harbour Station, Porthmadog, Gwynedd, North Wales) recruits volunteers from around the world for the summer season.

You'll find additional opportunities for all types of community service described in *Volunteer!: The Comprehensive Guide to Voluntary Service in the U.S. and Abroad* ($6.95), published by CIEE. Another good source of information is the Scottish Community Education Council (Atholl House, 2 Canning Street, Edinburgh EH3 8EG). This organization provides information on opportunities for voluntary community work in Scotland. Write for their brochure listing available opportunities (enclose an international postal reply coupon).

STUDY

"Studying in England allowed me to see and understand the country for what it really is. It is impossible to develop an accurate insight into the nation without experiencing it firsthand. I formed strong friendships and learned to understand English ways of thinking, behaving, and interacting."
—Kathryn L. Dixon, San Mateo, California

The British Council advises students who plan to study in Britain, makes available reference books in their offices, and publishes such informative brochures as *Postgraduate Study and Research in the United Kingdom*. To request information, contact the British Council's Education Information Service at the British Embassy, 3100 Massachusetts Avenue NW, Washington, DC 20008. Another good source of information is British Information Services at 845 Third Avenue, New York, NY 10022. British Information Services publishes several fact sheets, including *Study in Britain*, which lists courses, tuition fees, scholarships, and awards.

The study programs offered by CIEE-member institutions are listed below. Consult Appendix I for the addresses of the colleges and universities listed in this section. In addition to the programs below, Boston University, California State University, Cornell University, Guilford College, Illinois State University, Indiana University, Moorhead State University, New York University, Northern Illinois University, Pennsylvania State University, Pomona College, Southern Methodist University, Stanford University, the University of California, the University of Connecticut, the University of Pittsburgh, the University of Rhode Island, the University of South Carolina, the University of Tennessee, the University of Toledo, and Valparaiso University offer programs open to their own students only.

Semester and Academic Year

Art and Design

Beaver College.
"Architecture, Art, Craft, and Design at Glasgow School of Art." Glasgow, Scotland. Academic year, fall, or two spring terms. Juniors and seniors with 3.0 GPA. Apply by April 20 for year and fall; October 15 for spring.
"Studio Art at Sir John Cass School of Art, City of London Polytechnic." London. Academic year or semester. Juniors and seniors with 3.0 GPA. Apply by April 20 for year and fall; October 15 for spring.

University of Illinois. "Art and Design in Britain." Various sites in England and Wales. Students from institutions with programs in art and design only. Academic year or semester. Juniors and seniors. Apply by May 1 for fall and October 25 for spring.

Business Studies

Beaver College. "Business Studies at Middlesex Polytechnic at Hendon." London. Academic year or fall semester. Juniors and seniors with 3.0 GPA. Apply by April 20.

Communications

State University of New York at Brockport. "Middlesex Communications Program." London. Fall semester. Juniors and seniors with 2.5 GPA and 3.0 in Communications major. Apply by February 15.

University of Hartford. "Special Topics in British Media Systems." One week program in March. Freshmen to seniors. Apply by January 22.

Criminal Justice

State University of New York. "Criminal Justice Program." Brunel University in London. Fall semester. Juniors and seniors with 2.5 GPA. Apply by February 15.

Dance

Beaver College. "University of Surrey Department of Dance." Guildford. Academic year. Juniors and seniors with 3.0 GPA. Apply by April 20.

State University of New York at Brockport. "Middlesex Dance Program." London. Fall and spring semesters. Theory and practice. Junior and senior dance majors with 2.5 GPA. Apply by February 15 for fall; November 1 for spring.

East European Studies

Beaver College. "School of Slavonic and East European Studies, University of London." Academic year. Juniors and seniors with 3.0 GPA. Apply by April 20.

Economics

Beaver College. "Single-Term Program in the Department of Economics, University College London." Fall or spring term. Juniors and seniors with 3.0 GPA. Apply by April 20 for fall and October 15 for spring.

University of North Carolina—Chapel Hill.
"UNC at LSE." Academic year. Study at London School of Economics. Juniors and seniors with 3.5 GPA. Apply by February 12.
"LSE—Semester Honors Program." Fall. Juniors and seniors with 3.2 GPA. Apply by February 12.

English Literature

Michigan State University. "English Literature." Wimbledon. Fall quarter. Sophomores to graduate students. Apply by June 16.

State University of New York at Brockport. "Loughborough Academic Year Abroad," and "Loughborough Semester Program." Juniors and seniors with 2.5 GPA. Apply by February 15 for year; November 1 for spring only.

University of Minnesota. "Literature in London." Spring quarter. Freshmen to graduate students and adults. Apply by December 31.

General Studies

American Heritage Association. "Northwest Interinstitutional Council on Study Abroad—London." Fall, winter, and/or spring quarter. Sophomores, juniors, and seniors with 2.5 GPA. Apply by June 15 for fall, November 1 for winter, and January 15 for spring.

American University. "The London Semester." Internships available. Fall or spring. Sophomores, juniors, and seniors with 2.7 GPA. Apply six months ahead.

Beaver College.
"London Semester Program at City of London Polytechnic." Academic year or semester. Juniors and seniors with 3.0 GPA. Apply by April 20 for year and fall and October 15 for spring.
"Oxford Semester Program in Social Science and Humanities." Local faculty base specially arranged courses on Oxford-style teaching. Academic year or semester. Juniors and seniors with 3.2 GPA. Apply by April 20 for year and fall; October 15 for Spring.
University of Birmingham. Academic year, fall, or spring programs. Juniors and seniors with 3.0 GPA. Apply by April 20 for fall and year; October 15 for spring.
University of Bristol. Academic year. Juniors and seniors with 3.2 GPA. Apply by March 20.
University of Essex. Colchester. Academic year, fall or spring programs. Juniors and seniors with 3.0 GPA. Apply by April 20 for fall and year; October 15 for spring.
Royal Holloway and Bedford New College, University of London. Egham Hill, Surrey, England. Academic year, fall, or spring programs. Juniors and seniors with 3.0 GPA. Apply by March 20 for fall and year; October 15 for spring.
University College London. "JYA/Semester Exchange." London. Semester or academic year. Faculties of arts, life sciences (excluding medicine), mathematical and physical sciences, engineering, laws, environmental studies. Juniors, seniors, and graduate students with TOEFL score of 560 or higher. Apply by February 28.
University of Surrey. Guildford, England. Academic year. Social science and engineering. Juniors and seniors with 3.0 GPA. Apply by April 20.
University of Lancaster. Academic year, fall, or spring programs. Juniors and seniors with 3.0 GPA. Apply by April 20 for fall and year; October 15 for spring.
Goldsmiths' College, University of London. Academic year or spring program. Juniors and seniors with 3.0 GPA. Apply by April 20 for year; October 15 for spring.
Imperial College, University of London. Academic year, fall, or spring programs. Juniors and seniors with 3.3 GPA. Apply by April 20 for fall and year; October 15 for spring.
King's College, University of London. Academic year, fall, or spring programs. Juniors and seniors with 3.0 GPA. Apply by April 20 for fall and year; October 15 for spring.
London School of Economics and Political Science, University of London. Academic year, fall, or spring programs. Juniors and seniors with 3.3 GPA. Apply by March 10 for fall and year; October 15 for spring.
Middlesex Polytechnic at Trent Park. Greater London area. Academic year, fall, or spring program. Juniors and seniors with 3.0 GPA. Apply by April 20 for fall and year; October 15 for spring.
Queen Mary and Westfield College, University of London. Academic year, fall, or spring program. Juniors and seniors with 3.0 GPA. Apply by March 10 for fall and year; October 15 for spring.
City University. London. Academic year, fall, or spring programs. Juniors and seniors with 3.0 GPA. Apply by April 20 for fall and year; October 15 for spring.
University College, University of London. Academic year, fall, or spring program. Juniors and seniors with 3.0 GPA. Apply by March 10 for academic year; April 20 for fall; October 15 for spring.
University of Manchester. Academic year. Juniors and seniors with 3.2 GPA. Apply by April 20.
University of East Anglia in Norwich. Academic year, fall, or spring programs. Apply by April 20 for fall and year; October 15 for spring.

EUROPE: UNITED KINGDOM

University of Nottingham. Academic year, fall, or spring programs. Juniors and seniors with 3.0 GPA. Apply by April 20 for fall and year; October 15 for spring.
University of Reading. Academic year, fall, or spring programs. Juniors and seniors with 3.0 GPA. Apply by April 20 for fall and year; October 15 for spring.
University of Southampton. Academic year. Juniors and seniors with 3.0 GPA. Apply by April 20.
University of York. Academic year, fall, or spring programs. Juniors and seniors with 3.0 GPA. Apply by April 20 for fall and year; October 15 for spring.
The Queen's University of Belfast, Northern Ireland. Academic year, fall, and spring programs. Juniors and seniors with 3.0 GPA. Apply by April 20 for fall and year; October 15 for spring.
University of Aberdeen. Academic year, fall, or spring programs. Juniors and seniors with 3.0 GPA. Apply by April 20 for fall and year; October 15 for spring.
University of Edinburgh. Academic year, fall, or spring programs. Juniors and seniors with 3.0 GPA. Apply by March 20 for fall and year; October 15 for spring.
University of Glasgow. Academic year, fall, or spring programs. Juniors and seniors with 3.0 GPA. Apply by April 20 for fall and year; October 15 for spring.
University College of North Wales in Bangor. Academic year or spring programs. Juniors and seniors with 3.0 GPA. Apply by April 20 for year; October 15 for spring.

Brethren Colleges Abroad. Cheltenham, England. Excursions and study tour of Wales or Yorkshire. Semester or academic year. Sophomores, juniors, and seniors, with 3.0 GPA. Apply by April 15 for fall and year; November 1 for spring.

Brigham Young University. "BYU Study Abroad." London. Fall semester (July to December) and spring semester (January to June). Sophomores, juniors, and seniors. Apply by February 1 for fall; October 1 for spring.

Central University of Iowa.
"Central College London Program." Academic year or semester. Sophomores, juniors, and seniors with 2.5 GPA. Apply by March 15 for fall and October 15 for spring.
"Central College in Wales." Carmarthen, Wales. Semester or academic year (fall quarter option also available). Sophomores, juniors, and seniors with 2.5 GPA. Apply by October 15 for spring and March 15 for fall.

Central Washington University. "Northwest Interinstitutional Council on Study Abroad—London." See listing under American Heritage Association.

Colorado State University. Aberdeen, Scotland. Semester or academic year. Juniors and seniors.

Great Lakes Colleges Association. "GLCA Scotland Program, Wabash College." Aberdeen. Academic year. Sophomores, juniors, and seniors with 3.0 GPA and two faculty references. Apply by March 4. Contact GLCA Scotland Program, Wabash College, Crawfordsville, IN 47933; (317) 364-4410.

Grinnell College. "Grinnell-in-London." Fall. Juniors and seniors with 2.5 GPA. Apply by March 1.

Hiram College. "Cambridge Quarter." Fall quarter. Sophomores, juniors, and seniors with 2.5 GPA. Apply by March 15.

Hollins College. "Hollins Abroad London." Fall or spring semester. Juniors and seniors with 2.0 GPA. Apply by March 1 for fall and September 30 for spring.

International Student Exchange Program. Direct reciprocal exchange between U.S. universities and institutions in London, Cardiff, Northern Ireland, Glasgow, Plymouth, Sunderland, and Preston (Lancashire). Academic year. Full curriculum options. Open only to students at ISEP-member institutions.

Lake Erie College. "Academic Programs Abroad." Semester or academic year. Juniors and seniors with 2.5 GPA. Apply by June 1 for fall and October 1 for spring.

Lancaster University. Academic year or spring semester at Lancaster. Sophomores to graduate students. For applications contact: Ethel Sossman, 111 East 10th Street, New York, NY 10003; (212) 228-0321.

Michigan State University. "Humanities and Social Science in England and Scotland." London, Cambridge, York and the Lake District, and Edinburgh. Spring quarter. Freshmen to seniors. Apply by February 3.

Millersville University. "Humberside Exchange Program." Hull. Academic year. Sophomores to seniors with a 2.5 GPA. Apply by April 1.

Northern Arizona University. "Semester in London." Fall or spring semester. Sophomores, juniors, and seniors with 2.5 GPA. Apply by November 1 for spring and March 15 for fall.

Northern Illinois University.
"Academic Internships in London." Semester or academic year. Students take two courses plus internship. Wide range of internships available for own students; more limited selection for others. Sophomores to seniors with 3.0 GPA. Apply by April 4 for fall and November 1 for spring.
"Britain and the European Community." London. Politics, economics, sociology. Fall or spring. Sophomores to juniors with 3.0 GPA. Apply by June 1 for fall; November 1 for spring.

Portland State University. "Northwest Interinstitutional Council on Study Abroad—London." See listing under American Heritage Association.

Rosary College. "Rosary in London." Fall semester. Students take two courses: British Life and Culture (eight credits) and Independent Study (six to eight credits). Emphasis on experiential learning. Study tours to Edinburgh, York, the Lake District, and other important sites. Sophomore, juniors, and seniors. Apply by February 1.

Rutgers University. "Study Abroad in Britain." Academic year or spring semester. Exeter, Bristol, Reading, York, London, Brighton. Juniors with 3.0 GPA. Apply by February 1.

St. Lawrence University. "London Semester Program." Spring or fall semester. Internships or one-month Oxford course option can be arranged within the program. Sophomores to seniors with 2.8 GPA. Apply by February 20 for fall and October 10 for spring.

State University of New York at Albany.
"University of Glasgow Exchange." Academic year. Juniors and seniors with 3.3 GPA in major and 3.0 overall. Apply by March 15.
"Polytechnic Southwest Exchange." Academic year. Juniors and seniors with 3.3 GPA in major and 3.0 overall. Apply by March 15.
"University College of Swansea Exchange." Academic year. Juniors and seniors with 3.3 GPA in major and 3.0 overall. Apply by March 15.

State University of New York at Binghamton. "Semester in London." Literature and theater. Spring. Internships available. Sophomores to seniors. Apply by October 15.

State University of New York at Buffalo/College at Buffalo. "Manchester Polytechnic." Fall semester. Sophomores, juniors, and seniors with 2.5 GPA. Apply by March 1.

State University of New York at Cortland. "Polytechnic of North London." Fall or spring semester. Sophomores, juniors, and seniors with above average achievement in major. Apply by March 1 for fall and October 1 for spring.

State University of New York at Oswego. Imperial College, London. Academic year or semester. Broadcasting program offered in spring. Freshmen to seniors. Apply by April 1 for fall; November 1 for spring.

Stetson University. Nottingham. Academic year or semester. Sophomores, juniors, and seniors with 2.5 GPA (3.0 in major). Apply by March 1 for fall and October 15 for spring.

Syracuse University. "Syracuse in London." Fall or spring semester. Sophomores to graduate students with 3.0 GPA. Apply by March 15 for fall and October 15 for spring.

Texas Tech University. "London Semester." Fall or spring. Humanities and business programs. Sophomores to seniors with 2.5 GPA. Apply by October 15 for spring; April 1 for fall.

Tufts University. "Tufts in London." Academic year. Juniors with 3.0 GPA. Apply by February 1.

University of Colorado at Boulder. "Academic Year in Lancaster." Juniors and seniors with 2.75 GPA. Apply by March 1.

University of Essex. Colchester. Academic year or semester. Regular undergraduate courses for nondegree-program students, particularly students on junior year abroad. Sophomores to graduate students with 3.0 GPA. Apply by April for year or fall; November for spring.

University of Evansville. "University of Evansville's Harlaxton College." Grantham, England. Academic year or semester. Sophomores to seniors. Adviser's permission required. Apply by June 1 for fall semester and October 1 for spring.

University of Iowa. "Iowa Regents London Program." Fall or spring semester. Sophomores to juniors with 2.5 GPA. Preference given to students of Iowa Regents institutions. Apply by April 1 for fall; November 1 for spring.

University of Kansas. "Academic Year Abroad in Great Britain." East Anglia, Essex, Exeter, Hull, Leicester, Reading, St. Andrew's, Stirling, Strathclyde, Wales at Swansea, Wales at Aberystwyth. Full range of academic courses. (Semester or year at Stirling, Scotland.) Juniors with 3.0 GPA. Apply by March 1 for fall (KU students: February 15); October 15 for Stirling spring.

University of La Verne.
"Semester/Year in England." See listing under Brethren Colleges Abroad.
"Experiencing British Life and Culture." London and other cities. January interim. Juniors to graduate students with 2.5 GPA. Apply by October 31.

University of Maryland. "Study in London." Semester or academic year. Sophomores, juniors, and seniors with 2.5 GPA. Apply by May 1 for fall and October 15 for spring.

University of New Hampshire. "Study Abroad in Regent's College, London." Semester or academic year. Sophomores to graduate students with 2.5 GPA. Apply by mid-April for fall and mid-October for spring. Contact University of New Hampshire London Program, Hamilton Smith Hall, Durham, NH 03824; (603) 862-3962.

University of North Carolina—Chapel Hill.
"UNC Program to Bristol, England." Academic year. Sophomores, juniors, and seniors with 3.0 GPA. Apply by February 12.
"UNC Program to Leeds, England." Academic year. Juniors and seniors with 3.0 GPA. Apply by February 12.
"UNC Exchange Program to Manchester, England." Academic year. Juniors and seniors with 3.0 GPA. Apply by February 12.
"UNC Program to Sussex, England." Academic year. Juniors and seniors with 3.0 GPA. Apply by February 12.
"UNC Program to St. Andrews, Scotland." Academic year. Sophomores, juniors, and seniors. Apply by February 12.

University of North Texas. "Texas London Consortium." Fall or spring semester. Offered through AIFS in conjunction with the University of Texas at Arlington, the University of Houston and Texas Tech. Open only to students at schools in Texas. Sophomores through graduate students with 2.5 GPA. Apply by June 1 for fall and November 1 for spring.

University of Oregon. "Northwest Interinstitutional Council on Study Abroad—London." See listing under American Heritage Association.

University of Wisconsin—Madison. Coventry. Academic year. Sophomores to graduate students with 3.0 GPA. Open only to students at colleges or universities in the state or Wisconsin residents studying in other states. Apply by February 1.

University of Wisconsin—Platteville. "London Study Centre at Ealing College." Semester or academic year. Liberal arts, business administration, and criminal justice. Sophomores, juniors, and seniors with 2.5 GPA. Apply by April 15 for fall and October 20 for spring.

University of Wyoming. "London Semester." Spring semester. Second semester freshmen to seniors with 2.0 GPA. Apply by November 1.

Western Washington University. "Northwest Interinstitutional Council on Study Abroad—London." See listing under American Heritage Association.

Humanities

Beaver College. "London Humanities Semesters in Cooperation with City of London Polytechnic." Academic year or semester. Specially arranged courses for American students, with one-week co-curricular field-study trip to Paris or Berlin. Juniors and seniors with 3.0 GPA. Apply by April 20 for fall and year; October 15 for spring.

Boston University. "Modern British Studies at Oxford University." Academic year or semester. Choice of courses in British history, politics, and literature. Sophomores to seniors with 3.0 GPA. Apply by July 15 for year or fall; November 30 for spring.

State University of New York at Brockport.
"Middlesex Liberal Arts Program." London. Fall or spring semester. Juniors and seniors with 2.5 GPA. Apply by February 15 for fall; November 1 for spring.
"Oxford University Liberal Arts Program." Fall or spring semester. Juniors and seniors with 2.7 GPA. Apply by February 15 for fall; November 1 for spring.

Law

Beaver College. "Two-Term Spring Pre-Law Program at King's College, University of London." Juniors and seniors with 3.3 GPA. Apply by October 15.

Notre Dame Law School. "The Concannon Program of International Law." Academic year. Study at the Notre Dame London Law Centre. Law students who have successfully completed one year of law study. Contact Notre Dame Law School, Notre Dame, IN 46556.

Medicine

Beaver College. "Two Term Pre-Med Program at King's College, University of London." Spring only. Juniors and seniors with 3.0 GPA. Apply by October 15.

Nursing

University System of Georgia/Medical College of Georgia. "Nursing in England." Two weeks in spring. 2.5 GPA and students enrolled in BSN program or graduates. Apply by January 15.

Oriental and Asian Studies

Beaver College. "School of Oriental and Asian Studies, University of London." Academic year. Juniors and seniors with 3.0 GPA. Apply by April 20.

Physical Education

State University of New York at Brockport. "Chelsea College Physical Education Program." Brighton Polytechnic in Eastbourne. Spring semester. Junior and senior physical-education majors with 2.7 GPA. Apply by November 1.

Science

State University of New York at Brockport. Academic year at Leeds University. Natural sciences. Juniors and seniors with 3.0 GPA. Apply by February 15.

The University of Toledo. "Junior Year Studies in England." University of Salford, Manchester. Biology, chemistry, information systems, and operations management. Apply by February 28.

Social Sciences

American University. "London Semester." Fall or spring semester. British politics and society. Internships with British and international organizations. Second-semester sophomores, juniors, and seniors with 2.75 GPA. Apply six months prior to start of program.

Beaver College. "Single Term Program in the Faculty of Social Sciences at the University of Edinburgh." Fall or spring term. Juniors and seniors with 3.0 GPA. Apply by April 20 for fall; October 15 for spring.

State University of New York at Brockport.
"Brunel Political Science Exchange Program." London. Academic year. Juniors and seniors with 3.0 GPA. Only three students accepted annually. Apply by February 15.
"London Social Science Program." Brunel University. Fall or spring semester. Juniors and seniors with 2.5 GPA. Apply by April 1 for fall; November 1 for spring.

University of North Carolina—Chapel Hill. London. Academic year. Study at the London School of Economics. Juniors and seniors with 3.5 GPA. Apply by February 12.

Teacher Education

Hiram College. "Education in England." Cambridge. Fall quarter. Includes visits to English schools and cultural field trips. Sophomores, juniors, and seniors with 2.5 GPA. Apply by March 15.

Theater

University of Hartford. "London Theater." Two-week program in December and January. Freshmen to seniors with 2.5 GPA. Apply by October 19.

Summer

Art and Art History

Michigan State University.
"Art in London." Studio art and art criticism. Sophomores to graduate students. Apply by April 20. "History of Art." London. Instruction and visits to museums. Sophomores to graduate students. Apply by April 20.

New York University. "Tisch School of the Arts Summer in London." Freshmen to graduate students for independent study. Apply by April 15. Contact: TSOA Student Affairs Office, 721 Broadway, Seventh floor, New York, NY 10003, attn: Elena Pinto Simon; (212) 998-1900.

British Studies

American Heritage Association. "American Heritage Cultural Summer Program." London. British culture and history. Apply by April 15.

State University of New York at Brockport. "Oxford University Summer Program." Juniors and seniors with 2.5 GPA. Apply by May 1.

University Systems of Georgia/Armstrong State College. London. Undergraduates with 2.5 GPA and graduate students with 3.0 GPA. Apply by April 1.

Western Washington University. London. See listing under American Heritage Association.

Broadcasting

Syracuse University. "Media Drama in Britain." London. Juniors to graduate students. Apply by March 15.

Southern Illinois University at Carbondale. "British Television Programing, Policy and Production." London, Bristol, Manchester. Seminar focusing on the differences in programming, production, and administration between the British and American broadcasting systems. Sophomores to graduate students, and qualified professionals. Apply by March 1.

State University of New York at Oswego. Imperial College. London. Contemporary British culture. High-school graduates to graduate students. Apply by April 1.

Business

Syracuse University.
"Europe 1992: An International Business Perspective." London with trip to Brussels. Seniors and graduate students. Apply by March 15.
"Management Internships in London." Placement in English financial institutions. Research paper to be submitted after internship. Undergraduates and graduates with basic accounting and computing skills. Apply by February 15.

University of Colorado at Boulder. "London Seminar in International Finance and Business." Undergraduate/graduate seminar focusing on the planned integration of the European Community and its effects on the nations of the Community and on world finance. Juniors to graduate students with previous international finance or international economics. Apply by March 1.

University of Louisville. "Business Studies in Southampton." Freshmen to graduate students. Apply by April 30.

Communications

Michigan State University. "Mass Media and Reporting in Britain." London. Working seminars with British media professionals. Juniors, seniors, and graduate students. Apply by April 20.

Southern Methodist University. "SMU-in-London: Communications." International communications, public relations, and advertising. Sophomores to seniors. Apply by March 15.

Computer Science

University System of Georgia/Southern College of Technology. "Computer Science in Leicester." Undergraduate students with 2.5 GPA and previous courses in computer science including structured programming. Apply by April 1.

Criminal Justice

Michigan State University. "Forensic Anthropology and Human Identification." London and Cambridge. Instruction and field experiences in forensic anthropology in the study of skeletal biology and forensic identification. Juniors, seniors, and graduate students. Apply by April 20.

Drama

Michigan State University. "Acting and Theatre in Great Britain." London and Stratford-on-Avon. Seminars, plays, classes in acting and theater history, and class trips. Sophomores to graduate students. Apply by April 20.

Mary Baldwin College. "Contemporary Theatre in London." May term. Undergraduates. Apply by December 1.

New York University. "Educational Theatre." Graduate students. Apply by April 15. Contact: 32 Washington Place, Second floor, NY, NY 10003; (212) 998-5030.

University of Pennsylvania. "Penn-in-London I & II." British theater and literature. Apply by March 1.

Economics

University of Kansas. "International Summer School in Economics at the London School of Economics." Juniors and seniors with 3.0 GPA. Apply by March 18.

Education

State University of New York at Brockport. "British Educational Methods Program." London. Juniors to graduate students. Apply by March 15.

University of Louisville. "Education in Edinburgh." Freshmen to graduate students. Apply by April 30.

New York University. "Science Education in England." London. Seniors and graduate students. Apply by April 15. Contact: Graduate Admissions, 32 Washington Place, New York, NY 10003.

English Literature

Michigan State University. "English Literature in London." The course also involves theater productions and museum resources. Sophomores to graduate students. Apply by April 20.

New York University. "Cambridge University: Victorian Literature." Open to graduate students and adult members of the public. Apply by May 1.

State University of New York at Brockport. "British Writers Summer Program." Various sites in England and Ireland. Sophomores to seniors with 2.5 GPA. Apply by May 1.

University of Alabama. "Alabama at Oxford." Trips to London and Scotland. Freshmen to graduate students. Apply by March 31.

University of Louisville. "Study in London: Shakespeare and His Times." Freshmen to graduate students. Apply by April 30.

University of Massachusetts—Amherst. "Oxford Summer Seminar." Juniors, seniors, and graduate students, with 3.0 GPA. Apply by March 31.

University of North Carolina—Chapel Hill. "UNC Summer Program to London." Sophomores, juniors, and seniors. Apply by February 1.

Film Studies

Michigan State University. "Film in Britain." London and Edinburgh. Sophomores to graduate students. Apply by April 20.

General Studies

American Heritage Association. ISIS at Kingston-upon-Thames. Apply by May 1.

Boston University. "Summer Program in London." Choice of courses in advertising, public relations, the arts, comparative legal systems, management, finance, the media, politics and psychology, and the European economy. Sophomores to seniors with 3.0 GPA in major. Apply by April 15.

Brigham Young University. "British Literary Masterworks Study Abroad Program." Sophomores, juniors, and seniors. Apply by February 1.

Lake Erie College. "Academic Programs Abroad." Juniors and seniors with 2.5 GPA.

Louisiana State University. "LSU in London." Six weeks of coursework in theater, history, philosophy, and art history, supplemented by field trips to castles, gardens, museums, and cathedrals. Sophomores to seniors with 2.5 GPA; graduate students with 3.0 GPA. Apply by April 1.

Mary Baldwin College. "Virginia Program at Oxford." Sophomores, juniors, and seniors at Hampden-Sydney College, Mary Baldwin College, Roanoke College, Sweet Briar College, Virginia Military Institute, and Washington and Lee University who have completed intermediate French. Apply by March 1.

Michigan State University. "Cambridge University International Summer School." Juniors and seniors with 3.0 GPA. Apply by April 20.

New York University. "NYU in London—Summer Study Abroad." Freshmen to seniors. Apply by March 29. Contact: Director, NYU in London, English Department, Faculty of Arts and Science, New York University, 19 University Place, 2nd floor, New York, NY 10003; (212) 998-8817.

North Carolina State University.
"The London Experience." Freshmen to graduate students with 2.0 GPA. Apply by March 1.

Southern Methodist University. "SMU-in-Oxford." Sophomores, juniors, and seniors. Apply by March 15.

University of Hartford. "Discovering Britain." London, Bristol, and Oxford. Freshmen to seniors with 2.5 GPA. Apply by May 20.

University of New Hampshire. "A Summer of Study in Cambridge." Freshmen to graduate students. Apply by March. Contact Department of English, Hamilton Smith Hall, University of New Hampshire, Durham, NH 03824; (603) 862-3962.

University of Utah. "Cambridge International Summer School." Two, four, or six weeks. Students welcome from all over the West. Sophomores to seniors, and community. Cumulative 3.0 GPA required for students. Apply by March 20.

University of Wisconsin—Platteville. "Summer Session in London at Ealing College." Courses in theater, art, history, and culture. Sophomores to seniors with 2.0 GPA. Apply by March 31.

Western Michigan University. "Oxford Seminar." Literature and culture. Freshmen to graduate students, and community members (especially teachers). Apply by May 1.

History

Michigan State University. "History in Britain." London and Edinburgh. Sophomores to graduate students. Apply by April 20.

New York University. "Cambridge Study Program/Victorian Britain." All students and nonstudents interested in Victorian Britain. Apply by April 28. Contact NYU/SCE, International Programs, 331 Shimkin, Washington Square, New York, NY 10003; (212) 998-7133.

State University of New York at Oswego. "Historical Study of the British Isles." England, Scotland, and Wales. High-school graduates to graduate students. Apply by April 1.

Rutgers University. "Summer Institute in Sussex." Falmer. English Social History. Sophomores with 2.7 GPA. Apply by March 1.

Humanities

Beaver College. "London Humanities Summer Session." In cooperation with City of London Polytechnic. Eight weeks, two courses with co-curricular field-study excursions. Juniors and seniors with 3.0 GPA. Apply by March 1.

Michigan State University. "Humanities in London." A study of Western civilization drawing from the arts, history, literature, philosophy, and religion. Freshmen to seniors. Apply by April 20.

University of Kansas. "Humanities in Great Britain." London, Edinburgh, York, Oxford, Stratford-on-Avon, Exeter. Freshmen to seniors with 2.5 GPA. Apply by February 1.

Law

Mary Baldwin College. "Crime and Justice in England." May term. Undergraduates. Apply by December 1.

Notre Dame Law School. "Live and Learn Law in London." Study at Notre Dame Law Centre. Law students who have successfully completed one year of law study. June 26–August 2. Apply by April 1.

Ohio State University.
"Oxford—Law." Law students with one year of law school. Apply by April 10.
"Oxford—Pre-Law." Introduction to American law, with emphasis on the heritage of English culture and legal institutions. Juniors and seniors with 3.0 GPA. Apply by April 15.

Marketing

Michigan State University. "Packaging in England." London. Explore packaging and development of packages for the European market. Juniors and seniors. Apply by April 20.

Syracuse University. "Marketing Strategies in a Changing Environment." London. Juniors and seniors. Apply by March 15.

Nursing

Michigan State University. "Nursing Program in London." Role and responsibilities of nurses in different health-care organizations. Juniors to graduate students, and professional nurses. Apply by April 21.

State University of New York at Brockport. "Comparative Health Systems Overseas Study Programs." England and Scotland. Open to graduate students in health administration with 2.5 GPA. Apply by May 1.

University of Louisville. "Nursing in London." Course designed to guide registered nurses and nursing students in making personal choices in daily dilemmas. Freshmen to graduate students and registered nurses. Apply by April 30.

Philosophy

Michigan State University. "Medical Ethics and History of Health Care." London. Program is designed for medical and nursing students as well as students in philosophy, health policy, and international relations. Juniors, seniors, and graduate students. Apply by April 20.

Photography

Michigan State University. "Photo Communication in England and Scotland." London, Bath, York, Bradford, Edinburgh, and Glasgow. Freshmen to graduate students. Apply by April 20.

Political Science

Michigan State University.
"Political Science in London." Sophomores to graduate students. Apply by April 20.
"James Madison/Cambridge Program." Juniors and seniors. Apply by April 20.

Syracuse University. "Politics in England." London. Sophomores to seniors. Apply by March 15.

Social Sciences

Michigan State University. "Social Science in London." Political, economic, and social processes in the industrial world. Sophomores, juniors, and seniors. Apply by April 20.

Sociology

Michigan State University. "Comparative Health Care Systems." Juniors, seniors, and graduate students. Apply by April 20.

Speech Science

Michigan State University. "Speech-Language Pathology and Audiology in London." Juniors, seniors, and graduate students. Apply by April 20.

New York University.
"Elementary Education." Oxford. Graduate students only. Apply by April 15. Contact: School of Education, Health, Nursing, and Arts Professions. 32 Washington Place, Second floor, New York, NY 10003; (212) 998-5030.
"English Education." London and Oxford. Graduate students only. Apply by April 15. Contact: see above.

Writing

Michigan State University. "American Thought and Language—Writing." London. Freshmen and sophomores. Apply by April 20.

EXPLORING BRITISH CULTURE

Readings

Social and political issues dominate British writing, making it more concrete and less metaphysical than much European writing. If the French are preoccupied with philosophical issues, the British concern is with social manners and political morality. For example, in *Pride and Prejudice* (1813), Jane Austen explores social convention; in *Hard Times* (1854), Charles Dickens confronts the devastating impact of industrialization on Great Britain; and in *The Mill on the Floss* (1860), George Eliot traces a young woman's efforts to free herself from the restrictive pressures of family life. Alan Sillitoe confronts the mores and institutions of British society in the short story *The Loneliness of the Long-Distance Runner* (1959), a 20th-century example of this type of literature.

Novelists from the United States and the United Kingdom have found the meeting of the two societies a source for both serious cultural exploration and comedies of profound bewilderment. *Changing Places* (1975), David Lodge's novel of Anglo-American academic exchange, is an amusing example of this sort of cultural confusion. So is Malcolm Bradbury's *Stepping Westward* (1965). Alison Lurie's *Foreign Affairs* (1985) provides an example of an American version of the experience.

Perhaps the most interesting development in British literature has been the emergence of a number of younger writers from immigrant backgrounds. Timothy Mo, an Anglo-Chinese novelist, examines the trauma and comedy of one family's cultural adjustment in *Sour Sweet* (1982). Salman Rushdie, the product of an Anglo-Indian background, also represents this aspect of contemporary British writing: a growing cosmopolitanism and a movement away from the purely British landscape to the more complex and dangerous world of intercultural relations. His novel *Midnight's Children* (1981), like *The Satanic Verses* (1988), draws its considerable energy from a sense of being caught between two worlds and feeling at home in neither. Kazuo Ishiguro is a contemporary writer who was born in Japan and moved to Britain as a small child. His novel, *Remains of the Day* (1989), is written in the voice of a deceased English aristocrat's valet and provides insight into the British class system. Mo, Rushdie, and other writers of immigrant backgrounds have given voice to a new Britain characterized by cultural contrast, ethnic diversity, and, at times, unsettling discord.

Films

Not surprisingly, many of the most memorable films of the early British cinema were based either on British theater productions or works of British literature. Among the best known were re-creations of works by Dickens and Emily Brontë, in particular, Brontë's *Wuthering Heights* (1939), starring Lawrence Olivier and Merle Oberon. Other notable films of the period include a couple of Alfred Hitchcock's early thrillers, *The Man Who Knew Too Much* (1934; the first version, starring Leslie Banks and Peter Lorre) and *The Thirty-nine Steps* (1935).

A number of films made during and immediately after the war by the team of Michael Powell and Emeric Pressburger are worth seeing, among them *One of Our Aircraft Is Missing* (1942), *Stairway to Heaven* (1946), *Black Narcissus* (1947), and *The Red Shoes* (1948). Typically, the films of Powell and Pressburger were marked by a personal, quirky sense of humor and striking cinematography.

Many of the films of the 1950s and 1960s, a period of the disintegration of the British empire, looked back at times of greater glory. David Lean's *Bridge Over the River Kwai* (1957) is the best example of a number of 1950s films that depicted British heroism during the Second World War. This look backward continued in the 1960s with films such as Lean's epic *Lawrence of Arabia* (1962), the story of an enigmatic British adventurer in the First World War, and Tony Richardson's *Tom Jones* (1963), an adaptation of Henry Fielding's novel about the exploits of a rustic playboy in 18th-century England.

Since the early 1970s a great number of relatively low-budget independent films have been produced in Great Britain, many with the help of funding from the BBC. These films often have a curious relationship to current British social ills and the continuing decline of "British Eminence." Dennis Potter's fantasy transformation of the "hard-boiled detective" genre, *The Singing Detective*, is a particularly good example. Others also receiving attention in the U.S. are Mike Leigh's *High Hopes*, Stephen Frears's *My Beautiful Launderette*, *Prick Up Your Ears*, and *Sammy and Rosie Get Laid*, Neil Jordan's *Mona Lisa*, and Bill Forsyth's *Local Hero* and *Gregory's Girl*. Monty Python classics are a good introduction to wacky British humor, as is Charles Crichton's recent hit *A Fish Called Wanda*.

THE U.S.S.R.

The grim faces of Muscovite commuters at rush hour, a lunch of overcooked canned peas and gristly meat at a restaurant in Kiev, and the ubiquitous lines bending around buildings like serpents are typical images of life in the Soviet Union that most travelers take back—not to mention the national trend toward disorganization, which confronts the traveler at every juncture. Yet behind the exterior of an officious, cold, and bureaucratic (albeit chaotic) society is a nation as vast and varied as any country in the world.

The Soviet Union is two and a half times the size of the United States. Stretching from the Baltic across Europe and Asia to the Pacific, it contains an incredibly diverse population speaking dozens of different languages—Armenian and Azerbaijanian, Ukrainian and Uzbek, to name just a few. The Russians, who ruled this vast territory under the czars and continued their domination during the Soviet era, are now facing challenge: almost all of the republics, in which the majority populations are comprised of nationalities other than Russian, have risen up and demanded various forms of sovereignty and independence. The Baltic republics—Estonia, Latvia, and Lithuania—have declared themselves sovereign states, which have been recognized by the international community.

From the wooden Russian Orthodox churches of the north to the ancient minarets and mosques of central Asia, almost everyone can find in the country's vast size and long history some treasures especially of interest to them. For the specialist and nonspecialist alike, now is an especially exciting time to visit this enigmatic country in the process of fundamental change.

Led by President Mikhail Gorbachev, the Soviet Union has undergone a profound cultural thaw in which the people have been freed to reexamine their past and to criticize the injustices, failures, and self-inflicted atrocities of the last 75 years. Some of the contemporary theater, literature, and visual arts, which formerly were stilted and contrived (unless part of the underground movement) and followed the strict party line genre of Soviet Realism, have become far more daring and entertaining. Rock music, once an obscure movement of avant garde youth, has become a national obsession.

Yet the country remains as enigmatic as ever. Not even the gypsies who approach foreigners in the cities, dressed in colorful garb, claiming to tell fortunes for a small hard-currency fee, can read the future of the Soviet Union. Will Russia and the Russians continue to dominate? What groups will rise to power? How will the economy and the society be structured? One may not find definitive answers to these questions on a trip to the Soviet Union, but all travelers will come back far more informed and with a sense that they have seen history being written.

However, in spite of all the change and uncertainty, it is that which endures irrespective of the political era that is most compelling about the Soviet Union. Among the timeless qualities of the Soviet people are their warm hospitality, their ironic sense of humor, and their boundless faith, which has seen them through the best and the worst of times.

—*Julie Raskin, St. Petersburg, U.S.S.R.*

Official name: Union of Soviet Socialist Republics. **Area:** 8,649,496 square miles (about two and a half times larger than the U.S.). **Population:** 290,939,000. **Population density:** 33 inhabitants per square mile. **Capital and largest city:** Moscow (pop. 8,500,000). **Language:** Russian, Ukrainian, Byelorussian, Turkic, Tungusic, Georgian, Armenian. **Religion:** Atheism (official), Russian Orthodox, Islam. **Per capita income:** US$3,000. **Currency:** Ruble. **Literacy rate:** 99%. **Average daily high/low*:** Leningrad: January, 23°/12°; July, 71°/57°. Moscow: January, 21°/9°; July, 76°/55°. **Average number of days with precipitation:** Leningrad: January, 17; July, 13. Moscow: January, 11; July, 12.

TRAVEL

U.S. citizens will need a passport and a visa to enter the Soviet Union. To get a visa you must make advance travel arrangements for the entire time you plan to spend in the Soviet Union. The following documents must be submitted to the Soviet Consular Office no fewer than 14 days—but not more than three months—prior to arrival in the U.S.S.R. when applying for a tourist visa:

- photocopies of pages two and three of a U.S. passport, which should be valid at least one month after the date of *departure* from the Soviet Union
- four 1½ × 1¾-inch photographs made on matte or dull paper with white background (all four photos must be identical and made during the last 12 months)
- one copy of the visa application form duly filled out, typed, and signed (date of departure from the U.S. as well as complete travel itinerary in the U.S.S.R. must be indicated on application form)
- INTOURIST reference number (confirmation number)
- a copy of a telex from INTOURIST with confirmation of hotel accommodation and domestic transportation in the Soviet Union.

All visa documents must be accompanied by a letter from the travel agency arranging travel to the U.S.S.R. Tourist visas are valid for the duration of the tour that has been booked plus the time required for travel to/from the Soviet border. Visas for Americans traveling in the U.S.S.R. are granted by the Consular Division of the U.S.S.R. Embassy in the USA, 1825 Phelps Place NW, Washington, DC 20008 (202-939-8907), and by

---

*All temperatures are Fahrenheit.

the U.S.S.R. Consulate General, 2790 Green Street, San Francisco, CA 94123; (415) 922-6642.

"Your visa specifies the dates you will be in the U.S.S.R., the cities you are going to visit, and how long you will be in those cities. You are expected to comply with what is on the visa. It is virtually impossible to extend your stay in any city or to travel to a city that is not on your approved itinerary. It is also next to impossible to extend your stay in the U.S.S.R., so be sure to plan your itinerary carefully before you go."
—Brenda Richardson, Pasco, Washington

Getting Around

It is difficult to travel independently within the U.S.S.R. If you choose to travel on your own, you'll have to make all arrangements in advance through a travel agency that is affiliated with the official Soviet travel agency, Intourist (630 Fifth Avenue, Suite 868, New York, NY 10111). Intourist-affiliated travel agencies are listed in *Welcome to the U.S.S.R.*, a booklet available free of charge from the Intourist information office. Working with Intourist, the travel agent will make arrangements for you to travel independently or, if you prefer, will book you on an Intourist-sponsored tour. Before entering the country you must arrange prepaid accommodations for every night you will be there. This usually entails staying at Intourist facilities, which aren't cheap. Campgrounds are a lower-priced option available in the summer season. Inquire about these with your booking agent. Whether you decide to go with a group or make individual arrangements, your plans should be made well in advance, since your visa will not be issued until all arrangements have been duly confirmed by Intourist in Moscow.

Many students choose a third option—an organized youth or student tour—over individual travel or a tour arranged by Intourist. Student and youth tours are planned through SPUTNIK, the Soviet youth travel bureau, and are much less expensive than independent travel or tours arranged through Intourist. A number of U.S. colleges and universities offer organized group tours of the Soviet Union arranged by SPUTNIK. For tours offered by CIEE-member institutions and open to students at all colleges and universities see "Organized Tours," page 66.

Council Travel offices can book you on several types of organized tours in the Soviet Union ranging from kayaking an untamed river to crossing the country on the Trans-Siberian Express. Two travel organizations that specialize in Soviet tours are Rahim Tours (800-556-5305) and Inter-Tours Corp. (800-366-5458); both handle independent traveling arrangements and low-budget tours.

Homestays have recently emerged as another option for travel in the U.S.S.R. Homestay travelers stay in the homes of English-speaking Soviets eager to share their lives—and homes—with Westerners. Accommodations vary depending on the program, but you can generally expect your own bedroom in a small Soviet flat, three home-cooked meals per day, and an English-speaking host to show you the sights. The cost for a homestay depends on length and location. Homestay travel is not necessarily the cheapest option for seeing the U.S.S.R., because hosts must be compensated for their time and energy, but it is probably one of the best ways to meet the people. This type of travel must also be arranged in advance; contact Global Social Venture Network, 721 Montecillo Road, San Rafael, CA 94903 (415-491-1532), for more information.

Those who really want to see the Soviet Union from one end to the other can travel the Trans-Siberian Railroad, one of the longest and most famous railways in the world. Council Travel offices can arrange a tour that includes a train journey from Beijing to Leningrad with several days of sightseeing in Irkutsk, Moscow, and Leningrad. However, most travelers who make this train trip on their own start from Budapest, which is the cheapest place to book passage and obtain visas. From Moscow you can ride the Trans-Siberian Express to Beijing (through either Mongolia or Manchuria) or to the Soviet city of Nakhodka, where you can get a ferry to Japan. Many travelers make the journey across the U.S.S.R. on a transit visa, which is less expensive than a tourist visa. To get a transit visa, you must start your trip from a country that borders the U.S.S.R. and exit into a different nation. Transit visas for the U.S.S.R. are available only from Soviet consulates in Eastern Europe and Asia; you can't get them in the United States. With a transit visa, you can leave the train for up to three days in any city en route, as long you have the proper train tickets. Travel agents in Budapest should be able to process tickets and visas in about two weeks; elsewhere it may take longer. Required reading for anyone considering a journey abroad the Trans-Siberian Express is Paul Theroux's account of his journey in *The Great Railway Bazaar.*

"Even with its rich cultural and historical tradition, the Soviet Union is not rich economically. Everywhere there are people lining up to buy everyday necessities of life such as fruit, meat, vegetables, and bread along with other material needs. The traveler to the Soviet Union who must fend for himself will have trouble dealing with the crowds, lines, and frequent shortages, but anything can be gotten used to with a little patience."
—Laura K. Cummings, Old Lyme, Connecticut

Money Matters

There is no mandatory currency-exchange requirement in the U.S.S.R. However, travelers are prohibited from exchanging currency at any rate other than the official one, as well as from taking rubles in or out of the country. When you enter the U.S.S.R., you'll be given a currency declaration form on which each exchange transaction will be entered during your stay. You must keep this form, together with all receipts from transactions involving the spending or exchange of money, since they will be checked and the form turned in to a customs agent on departure. You can spend your money without changing it into rubles at the Beryozka shops, which offer souvenirs and a limited range of imported goods not generally available in regular Soviet stores.

"The economy has developed increasingly severe problems resulting in shortages of goods, certain foods, and inflated prices. For the visitor this means that their exposure to the massive Soviet counter-economy will be intensive and unrelenting. An individual on a two-hour stroll along Nevesky Prospect in Leningrad may be offered the opportunity to trade 15 or 20 times. Trading (particularly currency exchanges) is against Soviet law and the visitor should always obey all Soviet laws. However, it is a fact that many travelers to the U.S.S.R. do trade occasionally for a variety of items, and the laws prohibiting such activities are not rigorously enforced. If one should succumb to temptation, then the value of the deal should definitely not exceed $20 since severe penalties can be imposed."
—John O. Lindell, Oneonta, New York

Especially for Students

SPUTNIK (15 Kosygin Street, 117946 Moscow) is the Soviet Union's student travel bureau. It organizes travel for student groups visiting the U.S.S.R. but does not make travel arrangements for individual students. The International Student Identity Card provides free admission to most museums in the Soviet Union.

Meeting the People

The Citizen Exchange Council, a private nonprofit and nonpartisan organization devoted to U.S.-Soviet cultural exchange, sponsors educational travel programs that enable students to experience the Soviet Union by meeting its people. Personal contacts are arranged through "counterpart meetings" where participants can exchange ideas and experiences with Soviets who share similar interests. Other program features include predeparture orientation, home visits, and excursions to sites of historical and cultural interest. Individuals can travel with groups of high school students, college students, or educators; another option is traveling on a special-interest program focusing on the arts, the media, or public diplomacy. Programs are two to three weeks in length and take place throughout the year. Special summer church-restoration and voluntary service projects, whereby Americans live and work with their Soviets hosts, are offered periodically. There is no Russian language requirement. For more information, contact Citizens Exchange Council, 12 West 31st Street, Fourth floor, New York, NY 10001, or by phone: (212) 643-1985.

"The most important thing a visitor to the Soviet Union will experience beyond the history and culture is the deep and almost fanatical interest Soviets have in Americans. Language barrier or not, Soviets will find ways to talk with Americans. The subjects range from current events to the cost of dinner in New York City and what teenagers do for fun after school. Potential travelers to the Soviet Union are cautioned to study up on their own country before leaving."
—Laura Cummings, Old Lyme, Connecticut

For Further Information

You can get a copy of *Tips for Travelers to the U.S.S.R.*, published by the Department of State's Bureau of Security and Consular Affairs, by sending $1 to the Superintendent of Documents, U.S. Government Printing Office, Washington, DC 20402. Intourist (630 Fifth Avenue, New York, NY 10111) is the official organization responsible for travel arrangements for foreigners in the U.S.S.R. Contact the New York office for general travel information as well as specific information about tours and travel agents in the United States authorized to work with Intourist.

There are a growing number of travel guidebooks for the Soviet Union. Among the most recent is *USSR—A Travel Survival Kit*, available for $21.95 (plus $1.50 book-rate postage; $3 for first-class) from Lonely Planet Publications, Embarcadero West, 112 Linden Street, Oakland, CA 94607. Hippocrene Books (171 Madison Avenue, New York, NY 10016) publishes *Moscow at Your Fingertips*, which lists everything you would ever want to know about the Soviet capital, and the *Hippocrene Companion Guide: The Soviet Union*, which includes background information and city guides to Kiev, Tallinn, Moscow, and Leningrad. Finally, another good guidebook is Moon Publications' *Moscow-Leningrad Handbook*, available for $12.95 from Moon Publications, 722 Wall Street, Chico, CA 95928-5629.

"Few people in the U.S.S.R. speak English, so unless you speak Russian, independent wandering, even if it's only to the bread store, would be impossible without a phrasebook like the Berlitz book on Russian for travelers."
—Kyle Knauer, Fargo, North Dakota

WORK

Americans are not permitted to work in regular, paid jobs in the U.S.S.R. unless the job is part of a joint venture with a company outside the Soviet Union.

With the thaw in U.S.-Soviet relations, however, a limited number of teaching positions are now open to Americans. For a placement fee of $650, the Global Social Venture Network will set you up with a teaching position in the cities of Yalta, Ryazan, or Pskov. For more information, contact Global Social Venture Network, 721 Montecillo Road, San Rafael CA, 94903 (415-491-1532). *Surviving Together*, published by the

Institute for Soviet-American Relations (1608 New Hampshire Avenue NW, Washington, DC 20009) also offers information on teaching positions in the U.S.S.R.

Internships/Traineeships

Programs offered by members of the Council on International Educational Exchange are listed below.

AIESEC-US. Reciprocal internship programs for students in economics, business, finance, marketing, accounting, and computer science. See page 18 for more information.

Association for International Practical Training. "IAESTE Trainee Program." On-the-job training for undergraduate and graduate students in technical fields such as engineering, computer science, agriculture, architecture, and mathematics. See page 18 for more information.

Voluntary Service

CIEE places young people in voluntary service workcamps in the U.S.S.R. organized by a variety of youth organizations. At these workcamps, groups of volunteers from different countries work on community-service projects of various types. Volunteers receive room and board in return for their labor. The applications of U.S. residents are processed by CIEE. For more information contact the Voluntary Service Department at CIEE.

Mir Initiative, a U.S. organization working in partnership with the Cooperation Project in the U.S.S.R., places volunteers in workcamps in the Irkutsk region of southern Siberia. Most projects take place around Lake Baikal, the world's deepest freshwater lake. For more information, contact Mir Initiative, PO Box 28183, Washington, DC 20038-8183.

STUDY

Persons considering study in the Soviet Union might want to check out the *AAASS Directory of Programs in Soviet and East European Studies*, which lists close to 75 academic programs in the Soviet Union, including addresses and information on deadlines and costs. The directory also lists Soviet studies programs in the U.S. and can be ordered prepaid from the American Association for the Advancement of Slavic Studies, 128 Encina Commons, Stanford, CA 94305. The price is $25 for nonmembers, $10 for members; you might be able to find it in libraries or study-abroad offices.

In addition to the programs listed below, there is the option of summer study in the U.S.S.R. in one of several Russian-language seminars arranged by Intourist. The seminars last either 12 or 24 days and are held in one of 12 cities in the Soviet Union. Seminars are offered at various levels and are supplemented by other activities such as social events, excursions to museums and beaches, and a theater visit, all planned by Intourist. For information, write Intourist at 630 Fifth Avenue, Rockefeller Center, New York, NY 10111, or call Academic Travel Abroad at (800) 556-7896 or Global Tour Associates at (203) 651-2365.

Educational programs offered by CIEE member institutions are listed below. Consult Appendix I for the addresses of the colleges and universities that sponsor these programs. In addition to those listed below, Lewis and Clark College, Pennsylvania State University, and the University of California offer programs open only to their own students.

Semester and Academic Year

Russian Language/Area Studies

Associated Colleges of the Midwest. "Semester in the Soviet Union." Krasnodar. Fall semester. Preference given to students at institutions that are members of ACM or the Great Lakes Colleges Association. Juniors and seniors with two years of college Russian. Apply by February 15.

Council on International Educational Exchange. "Cooperative Russian Language Program." St. Petersburg. Academic year at Leningrad State University, semester at LSU or at Leningrad Gornyi Institute. Undergraduates and graduate students with three years of Russian. Apply by March 1 for fall and October 1 for spring. Contact University Programs Department.

Experiment in International Living/School for International Training.
"College Semester Abroad." St. Petersburg. Fall or spring semester. Intensive language, life and culture seminar, field-study methods seminar, independent-study project, excursions, and homestays. Sophomores to seniors with 2.5 GPA and two years of college Russian. Apply by May 15 for fall and October 15 for spring.
"College Semester Abroad." Volgograd. Fall or spring semester. Intensive language, life and culture seminar, field-study methods seminar, independent-study project, excursions, and homestays. Sophomores to seniors with 2.5 GPA. No language prerequisite. Apply by May 15 for fall and October 15 for spring.
"Contemporary Issues in the U.S.S.R." Moscow. Intensive language, seminars on contemporary issues in the U.S.S.R., and field study methods. Homestay, independent study, excursions to St. Petersburg and the Golden Ring. Sophomores to seniors with 2.5 GPA, two years of college Russian, and previous Soviet studies. Apply by October 31 for spring and May 31 for fall.

Middlebury College. Moscow. Sophomores to graduate students fluent in Russian. Rolling admissions.

Northeastern University. "Moscow University Exchange." Fall quarter. Exchange with School of Journalism at Moscow State University. Courses in journalism, culture, and language. Juniors and seniors with completion of elementary Russian and 3.0 GPA. Apply by April 15.

Ohio State University. Moscow. Russian Language Program at the Pushkin Institute. Academic year or semester. Juniors to graduate students with three years of college Russian. Apply by October 1 for spring and March 1 for fall or year.

State University of New York at Albany.
"Thorez Institute Exchange." Moscow. Fall semester. SUNY students only. Juniors and seniors with three years of college Russian. Apply by December 1 for fall.
"Moscow State University Exchange." Semester or academic year. Graduate students enrolled at a SUNY school only. Three years of college Russian. Apply by December 1.

Stetson University. "Semester in Moscow." Fall or spring. Moscow State University. All courses taught in Russian. Sophomores to seniors with 2.5 GPA and two years of college Russian. Apply March 1 for fall, and October 15 for spring.

University of Alabama. "Study Tour of the Soviet Union." Russia, Ukraine, Georgia. Three-week program in May. Undergraduates and graduates.

University of Illinois at Urbana-Champaign. "Semester in St. Petersburg." Fall or spring. Juniors and seniors with one year of Russian language studies and 4 (out of 5) GPA. Apply by March 15 for fall; October 15 for spring.

University of La Verne. "Comparative Cultures: The U.S.S.R." Moscow, St. Petersburg, Kiev. January interim. Juniors to graduate students with 2.5 GPA. Apply by October 31.

University of Massachusetts—Amherst. Leningrad State Technical University. Fall semester. Three years Russian language study required. Program limited to 12 students. Apply by March 15.

World College West. "World Study in the U.S.S.R." Pyatigorsk. Semester or academic year. Intensive cultural immersion. Language, culture, field-study methods, independent-study project, some homestay, potential internships. Juniors and seniors with one year of Russian language and one cultural studies class. Apply by March 15.

Summer

Eastern Michigan University. "Labor Studies in Moscow." One month residential seminar focusing on Soviet trade unions and the changing economy of the U.S.S.R. No language prerequisite. Undergraduates with 2.5 GPA. Apply by February 15.

Archaeology

University of Illinois at Urbana-Champaign. "Laboratory School in Experimental and Usewear Analysis." Orgreev region of Moldova. Experimental production and use of lithic and bone tools. Juniors to graduate students with 3.0 GPA. Apply by March 1.

Business

Council on International Educational Exchange. "Moscow Summer Business Program." Cosponsored with the University of Illinois at Urbana-Champaign. Plekhanov Institute of National Economy in Moscow. Juniors to graduate students with business/economics background. Apply by March 15. Contact University Programs Department.

Economics

Illinois State University. "ISU Summer in the Soviet Union." Various cities. Sophomores, juniors, and seniors. Apply by February 13.

Russian Language and Culture

Council on International Educational Exchange.
"Cooperative Russian Language Program." Leningrad State University or Leningrad Gornyi Institute. Sophomores to graduate students with two years of Russian. Apply by January 20. Contact University Programs Department.
"Cooperative Russian Language Program for Science Students." Novosibirsk. Freshmen to graduate students with one year of college Russian. Apply by January 20. Contact University Programs Department.
"Cooperative Russian Language and Area Studies Program." Tver. Freshmen to graduate

students with three to five semesters of Russian. Apply by January 20. Contact University Programs Department.

"Russian Language for Research." U.S.S.R. Academy of Science and Leningrad State University. Graduate students with four semesters of college Russian. Apply by January 20. Contact University Programs Department.

Indiana University. "Overseas Study in St. Petersburg." Freshmen to seniors with one year of Russian and 3.0 GPA. Apply by February 6.

University of Louisville. "The Soviet Union: Political Science and Art History." Freshman to graduate students. Apply by April 31.

Miami University. Moscow and St. Petersburg. Russian Language study tour. Freshman to graduate students (and alumni). Apply by April 1.

Theater

New York University. "Circle Summer Sessions in Moscow." Four weeks of study at Shepkin Theater School. Auditions required. Contact Circle in the Square Theatre School; (212) 307-2732.

EXPLORING SOVIET CULTURE

Readings

In the past several years, as a result of Mikhail Gorbachev's policy of *glasnost*, literary works that were previously considered "inappropriate" for publication are now being read by the Soviet public. Some of these literary works have already received wide acclaim in the West, such as Boris Pasternak's *Doctor Zhivago* (1959), which chronicles the period of the Revolution, the proletariat upheaval and the Communist secession; Alexander Solzhenitsyn's *Gulag Archipelago*, Evgeny Zamyatin's *We* (1983), and Andrei Platonov's *The Foundation Pit*. Other authors are being published for the first time in both the U.S.S.R. and the West. Anatoly Rybakov's *Children of the Arbat* (1988), which tells the story of a group of young adults in Moscow at the outset of the Second World War, and *Life and Fate* (1987), by Vasily Grossman, are stellar examples. One of the best known of contemporary Soviet writers is Tatyana Tolstaya, the great-grandniece of Leo Tolstoy. Her collection of short stories, *On the Golden Porch*, was translated into English in 1989. Fazil Iskandar is the current rave of the avant-garde scene: His latest collection of short stories is entitled *Rabbits and Boa Constrictors* (1989).

These contemporary authors have quite a foundation to build upon. The U.S.S.R. has a complex history, and much of the stoic vitality of the Russian character can be traced back to the social and political climate as documented in the writings of classic Russian masters such as Dostoyevsky, Gogol, and Tolstoy. Nikolay Gogol's works had an enormous impact on Russian society, in part because he was a Ukrainian by birth and saw Russian society as an outsider. By revealing the Russians to themselves, he created humorous, honest pieces that retain their freshness after a century and a half. *The Inspector General*, his satirical comedy written in the 1870s, is still eminently readable. Fyodor Dostoyevsky is another strong force in Russian literature: His intellectual, moody novels are considered by many to be among the best ever written. Many of the settings, characterizations, symbolism, and attitudes found in his two major works, *Crime and Punishment* and *The Brothers Karamazov*, endure in the country today.

The recent political changes in the Soviet Union have elicted a healthy capitalistic response from the West: there are now dozens of *glasnost*-variety books on the market.

Hedrick Smith's 1983 collection of essays, *The Russians*, however, remains one of the best. The recently updated version consists of reworked pieces from the years he spent in the Soviet Union as a correspondent for *The New York Times*. Another good book along these lines is by Pulitzer Prize–winning journalist David Shipler, *Russia: Broken Idols, Solemn Dreams*. Stephen Cohen and Katrina Vandem Heuvel have edited a recent anthology of well-written essays called *Voices of Glasnost: Gorbachev's Reformers Speak*. Paul Theroux's *The Great Railway Bazaar* is recommended by many; in this work, Theroux travels the Trans-Siberian Express.

Films

The cinema has been an integral part of modern Soviet culture. Consistent with the ideas of industrialization, mass culture, and modernity associated with the Russian Revolution, film was idealized as the art form of the proletariat in the decades that followed the overthrow of the czarist order. Montage stylistics, the epitome of machine-age experience, is the hallmark of Sergei Eisenstein's *The Battleship Potemkin* (1925), *October* (1928), and *Que Viva Mexico*! (1932), as well as *Man with a Movie Camera* (1929) by Dziga Vertov. In addition to their then-revolutionary technique, these films took an aggressive, confrontational look at the intricacies of class difference, revolution, and the role of cinema.

Governmental restrictions on filmmaking and the rehashing of traditional themes of patriarchy and patriotism faded with the post-Stalinist "thaw" in the 1950s. Socialist realism fell from grace when this "thaw" developed into what became known as the "spring" or "ice-breaking." Andrei Tarkovksy's cryptic and fantastic interpretations of personal identity in the modern Soviet Union, with all their beauty and spareness, are mapped out in his films, including *Ivan's Childhood* (1962), *Andrei Rublev* (1966), *Solaris* (1972), and *Mirror* (1975–78). Mikhail Kalatozov's *The Cranes Are Flying*, lauded at Cannes in 1957, is the story of youthful ambitions and love shattered by the intervention of war. Nikita Mikhalov's *An Unfinished Piece For a Player Piano* (1977) is a dramatic film based on Chekhov's incomplete last work.

The Soviet cinema is currently booming both abroad and at home. A multitude of films probing historical questions, the malaise of Soviet youth, the meaning of *glasnost*, and a range of social problems have received international attention. Typical of this trend is Vassili Pitchul's film, *Little Vera* (1988), a witty look at the bleak prospects for Soviet youth. *Moscow Does Not Believe in Tears*, Menshov's 1980 film, is a funny, charming story of three provincial young women who travel to Moscow in search of husbands; as always, though, complications arise. *Freeze, Die, Come to Life* (1990), the story of a young boy growing up in Siberia during World War II, is also worth seeing.

YUGOSLAVIA

Yugoslavia is a patchwork quilt of peoples, languages, and customs as well as a land of incredible scenic beauty. Situated in the heart of the Balkan peninsula along the Adriatic Sea, it has been a strategic crossroads between Europe and the Near East for centuries. As a result, Yugoslavia encompasses amazing contrasts. In a few hours you can travel from the fashionable boutiques and coffeehouses of Slovenia to the mysterious world of Bosnia, where the five-times-daily Moslem call to prayer transports you to a world far removed from Western Europe.

The enchanting coast and islands of the Adriatic are popular with tourists. More remote and exotic are the villages in the rugged mountains that cover two-thirds of the country. The nation's capital, Belgrade, lies in the fertile lowlands along the Danube River in the eastern part of the country.

Yugoslavia has existed as a nation only since 1919. After the First World War brought about the final collapse of the Austro-Hungarian and Ottoman empires, the two powers that had long dominated the region, Yugoslavia was created by the victorious Allied powers, who decided that the various Slavic peoples of the region should be united in a single country. This state fell apart during the Second World War but was reunited as a new socialist federated republic by the communist leader Josip Broz Tito in 1945. During the Cold War era, the country walked the tightrope between the capitalist West and the Soviet bloc.

The complex history of the region has resulted in a nation of great differences. Today Yugoslavia is made up of six republics (Serbia, Macedonia, Bosnia and Herçegovina, Montenegro, Croatia, and Slovenia) and two autonomous regions (Vojvodina and Kosovo)—each with its own particular ethnic mix. Serbo-Croatian, Slovenian, and Macedonian are the principal languages. Communication is further complicated by the fact that although the Serbs and Croats speak the same language, they use different alphabets (Cyrillic and Roman respectively). Islam and Christianity—both Eastern Orthodox and Roman Catholic—are the most prominent religions. To make it even more confusing, and fascinating, there are numerous smaller minorities: Slovaks, Czechs, Jews, Romanians, Gypsies, Hungarians, Albanians, and Italians.

Today, noncommunist, independence-minded governments elected in Slovenia and Croatia and violent ethnic clashes in Kosovo challenge the continued existence of the state of Yugoslavia. To compound the problem, the country's economy has fallen on difficult times. Extraordinary inflation, severe unemployment, an increasing number of strikes, a renewal of ethnic rivalries, and the legacy of one-party government have all contributed to an impending crisis. Some observers are suggesting that the fragile union is ready to fall apart while others think a restructured, maybe even revitalized, Yugoslavia will emerge. Everyone agrees that the next few years are crucial.

—*Thomas A. Emmert, St. Peter, Minnesota*

Official name: Socialist Federal Republic of Yugoslavia. **Area:** 98,766 square miles (about the size of Wyoming). **Population:** 23,864,000. **Population density:** 240 inhabitants per square mile. **Capital and largest city:** Belgrade (pop. 1,300,000). **Language:** Serbo-Croatian, Slovene, Macedonian. **Religion:** Eastern Orthodox, Roman Catholic, Islam. **Per capita income:** US$6,540. **Currency:** New dinar. **Literacy rate:** 90%. **Average daily high/low*:** Belgrade: January, 37°/27°; July, 84°/61°. **Average number of days with precipitation:** Belgrade: January 8; July, 6.

TRAVEL

A valid passport is required for U.S. citizens traveling to Yugoslavia. For specific requirements, check with the Yugoslav Consulate General, 767 Third Avenue, 17th floor, New York, NY 10017.

Getting Around

An assortment of boats—ferries, hydrofoils, steamers, and so forth—link the cities along Yugoslavia's popular Adriatic Coast with Italy. International train and bus service connects Yugoslavia to the rest of Europe. Eurail passes are not valid within Yugoslavia; however, the InterRail pass is. Trains are inexpensive, and although travel on many lines is slow, the rail network extends to all parts of the country. Students also get a discount on the already cheap intercity fares on JAT, the state airline.

---

*All temperatures are Fahrenheit.

Especially for Students and Young People

Yugotours-NAROM is Yugoslavia's student travel bureau. Their main office is located at Djure Djakovica 31, 11000 Belgrade, and they also have offices in Zagreb and Skopje. Students with the International Student Identity Card get 10 percent off domestic airfares, as well as reductions on rail travel to other Eastern European countries, international airfares, and accommodations. They are also entitled to a 50-percent discount at many museums and galleries. The International Youth Card is good for discounts on accommodations and some museums.

For Further Information

For more background information about the country, contact the Yugoslav Press and Cultural Center, 767 Third Avenue, New York, NY 10017. Tourist information is available from the Yugoslav National Tourist Office, 630 Fifth Avenue, Suite 280, New York, NY 10111. *The Real Guide: Yugoslavia* offers advice on combatting red tape, what to drink and when, and whether or not consulates will lend you money in an emergency (they won't). Frommer's *Eastern Europe & Yugoslavia on $25 a Day* is also recommended for students and young people traveling on a budget. For those who prefer to exercise as they travel, look for a copy of *Yugoslavia: A Climbing, Walking and Cultural Guide*, published by Hunter Publishing and available in most bookstores for $13.95.

WORK

It is difficult for U.S. citizens to get the work permit needed for regular, paid employment in Yugoslavia. You can contact the Embassy of Yugoslavia for specific regulations on the subject, however. As an alternative to regular employment, you might be interested in a trainee program or participation in a workcamp.

Internships/Traineeships

Two programs offered by members of the Council on International Educational Exchange are listed below.

AIESEC-US. Reciprocal internship program for students in economics, business, finance, marketing, accounting, and computer science. See page 18 for more information.

Association for International Practical Training. "IAESTE Trainee Program." On-the-job training for undergraduate and graduate students in technical fields such as engineering, computer science, agriculture, architecture, and mathematics. See page 18 for more information.

Voluntary Service

CIEE places young people in voluntary-service workcamps in Yugoslavia organized by Voluntary Service Yugoslavia (Mestni TRG 13, 61000 Ljubljana). At these workcamps, groups of volunteers from various countries work together on projects that involve reforestation efforts, recreation for people with muscular diseases, and conservation of historical sites. Volunteers must be at least 18 years old. Room and board are provided by the camp. The applications of U.S. residents are processed by CIEE. For further information, contact the International Voluntary Service Department at CIEE.

STUDY

A study program offered by a CIEE-member institutions is described below. Consult Appendix I for the address to write for more information. In addition to the program below, Indiana University offers a program open only to its own students.

Summer

General Studies

Michigan State University. "The Roman Frontier in Yugoslavia." Molsia. Archaeological field training, research, and lectures on the Roman frontier in Maesia. Juniors, seniors, and graduate students. Apply by April 20.

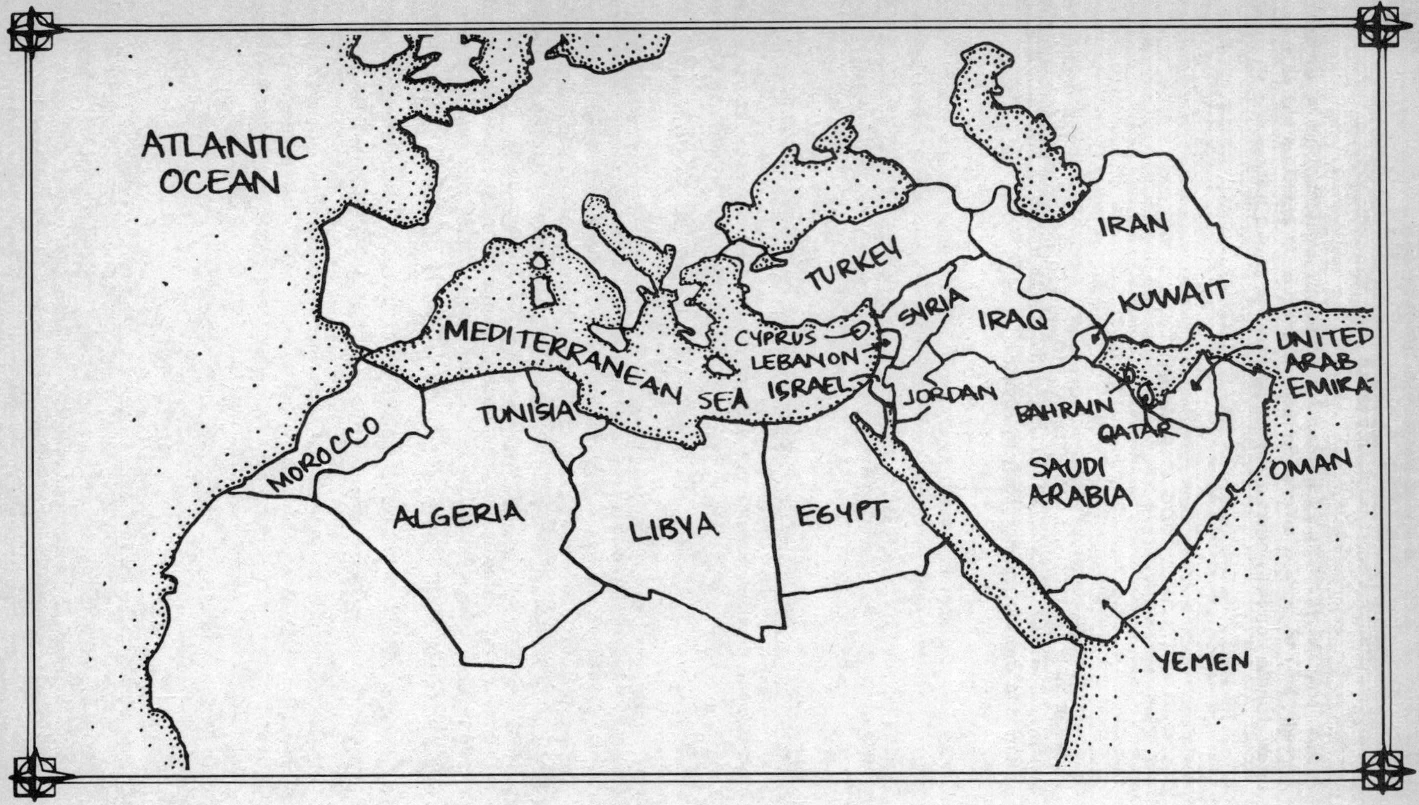
ATLANTIC
OCEAN
MEDITERRANEAN SEA
CYPRUS
LEBANON
ISRAEL
TURKEY
SYRIA
IRAQ
IRAN
KUWAIT
JORDAN
BAHRAIN
QATAR
UNITED
ARAB
EMIRA
SAUDI
ARABIA
OMAN
YEMEN
EGYPT
LIBYA
TUNISIA
ALGERIA
MOROCCO

CHAPTER SEVEN
THE MIDDLE EAST AND NORTH AFRICA

This chapter encompasses a broad range of countries lying between the Caucausus Mountains and the Sahara, between the Mediterranean Sea and the Indian Ocean. A number of powerful bonds unite this region: most of these countries share a common religion (Islam) and many share a common language (Arabic). Nevertheless, cultural diversity—rather than unity—is the dominant characteristic of the area.

Located at the juncture of Europe, Africa, and Asia, this area has long been of vital importance in world history. The region also encompasses a number of strategic waterways—the Bosporus, the Strait of Gibraltar, the Strait of Hormuz, and the Suez Canal—guaranteeing the area's continued importance as a crossroads of the world's commerce. The historic significance of the region has been further enhanced in this century by the discovery of vast petroleum reservoirs.

The Middle East

It is not only by virtue of its geographic location that the Middle East is crucial to world history; many of the world's peoples trace the roots of their religion and culture to the region. The fertile river valleys of the Tigris, the Euphrates, and the Nile were home to some of the world's earliest civilizations. The surrounding land is rich with the artifacts of the ancient cultures of Egypt, Babylon, Assyria, and Persia.

While most of the countries of the Middle East share the religion of Islam, the region was also the birthplace of Judaism and Christianity. But while these three religions have a history of mutual antagonism, regional violence has escalated since the creation of the state of Israel in 1948 and the ensuing displacement of the Palestinian population. While the Palestinian-Israeli dispute continues to dominate international politics in the Middle East, it is not the only cause of the continuing war and violence in the region. Many complex rivalries and animosities combined to produce the most region's most recent conflict, the Persian Gulf War of 1991, which involved Arab, European, Canadian, Australian, and American forces.

Peace in this region has yet to be achieved. For this reason, many Americans are hesitant to travel or study here; yet the need for Americans to gain an understanding of the people, cultures, and languages of the region has never been greater. While there are good reasons you may want to avoid countries like Lebanon, Iraq, and Iran at the present time, it is also important not to make broad generalizations about all the different countries of the Middle East. Those who consider their options and travel wisely have an unequalled chance to witness some of today's most important world events unfold from an entirely different perspective. They will also have the opportunity to gain insight into a fascinating world that few Americans have seen and even fewer understand.

North Africa

For thousands of years civilization has flourished in the fertile strip between the Sahara and the Mediterranean. Rome and Carthage left their mark, but the greatest influence is that of the Arabs whose language, religion, and culture still pervade the region. More recent foreign influences have been those of Europeans; the colonial powers of France, Italy, Spain, and Britain controlled the region during the first half of this century. Today's nations of North Africa did not gain their independence until the 1950s.

While North Africa shares many characteristics with the Middle East, it is more accessible to Western tourists, and more familiar with Western ways. Thousands of Europeans visit Egypt, Tunisia, and Morocco, attracted by sunny beaches, ancient ruins, vibrant cities, and exotic cultures. Fewer Americans travel to the region, but those making the trip will be well rewarded.

GETTING THERE

The cheapest fares available from the U.S. to the Middle East and North Africa are generally APEX fares (see Chapter Five for a general explanation of air fares). There are also student fares to a limited number of destinations. Listed below are some examples of *one-way* summer fares that were in effect during 1991. More up-to-date information is available at Council Travel offices (see listing on pages xix–xxi).

New York–Istanbul	$425
New York–Casablanca	$425
New York–Cairo	$425

In addition, student/youth flights are available from several European cities to the Middle East and North Africa. These can be booked at any Council Travel office or at a student travel bureau in Europe. Regulations vary depending on the airline, but generally holders of the International Student Identity Card (see page 8) or the International Youth Card (see page 10) are eligible. Listed below are sample *one-way* student fares for the 1991 peak summer season.

London–Tel Aviv	$209
Paris–Tel Aviv	$255
London–Istanbul	$195
Frankfurt–Tel Aviv	$285

Several nations around the Mediterranean are but a short trip from Europe. From Algeciras, Spain, a variety of boats (including car ferries and hydrofoils) depart for the cities of Ceuta and Tangiers on the African continent, only a couple of hours away. From Palermo and Trapani in Sicily, you can find various types of passenger boat service to Tunisia. And several Greek islands, including Rhodes and Samos, are only a short boat trip from Turkey's Aegean coast. Ferry service is also available from Greece to Cyprus and from there on to Lebanon and Israel. Student travel bureaus in Europe will be happy to provide you with more information.

Travel in the Middle East and North Africa

U.S. citizens may encounter travel restrictions in several countries. Currently, all travel to Libya and Lebanon by U.S. citizens is prohibited by the Department of State. For up-to-date information on this policy, contact the U.S. Treasury Department's Office of Foreign Assets Control, (202) 376-0922. For travel advisories on possible dangers in other countries, contact the State Department's Citizens Emergency Center, (202) 647-5225.

Because of the recent war and continuing reconstruction of Iraq and Kuwait, travel in these two countries is nearly impossible. At press time, neither Iraq nor Kuwait were issuing tourist visas to American citizens, although Kuwait plans to issue them again in the near future.

Historically, most Persian Gulf states have discouraged tourism. Unless you have official business, you can obtain only short-term transit visas for Bahrain, Saudi Arabia, and the United Arab Emirates. However, some Gulf states have begun to change their policy. Qatar and Oman both grant tourist visas, though these are valid only for a few weeks.

Currently, Jordan and Syria welcome U.S. tourists a little more eagerly. Syria grants tourist visas valid for either three or six months. Jordan issues multiple-entry visas; the length of time you can stay in the country is determined at the airport, but generally you will be allowed to stay as long as you want and to extend your visa at a later date.

The U.S. Department of State discourages but does not prohibit travel by U.S. citizens to Iran. For information on visa requirements, contact the Iranian Interests Section of the Algerian Embassy, 2137 Wyoming Avenue NW, Washington, DC 20008; (202) 965-4990.

In addition, many Arab countries refuse to admit persons who have Israeli stamps or notations in their passports, or who are travelling to or from Israel. To avoid this problem, it's possible to have Israeli visa, entry, and exit stamps put on a separate sheet that can be stapled to the passport and removed on departure. For more detailed information, contact the embassies of the countries you wish to visit (see addresses in the individual country sections that follow).

In predominately Muslim countries, travelers of both sexes—but women in particular—will feel more comfortable if they are sensitive to local customs and act and dress accordingly. Remember, too, that there is a tremendous difference between urban and rural areas; what is acceptable in the city may not be acceptable in the country.

Most people seem to agree that in most Muslim countries, with some exceptions, single women travelers will find it difficult to go out at night or to certain areas without attracting unwanted attention. One option is to travel with others; dressing in a conservative fashion is another. Local women are often protective of foreign women, and you can always hire a local male guide who can both show you the sights and discourage harassment. Women should not shirk from exploring the region; they should, however, be prepared for uncomfortable situations and unfamiliar restrictions.

"Although everyone noticed me, I encountered no problems taking evening walks in Damascus, Cairo, Baghdad, or Amman. It was safer than my own neighborhood in Minneapolis. I found the average male, especially of university age, very protective towards the woman traveler."
—Ramita Jaravayan, Minneapolis, Minnesota

"Women should take light, ankle-length skirts and long-sleeved shirts or loose tunic/pants outfits with them as well as one large scarf that can be used as a head covering. These clothes suit local custom, and are most comfortable for the climate."
—Ann Waters, Flagstaff, Arizona

Ramadan is the ninth month of the Islamic calendar, during which Moslems fast from dawn to sunset, in commemoration of the revelation of the *Koran* to Mohammed. (In 1992, *Ramadan* begins on March 6; because the Islamic calendar is 11 days shorter than ours, *Ramadan* begins 11 days earlier in each successive year.) If you try to get a meal in a restaurant during daylight hours in this month, you may be frowned upon or even refused service. Fasting includes no eating, drinking, or smoking, and since it is adhered to strictly in a number of countries, it is a simple matter of respect for a tourist to refrain from breaking the custom in public. If you want to eat during daylight hours, do so in private. The best solution is to adhere to local custom; at nightfall festive crowds fill the streets and the resturants and cafes stay open late.

For Further Information

There are many guidebooks for the countries most often visited by tourists, such as Egypt, Israel, Morocco, and Turkey (see the individual country sections that follow for some of these books). Among the few guides to less-visited countries, Lonely Planet Publications' *Jordan and Syria: A Travel Survival Kit* and *Yemen: A Travel Survival Kit* (both $8.95) are among the best. An excellent regional guide, especially for those traveling farther east, is *West Asia on a Shoestring* ($14.95). If you can't find these titles in bookstores, you can order them by mail (include $1.50 postage and handling) from Lonely Planet Publications, Embarcadero West, 112 Linden Street, Oakland, CA 94607.

Students traveling in Europe who want to make a side trip to a nearby North African nation will find several *Let's Go* guides helpful. Chapters on Morocco are included in *Let's Go: Spain and Portugal* and *Let's Go: Europe*. A chapter on Tunisia is included in *Let's Go: Italy*; Turkey is covered in *Let's Go: Greece and Turkey* and *Let's Go: Europe*. The *Let's Go* books are available in bookstores and Council Travel offices.

For persons interested in staying at youth hostels in the region, volume two of the *International Youth Hostel Handbook* lists hostels in Israel, Lebanon, Morocco, Syria, Tunisia, and Egypt. The government tourist offices of Egypt, Israel, and Turkey will also be happy to send you free hostel information for their countries.

Those unfamiliar with regional social etiquette may want to prepare themselves by reading *The Traveler's Guide to Middle Eastern and North African Customs & Manners*, written in 1991 by Elizabeth Devine and Nancy L. Braganti. Published by St. Martin's Press, it's available in bookstores for $13.95.

American travelers going to the Middle East should be prepared for discussions of the region's disputes and problems and the U.S. role in these. One of the sources of materials on this subject is the Foreign Policy Association (see page 12). Among the better books concerning Arab-Israeli relations is *Arab and Jew*, a historical study of the conflict between the two peoples by former *New York Times* correspondent David Shipler. For a penetrating look at the lives of foreign workers in the Middle East, as well as the repurcussions of the Iran-Iraq war, read *Expats* by *Newsweek's* ex–Paris bureau chief Christopher Dickey.

"It is important for students planning to travel to the Middle East to generally prepare before departing the United States. There are many Middle Eastern organizations in the U.S., especially on college campuses, which you can use to help familiarize yourself with the country you intend to visit. American students will have a much more complete experience if they possess some rudimentary knowledge of what to expect."
—Elizabeth Andersen, Greenville, South Carolina

Listed below are addresses where you can write for general information as well as details on visa requirements for the nations we do not cover later this chapter:

- Embassy of Bahrain, 3502 International Drive NW, Washington, DC 20008
- Embassy of Iraq, 1801 P Street NW, Washington, DC 20036
- Embassy of the Hashemite Kingdom of Jordan, 3504 International Drive NW, Washington, DC 20008
- Embassy of the Republic of Kuwait, 2940 Tilden Street NW, Washington, DC 20008
- Embassy of Lebanon, 2560 28th Street NW, Washington, DC 20008
- People's Bureau of the Diplomatic Mission of the Socialist People's Libyan Arab Jamahiriya, 1118 22nd Street NW, Washington, DC 20037
- Embassy of Oman, 2342 Massachusetts Avenue NW, Washington, DC 20008
- Embassy of Qatar, 600 New Hampshire Avenue NW, Washington, DC 20037
- Embassy of Saudi Arabia, 601 New Hampshire Avenue NW, Washington, DC 20037
- Embassy of the Syrian Arab Republic, 2215 Wyoming Avenue NW, Washington, DC 20008
- Embassy of the United Arab Emirates, 600 New Hampshire Avenue NW, Washington, DC 20037
- Embassy of the Republic of Yemen, 600 New Hampshire Avenue NW, Suite 860, Washington, DC 20037

WORK

For U.S. citizens, the chances of obtaining salaried employment in the Middle East and North Africa are not very good unless they are fluent in the local language. Teaching is one area, however, where there are a few openings for Americans. Anyone interested in teaching in the region should write for a copy of AMIDEAST's *Teaching Opportunities in the Middle East and North Africa*, available for $14.95 from AMIDEAST, 1100 17th Street NW, Washington, DC 20036.

You'll find internships and traineeships in Cyprus, Egypt, Israel, Morocco, Tunisia, and Turkey listed in the individual country sections later in this chapter. In addition, there are internship possibilities in the IAESTE program in Iraq, Jordan, Lebanon, Libya, and Syria; see page 18 for more information.

As a result of the destruction the Persian Gulf War brought to Kuwait, programs for overseas workers are available in the Persian Gulf through U.S. Government organizations such as the Agency for International Development (AID), the Army Corps of Engineers, and the Department of Defense. See "Jobs with the U.S. Government" on page 29 for more information.

STUDY

You'll find study programs listed for Egypt, Israel, and Morocco later in this chapter. In this section, we've listed only those study programs offered by CIEE members that take place in more than one country of the region. Consult Appendix I for the addresses of the colleges and universities listed below.

Semester and Academic Year

General Studies

St. Olaf College.
"Term in the Middle East." Istanbul, Turkey; Cairo, Egypt; Jerusalem, Israel; and Rabat, Morocco. Fall semester plus January. Social and political issues of the contemporary Middle East. Sophomores, juniors, and seniors. Apply by March 1.
"Global Semester." Cairo, Egypt; Bangalore, India; Taipei, Taiwan; and Kyoto, Japan. Fall semester plus January. Cultures, political and social issues of selected non-Western countries. Sophomores, juniors, and seniors. Apply by March 1.

University of Pittsburgh. "Semester at Sea." Fall or spring semester. Students, based aboard the S.S. *Universe*, attend classes on board and travel to various countries in Europe, the Middle East, Africa, and Asia. Sophomores, juniors, and seniors with 2.75 GPA. Contact: Semester at Sea, Eighth floor, William Pitt Union, University of Pittsburgh, Pittsburgh, PA 15260; (412) 648-7490.

Summer

History

University of Louisville. "Egypt and Greece." Various cities. Ancient history. Freshmen to graduate students. Apply by April 31.

ALGERIA

A nation of wine, Islam, and oil, Algeria is the second-largest nation of Africa. It is divided by the Atlas Mountains into arable land along the northern coast and the vast desert that covers the south. Arabic is the prevailing language but many educated Algerians also speak French. As you go south into the Atlas Mountains and the Sahara, Berber languages predominate.

One hundred and thirty years of French occupation ended when independence was granted in 1962. In fact, it was the eight-year guerrilla war waged by Algerians against the French that prompted France to give up its holdings all over the African continent. Perhaps because of this long struggle against colonialism, independent Algeria has become a leading voice of the Third World. The government supports "liberation" struggles around the world, including a deep commitment to the Polisario guerrilla force fighting to drive Morocco out of Western Sahara. As a result, tensions between Morocco and Algeria are high and crossing the border between these two nations may take some time—there are only two crossing points along their 800-mile frontier.

The socialist agenda adopted by Algeria's first president, Ahmed Ben Bella (and his successors), has given rise to an extensive campaign to modernize traditional Arab gender relations and reconstruct the economy of the country. The exploitation of natural gas and petroleum deposits in the Sahara has helped strengthen the economy and fund the reforms of the postindependence period. Today Algeria continues its commitment to socialism and is also moving towards the gradual democratization of political life.

—*Esther Langley, Charlottesville, Virginia*

Official name: Democratic and Popular Republic of Algeria. **Area:** 918,497 square miles (more than three times the size of Texas). **Population:** 25,714,000. **Population density:** 27 inhabitants per square mile. **Capital and largest city:** Algiers (pop. 1,483,000). **Language:** Arabic, various Berber languages. **Religion:** Islam. **Per capita income:** US$2,760. **Currency:** Dinar. **Literacy rate:** 52%. **Average daily high/low*:** Algiers: 59°/49°; July, 83°/70°. **Average number of days with precipitation:** Algiers: January, 11; July, less than 1.

TRAVEL

U.S. citizens need both a passport and a visa to visit Algeria. For applications and further information, contact the Embassy of the Democratic and Popular Republic of Algeria, 2137 Wyoming Avenue NW, Washington, DC 20008.

Getting Around

Domestic air service, radiating from Algiers, is used almost as frequently as the bus system. Due to large government subsidies, local air transport is quite inexpensive for most Algerians. For foreigners required to exchange currency at official rates, however, the cost is somewhat higher.

Getting around at ground level is no problem on the well-paved roads of the north; but in the south, with fewer roads and services, it's slower and less comfortable. Buses, operated by the national company TVE, travel to all parts of the country. Train service, slower and less frequent than buses, is confined to the north. Hitching is also an easy way to get around, although again this is only true in the north.

---

*All temperatures are Fahrenheit.

For Further Information

The best guide to Algeria and its North African neighbors is *Morocco, Algeria and Tunisia: A Travel Survival Kit*, available for $13.95 (plus $1.50 book rate postage; $3 first-class) from Lonely Planet Publications, Embarcadero West, 112 Linden Street, Oakland, CA 94607.

WORK

It is extremely difficult for Americans to obtain permission for regular employment in Algeria. More information is available from the Algerian embassy (address above).

Voluntary Service

CIEE places young people in voluntary-service work camps in Algeria organized by the Association Culturelle des Activities d'Amitie d'Echanges entre Jeune (ACAAEJ Centre Culturel, Naciria 35250, Boumerdes). These workcamps bring together volunteers from various countries to accomplish a range of construction and renovation projects. Volunteers must be 18 years of age or older and speak French; room and board are provided. The applications of U.S. residents are processed by CIEE. For more information, contact the Voluntary Service Department at CIEE.

EGYPT

When most Americans envision Egypt, they think of the pyramids, the Sphinx, and King Tut. Indeed, the thousands of American tourists who visit Egypt each year come almost exclusively to visit Pharaonic Egypt. The monuments of ancient Egypt attract even larger numbers of European tourists, who also come for the Egyptian sun and Mediterranean and Red Sea beaches. However, to those who really want to get to know and understand the Arab world, Egypt offers the opportunity to study Arabic and gain insights into Islam, Arab history, and the politics, economics, and culture of the contemporary Middle East.

The roll call of civilizations and cultures in Egypt actually has been much more diverse than simply the Pharaonic and Arab. There are traces of ancient Persia in Egypt; the ancient Greek and Roman civilizations are visible in Egyptian monuments; and the Byzantine and Coptic Christian cultures are evident as well. Indeed, although today 85 percent of the population is Moslem, 15 percent remains Coptic Christian. In fact, the word Copt comes from the same root word as Egypt, and the Copts regard themselves as the true Egyptians, undiluted by the intermingling of later Moslem conquerors. Throughout the 19th and early decades of the 20th century, France and Great Britain were the foreign powers that extended their influence over Egypt. Finally, in 1952, after a nonviolent revolution, Egyptians once again ruled Egypt. Thus Egypt, although one of the world's oldest civilizations, is a relatively new independent nation-state.

Though a trite phrase, "Egypt, the gift of the Nile" is essential to understanding the nation. Ninety-six percent of Egyptian territory is uninhabited desert. In the remaining four percent live 50 million Egyptians, making the Nile valley and delta among the most intensely farmed and densely populated areas on earth.

A quarter of all Egyptians live in metropolitan Cairo, which has been described as the ultimate urban experience—one of the noisiest and most crowded cities on earth. It is also a city where the vast majority of the population is poor, yet there is very little crime. This fact can be ascribed to the importance of the family and religion in Egyptian life. Both Moslems and Christians believe that individual behavior must ultimately be judged by family and God.

God is in every Egyptian's conversation: "See you tomorrow, *ensha'allah* (God willing)"; "My mother is recovering nicely, *el hamduli'lah* (thanks be to God)." Both

Moslems and Christians use the same phrases and acknowledge the same God's influence in their lives. But religion in Egypt is neither puritanical nor gloomy. Egyptians are optimistic, exuberant, possess a sense of humor, and have a great capacity for enjoying themselves.

—*Molly Bartlett, Eugene, Oregon*

Official name: Arab Republic of Egypt. **Area:** 386,650 square miles (¾ the size of Alaska). **Population:** 54,139,000. **Population density:** 141 inhabitants per square mile. **Capital and largest city:** Cairo (pop. 12,560,000). **Language:** Arabic. **Religion:** Islam. **Per capita income:** US$490. **Currency:** Egyptian pound. **Literacy rate:** 44%. **Average daily high/low*:** Cairo: January, 65°/47°; July, 96°/70°. **Average number of days with precipitation:** Cairo: January, 1; July, 0.

TRAVEL

U.S. citizens are required to have a passport and a visa to enter Egypt. Applications for tourist visas, which are valid for six months from date of entry, must be accompanied by a passport-sized photograph and a $12 fee. For specific requirements, check with the Embassy of the Arab Republic of Egypt (2310 Decatur Place NW, Washington, DC 20008), or with the Egyptian consulates in Chicago, Houston, San Francisco, or New York.

Getting Around

One of the best ways to get around Egypt is by train. Trains connect Cairo with Alexandria and Port Said and will take you south up the Nile Valley to Luxor and Aswan. Good overnight service with sleeping cars is provided on the longer runs and discounts are available to students (see "Especially for Students and Young People" below).

Buses are also another option between the major cities, and are preferable to trains for shorter trips. They also provide service to areas not accessible by train, such as the Sinai and the Oases. Shared taxis, which travel on a fixed route dropping off and picking up passengers along the way, serve virtually every town and village in the Nile Valley. If you hitchhike, you will be expected to pay the equivalent of the shared taxi fare. As always, women should not hitchhike alone.

You can also rent a car; Hertz, Avis, and Budget are among the companies operating in Egypt. Driving is on the right side of the road, and you will need an International Driving Permit.

Probably the most relaxing and scenic way to get around the country is by traveling on the Nile, which has served as the country's major highway for thousands of years. Numerous passenger boats make the three- to four-day trip between Aswan and Luxor, which has become a standard part of most organized tours to Egypt. You can also choose to make this trip by *felucca*, the traditional sailboats that still provide local transportation up and down the river for many Egyptians, for much less money.

"*All transportation within Egypt is heavily crowded but inexpensive. Buses will have people hanging on them while trains have passengers in the coaches, on top of the cars and on the locomotive. However, Port Said and Alexandria can both be reached from Cairo for only a few dollars.*"

—*Paul Estenskar, Chicago, Illinois*

---

*All temperatures are Fahrenheit.

Especially for Students and Young People

ESC/STSD at the Medical Faculty of the Egyptian Scientific Centre (PO Box 58, El-Malek El-Saleh, Cairo) provides students and young people with tourist information such as tours and youth hostel accommodation. Holders of the International Student Identity Card receive reduced airfares from Egypt to a number of international destinations, discounts on train travel (except first class) within Egypt, and 50 percent off admission to museums and historical sites.

"In Egypt, be prepared to haggle over everything from the price of a bottle of water to the availability of space on trains. Haggling is not only common, it is expected; tourists will be treated with more respect if they start by haggling."
—Ellis Kendrick, Denver, Colorado

For Further Information

Let's Go: Israel and Egypt is one of the best budget-travel guidebooks to the region. It's available for $14.95 in most bookstores and at Council Travel offices. Another very good guide to Egypt is Lonely Planet's *Egypt and the Sudan: A Travel Survival Kit*. If you can't find it in a bookstore, you can order it for $14.95 (plus $1.50 book-rate postage; $3 first-class) from Lonely Planet Publications, Embarcadero West, 112 Linden Street, Oakland, CA 94607.

You'll also want to contact the Egyptian Tourist Authority (630 Fifth Avenue, New York, NY 10111), which can provide you with information on youth hostels, budget hotels, restaurants, and study opportunities in Egypt; there's an Egyptian Tourist Authority office in San Francisco as well. The Egyptian embassy (2310 Decatur Place NW, Washington, DC 20008) will provide copies of *Prism: Quarterly of Egyptian Culture* upon request.

WORK

Finding regular salaried employment in Egypt is difficult for foreigners. A contract offer from an Egyptian company is required for starters, and then you must apply for a work permit at a labor office in Egypt.

Internships/Traineeships

Programs offered by members of the Council on International Educational Exchange are listed below.

AIESEC-US. Reciprocal internship program for students in economics, business, finance, marketing, accounting, and computer science. See page 18 for more information.

Association for International Practical Training. "IAESTE Trainee Program." On-the-job training for undergraduate and graduate students in technical fields such as engineering, computer science, agriculture, architecture, and mathematics. See page 18 for more information.

STUDY

For information on Egyptian universities that offer courses for foreign students in Arabic language, Islamic history, Islamic religion, and Egyptology, contact the Cultural Counselor, Egyptian Educational Bureau, 2200 Kalorama Road NW, Washington, DC 20008.

The American University in Cairo, a private university founded in 1919, welcomes students from American colleges and universities for a semester or full year. The aim of the university is to offer an American-style education to Egyptian, Middle Eastern, African, American, and other students and to serve "as a bridge of understanding between the U.S. and the Middle East." Eighty percent of its students are Egyptian, and there are normally 150 to 200 American students on campus studying Middle Eastern politics, economics, anthropology and sociology, Egyptology, and other subjects. The language of instruction is English, but an intensive Arabic language program is also available. Apply by May 31 for the fall term and October 31 for the spring term. In addition, the American University in Cairo offers summer courses in Arabic language and general studies. Apply by March 31. Consult Appendix I for the address you can write to for more information.

In addition to the programs of the American University in Cairo, two other CIEE-member institutions, the University of California and Pennsylvania State University, offer study programs open only to their own students.

Semester and Academic Year

Arabic Language

American University in Cairo. "Intensive Arabic." Fall. Freshman to graduate students and adults interested in studying Arabic intensively. Apply by May 31.

General Studies

American University in Cairo. "Study Abroad for a Semester or a Year." Sophomores to graduate students. Instruction in English. Apply by May 31 for fall or academic year; October 31 for spring.

Antioch University. "Egyptian and Islamic Culture and History." Cairo. Winter quarter. Six weeks of class, three weeks of travel, and two weeks of independent study. Some knowledge of Arabic recommended. Sophomores to graduate students. Apply by August 1.

Summer

Arabic Language

American University in Cairo. Freshman to graduate students and adults interested in studying Arabic intensively. Apply by March 31.

Egyptology

American University in Cairo. "Summer Seminar in Egyptology." Undergraduates, graduates, and adults. Apply by March 31.

General Studies

American University in Cairo. Freshman to graduate students. Instruction in English. Apply by March 31.

EXPLORING THE CULTURE OF EGYPT

Readings

The most internationally recognized of Egypt's contemporary writers is Naguib Mahfouz, winner of the 1988 Nobel Prize for literature. Mahfouz is noted for his ability to paint a vivid picture of Egyptian daily life. His *Midaq Alley* depicts working-class Cairo; *Children of Gebelawi*, set in a Cairo alley, is an allegory that retells the stories of Mohammed, Moses, Jesus, and Adam and Eve. The first two volumes of Mahfouz' famous *Cairo Trilogy*, first published in 1956, have just appeared in English as *Palace Walk* and *Palace of Desire*. The trilogy is about a Cairo family in the early 20th century and the ways they adapt to changing Egyptian society.

Although he lacks Mahfouz's international reputation, Yusuf Idris is widely read and appreciated by Egyptians themselves. A novelist who once worked as a doctor in the Nile delta, his books, such as *Rings of Burnished Brass*, are sharp, gritty stories that portray rural life in Egypt. Fathey Ghanem, author of *The Man Who Lost His Shadow*, is a writer of more popular, commercial fiction. The most important Egyptian playwright is Tawfiq Al-Hakim, whose plays include *The Tree Climber* and *Fate of a Cockroach*.

For a vivid portrait of life in Egypt today, you might try reading a biography. *Shahhat, an Egyptian*, is an account of the life of an Egyptian peasants as told to Richard Critchfield. In *Khul-Khaal: Five Egyptian Women Tell Their Stories*, Nayra Attiya portrays the strength and spirit of five contemporary women of the lower and lower-middle classes.

Films

Since World War II, there has been a rapid expansion of filmmaking in Egypt, particularly of commercial melodramas and farces with dreamy settings. Most of these are stories of love and jealousy dripping with wealth, glamour, and the usual touch of song and dance. This successful formula may explain the enormous popularity of Egyptian films throughout the rest of the Arab world. Alongside the commercial industry is a relatively small number of independent filmmakers who, beginning in the 1950s, wanted to make films accessible to their audience, but without strictly adhering to the formulaic rigidity of most Egyptian commercial films.

Chief among these independent filmmakers is Youssef Chahine, whose films *Cairo Station* and *Black Waters* are portraits of the workers and lower classes of Egypt. Two of his later films, *The Land* and *The Sparrow*, are insightful, political impressions of conflicting Egyptian social forces. *The Land* is a story about a land-and-water dispute between a village and a wealthy bey; *The Sparrow* investigates the 1967 war with Israel. The maturation of Chahine's style continues with two of his more recent films, *Alexandra . . . Why?* and *An Egyptian Story*, both heavily autobiographical films detailing the experience of attempting to balance the cultural influences of Egypt with those of the dominant Western world.

ISRAEL

For centuries, Muslims, Christians, and Jews have fought to control this small piece of relatively arid land. Today, the continuing struggle pits Arab against Jew for control of the homeland the Arabs call Palestine and the Jews call Israel.

Late in the 19th century, the Zionist movement was founded in Europe. Its goal was to create a Jewish state on the land the Hebrews inhabited in biblical times. During the first half of this century, Jews from Europe began immigrating to Israel—an immigration that swelled after 1945 with survivors of the Holocaust. In 1948, the State of Israel was born. Ever since, the politics of the region have been dominated by the competing claims of Arabs and Jews to this piece of land situated between the Jordan River and the Mediterranean Sea.

Israel—partly as a result of wars with its Arab neighbors in 1948, 1956, 1967, and 1973—now controls the disputed territory. But Arab Palestinians comprise nearly half the population of the land under Israeli administration (Israel proper and the occupied territories of the West Bank, Gaza, and the Golan Heights). A Palestinian uprising that began in 1987 in the occupied territories continues to challenge the political and moral authority of the Israeli occupation. Unrest in the occupied territories and Iraqi missile attacks during the Persian Gulf War serve as a reminder of the uncertain future of Israel, a nation that in spite of its impressive military victories still finds security to be an elusive goal.

Today, for an insider's look at the "real" Israel, push and shove your way on to a bus. Each ride presents a microcosm of Israeli society as varied as the landscape stretching before you. An ultra-orthodox Hasid, dressed in the black garb of his 18th-century Polish ancestors, sits next to a soldier on his way home for a short leave. An Arab woman in white headdress sits next to an *oleh hadash* (new immigrant) from Argentina, eating felafel. Suddenly the multilingual cacophony dies down. Six piercing beeps signal the beginning of the hourly news broadcast. The bus driver raises the volume on the radio so that passengers can follow world events.

With the places along your route—names like Jericho, Jerusalem, Bethlehem, and Masada—serving as constant reminders that this is an ancient land, it is easy to forget that the State of Israel is a relative newcomer to the family of nations. Many Israeli Jews are recent immigrants. The new nation absorbed first the Ashkenazi Jews, refugees from central and eastern Europe, then the Sephardic Jews of the Middle East and North Africa, and next the Falashas, or Ethiopian Jews. The latest wave of immigrants is from the Soviet Union; Israel's efforts to absorb the newest arrivals—half a million in 1990 alone—have strained its limited resources. Each group of immigrants has brought with it its own language, food, music, dress, and traditions, but the renaissance of the Hebrew language has done much to unify these disparate groups. In fact, the efforts of the lexicographer Eliezer Ben Yehuda, the "father of Modern Hebrew," to fashion a modern language out of a biblical tongue are celebrated in a popular song.

The Israeli Defense Forces have also played a significant role in the absorption effort. Men and women alike are drafted at the age of 18, women for two years, men for three. Then there is reserve duty—until the women become mothers and the men reach the age of 55—for up to 45 days a year. As a result, the army is more than a formidable defense force; it is "the great equalizer."

It may surprise you to learn that the overwhelming majority of Israeli Jews are secular. Nevertheless, religion pervades every aspect of life. Part of the reason for this is rooted in Israel's parliamentary democracy. Since no one party ever wins the majority necessary to take control of Israel's 120-member Knesset (parliament), small religious parties holding no more than three or four seats can force concessions that affect the whole country. Their influence has resulted in unusual situations and arrangements: there is no bus service on the Sabbath (except in the northern city of Haifa) and on the day before Passover, the State of Israel sells the contents of its granaries to a wealthy Israeli Arab so as to not knowingly be in possession of any leavened substance during the eight-day festival.

A trip to Israel offers the chance to visit important religious sites, ancient archaeological digs, and modern cities. You can relax on Mediterranean beaches, explore the Negev Desert, scuba dive in the Gulf of Aqaba, or ski on Mount Hermon. It also provides a chance to better understand the contemporary struggles of the different peoples who inhabit this ancient land.

—*Carina Klein, New York, New York*

Official name: State of Israel. **Area:** 7,847 square mile (about the size of Massachusetts). **Population:** 4,371,000. **Population density:** 570 inhabitants per square mile. **Capital:** Jerusalem (the United States and most of the international community recognize Tel Aviv as the capital). **Largest city:** Jerusalem (pop. 468,400, including East Jerusalem). **Language:** Hebrew, Arabic. **Religion:** Judaism, Islam. **Per capita income:** US$5,995. **Currency:** Shekel. **Literacy rate:** 88%. **Average daily high/low*:** Jerusalem: January, 55°/41°; July, 87°/63°. **Average number of days with precipitation:** Jerusalem: January, 9; July, 0.

---

*All temperatures are Fahrenheit.

TRAVEL

A passport valid for nine months from the date of your arrival is required for U.S. citizens. Onward or return tickets are also required; however, a visa is not needed for tourists stays of less than three months. For specific requirements, check with the Embassy of Israel (3514 International Drive NW, Washington, DC 20008) or with an Israeli consulate in New York, Chicago, Boston, Houston, Los Angeles, New Orleans, Philadelphia, San Francisco, Detroit, or Newark. Remember that many Arab countries will not let you enter if you have evidence of a visit to Israel in your passport. Israeli passport officials, however, can put your visa stamp on a removable piece of paper if you ask when you enter the country.

Traveling in Israel itself has been little affected by Palestinian unrest in the occupied territories. However, travel into the West Bank or Gaza Strip may not always be advisable. Before you go, contact the Citizens Emergency Center (see page 8) at the U.S. State Department for any travel warnings that may be in effect. You might also want to become more informed about the *intifadeh* and the political situation in the Middle East. *Conflicts and Contradictions*, by Meron Beneviste (an Israeli geographer), is a good examination of the dilemma of Israel/Palestine and the legitimate and powerful claims of two ancient peoples for the same land. One of the best analyses of the Palestinian uprising in the West Bank and Gaza Strip is "Intifadeh," by Don Peretz, in the Summer 1988 issue of *Foreign Affairs*.

"Living in Israel, I got a much better understanding of a country that is controversial. You get a much different perspective when you're on the other end of the U.S. news stories. It's very interesting to see how people live in a country where war and conflict seem ever-present."
—Christopher Shern, New Hope, Minnesota

Getting Around

It's easy to get around Israel; distances are short and there is good and inexpensive bus service. Be aware, however, that there is no bus service between Friday afternoon and Saturday night except in Haifa. Holders of the International Student Identity Card receive a 10-percent discount on Egged buses, which serve nearly every city and settlement in the country. Egged also runs a line of tour buses to various tourist sites in Israel, including jaunts to the Sinai Desert, the Red Sea, and the Tiberias Hot Springs. The Egged tour office in the U.S. (800-682-3333) can send you a pamphlet listing all the possibilities. Trains offer another travel option, though service is limited and, like buses, trains don't run during the *shabbat*. Holders of the International Student Identity Card receive a 20-percent discount on train tickets. Another option is the *sherut* taxis that operate between cities and towns, leaving when filled and dropping off and picking up passengers along the way. They are cheaper than regular taxis but more expensive than buses; they operate on Saturday and late at night, when buses don't. Try to agree on a price before setting out.

Most people find that the extensive public transportation system makes renting a car unnecessary. Renting a car is fairly easy, however, although you'll need the International Driving Permit (see page 52). The leading car rental agencies are Hertz, Avis, and Eldan; you can get further information by calling the toll-free numbers for Hertz or Avis in the United States.

Especially for Students and Young People

Israel Students Tourist Association (ISSTA), with offices in Tel Aviv (109 Ben Yehuda Street, Tel Aviv 63401), as well as in Jerusalem, Haifa, and Beer Sheba, is the nation's student travel bureau. They provide travel information and book accommodations for both Israel and other countries; they also sell plane, train, and bus tickets. Mail may be sent to travelers c/o ISSTA Poste Restante at the above address. ISSTA's direct information lines (03-5230696 and 03-5230697) are open Sunday to Thursday, 8:30 A.M. to 6:00 P.M. and Friday 8:30 A.M. to 1:00 P.M.

Holders of the International Student Identity Card receive a discount on trains, buses, and international ferries and get reduced admission to most museums and archaeological sites. There is also a discount on tours of Israel and Egypt organized by ISSTA. The International Youth Card is valid for discounts on some accommodations, restaurants, tours, and excursions.

Meeting the People

Through the "Meet the Israelis" program, get-togethers are arranged during the day or evening with Israeli families or individuals with similar interests or professions. Israeli government tourist offices in Israel can arrange these visits for individual travelers on a day's notice. For a list of addresses of tourist offices in Israel, write to the Israel Government Tourist Office, 350 Fifth Avenue, New York, NY 10118.

"The sabra (a cactus fruit that is hard and prickly on the outside and soft and sweet on the inside) is the nickname for a native Israeli. It is quite appropriate for a nation that has suffered through five wars during its brief existence and centuries of persecution before that. To get through the rugged skin and meet the person inside takes some persistence and patience, but the rewards and insight into the Middle East one gains are worth the effort."
—Kenneth L. Milman, New York, New York

For Further Information

For general tourist information, contact the Israel Government Tourist Office (address above), which can provide you with information on camping and youth hostels, among many other topics.

One of the best guidebooks for the independent traveler on a budget is *Israel: A Travel Survival Kit*, which combines practical travel facts with authoritative historical references and covers both the modern state and the ancient biblical country. If you can't find it in a bookstore, you can order it for $13.95 (plus $1.50 postage; $3 for first-class) from Lonely Planet Publications, Embarcadero West, 112 Linden Street, Oakland, CA 94607. Another helpful guide for the student is *Let's Go: Israel and Egypt*, which includes the West Bank and Jordan. It's available for $14.95 in most bookstores and at Council Travel offices. A helpful pamphlet entitled *A Youth and Student Travel Adventure in Israel* can be ordered from the Israel Government Tourist Office.

The American Zionist Youth Foundation provides information on institutions and organizations in Israel with programs open to American students. Their free 142-page booklet entitled *Higher Education in Israel* lists general information about study in Israel and includes a list of the Israeli universities and other diploma-granting institutions that accept foreign students. Another publication, *A Guide to 3-Month to 1-Year Programs in Israel*, lists other alternatives to traveling, such as work options, internships, and kibbutz contacts. Call the American Zionist Youth Foundation at 800-274-7723 (800-27-ISRAEL) or write University Student Department, American Zionist Youth Foundation, 110 East 59th Street, New York, NY 10022.

WORK

"Working in Israel showed me some of the less glamorous aspects of the country—the Tel Aviv Central Bus Station every morning, trying to stretch each paycheck to pay for everything, and only having one and a half days for the weekend."
—Joanne Abraham, Youngstown, New York

Internships

Programs offered by members of the Council on International Educational Exchange are listed below.

AIESEC-US. Reciprocal internship program for students in economics, business, finance, marketing, accounting, and computer science. See page 18 for more information.

Association for International Practical Training. "IAESTE Trainee Program." On-the-job training for undergraduate and graduate students in technical fields such as engineering, computer science, agriculture, architecture, and mathematics. See page 18 for more information.

Working on a Kibbutz

Kibbutz Aliya (27 West 20th Street, New York, NY 10011) is the U.S. representative for kibbutzim in Israel, and offers young Americans (ages 18 to 32) the opportunity to live and work in one of these unique communities that accept volunteer workers from all over the world. One option offered by the organization is the Temporary Worker Program, in which participants must make a commitment to remain on the kibbutz for at least one month (the maximum commitment is one year). Another option is the Kibbutz Ulpan Program, one half of which consists of work and the other half of intensive study of Hebrew. The program lasts six months, although a special ten-week course is available in the summer. (Academic credit from Haifa University can also be arranged.) The Kibbutz University Semester Program, an eight- to ten-week kibbutz period and a full semester at Haifa University, is still another possibility. A summer semester combining a month at Hebrew University in Jerusalem and a month on a kibbutz is also available. Further information is available from Kibbutz Aliya upon request.

The American Zionist Youth Foundation (110 East 59th Street, New York, NY 10022) sponsors a variety of programs that bring young people to Israel for periods of a summer, a semester, six months, or a year. The summer programs offer special experiences in the areas of science, nature study, and kibbutz life—all combined with extensive touring of the country. The long-term programs range from six months to a year and combine work with intensive Hebrew language study. Other options include a semester at an Israeli university and a work/study program on kibbutzim, as well as leadership development programs.

"The communal experience requires a great deal of determination and persistence. It is extremely difficult to live with and depend on total strangers, but work provided a common ground for us to get to know each other. At first it was a lonely situation, but after a week I felt completely at home."
—William Bonney, New York, New York

Working on an Archaeological Dig

Another work possibility in Israel is volunteering for an archaeological dig. A listing of archaeological excavations open to volunteers is put together each January by the Ministry of Education and Culture, Department of Antiquities (PO Box 586, Jerusalem 91004). You must be at least 17 years of age, however, and be prepared to work for at least a week or two. In addition, volunteers must be physically fit and capable of doing strenuous work in a hot climate. The listing of such digs is also available from the Israel Government Tourist Office (350 Fifth Avenue, New York, NY 10118) or the American Zionist Youth Foundation (110 East 59th Street, New York, NY 10022).

WORK, STUDY, TRAVEL ABROAD

STUDY

If you are interested in enrolling at an Israeli university, you can contact the New York offices of the following organizations: American Friends of the Hebrew University (11 East 69th Street, New York, NY 10021), American Friends of Tel Aviv University (360 Lexington Avenue, New York, NY 10017), American Friends of Haifa University (168 Fifth Avenue, New York, NY 10010), American Technion Society (810 Seventh Avenue, New York, NY 10019), American Associates of Ben-Gurion University of the Negev (342 Madison Avenue, Room 1924, New York, NY 10173), and the American Committee for the Weizman Institute of Science (51 Madison Avenue, New York, NY 10010). The Hebrew University of Jerusalem offers scholarships to U.S. students in a number of different fields. For applications and information, contact the Office of Academic Affairs, 11 East 69th Street, New York, NY 10021.

The following academic programs are offered by CIEE-member institutions. Consult Appendix I for the addresses of the colleges and universities listed in this section. In addition to the programs below, Boston University, California State University, Cornell University, New York University, Pennsylvania State University, and the University of California offer programs open to their own students only.

Semester and Academic Year

General Studies

Boston University. "Boston University at the University of Haifa." Academic year or semester. Academic program preceded by intensive Hebrew instruction during two-month Kibbutz stay. Courses in English and/or Hebrew. Freshmen to seniors with 3.0 GPA. One semester Hebrew language study recommended but not required. Apply by March 15 for academic year or fall semester; October 15 for spring.

Friends World College. "Middle East Studies." Jerusalem, with field trip to Egypt. Academic year or semester. Middle East and Israel studies, Hebrew or Arabic, and individualized program combining independent study with fieldwork or internships. Sophomores, juniors, and seniors. Others may participate but will not receive credit. Apply by May 15 for fall and November 15 for spring.

Hebrew University of Jerusalem.
"Freshman Year Program." Open to high-school graduates for the first year of college studying in English and/or Hebrew. Apply by April 10.
"One Year Program." Sophomores, juniors, and seniors. Students can earn a full year of college credit for studying in English and/or Hebrew. Apply by April 10.
"Four-Year Program." Offers high-school graduates a foundation in Hebrew language, Jewish studies, and sciences in preparation for entrance into three-year bachelor's programs. Apply by April 10.
"Undergraduate Studies." Direct entrance into three-year bachelor's degree programs for students with at least one year at an accredited American university and some Hebrew proficiency. Apply by February 20.
"Visiting Graduate Study." Qualified students, holders of bachelor's or master's degrees or students currently enrolled in a graduate program may enroll for one year of study in English and/or Hebrew at Hebrew University. Apply by April 10.
"Graduate Studies." Master's degree program open to students with bachelor's degree. Apply by February 20.

Rutgers University. "Junior Year in Israel." Haifa. Juniors with 3.0 GPA. Apply by March 1.

State University of New York at Albany. Academic year or semester. Juniors and seniors; residents of New York State only. Apply by October 7 for spring; March 1 for fall.

State University of New York/Empire State College. "Semester Program in Israel." Individualized tutorials and field studies. Internship and voluntary service opportunities available. Sophomores to graduate students and adults.

Syracuse University. "Hebrew University—Rothberg School for Overseas Students." Jerusalem. Academic year or spring semester. Syracuse University sophomores, juniors, and seniors with 3.0 GPA. Apply by March 15 for academic year; by October 15 for spring.

University of North Carolina—Chapel Hill. "UNC Program to Hebrew University in Jerusalem." Sophomores to graduates with 3.0 GPA. Apply by March 15.

University of Notre Dame. "International Study Program in Jerusalem." Spring semester, with special focus on Arabic, theology, history, and government. Freshmen to graduate students with 2.5 GPA. Apply by October 15.

University of Oregon. "UO—Hebrew University Exchange Program." Sophomores, juniors, and seniors with 3.0 GPA. Apply by April 1.

University of Wisconsin—Madison. Jerusalem. Academic year. Sophomores to graduate students with two years of college Hebrew and 3.0 GPA. Open only to students at the University of Wisconsin. Apply by February 1.

Middle Eastern Studies

Syracuse University. Tel Aviv. Fall or spring semester. Sophomores, juniors, and seniors with 3.0 GPA. Apply by March 15 for fall and October 15 for spring.

Wesleyan University. "Spring Semester in Israel." Jerusalem. A program in the anthropology of religion and the political cultures of Christians, Muslims, and Jews in the region. Sophomores, juniors, and seniors. Apply by November 1.

Summer

Archaeology

University of Massachusetts—Amherst. "Field Program in Israel." Tal Nami. Juniors and seniors. Apply by April 24.

Michigan State University. "Archaeology, Modern Hebrew, and History of Religion." Haifa. Study at Haifa University. Sophomores to graduate students with elementary Hebrew. Apply by April 21.

Communications

New York University. "Journalism Program in Israel." Juniors to graduate students. Apply by April. Contact: Marcia Rock, Department of Journalism, 10 Washington Place, New York, NY 10003; (212) 998-7985.

General Studies

Hebrew University of Jerusalem. Sophomores to graduate students. Apply by May 15 for July and June 15 for August.

University of North Carolina—Chapel Hill. Jerusalem. Sophomores to graduate students with 3.0 GPA. Apply by March 15.

University of Wisconsin—Madison. Archaeological Summer Program at Caesarea Maritima. Open to sophomores, juniors, and seniors. Apply by March 15.

EXPLORING THE CULTURE

Readings

The works of a number of Israeli writers are readily available in translation in the United States. In 1947, as Jews from all over the world were settling in Israel, Shmuel Agnon, who later won the Nobel Prize for literature, published *In the Heart of the Seas*, about a journey to Israel. Another major Israeli novelist is Abraham B. Yehoshua, whose most recent work, *Five Seasons*, deals with a widower coming to terms with his changed life. *The Fifth Heaven*, by the novelist Rachel Eytan, is the story of a young girl's coming of age in a Tel Aviv orphanage during the Second World War. A best-seller when first published in 1962, it is regularly reissued and still widely read in Israel.

Another influential Israeli writer is Amos Oz, whose most recent book, *Black Box*, explores the breakdown of a marriage. Oz's *Elsewhere, Perhaps* (1966) depicts life on a kibbutz; his novel *In the Land of Israel* (1983) chronicles the author's journey through Israel and the West Bank and presents his conversations with people from all walks of life about the Israel of yesterday, today, and tomorrow.

In David Grossman's *The Smile of the Lamb* (1983), a young Israeli soldier is forced to grapple with the impossible task of living according to traditional values of morality and justice while enforcing the Israeli occupation of the West Bank. This novel echoes many of the same themes treated in Grossman's earlier nonfiction work, *The Yellow Wind*, which was first published as a series of articles in an Israeli newspaper. In Grossman's *See Under: Love* (1989), set in Israel in the late 1950s, a child tries to make sense of the "Nazi Beast" he hears talked about all around him.

Arabesques, by Anton Shammas, is the story of an Israeli-Arab family and focuses on the Palestinian-Israeli conflict. It was the first novel written in Hebrew by an Israeli Arab and caused a sensation when it was first published in 1986. Since the publication of *Arabesques*, Shammas has emerged as a key Palestinian voice on the international scene; in "A Lost Voice" (*New York Times Magazine*, April 28, 1991) he argues that cultural misunderstanding—especially of how language is used—lay at the heart of the Persian Gulf War.

MOROCCO

Although Morocco is closer to the United States than most of the nations of Europe, few Americans are familiar with this land of dramatic landscape, colorful history, and ancient traditions. Morocco lies in the northwest corner of Africa, only an hour's ferry ride from Spain across the Strait of Gibraltar. It is bordered by the Mediterranean and the Atlantic to the north and west, and the Sahara desert to the south and east. Great mountain peaks, hills, fertile valleys, and expansive plains provide the backdrop for the villages and farmland that make up rural Morocco. This exotic scenery has long attracted Hollywood directors and many well-known films have been made there, including *Lawrence of Arabia*, and more recently, *The Last Temptation of Christ*.

In ancient times the Phoenicians, Carthaginians, and Romans all made use of these shores. But Morocco's national history began in the eighth century with the arrival of the Arabs from across North Africa, making Morocco "Al Maghrib Al Aqsa," Islam's westernmost territory. The indigenous Berbers gradually converted to Islam, as a series of Arab dynasties ruled Morocco until the twentieth century.

Part of Morocco was annexed by Spain in the 19th century and the rest of Morocco became a protectorate of France in 1912; the country regained is independence in 1956. The current form of government is a constitutional monarchy, although King Hassan II has enjoyed almost complete power since 1961 when he inherited the throne. He leads a country of 26 million Moroccans who are predominantly Sunni Moslems and a mixture of Berber and Arab heritages. The national language is Arabic, although French is taught in schools and spoken by many Moroccans. Berber languages can still be heard in the more remote areas.

While Morocco remains largely a rural society, a major effort towards industrialization is well underway. A consistently high birth rate has created a population that is largely young, and unemployment has been a major issue in recent years, particularly in the major cities.

Elements of the old and the new often appear in striking juxtaposition. It is typical to see a mother in a long caftan with a veil walking with her daughter who wears blue jeans and high heels. Men wear western suits under their djellabahs. In the valleys of the Atlas Mountains, the way of life for the Berbers in fortress towns has remained unchanged for centuries, while their counterparts in Casablanca make their homes in high-rise apartments.

The influence of the French is everywhere, but because they built modern facilities outside the old town walls, Morocco's imperial cities remain much as they were in previous centuries. Fez was a powerful center of art, intellectual life, and commerce in medieval times. Today, to wander its narrow winding streets—only accessible on foot or by mule—is truly to take a trip back in time. To the south, the city of Marrakesh stands in a palm-covered plain at the foot of the snowcapped High Atlas. Rabat, Morocco's capital, boasts well-preserved monuments and an imposing fortress that faces the Atlantic.

The medina—the old Arab quarter, usually including a market—of any Moroccan city dazzles the visitor with fortune-tellers, hustlers, and merchants in their seemingly endless throng of activity. Traditional ceramics, textiles, wood and metal work can be purchased by anyone willing to venture into a lively bargaining process. Getting around Morocco takes energy, but a quiet moment in the evening can bring the smell of saffron in the air, friendly conversation over mint tea, and the call to prayer echoing from the minaret of a nearby mosque.

—*Brooke Pickering, New York, New York*

Official name: Kingdom of Morocco. **Area:** 172,413 square miles (about the size of New Mexico). **Population:** 26,249,000. **Population density:** 147 inhabitants per square mile. **Capital:** Rabat (pop. 556,000). **Largest city:** Casablanca (pop. 2,600,000). **Language:** Arabic, various Berber languages. **Religion:** Islam. **Per capita income:** US$630. **Currency:** Dirham. **Literacy rate:** 35%. **Average daily high/low*:** Casablanca: January, 63°/45°; July, 79°/65°. **Average number of days with precipitation:** Casablanca: January, 8; July, 0.

---

*All temperatures are Fahrenheit.

TRAVEL

U.S. citizens will need a passport in order to travel to Morocco; however, a visa is not required for a stay of up to three months. Check with the Embassy of Morocco (1601 21st Street NW, Washington, DC 20009) for specific requirements.

"Morocco generally isn't recommended for women traveling alone, but if you have a high adventure threshold, a low budget, and are willing to leave city comforts behind, a unique experience awaits you."

—Louise Shaughnessy, Ottawa, Ontario

Getting Around

Algeciras, Spain, is the jumping-off point for most travelers going to Morocco. The ferry across the Strait of Gibraltar from Algeciras to Ceuta takes about 90 minutes or about 2½ hours to Tangier.

InterRail passes are valid on Moroccan trains. Eurail passes are valid only for a 20-percent discount off the cost of passage. The main north-south rail line connects Tangier, Rabat, Casablanca, and Marrakesh. Another line runs from Casablanca and Rabat to Fez and on to the Algerian border. Train travel in first- or second-class compartments is definitely the most comfortable means of public transportation and only a little more expensive than bus fare. Third- and fourth-class cars, while cheap, are extremely cramped.

Morocco's bus network is much more extensive, and less expensive, than its rail system. On the down side, buses are usually crowded, poorly ventilated, and slow-moving, making frequent roadside stops to pick up and discharge passengers. The fastest and most comfortable service is offered by the national bus company, Compagnie de Transports du Maroc (CTM).

Intercity service is also provided by *grandes taxis* (as opposed to *petits taxis*, which provide service only within city boundaries). Also, *collective taxis* provide long-distance service for groups. *Collective taxis*, bound for specific destinations, board at designated taxi stands. They are faster than buses and perhaps safer than *grandes taxis*, as passengers pay a common fixed fare.

Morocco's road system is comprised of generally good but narrow roads, with signs in both Arabic and French. Primary roads (marked with a "P") are in better condition than secondary roads (marked with an "S"). Car rentals are available in major cities from international companies such as Hertz, Avis, and Europcar. If you rent from a local company, you'll have to haggle over the price. Hitchhiking is difficult in Morocco and sometimes expensive—offers of a lift may end up costing you more than a bus fare.

"Campgrounds can usually be found in most cities and cost very little. However, if you prefer camping away from regular campgrounds, the southern coast is best. People who really want to get to know Morocco should go south anyway, as the north is extremely tourist-oriented."

—Mark C. Eddy, Protomunster, Arizona

Especially for Students and Young People

The student travel bureau OYED (18 Rue Tansift, #21, Rabat) distributes information on travel in Morocco and sells plane, train, and bus tickets. Holders of the International Student Identity Card are entitled to reduced rates on airfare within the country, as well as from Casablanca, Marrakesh, Fez, Agadir, Tangier, and Rabat to a number of international destinations. OYED also arranges accommodations in university residences during the summer vacation (from July 15 to September 15). The International Youth Card is good for discounts at a number of accommodations, restaurants, recreational facilities, shops and stores, plus some tours, excursions, and car rentals.

Meeting the People

OYED can arrange for a limited number of foreign students to live with Moroccan families in either Safi, Marrakesh, Rabat, Fez, or Casablanca. Write the OYED office in Rabat (address above) at least two months in advance.

For Further Information

There is no shortage of travel guidebooks written for the young independent budget traveler to Morocco. *Let's Go: Spain and Portugal* includes a section on Morocco and is available for $14.95 in most bookstores and at Council Travel offices. One of the best guidebooks for the independent traveler is *Morocco, Algeria and Tunisia: A Travel Survival Kit*. If you can't find it in a bookstore, you can order it for $13.95 (plus $1.50 book-rate postage; $3 for first-class) from Lonely Planet Publications, Embarcadero West, 112 Linden Street, Oakland, CA 94607. You might also check out *The Real Guide: Morocco* ($12.95), published by Prentice-Hall. In addition, general tourist information is available from the Moroccan National Tourist Office (20 East 46th Street, Suite 503, New York, NY 10017).

WORK

It is necessary for a foreigner to obtain a work permit to work in Morocco. Application for the permit must be made by the employer. First priority for employment is given to Moroccan citizens.

Internships/Traineeships

Programs sponsored by members of the Council on International Educational Exchange are described below. Consult Appendix I for the addresses of the institutions listed in this section.

AIESEC-US. Reciprocal internship program for students in economics, business, finance, marketing, accounting, and computer science. See page 18 for more information.

University of Minnesota. "Minnesota Studies in International Development." Academic year. Predeparture coursework at the U of M fall quarter with internship in development-related research or action project in winter and spring quarters. Juniors to graduates and adults with interest in development; 2.5 GPA and two years of French or one year of Arabic required. Apply by May 15.

Voluntary Service

CIEE places young people in voluntary-service workcamps in Morocco organized by Chantiers Jeunnesse Maroc (B.P. 1351 Rabat). These workcamps bring together volunteers from various countries for a three-week period to do gardening and environmental work. Volunteers must be 18 years of age or older and speak French. Room and board are provided. The applications of U.S. residents are processed by CIEE. For more information, contact the Voluntary Service Department at CIEE.

STUDY

Programs offered by CIEE-member institutions are listed below. Consult Appendix I for the addresses of the colleges and universities listed in this section.

Semester and Academic year

General Studies

Experiment in International Living/School for International Training. "College Semester Abroad." Rabat. Fall or spring semester. Arabic language study, life and culture seminar, field-study methods seminar, independent-study project, homestay, and educational travel to Fez, Meknes, and Marrakesh. Sophomores to seniors with 2.5 GPA. Apply by May 15 for fall and October 15 for spring.

State University of New York at Binghamton.
Arabic Studies in Tangier. Academic year or semester. Intensive language study. Sophomores to graduate students with elementary proficiency in modern standard Arabic. Apply late spring for fall semester and mid-fall for spring semester.

TUNISIA

Even the name of Tunisia's main airport, Tunis-Carthage International, reminds arriving visitors that this nation, located at the crossroads of the Mediterranean, has a long and proud history. Phoenicians, Carthaginians, Romans, Arabs, Turks, French—all have left their mark on Tunisia.

Arab conquerors, arriving in the seventh century, called Tunisia "the green land." In fact, the relatively well-watered north, once the granary of Rome, still grows produce such as oranges and olives for the tables of Europe. But today, agriculture has been supplanted by the tourist industry and petroleum from the nearly uninhabited desert that comprises the southern two-thirds of the country as the leading contributor to the economy.

Everywhere you go, you'll find streets, schools, mosques, and what-have-you named after Habib Bourguiba, the national hero who led Tunisia in its drive for independence from France in 1956 and then served as president for 31 years. Although ousted from power in 1987, his political legacy lives on in such things as the equal legal status of women and the country's ties with the West.

Today, Tunisia is a North African nation with cultural, racial, and linguistic ties to both Europe and the Middle East. This delicate balance is evident everywhere. The Avenue Habib-Bourguiba, hub of the cosmopolitan capital city of Tunis, is lined with cafés serving mint tea and French pastries, while just a few blocks from the city center is the entrance to the medina and the world of the souks, or traditional outdoor markets, which offer a dizzying array of colors, sights, and smells as well as a chance to test your bargaining skills (most Tunisians speak both Arabic and French).

But you won't want to spend all of your time in Tunis. The electric train known as the TGM is an easy and inexpensive way to get out of the city, and the ride offers a slice of Tunisian life most tourists never see. Your fellow passengers will probably strike up a conversation with you as the train whisks past the ruins of Carthage and the picturesque port city of Sidi Bou Said. The last stop will be the beaches of La Marsa. Don't be surprised to see women in bikinis, or even topless. While Islam is the religion of Tunisia, 75 years of mostly French rule and 1.3 million tourists annually, mostly from Western Europe, have had an impact.

—*Carina Klein, New York, New York*

Official name: Republic of Tunisia. **Area:** 63,170 square miles (about the size of Missouri). **Population:** 8,094,000. **Population density:** 125 inhabitants per square mile. **Capital and largest city:** Tunis (pop. 1,000,000). **Language:** Arabic. **Religion:** Islam. **Per capita income:** US$1,163. **Currency:** Tunisian dinar. **Literacy rate:** 46%. **Average**

daily high/low*: Tunis: January, 58°/43°; July, 90°/68°. **Average number of days with precipitation:** Tunis: January, 13; July, 2.

TRAVEL

U.S. citizens will need a valid passport to travel to Tunisia; however, visas are not required for stays of up to four months. Check with the Embassy of Tunisia (2408 Massachusetts Avenue NW, Washington, DC 20008) for specific requirements.

"Tunisia is easily reached by ferry from Genoa, Marseille, Palermo, or Trapani. A week here can make the usual trip through Europe more of an adventure."
—Matt Lussenhop, Minneapolis, Minnesota

Getting Around

The Tunisian rail network serves the major intercity routes and links the country to Algeria. Tunisian trains are comfortable and convenient, but service is less frequent than on buses, the most common mode of transport. Buses, however, can be crowded and slow. Perhaps the fastest mode of transportation is the *louage*, intercity taxis serving fixed routes. *Louages* display their destination on a sign and usually carry five people at a posted per person rate.

Tunisian roads, both surfaced and unsurfaced, remain in relatively good condition. With the exception of the Tunis-Hammamet superhighway, however, they tend to be narrow. Road signs everywhere are in Arabic and French. Renting a car is relatively easy, although advance reservations are advisable during the summer tourist season. Rental cars are practically the only way to see the southern Sahara region of Tunisia. Bicycles and motorcycles are also available to rent.

"Because I took the bus most of the time, I often ended up spending hours in small towns waiting for connections. People were extremely helpful and friendly. They would crowd around me to talk to me—some even offered to buy lunch so that they could talk to me alone. In one town, a boy ran home and returned with a steaming pot of food. I don't know what it was, but it was delicious."
—Eleanor LaVish, Coffeyville, Kansas

Especially for Students and Young People

Sotutour/STAV (2 Rue de Sparte, Tunis) is Tunisia's student travel bureau. The organization provides information on student travel and offers a variety of one-week tours, including one that involves four days of camel-trekking in the Sahara. Holders of the International Student Identity Card receive a discount on air travel from Tunis to many international destinations. The International Youth Card is good for discounts on limited accommodations.

For Further Information

One of the best guidebooks for the independent, budget-minded traveler is *Morocco, Algeria, and Tunisia: A Travel Survival Kit*. If you can't find it in bookstores, you can order it for $13.95 (plus $1.50 book-rate postage; $3 for first-class) from Lonely Planet Publications, Embarcadero West, 112 Linden Street, Oakland, CA 94607. Travelers

---

*All temperatures are Fahrenheit.

coming from Italy will find the Tunisia chapter in *Let's Go: Italy* full of useful information. Annually revised by Harvard Student Agencies and published by St. Martin's Press, *Let's Go: Italy* is available for $14.95 in bookstores and at Council Travel offices.

WORK

To hold a regular job in Tunisia, you will need a work permit; a job contract is required before applying. Generally, permits are only granted for those with skills that are not readily obtainable in Tunisia itself.

Internships/Traineeships

Programs offered by members of the Council on International Educational Exchange are listed below.

AIESEC-US. Reciprocal internship program for students in economics, business, finance, marketing, accounting, and computer science. For more information see page 18.

Association for International Practical Training. "IAESTE Trainee Program." On-the-job training for undergraduate and graduate students in technical fields such as engineering, computer science, agriculture, architecture, and mathematics. See page 18 for more information.

Voluntary Service

CIEE places young people in voluntary service workcamps in Tunisia organized by the Association Tunisienne d'Action Volontaire (Maison de RCD, B1 9 Avril 1938, La Kasbah, Tunis). These workcamps bring together volunteers from various countries for two weeks to accomplish a range of construction and restoration projects. Volunteers must be 18 years of age or older and speak French. Room and board are provided. The applications of U.S. residents are processed by CIEE. For more information contact the Voluntary Service Department at CIEE.

STUDY

Although there are no study programs offered by CIEE members in Tunisia, a short term of study in the country is easy to arrange, especially at language schools, where you can take courses in French or Arabic.

"The Institut Bourguiba des Langues Vivantes (or 'Bourguiba School') is a good place to study Arabic. I was able to improve my knowledge of Arabic a great deal due to the class but mostly due to my interaction with the people. Another possibility is trading Arabic lessons for English lessons. Contacts can be made at the American Cultural Center or the British Council Library, both in downtown Tunis."
—Matt Lussenhop, Minneapolis, Minnesota

TURKEY

Turkey is a country very much in transition. It is a Muslim country, but one receptive to Western influence. On the same beach, you may see a Turkish woman sunbathing in a bikini while nearby in the shallow water another wades fully dressed in heavy layers of clothing, including the traditional head scarf and long, full Turkish pants. Both will point to different interpretations of the Koran to explain their attire—or relative lack thereof. And although bars are still rare in Turkey (in most Muslim countries, drinking alcohol is frowned upon), beer and an anise-like liquor called raki are produced and consumed here. For the most part, however, teahouses, rather than bars, are where people gather socially. Traditional teahouses are almost exclusively male, but, especially in the larger cities, there are many that have become used to and even cater to male and female tourists.

Turkey, one of the largest countries in the Middle East, borders on Greece, Bulgaria, the Soviet Union, Iran, Iraq, and Syria. Culturally, it is as varied as the six different countries it adjoins. Istanbul, the former capital of the Ottoman Empire and a gateway connecting Europe and Asia, is a cosmopolitan city, at once an architectural mosaic of ancient mosques and palaces, working-class neighborhoods with traditional wooden houses, and modern areas complete with skyscrapers. In the western part of the country, tourism has become an important part of the economy. This is most noticeable on the Aegean coast, with its impressive beaches and historic ruins. As you head east, the country becomes poorer and more traditional, although Ankara, the capital city located in the center of the country, is a notable exception. The villages along Turkey's northern coast, on the Black Sea, are farming and fishing communities, and the northeast is a rainy mountainous region where most of the tea that is drunk in Turkey is grown. The deserts of the southeast, near Iran and Iraq, are the home of the Kurdish-speaking people.

Though attitudes toward Westerners vary in different regions of the country, in general, Turks are friendly and interested in meeting people from other countries. One of the most interesting ways to meet them is to go shopping. There are plenty of interesting goods to be bought in flea markets and shops, including the brightly colored, handwoven carpets for which the country is famous. Many areas in Turkey are known for their characteristic styles of carpets and kilims. If you express interest in one, the owner will most likely invite you to sit down and have tea with him as you discuss the carpet. Turks are great businessmen and love to haggle; you'll want to break out your best bargaining skills and match wits with the owner of the carpet. Even if you don't buy it, chances are you'll wind up having a very interesting conversation while learning a lot about carpets. But watch out: you may end up the proud owner of a carpet you never realized you needed!

—*Mary Leonard, New York, New York*

Official name: Republic of Turkey. **Area:** 301,381 square miles (slightly larger than Texas). **Population:** 56,549,000. **Population density:** 183 inhabitants per square mile. **Capital:** Ankara (pop. 1,700,000). **Largest city:** Istanbul (pop. 5,800,000). **Language:** Turkish. **Religion:** Islam. **Per capita income:** US$1,160. **Currency:** Turkish Lira. **Literacy rate:** 70%. **Average daily high/low*:** Istanbul: January, 45°/35°; July, 81°/65°. **Average number of days with precipitation:** Istanbul: January, 12; July, 3.

TRAVEL

A passport is required for U.S. citizens traveling to Turkey; however, a visa is not needed for tourists staying less than three months. Persons traveling to Turkey for reasons other than tourism are required to obtain a visa in advance, regardless of their length of stay. Check with the Embassy of the Republic of Turkey (1606 23rd Street NW, Washington, DC 20008), or with the Turkish consulate in New York or Chicago, for specific requirements.

---

*All temperatures are Fahrenheit.

GETTING AROUND

Travel in Turkey is inexpensive, whatever way you go. Bus service is quick, comfortable, and cheap. Trains are even less expensive than buses, but they are generally slower and don't serve Turkey's popular western coast. Shared taxis (called *dolmus*) follow fixed routes between cities and allow you to get off and on wherever you like. *Dolmus* can be identified by their yellow bands (regular taxis have checkered bands). Hitchhikers, too, have an easy time in Turkey, where autos stop for waving hands. Drivers may ask for payment, but will charge you less than the bus.

Those traveling to eastern Turkey from Istanbul or any other western city are well advised to check out Turkish Airlines. Domestic fares on Turkish Airlines are more than reasonable, and flying will save you from a 36-hour ordeal by bus. Another option is Turkish Maritime Lines, which operates passenger ships along the Black Sea coast from Istanbul to Trabzon and along the Aegean Sea from Istanbul to Izmir.

"Northern Europeans have been flocking to the warm beaches of western and southern Turkey. Many tourists also come for the historical, archaeological, and cultural attractions of this ancient land which has harbored varied civilizations for 30 centuries."
—Ugur Aker, Hiram, Ohio

Especially for Students and Young People

There are two student/youth travel organizations in Turkey:

- GENCTUR, Yerebatan Caddesi 15/3, 34410 Sultanahmet, Istanbul
- 7 TUR, Inonu Caddesi 37/2, Gumussuyu-Taksim, Istanbul

The International Student Identity Card is valid for a 10-percent reduction on some domestic ferries as well as reductions on international train and plane fares. The International Youth Card is widely accepted in Turkey and good for discounts on numerous accommodations, all kinds of transportation, and entrance fees at state museums.

Turkey's only International Youth Hostel, the Yucelt Interyouth Hostel, is also located in Istanbul, at Caferiye Sk. 6/1, 34400 Sultanahmet. At the foot of the Sofia mosque, the hostel is a good place to meet fellow travelers. The International Youth Card is good for discounts on an extensive range and number of accommodations and museums, and, to a lesser extent, on restaurants, tours, and excursions.

For Further Information

The most complete guide to the country is *Turkey: A Travel Survival Kit*, which can be ordered from Lonely Planet Publications (Embarcadero West, 112 Linden Street, Oakland, CA 94607) for $14.95 (plus $1.50 book-rate postage; for first-class). Lonely Planet's *West Asia on a Shoestring* includes Turkey and is a valuable resource for those planning to travel eastward from Turkey. *Let's Go: Greece and Turkey* includes extensive information on traveling in all parts of the country. It's available for $14.95 in most bookstores and at Council Travel offices. General tourist information is available from the Turkish Government Tourism and Information Office, 821 United Nations Plaza, New York, NY 10017.

WORK

If you want to work in Turkey, you'll have to obtain a work visa prior to entering the country, and to get a work visa, you'll already need to have a job in Turkey. If you'll be staying less than six months (or working for the government), you must submit a copy of the employment contract and an official letter with a description of your position (including the duration of the job) when applying for the visa. If you're planning to stay more than six months in an advisory, technical, or managerial capacity in the private sector, you must obtain the approval of the State Planning Organization and submit this along with the contract and letter at the time of application. For more information contact the Turkish Embassy, Consular Section, 1714 Massachusetts Avenue NW, Washington, DC 20036.

Internships/Traineeships

Programs offered by members of the Council on International Educational Exchange are listed below.

AIESEC-US. Reciprocal internship program for students in economics, business, finance, marketing, accounting, and computer science. See page 18 for more information.

Association for International Practical Training. "IAESTE Trainee Program." On-the-job training for undergraduate and graduate students in technical fields such as engineering, computer science, agriculture, architecture, and mathematics. See page 18 for more information.

Voluntary Service

CIEE places young people in voluntary-service workcamps in Turkey organized by Genctur (see address above). At these workcamps, groups of up to 20 people from various countries work on projects involving construction, gardening, or archaeology. Most camps are two weeks in length. Volunteers must be at least 18 years old and willing to work an average of eight hours a day for two to three weeks. They receive room and board in return. The applications of U.S. residents are processed by CIEE. For more information contact the Voluntary Service Department at CIEE.

EXPLORING TURKISH CULTURE

Films

Although a large portion of Turkish filmmaking has consisted of attempts to recreate the commercial successes of Hollywood, Turkey has also produced a number of adventurous attempts to create its own film culture.

Yilmaz Guney, a leading actor in over 100 Turkish films, many of them the Hollywood imitations, was also a prolific screenwriter and director. In his own films he addressed the social concerns of modern-day Turkey. The contradictions and conflicts of values in modern Turkey are the focus of much of his work, including *Yol, The Herd*, and *The Enemy*. Internal immigration in search of a means of living is a recurring theme in *Elegy, Hope, Anxiety, The Herd*, and *The Father*. Other themes pervading his films are social attitudes toward sexuality, women, revolt, and responsibility.

Other directors attempting to forge a specifically Turkish film culture include Metin Erksan (*Dry Summer* and *I Cannot Live Without You*) and Omer Kavur (*Yusuf* and *Kenan*). In addition, several Turkish filmmakers have taken to making films in exile in response to the political restrictions at home. Significant among these is Tunc Okan, whose film, *The Bus*, is a story about migrant Turkish workers in Germany who are swindled by a fellow countryman and end up isolated and deserted in Sweden.

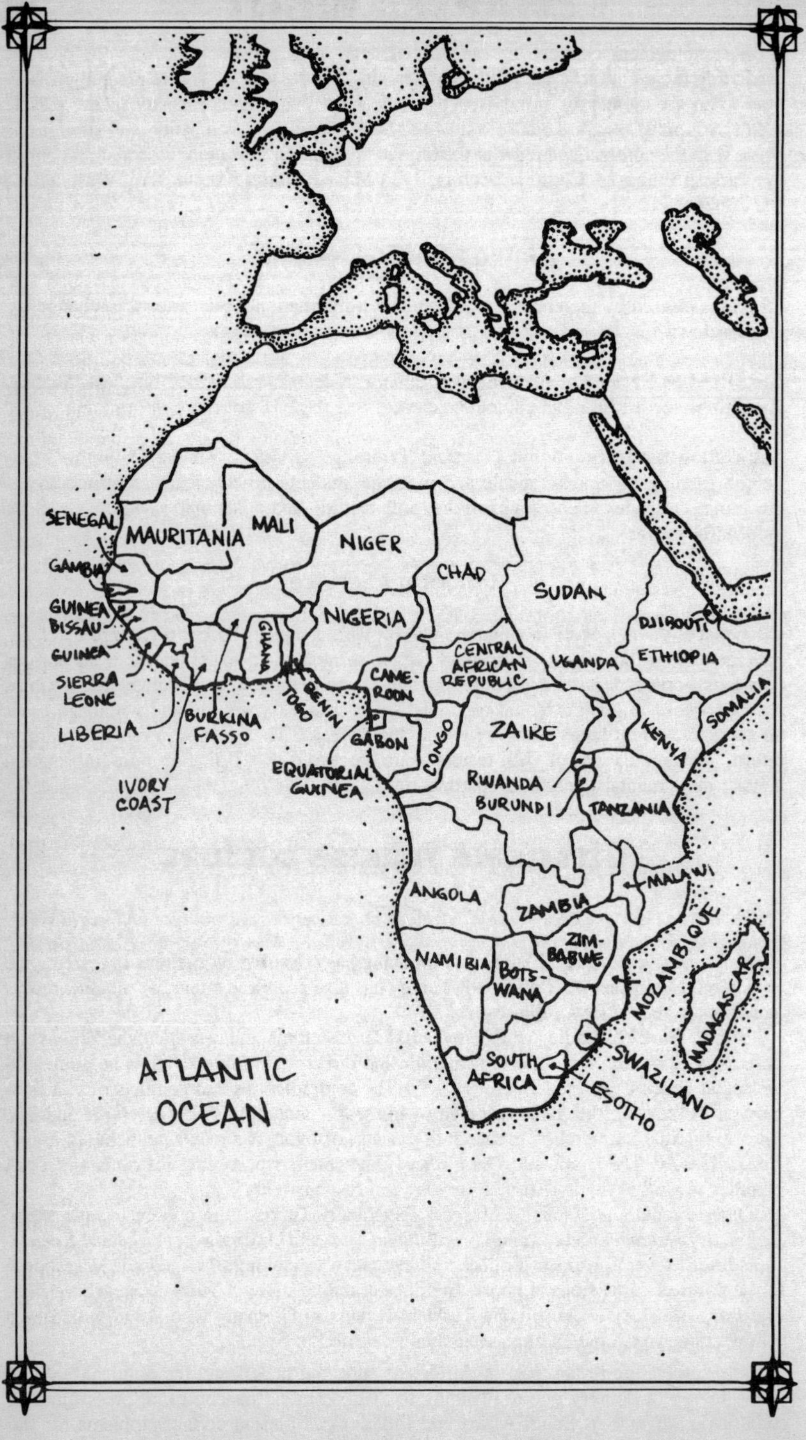
SENEGAL
MAURITANIA
MALI
NIGER
CHAD
SUDAN
GAMBIA
GUINEA BISSAU
GUINEA
SIERRA LEONE
LIBERIA
GHANA
NIGERIA
DJIBOUTI
ETHIOPIA
CENTRAL AFRICAN REPUBLIC
UGANDA
CAME-ROON
BENIN
TOGO
BURKINA FASSO
IVORY COAST
GABON
EQUATORIAL GUINEA
CONGO
ZAIRE
SOMALIA
KENYA
RWANDA
BURUNDI
TANZANIA
MALAWI
ANGOLA
ZAMBIA
ZIM-BABWE
MOZAMBIQUE
MADAGASCAR
NAMIBIA
BOTS-WANA
SOUTH AFRICA
SWAZILAND
LESOTHO
ATLANTIC OCEAN

CHAPTER EIGHT

AFRICA SOUTH OF THE SAHARA

A vast continent, Africa offers the visitor an array of impressions and experiences not easily forgotten. It is a region of immense cultural and linguistic diversity; in fact, more than 800 languages are spoken. Virtually all African countries encompass a variety of languages, cultures, and religions within artificial boundaries that follow the lines arbitrarily drawn by the European colonial powers early in this century. As a result, African nations—most of which have come into existence as independent states only within the last 35 years—are still struggling to forge a sense of nationhood among disparate ethnic groups.

Substantial economic growth continues to elude most African nations, a disproportionate number of which are classified in the lowest economic bracket by the United Nations. As these nations have matured, however, the showy industrial projects of the 1960s and early 1970s have given way to a more realistic emphasis on agrarian development. Still, some regions have been hit hard by a deadly mixture of recurring drought, poor land management, political conflict, and rapid population growth that has often resulted in famine. As a result of the media campaign surrounding the "Live Aid" concert of 1985 and the international attention it brought to African famine, images of hunger and starvation remain the most prevalent images of Africa among Americans. Famine continues to be a problem in the Horn of Africa and along the southern fringes of the Sahara; however, a visit to Africa can do much to broaden one's image of this complex and rapidly changing continent.

Africa offers the perceptive student, volunteer worker, and traveler the chance to experience a radically different way of life while gaining a new perspective on oneself and the world. Among those who have had the chance to experience Africa as more than just a casual tourist, few leave the continent unchanged.

"Nothing can compare to being challenged by an entirely foreign culture and world view. Rather than monuments of the past or obsession with future constructions and acquisitions, life itself is the attraction in Africa. At first, I was incredibly impatient at the slow pace of daily life, but once I got used to it I could not understand how anyone could live any other way. There is nothing like seeing it for oneself."
—James Tho, Baltimore, Maryland

TRAVEL

The Essentials

A trip to sub-Saharan Africa will be a trip off the beaten tourist path and will require some initiative and preparation. One way you can prepare is to talk to people who have traveled there, as well as to Africans who are living and studying in your community. Another way is to read some of the books you'll find recommended in this chapter. These, especially the literary works by Africans authors, will help put you in touch with the worlds you are about to encounter.

Before traveling to any part of Africa, be sure you understand the political realities of the region or country you're planning to visit. Political instability (at press time, in countries as diverse as South Africa and Liberia) can present certain problems for the traveler. It is important to stay informed and to be flexible in your travel plans. Unfortunately, coverage of African political news in the U.S. press is notoriously poor. Instead, you might need to turn to *Jeune Afrique, Africa News*, and *South*, periodicals that should be available in most libraries. For daily newspaper coverage of events in Africa, we refer you to *Le Monde*, the *Manchester Guardian*, the *Nairobi Times*, and the *Christian Science Monitor*.

From time to time, the State Department issues travel advisories for African countries. Borders close, governments restrict travel, borders open, and restrictions are raised. You can contact the department's Citizens Emergency Center (see page 8) for current travel advisories that may have been issued concerning areas you are planning to visit.

Other preparations you'll need to make involve health. For travel to many of the countries of sub-Saharan Africa, you are required to be vaccinated against yellow fever, cholera, typhoid, and polio. It is best to contact your local public health office for details on the latest health requirements for individual countries; information is also available from the major international air carriers as well as from the consulates of each country. Be sure your doctor records your shots on an International Vaccination Card. Then carry it with you at all times; failure to present this card at some borders may lead to your having to be needlessly inoculated again. Further information about health problems and precautions for travelers can be found in the "Health" section of Chapter Two.

Travelers to the region should also be aware of the prevalence of AIDS in Burundi, Rwanda, Uganda, Zaire, and—to a lesser degree—Kenya and Tanzania. Unlike in the U.S., AIDS in sub-Saharan Africa is spread almost entirely by heterosexual intercourse; men and women are equally infected. Transmission of AIDS through contaminated blood and blood products is common because some countries do not screen blood for HIV before transfusion. Travelers to the region should try to avoid blood transfusions unless they know HIV-antibody screening has been done. It is also possible to pick up the virus from an unsterilized needle, so if you need an injection in Africa make sure the needle either is new or has been properly sterilized. More information on precautions against AIDS can also be found in Chapter Two of this book.

"Having been in Africa for some time, I feel a great need to stress health precautions. Often governments out here will not admit that an outbreak of some epidemic exists for fear that it will keep out tourists or show that the government can't cope with health affairs. There are often outbreaks of cholera and polio. Walking barefoot should be discouraged because of the danger of catching hookworms and the Chigoe flea. Furthermore, most fresh water bodies south of the Sahara are infested with bilharzia—you can't just jump in for an impromptu swim. And malaria pills are a must out here."
—Edward Okonkwo, Brooklyn, New York

Traveling from country to country in Africa, you may have to contend with an imposing bureaucratic network. Not only do entry requirements periodically change but border and consular officials can, for whatever reason, play havoc with your travel plans. For example, some officials in southern Africa may object to travelers coming from the nation of South Africa. Others may decide you don't have enough money. The most one can do in such situations is to remain calm and polite.

In addition to your passport, you'll need a visa to enter most countries of sub-Saharan Africa. Visas can be obtained in the United States at the embassy or a consulate of the country you are traveling to; in most cases, your passport must accompany the visa application. Since it may take from ten days to three weeks for a visa to be processed, you will want to start collecting the necessary visas well before your departure date. If you don't have a well-planned itinerary, however, it might be best to obtain the necessary visas at the appropriate consulates as you travel through Africa. In this case, be sure to pack plenty of extra passport photos, and keep your ears open as to which consulates are most hospitable.

You may also be required to show an onward ticket out of the country when crossing the border. In this regard, booking an airline ticket with plenty of stopovers is a good idea (see the "Getting Around" section below). In lieu of an onward ticket, however, proof of sufficient funds should gain you passage. While "sufficient funds" may vary from country to country, major credit cards are widely recognized as proof.

"Some borders are easy and some are hard. I met someone who was turned back at the Zimbabwe border for insufficient funds—she had $900 and a ticket for an overland truck trip back."

—William Savittola, Philadelphia, Pennsylvania

Getting There

There are APEX fares from the U.S. to major African cities such as Lagos and Nairobi. Sample fares available during the summer of 1991 are listed below. For more up-to-date information, check with a Council Travel office (see listing of locations on pages xix–xxi).

	Round-trip	One-way
New York–Nairobi	$1,105	$605
New York–Johannesburg	$1,425	$759
Los Angeles–Nairobi	$1,265	$705

If you already are in Europe, it is relatively inexpensive to fly to most major African cities. Students and young people are eligible for special discounted fares between Europe and Africa. These can be booked at any Council Travel office or a student travel bureau in Europe. Regulations vary depending on the airline but generally holders of the International Student Identity Card (see page 8) or the International Youth Identity Card (see page 10) are eligible. Sample *one-way* student fares available during the summer of 1991 are listed below.

Berlin–Nairobi	$519
Berlin–Johannesburg	$969
Amsterdam–Johannesburg	$895
Paris–Abidjan	$455
Paris–Lagos	$455
Paris–Douala	$479
London–Lagos	$529

Traveling around Africa

"I spent a great deal of time in West Africa: Senegal, the Ivory Coast, Cameroon, and the Gambia are among the most stable and best organized countries on the continent. There's a good tourist infrastructure at various price levels throughout these countries. Attractions include the rich local traditions maintained in the interior, game preserves, vibrant modern cities, and attractive beaches with camping on some. The confluence of Islam, colonial Western civilization, and a quest for an appropriate indigenous modernity make West Africa especially compelling for visitors."

—Holly Burgess, Tappan, New Jersey

If you're going to cover long distances within Africa and your time is short, you'll probably have to fly. Air travel within Africa is fairly expensive, so it's important when you make your initial reservation that you book a seat to the farthest point you are traveling to and arrange your intermediary travel via stopovers. If you wait until you're in Nairobi to decide you want to go to Johannesburg, your costs may be double what they'd have been if you'd booked through to Johannesburg with a stopover in Nairobi.

Train travel in Africa is reasonably inexpensive, but slow. The railroads were built for colonial purposes—to transport raw materials from the interior of Africa to the coast, where they could be shipped off to other parts of the world. As a result, you won't be able to travel along the coast by rail, but in most countries you will find lines running from the coastal capital cities into the interior. Some of these lines will treat you to some spectacular scenery along the way. If you want to meet Africans and travel cheaply, trains are perhaps your best bet.

Road conditions vary throughout Africa but generally follow predictable patterns. Roads around and between major cities are usually paved and in good repair. Outside of the main intercity routes, road conditions are dictated by the relative stability of each country and the economic state of affairs. Always place greater value on word of mouth than on maps. Bus service of some type covers all parts of the continent and many routes have frequent service. However, buses tend to be crowded and make many stops along the way to pick up and discharge passengers, which means slow going.

Another, often speedier option is the shared taxi. Called by different names in different countries, the shared taxi can also take many forms: car, truck, or van. Basically, a shared taxi is any vehicle running between two points along a fixed route, waiting at designated spots to fill up with passengers before departing for its destination. Taxis generally are more expensive than buses, but in some countries the difference is very little.

Hitching, too, is a recognized form of travel in Africa. Trucks are most likely to pick up hitchhikers, which they carry in back, on top of the load. But while it is easy to get a ride, you will be expected to pay. Normally, the fare is less expensive than it would be on a bus travelling the same distance. In Africa, it is impolite to stick out your thumb. Hitchhikers wave their hands.

"I like traveling on top of trucks—the fresh air is nice. Just be sure to watch for low-lying branches."

—Jerry Rivers, Hudson, Wisconsin

"One thing you must have in order to survive a long trip overland in Africa is patience. It is rare that anything arrives on schedule; people with strict itineraries will face nothing but frustration. Generally you have to wait at least a day or two for a connecting bus, train, or ship, and must make the best out of unwanted or unplanned delays. However, the locals are used to it—you may find yourself a several-night guest at someone's house in a town you never planned to set foot in."

—Samuel Barka, St. Louis, Missouri

Eating and Sleeping

Africa has an abundance of cheap places to stay, many of which are listed in the guidebooks published by Lonely Planet Publications (see page 55). Another source of information on accommodations in most major cities is the local tourist office, which will be centrally located and easy to find. In addition, the second volume of the *International Youth Hostel Handbook* lists hostels in Kenya, Namibia, and Zimbabwe (see page 53). For information on youth hostels in South Africa, write to the South African Youth Hostels Association, PO Box 4402, Cape Town 8000.

Especially for Students and Young People

Aside from South Africa and Ghana (see information in the individual country sections that follow), there are no national student travel bureaus operating in Africa south of the Sahara. Thus, unless you are going to one of these two countries, you won't find student discount programs specially designated for holders of the International Student Identity Card. However, obtaining the card will allow you to take advantage of student air fares from Europe to Africa. And although you certainly won't be able to count on it being as widely recognized in Africa as it is in Europe, the International Student Identity Card may allow you to take advantage of any special discounts for students that you do come across. Air Afrique, for example, offers special youth fares on international flights within West Africa.

Organized Tours

Given the uncertainties of travel in many parts of Africa, many people select the more expensive option of an organized tour. A wide variety of tours are offered to popular destinations like the game parks of Kenya; Council Travel offices and other travel agents have more information. For persons interested in an organized educational tour to Africa, Western Michigan University, a member of CIEE, offers two different programs:

- "East Africa: Journey of Discovery." Kenya and Tanzania. A one-month summer tour for physically fit students and adults. Apply by May 1.
- "Kenya Adventure." Nairobi and various national parks. A two and a half-week summer tour for adults and students over 18. Apply by May 1.

For Further Information

The best guidebooks on Africa are those published by Lonely Planet. *Africa on a Shoestring* ($24.95), by Geoff Crowther, contains more than 1,000 pages of detailed information on 55 African countries. Like all Lonely Planet publications on Africa, it's geared to independent travelers on a budget. Those who don't want to carry around a big book, however, should check out Lonely Planet's more focused regional guides: *West Africa: A Travel Survival Kit* ($12.95) and *Central Africa: A Travel Survival Kit* ($10.95), by Alex Newton; *East Africa: A Travel Survival Kit* ($21.95), by Geoff Crowther; and *Madagascar and the Comoros: A Travel Survival Kit* ($10.95), by Robert Wilcox. If you can't find these in a bookstore, you can order them (adding $1.50 postage per book; $3 first-class) from Lonely Planet Publications, Embarcadero West, 112 Linden Street, Oakland, CA 94607. If you plan to do a lot of overland traveling, you'll probably want to get some maps. The most accurate maps of Africa are those published by Michelin, including *North East Africa, North West Africa, Southern Africa,* and *Côte d'Ivoire*.

You'll find information about visas and other requirements in the individual country sections later in this chapter. Listed below are the addresses of embassies of countries not covered in the separate sections of this chapter:

- Embassy of the People's Republic of Benin, 2737 Cathedral Avenue NW, Washington, DC 20008
- Embassy of the Republic of Botswana, 4301 Connecticut Avenue NW, Suite 404, Washington, DC 20008
- Embassy of the Republic of Burkina Faso, 2340 Massachusetts Avenue NW, Washington, DC 20008
- Embassy of the Republic of Burundi, 2233 Wisconsin Avenue NW, Suite 212, Washington, DC 20007
- Embassy of the Republic of Cape Verde, 3415 Massachusetts Avenue NW, Washington, DC 20007
- Embassy of the Central African Republic, 1618 22nd Street NW, Washington, DC 20008
- Embassy of the Republic of Chad, 2002 R Street NW, Washington, DC 20009
- Embassy of the People's Republic of the Congo, 4891 Colorado Avenue NW, Washington, DC 20011
- Permanent Mission of Djibouti to the United Nations, 866 United Nations Plaza, Suite 4011, New York, NY 10017
- Permanent Mission of Equatorial Guinea to the United Nations, 801 Second Avenue, New York, NY 10017

- Embassy of Ethiopia, 2134 Kalorama Road NW, Washington, DC 20008
- Embassy of the Gabonese Republic, 2034 20th Street NW, Washington, DC 20009
- Permanent Mission of Gambia to the United Nations, 19 East 42nd Street, New York, NY 10017
- Embassy of the Republic of Guinea, 2112 Leroy Place NW, Washington, DC 20008
- Permanent Mission of Guinea-Bissau to the United Nations, 211 East 43rd Street, Suite 604, New York, NY 10017
- Embassy of the Kingdom of Lesotho, 2511 Massachusetts Avenue NW, Washington, DC 20008
- Embassy of the Republic of Mali, 2130 R Street NW, Washington, DC 20008
- Embassy of the Islamic Republic of Mauritania, 2129 Leroy Place NW, Washington, DC 20008
- Embassy of the People's Republic of Mozambique, 1990 M Street NW, Suite 570, Washington, DC 20036
- Embassy of the Republic of Namibia, 1413 K Street NW, Seventh floor, Washington, DC 20005
- Embassy of the Republic of Niger, 2204 R Street NW, Washington, DC 20008
- Embassy of the Republic of Rwanda, 1714 New Hampshire Avenue NW, Washington, DC 20009
- Permanent Mission of Sao Tome and Principe to the United Nations, 801 Second Avenue, Room 1504, New York, NY 10017
- Permanent Mission of Seychelles to the United Nations, 820 Second Avenue, Suite 900S-F, New York, NY 10017
- Embassy of the Somali Democratic Republic, 600 New Hampshire Avenue NW, Washington, DC 20037
- Embassy of the Republic of the Sudan, 600 New Hampshire Avenue NW, Washington, DC 20037
- Embassy of the Kingdom of Swaziland, 4301 Connecticut Avenue NW, Washington, DC 20008
- Embassy of the Republic of Uganda, 5909 16th Street NW, Washington, DC 20011
- Embassy of the Republic of Zaire, 1800 New Hampshire Avenue NW, Washington, DC 20008

WORK

The ministries of education of the various African countries often have information on teaching positions in their high schools and universities. A university degree is required, and teaching certification or experience is helpful; three-year contracts are common. For the address of the ministry of education in the country you are interested in, contact its embassy or a consulate.

"College students interested in teaching should think about the option of teaching in Africa for a few years. African students are hardworking, appreciative, and eager to know about America. Teaching in Zimbabwe, I got valuable teaching experience, an inside look at a fascinating continent, lasting friendships with Africans, and the opportunity to travel to neighboring countries. There were some hardships to face—you have to be resourceful—but, beyond a doubt, it was the most interesting two years of my life."
—Elizabeth Grossi, New York, New York

Another option is voluntary service. To help fill the great need for technical and educational assistance in Africa, a number of organizations based in the United States operate programs there, and many place volunteers in these programs. Some of these are church related, while others are privately run or government agencies. Most of the voluntary service organizations listed in Chapter 3 (including the Peace Corps) make placements in African countries. The Council's publication *Volunteer!: The Comprehensive Guide to Voluntary Service in the U.S. and Abroad* (see page 20) will also give you excellent leads on voluntary-service programs in Africa. While some service programs will require you to have technical skills and/or teaching experience, others will accept you without any previous experience.

There are also a number of internship/traineeship possibilities in Africa. In the individual country sections that follow, you'll find information on programs offered by member institutions and organizations of CIEE. In addition to these listings, there are IAESTE trainee programs in Lesotho and the Sudan; see page 18 for more information.

STUDY

There are a growing number of study programs in Africa sponsored by U.S. institutions and designed primarily for American students. You'll find the study programs of CIEE-member institutions listed in the country sections that follow. It's also possible for a well-qualified American undergraduate to enroll directly in an African university. Graduate students planning to conduct research in an African country must notify its government of their plans and obtain the proper visa before going; in most African countries, research is not possible on a tourist visa.

Semester and Academic Year

University of Pittsburgh. "Semester at Sea." Fall or spring semester. Students, based aboard the SS *Universe*, attend classes on board and travel to various countries in Europe, the Middle East, Africa, Asia, and South America. Sophomores, juniors, and seniors with 2.75 GPA. Contact: Semester at Sea, Eighth floor, William Pitt Union, University of Pittsburgh, Pittsburgh, PA 15260; (412) 648-7490.

EXPLORING THE CULTURES OF AFRICA

Readings and Films

In many of the individual country sections that follow, you'll find recommendations of books to read and films to see. However, the notion of African national literatures is somewhat misleading since European colonizers created the present "nations" of Africa without regard for indigenous ethnic patterns. Many of today's African writers actually represent a region, rather than an individual country. Thus, to get a listing of applicable readings or film suggestions, be sure to check not only the specific country you are going to but also that of neighboring countries with similar cultures.

There are a number of anthologies that include works of African authors from different regions of the continent. *Stories from Central & Southern Africa* (1983), edited by Paula Scanlon, illustrates the art of short fiction and the short story in Zambia, Zimbabwe, Malawi, and South Africa. *African Short Stories* (1985), edited by Nigerian novelist and poet Chinua Achebe and C. L. Innes, is an excellent anthology of African short stories from the last 25 years. *Unwinding Threads* (1983), edited by Charlotte H. Bruner, is a collection of African women fiction writers, both short stories and extracts from novels. Finally, *Ten One-Act Plays* (1968), edited by Cosmo Pieterse, contains plays from East, South, and West Africa, while *Woza Afrika*! (1986), edited by Duma Ndlovu, is a collection of contemporary plays from Southern Africa.

If you have trouble finding works referred to in this chapter at your local bookstore or library, you can contact Heinemann Publishers, Three Continents Press, and Africa

World Press/Red Sea Press, each of which publishes a variety of African literature, including novels and collections of stories. Heinemann Publishers is located at 361 Hanover Street, Portsmouth, NH 03801; Three Continents Press is located at 1901 Pennsylvania Avenue NW, Suite 407, Washington DC 20006; and Africa World Press/Red Sea Press is located at 15 Industry Court, Trenton, NJ 08638.

CAMEROON

Cameroon has a long history of European involvement that reads like a sort of *Who's Who* of Western imperialism. European contact with Cameroon dates from the 15th century, when the Portuguese arrived. In fact, although the predominant European influence in Cameroon today is French, Cameroon's name comes from the Portuguese *camaroes*, or "giant shrimp," which live in abundance on the country's Atlantic coastline. Later, slave traders—chiefly Dutch and American—were active in the area. In the nineteenth century the Germans took control of the territory and created Cameroon's present boundaries. After Germany's defeat in the First World War, Britain and France divided the territory, with France controlling the largest portion. Finally, in 1960 Cameroon emerged as an independent nation.

Cameroon stretches from the central African coast to the banks of the largely evaporated Lake Chad in the Sahel, encompassing tropical rain forest, desert, and cool mountain highlands. More than one hundred ethnic groups live within its borders. There are religious differences between the north and the south; the north is Muslim and the south either ascribes to traditional religions or to Christianity. The south is more commercial and European-influenced than the north.

While not immune to political unrest, especially between north and south during the early sixties, Cameroon has had a relatively stable, albeit authoritarian, government. Tension remains between the northern and southern regions of the country, and there is sometimes violent intragovernmental jockeying for position. However, the social and economic life of Cameroon continues undisturbed.

Relative stability has prevailed in the economic arena as well. Cameroon is one of the few African nations that is a self-sufficient food producer, and it exports its flourishing cocoa and coffee crops. By avoiding the conspicuous "show" projects, such as large international centers and superhighways, that many newly independent African nations produced in quantity and concentrating instead on long-term yield projects such as education and agriculture, Cameroon avoided the heavy borrowing that has come back to haunt much of Africa. Cameroon now has a sufficient economic base and has recently embarked on a number of internationally and commercially-oriented ventures.

—*Mario Miraldi, New York, New York*

Official name: Republic of Cameroon. **Area:** 185,586 square miles (somewhat larger than California). **Population:** 11,109,000. **Population density:** 58 inhabitants per square mile. **Capital:** Yaoundé (pop. 700,000). **Largest city:** Douala (pop. 852,000). **Language:** French and English (both official), Foulbé, Bamiléke, Ewondo, Donala, Mungaka, Bassa. **Religion:** Christianity, Islam, animism. **Per capita income:** US$1,171. **Currency:** CFA Franc. **Literacy rate:** 65%. **Average daily high/low*:** Yaounde: January, 85°/67°; July, 80°/66°. **Average number of days with precipitation:** Yaounde: January, 3; July, 11.

---

*All temperatures are Fahrenheit.

AFRICA SOUTH OF THE SAHARA: CAMEROON

TRAVEL

U.S. citizens visiting the country need a passport and a visa. In addition, a return/onward ticket is required as well as a financial guarantee from a bank. You will need to be inoculated against cholera and yellow fever. For specific regulations, check with the Embassy of the Republic of Cameroon (2349 Massachusetts Avenue NW, Washington, DC 20008).

Getting Around

The road system in Cameroon is fair and improving. The major arteries in the north and the southwest are paved but roads into the southeastern portion of the country are not as good and often damaged after heavy storms. Car rentals can be arranged from Hertz, Avis, and Eurocar. Cameroon Airlines offers good service from Douala and Yaounde to all major towns. Buses are few and far between; public transport consists mainly of shared taxis or trucks. A rail line links Douala and Yaoundé and goes on into the interior; service is slow and infrequent, but provides a cheap and interesting way to travel.

WORK

It is very difficult for foreigners to secure regular, salaried employment in Cameroon. For more information, contact the Embassy of the Republic of Cameroon, 2349 Massachusetts Avenue NW, Washington, DC 20008.

Internships/Traineeships

The program described below is offered by a member of the Council on International Educational Exchange.

AIESEC-US. Reciprocal internship program for students in economics in business, finance, marketing, accounting, and computer science. See page 18 for more information.

STUDY

A program offered by a CIEE-member institution is described below. Consult Appendix I for the address of the school listed in this section.

Semester and Academic Year

General Studies

Experiment in International Living/School for International Training. "College Semester Abroad." Yaoundé. Fall or spring semester. French language training, excursions, village stay, seminar on Cameroonian culture, development issues, field-study methods seminars, homestay, and independent-study project. Three semesters of college French required. Sophomores to seniors with a 2.5 GPA. Apply by May 15 for fall and by October 15 for spring.

EXPLORING THE CULTURE OF CAMEROON

Readings

Mongo Beti is probably the best-known Cameroonian writer; *Mission to Kala* (1964) is a satiric tale about a man who must retrieve a fellow villager's wife after she has run off. His other works include *Perpetua and the Habit of Unhappiness* (1978), which conveys Beti's concerns about postindependence Africa, and *Remember Ruben* (1980), set just prior to Cameroonian independence.

Ferdinand Oyono used colonial Cameroon as his canvas in *Houseboy* (1966) and *The Old Man and the Medal* (1969). The former is written as the diary of a Cameroonian houseboy and tells of his fascination with the French colonials he serves. The latter is a satiric story of a villager who is awarded a medal by the French. His pride turns to doubt and finally contempt for the system that the medal represents.

Also set in colonial Cameroon is Kenjo Jumbam's book *The White Man of God* (1980), which describes the confusion of a boy trying to come to terms with the grown-up world and the Christian Western world presented to him through a local priest. Another novel, Mbella Sonne Dipoko's *Because of Women* (1969), is a delicate story of a man who quarrels with his pregnant wife over another woman.

CÔTE D'IVOIRE

Côte d'Ivoire, or the Ivory Coast, is probably the most cosmopolitan nation in West Africa. Centrally situated on the Gulf of Guinea and dominated by the French for more than three centuries, it was once a major export center for ivory, slaves, and other "commodities." Today its residents include about 30,000 French nationals, many Lebanese and Vietnamese, and even ambassadors from both the P.L.O. and Israel.

In Abidjan, the nation's capital, the shining clusters of skyscrapers, the luxurious hotels, the dozens of European banks, and the superhighways swooping over estuaries cannot quite obscure the city's slums. No other nation in West Africa so dramatically embodies the contrasts between rich and poor, new and old.

The contrast is particularly dramatic because of the enormous wealth of those who are rich. Imported luxury cars are surprisingly common in the streets of Abidjan. Cash crops such as cocoa, rubber, pineapples, and bananas are grown on giant plantations near the coast—many of them owned by President-for-life Félix Houphouët-Boigny, who is believed to be a billionaire. The president recently has been busy overseeing the relocation of the capital from Abidjan to Yamoussoukro, the former village—now a city—where he was born, and the government is spending hundreds of millions of dollars to make the new capital a monument to his rule. Meanwhile, political groups and the press are struggling for freedom of expression, and no one knows what will happen when the president, who is in his late eighties, eventually dies.

Houphouët's rule has achieved some notable successes, however. Poverty in Côte d'Ivoire is less severe than in nearby countries such as Guinea and Liberia. Most years, villagers are able to grow ample supplies of staples such as corn and yams, cassavas, and tomatoes. In addition, most of the country has electricity, potable water supplies, and well-funded schools run by government-supplied teachers.

Ivorians are justifiably proud of their artisanship. They specialize in linen tapestries painted with folk-art animal designs, cotton textiles in bright colors, silver filigree jewelry, and striking wooden sculptures of animals. However, stores aren't limited to traditional merchandise; Abidjan also has some of the largest cassette-tape outlets you may ever come across.

Any traveler to Côte d'Ivoire should try to get out of Abidjan to see the rest of the country. The intercity bus system is excellent. And urban Ivorians will jump at the chance to take a visitor to their ancestral village. Don't turn them down.

—*Jason Zweig, New York, New York*

Official name: Republic of Côte d'Ivoire. **Area:** 124,503 square miles (about the size of New Mexico). **Population:** 12,070,000. **Population density:** 94 inhabitants per square mile. **Capital and largest city:** Abidjan (pop. 1,850,000). **Language:** French, Diaula. **Religion:** Animism, Christianity, Islam. **Per capita income:** US$921. **Currency:** CFA Franc. **Literacy rate:** 35%. **Average daily high/low*:** Abidjan: January, 88°/73°; July, 83°/83°. **Average number of days with precipitation:** Abidjan: January, 3; July, 12.

TRAVEL

U.S. citizens will need a passport and a visa. An onward or return ticket, a financial guarantee from a bank, and proof of yellow-fever vaccination are also required. For specific requirements contact the Embassy of the Republic of Côte d'Ivoire (2412 Massachusetts Avenue NW, Washington, DC 20008).

Getting Around

Côte d'Ivoire has one of the best internal transportation systems in all of West Africa. Air Ivoire provides regular service from Abidjan to the country's other major cities. Luxury express buses also link the major cities, which are connected by a relatively well-maintained system of roads. Bush taxis provide service throughout the country. In addition, a single rail line crosses the country north from Abidjan to Ouagadougou in Burkina Faso, and is a good way of getting to many towns in the interior.

WORK

It is very difficult for foreigners to secure regular, salaried employment in the Côte d'Ivoire. For more information contact the Embassy of the Republic of the Côte d'Ivoire, 2424 Massachusetts Avenue NW, Washington, DC 20008.

Internships/Traineeships

A program offered by a member of the Council on International Educational Exchange is listed below.

AIESEC-US. Reciprocal internship program for students in economics, business, finance, marketing, accounting, and computer science. For more information see page 18.

STUDY

Programs offered by CIEE-member institutions are described below. Consult Appendix I for the addresses you can write for more information.

---

*All temperatures are Fahrenheit.

Semester and Academic Year

General Studies

International Student Exchange Program. Direct reciprocal exchange between U.S. universities and the Université Nationale de Côte d'Ivoire. Academic year. Full curriculum options. Open only to students at ISEP-member institutions.

Summer

Public Health

Boston University. "International Health Program in West Africa." Twelve-week study program in Abidjan with excursions. Graduate-level seminars on public-health issues in developing countries, planning and financing of services, and common delivery strategies. Intensive French language instruction and/or opportunity to study a local language. Six-week internship with local health facility. Apply by March 1. Contact the Program Coordinator, Center for International Health, 53 Bay State Road, Boston, MA 02215.

GHANA

In 1957, Ghana, formerly the British colony of the Gold Coast, was the first black nation of Africa to gain independence from colonial rule. Its first president, Osagyefo Dr. Kwame Nkrumah, followed a pan-African political agenda and was respected as the voice of Africa in the late fifties and early sixties. Nkrumah's pan-African ideals, however, caused him to neglect Ghana itself and he was overthrown in 1966. Since then, Ghana has been ruled by a succession of civilian and military regimes.

Numerous ethnic and language groups inhabit Ghana. In the north, there are the Dagomba, Nanumba, Dagarti, and Frafra groups, and in the south, there are the Akan, Ewe, and Ga groups. About 46 languages and dialects are spoken by the people; however, the principal languages are Ewa, Ga, Hausa, Dagbani, Kasem, and Dagaare. English is the official medium of expression and is spoken widely in urban areas, where visitors are made to feel welcome. Nevertheless, Ghana, more so than many other African nations, has a strong sense of national identity.

Economically, Ghana has experienced economic booms and busts but has always survived. Ghana went from being one of the richest African colonies to a country plagued by huge debts, failed projects, and a dwindling GNP. Recently, however, a remarkable turnaround has been achieved. In 1983, the government launched an economic recovery program under which the private sector has received support from the government and the international donor community. As a result, exports of minerals, forest resources, and agricultural products have shown encouraging gains.

The people of Ghana have elaborate rituals to mark important events. There are rites of child naming, rites of puberty, rites of initiation and marriage, and rites of death. The most important rituals take place in the annual festivals, which bring whole towns and tribes together. During the festivals people remember their past leaders and ask for their help and protection. Even the state undergoes ritual purification, preparing it for the new season.

—*Lloyd Ledlum, Brooklyn, New York*

Official name: Republic of Ghana. **Area:** 92,098 square miles (about the size of Wyoming). **Population:** 15,310,000. **Population density:** 160 persons per square mile.

Capital and largest city: Accra (pop. 949,000). **Language:** English, Twi, Fanti, Ga, Ewe, Dagbani. **Religion:** Christianity, animism, Islam. **Per capita income:** US$390. **Currency:** Cedi. **Literacy rate:** 30%. **Average daily high/low*:** Accra: January, 87°/73°; July, 81°/73°. **Average number of days with precipitation:** Accra: January, 1; July, 4.

TRAVEL

For U.S. citizens, both a passport and a visa are required. You'll also need an onward or return ticket and a guarantee of financial support from a bank or employer to cover your stay in the country. Finally, a certificate of immunization against yellow fever is required. For specific regulations, check with the Embassy of the Republic of Ghana, 2460 16th Street NW, Washington, DC 20009.

Getting Around

Ghana is known for extremely poor road and rail systems. Ten years ago the transport system was in a state of near-total collapse. Conditions have since improved, but overland travel is generally slow and uncomfortable. The rail system is limited to the southern portion of the country and is subject to frequent interruptions in service. The most prevalent form of transport is the private bus, which is usually a modified truck or van fitted with benches and stuffed full of people. You're in for a bumpy ride. Fortunately, the government has recently invested in a new fleet of buses which are comfortable, reliable, and fast when roads permit. Unfortunately, lines to purchase state bus tickets are very, very long.

The traveler who wishes to avoid these obstacles can find inexpensive domestic flights between the cities of Accra, Tamale, and Kumasi. Another, more interesting alternative is to travel along Lake Volta. Passenger boats, freighters, and smaller vessels regularly depart Akosombo for northern ports.

Especially for Students

Ghana is one of the few African countries with a student travel organization. Student and Youth Travel Services (SYTAG), PO Box 14337, Accra (located at the Accra Community Centre, High Street, Accra), can book cheap accommodations in several cities in Ghana, issue the International Student Identity Card, and arrange local tours. Holders of the International Student Identity Card are entitled to reduced domestic and international airfares as well as discounts at some shops, museums, theaters, and cultural events.

WORK

It is very difficult for foreigners to secure regular, salaried employment in Ghana. For more information, contact the Embassy of Ghana, 2460 16th Street NW, Washington, DC 20009. For another type of work experience, see the internship and voluntary-service sections below.

Internships/Traineeships

Programs offered by members of the Council on International Educational Exchange are listed below.

---

*All temperatures are Fahrenheit.

AIESEC-US. Reciprocal internship program for students in economics, business, finance, marketing, accounting, and computer science. See page 18 for more information.

Association for International Practical Training. "IAESTE Trainee Program." On-the-job training for undergraduate and graduate students in technical fields such as engineering, computer science, agriculture, architecture, and mathematics. See page 18 for more information.

Voluntary Service

CIEE places young people in voluntary service workcamps in Ghana organized by the Voluntary Workcamp Association of Ghana (VOLU), PO Box 1540, Accra. These workcamps bring together international and Ghanian youth for three-week periods during July, August, September, and December to build schools, health clinics, drains, and public latrines in rural areas. Volunteers must be 18 years of age or older. The applications of U.S. residents and an orientation are handled by CIEE. For more information, contact the Voluntary Service Department at CIEE.

The International Ecumenical Workcamp, a voluntary service workcamp in Ghana, gives young people (ages 18 to 35) from all over the world the opportunity to work on a rural-development construction project. The term of service is four weeks. Apply by May 1 to International Christian Youth Exchange (see Appendix I for address). For persons interested in longer-term voluntary service work, the same organization's Year Abroad Program offers persons ages 18 to 24 voluntary-service opportunities in the fields of health care, education, the environment, construction, et cetera. See page 23 for more information.

STUDY

The following programs are offered by CIEE-member institutions. Consult Appendix I for the addresses of the colleges and universities listed in this section. In addition, the University of California offers a program open only to students at its own schools.

Semester and Academic Year

State University of New York at Brockport.
"Accra Academic Year Program." Institute of African Studies at the University of Ghana. Juniors and seniors with 2.5 GPA. Apply by February 15.
"West Africa Seminar Intersession Program." Accra. January interim. Juniors and seniors with 2.5 GPA. Apply by November 1.

Summer

Pan-African Studies

University of Louisville. "Pan-African Studies in Ghana." Freshmen to graduate students. Apply by April 30.

Performing Arts

University of Maryland. "Performing Arts in Ghana." In cooperation with the School of Performing Arts, University of Ghana. Five-week program. Undergraduate credit. Apply by March 15.

EXPLORING THE CULTURE OF GHANA

Readings

A number of novels by contemporary Ghanaian authors are available in English. Ayi Kwei Armah, one of Ghana's most prominent writers, is the author of *Two Thousand Seasons* (1979), in which he reconstructs one thousand years of African history, and *The Beautyful Ones Are Not Yet Born* (1969), which deals with political corruption in a newly independent African nation, among other books. *This Earth, My Brother* (1972), by the poet and novelist Kofi Awoonor, is an allegorical novel in which a lawyer searches for meaning and identity in postcolonial Africa.

Those interested in poetry and theater should read J. C. DeGrafts's *Beneath the Jazz and Brass* (1975) and *Muntu: A Play* (1983). Kojo Laing's book of poetry *Godhorse* (1989) is varied, evocative, and humorous. The play *The Blinkards* (1974), by Kobina Sekye, is a witty send-up of the pretensions of the Ghanian nouveaux-riches. For a look at many of the concerns of contemporary Ghanian theater, read the plays of Asiedu Yirenki, especially the collection *Kivalu and Other Plays* (1980).

KENYA

Friendly people, a stable government, and spectacular natural beauty have made Kenya one of Africa's most popular tourist destinations. Vital to the country's economy, tourism is promoted by the government and fairly well developed. But while thousands of tourists visit the large game parks, most parts of the country still offer adventuresome travelers the opportunity to explore Africa well off the beaten tourist circuit.

Throughout the country you'll be greeted by a warm and friendly "jambo," the customary Swahili greeting. Kiswahili is the official language, but English is widely spoken, especially in Nairobi, one of the larger metropolitan centers on the African continent. While most of the population is Christian, many people continue to adhere to traditional religious beliefs and there is a sizable Muslim community along the coast.

Although there are more than 40 different ethnic groups in the country, political stability has been the rule over the 27 years since Kenya gained its independence from Great Britain in 1963. The first president, Jomo Kenyatta, instituted a policy of *harambee*, or a pulling together of all people, to build a unified independent state, and Kenya emerged as a pro-Western country with a capitalist economy. But poverty is everywhere. There has been, in addition, an enormous population increase, and some experts estimate its rate of population growth to be the highest in the world. Despite its many ties with the West, today Kenya must look inward, examine pressing domestic problems, and find the keys to furthering its economic development while maintaining its natural beauty and ethnic diversity.

—*Liz MacGonagle, Annandale, New Jersey*

Official name: Republic of Kenya. **Area:** 224,960 square miles (slightly smaller than Texas). **Population:** 25,393,000. **Population density:** 105 inhabitants per square mile. **Capital and largest city:** Nairobi (pop. 969,000). **Language:** Kiswahili (official), Bantu, Kikuyu, English. **Religion:** Christianity, traditional African religions. **Per capita income:** US $322. **Currency:** Kenyan shilling. **Literacy rate:** 50%. **Average daily high/low*:** Nairobi: January, 74°/54°; July, 69°/51°. **Average number of days with precipitation:** January, 5; July, 6.

---

*All temperatures are Fahrenheit.

TRAVEL

U.S. citizens need a passport and a visa. A yellow-fever vaccination is recommended, but not required. A copy of a return or onward ticket or a letter from a travel agent is also needed. For specific requirements, check with the Embassy of the Republic of Kenya, 2249 R Street NW, Washington, DC 20008.

Getting Around

Bus service extends to all parts of the country, and is provided by an array of vehicles, ranging from comfortable air-conditioned buses on a few main routes to *matatus*, rundown and crowded minibuses usually owned by the driver that provide cheap, albeit risky, transportation on local routes. Limited train service is also available, although most only travel at night and are fairly slow. The major exception to this is the famous run between Mombasa and Nairobi; the overnight trains offer a fascinating view of the landscape as it changes from safari to ocean to desert. Taxis are also a travel option for local trips. They usually drive from one point to another with a carful of passengers. Don't pay until the cab starts moving, and try to choose one that is already full of people—otherwise you'll have to wait around until some are rounded up. In addition, there are a number of small domestic airlines that provide fairly inexpensive service to the various regions of the country—a timesaver and also an opportunity to see the startling African landscape from above.

The majority of people in rural areas travel by flagging down a vehicle—whether it's a *matatu*, a truck, or a car. Generally speaking, when offered a ride you are expected to pay a small amount to the driver. At the other extreme in price, you can rent your own car or jeep in Nairobi or Mombasa (the minimum age is usually 23). Be warned: gas is expensive and accidents can be costly if your insurance is not comprehensive. Your U.S. driver's license is valid in Kenya, but remember to stay on the left-hand side of the road. Kenya's famed game reserves and national parks are accessible to motorists driving their own cars, but most choose to see the sights as part of an organized tour.

"Be ready for adventure! Leave your curling irons and hairspray at home. This is a country where material possessions don't matter except for your camera and a lot of film. Be prepared for a challenge. People are friendly, and you may find yourself overwhelmed with people willing to give you the shirts off their backs. The final challenge comes when you have to return home."

—Sean P. Hinchey, Glastonbury, Connecticut

For Further Information

General information is available from the Kenya Tourist Office, 424 Madison Avenue, New York, NY 10017. The best guidebook for adventurous travelers who really want to get to know the country is *The Real Guide: Kenya*, by Richard Trillo. It's published by Prentice-Hall and sells for $12.95 in bookstores.

WORK

In order to work in Kenya, it is necessary to obtain a work permit; application for the permit must be made by the employer. Permits are only issued when there are no Kenyan applicants for the job. For further information, contact the Embassy of Kenya, 2249 R Street NW, Washington, DC 20008.

AFRICA SOUTH OF THE SAHARA: KENYA

Internships/Traineeships

Programs sponsored by CIEE members are described below. Consult Appendix I for the addresses of the institutions listed in this section.

AIESEC-US. Reciprocal internship program for students in economics, business, finance, marketing, accounting, and computer science. See page 18 for more information.

University of Minnesota, "Minnesota Studies in International Development." Academic year. Predeparture coursework at the U of M fall quarter with internship in development-related research or action project in winter and spring quarters. Juniors to graduates and adults with interest in development. A 2.5 GPA is required; apply by May 15.

STUDY

The following programs are offered by member institutions of the Council on International Educational Exchange. Consult Appendix I for the addresses where you can write for more information. In addition to those listed below, Lewis and Clark College, Pennsylvania State University, and the University of California system offer programs open to their own students only.

Semester and Academic Year

Coastal Studies

Experiment in International Living/School for International Training. Lamu, Nairobi, Zanzibar (Tanzania). Fall or spring semester. Intensive Swahili language, development studies seminar, independent-study project, village stays, educational travel, and homestays. Sophomores to seniors with 2.5 GPA. Apply by May 15 for fall and October 15 for spring.

General Studies

Experiment in International Living/School for International Training. Nairobi. Fall or spring semester. Intensive language study, independent-study project, seminar in Kenyan life and culture, field-study methods seminar, and rural development seminar. Excursions to Tanzania and rural Kenya and homestays. Sophomores to seniors with 2.5 GPA. Apply by May 15 for fall and October 15 for spring.

Friends World College. "East African Studies." Machakos, Nairobi, and Lamu. Semester or academic year. African studies, Swahili language, and individualized program combining independent study and fieldwork or internships. Sophomores, juniors, and seniors. Others may participate on noncredit basis. Apply by May 1 for fall and November 15 for spring.

International Student Exchange Program. Direct reciprocal exchange between U.S. universities and Kenyatta University. Academic year. Full curriculum options. Open only to students at ISEP-member institutions.

Kalamazoo College. "Kalamazoo College in Kenya." Nairobi. Study at the University of Nairobi. Academic year or fall semester. Juniors and seniors with 3.0 GPA. Residence in Kalamazoo during summer prior to study abroad. Apply by February 15.

St. Lawrence University. "Kenya Semester Program." Nairobi. Fall or spring semester. Includes a one-month internship with a private or public agency. Apply by February 20 for fall and October 10 for spring.

University of La Verne. "Comparative Cultures: East Africa." January interim. Juniors to graduates students with 2.5 GPA. Apply by October 31.

University of Massachusetts—Amherst. Nairobi. Academic year and semester. Junior or above. Study in Swahili preferred. Apply April 1 for fall, November 1 for spring, but preferably much earlier for both.

Summer

General Studies

Experiment in International Living/School for International Training. "Summer Academic Study Abroad." Nairobi, Lamu, and field sites. Survival, Swahili language, interdisciplinary seminar, development studies, homestay, field visits. Freshmen to seniors. Apply by March 15.

EXPLORING THE CULTURE OF KENYA

Readings and Films

The works of Ngugi Wa Thiong'o, the best-known Kenyan writer of today, have been highly influential for the last 30 years. Many are considered so volatile by the Kenyan government that he has been imprisoned and was ultimately exiled. Among his most important works are *Ngaahika Ndeenda: I Will Marry When I Want* (1982), written with Ngugi Wa Mirii, and *Matigari* (1986), about a fictional freedom fighter who emerges from the forest after the rebellion to look for the "new" Kenya. After its publication, rumors spread that a man, Matigari, was circulating militant propaganda in the Central Highlands. Police launched a manhunt before they realized their mistake. Other novels by Thiong'o are *Weep Not, Child* (1964), an early work set before and during the Mau Mau insurgency, and *Petals of Blood* (1978), which presents his view of contemporary Kenya. The novel *Devil on the Cross* (1982), which shows Thiong'o's increasing political committment, was written on scraps of toilet paper during his imprisonment.

The Mau Mau rebellion, which helped end colonial rule in Kenya, is further dealt with in *Mau Mau Detainee* (1975), by J. M. Kariuki, a Kikuyu tribesman and participant in the uprising. Meja Mwangi's *Carcass for Hounds* is also set in the Laikipia district during the rebellion. Other books by Mwangi include *Kill Me Quick* (1973), about two unemployed youths in Nairobi, and *Going Down River Road* (1976), a story of vivid desperation about a construction worker whose life crumbles around him. Recently, both Thiong'o and Mwangi have turned towards film in order to communicate more directly with their audiences. *Carcass of Hounds* was made into a film entitled *Cry Freedom* (1980, not to be confused with the Hollywood treatment of Stephen Biko's life of the same name) by Nigerian film director Ola Balogun.

Taban Lo Liyong's poetry—notably *Eating Chiefs* (1970) and *Another Nigger Dead* (1972)—is highly controversial and inspiring. Thomas Akare writes from the similar inspiration, but his work is hardened and unsentimental. In *The Slums* (1981), he presents a powerful look at the "other" Nairobi to which the rich bring their cars to be washed by the novel's protagonists.

When many Westerners want to read "Kenyan" literature, they think of Elspeth

Huxley (*Flame Trees of Thika*) and Isak Dinesen (*Out of Africa*). Though these books use the Kenyan countryside as their setting, they have little to do with the people and culture of Kenya today; they present only a European look at transplanted Europeans in Kenya in the early part of the century. A book that does look at the relationships of Africans and Europeans under colonialism is Mugu R. Gatheru's autobiography, *Child of Two Worlds* (1964). Gatheru, the son of a tribal ritualist, became a professor of African history after studying in Kenya, India, Britain, and America.

In addition, a couple of nonfiction works are worthy of mention for the insights they provide into the lives of today's Kenyans. Tepit Ole Saitoti's *The Worlds of the Maasai* examines the complexities of that traditional society as it struggles to survive in the midst of contemporary Kenya. *Three Swahili Women: Life Histories* (1989), by Sarah Mirza and Margaret Strobel, presents a picture of life in the coastal region of the country.

NIGERIA

Nigeria is not for the faint of heart. The incessant barrage of intense heat, color, sounds, and tastes tests the culture shock threshold of all but the most resilient. The country—Africa's most populous—shows the strains of a large population competing for scarce resources at almost every turn; however, in this somewhat hostile environment you'll also see an aggressive enjoyment of life.

The Niger and Benue Rivers form a Y that divides the country into north and south, and the south into distinct southeastern and southwestern regions. The south is home to the traditional capital, Lagos (soon to be moved to the more central city of Abuja) as well as most of the country's larger cities; it is also the focus of the government's efforts toward social and economic development. Each of the major regions is populated by different ethnic groups, the chief of which are the Yoruba in the southwest, the Ibo in the southeast, and the Hausa-Fulani in the north. Nigeria has struggled with these ethnic division since its amalgamation into one territory under British control, but especially since independence in 1960. In 1967 ethnic animosities culminated in a civil war that left an estimated one million Nigerians (mostly Ibos) dead. Today Nigeria maintains a fragile national unity, but the federal government remains shaky—six military coups since independence, a record for Africa.

Although Nigeria is the second largest African oil-producing nation (after Libya), massive migration from rural to urban areas, a shaky industrial base, rampant inflation, and governmental corruption and mismanagement have created immense poverty and one of the most precarious economies in Africa. Social reform has been frustratingly slow, and the cities to which rural migrants flock have become dangerous, overcrowded, and out of control.

Despite these modern ills, Nigeria has succeeded in preserving its traditional cultures. Indigenous beliefs are much in evidence, although most contemporary Nigerians profess to be adherents of Islam or Christianity. And despite the influx of Western-style stores, the Nigerian love of bargaining is still on display in the open-air markets. You will also have the opportunity, especially in the south, to experience colorful traditional festivals on every occasion, be it a birth, a funeral, the time for planting, or the harvest. In fact, no matter how much you learn about Nigeria before your departure, prepare to be surprised by its contradictions and amazing diversity.

—*Sarah Wood, New York, New York*

Official name: Federal Republic of Nigeria. **Area:** 356,667 square miles (about three times the size of Nevada). **Population:** 118,865,000. **Population density:** 322 inhabitants per square mile. **Capital and largest city:** Lagos (pop. 1,243,000). **Language:** English (official), Hausa, Yoruba, Ibo. **Religion:** Islam, Christianity. **Per capita income:** US$790.

Currency: Naira. **Literacy rate:** 42%. **Average daily high/low*:** Lagos: January, 88°/74°; July, 83°/74°. **Average number of days with precipitation:** Lagos: January, 2; July, 16.

TRAVEL

U.S. citizens need a passport and a visa. An onward/return ticket is required, as well as a letter of proposal stating why one is visiting Nigeria. For specific requirements, check with the Embassy of the Federal Republic of Nigeria (2201 M Street NW, Washington, DC 20037) or the Nigerian consulate in New York.

Getting Around

Nigeria's road system is one of the best in Africa and includes an expressway linking Ibadan and Lagos, the country's two largest cities. Buses connect the main cities, but are not cheaper than taxis—only safer. The fastest means of transport is provided by shared taxis (cars and minibuses), which speed along fixed routes, leaving when full and picking up and dropping off passengers along the way. Hitchhiking is relatively easy, but the driver will expect anyone hitching to pay something for the ride. A limited rail system provides a cheap but slow alternative for those with more time. You can also find cheap internal flights.

WORK

It is not necessary to secure a job before going to Nigeria, but you must obtain a work permit for employment. For more information, contact the Consulate of Nigeria, 515 Lexington Avenue, New York, NY 10022.

Internships/Traineeships

A program offered by a member of the Council on International Educational Exchange is listed below.

AIESEC-US. Reciprocal internship program for students in economics, business, finance, marketing, accounting, and computer science. See page 18 for more information.

Voluntary Service

For persons interested in voluntary service work the Year Abroad Program sponsored by the International Christian Youth Exchange offers persons ages 18 to 24 voluntary service opportunities in the fields of health care, education, the environment, construction, et cetera. See page 18 for more information.

STUDY

The following programs are offered by CIEE-member institutions. Consult Appendix I for the addresses of the colleges and universities listed in this section.

---

*All temperatures are Fahrenheit.

Semester and Academic Year

General Studies

Experiment in International Living/School for International Training. "College Semester Abroad." Lagos. Fall or spring semester. Intensive language study with excursions to sites in northern Nigeria, seminar on Nigerian life, field-study methods seminar, culture, and development, independent-study project, homestay, and educational tour. Sophomores to seniors with 2.5 GPA. Apply by May 15 for fall and October 15 for spring.

International Student Exchange Program. Direct reciprocal exchange between U.S. universities and the University of Ibadan. Semester or academic year. Full curriculum options. Open only to students at ISEP-member instiions.

Summer

University of Pennsylvania. "Penn-in-Ibadan." Examination of indigenous traditional culture and contemporary society. Apply by April 1.

EXPLORING NIGERIAN CULTURE

Readings

Nigeria has produced many of the more popular African writers writing in English today. Chinua Achebe, probably the most famous African novelist, is best known for *Things Fall Apart* (1962), which explores what happens to traditional life as it falls under the influence of Western culture. *Arrow of God* and *No Longer of Ease* (1963) continue his exploration of this theme, while *Man of the People* is a novel about politics and government corruption in the Nigeria in the 1960s.

Wole Soyinka, winner of the 1985 Nobel Prize for literature, also addresses problems of contemporary life. The autobiography of his childhood, *Ake* (1983) provides a window into the complexities of a life lived between the traditional and contemporary worlds. A more recent work of his is *A Play of Giants* (1984), which portrays a group of dictatorial African leaders in an embassy in New York. Soyinka has turned to film in the last few years. His directorial debut was the film *Blues for a Prodigal* (1984).

Amos Tutuola should also be included in any list of prominent African writers. His *The Palm-Wine Drinkard* (1953) is a Nigerian folktale drawn from Yoruba myths and legends, while *My Life in the Bush of Ghosts* (1954), perhaps his most popular book, is the story of a small boy in the bush who faces many of the spirits of African mythology.

A number of other Nigerian writers have also distinguished themselves. T. Obinkaram Echewa's novel *The Crippled Dancer* (1986) concerns feuding and intrigue within an Igbo village. Buchi Emecheta's *In the Ditch* (1987), about the problems of a Nigerian woman living in London, and *Second Class Citizen* (1983), which tells the story of the same woman's early years in Nigeria, have found a large audience in Nigeria and abroad. Flora Nwapa writes about unconventional African women in books such as *Efuru* (1966).

Those who seek to understand something of the civil war that tore at Nigeria's fabric in the 1960s should read Cyprian Ekwensi's novel *Survive the Peace* (1976). The same author vividly portrays Nigerian city life in *Lokotown* (1966) and *Jagua Nana* (1975), and his *Burning Grass* (1962) is about the herding peoples of northern Nigeria.

SENEGAL

Senegal, the westernmost nation on the African mainland, was the point of embarcation for slaves being shipped to the New World. Today it is the point of arrival for most travelers to West Africa.

Until independence in 1958, France controlled Senegal for the better part of three centuries. The French colonial agenda, however, was only a partial success. Today, while many Senegalese speak French and are Catholic, most are Muslims who speak African languages such as Wolof, Malinke', or Pulaar. Unfortunately, the most visible legacies of French colonialism are also the most tragic: the slave warehouse on the island of Goree' and an environment ravaged by the French focus on the cultivation of peanuts.

The central district of Dakar, Senegal's capital, is clean and open to the sun and sea. It bears the imprint of Leopold Senghor, the nation's president for its first 20 years of independence. Senghor, who loved France, had many of the public buildings designed in French style and named the streets after French heroes. But the rest of Dakar—and the rest of Senegal—are marked by its African heritage. Herds of goats pass through city streets, urban dwellers cook over open charcoal stoves, and brightly dressed nomads drive their flocks through the sandy northern savannah.

The transformation of Senegal into a multiparty democracy in 1983 has encouraged political activity and a freer press. There are several independent newspapers, and European and American papers are often available in Dakar.

The Senegalese love music, and a few of their stars—reggae performer Alpha Blondy and rock star Youssou N'Dour among them—are already well known in the United States. In Senegal itself, cassette tapes play everywhere and the periodic village festivals are full of music and dance. Much of the music is unforgettably beautiful.

Sadly, in the extreme north, along the Senegal River, the savannah is being transformed into desert. In the 19th century the French covered northern Senegal with peanut farms. This had the effect of turning the Senegalese away from traditional farming methods and crops of vegetables and grains and, ultimately, turning thousands of acres of rich land into desert. Seeing this is essential to understanding one of Senegal's most pressing problems.

If your French is weak, get a visa to enter The Gambia, a tiny English-speaking country surrounded by Senegal. An express bus links Dakar and Banjul, the Gambian capital. The Gambia is a sliver of a nation, 200 miles long and as little as 10 miles wide, that stretches along the banks of the River Gambia in central Senegal and boasts fine beaches, picturesque towns reminiscent of the Caribbean, markets buzzing with commerce, and villages with a lively traditional life.

—*Jason Zweig, New York, New York*

Official name: Republic of Senegal. **Area:** 75,750 square miles (about the size of Utah). **Population:** 7,740,000. **Population density:** 101 inhabitants per square mile. **Capital and largest city:** Dakar (pop. 1,300,000). **Language:** French (official); Wolof, Serer, and other regional languages. **Religion:** Islam. **Per capita income:** US$380. **Currency:** CFA Franc. **Literacy rate:** 10%. **Average daily high/low*:** Dakar: January 79°/64°; July 88°/76°. **Average number of days with precipitation:** Dakar: January, 0; July, 7.

TRAVEL

U.S. citizens need a passport and a visa. Proof of yellow-fever vaccination is also required. Prospective visitors must pick up the visa application at the embassy in Washington in

---

*All temperatures are Fahrenheit.

person. For specific requirements, check with the Embassy of the Republic of Senegal (2112 Wyoming Avenue NW, Washington, DC 20008).

Getting Around

Senegal's main roads run north-south from Mauritania to Guinea-Bissau, but they are mostly concentrated on the western side of the country, near the coast. The roads are well-served by buses and taxis. For travel westward, the train from Dakar to Bamako is most convenient. A shorter line runs between Dakar and St. Louis to the north.

Boat travel is a good alternative for travel along the coast. The weekly "Casamance Express" runs between Dakar and Ziguinchor (The Gambia).

WORK

It is very difficult for foreigners to obtain regular, salaried employment in Senegal. For more information, contact the Embassy of the Republic of Senegal, 2112 Wyoming Avenue NW, Washington, DC 20008.

Internships/Traineeships

Programs offered by members of the Council on International Educational Exchange are described below. Consult Appendix I for the addresses of the institutions listed in this section.

AIESEC-US. Reciprocal internship program for students in economics, business, finance, marketing, accounting, and computer science. For more information see page 18.

University of Minnesota. "Minnesota Studies in International Development." Academic year. Predeparture coursework at the U of M fall quarter with internship in development-related research or action project in winter and spring quarters. Juniors to graduates and adults with interest in development; 2.5 GPA and two years of French. Apply by May 15.

STUDY

Programs sponsored by CIEE-member institutions are described below. Consult Appendix I for the addresses you can write for more information.

Semester and Academic Year

General Studies

Kalamazoo College. "Kalamazoo College in Senegal." Dakar. Academic year at University of Dakar. Summer orientation at Kalamazoo prior to going abroad. Juniors and seniors with 20 quarter-hours of French and 3.0 GPA. Apply by February 15.

University of La Verne. "Comparative Cultures: West Africa." Senegal and the Gambia. January interim. Juniors to graduate students with 2.5 GPA.

EXPLORING SENEGALESE CULTURE

Readings

Leopold Sedar Senghor, the first president of Senegal, was also a founder of the "negritude" school of literature, which became important in the French-speaking African countries during the 1960s and 1970s. The idea behind "negritude" was to establish a literature separate from traditional French literature that reflected the lives and concerns of black Africans. More recently, black writers have gone beyond this rather moderate "negritude" approach. For example, Camara Laye, born in Guinea but now living in Senegal, has written *The Dark Child* (1954, also translated as *The Black Child*), an autobiographical novel about growing up in Guinea. He is also author of *The Guardian of the Word: Kouma Lafolo Kuoma*, a historical novel about the great Mali Emperor Sundiata narrated by a griot, a kind of African troubadour.

Another Senegalese writer worth reading is Sembene Ousmane. His novel *Xala* (1983) is about a Senegalese businessman caught between the traditional way of life and the modern world. In *God's Bits of Wood* (1970), considered a classic, Ousmane looks at Africa through the prism of a 1948 railroad strike on the Senegal-Niger. And his recently reissued book of short stories, *Tribal Scars and Other Stories* (1974), illustrates Ousmane's social conscience as well as his irony and wit. Ousmane works mostly with film at present; like other prominent contemporary African authors, he has found it a more expressive medium for his work.

SIERRA LEONE

Sierra Leone (which means "Lion Mountains") was named by Portuguese explorers. In the 18th century the British wanted to expand trade in West Africa as well as to find a place for freedmen to settle after slavery was abolished in the British Empire. The first settlements in Sierra Leone of freed slaves from the Americas were made in 1787; however, most of the original settlers fell prey to either disease or hostile locals. While the freedmen settlers and their descendants, or "Krios" as they came to be called, enjoyed a privileged status under British rule, they never made up more than a small percentage of the population and currently do not have much political power, although they comprise a disproportionately large percentage of the country's intellectuals and professionals.

Today, some 18 different ethnic groups call Sierra Leone home. But since independence in 1961, its politics have been characterized by a struggle between the two largest groups, the Temnes and the Mendes, which are about equal in numbers. The result has been political instability, including a high incidence of civil violence and military coups.

Corruption and mismanagement have led to Sierra Leone's transformation from one of Africa's richest nations to one of its poorer nations. The diamond industry, from which Sierra Leone derives much of its export wealth, is crippled by the fact that one-third of the gems produced are smuggled out of the country.

Sierra Leone is noted for its lush tropical vegetation, beautiful mountains, and unspoiled beaches. Tourism has grown rapidly along the mountainous Freetown peninsula, where during the winter season the limited number of resort hotels fill to capacity with Europeans seeking warm weather, beaches, and cheap prices. Tourist enclaves have also cropped up at Bo, a city southeast of Freetown. However, you'll encounter few tourists in other areas of the country, including the mountainous interior, where roads are poor and tourist facilities are virtually nonexistent. Tourism is an important source of income, one that is being expanded with the hopes of turning around Sierra Leone's economic downslide.

—*Raquel Hodgson, Berkeley, California*

Official name: Republic of Sierra Leone. **Area:** 27,925 square miles (slightly larger than West Virginia). **Population:** 4,168,000. **Population density:** 154 inhabitants per square mile. **Capital and largest city:** Freetown (pop. 469,000). **Language:** English (official); Mende, Temne, Creole. **Religion:** Animism, Islam, Christianity. **Per capita income:** U.S. $320. **Currency:** Leone. **Literacy rate:** 15%. **Average daily high/low*:** Freetown: January, 88°/72°; July, 83°/72°. **Average number of days with precipitation:** Freetown: January, 1; July, 29.

TRAVEL

U.S. citizens need a passport and a visa. A return or onward ticket and proof of financial support from a bank or employer is also required. In addition, currency restrictions are enforced: a minimum of $100 must be changed in the airport by all adult travelers over the age of 16 upon entry. The purpose of the trip must be specified before arrival in Sierra Leone. Proof of immunizations against cholera and yellow fever are needed. For specific requirements, contact the Embassy of the Republic of Sierra Leone (1701 19th Street NW, Washington, DC 20009).

Getting Around

Despite its small size Sierra Leone is not always easy to get around, especially in the rainy season. The transport system is limited to government buses and *poda podas* (local trucks). Bus service is reasonably good between Freeport and the larger centers of population. Pickup trucks or vans tend to be slow, crowded, unreliable, and uncomfortable. Roads (not entirely paved and sometimes impassable) connect Sierra Leone to the neighboring countries of Liberia and Guinea.

WORK

It is very difficult for foreigners to obtain regular, salaried employment in Sierra Leone. For more information, contact the Embassy of Sierra Leone, 1701 19th Street NW, Washington, DC 20009. For another type of work experience, see the internship and voluntary-service sections below.

Internships/Traineeships

Programs offered by members of the Council on International Educational Exchange are listed below.

AIESEC-US. Reciprocal internship program for students in economics, business, finance, marketing, accounting, and computer science. For more information see page 18.

Association for International Practical Training. "IAESTE Trainee Program." On-the-job training for undergraduate and graduate students in technical fields such as engineering, computer science, agriculture, architecture, and mathematics. See page 18 for more information.

Voluntary Service

For persons interested in voluntary service work, the Year Abroad Program sponsored by the International Christian Youth Exchange offers persons ages 18 to 24 voluntary

---

*All temperatures are Fahrenheit.

service opportunities in the fields of health care, education, the environment, construction, et cetera. See page 23 for more information.

STUDY

The following programs are offered by members of the Council on International Educational Exchange. Consult Appendix I for the addresses of the institutions listed in this section.

Semester and Academic Year

General Study

Kalamazoo College. "Kalamazoo College in Sierra Leone." Freetown. Study at Fourah Bay College (University of Sierra Leone). Fall and winter quarter, with summer orientation at Kalamazoo College. Juniors and seniors with 2.75 GPA. Apply by February 15.

University of Wisconsin-Madison. Freetown. Academic year. Open to juniors, seniors, and graduate students with 3.0 GPA. Instruction is in English. Apply by February 1.

EXPLORING THE CULTURE OF SIERRA LEONE

Readings

William Conton's book *The African* was published in 1960 but it remains the best-known Sierra Leonean work. It tells the story of a young man's education and his eventual rise to power as a nationalist leader. Recently, poet and novelist Syl Cheney-Coker has also risen to some prominence, drawing not just on Sierra Leone for his material, but on all of Africa as well as Europe and the United States. *The Graveyard Also Has Teeth* (1980) is a collection of some of his poems. For an example of his fiction, read *The Last Harmattan of Alusine Dunbar* (1991), which traces black pioneers returning from America just after the Revolution to the West African coast, and tells the story of their settlement up until today.

SOUTH AFRICA

South Africa has established itself as one of the chief economic powers of the continent by taking advantage of its mineral wealth, location, and fair climate. Unfortunately, because of the traditional governmental policy of apartheid, this wealth has been concentrated almost exclusively in the hands of white South Africans.

Apartheid—formally implemented in South Africa in the late 1940s and now on the path to abolition—is a concept of government that segregates the population according to four main racial categories: black, white, "colored" (an ambiguous grouping comprising Indians and biracial persons, although interracial marriage was strictly outlawed until recently), and Asian.

Most notable among the recent changes in the structures of apartheid have been the repeal of the Pass Laws, which required every nonwhite citizen to carry an internal passbook. The Land Areas Act has also been repealed, making it legal for black South Africans to leave the infamous homelands, where they have been internally exiled since apartheid's inception. However, though these policies are now the official government line, the country still has a long way to go before it eliminates apartheid.

Black South Africans, almost three-quarters of the country's population, are still excluded from the South African government. Only whites are allowed to vote for the president. The current South African government—acting in concert with the African National Congress, led by Nelson Mandela, and Inkatha, the primary Zulu organization—is moving toward convening a constitutional conference assigned the task of producing a democratic nonracial constitution within the next three years.

Cape Town, with one of the world's most beautiful settings, is probably South Africa's friendliest and most loved city. Cape Town is on a peninsula nestled between the mountains and two great oceans, the Indian and the Atlantic. Known for its superb beaches, climate, food, and wine, Cape Town is also the home of two of South Africa's greatest schools, the Universities of Cape Town and Stellenbosch.

On the opposite side of the country, easily accessible by frequent and inexpensive train service, lies the city of Durban. While Cape Town is considered relaxed and slow-paced, Durban is wild and crazy. It is here that one finds the best nightlife in the country. The land surrounding Duran is often referred to as The Valley of a Thousand Hills. This is Zulu country, where one is just as likely to find a man driving a team of oxen pulling a cart or an ordinary automobile.

Inland, in the Afrikaaner-cominated Transvaal, is Johannesburg, the largest city in Africa south of Cairo and the industrial and financial center of South Africa. In 1886, one of the richest gold veins in the world was discovered there. Jo'burg, as it is commonly called, was strictly segregated until recently. Most black workers still have to travel back to the townships every night after working in the mines around Johannesburg.

On the border with Mozambique is Kruger National Park, where the nature enthusiast will find more than 122 species of mammals, ranging from elephants and rhinoceros to zebra and impala.

While South Africa has a great many things to offer the tourist, it is still not a free country and it is impossible to ignore this fact. The only certain thing is that South Africa is in a difficult period of adjustment.

—*Gregory F. Ferro, Tucson, Arizona*

Official name: Republic of South Africa. **Area:** 472,359 square miles (about twice the size of Texas). **Population:** 39,550,000. **Population density:** 75 inhabitants per square mile. **Capitals:** Pretoria (pop. 822,000) administrative, and Capetown (pop. 1,000,000), legislative. **Largest city:** Johannesburg (pop. 1,900,000). **Language:** Afrikaans, English (both official), various Bantu languages. **Religion:** Protestant, Roman Catholic. **Per capita income:** US$1,890. **Currency:** Rand. **Literacy rate:** 99% (whites), 69% (Asians), 62% (Indians and biracial persons), 50% (Africans). **Average daily high/low*:** Cape Town: January 78°/60°, July 65°/45°; Johannesburg: January 78°/58°, July 63°/39°. **Average number of days with precipitation:** Cape Town: January, 3; July, 10. Johannesburg: January, 12; July, 1.

TRAVEL

U.S. citizens need a passport and visa. Proof of onward or return transportation is also required. For specific regulations, check with the Embassy of the Republic of South Africa, 3051 Massachusetts Avenue NW, Washington, DC 20008. It is advisable to get your passport stamped on a detachable piece of paper if you are planning on travelling anywhere else in Africa. Otherwise you will have a difficult time entering most countries and may be refused outright in others, specifically Zambia and Tanzania.

---

*All temperatures are Fahrenheit.

Getting Around

South Africa has a good modern system of highways ranging from expressways to an extensive network of secondary roads, most of which are paved. There are numerous bus companies, and Greyhound covers long-distance routes. South Africa is also is said to be one of the easiest countries to hitchhike in; this, however, is true only if you are white. While South Africa has an extensive railway network, rail travel is generally slow owing to smaller guage lines. The Blue Line express train operates between Johannesburg and Cape Town. Another option for getting around is South African Airways' comprehensive system of flights between the country's major cities.

Owing to the existence of interfactional violence, care should be taken on visits to townships. Travel in the company of persons familiar with the area is advised.

"If you go to South Africa, visit the black townships and poverty-stricken rural areas as well as the big tourist draws (beaches, wildlife parks, et cetera). Read about South Africa before you go—a broader range of materials is available outside than in. Talk to people as you eat, relax, and sightsee. Everyone will tell you their opinions on politics. It's an interesting and beautiful country but come prepared."
—Derek Grebdor, Ithaca, New York

Especially for Students and Young People

SASTS (Second floor, Thibault House, Hans Strijdom Avenue, Foreshore, Cape Town) is South Africa's student and youth travel agency. Other SASTS offices are located on these campuses: the University of Cape Town, the University of Natal at Durban, the University of Natal at Pietermaritzburg, the University of the Witwatersrand in Johannesburg, and Rhodes University in Grahamstown. All of these offices provide a variety of services, including booking accommodations, providing travel information, and selling plane, train, and bus tickets. In South Africa, holders of the International Student Identity Card receive discounts on international and domestic airfares.

For Further Information

General tourist information is available from the South African Tourist Corporation, 747 Third Avenue, New York, NY 10017.

WORK

It is necessary to obtain a temporary employment visa in order to work in South Africa. Applicants must submit an offer of employment from the prospective employer to the South African Consulate three months before the date of departure. For more information, contact the South African Consulate General, 326 East 48th Street, New York, NY 10017.

Internships/Traineeships

Programs offered by members of the Council on International Educational Exchange are listed below.

AIESEC-US. Reciprocal internship program for students in economics, business, finance, marketing, accounting, and computer science. See page 18 for more information.

Association for International Practical Training. "IAESTE Trainee Program." On-the-job training for undergraduate and graduate students in technical fields such as engineering, computer science, agriculture, architecture, and mathematics.

AFRICA SOUTH OF THE SAHARA: SOUTH AFRICA **291**

EXPLORING SOUTH AFRICAN CULTURE

Readings

Woza Albert! by Percy Mtwa, Mbongeni Ngema, and Barney Simon (first performed in 1984, published in 1988) is a play that illustrates both the ridiculous and the tragic contradictions of apartheid. It is based on the idea that Christ will make his Second Coming in South Africa, and it brilliantly illustrates the concept of "laughing to keep from crying." Powerful and more strictly tragic than *Woza Albert!* are D. M. Zwelonke's *Robben Island* (1973) and Hugh Lewin's *Bandiet—Seven Years in a South African Prison* (1981). *Bandiet* is an account of the author's imprisonment and the novel, *Robben Island*, is set in South Africa's harsh island prison where a leader of the Poko branch of the resistance does not crack under torture, although his body gives out.

For books written within the last couple of years, read *Coming Home and Other Stories* by Farida Karodia (1988), and *Have You Seen Zandile?* (1990), a play by Gcina Mhlophe, Thembi Mtshali, and Maralin Vanrenen. Though Karodia now lives in Canada, she was raised in South Africa and it is the setting for her work, including her novel *Daughters of the Twilight* (1986). *Have you Seen Zandile?* is about a child living with her grandmother in Durban, who is forced to come live in the Transkei homeland by her mother.

For a historical perspective on South Africa, read Thomas Mofolo's *Chaka*. Contemporary issues dominate most works by prominent African writers. Among these are Eskia Mphahlete's *Down Second Avenue* (1985) and Alex La Guma's novel *Time of the Butcherbird* (1979) and his short stories "A Walk in the Night" and "The Stone Country." You might also want to read *Ushaba: The Hurtle to Blood River* (1974), by Jordan K. Ngubane, South Africa's leading Zulu novelist.

In white South African fiction, apartheid is also the dominant theme. The late Alan Paton's *Cry the Beloved Country* (1948) was one of the first internationally acclaimed books to deal with apartheid, and was followed by his *Ah! But Your Land Is Beautiful*. Other important white South African writers include Athol Fugard (*Master Harold and the Boys*), Peter Abrahams (*Tell Freedom* and *Mine Boy*), Nadine Gordimer (*A Soldier's Embrace* and *Crimes of Conscience*), and Andre Brink (*A Dry White Season*).

The most important white South African writer today is probably the Afrikaaner J.M. Coetzee. *The Life and Times of Michael K.* (1984) is a black man's odyssey from municipal gardening to an abandoned farm, war, labor camps, and finally back to Cape Town. *From the Heart of the Country* (1977) is a tale of madness set in the African veldt.

Films

A Dry White Season (1990), based on the novel by Andre Brink and directed by Euzhan Palcy, is a tragic and moving story about apartheid. It is told through an Afrikaaner narrator, though the main actors in the tragedy are black. *Come Back, Africa* (released on video), by Rogosin, is a documentary-style feature that was secretly shot while the director was supposed to be making a commercial musical. It dramatizes the squalor and desperation of the slums, as well as concentrated oppression specifically aimed at breaking up black family and community. Although the major historical figure in *Cry Freedom* (1987) was Stephen Biko, the movie actually tells the story of Donald Woods, a white journalist who has contact with the South African martyr. Because the film reduces Biko to a marginal character in his own story in favor of a white character who was a minor player in the actual history, and because of popular local opposition to the film, *Cry Freedom* was poorly received in South Africa. Two films that were originally banned, *Mapantsula* (1989), directed by Oliver Schmitz, written by and starring Thomas Mogotlane, and *The Stick* (1989), directed by Darrell Roodt, are now due to be released publicly.

TANZANIA

Tanzania is a land of rare beauty and unusual interest, boasting such world famous sites as Mount Kilimanjaro, Lake Victoria, the Great Rift Valley, Olduvai Gorge, and the Serengeti Plain. It also has a variety of ethnic groups, the most widely known being the Masai, who have proudly retained their nomadic lifestyle. But the attraction for which Tanzania is most famous is neither its topography nor its people, but its wildlife. In fact, more than a quarter of the country's area is protected as national parks and game preserves. Yet in spite of these well-known attractions, little has been done to develop tourism and only a few adventurous travelers visit Tanzania.

For most of the last five hundred years, Tanzania has been dominated by foreign powers—Arab, Persian, Portuguese, German, and British. After gaining its independence from Britain in 1961, Tanganyika annexed the island of Zanzibar off the East African coast and became Tanzania in 1964.

For most of its short history as an independent nation, Tanzania was led by Julius Nyerere, or *Mwalimu* (teacher), as he was often called. Under Nyerere's leadership, Tanzania experimented with an African style of socialism called *Ujamaa*. Major corporations were nationalized and private enterprise discouraged. And Tanzanians, a diverse group of over 120 tribes, each with its own language and culture, were encouraged to further national unity by learning Swahili, a language that has long served as a lingua franca among traders on the East African coast. Ironically, a language that developed in conjunction with the Arab and Persian exploitation of Africans has become the language of an African nation trying to assert its freedom and identity.

The Tanzanian socialist experiment, however, has not been notably successful. In spite of receiving the highest per capita foreign assistance in Africa, Tanzania is one of the 25 poorest countries in the world. Agriculture dominates the economy and over 90 percent of the population lives in rural areas. But under the leadership of Ali Hassan Mwinyi, who assumed the presidency after Nyerere stepped down in 1985, the country has gradually moved toward a more open economic system, with positive results.

Tanzanians are a peaceful and friendly people who rarely criticize one another either publicly or privately. They treat each other, and especially the elderly, with respect. Women are regarded as subservient to men and do most of the work. And the lives of most Tanzanians are heavily influenced by witchcraft, spirits, and magic.

—*Erna Loewen-Rudgers, Mbeya, Tanzania*

Official name: United Republic of Tanzania. **Area:** 364,886 square miles (three times the size of New Mexico). **Population:** 26,070,000. **Population density:** 67 inhabitants per square mile. **Capital and largest city:** Dar es Salaam (pop. 1,400,000). **Language:** Swahili, English (both official). **Religion:** Christianity, Islam, Animism. **Per capita income:** US$258. **Currency:** Tanzanian shilling. **Literacy rate:** 85%. **Average daily high/low*:** Dar es Salaam: January, 87°/77°; July, 83°/66°. **Average number of days with precipitation:** Dar es Salaam: January, 8; July, 6.

TRAVEL

U.S. citizens are required to have a passport that is valid for at least six months beyond their date of entry, as well as a visa. Return or onward transportation plus proof of financial support from a bank, employer, or travel agent is also required. Proof of yellow-fever vaccination is required for all of Tanzania; proof of cholera vaccination is required

---

*All temperatures are Fahrenheit.

only for visiting the island of Zanzibar. Every visitor must exchange $50 at point of entry. For specific requirements, check with the Embassy of the United Republic of Tanzania (2139 R Street NW, Washington, DC 20008).

Getting Around

Major urban centers within Tanzania are connected by roads; however, due to the economic situation in the country, maintenance of roads has been neglected. In addition, a shortage of fuel and spare parts for vehicles has severely affected public transport. Bus service along certain routes is liable to be canceled at any point for indefinite periods of time. The three main rail lines radiate from Dar es Salaam north to Arusha (near Mount Kilimanjaro and the Kenyan border), west to Lake Tanganyika, and southwest into Zambia. Whichever way you go, be prepared for long delays.

Ferries generally are more reliable than ground transportation. They operate along the coast of Lake Tanganyika, providing service to Burundi and Zambia (cargo boats provide connections to Zaire) and along Lake Victoria, providing service to Uganda and Kenya. Boats also connect Dar es Salaam to the islands of Zanzibar, Mafia, and Pemba in the Indian Ocean.

For Further Information

General tourist information is available from the Tanzania Tourist Corporation, 201 East 42nd Street, New York, NY 10017.

WORK

It is very difficult for foreigners to obtain regular, salaried employment in Tanzania. For more information, contact the Embassy of the United Republic of Tanzania, 2139 R Street NW, Washington, DC 20008.

Voluntary Service

Global Volunteers places participants in rural communities to work on economic and human development projects in Tanzania. Projects include tutoring, construction work, health care, and business planning. Volunteers serve for two to three weeks; no special skills are required. For more information, contact Global Volunteers, 2000 American National Bank Building, St. Paul, MN 55101.

STUDY

Study programs offered by CIEE-member institutions are listed below. Consult Appendix I for the addresses where you can write for more information.

Semester and Academic Year

General Studies

International Student Exchange Program. Direct reciprocal exchange between U.S. universities and the University of Dar es Salaam. Academic year. Full curriculum options. Open only to students at ISEP-member institutions.

Wildlife Conservation and Ecology

Experiment in International Living/School for International Training. "College Semester Abroad." Arusha, Moshi, Serengeti National Park, and other sites. Intensive Swahili, wildlife ecology and field-study methods seminars, homestays, field visits, and independent-study projects. No language prerequisite. Sophomores to seniors with 2.5 GPA and previous coursework in environmental studies or biology. Apply by October 31 for spring; May 31 for fall.

TOGO

Togo is a splinter-thin strip of land wedged between Ghana and Benin. It was part of Germany's only West African colony from 1894 to 1919, when France and Great Britain split the territory between them. Britain took the western area and added it to Ghana. The French granted Togo independence in 1960.

Togo's population of a little over three million people is divided among almost 40 ethnic groups. The climate ranges from the scorching savannah of the north to breezy inland lakes to a lush semitropical zone along the coast. From lagoons on the Atlantic, the land rises to a peak of more than three thousand feet in the central mountains. The port cities—including the capital, Lomé—are full of a profusion of fresh seafood, including some of the finest lobster you will ever taste. Game reserves in the north shelter herds of antelope and buffalo—and, if you are very lucky, you may even spot one of West Africa's last remaining elephants. All this in a country only 350 miles long and 32 miles wide at the seashore.

Unlike some of West Africa's larger, dirtier capitals that ring with constant clanging and honking, Lomé is a city built on a comfortably human scale. It is a thriving port and market center; goods pour ashore through its free-trade zone, then fan out through the region along traditional trading routes. Lomé's pristine, relatively uncrowded beaches attract tourists from Europe and elsewhere. Everything from luxury hotels to cheap corner cafés caters to the traveler, and all are welcome.

Togo is opening up further. The autocratic president, General Gnassingbé Eyadema, who seized power in 1967, announced in April 1991 that he would allow multiparty elections and a new, democratic constitution. That could provide, at long last, a legal outlet for dissent and free political expression. If Africa, like Eastern Europe, can move peacefully toward greater democracy, Togo could become an even more interesting place to visit.

—*Jason Zweig, New York, New York*

Official name: Republic of Togo. **Area:** 21,622 square miles (about the size of West Virginia). **Population:** 3,556,000. **Population density:** 158 inhabitants per square mile. **Capital and largest city:** Lomé (pop. 300,000). **Language:** Ewé, Mina, Kabyé, Cotocoli, French (official). **Religion:** Animism, Christianity, Islam. **Per capita income:** US $240. **Currency:** CFA Franc. **Literacy rate:** 45% (males). **Average daily high/low*:** Lomé: January, 88°/74°; July, 83°/74°. **Average number of days with precipitation:** Lomé: January, 2; July, 16.

TRAVEL

U.S. citizens need a passport, but Togo is one of the few African countries that does not require a visa for stays of up to three months. However, the government does require

---

*All temperatures are Fahrenheit.

yellow-fever vaccinations. For specific regulations, check with the Embassy of the Republic of Togo, 2208 Massachusetts Avenue NW, Washington, DC 20008.

Getting Around

Main roads in Togo are excellent. Paved roads link the different regions of the country, making it possible to drive from Lomé to the capital cities of neighboring Benin or Ghana in just a few hours. Traveling these roads is cheap and comfortable, with minibuses being the chief means of public transport. There are also two short rail lines from Lomé into the interior, but trains are infrequent and slow. Except for small chartered planes, there is no domestic air service in Togo.

WORK

It is very difficult for foreigners to obtain regular, salaried employment in Togo. For more information, contact the Embassy of the Republic of Togo, 2208 Massachusetts Avenue NW, Washington, DC 20008.

Internships/Traineeships

The program listed below is sponsored by a member of the Council on International Educational Exchange.

AIESEC-US. Reciprocal internship program for students in economics, business, finance, marketing, accounting, and computer science. See page 18 for more information.

STUDY

The following programs are offered by CIEE-member institutions. Consult Appendix I for the addresses where you can write for more information. In addition to those listed below, the University of California system offers a program open only to students enrolled at its various schools.

Semester and Academic Year

General Studies

International Student Exchange Program. Direct reciprocal exchange between U.S. universities and the Université du Bénin in Lomé. Semester or academic year. Full curriculum options. Open only to students at ISEP-member institutions.

Summer

French Language

North Carolina State University/Raleigh. "Summer in Togo." Lomé. Sophomores to graduate students with 2.0 GPA; no language prerequisite. Apply by February 15.

ZAMBIA

Zambia was originally organized by the British South Africa Company as Northern Rhodesia during the late nineteenth century. But as was so often the case with other African countries, its borders unified neither tribal nor linguistic groups. However, in this century a nationalistic movement was able to transcend internal differences and eventually bring about the bloodless revolution that resulted in the creation of an independent Zambia in 1964.

More than 25 years after independence, Zambia still sees itself as a "front-line" state battling the legacies of colonialism—most notably poverty—while at the same time risking its own security and economic stability to help neighboring countries: Zimbabwe in the 1970s, and now black South Africans. Today, the same man who led Zambia to independence, Kenneth Kaunda, is president under a "one-party participatory democracy." All opposition parties were banned in 1972.

Much of Zambia's economy is based on copper mining; a decline in world copper prices over the last 20 years has caused Zambia's economy to spiral downward. Recently, new cash crops have been introduced to supplement Zambia's traditional agricultural exports of maize, tobacco, and cotton. But Zambia, faced with a large international debt, remains in economic difficulty.

There is a great deal of political unrest in Zambia; however, Zambians are quick to point out that the soldiers and the government cause most of the trouble for tourists, while the people themselves are quite friendly. Do not wear khaki or military-style clothing, and do not take pictures of borders, post offices, or other government establishments. As long as you show deference and do not challenge soldiers' authority, they will probably leave you in peace requiring only a bribe or other "present."

—*Kimberly Lamour, Baton Rouge, Louisiana*

Official name: Republic of Zambia. **Area:** 290,586 square miles (about three times the size of Oregon). **Population:** 8,119,000. **Population density:** 26 inhabitants per square mile. **Capital and largest city:** Lusaka (pop. 870,000). **Language:** English (official), various Bantu dialects. **Religion:** Animism, Christianity. **Per capita income:** US$304. **Currency:** Kwacha. **Literacy rate:** 54%. **Average daily high/low*:** Lusaka: January, 78°/63°; July, 73°/49°. **Average number of days with precipitation:** Lusaka: January, 21; July, 1.

TRAVEL

U.S. citizens visiting Zambia need a visa and passport. Yellow-fever and cholera vaccinations are required. For specific requirements, check with the Embassy of the Republic of Zambia, 2419 Massachusetts Avenue NW, Washington, DC 20008.

Getting Around

The main roads are quite good but many of the rural routes are often impassable in the rainy season. Hitching in Zambia is not as safe as it is in other African countries due to crime caused by the poor economy. Zambia Railways runs passenger trains from Lusaka north to Zaire, northeast to Tanzania, and south to Victoria Falls and Zimbabwe. Zambia Airways serves all major cities and tourist centers. Ferry service across Lake Tanganyika connects Zambia with Tanzania.

---

*All temperatures are Fahrenheit.

"For a sense of the Zambian people—there are some 74 different tribal groups—time is better spent in the rural areas than in Lusaka, a capital city that's not especially known for its character. Victoria Falls is both vast and stunning and should not be missed. The unusual wildlife in Luangwa and Katue parks make them well worth the visit."
—Denis Choiniere, Hull, Quebec

For Further Information

General tourist information is available from the Zambian National Tourist Board, 237 East 52nd Street, New York, NY 10022.

STUDY

A program offered by a CIEE-member institution is described below. Consult Appendix I for the address where you can write for more information.

Semester and Academic Year

General Studies

International Student Exchange Program. Direct reciprocal exchange between U.S. universities and the University of Zambia. Academic year. Full curriculum options. Open only to students at ISEP-member institutions.

ZIMBABWE

Zimbabwe, a landlocked country in Southern Africa, is peaceful now but still bears the scars of a bloody interracial war. Zimbabwe was the British colony of Southern Rhodesia until 1965, when white Rhodesians declared independence from Britain and formed a government dominated by whites. Blacks, who comprise over 95 percent of the population, fought a guerrilla war against the white Rhodesian regime, until a 1980 settlement renamed the nation Zimbabwe, ruled by a black majority government headed by Robert Mugabe. Today, blacks and whites work alongside each other. Although racial tensions persist, one is more likely to encounter a widespread feeling of reconciliation and determination to build a better country together.

An American may be surprised by the lingering British influence on the customs, language, and school system in Zimbabwe. Many Zimbabweans still celebrate British holidays such as Boxing Day and take their tea with milk, and English is still the primary language taught in high schools and used in newspapers (in part because the two main ethnic groups, the Shona and Ndebele, speak different languages). In addition, the capital, Harare, is quite cosmopolitan and boasts nightclubs, large hotels, department stores, and public gardens.

But in the countryside, where over three-quarters of the black population lives, Zimbabwe's traditional way of life is much more evident. Most rural blacks are farmers or livestock herders, their life an economic struggle. The majority government's efforts to live up to its promises of education, health care, and other basic services for all are hindered by its dependence on the military and industrial giant to the south. Zimbabwe relies on South Africa for most of its trade as well as for access to the ports necessary for its imports and exports.

Despite economic hardships, however, Zimbabweans are proud of their past and eager to show visitors the beauty of their country. The tropical savannah landscape encompasses some stunning highlights, including Victoria Falls, an abundance of ancient cave paintings, and game parks alive with elephants, lions, and giraffes. The ruins of Great Zimbabwe, capital of a fourteenth-century gold-trading empire, are also a spectacular sight. Traveling to these spots is made easy by a network of reliable buses.

Zimbabweans are family-oriented; a visit to someone's home usually includes a hearty meal and plenty of conversation. While foreigners can get by without fluency in Shona or Ndebele, communication in the rural areas is easier if you can manage a simple conversation. And, as is true in most African countries, Zimbabweans will appreciate your efforts to learn their language. They will also share with you the struggles of their past and the hopes for the country's future. For a new nation that enjoys internal stability and increasing economic growth based on agriculture, gold, and chromium, the future looks promising.

—Elizabeth Grossi, New York, New York

Official name: Republic of Zimbabwe. **Area:** 150,803 square miles (about the size of Montana). **Population:** 10,205,000. **Population density:** 66 inhabitants per square mile. **Capital and largest city:** Harare (pop. 730,000). **Language:** English (official), Ndebele, Shona. **Religion:** Traditional African religions, Christianity. **Per capita income:** US$275. **Currency:** Zimbabwean dollar. **Literacy rate:** 50%. **Average daily high/low*:** Harare: January, 78°/60°; July, 70°/44°. **Average number of days with precipitation:** Harare: January, 18; July, less than 1.

TRAVEL

U.S. citizens need a passport (but not a visa) for travel in Zimbabwe. An onward or return ticket is also required. Visitors must also declare currency upon arrival. For specific requirements, check with the Embassy of Zimbabwe, 1608 New Hampshire Avenue NW, Washington, DC 20009.

"Come with an awareness of the history of Zimbabwe. You should know something about its recent liberation struggle, the impact of apartheid in South Africa on Zimbabwe, and the role the U.S. has played in the region."
—Melanie Gorehund, St. Louis, Missouri

Getting Around

A good rail network connects the major regions of the country and links Zimbabwe to South Africa. There is also an extensive road system, most of which is well maintained. Various types of buses serve the country, providing everything from intercity express service to local service in the cities and countryside. They are slow and usually crowded, but cheap and serve most of the country. In addition, Air Zimbabwe (800-228-9485) connects the country's major urban centers and tourist attractions, including Victoria Falls.

"People are looking for pen pals, especially American pen pals, all the time. Some will ask for an address without even saying hello. They are serious. If you aren't serious, don't give your address. An unanswered letter is much more of an insult than refusing to give your address. Often, saying, 'I'd like to know you better before I give you my address' is a polite way of doing this."
—Megan McShea, Moorestown, New Jersey

---

*All temperatures are Fahrenheit.

For Further Information

An excellent guide to Zimbabwe and neighboring countries is *Zimbabwe, Botswana and Namibia—A Travel Survival Kit*, available for $16.95 (plus $1.50 book-rate postage; $3 for first-class) from Lonely Planet Publications, Embarcadero West, 112 Linden Street, Oakland, CA 94607.

WORK

It is very difficult for foreigners to obtain regular, salaried employment in Zimbabwe. For more information, contact the Embassy of Zimbabwe, 1608 New Hampshire Avenue NW, Washington, DC 20009.

Internships/Traineeships

A program sponsored by the Council on International Educational Exchange is listed below.

AIESEC-US. Reciprocal internship program for students in economics, business, finance, marketing, accounting, and computer science. For more information see page 18.

An internship program is also offered by Overseas Development Network (ODN); for more information see page 29.

STUDY

Programs sponsored by CIEE-member institutions are described below. Consult Appendix I for the addresses you can write for further information. In addition, Michigan State University offers a study program open only to its own students.

Semester and Academic Year

General Studies

Associated Colleges of the Midwest. "Zimbabwe Program." Harare. Spring semester. Courses in language, culture, development issues. Independent field project, homestays, and field trips. Sophomores, juniors, and seniors. Apply by October 15.

Experiment in International Living/School for International Training. "College Semester Abroad." Harare. Fall or spring semester. Language training, seminar in Zimbabwe life and culture and southern Africa studies, independent-study project, homestay, and educational tour. Sophomores to seniors with 2.5 GPA. Apply by May 15 for fall and October 15 for spring.

Michigan State University. "Undergraduate Student Exchange Program." University of Zimbabwe in Harare. Academic year from April to December. Sophomores to seniors. Apply by November 2.

Pitzer College. "Scripps-Pitzer in Zimbabwe." Various locations in Zimbabwe. Spring semester. Six-month intensive-study program featuring rural and urban components, a seminar in political and social change and the opportunity to enroll in regular courses at the University of Zimbabwe. Sophomores to seniors with 2.75 GPA. Apply by October 1.

EXPLORING THE CULTURE OF ZIMBABWE

Readings

Among the many books that explore the colonial period and its injustices is Wilson Katiyo's *A Son of the Soil* (1976), about a black boy growing up in colonial Rhodesia. The difficult, unequal relationships between the few whites and many blacks there creates a tension that finally leads to madness. The underside of colonial Rhodesia is starkly presented in Dambudzo Marechera's *The House of Hunger* (1978).

Bones (1990), by Chenjerai Hove, is a novel about the guerilla war for freedom in Zimbabwe. It is told through the device of interior monologues, by representative colonial "types," and by spirits. Hove captures the conflicts and ambivalence between the peasants and guerillas, and between the state and the people. *Harvest of Thorns* (1991), by Shimmer Chinodye, is another take on conflict in the Zimbabwean consciousness; Benjamin Tichifa, the protagonist, is torn between the old colonial regime and the new African one.

Since independence, more of an interest has emerged in books that deal with modern Zimbabwean issues as well as in books that reinforce Zimbabwean identity by celebrating its history, culture, and heroes. Solomon Mutswairo's *Chaminuka: Prophet of Zimbabwe* (1983) is a historical novel about Zimbabwe's legendary 19th-century man of peace. In a similar vein, Mutswairo's *Mapondera: Soldier of Zimbabwe* (1978) tells the story of this man's struggle against the British in the 19th century. *The Polygamist* (1972), by Ndabaningi Sithole, is an essentially autobiographical novel that tells the story of a man who returns to his people (the Ndebele) as a converted Christian.

CHAPTER NINE
SOUTH ASIA

South Asia, separated from the rest of Asia by the Himalayas, is also known as the Indian subcontinent. The region is dominated by India, which at its present rate of growth is projected to become the world's most populous nation early in the next century. India contains a great diversity of peoples, religions, languages, and cultures, as well as some of the world's greatest topographic and climatic extremes. The smaller nations on its borders—Bangladesh, Bhutan, Nepal, and Pakistan—as well as the island-nation of Sri Lanka, add to the rich cultural diversity of the region. This diversity, while a source of much that is honored and cherished, has also been at the root of the civil and political strife that has produced a number of bitter conflicts both within and between the nations of the region.

With the exception of landlocked Nepal and Afghanistan, the modern nations of South Asia have only emerged as independent states since the end of the Second World War. However, the peoples and cultures of the region have a long history; in fact, the Indus River valley was one of the earliest centers of civilization. Here, in the third millenium B.C., the Hindu religion emerged. Islam spread to the region from the Middle East in the eleventh century and remains a major religion in the area. Buddhism, which had its origins in India, is not widely practiced except in Nepal, Bhutan, and the northernmost parts of India.

In 1947, Britain relinquished its colonial control of the region. The British presence thoroughly infiltrated all levels of society through its transformation of the education system and the bureaucracy in the 19th century. In most nations of South Asia, English remains the language by which people from different linguistic groups communicate with each other. Britain's worldwide empire also uprooted many, transporting South Asian workers to the Caribbean, Africa, and the South Pacific islands as well as to England itself. For these reasons, the nations of the Indian subcontinent, which in antiquity bore the germ of a broader Asian culture, have in many ways developed a closer relation to the West than most other Asian countries.

Getting There

Food, lodging, and land transportation in South Asia are generally inexpensive. Getting there will be your main expense. From the U.S., the cheapest air fares to South Asia are APEX or other excursion fares. You'll find up-to-date information on such fares at Council Travel offices. To give you some idea of cost, we've listed sample *one-way* fares in effect during the summer of 1991 below:

Los Angeles–Bombay	$1,628
New York–Delhi	$1,448
San Francisco–Calcutta	$1,219

From Europe, special student/youth fares, which enable you to save up to 50 percent on regular commercial fares, are available from several European cities to destinations in South Asia. These can be booked at any Council Travel office or a student travel bureau in Europe. Regulations vary depending on the airline, but generally holders of the International Student Identity Card (see page 8) or the International Youth Card (see page 10) are eligible. These are some sample *one-way* fares in effect during 1991:

| Frankfurt–Delhi | $445 |
| Paris–Karachi | $485 |

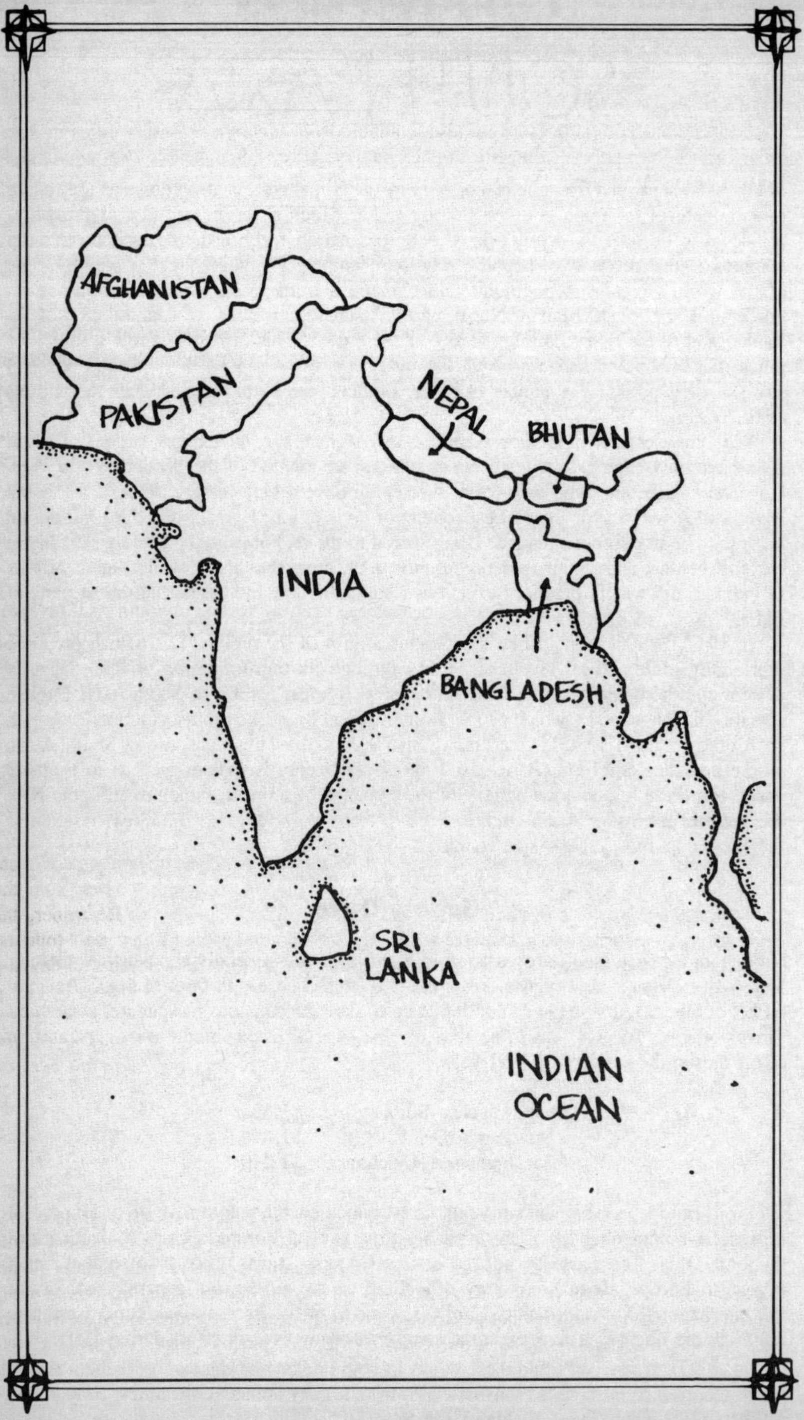
AFGHANISTAN
PAKISTAN
NEPAL
BHUTAN
INDIA
BANGLADESH
SRI LANKA
INDIAN OCEAN

Frankfurt–Bombay	$445
Paris–Delhi	$485

Special student/youth fares are also available from a number of other cities in Asia. For further information, contact a Council Travel office. Some sample *one-way* fares in effect during 1991 are:

Bangkok–Calcutta	$159
Hong-Kong–Bombay	$459
Bangkok–Kathmandu	$229

Overland trips from Europe to India and Nepal and beyond were once quite popular among more adventurous travelers. "Overlanding" is still an option, although conditions in the Middle East have narrowed the options. Today the only viable routes are through Turkey and the Soviet Union. Many such tours are operated by British groups. One such organization, Trailfinders Travel Center (42–48 Earl's Court Road, London W8, England), also puts out a free magazine, *Trailfinder*, which focuses on unusual adventure-travel tours around the world.

Getting Around South Asia

India comprises more than half of South Asia and is, geographically speaking, the most important country in the region. For the most part, getting around in South Asia involves travel in India, which will be discussed later on in this chapter. If you plan on visiting several distant points within the region and want to make the most of your time, you might consider an airline ticket. Below are listed some sample *one-way* fares in effect during 1991:

Delhi–Kathmandu	$249
Calcutta–Karachi	$145
Delhi–Dhaka	$108

Traveling conditions will also be affected by the weather. The Indian subcontinent experiences two monsoon seasons. Beginning in June, the monsoon comes from the southwest and blows northward during the summer. From October to December, the monsoon comes from the northeast. While the downpours frighten away most tourists, travel during the monsoon seasons can be a pleasant surprise. It seldom rains all day and the rains break the humidity and heat and bring the vegetation to full bloom.

"In Pakistan and India, you should never be surprised to find things not working out the way you expected. Be sure to have an alternative plan or two (or three!) to fall back on at a moment's notice."
—Debbi D. Harris, White Plains, New York

For Further Information

A useful guide to a number of countries in the region is Lonely Planet's *West Asia on a Shoestring* ($14.95). Almost half the book is devoted to India and its neighbors while the rest deals with countries further west (from Afghanistan to Turkey). Lonely Planet also publishes a variety of more detailed books on specific countries and regions. Among those focusing on countries not covered in this chapter are *Pakistan: A Travel Survival Kit* ($8.95), *Bangladesh: A Travel Survival Kit* ($10.95), and *Sri Lanka: A Travel Survival Kit* ($8.95). If you can't find these books in your bookstore, you can order them (include $1.50 book-rate postage; $3 for first-class) from Lonely Planet Publications, Embarcadero West, 112 Linden Street, Oakland, CA 94607.

A good source for books and information on all Asian nations is The Asia Society, 725 Park Avenue, New York, NY 10021. Write for a current publications catalog.

Travelers interested in staying in youth hostels in South Asia might want to take a look at volume two of the *International Youth Hostel Handbook* (see page 53), which lists hostels in India, Sri Lanka, Pakistan, and Nepal.

Listed below are the embassies you can write for information on the visa requirements of the countries not covered in individual sections later in this chapter:

- Embassy of the Republic of Afghanistan, 2341 Wyoming Avenue NW, Washington, DC 20008
- Embassy of the People's Republic of Bangladesh, 2201 Wisconsin Avenue NW, Washington, DC 20007
- Consulate of the Kingdom of Bhutan, 2 United Nations Plaza, New York, NY 10017
- Embassy of Pakistan, 2315 Massachusetts Avenue NW, Washington, DC 20008
- Embassy of the Democratic Socialist Republic of Sri Lanka, 2148 Wyoming Avenue NW, Washington, DC 20008

Working in South Asia

It is generally quite difficult for Americans to get any type of regular employment in the region. However, voluntary service opportunities and internship positions are available and are discussed in the individual country sections that follow. In addition the Association for International Practical Training's "IAESTE Trainee Program" operates in Pakistan; see page 18 for more information.

Studying in South Asia

You'll find a number of study programs listed in the individual country sections later in this chapter. In the section below we've listed study programs offered by CIEE-member institutions that take place in more than one country of the region. Consult Appendix I for the addresses of the sponsoring institutions.

Semester and Academic Year

General Studies

St. Olaf College. "Global Semester." Cairo, Egypt; Bangalore, India; Taipei, Taiwan; and Kyoto, Japan. Fall semester plus January. Cultures, social and political issues of selected non-Western countries. Sophomores, juniors, and seniors. Apply by March 1.

University of Pittsburgh. "Semester at Sea." Fall or spring semester. Students, based aboard the S.S. *Universe*, attend classes on board and travel to various countries in Europe, the Middle East, Africa, Asia, and South America. Sophomores, juniors, and seniors with 2.75 GPA. Contact: Semester at Sea, Eighth floor, William Pitt Union, University of Pittsburgh, Pittsburgh, PA 15260; (412) 648-7490.

Tibetan Studies

Experiment in International Living/School for International Training. "College Semester Abroad." New Delhi and Dharamsala, India; Kathmandu, Nepal; and Tibet. Fall or spring semester. Intensive language, seminar in Tibetan studies, field-study methods, village excursions and homestay, and independent-study project. Sophomores to seniors with 2.5 GPA. Apply by May 15 for fall and October 15 for spring.

INDIA

The quiet inside of a temple contrasts with the chaos of traffic outside. High-rise office buildings coexist with slums. Nuclear power plants stand beside fields plowed by oxen. As a traveler, you will undoubtedly be struck by the multitude of landscapes, cultures, and ways of thinking that India encompasses.

Perhaps the best way to understand India's provocative contrasts is to look at its history. The subcontinent has experienced a series of invasions, beginning in 1500 B.C. with the Aryan invasion and finally ending in 1947 when the British granted the country its independence. Each successive group brought changes to the subcontinent, enriching its culture with new religions, forms of government, customs, and art. Aryans introduced the caste system as well as a variety of religious practices and beliefs that influenced Hinduism. Moghul invasions beginning in the 16th century ushered in a long period of Muslim rule, with new architectural, artistic, and governmental forms. British colonial rule built the bureaucracy, cemented India's ties with the West, and left a legacy readily seen in the nation's educational system and parliamentary democracy.

As a result of these foreign influences, India is home to many religions: Islam, Hinduism, Parsi, Sikhism, Christianity, Buddhism, and Jainism. There is always a festival or celebration going on, and Westerners are welcomed into most temples and mosques —but take off your shoes and don't take photos! Inside, you can observe the daily prayers, and probably talk with an English-speaking guide about the details of the religious rituals.

Equal to the importance of religion in Indian society is the dominance of the family unit, which is extended to include perhaps three or four generations. The family is a critical social component in India; family members rely on and care deeply about each other.

Indians are friendly toward foreigners; learn to be patient and to put aside inhibitions about accepting invitations. The bazaar gives foreigners an opportunity to see most Indians in their element. Tea stalls, sweet shops, vegetable stands, and cold-drink counters are colorful and fragrant, and their merchandise, delicious.

Whether exploring the Ganges plain, climbing the Himalayas, or visiting the Taj Mahal, the Westerner will everywhere encounter the unique and exotic. Visiting the land of Mahatma Gandhi and Mother Teresa will expose the traveler not only to the nation's religious, language, cultural, and class differences, but also to one of the world's oldest and most dynamic civilizations.

—*Laryn E. Callaway, St. Louis, Missouri*

Official name: The Republic of India. **Area:** 1,266,595 square miles (about ⅓ the size of the U.S.). **Population:** 850,067,000. **Population density:** 658 inhabitants per square mile. **Capital:** New Delhi (pop. 7,200,000). **Largest city:** Calcutta (pop. 9,900,000). **Language:** Hindi and English. **Religion:** Hindu, Islam, Christianity, Sikh. **Per capita income:** US$300. **Currency:** Rupee. **Literacy rate:** 36%. **Average daily high/low*:** Bombay: January, 83°/67°; July, 85°/77°. New Delhi: January, 70°/41°; July 96°/81°. **Average number of days with precipitation:** Bombay: January, 1; July, 21. New Delhi: January, 2; July, 8.

TRAVEL

U.S. citizens traveling to India will need a passport and visa. The visa, valid for stays of up to three months, must be obtained before your arrival in the country. For this you'll need two photographs, your passport, and proof of onward transportation. Be sure to

---

*All temperatures are Fahrenheit.

request a multiple-entry visa if you wish to visit neighboring countries and then return to India. An AIDS test is required for all students and anyone over 18 staying more than one year (U.S. test sometimes accepted). For specific requirements, check with the Embassy of India (2107 Massachusetts Avenue NW, Washington, DC 20008) or an Indian consulate in New York, Chicago, or San Francisco. (Note: Holders of a three-month tourist visa are given a liquor permit, which allows them to purchase liquor in some of the "dry" states of India.)

Keep all official bank receipts for money exchanged so that you'll be able to convert your rupees back into American dollars when you leave. When you pay in rupees for your transportation out of India, you'll be asked to show a receipt to prove that you have obtained your rupees officially.

Getting Around

The Indian subcontinent covers so vast a territory that you may well want to fly between certain major cities rather than make arduous journeys overland. Domestic air service is provided by Indian Airlines, which connects more than 70 cities around the country. If you have only a little time to spend and want to see a lot of the country, you can purchase a Discover India pass, which entitles you to 21 days of unlimited travel on Indian Airlines for $400. Passes are available only to foreigners, however, and must be purchased outside the country in conjunction with your plane ticket to India. For further information, contact a Council Travel office.

India's rail network connects even the most remote areas of the country (except Kashmir). Since rail travel is popular among Indians, it's a good way to meet the people and experience the diversity of India's different cultures. Although there are no student discounts on rail travel in India, trains are generally inexpensive. If you plan to travel long distances, it might be worthwhile to invest in an Indrail Pass, which entitles the bearer to unlimited travel for a fixed period of time. Indrail passes can be purchased only by foreigners and must be paid for in U.S. dollars, although they may be purchased within India itself. For further information, contact Hariworld Travels, 30 Rockefeller Plaza, Suite 21, North Mezzanine, New York, NY 10012. The following prices (including night-sleeper charges, but excluding reservation fees) were in effect in 1991 for Indrail passes:

Period	Air-Conditioned Class	First Class	Second Class
1 day	$ 65	$ 29	$ 12
7 days	$220	$110	$ 55
15 days	$270	$135	$ 65
21 days	$330	$165	$ 75
30 days	$410	$205	$ 90
60 days	$600	$300	$135
90 days	$800	$400	$175

The labeling of these three classes is somewhat misleading. Many second-class cars are also air-conditioned and may be the best bargain. With the Indrail pass, it's possible to stay overnight in the railroad stations, either for a fee in the "retiring rooms" (beds and private rooms) or for free on couches in the first-class or second-class waiting rooms.

"You can expect your fellow passengers to be extremely hospitable, offering to share the copious amounts of food and drink they bring along with them for the journey. It's always a good idea to pack your own food, and to offer it in turn. Though some may refuse in keeping with their dietary laws, all will appreciate the gesture."
—Johnson Burns, Detroit, Michigan

Buses in India are used primarily for local transportation. In urban areas, buses are the primary component of the mass transit system. In rural areas, buses complement the rail system, fanning out to villages from train stations. An increasing number of air-conditioned, long-distance buses provide links between the country's major cities, creating a comfortable alternative for getting around India.

Rental cars are not readily available in India; however, cars with drivers can be arranged. The price, which may be negotiable, depends on the size of the car, the time spent, and the distance covered.

In the major cities, taxis are readily available. An alternative to taxis are "scooters," three-wheel vehicles that are usually metered, with fares running about half those of regular taxis. In addition, pedal trishaws still operate in many cities and smaller towns. And nearly everyone has a bicycle—perhaps the most efficient way to travel locally.

Eating and Sleeping

Accommodations and meals in India are inexpensive. Cheap or modest hotels can be found in most towns, and are listed in the various publications of the government tourist offices in addition to more expensive Western-style hotels. In addition, you'll find accommodations in YM/YWCAs in major cities, and Salvation Army guesthouses in Calcutta, Bombay, and Madras are popular with foreigners as well. The Government of India Tourist Offices (30 Rockefeller Plaza, Suite 15, North Mezzanine, New York, NY 10112) can also provide you with a list of youth hostels set up by the Department of Tourism.

"It may take some time for your stomach to get accustomed to the spicy food of India. If the food is too hot at first, try mixing curd or yogurt with everything. If you must eat western food, you'll find it in most major cities, though prices will be much higher than for Indian food."
—Susan Bryce, Seattle, Washington

Especially for Students

India's student travel agency and issuer of the International Student Identity Card is the Student Travel Information Centre (STIC) located at the Hotel Imperial, Room 6, Janpath, New Delhi 110001, with branch offices in Bombay, Calcutta, and Madras. STIC issues Indrail Passes, distributes lists of inexpensive hotels and guesthouses, and has information on low-cost flights within India and the region. In India, the International Student Identity Card entitles the holder to discounts on some accommodations and on STIC-operated tours.

Meeting the People

The Government of India Tourist Office sponsors a meet-the-people program. For further information, contact any of the following tourist offices upon arrival: 123 Maharishi Karve Road, Churchgate, Bombay; Embassy No. 4 Shakespeare Sarani, Calcutta; 88 Janpath, New Delhi; and 154 Anna Road, Madras. These offices can also direct you to Indian homes that welcome paying guests.

"Indians feel a real sense of duty towards their guests, and they will go to great lengths to take care of you. Such attention may seem awkward to most Americans, but it's best to simply accept this hospitality and appreciate a different way of life."
—Abbas Raghaban, Akron, Ohio

For Further Information

The Government of India Tourist Office (30 Rockefeller Plaza, Suite 15 North Mezzanine, New York, NY 10112) has brochures on places to see and stay throughout India. For an analysis of the past year's social, political, and economic events, read *India Briefing*, an annual survey of contemporary Indian affairs published by The Asia Society, 725 Park Avenue, New York, NY 10021.

India—A Travel Survival Kit is an excellent travel guide. It's available for $19.95 (plus $1.50 book-rate postage; $3 for first-class) from Lonely Planet Publications (Embarcadero West, 112 Linden Street, Oakland, CA 94607). Lonely Planet also publishes *Kashmir, Ladakh and Zanskar: A Travel Survival Kit* ($10.95), which provides practical information on all three Himalayan regions, and *Trekking in the Indian Himalaya* ($13.95), a hiker's guide.

WORK

It is necessary for foreigners to obtain a work permit to be employed in India. Though you don't have to secure a job before going to the country, it is advisable to do so. For more information, contact the Ministry of Labor and Employment, Shral Shakti Bhavan Rafi Marg, New Delhi 110001.

Internships and Traineeships

Programs sponsored by members of the Council on International Educational Exchange are described below. Consult Appendix I for the addresses of the institutions listed in this section.

AIESEC-US. Reciprocal internship program for students in economics, business, finance, marketing, accounting, and computer sciences. See page 18 for more information.

University of Minnesota. "Minnesota Studies in International Development." Academic Year. Predeparture coursework during the fall quarter at the U of M; internship in development-related research or action project in winter and spring quarters. Juniors to graduates and adults with interest in development; 2.5 GPA required. Apply by May 15. See Appendix I for address.

Voluntary Service

Sisters of Charity of Nazareth sponsors a volunteer program in India for those interested in health care, social service, education, and ministry. Participants serve from two weeks to three months. Room and board are provided. For service periods of three months or more, at least nine months prior notification is required. For more information, contact Sisters of Charity of Nazareth, SCNA Center, Nazareth, KY 40048.

In addition, the Partnership for Service Learning and the Overseas Development Network (ODN) sponsor service opportunities in India; for more information see page 29.

STUDY

The American Institute of Indian Studies (AIIS) is a cooperative organization comprised of 40 American colleges and universities with a special interest in Indian studies. The organization offers a variety of research fellowships to graduate students, researchers, and university faculty members. AIIS also operates a nine-month intensive language training program from September to May. For further details, write AIIS, 1130 East 59th Street, Chicago, IL 60637.

For an overview of Indian educational institutions and advice for the foreign student, ask for the booklet *Studying in India*, available from the Minister of Education and Culture at the Embassy of India (address above).

The following academic programs are offered by CIEE-member institutions. Consult Appendix I for the addresses of the colleges and universities listed below. In addition, the University of California offers a program open only to its own students.

Semester and Academic Year

Buddhist Studies

Antioch University. "Comparative Buddhist Studies." Bodh Gaya. Fall quarter. Courses in philosophy, contemporary culture, history, beginning Hindi or Tibetan, and meditation. Orientation held in London. Sophomores to graduate students in good academic standing. Apply by March 15.

General Studies

Associated Colleges of the Midwest. "India Studies." Pune. Spring term at an ACM College and six months in India. Priority given ACM students. Freshmen to graduate students, with priority to sophomores or juniors. Apply by April 1; final deadline is November 1.

Experiment in International Living/School for International Training. "College Semester Abroad." New Delhi and Udaipur, Rajsthan. Fall or spring semester. Intensive Hindi language, life and culture, rural development and environment seminar, village stay, field-study seminar, homestays, and independent-study project. Sophomores, juniors, and seniors with 2.5 GPA. Apply by May 15 for fall and October 15 for spring.

Friends World College. "South Asian Studies." Bangalore, with trips to other locations in India and Nepal. Academic year or semester. South Asian studies, language, and individualized program combining independent study with fieldwork or internships. Sophomores, juniors, and seniors. Others may participate without credit. Apply by May 15 for academic year and fall semester and November 15 for spring semester.

University of Wisconsin—Madison. Madurai, Varanasi, or Waltair. Academic year. Sophomores to graduate students with 3.0 GPA. Participants normally complete summer course in Tamil, Hindu, or Telugu at Madison prior to departure. Apply by February 1.

South Asian Studies

Davidson College. "Davidson College Fall Semester in India." Madras. Fall only (in even-numbered years). Courses in India past and present, issues in contemporary India, art history seminar, independent study. Program-related travel. Juniors and seniors with 2.75 GPA. Preference given to those with previous course work relating to South Asia. Apply by March 1.

Summer

Peace Studies

Lisle Fellowship. "Creating Alternatives to Violence." Cosponsored by Gandhi Peace Foundation. Six weeks in midsummer. Open to recent high-school graduates, college students, and adults. Apply by April 1.

New York University. "Asian Studies in India." Bombay. Even years. Seniors and graduate students. Apply by April 15. Contact: Graduate Admissions Office, 32 Washington Place, New York, NY 10003.

EXPLORING INDIAN CULTURE

Readings

Most of the literature of India consists of works in Hindi or Tamil. Noteworthy among the authors writing in Tamil who have been translated into English is Thakathi Pillai, whose novels are mostly set in the state of Kerala on India's southwest coast. These include *The Unchaste*, which addresses the problems women face in Indian society, and *Rungs of the Ladder*, a story of simple people corrupted by the desire for power. Available in translation from the Hindi original is Bibhutibhushan Banerjee's *Pather Panchali*, the realistic story of a poverty-stricken family in the state of Bengal.

There is also a vast amount of literature written in English. Ruth Prawer Jhabvala uses English to express her theme of conflict between Indian life and Western influence. Her book *Travelers* offers an instructive contrast to E. M. Forster's classic *A Passage to India*. Anita Desai's *Clear Light of Day* is about a middle-class Hindu family forced to confront the increasingly problematic world. Another woman writer who has chosen the English language, Meena Alexander, tells the story of a woman who returns to India to teach after studying in Europe in *Nampally Road*.

Among English-language novels by men, there is a steady tradition of exploring the lives of the poor. Kamala Markandaya's *Nectar in a Sieve* is a powerful and sensitive novel about a rural family on the margins of survival. Saadat Hasan Manto, explores the lower castes of Bombay in *Kingdom's End and Other Stories*. The title story of O. J. Vijayan's *After the Hanging and Other Stories* describes a poor farmer's visit to the prison where his son is about to be executed.

India's best-known author, R. K. Narayan writes of the lives of middle-class people in the imaginary town of Malgudi. In *The Dark Room* he deals with the problems faced by a traditional Hindu wife; *The Guide* explores the transformation of a guide into a guru; and *The Vendor of Sweets* contrasts the views of an old Gandhian with those of his son just returned from the United States. A collection of Narayan's shorter works—essays, stories, and travel pieces—can be found in *A Story-Teller's World*.

Some of the keenest observers of Indian society are those who have been removed from it. V. S. Naipaul, a Trinidadian of Indian descent, has made several journeys through India, chronicling the people along the way. *India: A Million Mutinies Now* is his most recent book. Salman Rushdie, the Pakistani English writer famous for *The Satanic Verses*, has also written insightfully of India. *Midnight's Children* is the story of 1,001 children born in the first hour of Indian independence.

Films

India's movie industry, supported by the world's largest film-going public, annually produces more films (over 700) than any other country in the world. In the opinion of many Westerners, it also produces the world's worst films; however, this judgment as often as not indicates a misunderstanding of the cultural roots of commercial Indian cinema. Indian films, predominantly produced in the Hindi language, emphasize spectacular and emotional excess at the expense of strong story lines and narrative realism, and they are usually grouped under the following genres: mythologicals, historicals, song and dance, and super-hero films. Two particularly popular and typical examples of the latter category are Manmohan Desai's superheroic *Naseeb* (1981) and Mehboob Khan's more folklorically tinged *Mother India* (1957). In addition, many of the song-and-dance spectacles can be found on cable television's arts and culture channels on Sunday mornings.

Since the early 1950s, more and more Indian films have been made in opposition to the economic and cultural dominance of the commercial tradition, with a number of independent filmmakers following the example of Satyajit Ray, India's most internationally renowned filmmaker. Ray's own Apu Trilogy—*Pather Panchali* (1955), *The Unvanquished* (1956), and *The World of Apu* (1959)—presents the stories of a succession of young rural characters trapped between Indian traditions and Western ideas. Other well-known figures in the "New Indian Cinema" are Ritwak Ghatak, who explored rural and urban social attitudes in *Ajantrik*, and Shyam Benegal, whose *The Role*, ostensibly the biography of a popular female film star, is an important commentary on the postion of women in Indian culture as well as an encapsulation of the history of Indian film genres.

NEPAL

A rapidly developing tourist industry has brought far-reaching changes to this once-isolated kingdom, situated between India and China in the middle of the Himalayan Mountains. As a result, today you can find five-star hotels and Western restaurants serving pizza and linguine in Kathmandu, the country's capital. While these amenities bring the comforts of home to the Westerners who visit Nepal, they can also shelter the traveler from the rustic but far more interesting conditions typical of the country.

By Western standards, Nepal is an impoverished country, its average annual per capita income only about $120 per year. However, this poverty is rarely oppressive, and few sick or starving people wander the streets. Kathmandu is bustling, muddy, and polluted; yet it remains a beautiful city filled with temples, open-air markets, and merchants peddling mangoes and oranges on their bicycles. Barefooted, bare-bottomed children run through the streets playing with discarded bicycle tires and asking unsuspecting tourists for "one rupee," "pen," or "balloon." Women in colorful saris, *lungis*, or Punjabi suits battle the flies for the perfect tomato or head of cauliflower. Many of the side streets reek of rotting meat, courtesy of the merchants who sell chunks of fresh goat and buffalo to loyal customers, and major thoroughfares are filled with dilapidated taxis, bicycles, rickshaws, cows, and city buses overflowing with gaudy decorations and passengers who sit on the dashboards, hang out of the windows, or stand on the bumpers.

Despite the crowds and often oppressive smells of the city, the most pervasive feeling in Kathmandu is one of warmth and friendliness. The Nepalese people exude goodwill and will do anything to help a confused visitor. Perhaps it is due to the influence of the two dominant religions in Nepal, Hinduism and Mahayana Buddhism, with most people practicing a combination of the two.

The countryside beyond Kathmandu is even more rustic, friendly, and beautiful. In the monsoon season, from July to mid-September, the white-capped Himalayas are obscured by mist and clouds. Even then, however, breathtaking scenery is provided by the green-terraced hillsides that the locals plant with rice paddies and banana trees.

Much of the country is inaccessible by road. Instead, the footpaths that crisscross the mountains are literally the highways of Nepal. Not surprisingly, the Nepalese people are exceptionally strong and surefooted, and even small children scramble along the mountain paths with fifty-pound loads of firewood and fodder on their backs. People will think nothing of walking several days to visit a friend or relative. Tea shops dot the roadsides, and weary travelers are always welcome to sit down to the typical Nepalese meal of *dal bhaat*, which consists of rice, lentils, and vegetables such as potatoes or green beans.

The friendliness of the Nepalese people is an overwhelming as the mountains that attract most visitors to Nepal. And the lack of electricity, running water, and toilet paper hardly seems to matter in this small country with an enormous heart.

—*Victoria R. Clawson, Bernardsville, New Jersey*

Official name: Kingdom of Nepal. **Area:** 56,136 square miles (about the size of Wisconsin). **Population:** 19,158,000. **Population density:** 334 inhabitants per square mile. **Capital and largest city:** Kathmandu (pop. 422,000). **Language:** Nepali (official). **Religion:** Hindu. **Per capita income:** US$160. **Currency:** Nepalese rupee. **Literacy rate:** 29%. **Average daily high/low*:** Kathmandu: 65°/35°; July, 84°/68°. **Average number of days with precipitation:** Kathmandu: January, 1; July, 21.

TRAVEL

U.S. citizens need a passport and a visa. A visa valid for 30 days can be obtained before leaving the United States from the Nepalese embassy. Short-term visas for 15 days are also issued on arrival at the Kathmandu airport. For specific information, contact the Royal Nepalese Embassy (2131 Leroy Place NW, Washington, DC 20008) or any Nepalese embassy abroad.

Getting Around

Nepal has no railroads and a limited number of roads passable to motor vehicles. However, if there's a road leading where you want to go, you can be sure there's a bus going there. Bicycles are an excellent way of seeing the towns and countryside in the area around Kathmandu and can be rented in Kathmandu itself. Motorbikes can also be rented by the hour. If you're in a hurry, Royal Nepal Airlines operates flights to all areas of the country. While in Kathmandu, you can get around by bus, taxi, or rickshaw; but because the city is quite compact, perhaps the best—and certainly the cheapest—alternative is simply to walk.

"The diversity of religions, ethnic groups, and even topography can be overwhelming, especially for one who goes to Nepal to study. If you stay long enough, you will be duly impressed by the tolerance and patience that mark the nature of most Nepali people, a nature which has evolved to allow them to survive in this diverse cultural climate. It may even rub off on you."
—Sam Davol, Concord, Massachusetts

"One of the saddest things I see happening is a booming tourism industry that breeds disrespect for the host culture. Women should not wear shorts, sleeveless shirts, or other tight-fitting or revealing clothes. Doing so only furthers the negative image of Western women already brought to this culture by television and film."
—Jane Olson, Parkersburg, West Virginia

Trekking

Trekking in Nepal is an unforgettable experience; the scenery is beautiful, the paths are safe, and villagers are hospitable. It is hard work, especially at higher altitudes, so make sure you're in good health and try to travel with as little gear as possible. You'll need to get a trekking permit from the Central Immigration Office in Kathmandu; it will take a minimum of three working days. All your trekking equipment—down jacket, pack, boots, and bags—can be rented right in Kathmandu or Pokhara. There are many trekking agencies in Nepal that can arrange a trek for you in which all you have to do is carry your camera and walk. If you want to organize your own trek, for a nominal fee you

---
*All temperatures are Fahrenheit.

can hire porters to carry your gear. Porters can also serve as guides and organizers if you want to avoid prearranged tours. For safety reasons, you should not trek alone. There have been a number of robberies and even attacks on trekkers over the last couple of years.

The trekking season in Nepal is governed by the monsoon season which begins in mid-June and lasts until mid-September. Therefore, the months between October and May are good months to trek. Blue skies and clear views make autumn the best season for trekking, but springtime (February and March) treks will yield breathtaking views of hillsides covered with wildflowers and rhododendrons. And, as the the government's *Trekking in Nepal* brochure puts it, "The botanists and students of leeches will enjoy the summer season (July to September)."

The previously quoted *Trekking in Nepal* brochure, which includes general tourist information, is available free from the Royal Nepalese Embassy (address above). They will also send you a copy of *Travellers' Information: Nepal*, which covers basic information like currency exchanges, airport taxes, and goverment office hours. A valuable source of information is *A Guide to Trekking in Nepal*, by Stephen Bezrucha, available from Mountaineers Books, 1011 S.W. Klickitat Way, Suite 107, Seattle, WA 98134 ($12.95). The book includes maps of various treks and lists items that you will need to take with you. *Trekking in the Nepal Himalaya*, by Stan Armington, provides route descriptions as well as recommendations for equipment. It's available for $14.95 (plus $1.50 book-rate postage; $3 for first-class) from the publisher, Lonely Planet Publications, Embarcadero West, 112 Linden Street, Oakland, CA 94607. Another guide to trekking in Nepal is *The Nepal Trekker's Handbook*, by Amy Kaplan, published by Mustang Publishing and available in bookstores for $9.95. It can also be ordered by phone (800-462-6420).

For Further Information

Nepal: A Travel Survival Kit ($16.95) is a thoroughly researched and recently updated guide by Lonely Planet, covering everything from trekking in the Himalayas to the best restaurants on Freak Street, Kathmandu. Lonely Planet also publishes *The Nepal Phrasebook* ($2.95), which includes a special chapter for use while trekking. Both are available from the address above (see "Trekking").

WORK

Work permits are required for Nepal, and obtaining one is extremely difficult. Generally, they are only issued to embassy staff, to those working on government projects, or to foreigners working with the airlines.

Voluntary Service

Sisters of Charity of Nazareth sponsors a volunteer program in Nepal for those interested in health care, social services, education, or ministry. Participants serve from two weeks to three months; room and board are provided. For service periods of three months or more, at least nine months prior notification is required. For more information contact the Sisters of Charity of Nazareth, SCNA Center, Nazareth, KY 40048

STUDY

The following programs are offered by CIEE-member institutions. Consult Appendix I for the addresses of the colleges and universities listed in this section.

Semester and Academic Year

General Studies

Experiment in International Living/School for International Training. "College Semester Abroad." Kathmandu. Fall or spring semester. Intensive language, life and culture seminar, field-study methods seminar, village and urban homestays, educational travel and independent-study project. Sophomores to seniors with 2.5 GPA. Apply by May 15 for fall and October 15 for spring.

Pitzer College. "Experience in Nepal." Various locations. Cultural-immersion program featuring 250 hours of language instruction, homestays with rural families throughout the stay, trek, independent study and a community-development project. Fall or spring semester. No language prerequisite. Apply by March 15 for fall and October 1 for spring.

University of Wisconsin—Madison. Kathmandu. Academic year. Participants normally complete a summer course in Nepali and Tibetan at Madison prior to departure. Sophomores to graduate students with 3.0 GPA. Apply by February 1.

World College West. "World Study in Nepal." Kathmandu and rural areas. Semester or academic year. Intensive cultural immersion. Language, culture, field-study methods, independent-study project, urban and village homestays. Juniors and seniors with one year of Nepali language studies and one cultural studies class. Apply by March 15.

CHAPTER TEN
EAST ASIA

Terms such as "the Orient" or "the Far East" still conjure up images of a faraway and mysterious land, but these terms are heard less frequently today as the use of "the Pacific Rim" become more common. Thinking in terms of a Pacific Rim suggests commonalities and linkages rather than distance and differences. It is because of the growing importance of the economic, political, and cultural linkages between the U.S. and East Asia that the American government, business establishment, educational system, and public are all focusing increasing attention on the region.

East Asia encompasses a diversity of peoples that account for nearly a third of the world's population. In fact, almost a fourth of the earth's people live in China alone. Due to China's historically dominant position within the region, all the countries and cultures of East Asia have been greatly influenced by China in language, religion, and social structure. Today, however, a number of smaller Asian nations on China's periphery—Taiwan, South Korea, Japan, and the British colony of Hong Kong—have surpassed China economically. Politics within the region since the Second World War have been conditioned by tensions between China and these neighboring developing capitalist nations protected by an American military presence. Today, the border between North and South Korea is a final vestige of the Cold War.

The countries of East Asia are fast becoming more prominent in the picture Americans have of the world. In large part, this interest arises from the increasing economic power of Hong Kong, Japan, South Korea, and Taiwan, whose products now flood Western markets. Today, U.S. trade with Asia surpasses its trade with Europe, and U.S. banks and corporations face growing competition from their Asian counterparts. The greater portion of the world's economy now circulates about the Pacific Rim, bringing together two cultural spheres which are only beginning to know each other.

Getting There

Today, a variety of excellent airfares have brought down the price of travel to Asia. Many carriers to Asia offer APEX and promotional fares, and student fares are available to a number of cities. Sample *one-way* fares from the U.S. to Asia in effect for the summer of 1991 are listed below. For more up-to-date information on fares to Asia, contact any Council Travel office (see pages xix–xxi).

Seattle–Tokyo	$589
San Francisco–Hong Kong	$439
New York–Beijing	$599
Los Angeles–Seoul	$499

From Europe, persons with the International Student Identity Card (see page 8) or the International Youth Card (see page 10) can get special discounted fares on scheduled flights from a number of European capitals to Hong Kong, Osaka, Seoul, Taipei, or Tokyo. Sample *one-way* student/youth fares in effect during 1991 are listed below:

London–Hong Kong	$655
Paris–Seoul	$835
London–Osaka	$815

Many of these student/youth fares allow stopovers in Bangkok, Thailand. Contact a Council Travel office or a student travel bureau in Europe or Asia for complete information.

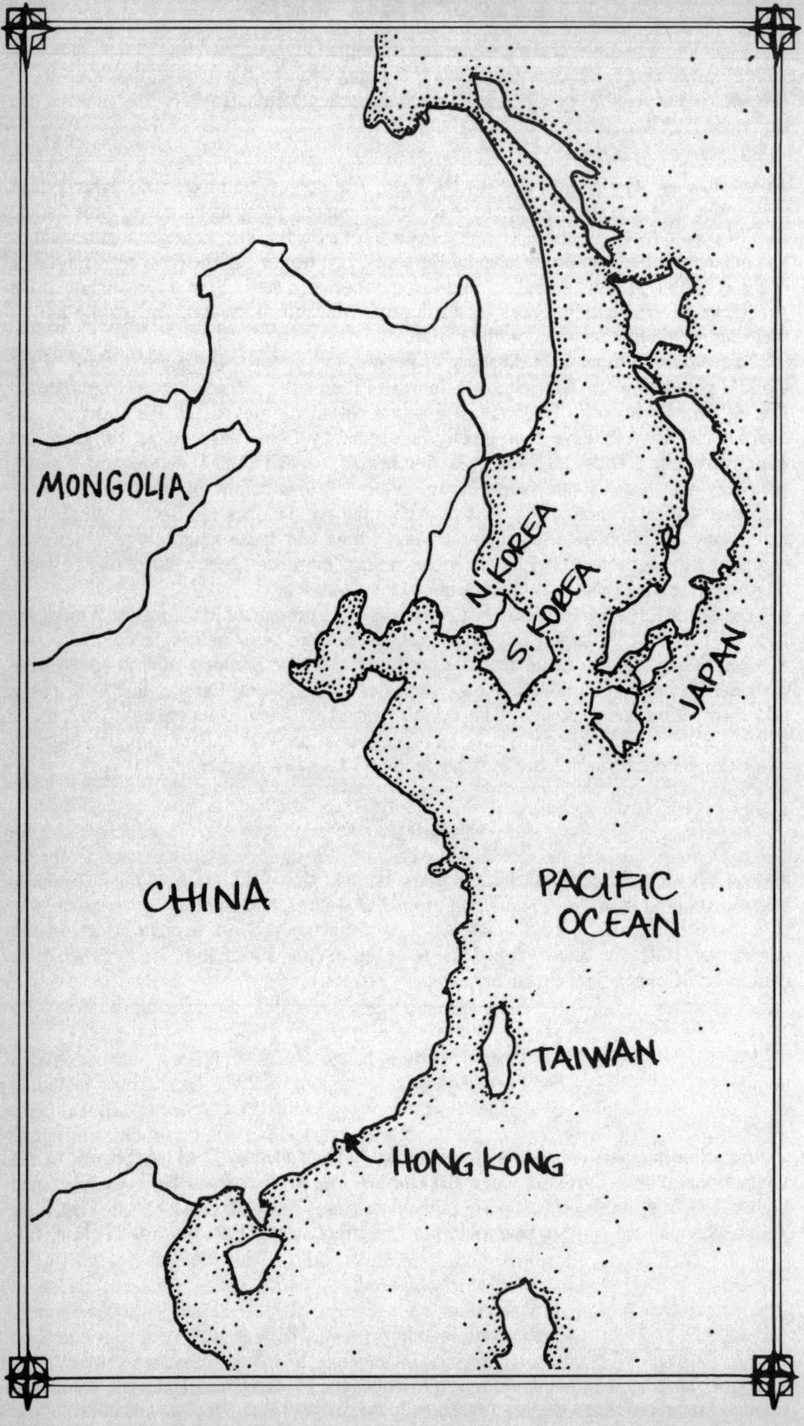
MONGOLIA
N. KOREA
S. KOREA
JAPAN
CHINA
PACIFIC
OCEAN
TAIWAN
HONG KONG

Student/youth fares are also available on scheduled flights connecting East Asian cities with cities in South and Southeast Asia. On some of these flights you'll save up to 50 percent on the regular fares. Sample *one-way* student/youth fares in effect during the summer of 1991 are listed below:

Bangkok–Tokyo	$145
Bangkok–Hong Kong	$165
Hong Kong–Singapore	$279

If you want to travel overland between Europe and East Asia, you might consider traveling through the Soviet Union on the Trans-Siberian Railroad. The world's longest train route, the Trans-Siberian makes 91 stops, takes you one-quarter of the way around the globe, and passes through seven time zones and 100 degrees of longitude. Nonstop, from Moscow to Nakhodka, the trip takes eight days. From Nakhodka, ship passage can be arranged to Yokohama, Japan. Two other routes take you to Beijing, China, via Manchuria or Mongolia. Soviet transit visas are considerably less expensive than tourist visas, but you can only arrange them in Soviet consulates in eastern Europe and Asia. For further information, see "Getting Around" in the U.S.S.R. section.

Another popular overland route is to cross China from India or Nepal to Hong Kong or Beijing. Traveling across China is an experience in itself, and one for which you'll want to allow plenty of time. You'll frequently have to change trains and buses and might have to deal with some official red tape, even if your papers are in order. But if you don't mind delays, you'll have a great trip.

Traveling around East Asia

Largely because of geography, but also because of politics, most travel between the countries of East Asia is by air. Of the five nations covered at length in this chapter, only China and Hong Kong share a common border. Thus, for the most part, overland transport—while viable within individual countries—is simply not an option for international travel in the region.

Air service between the nations of East Asia is convenient and fairly inexpensive for persons eligible for student/youth fares; eligibility for these fares is the same as for the student fares discussed above. Sample *one-way* fares available from Council Travel in 1991 are listed below:

Tokyo–Hong Kong	$369
Tokyo–Seoul	$310
Seoul–Hong Kong	$265

But if travel by air doesn't appeal to you, you can also travel by boat between several countries. From Hong Kong, vessels depart for a number of Chinese cities, including Guangzhou (Canton) and Shanghai, as well as the island of Taiwan. From Taiwan, boats travel to Okinawa, where you can get connecting service to a number of cities in Japan; several of these boats make stops on some of the smaller islands which are part of the Japanese archipelago. There is also frequent ferry service between Shimonoseki, Japan and Pusan, South Korea. Combined, these various shipping lanes make a nice circuitous route. And boat service can be surprisingly cheap.

The United States government does not recommend travel to North Korea by U.S. citizens (for U.S. government restrictions, contact the Licensing Division, Office of Foreign Assets Control, Department of the Treasury, 1331 G Street NW, Washington, DC 20220). The North Korean government, however, has eased its own restrictions on foreign tourism. U.S. citizens interested in traveling to North Korea must apply for a visa at a North Korean embassy in a third country such as Denmark, Egypt, Malaysia, Norway, Pakistan, or Singapore.

For Further Information

While there are many excellent guidebooks to the separate countries of east Asia (which will be noted later in this chapter), one of the few general guides to the entire region is Lonely Planet's *North-East Asia on a Shoestring*. While this book doesn't go into great depth on any one country, it's useful for getting around between countries. It can be ordered from Lonely Planet Publications (Embarcadero West, 112 Linden Street, Oakland, CA 94607) for $11.95, plus $1.50 book-rate postage ($3 for first-class).

Persons interested in staying in youth hostels in East Asia will find volume two of the *International Youth Hostel Handbook*, which lists nearly 500 youth hostels in Japan as well as ones in Hong Kong and South Korea, indispensable.

Since the countries and cultures of East Asia are so different from those most Americans are accustomed to, most travelers will find some sort of cultural introduction as useful as a travel guide. *A Traveller's Guide to Asian Culture*, by Kevin Chambers, gives a broad overview of cultural trends from India to Japan, from antiquity to the present century. Published by John Muir Publications, it's available for $13.95 in bookstores.

The Asia Society, a nonprofit organization dedicated to increasing Americans' understanding of Asian cultures, publishes and distributes a variety of books and is generally an excellent source of information. For a publications catalog and information about the society's other services, write to The Asia Society at 725 Park Avenue, New York, NY 10021. Another good source for books on East Asia, especially Japan and Korea, is the Charles E. Tuttle Company, 26-30 Main Street, Rutland, VT 05701.

Studying in East Asia

You'll find a number of study programs listed in the individual country sections later in this chapter. In the section below we've listed only the study programs of CIEE-member institutions that take place in more than one country. Consult Appendix I for the addresses of the colleges and universities listed in this section.

Semester and Academic Year

Business

University of La Verne. "Analysis of Pacific Rim Business." Japan, Republic of Korea, Hong Kong, Singapore (sometimes substituting Thailand, Australia, and/or New Zealand). Six-week program (three weeks abroad) in January or August. Juniors to graduate students with 2.5 GPA. Apply in September for January; April for August.

General Studies

St. Olaf College.
"Term in the Far East." Japan, Taiwan, China, and Thailand. Fall semester plus January. Cross-cultural experience with academic study, including three-month family stay in Chaing Mai, Thailand. Sophomores, juniors, and seniors. Apply by March 1.
"Global Semester." Cairo, Egypt; Bangalore, India; Taipei, Taiwan; and Kyoto, Japan. Cultures, social and political issues of selected non-Western countries. Fall semester plus January. Sophomores, juniors, and seniors. Apply by March 1.

University of Pittsburgh. "Semester at Sea." Fall or spring semester. Students, based aboard the S.S. *Universe*, attend classes on board and travel to various countries in Europe, the Middle East, Africa, and Asia. Sophomores, juniors, and seniors with 2.75 GPA. Contact: Semester at Sea, Eighth floor, William Pitt Union, University of Pittsburgh, Pittsburgh, PA 15260; (412) 648-7490.

Special Education

Southern Illinois University at Carbondale. "Special Education in Japan and Hong Kong." Program features site visits to facilities for the mentally and physically handicapped. Juniors, seniors, graduate students, and special education teachers. Apply by April 1.

Summer

Agriculture

Michigan State University. "Food and Agricultural Systems in China and Japan." Tokyo, Mt. Fuji, and Osaka, Japan; Beijing, Harbin, and Changdu, China. Juniors to graduate students. Apply by April 20.

Asian Studies

New York University. China, India, and Hong Kong. Interaction of tradition and modernity. Graduate students, teachers, and specialists. Apply by April 15. Contact: School of Education, Health, Nursing and Arts Professions. 32 Washington Place, Second floor New York NY 10003; (212) 998-5030.

Humanities

New York University.
"Deafness Rehabilitation." Japan and Thailand. Graduate students only. Apply by April 15. Contact: see below.
Hong Kong, Taiwan, and China. Graduate students. Apply by April 15. Contact: School of Education, Health, Nursing and Arts Professions. 32 Washington Place, Second floor, New York, NY 10003; (212) 998-5030.

CHINA

China, the world's oldest living civilization, has an indomitable heritage, culture, and tradition. Foreigners visiting China today will find themselves witness to a turning point in the nation's long history, as the government continues to support far-reaching social and economic changes while repressing demands for democracy and political change. We have yet to see if, after a century of cultural and economic isolation, China will embrace the capitalist ideals of internationalism and modernity.

Much of the turmoil of Chinese history is written on the faces of the Chinese people. The older generation remains fearful and cautious of politics. In 1949, the Communist government under Mao Zedong declared a Chinese nation at last independent of foreign domination and internal chaos. But domestic politics soon turned to repression, particularly during the Cultural Revolution of the late 1960s and 1970s. As a result, older Chinese have witnessed family and friends being subjected to accusations, jailed, shipped off to labor camps, and in many cases killed. Now, young people, too—as a result of the government's bloody repression of the student prodemocracy movement in 1989—have become victims of a party leadership intent on enforcing its claim to authority. The Chinese people have been numbed by innumerable swings of the political pendulum and masterful manipulation of "truth" for political ends. If fear and apathy seem to be dominating the nation's political life, at the moment it is because the Chinese are tired of sacrificing for the political elite in the name of China.

Over the last decade, greater economic freedom has resulted in an improved standard of living and more contact with the outside world. The young have been at the forefront of this trend. Free markets, black markets, "strange" clothes, "decadent" ways, and foreign ideas, music, and language have been heartily embraced. The world's largest Kentucky Fried Chicken outlet was built 100 meters from Mao's memorial. Material rewards have also been adopted to provide incentive for higher economic productivity. Slowly and expensively, the Chinese are being introduced to the luxuries of TVs, refrigerators, and washing machines.

Social changes are also evident. Lovers, previously invisible in public areas, crowd parks, benches, boating houses, and any space they can find—something that would not have been possible a few years ago. More fundamental social change is resulting from the government's strict enforcement of the controversial one-child-per-family policy implemented to control population growth—a policy that challenges the age-old Chinese tradition of the extended family.

However dramatic China's economic and social reforms have been, political reform has lagged behind. This fact fueled much of the popular frustration that led to the student prodemocracy movement in the spring of 1989. TV images of Chinese citizens in open defiance of the regime granted the world an opportunity to transform its stereotypical preconceptions of China. No longer are the Chinese seen as a vast, passive population, a people who are undistinguished in all but their reliance on the glories of their past.

The foreigner drawn to China should try to understand China's attraction to the West as well as the history behind its urgency to "catch up" to its Western counterparts. China was once the world's leading civilization. When it reopened its doors to the world in the late 19th century, however, it was stunned to discover that the industrial civilizations of the West had long surpassed it in almost every dimension. Nor was this discovery without its irony. It was, after all, the Chinese who invented the compass, which enabled the European powers to extend their empires and cultural influence all over the globe. It was the Chinese who invented gun powder as well, which armed the West to conquer and colonize. And it was also the Chinese who invented paper currency, which facilitated international trade and the growth of capitalism. Today, the awakened sleeping giant that is China is reaching another vital juncture. The course it will take, both in pace and direction, is unpredictable but of critical importance to the rest of the world.

—*Ching-Ching Ni, Oberlin, Ohio*

Official name: People's Republic of China. **Area:** 3,705,390 square miles (slightly larger than the U.S.). **Population:** 1,130,065,000. **Population density:** 288 inhabitants per square mile. **Capital:** Beijing (pop. 9,330,000). **Largest city:** Shanghai (pop. 11,940,000). **Language:** Chinese (Mandarin, Cantonese, Wu, Kan-Hakka, Amoy-Swatow, Foochow). **Religion:** Atheism (official), Confucianism, Buddhism, Taoism (traditional). **Per capita income:** US$330. **Currency:** Renminbi (yuan). **Literacy rate:** 70%. **Average daily high/low*:** Beijing: January, 35°/15°; July, 89°/71°. **Average days with rain:** Beijing: January, 3; July, 13.

TRAVEL

U.S. citizens will need both a passport and a visa for travel to China. Travel arrangements are usually made by China International Travel Service (CITS), the agency with exclusive responsibility for all foreign tourism in China (excluding Chinese people living abroad). CITS tours may be booked through travel agencies and airlines in the United States and abroad. Visas for tour group members are usually obtained by the travel agents as part of the tour package.

---

*All temperatures are Fahrenheit.

It is also possible for individuals to travel on their own in China. Visa applications may be submitted to the Embassy of the People's Republic of China (2300 Connecticut Avenue NW, Washington, DC 20008) or the Chinese Consulates General in Chicago, Houston, New York, Los Angeles, or San Francisco. The current visa fee is $7, and two passport-size photos are required. Allow at least one week for processing.

Tourism in China

"There is no need to announce your presence or take an aggressive role in trying to 'experience' Chinese culture. A smile and a nod are about as forward as you should get, but if someone wants to speak to you (usually in order to practice their English), they may just start up a conversation without any introduction."
—Fraser Brown, New York, New York

During the past decade China's interest in attracting Western currency and many Americans' interest in seeing and experiencing a long-inaccessible nation rich in culture and history have combined to produce skyrocketing growth in tourism in China. The Chinese government continues to encourage tourism from the West, though it limits the number of cities open to foreigners.

The official brand of tourism in China has always focused on seeing the sights and seldom involves significant contact between foreigners and Chinese. Contact is limited both by language and cultural barriers as well as government policies. Tourists—as well as students, businessmen, and diplomats—are generally placed in accommodations exclusively for foreigners rather than being allowed to mingle freely with Chinese.

A special currency has been developed for foreigners in China. *Renminbi* (people's money) is the currency of China, but foreign-exchange certificates (FECs) are supposed to be used by foreigners for all expenses. In practice, FECs must be used for accommodations, train and plane tickets, hotel restaurants, and Friendship stores, while renminbi can be used for everything else. If a person insists, renminbi will sometimes be accepted when they shouldn't be. Both FEC and renminbi are made up of fen, jiao, and yuan. Ten fen equals one jiao, ten jiao equals one yuan.

The host of most tourist programs in the PRC is the China International Travel Service (CITS—the Chinese name is Luxingshe), located at 6 East Ch'ang-an Avenue, Beijing. In New York, the China National Tourist Office (60 East 42nd Street, Suite 3126, New York, NY 10165-0163) handles CITS promotion and information activities.

"You will always be foreign in China. You must accept your status and, at the same time, try to mix with the Chinese. It is a very wide gap to bridge, but persist and you will most likely be rewarded with friendship."
—John L. Steers, Columbus, Ohio

Organized Tours

Council Travel, in cooperation with the Hong Kong Student Travel Bureau (HKSTB), offers a number of tours to China, ranging from a few days to several weeks, with regular departures throughout the year. These include traditional "grand" tours that visit the main tourist destinations of Beijing, Shanghai, Guangzhou, Luoyang, and Xi'an to ones that focus on special interests such as bicycling or living on an agricultural commune. Tours are designed especially for students but are open to people of any age. HKST can also arrange itineraries for solo travelers. Council Travel offices (see pages xix–xxi) have the details.

CIEE conducts a summer program for educators interested in visiting schools and meeting with their counterparts in the People's Republic of China. Participants in the U.S.-China Educator Exchange also visit sites of historic and cultural interest in various cities and regions throughout China. In a reciprocal program, a delegation of Chinese educators visits the U.S. each fall. For more information, contact CIEE's Professional and Secondary Education Programs Department.

Also, Ohio University offers a four-week summer tour to Beijing and Xi'an, entitled "Chinese Art and Architecture." For information on this program, contact the Office of Continuing Education, (614) 593-1776. Applications must be made by April 1.

Getting Around

Westerners can travel around the country with a minimum of restrictions. From a practical point of view, however, those unable to speak Chinese will find independent travel difficult. Learning a little Chinese—even a limited number of phrases—will make things easier, and more enjoyable.

China's extensive railway network has in recent years been submitted to heavier use than ever before, both by tourists and the increasingly mobile Chinese population. Unfortunately, the rail system has not been sufficiently upgraded to handle the strain, nor has the number of cars been proportionately increased. You may have to wait several days to find a seat on the train you want. Be patient.

Intercity trains have two classes of service: hard seat and soft seat. Hard seats are wood or vinyl-covered benches seating three across; soft seats are linen-covered seats in a private car or compartment. Soft-seat prices are double that of hard seats. Overnight trains have hard sleeper and soft sleeper in addition to seats. Foreigners are charged somewhat more for tickets than Chinese locals and are usually directed into special lines at train stations. Students studying in China may be allowed to pay the local price. It should also be noted that a person can only buy tickets for trains originating in that city (i.e., you can't buy a ticket from Shanghai to Nanjin in Beijing).

Intercity air service often runs late and service onboard is minimal, but it will get you where you want to go. The national airline has recently split up into several regional domestic carriers: China Eastern Airlines, China Southern Airlines, and China Northwest Airlines. Service to Hong Kong and other Asian cities is provided by Dragon Air. Regular tickets are fairly inexpensive, but foreigners must pay twice the regular fare on domestic flights.

The bicycle is probably the most popular form of transportation in China. Chinese bicycles are basic and can be rented everywhere by the hour, day, or week. They can also be loaded on the luggage racks on top of buses with no questions asked; but taking them on a train will involve more red tape.

Eating and Sleeping

Lodging for foreigners and Chinese are separate, either by hotel, as is usually the case, or by rooms or floors in a single hotel. At least one hotel in each major tourist city provides dormitory-style accommodations for a small fee per night. Also, men and women are generally not allowed to share a room unless they say they are married.

Especially for Students and Young People

The People's Republic of China does not have an organization that issues the International Student Identity Card and promotes student travel and student travel discounts. As a result, the International Student Identity Card often is not recognized for special discounts in China. However, saying that you are a student may be a useful bargaining tool in obtaining cheaper prices.

For Further Information

The National Committee on U.S.-China Relations, 777 United Nations Plaza, New York, NY 10017, has developed a *Briefing Kit on the People's Republic of China* ($20) designed to meet the special interests of individual visitors or delegations going to China. It includes three sections: (1) a travel guide, which provides basic information on sightseeing, food, hotels, and transportation; (2) a collection of background materials such as annotated bibliographies, maps, a profile on the economy, and biographies of Chinese leaders; and (3) reprinted articles on topics of concern. Because these kits are individualized, allow four weeks for their preparation in advance. Orders should include the dates of your trip, your itinerary, and any special interests in China that you may have.

Budget travelers will find *China: A Travel Survival Kit* the most helpful guidebook to take along. This book can be ordered from Lonely Planet Publications (Embarcadero West, 112 Linden Street, Oakland, CA 94607) for $19.95 (plus $1.50 book-rate postage; $3 for first-class). Information on sightseeing in China is readily available in a number of other guidebooks. *The China Guidebook*, updated annually and published by Eurasia Press (168 State Street, Teaneck, NJ 07666), is available for $16.95. One of the most complete cultural guides is *Magnificent China*, by Petra Häring-Kuan and Kuan Yu-Chien. *Magnificent China* can be ordered for $4.99 (plus $2.25 postage and handling) from the publisher, China Books and Periodicals, 2929 24th Street, San Francisco, CA 94110. China Books publishes and distributes many other books of interest; ask for their catalog.

For an excellent summation of recent Chinese affairs, read *China Briefing*, prepared annually by the China Council of the Asia Society. It can be ordered for $14.85 (plus $3 postage) from the Asia Society, 725 Park Avenue, New York, NY 10021.

WORK

Westerners are not permitted to work in China unless they are teachers or technicians working under contract with an agency related to the Chinese government. Chinese institutions of higher learning offer year-long teaching posts to foreign applicants in the fields of English language and linguistics, literature, basic and engineering sciences, finance, business and management, law, and so on. Applicants should have a master's degree or higher and at least two years' teaching experience. Applicants are encouraged to contact individual colleges and universities in China directly. For further information, contact the Consulate General of the People's Republic of China, 520 12th Avenue, New York, NY 10036.

Western Washington University sponsors a China Teaching Program for people who want to teach English as a second language in the PRC. Participants are required to attend one of the two short-term training sessions offered annually. Chinese language, geography, history, culture, and TESOL methodology, as well as preparation for living in China are covered. Teaching positions are negotiated with institutions of higher learning in China and participants are placed twice a year (spring and fall). An undergraduate degree is required; applicants from a variety of fields are accepted. In addition, a placement-only option, which enables qualified individuals to forego the training session, is available to people who have teaching experience and extensive knowledge of China. Participants are typically placed in one-year assignments. For more information contact China Teaching Program/Western Washington University, Old Main 530, Bellingham, WA 98225-9047.

Voluntary Service

For persons interested in voluntary-service work, the Year Abroad Program sponsored by the International Christian Youth Exchange offers persons ages 18 to 24 voluntary service opportunities in the fields of health care, education, the environment, construction, et cetera. See page 23 for more information.

In addition, WorldTeach sponsors a volunteer teaching program in China (for more information see page 26) and Goshen College offers a study-service term open primarily to Goshen students with a limited number of spaces sometimes available to other students.

STUDY

A publication that might be of help to persons planning to study in China, *China Bound: A Guide to Academic Life and Work in the PRC*, is written for Americans traveling to China to live and work in an academic setting. Although it's designed mainly for graduate students, researchers, and professors, it is also useful for undergraduate students. *China Bound* is available for $14.95 from the National Academy Press, 2101 Constitution Avenue NW, Washington, DC 20418. If you are thinking of enrolling in a Chinese university, contact the Consulate General of the People's Republic of China (address above) for its fact sheet on the enrollment of foreign students in China.

A new book, *Chinese Universities and Colleges*, has information on 644 institutions of higher education in China. Published by the Chinese Education Organization and distributed in the U.S. by the Institute of International Education, this hardcover directory costs $59.95. Look for it in your library or study abroad office.

The following programs are offered by CIEE-member institutions. Consult Appendix I for the addresses of the institutions listed in this section. In addition to the programs below, the American Graduate School of International Management, Lewis and Clark College, Northern Arizona University, Ohio State University, the University of the Pacific, and the University of California offer study programs open only to their own students.

Semester and Academic Year

Chinese Language and Culture

Beloit College. "Fudan Exchange Program." Shanghai. Academic year or fall semester. Sophomores to graduate students with intermediate-level Chinese and a 2.5 GPA. Apply by April 1.

Brethren Colleges Abroad. Dalian Foreign Languages Institute. Semester or academic year. Chinese language from beginning to advanced levels, literature, history, and arts; three weeks of study tours. Sophomores, juniors, and seniors with 2.7 GPA. Apply by December 1 for spring and May 1 for fall and year.

Central University of Iowa. "Central College in China." Zhejiang University in Hangzhou. Spring quarter. Chinese language and culture. Sophomores to seniors with 2.5 GPA. Apply two months before beginning of term.

Cornell University. "Cornell Abroad in Xiamen." Xiamen, with field trips in Fujian Province and Shanghai. Fall semester. Juniors to graduate students with one year of Chinese and 3.0 GPA. Apply by April 1.

Council on International Educational Exchange.
"Advanced Graduate Students Program." Peking University. Supplementary studies or research after the completion of a master's degree and for students currently enrolled in a doctoral program who would like to further their primary research. Students attend Peking University classes and are assigned a supervisor/mentor to aid them. Students may request assignment to a specific professor. Contact University Programs Department.
"China Cooperative Language and Study Program." Beijing. Fall or spring semester. Study at Peking University. Sophomores to graduate students with two years of Mandarin. Apply by March 1 for fall and October 10 for spring. Contact University Programs Department.
"China Cooperative Language and Study Program." Nanjing. Academic year or semester. Study at Nanjing University. Sophomores to graduate students with at least one year of

college Mandarin. Apply by March 1 for fall and academic year; October 10 for spring. Contact University Programs Department.
"The Research Program for Scholars." Peking University. For post-doctoral scholars to further research their fields of specialities. Program participants work in close contact with Peking University faculty members. Contact University Programs Department.

Experiment in International Living/School for International Training. "College Semester Abroad." Shijiazhuang, with excursions to Qufu, Beijing, and Chengde. Intensive language, life and culture, field-study methods seminar, home hospitality, and independent study. No language prerequisite. Sophomores to seniors with 2.5 GPA. Apply by October 31 for spring; May 31 for fall.

Moorhead State University. "China Program." Nankai University in Tianjin. Academic year. Juniors and seniors with some Chinese language study. Open only to students at National Student Exchange participants schools. Apply by April 1.

Portland State University. "Study in China." Zhengzhou. Academic year or semester. Juniors to graduate students with two years of college Chinese. Flexible deadline.

State University of New York at Albany. Beijing and Tianjin, Nanjing, Shanghai, Taipei. Academic year. Juniors, seniors, and graduate students with one year of Chinese. Apply by February 15.

State University of New York at Oswego. Beijing. Semester or academic year. Undergraduates with 2.8 GPA. Apply by April 1 for fall and November 1 for spring.

University of Alabama. "Study Tour of the People's Republic of China." Giuzhou University. In Huaxi, Shanghai, Xian, Beijing. Freshmen to graduate students. Apply by April 1.

University of La Verne. "Semester/Year in China." See listing under Brethren Colleges Abroad.

University of Massachusetts—Amherst. "University of Massachusetts in China." Beijing. Juniors, seniors, and graduate students with two years of college Mandarin. Apply by March 1.

University of North Carolina at Chapel Hill. "UNC Program to China at Beijing." Academic year. Juniors and seniors; no previous Chinese required. Apply by February 12.

University of Oregon.
"OSSHE Beijing Program." Fall semester. Sophomores above with 2.75 GPA. Preference given to Oregon State System of Higher Education (OSSHE) students. Apply by March 1.
"OSSHE Fujian Program." Winter and spring terms. Sophomores, juniors, and seniors with one year of Chinese and 2.75 GPA. Preference given to Oregon State System of Higher Education (OSSHE) students. Apply by November 1.

University of South Carolina. "USC/Shanxi Exchange Program." Semester or academic year. Juniors to graduate students; undergrads must have two semesters Chinese language studies and a 3.0 GPA. Apply by March 15.

Valparaiso University. "Hangzhou Semester." Fall. Sophomores to seniors with 3.0 GPA. Apply by March 21.

General Studies

American University. "Beijing Semester." Fall semester. Intensive Mandarin and courses on Chinese politics, business, culture, and civilization. Juniors and seniors; knowledge of Mandarin not necessary. Apply six months prior to start of program.

Brigham Young University. "BYU Study Abroad." Nanjing. Spring term. Sophomores, juniors, and seniors with some knowledge of Chinese. Apply by February 1.

Friends World College. "Chinese Studies." Hangzhou (Zhejiang province), with three-week orientation in Hong Kong; optional semester on Taiwan. Academic year; semester option for language study. Chinese studies, Mandarin, TESL, and individualized program combining independent study and field research. Juniors and seniors. Apply by May 15 for fall and November for spring.

State University of New York at Cortland. Beijing. Semester or academic year. Juniors, seniors, and graduate students with one year of Mandarin and 2.5 GPA in major. Apply by March 1 for fall and October 15 for spring.

Physical Education

State University of New York at Cortland. Beijing. Semester or academic year. Juniors, seniors and graduate students with one year of Mandarin and 3.5 GPA in major. Apply by March 1 for fall and October 15 for spring.

Summer

Chinese Language and Culture

American Heritage Program. "American Heritage Cultural Summer Program." Jolin. Chinese culture and history. No language requirement. Apply by April 15.

AFS Intercultural Programs. "Chinese Studies." Six-week program in Kunming. Three-week program in Shanghai and Hangzchou. Undergraduates, graduates, and adults. Apply by May 1.

Council on International Educational Exchange.
"China Cooperative Language and Study Program." Study at Peking University in Beijing. Sophomores to graduate students with at least one year of college Mandarin for program in Beijing. Apply by March 1. Contact University Programs Department.
"Shanghai Summer Language and Culture Program at Fudan University." Language and area studies. No language prerequisites. Apply by March 1. Contact University Programs Department.

Michigan State University. Shanghai. "Intensive Chinese Language and Culture Studies Program." Summer. Juniors, seniors, and graduate students with one year of college Chinese. Apply by April 20.

University of Minnesota. "Minnesota-Nankai Summer Intensive Chinese Language Institute." Tianjin. High school students to college graduates. Nonstudents can also apply. One year of standard Chinese required. Apply by February 24. Contact Minnesota-Nankai Institute, 113 Folwell Hall, 9 Pleasant Street SE, Minneapolis, MN 55455; (612) 624-0386.

Washington State University. "Chinese Intensive Language and Culture Program." Chengda, Sichuan, Xian, Beijing. Juniors to graduate students and others. 3.0 GPA. Apply by April 15.

Western Washington University. See listing under "American Heritage Association."

General Studies

Portland State University. "Summer Session in Zhengzhou, China." Month-long program designed for intensive language acquisition and cultural immersion. High-school graduates to graduate students and nonstudents.

Political Science

The University of Toledo. "Summer Study in China." Beijing, Shanghai, Hangzhou, Xian, Guilin, and Guangzhou. Study Chinese political system through lectures by government and party officials and by Chinese professors. High school students, college students, and adults. Apply by May 1.

EXPLORING CHINESE CULTURE

Readings

One of the earliest Chinese novels has been given the English title *Monkey* (although the Chinese title means "Journey to the West"). Written in the sixteenth century by Wu Cheng-en, *Monkey* retells the legendary pilgrimage of a famous Buddhist monk to India. Only in this version, the monk takes a back seat to the hilarious misadventures of his disciples, which include an immortality-seeking monkey. This book has enjoyed immense popularity for ages.

The last great novel of pre-Revolution China, written in the eighteenth century by Ts'ao Hsueh-ch'in, *The Story of the Stone* chronicles the rise and fall of a family with numerous children. The central love story is entwined with hundreds of other stories and evokes the glory of classical China while documenting its decay. Still widely read, this novel has become a window through which present generations view their nation's past.

There have been two particularly fertile periods in 20th-century Chinese literature. The first, ushered in by the May Fourth Movement of 1919, was characterized by the revolutionary use of modern spoken Chinese instead of classical language, permitting many social issues to be addressed. The most famous writer of this generation, Lu Hsun (1881–1936), was named Commander of the Cultural Revolution. His stories, which deal with proletarian life and the decay of Chinese intellectual culture, have been collected in a number of volumes. *Family* (1931), by Pa Chin, is an epic saga that contrasts traditional Chinese values with the modern ideas of the Nationalist May Fourth Movement. Mao Dun's *Midnight*, written in 1933, deals with corruption in pre-revolutionary Shanghai. *I Myself Am a Woman* brings together writings of Ding Ling, one of the first Chinese writers to explore women's thoughts and feelings in fiction.

The second flowering of literary expression occurred after the death of Mao in 1976 as Chinese writers began to reflect on the country's recent history. *Roses and Thorns: The Second Blossoming of the Hundred Flowers in Chinese Fiction 1979–80*, an anthology of post-Mao writing, shows the evolution of the politically oriented writing of the Mao era to a more personal and experimental style. *Chrysanthemums and Other Stories*, a collection of pieces by Feng Ji Cai, examines the lives of ordinary people and how they were affected by the Cultural Revolution. Gu Hua's *A Small Town Called Hibiscus* (1982) shows the effect of political events on ordinary country people, starting in the early 1960s and ending with the fall of the "Gang of Four" in the late 1970s. In the controversial

Half of Man Is Woman (1988), Zhang Xian-Liang depicts sexual contact inside a labor camp. In *Lapse of Time*, (1988) Wang Anyi, an important younger writer, addresses the problems of young people returning to the cities after years of "reeducation" in the countryside during the Cultural Revolution.

A picture of the political ferment that led up to the Tiananmen demonstrations can be found in *Seeds of Fire: Chinese Voices of Conscience* (1989), an anthology of protest and political commentary in various forms, including stories, essays, cartoons, and rock lyrics, organized into sections dealing with different contemporary issues. Among the newest voices, Ai Bei resides in the United States, having fled China after the Tiananmen incident. Several of her stories and a novella are collected in *Red Ivy, Green Earth Mother* (1990).

Of course, China has also captured the imagination of outsiders for many centuries. Marco Polo's *Travels* is only the beginning of a long list of western perspectives on this great nation. For a look at China during the Japanese occupation, read *Empire of the Sun* (1985), by J. G. Ballard, an autobiographical account of the authors's boyhood in Shanghai and his time in the internment camps. Among more recent visitors, Vikram Seth takes a complicated stance as an Indian educated in the West and living in China. *From Heaven's Lake* (1983) takes the reader along on Seth's overland route home from Nanjing. From the U.S., Mark Salzman tells of his time in China as a teacher of English and a student of martial arts in *Iron and Silk*. For a penetrating look at Chinese youth, read *Broken Portraits*, by Michael David Kwan, a Chinese-Canadian English teacher's detailed account of life with his Beijing students.

Films

While the Chinese film industry has always been prolific, it is not until recently that Chinese films have begun to appear in the U.S., this market being dominated by Hong Kong productions of the martial-arts type.

Some extremely interesting films have been co-produced by teams from the People's Republic of China and Japan. *The Go Masters* (1984), directed by Junya Sata and Duan Jishun, is a historical film about a Chinese *go* player who travels to Japan in the 1930s but becomes trapped there during wartime. *Shadow of China* tells the story of a former member of Mao's Red Guard who becomes a powerful businessman in Hong Kong and whose life is transformed when he discovers his father was a Japanese spy in World War II.

China's brightest young director is Zhang Yimou, who became widely known in the U.S. through his movie *Red Sorghum* (1988). This film, a love story set in the poor, rural sorghum fields, is especially notable for its visual appeal. Zhang's latest film, *Judou* (1990), is a tragedy of family love and violence set in a dye factory. *Judou* is the first Chinese film to have been nominated for an Academy Award, but the Chinese government, uncomfortable with the image represented, has called for its suppression.

China has also become an attractive subject for Western filmmakers. Bernardo Bertolucci's production of *The Last Emperor* (1987) depicts the life of Pu Yi, the last of China's imperial line, who comes of age during the revolution. Steven Spielberg's *Empire of the Sun* (1987) is a film adaption of J. G. Ballard's autobiographical account of Japanese prison camps in World War II. One of the few American movies to deal with contemporary Chinese culture, Peter Wang's and Shirley Sun's *A Great Wall* humorously chronicles the return of native Chinese Leo Fang and his American-born wife to China.

HONG KONG

Flying into Hong Kong's Kai Tak Airport, the traveler sees both the spectacular natural beauty of Hong Kong harbor and the drabness of the crowded tenements that fan out from the landing strips. The thriving business districts on both sides of the harbor are full of modern skyscrapers buzzing with commerce. Beyond this core is the other side of Hong Kong: the overloaded apartments that characterize one of the most densely populated cities in the world. Hong Kong has so many immigrants that it regularly repatriates people to China and must keep Vietnamese boat people in closed refugee camps for resettlement overseas.

By virtue of its natural harbor, Hong Kong has long been a center of commerce in South China. The British took advantage of this strategic position when they made Hong Kong a colony in the mid-19th century. On July 1, 1997, however, the British have agreed to return sovereignty of Hong Kong to the People's Republic of China. The transfer of one of the world's showcases of capitalism to the world's largest Communist nation has caused anxiety among Hong Kong residents and international businesses alike. As a result, the rate of emigration has increased, with many Hong Kong residents applying for residency in other countries, such as the United Kingdom, the United States, Canada and Australia. But this same anxiety has also caused some businesses to develop more rapidly and to build factories on the other side of the Chinese border.

Hong Kong is a cosmopolitan city, where Chinese, British, and American influences are evident in language, cuisine, commercial style, and social life. Still, the population is 98 percent Chinese with the majority coming from Southern China and speaking Cantonese. On weekend mornings, Chinese families go on outings to the outer islands of Hong Kong, visit a temple to burn incense, or just have tea and *dim sum* (traditional Chinese delicacies) at the large restaurants overlooking the harbor. After dark, the younger crowd dominates the night life in this paradoxical Chinese city where the latest fad coexists with time-worn traditions. As Hong Kong approaches 1997, the pace of life, day and night, becomes ever more hectic. Hong Kong today is one of the world's most exciting cities.

—*Ellen S. Lautz, New York, New York*

Hong Kong is a dependency of the United Kingdom. Area: 403 square miles (about ¼ the size of Rhode Island). **Population:** 5,656,000. **Population density:** 14,035 inhabitants per square mile. **Capital and largest city:** Victoria (pop. 767,000). **Language:** English (official), Chinese (Cantonese). **Religion:** Buddhism, Taoism, Christianity. **Per capita income:** US$4,000. **Currency:** Hong Kong dollar. **Literacy rate:** 90%. **Average daily high/low*:** January, 64°/56°; July, 87°/78°. **Average number of days with precipitation:** January, 4; July, 17.

TRAVEL

U.S. citizens are required to have a passport; however, a visa is not required for stays of up to one month with proof of onward transportation by sea or air. For study or work, a visa is required in addition to a passport. For specific requirements, check with the British Embassy (3100 Massachusetts Avenue NW, Washington, DC 20009) or with British consulates in New York, Atlanta, Houston, or Los Angeles.

Getting Around

The city center is located on Hong Kong Island, which is connected to the surrounding islands by ferry service. The mainland peninsula known as Kowloon, across from Hong Kong Island, is also a busy commercial district. Beyond Kowloon, the New Territories include a number of new cities and smaller villages punctuating rural land. You can travel between Hong Kong Island and Kowloon either by boat, by train, or by car or bus via the Cross-Harbour Tunnel.

---

*All temperatures are Fahrenheit.

Train service in Hong Kong is fast, extensive, and easy to use. And all station signs are printed in Chinese and English. The three-line MTR (Mass Transit Railway), which serves Hong Kong Island and Kowloon, operates from 6 A.M. to 1 A.M. Hong Kong's second main railway, the KCR (Kowloon-Canton Railway) runs through the New Territories to the Chinese border at Lo Wu. A third line, the LRT (Light Rail Transit) connects the New Territories cities of Tuen Mun and Yuen Long.

While there are no student discounts on the public transportation system, you will save money and time if you purchase a Tourist Ticket. Available at all ticket offices and other locations, the Tourist Ticket is valid for HK$20 (about US$3) worth of travel on the MTR and KCR. The "last ride bonus" allows the bearer to travel anywhere on these lines on the final trip regardless of the ticket's remaining value. For long stays in Hong Kong, you might want to invest in a Common Stored Value Ticket, available in denominations of HK$50 (US$6), HK$100 (US$13), and HK$200 (US$26). For help in getting around, pick up a free copy of the MTR Guidebook, which explains the proper buses and trams to use when the trains don't go directly to your destination.

Buses in Hong Kong fall into three types: double-deckers, minibuses, and maxicabs. Minibuses and maxicabs are smaller and faster and most commonly used by local residents. On Hong Kong Island, the cheapest mode of transportation is the tram system, still operating after 80 years.

"Hong Kong is the greatest place to shop! There's a great variety of merchandise and it's all tax free. You really get your money's worth."
—Amy Shum, New York, New York

Boat service between the outlying islands and along the mainland coast is widespread and inexpensive. In fact, crossing the harbor via the Star Ferry is cheaper than taking the train across. There is also a multitude of small, motorized boats known as *kaidos* which serve as waterborne taxis. If you get tired of the pace of the city and want a change, take a ferry ride to some of Hong Kong's outer islands, where you can spend some time in a sedate farming village, or on a beautiful beach. Another trip popular with tourists is the ferry to Macao, a tiny Portuguese outpost on the coast of China scheduled to revert to Chinese control in 1999. Ferries also take passengers to the Chinese city of Guangzhou.

Bicycle rental is another attractive way to get around outside of the busy streets of Hong Kong Island and Kowloon. The country roads of the New Territories are worth exploring by bike but the less-populated islands are probably the best places to bike. For information on bicycle rentals, contact the Hong Kong Tourist Association (35th floor, Jardine House, 1 Connaught Place, P.O. Box 2597, Central, Hong Kong) or the Hong Kong Cycling Association (Queen Elizabeth Stadium, 18 Oi Kwan Road, Wan Chai).

For persons interested in seeing Hong Kong as part of a group tour, the Hong Kong Student Travel Bureau (see address in "Especially for Students and Young People" below) offers a selection of tours available throughout the year. Options include half-day and one-day tours by bus, ferry, or junk. The organization also offers an array of tours into the People's Republic of China geared to students and young people; details are available at Council Travel offices.

Especially for Students and Young People

The Hong Kong Student Travel Bureau (Room 1021, Star House, 3, Salisbury Road, Tsim Sha Tsui, Kowloon, Hong Kong) has seven offices scattered about the city. This organization performs a variety of services for students and youths, including providing information, arranging tours, booking accommodations, and selling plane, rail, and bus tickets.

Holders of the International Student Identity Card get reduced fares on international flights from Hong Kong and discount rates on a selection of accommodations including the YMCA International House, the Student Travel Bureau's hostel, and a number of hotels. In addition, a number of retail stores and restaurants offer discounts to cardholders; a list of these discounts is available at Hong Kong Student Travel Bureau offices. The organization also distributes free maps and lists of cultural events.

While Hong Kong boasts a large number of budget youth hostels, especially on Nathan Road in Kowloon, many of these are in extremely poor repair. YMCAs are considered a better option. Hong Kong Student Travel Bureau has a list of other inexpensive accommodations in the city.

Meeting the People

There are several organizations in Hong Kong that can help you meet people with interests similar to your own. The Hong Kong Tourist Association (see address above) has further information.

For Further Information

The newest and most up-to-date guidebook to Hong Kong is *The Real Guide: Hong Kong and Macau*, available in bookstores for $11.95. Lonely Planet's *Hong Kong, Macau and Canton: A Travel Survival Kit* is also useful for the budget traveler. It's available in many bookstores, or you can order it for $12.95 (plus $1.50 book-rate postage; $3 for first-class) from Lonely Planet Publications, Embarcadero West, 112 Linden Street, Oakland, CA 94607.

For general information, write the Hong Kong Tourist Association (590 Fifth Avenue, New York, NY 10036) which also has two information centers in Hong Kong: in Kowloon (Star Ferry Concourse, Tsimshatsui) and on Hong Kong Island (Shop 8, Basement, Jardine House, Central District).

WORK

U.S. citizens interested in regular employment in Hong Kong will need a work permit. Applications for permits can only be made by employers wishing to hire foreigners residing outside the colony. Review of applications requires six to eight weeks.

Internships/Traineeships

Programs offered by members of the Council on International Educational Exchange are listed below. For further information, consult Appendix I for the appropriate addresses.

AIESEC-US. Reciprocal internship program for students in economics, business, finance, marketing, accounting, and computer science. See page 18 for more information.

Syracuse University "Retailing and Fashion Internships in Hong Kong." Summer. Undergraduate students are placed in American retailing or fashion companies. Round-trip transportation, housing, and tuition for six credits are included in program fee. Apply by March 15. See Appendix I for address.

STUDY

The following academic programs are offered by CIEE-member institutions. Consult Appendix I for the addresses of the institutions listed in this section. In addition to the programs below, the University of California and New York University offer programs open only to their own students.

Semester and Academic Year

General Studies

International Student Exchange Program. Direct reciprocal exchange between U.S. universities and the Chinese University of Hong Kong. Academic year. Full curriculum options. Open only to students at ISEP-member institutions.

University of La Verne. Semester in Hong Kong/People's Republic of China. Spring. Hong Kong and Guangzhou with tour of China. Juniors to graduate students with 2.5 GPA. Apply by October 1.

JAPAN

One of the first things many Americans notice when visiting Japan is the proliferation of vending machines along most city streets. Even more surprising than their sheer number is the fact that many of them dispense beer and whiskey. Yet far from what one might expect to see in America, Japanese youths do not line up illicitly at these beer machines after school. One has the queer, paradoxical sense of capitalism run wild within a society so well regulated that most citizens refrain from breaking its rules even when circumstances would seem to permit, even encourage them to stray.

Japan has a long history of careful authoritarian control. Although Japan's first contact with the West came with the landing of a Portuguese vessel in the 16th century, the reigning shoguns (warlords) made it their policy over the next 300 years to isolate their people from outside influences, in effect closing off their country from the world. The great change began in 1854, when Commodore Perry anchored American gunships in Tokyo Bay and persuaded the Japanese to open their ports to foreign trade. Internal conflict aroused by this event came to a head in 1868 with the Meiji Restoration, in which the shogunate was overthrown by an intelligentsia which perceived the advantages of assimilating Western technology and the corresponding political forms. Thus were the Japanese people thrown, in a very short time, from a culturally insular state to one in which they were systematically inundated with selected Western ideas.

Perhaps it was the shock of this transition that impelled Japan along the course of militarism which characterized the life of the nation for the first half of this century, a drive to control East Asia and the Pacific that ended with the detonation of atomic bombs in Hiroshima and Nagasaki, and the American occupation. Today, most of those who lived through the war remember the privation their families suffered and say that they were captive to a military government. For the younger generations, the history of Japanese aggression in Korea, China, and Southeast Asia remains distant and ill-understood, owing in part to the careful scrutiny to which history textbooks are subjected by the Ministry of Education. The moral fallout of the war is exemplified today by the ambiguous status of hundreds of thousands of Koreans, descendants of forcibly expatriated laborers, who are refused the rights of citizenship.

For better or worse, history has created a special relationship between Japan and the United States. During the occupation years, General Douglas MacArthur oversaw the establishment of a Western-style parliamentary democracy and more or less dictated Japan's current constitution, which bans forever the use of offensive military force. After the occupation's official end, the U.S. military remained behind, making Japan its foothold in East Asia. In exchange, Japan received U.S. reconstruction aid and favored trade status and, in the long run, was able to peacefully apply its industries to the production of consumer goods, a contributing factor in its emergence as a world technological leader. Exportable goods have bolstered the Japanese economy and allowed Japanese corporations to amass staggering amounts of worldwide capital. During this period, it appeared to many that Japan was making itself over in America's image. But now that the U.S. must confront Japan as an equal if not superior power, people are beginning to see how different these two countries really are.

Japan's new economic success can be seen in the massive shopping centers of gleaming metal, plastic, and glass that bejewel such cities as Tokyo and Osaka. At night, the avenues are transfigured by flashing walls of neon light and gigantic outdoor television screens, bringing to mind such science-fiction films as *Bladerunner*. Behind the glitzy facade, however, one notices that most city buildings have the plain, hastily constructed look of concrete bunkers, a reminder of the sweeping destruction wrought by American bombers in World War II and the rapid reconstruction that followed. Above all, one is amazed by the pure efficiency with which everything operates and impressed by the extraordinary effort involved in building this new Japan.

Despite a profusion of luxury items, the real living conditions of most Japanese are quite modest. Only a very few people own real estate; most live in what by Western standards are extremely cramped rented quarters. As only one-fifth of this extremely mountainous land is suitable for human development, the Japanese have always had to make the most of little space, a necessity that has contributed to a highly formal and restrained social manner and an acute sensitivity to human relationships. But as Japan burgeons into an economic empire, these traditions dictate sacrifice. The typical "salary man," for example, spends his life working for one corporation, to which he devotes sometimes 12 or 14 hours each day, maintaining his energy with "health tonics" loaded with nicotine and caffeine. Under such extreme pressure, more and more young people are expressing discontent with the Japanese system and its demands.

Japan is most certainly changing as Japanese people look increasingly outward and as the outside world increasingly looks to Japan. No longer entirely Eastern nor Western, Japan is becoming a hybrid culture. Whether this hybridization will result in a standardized commercial technocracy or an enlightened meeting of minds has yet to be seen. Whatever the case, modern Japan seems to bear the seeds of the future.

—*Max Terry, New York, New York*

Official name: Japan. **Area:** 145,856 square miles (about the size of Montana). **Population:** 123,778,000. **Population density:** 844 inhabitants per square mile. **Capital and largest city:** Tokyo (pop. 8,300,000). **Language:** Japanese. **Religion:** Shintoism, Buddhism. **Per capita income:** US$15,030. **Currency:** Yen. **Literacy rate:** 99%. **Average daily high/low*:** Tokyo: January: 47°/29°; July, 80°/70°. **Average number of days with with precipitation:** Tokyo: January, 5; July, 10.

TRAVEL

A passport is required, but U.S. citizens don't need a visa for stays of up to 90 days. Check with the Embassy of Japan (2520 Massachusetts Avenue NW, Washington, DC 20008) or with Japanese consulates for specific requirements.

When to Go

If you're planning only a short visit, the best times to go are in the spring or fall. The weeks at the end of March and early April encompass the cherry-blossom season, when the Japanese drink sake under the falling pink petals to welcome the spring. In the month of October the mountains are covered with orange and gold foliage, prompting many to take to the hiking trails and enjoy the beautiful scenery and the last of the warm weather.

---

*All temperatures are Fahrenheit.

June, however, begins the rainy season, which lasts until early July. During this season, rain falls almost continually, making even household interiors soggy. The rest of the summer is exceptionally humid and hot. In the middle of August, known as *O-Bon*, everybody goes on vacation; many leave the country. Transportation and lodging is at its most crowded, and most everything else shuts down during this time, making it an inconvenient time to visit.

Winters in Japan are cold but no colder than in the U.S. They may seem colder indoors, however, as few apartments are equipped with central heating. New Year celebrations begin January 1 and last about a week, during which businesses close down again as during *O-Bon*. New Year's celebrations are more subdued affairs than in the U.S., with most families spending time together. Christmas is a more raucous holiday.

Getting Around

The Japanese rail system is probably the world's most efficient. The government-owned Japan Railways (JR) operates 23,400 trains each day through nearly 5,000 stations across the country. There are also many privately-owned lines competing with JR to offer better service. The cheapest are the local trains, which stop at every station along the line; then come the express trains, the limited express trains, and the *shinkansen*, or "bullet trains," which travel at speeds of up to 130 miles per hour. Most JR trains (except locals) offer more comfortable "green car" service at extra cost.

JR's Japan Rail Pass offers unlimited travel on JR (not private) trains, ferries, and buses for periods of 7, 14, or 21 days. Passes can be purchased for either of two classes—ordinary or green (luxury). Following are 1991 prices for ordinary class: 7 days, $206; 14 days, $327; and 21 days, $419. The seven-day pass pays for itself even if you only take a round-trip excursion to Kyoto from Tokyo. Passes are available only to foreign visitors and must be purchased before your arrival in Japan; you can buy vouchers (exchanged for the actual pass upon arrival in Japan) through Japan Airlines or a travel agent. Persons traveling to Japan on a student visa are not eligible for the Japan Rail pass. Contact a Council Travel office for further information.

During peak travel seasons, train seats must be booked in advance, though at no extra cost. Peak seasons are April 28 to May 6, July 21 to August 31, December 25 to January 10, and March 21 to April 5.

Train and subway networks in Japan's major cities can be somewhat confusing for the foreigner. Once you board the right train, it's easy to tell where you get off, as station names are marked clearly in English on all platforms. On the other hand, locating your train in the first place, can be a challenge inside the larger stations, where signs are not so easy to read. Luckily, most Japanese passers-by are more than willing to point you in the right direction, and command sufficient English to do so. Since you have to buy most local tickets from machines with destination-names displayed in Japanese, you may not be sure how much to pay. The answer is to purchase the cheapest ticket: when you arrive at your destination, the ticket-collector will tell you how much you owe.

"The first thing you have to do, especially if you're living in Tokyo, is to buy a guide to the subway system. I recommend The Tokyo Transit Book, *by Gary Bassin, published by* The Japan Times.*"*

—Mickie Mossler, Clarkston, Washington

Buses make up an integral part of urban transportation networks. But because their routes are not marked in English, they can be somewhat difficult to use. Buses usually depart from the same area near major train stations. Just keep repeating the name of your destination and someone will point out the right bus. Or, if you know the characters, write them down. You're likely to use buses in the countryside and the mountains. However, take the train instead of the bus on major intercity routes, as the highways are often crowded and driving is slow.

Domestic airlines are almost prohibitively expensive, but if you're pressed for time, you'll find extensive air service between Japanese cities. Japan Airlines (JAL) flies only between the major cities, while two other carriers, All Nippon Airways (ANA) and Japan Air System (JAS) provide more comprehensive service to both major cities and the smaller provincial centers.

Many students traveling in Japan recommend bicycling and hitchhiking as good ways to get around. If hitching, take the train or bus out of town to the stop nearest the road you want, and have a map handy to trace your route. You can't hike on the shoulders of expressways, but you can meet drivers in rest areas. Once you're out on your own, or with a friend, away from the cities, you begin to experience more fully the kindness and hospitality of the Japanese people. Your driver is likely to offer you food and drink, but sometimes will think you simply want to get to the next train station. Some of the best rides you can get are with long-distance truckers.

Touring the countryside by bike is perhaps the best way to enjoy the lush, natural beauty of Japan. If you plan to tour, bring your own bicycle with you on the plane. Buying and even renting bicycles in Japan can be quite expensive. Two organizations can be of great help to cyclers: the Japan Bicycle Promotion Institute (Nihon Jitensha Kaikon Biru, 9-3 Akasaka, 1-chome, Minato-ku, Tokyo) and the Japan Cycling Association (Tokyo Cycling Association, c/o Maeda Industry Co. Ltd., 3-8-3 Ueno, Taito-ku, Tokyo). Also, there is a good cycling magazine published in English: *Oikaze* (Futatsubashi 26, 2-24-3 Tomigaya-cho, Shibuya-ku, 151 Tokyo).

"Bicycling in Japan is an unexpected treat. Though the mountainous terrain can be hard going, the Japanese landscape has a peculiar, hypnotic charm unlike anything I've ever seen. The Japanese people, too, seem especially fond of foreign cyclists and are eager to hear of their travels. They may even take you home with them!"
—Mitch Sattler, Tacoma, Washington

Even if you don't envision yourself making long trips through the mountains, a bicycle will be a useful friend. Everyone in Japan rides a bike, many using them for the first leg of their commute to work leaving them unlocked at the railroad station). If you only want a bicycle to get around your own neck of the woods, you'll need only a simple model. Chances are, you can buy one secondhand at a very good price. Another good way to get around—and one popular with many young Japanese—is by motor scooter, which will allow you to cover more territory than a bicycle.

"If you are going to Japan, remember to get an international driver's permit. Being arrested for driving a motor scooter without a license will definitely give you an opportunity to meet many of Tokyo's finest, but it is also a hassle to be avoided."
—Matthew Christian Hall, Laguna Niguel, California

Eating

Like many things, food is generally quite expensive in Japan, especially fruits and vegetables. Even for their staple food, rice, the Japanese pay about five times the world average price. As you may imagine, restaurant prices can be rather high, and servings are much smaller than what most Americans are used to. Even so, Japan is one country where preparing your own food at home is not necessarily less expensive than eating out.

Still, if you go to the right places, at the right times, you can eat well and cheaply. Many restaurants serve a fixed-price "lunch set" that usually includes a main dish, soup, salad, rice, and coffee or tea. A plastic replica of the lunch set is commonly displayed in a glass case outside the door (as are many other dishes, so you can point to what you want if you don't know the name).

Certain types of restaurants are known to be inexpensive. Among these are *ramen* shops, where you can eat big bowls of noodles with meat and vegetables for 300 to 500 yen ($2 to $4). You can find good, cheap sushi (slices of raw fish on vinegared rice) at a number of small counters. Yakitori stands, which serve chicken, meat, and vegetables grilled on skewers, are also good values, and their generally low beer prices make them an attractive alternative to regular bars.

When shopping for food, department stores, oddly enough, usually have better prices than the smaller grocery stores and ubiquitous convenience marts. Most large department stores have a vast food department on the basement level. Walking down the aisles, you can almost always snack on a few free samples. About an hour or so before closing, they drastically mark down such perishable goods as fish.

Sleeping

"If you want to do any real traveling in Japan, you need to have a youth hostel card. Unless you have loads of money or lots of friends with extra room, you won't be able to afford regular tourist accommodations. Youth hostels are quite inexpensive, and though many (but not all) have curfews, you get to meet all sorts of interesting people. In fact, many young Japanese travelers stay in youth hostels. Once I stayed up all night learning to play mah jongg (like Chinese dominos) with a Japanese little league team."
—Robert Moss, Des Moines, Iowa

There are over 450 youth hostels in Japan. About 75 of these are government-run and the rest are privately operated. A map that includes a complete listing of both types of hostels, "Youth Hostels Map of Japan," is available on request from the Japan National Tourist Organization (630 Fifth Avenue, New York, NY 10111). Likewise, you'll find a complete listing of Japanese youth hostels in the second volume of the *International Youth Hostel Handbook*. There are all sorts of youth hostels. Some are Japanese-style homes, with *tatami* floors and *futons*; others are Western-style dormitories, with cots or bunks. Generally for 1,000 to 2,000 yen (between $7 and $15), hostels are your best budget bet. For information about hosteling and youth hostel cards, see page 00. If you arrive in Japan without a hostel card, you can purchase one there; contact Japan Youth Hostels, Hoken Kaikan 3F, 1-2 Sadohara-cho, Ichigaya, Shinjuku-ku, Tokyo 162.

Other options, more expensive than youth hostels but less expensive than Western-style hotels, are *ryokan* and *minshuku*. Both are smaller, more traditional Japanese inns. While some *ryokan* cost as little as 5,000 yen (about $36) per night without meals, some are astronomically priced. The somewhat more comfortable *minshuku* are guest houses run by families, similar to American bed-and-breakfasts. The cost usually remains in the 5,000-yen range with two meals included. It is advisable to make reservations ahead of time. Contact the Japanese Inn Group (c/o Sawanoya Ryokan, 2-3-11, Yanaka, Taito-ku, Tokyo 110) or the Japan Minshuku Center (Tokyo Kotsu Kaikan Bldg. B1, 2-10-1 Yuraku-cho, Chiyoda-ku, Tokyo). The Japan National Tourist Organization in New York also has a list of recommended *minshuku* and *ryokan*.

Another possibility that might appeal to you, especially if you're interested in Japan's religious life, is an overnight stay in a Buddhist temple. You'll have an easier time finding room in a temple located in the countryside, however, since many of the temples in the larger cities have waiting lists. In most cases, if you stay in a temple, you will be expected to participate fully in the temple life. This may include getting up at 3 A.M., helping to clean the grounds, and meditating. If you don't speak Japanese, you should try to have someone with you who does. If at all possible, make arrangements ahead of time.

If you find yourself in a situation where you do not have reservations and need a place to stay, you'll find an information booth in nearly every train station—even in the smaller towns. The people staffing these booths are usually very helpful, and in many cases will call to arrange a room for you; usually you can pay for it right at the desk.

There are few organized campgrounds in Japan, so finding an isolated spot to pitch a tent or drop a sleeping bag can be difficult. Camping is not popular among the Japanese;

instead, the need for cheap accommodations is well supplied by the abundance of youth hostels.

"Those who are used to dropping a sleeping bag in any open space must remember that the Japanese are among the most efficient users of land in the world. The observant traveler will notice that there simply are no unused, clear, flat spaces of land in Japan. The only real possibilities for camping are along the beaches in some of the coastal areas. Anyone spending the night on what appears to be a remote, rural beach, however, should not be surprised to wake up at sunrise in the midst of a large crowd of villagers hauling in the shore nets."
—Paula McCoy, Chattanooga, Tennessee

If you're planning to stay in one city for some time but haven't arranged your accommodations, you will probably want to check into a gaijin house. Gaijin houses, usually found in larger cities, are boarding houses that cater to foreigners. You should be able to find a single room for $300 to $400 per month. As a rule, prices are higher in city centers, lower in the suburbs. Gaijin houses are generally well kept, some with Western-style and some with Japanese-style rooms. While living in a community of foreigners can sometimes isolate you from Japanese life, gaijin houses are good places to meet people and get your bearings.

Especially for Students and Young People

CIEE's Tokyo office (Sanno Grand Building, Room 102, 14-2 Nagata-cho, 2-chome, Chiyoda-ku, Tokyo 100) is a good source of student and youth travel information. The office also issues the International Student Identity Card and can book airline tickets for you.

Japan's student travel organization and issuer of the International Student Identity Card is the National Federation of University Cooperative Associations of Japan (NFUCA). Their main office is located in the Sanshin-Hokusei Building, 2-4-9 Yoyogi, Shibuya-ku, Tokyo 151, and they also have an office in Osaka. NFUCA sells plane and ferry tickets, books accommodations, and provides information on student discounts.

Holders of the International Student Identity Card can take advantage of student fares on flights from Tokyo or Osaka to other parts of Asia. Students are eligible for a 35-percent discount if they fly standby on domestic routes and also receive a discount on most ferries between Japan's various islands. In addition, student discounts are available for some cultural and sporting events as well as at selected hotels, museums, and shops. Contact NFUCA for further information.

The International Youth Card is good for a limited number of discounts on accommodations, recreational facilities, shops, car rental, and international flights.

Meeting the People

The Home Visit System, which now operates in 11 cities, gives foreigners a chance to visit a typical Japanese home and talk to the family for a few hours after the evening meal. Although there is no charge for a home visit, a small gift is appreciated. (The Japanese love to give and receive gifts.) The gift needn't be expensive, just a token of thanks to the family for their hospitality. If you'd like to participate in the Home Visit System (you can even bring up to three friends with you), you should contact one of the local tourist information offices after you've arrived in Japan. A list of offices is included in the brochure *Home Visit System*, available from the Japan National Tourist Office (630 Fifth Avenue, Suite 2101, New York, NY 10111). You'll have to visit the tourist office in advance, however, in order to fill out an application form and allow the office time to make the arrangements. Be sure to ask for specific directions to the house you visit, as the Japanese address system is quite different from what you're used to.

"I would definitely advise people going to Japan to thoroughly read up on Japanese customs and etiquette. In Japan, you can never know enough about the subtle nuances that are at work in all types of relationships."
—Matthew Christian Hall, Laguna Niguel, California

"Unlike China, where a foreigner will always be an outsider, Japan is less orthodox to a certain extent. A traveler who is conscious of the social fabric of Japan can weave him or herself into Japanese society."
—Harry Dauer, Osaka, Japan

For Further Information

The Japan National Tourist Organization (JNTO) operates three Tourist Information Centers (TIC): one in the Narita airport, one in Tokyo (Kotani Building, 1-6-6 Yurakucho, Chiyoda-ku), and one in Kyoto (Kyoto Tower Building, Higashi-Shiokojicho, Shimogyo-ku). It also operates a toll-free telephone line, the Japan Travel-Phone System, designed to help English speakers who need travel information or emergency medical aid. In Tokyo, the number is 3502-1461; in Kyoto, it's 371-5649; outside these two cities, dial 0120-222-800 for information on eastern Japan or 0120-444-800 for information about western Japan.

A number of helpful brochures on Japan are available free of charge from JNTO, which has offices in four U.S. cities in addition to its New York office (630 Fifth Avenue, New York, NY 10111). Of particular interest to students are *Economical Travel in Japan* and *Youth Hostels in Japan*.

A good book for the budget traveler is *Japan: A Travel Survival Kit*, recently updated by Ian McQueen, available for $21.95 (plus $1.50 book-rate postage; $3 for first-class) from Lonely Planet Publications, Embarcadero West, 112 Linden Street, Oakland, CA 94607. A new guidebook, *Gateway to Japan*, by June Kinoshita and Nicholas Palevsky, gives a very thorough summary of Japanese history and culture, as well as a detailed province-by-province guide to restaurants, hotels, and sights. Published by Kodansha International, the book costs $15.95. A good source for all types of hard-to-find books on Japan is the Charles E. Tuttle Company, 28 South Main Street, Rutland, Vermont 05701; send for a free catalog.

The Japan Information Center is located in the Japan Consulate General, 299 Park Avenue, 18th floor, New York, NY 10171. The center has an auditorium for film showings and lectures, a library and reading room, a photo and film library, and a number of free publications. Another organization devoted to promoting an understanding of Japan in the United States is the Japan Society (333 East 47th Street, New York, NY 10017), a private nonprofit organization that arranges various events for its members and the general public including lectures, classes, demonstrations, films, and concerts. The Asia Society (725 Park Avenue, New York, NY, 10021) is another good source of educational materials about Japan and its culture. Write these organizations for information about their publications and public-education programs.

WORK

Getting a Job

Foreigners need a commercial visa in order to land full-time paid employment in Japan. Unfortunately, obtaining a work visa is a complicated process that involves finding an employer willing to offer you a job and sponsor your application for a visa. Most Americans in Japan are employed by the U.S. government, Christian missions, schools, or U.S. companies with branch offices in Japan. Positions for English-speaking persons are often listed in the help-wanted sections of English-language newspapers such as the *Japan*

Times and the *Asahi Evening News*. English teachers usually have little trouble getting the necessary commercial visa; for others, it may be more difficult. Persons interested in working in Japan can enter as tourists, look for work, and, if a position is found, try to apply for the visa in Japan. In some cases, however, they'll have to leave Japan and apply for their visa in a Japanese consulate in another country (such as Korea), which can take some time as well as money. Generally, the ease with which foreigners receive visas depends upon their employer's connections with immigration officials.

If you're seriously considering working in Japan, get a copy of *Jobs in Japan*, a 266-page guide for English-speaking foreigners seeking work in Japan. Written by John Wharton, it's available for $9.95 (plus $1 postage) from Global Press, 1510 York Street, Suite F-204, Denver, CO 80206.

Teaching English

There are a number of possibilities for people interested in teaching English in Japan, including both regular salaried employment and informal tutoring. For those interested in either possibility, *Teaching Tactics for Japan's English Classrooms*, also written by John Wharton and available from Global Press (address above), is a useful primer filled with basic information on English-teaching methodologies as well as on popular classroom activities, on dealing with Japanese students, and so on. The book costs $6.95 (plus $1 postage).

"It's easy to find a teaching job in any number of conversation schools. All Japanese have to learn English grammar in school, so they have a background, but most are nervous about speaking. The most difficult task you'll face will be breaking the ice and getting strangers to talk."
—Candy Brown, Chicago, Illinois

"You can make the best money teaching privately to individuals, but you have to make the right connections and get introductions and that takes time. You can also put up advertisements on university bulletin boards, but that also takes time."
—Doug Adams, Philadelphia, Pennsylvania

Persons considering teaching in Japan should be aware of the Japan Exchange and Teaching Program, which offers 12-month positions as assistant English teachers assigned to public or private schools or local boards of education; participants are assigned duties related to English education at the secondary-school level. Applicants must be under 35 years of age, have a bachelor's degree, and excellent English-speaking skills. Some Japanese language ability and study of or living experience in Japan is preferred, in addition to some background in the teaching of English as a Second Language. The program is cosponsored by the Ministry of Foreign Affairs, the Ministry of Education, the Ministry of Home Affairs, and the local governments of Japan. For further information, contact the Embassy of Japan, Office of JET Program, 2520 Massachusetts Avenue NW, Washington, DC 20008.

For most salaried positions in language institutes, you will need to be a native speaker of English with experience or training in teaching English as a Second Language. For a complete list of the hundreds of English schools in Japan, see *Teaching Tactics for Japan's English Classrooms* (described above).

English teaching positions offered by CIEE-member organizations are described below. Consult Appendix I for the addresses where you can write for further information.

- Earlham College's Teaching English in Japan program involves two-year English teaching-assistant positions in rural junior high schools. Applicants should be college graduates with Japanese language preparation and some knowledge of TESOL principles.

- The Overseas Service Corps YMCA program sends people to teach conversational English as a Second Language in community-based YMCAs in Japan. A basic salary and housing are provided, along with round-trip transportation to and from the YMCA. Applicants must have a B.A. degree; teaching experience and training are desirable. Write to the International Office of Asia, YMCA of the U.S., 909 4th Avenue, Seattle, WA 98104.

Internships/Traineeships

Programs offered by members of the Council on International Educational Exchange are listed below.

AIESEC-US. Reciprocal internship program for students in economics, business, finance, marketing, accounting, and computer science. See page 18 for more information.

Association for International Practical Training.
"IAESTE Trainee Program." On-the-job training for undergraduate and graduate students in technical fields such as engineering, computer science, agriculture, architecture, and mathematics. See page 18 for more information.
"Hotel & Culinary Exchanges Program." On-the-job training for young people beginning a career in the hotel and food-service industries. Participants must have graduated, or be currently enrolled in a university or vocational school and possess at least six months of training or experience in the chosen field. Training usually runs 6 to 18 months. Consult Appendix I for the address where you can write for further information.

Voluntary Service

For persons interested in long-term voluntary-service work, the Year Abroad Program sponsored by the International Christian Youth Exchange offers persons ages 18 to 24 voluntary-service opportunities in the fields of health care, education, the environment, construction, and so on. See page 23 for more information.

STUDY

Admission to Japanese universities is based almost entirely on entrance examinations given by the respective institution. It should come as no surprise that it's very difficult for foreign students to compete with Japanese students in these entrance examinations. There are, however, a few national and private universities that will admit foreigners as long as they can prove that their command of the Japanese language is good enough to enable them to take courses given exclusively in Japanese. There are also several private universities in Japan—including International Christian University, Obirin University, Sophia University, Waseda University, Nanzan University, Kansai Gaidai University, Keio University, Nagoya Gakuin University, and Seinan Gakuin University—which offer special language programs and courses in Japanese and English for foreigners. (For more information about the programs of International Christian University, see the program listings at the end of this section.)

"Students who come to Japan to study should understand that after the rigorous secondary education and college entrance examinations, the academic demands on university students (except some women's colleges and science and engineering institutions) give way to an emphasis on personal and social development. Learning tends to be left up to the individual."

—Hallam C. Shorrock, Tokyo, Japan

Monbusho—the Ministry of Education, Science, and Culture of the Government of Japan—offers scholarships to those who want to pursue Japanese studies or study at a Japanese university as a research student. For further information, contact the Embassy of Japan (2520 Massachusetts Avenue NW, Washington, DC 20008).

Other possibilities for study in Japan include enrollment in one of the many institutions that offer intensive language instruction for foreigners who want to learn Japanese. Up-to-date information on language schools in Japan is available from the Japanese Language Division, Agency for Cultural Affairs, 3-1-1 Kasumigaseki, Chiyoda-ku, Tokyo 100. Another option is studying full- or part-time at one of the many cultural-arts schools in Japan, which offer many different courses, either in English or Japanese, in such subjects as martial arts, flower arrangement, tea ceremony, calligraphy, Zen, and shiatsu. Tourist information centers around Japan can provide information on the courses available and how to apply.

Following are the academic programs offered by CIEE-member institutions. Consult Appendix I for the addresses of the institutions listed. In addition to the programs listed below, the American Graduate School of International Management, California State University, Guilford College, Mary Baldwin College, New York University, Ohio State University, Pennsylvania State University, Stanford University, the University of California, the University of Notre Dame, the University of Oregon, and the University of Rhode Island offer study programs open only to their own students.

Semester and Academic Year

Business

Brethren Colleges Abroad. Sapporo. Japanese language, literature, and culture courses at Hokusei Gakuen University, plus independent study. Study tour to Tokyo, Kyoto, and Hiroshima. Academic year or semester. Sophomores, juniors, and seniors with 2.7 GPA. Apply by December 15 for academic year or spring; May 1 for fall.

Council on International Educational Exchange. "Cooperative Japanese Business and Society Program." Tokyo. Fall or spring semester. Sophomores to graduate students with basic business courses and 2.75 GPA. Apply by March 25 for fall and October 15 for spring. Contact University Programs Department.

University of Oregon. "OSSHE—Aoyama Gakuin University Exchange." Tokyo. Japanese academic calendar, April–November. Sophomores with one year of college Japanese and 3.0 GPA. Preference given to students at schools in Oregon State System of Higher Education. Apply by November 1.

General Studies

Associated Colleges of the Midwest. "Japan Study." Tokyo. Limited to students at member institutions of the Associated Colleges of the Midwest or Great Lakes Colleges Association. Academic year. Freshmen to graduate students with one year of Japanese and 2.5 GPA. Apply by February 1.

Experiment in International Living/School for International Training. "College Semester Abroad." Tokyo. Fall or spring semester. Intensive language, life and culture seminar, field-study methods seminar, independent-study project, homestays, and excursions. Sophomores to seniors with 2.5 GPA. Apply by May 15 for fall and October 15 for spring.

Friends World College. "Japanese/East Asian Studies." Kyoto. Academic year or semester. Japanese history, culture, and language; individualized program combining independent study with fieldwork or internships. Sophomores, juniors, and seniors. Others may participate but will not receive credit. Apply by May 1 for fall; November 15 for spring.

Great Lakes Colleges Association. See program listed under Associated Colleges of the Midwest.

International Christian University.
Tokyo. Academic year of study as regular student at ICU. Wide range of courses available; Japanese and English are languages of instruction. Sophomores, juniors, and seniors with 3.0 GPA. Apply by April 1. Graduate program and undergraduate degree program are also available to qualified U.S. students.
"International Studies." Academic year. Multidisciplinary division, international law, organizations, economics, business, communications, linguistics, and cooperative culture. English or Japanese. High-school graduates and up. Apply by April 1.

Michigan State University. "Year in Japan." Kobe. Academic year at Konan University. Juniors and seniors. Apply by March 1.

Southern Illinois University at Carbondale. "Year in Japan." Nakajo and Tokyo. Academic year or semester. Japanese language and culture. Housing with Japanese students. Freshmen to graduate students with 3.0 GPA. Apply by March 1.

Southern Methodist University. "SMU-in-Japan." Nishinomiya. Language, liberal arts, and business courses at Kwansei Gakuin University. Academic year or fall semester. Sophomores, juniors, and seniors. Apply by March 15.

State University of New York at Albany. Osaka. Juniors and seniors with 3.0 GPA and at least one year of college Japanese. Apply by February 15 for fall; October 1 for spring.

State University of New York at Buffalo. "Kansai Gaidai." Osaka. Academic year. Juniors and seniors with 3.0 GPA. Apply by March 1.

University of La Verne. "Semester/Year in Japan." See listing under Brethren Colleges Abroad.

University of North Carolina—Chapel Hill. "UNC in Kansai Gaidai." Academic year. Sophomores, juniors, and seniors with 3.0 GPA. Previous Japanese helpful. Apply by February 12.

University of Oregon.
"Meiji University Exchange Program." Tokyo. Japanese academic year (April to February). Juniors and seniors with 3.0 GPA and three years of college Japanese. Preference given to University of Oregon students. Apply by October 15.
"OSSHE—Waseda University Exchange." Tokyo. Sophomores with 3.0 GPA. One year of Japanese language required. Preference given to Oregon State Schools of Higher Education (OSSHE) students. Apply by February 1.

University of Pittsburgh. "A Year in Japan." Kobe. Academic year. Juniors and seniors with 2.75 GPA. Apply by March 1. Contact Department of East Asian Languages and Literatures, 1501 Cathedral of Learning, University of Pittsburgh, Pittsburgh, PA 15260.

University of Wisconsin-Madison.
Nagoya. Academic year at Nanzan University. Open to juniors, seniors, and graduate students with two college semesters of Japanese and 3.0 GPA. Apply by February 15. Tokyo. Academic year at Sophia University. Open to juniors and seniors with two college semesters of Japanese and 3.0 GPA. Apply by February 15.

Japanese Language and Culture

Brigham Young University. "Spring Term in Japan." Kyoto. Sophomores, juniors, and seniors. Some Japanese required. Apply by February 1.

Michigan State University. "Japan Center for Michigan Universities." Shiga. Academic year or semester. Program sponsored by consortium of public universities in Michigan. Open only to sophomores, juniors, and seniors at public colleges and universities in Michigan. Apply by February 1.

Stanford University. "Kyoto Center for Japanese Studies." Academic year. Sophomores, juniors, and seniors with two years of college Japanese. Apply by January 31.

State University of New York at Brockport. "Kansai Gaidai Japanese Language and Asian Studies Program." Osaka. Academic year. Juniors and seniors with 2.5 GPA. Apply by February 15.

Urban Planning

Michigan State University. "Real Estate Development in Japan." Tokyo. Technical and cross-cultural aspects of real-estate development critical to building and living in cities in highly urbanized societies. Spring quarter. Juniors to seniors. Apply by February 3.

Summer

Art

Southern Illinois University at Carbondale. "Studio Arts Studies in Japan." Niigata, Tokyo, and Kyoto. Study in one of five workshops: landscape drawing and painting, woodblock printing, raku ceramics, textiles, and stencil printing. Freshmen to adults. Apply by April 19.

Business

Council on International Educational Exchange. "Cooperative Japanese Business and Society Program." Tokyo. Juniors to graduate students with previous business courses and 2.75 GPA. Apply by March 1. Contact University Programs Department.

Japanese Language and Culture

International Christian University. Tokyo. Six-week intensive Japanese language program. College students and graduates with one year of college Japanese. Apply by April 1.

Michigan State University. "Intensive Japanese Language Study." Hikone and Otsu. Language and culture. Juniors and seniors with two years of college Japanese. Apply by April 20.

Portland State University. "Summer Session in Sapporo." High school graduates to graduate students, and nonstudents. Even years only.

University of Kansas. "Japanese Language/Culture and Business Studies in Hiratsuka." Beginning, intermediate, and advanced language offered. Freshmen to seniors. Apply by March 20.

University of Utah. "Kobe Japanese Language Program." Six or seven weeks. Freshmen to graduate students and others. One or two quarters of college-level Japanese or the equivalent is recommended but not required. Apply by March 1.

EXPLORING JAPANESE CULTURE

Readings

It is significant that the writer considered by many to mark the beginning of modern literature in Japan, Natsume Soseki, spent several years in England. His foreign perspective of English literature led him to see his own milieu with an increasingly critical eye. In *I Am a Cat* (1904–06), the narrator, a talking cat (who presumably writes as well), observes human society with humorous skepticism. *Botchan* (1906) tells the story of a young misfit from Tokyo who takes a teaching job in a country school and finds himself part of an intolerable community of busybodies. The comic frustrations of this malcontent immediately struck a chord with many Japanese, and today *Botchan* remains a national best-seller. Among Soseki's later novels, *Kojin* ("The Wayfarer," 1913) and *Kokoro* ("Heart," 1914) deal most powerfully with the struggles of an individual at odds with a repressive, utilitarian society.

Japan's rapid industrialization, often perceived as Westernization, moved many writers to embrace traditional values. In Jun'ichiro Tanizaki's *Some Prefer Nettles* (1928), various characters are drawn irresistably to the opposite poles of East and West, to ideas characterized as old or new. Tanizaki's most famous novel, *The Makioka Sisters* (1942–48), chronicles the disappearance of old ways of life in the years preceding World War II. Aside from his novels, Tanizaki published many essays; *In Praise of Shadows*, a short treatise on Japanese aesthetics published in book form, makes striking comparisons between eastern and western concepts of beauty and should be read by everyone who seeks a better understanding of Japan.

Yasunari Kawabata, Japan's first Nobel Laureate, is known for his depictions of ill-fated love affairs set in hot-spring resorts, the most famous of which is his novel *Snow Country* (1947). His protégé, Yukio Mishima, perhaps more than any of his contemporaries, personally internalized the conflicting ideals of East and West as he understood them. Born of a fallen samurai family, he acquired a deep knowledge of ancient Greek as well as the Japanese classics, lived a flamboyant "Western" lifestyle, and committed ritual *seppuku* to express his devotion to the emperor. *Confessions of a Mask* (1949) is a somewhat autobiographical novel of a young boy's homosexual coming of age. *The Temple of the Golden Pavilion* (1956) is based on the true story of a young Buddhist priest who burns down his temple. More accessible works are Mishima's short stories, of which there are many collections; the story *Patriotism* (1960), a tale of lovers' suicide, is among the best.

In stark contrast to the traditional aesthetic, the novels of Kobo Abe analyze the effects of technology and urbanization on human life, frequently employing the method of the detective story. *The Woman in the Dunes* (1962) and *The Ruined Map* (1967) both center on missing persons, the former from the point of view of the missing, the latter from that of the detective. Most recently, *Beyond the Curve*, Abe's first collection of short fiction to be published in English, reveals a somewhat lighter sense of humor than do his longer works.

Other writers have looked more realistically at postwar Japan. Masuji Ibuse's *Black Rain* chronicles the lives of ordinary citizens of Hiroshima in the aftershock of the atom bomb. Oe Kenzaburo studies the moral dilemma of Japan during and after the American occupation; in *A Personal Matter* (1965), the protagonist must choose between keeping or killing the deformed baby he and his wife have brought into the world. Yuko Tsushima, in *The Shooting Gallery* (1988), looks at the changing roles of women in modern Japan. The most recent Japanese best-seller translated into English is Murakami Haruki's *A Wild Sheep Chase* (1990).

Japanese comics—or *manga*—deserve a special mention. Unlike their counterparts in the United States, *manga* are truly popular, read by people of all ages. Surprisingly enough, these comics are now available with English subtitles through a magazine called *Mangajin*. With Japanese characters spelled out phonetically and translated, *Mangajin* is an entertaining device to help with language-learning. For more information, write *Mangajin*, PO Box 10443, Atlanta, GA 30319. The Charles E. Tuttle Company (28 South Main Street, Rutland, VT 05702-0410) also distributes *manga* in translation.

Special insight is provided by a few perceptive foreigners writing about the Japanese. An interesting study of Japanese popular culture has been written by British journalist Ian Buruma. *Behind the Mask* (1985) examines the Japanese character through the frames of comic strip, movie screen, and television tube. Those interested in the bizarre life of writer Mishima Yukio should read the biography, *Mishima* (1970), by John Nathan. This book, however, goes far beyond the personal, faithfully representing Japanese society during Mishima's lifetime, with especially interesting descriptions of Japan in the fifties and sixties. Finally, one of the more perceptive books to be written about Japan by a young Westerner, John Morley's *Pictures from the Water Trade* (1985), looks very closely at Japanese social habits, especially among salary-men after work.

Films

Japan's most widely known director is without a doubt Akira Kurosawa. Kurosawa weaves tales of action and suspense while maintaining a philosophical, almost mystical attitude toward the life he depicts. In *Seven Samurai* (1954), a village hires a group of warriors to defend against bandits who make an annual raid. *Ran* ("Chaos," 1985) is based at once on Shakespeare's *King Lear* and the feudal history of Japan. Kurosawa's most recent film, *Dreams*, pits five men against death when they are trapped together under an avalanche. This inspiring film flashes back through these men's lives and hauntingly implies the ways in which they could have taken different courses.

Hiroshi Teshigahara created one of the most popular films of the 1960s in *The Woman in the Dunes*. Based on Kobo Abe's novel, this film version portrays with hallucinatory effect a man's imprisonment in a village covered with sand. More recently, Teshigahara has directed *Rikyu* (1990), about the life of the man who invented the tea ceremony. Another excellent historical drama is Kenji Mizoguchi's *Forty-seven Ronin* (1942).

Japan's most comic director is Itami Juzo. *Tampopo* ("Dandelion," 1987) tells the story of one woman's struggle to improve her noodle recipe while revealing hilarious relationships between sex and food. A follow-up to *Tampopo*, Itami's *A Taxing Woman* (1987) pits a female tax collector against the wily owner of a "love hotel." Also good is *Funeral* (1986), the film that made Itami famous.

Of course, Japan is equally infamous for Tomoyuki Tanaka's mutant monster creations: *Godzilla, Rodan,* and *Mothra*. The preoccupation with nuclear radiation evident in such movies as these has once again been taken as a theme in Katsuhiro Otomo's animated film *Akira*. Otomo began his career as a comic-book illustrator, and *Akira* is an adaption of one of his illustrated masterpieces, set in the city of Neo-Tokyo after World War III.

SOUTH KOREA

Korea is a divided nation, split after the Second World War into a communist state in the north supported by the Soviet Union and a U.S.-backed state in the south. Although a slight thaw in relations may be occurring, the People's Democratic Republic of Korea in the north and the pro-Western Republic of Korea in the south remain bitter enemies.

Japanese colonialism (1910–45) and the Korean War (1950–53) left Korea a decimated nation. However, over the past two decades, South Korea has undergone an "economic miracle" that has resulted in an incredible rate of growth. Today it is one of the world's fastest-developing countries and the model after which many Third World nations are looking to fashion their own economic growth.

Politically, South Korea is in a sensitive and important stage of transition. After mass student-led demonstrations in June 1987 against the authoritarian rule of former president Chun Doo-Hwan, direct democratic elections were held for the first time in Korea's history. Chun's handpicked successor and the newly elected president, Roh Tae-Woo, is in the process of implementing democratic reforms and opening up South Korea's foreign relations. Although President Roh has been able to improve South Korea's international relations by warming up relations with China and the U.S.S.R., and by seeking membership in the United Nations, his domestic policies face strong opposition from a small yet vocal group of leftist students intent on pushing the pace of change.

The media has tended to portray student-led demonstrations in South Korea as dangerous, chaotic events. While this is not really the case, neither are they completely safe. However, they should not deter those interested from visiting the country. In fact, if you keep a reasonable distance from the demonstrations and observe, it becomes clear that they are actually carefully orchestrated events that present no real danger to the cautious.

Approximately a quarter of South Korea's population resides in the capital of Seoul, making it one of the most populated cities in the world. It is also a city of marked contrast and change, one whose modern technology and centuries-old traditions exist side by side. Huge skyscrapers and beautifully constructed ancient palaces and temples can be found in every part of the city, creating a varied and exciting atmosphere.

Koreans are an emotional and sincere people. They are concerned about their country's welfare and cultural heritage as Western influences penetrate and alter their society. Today, South Korea is striving to become a major economic power, while at the same time trying to cope with the political, social, and cultural changes brought about by its amazing strides toward accomplishing that goal.

—*Eugene W. Suh, Hartford, Connecticut*

Official name: Republic of Korea. **Area:** 38,025 square miles (about the size of Virginia). **Population:** 43,919,000. **Population density:** 1,189 inhabitants per square mile. **Capital and largest city:** Seoul (pop. 10,200,000). **Language:** Korean. **Religion:** Buddhism, Christianity. **Per capita income:** US$2,180. **Currency:** Won. **Literacy rate:** 92%. **Average daily high/low*:** Seoul: January, 35°/15°; July, 87°/71°. **Average number of days with precipitation:** Seoul: January, 8; July, 16.

TRAVEL

U.S. citizens need both a passport and a visa to visit South Korea; however, for stays of up to 15 days, no visa is required. A tourist visa is valid up to 90 days. Multiple entries are allowed with a re-entry permit, which requires an affidavit of support in addition to

---

*All temperatures are Fahrenheit.

the regular visa application process. Check with the Embassy of the Republic of Korea (2370 Massachusetts Avenue NW, Washington, DC 20008) for specific requirements.

Getting Around

The hub of every transportation network in Korea is Seoul, with highways, rail lines, and flight lanes fanning out from there to the rest of the country. From Seoul, Korean Air and Asiana Airlines provide direct domestic service to 10 cities.

Travel by rail has been facilitated by a new super-express train, the Saemaulho, which runs along three principal routes: Seoul–Pusan, Seoul–Yosu, and Seoul–Kwangju. In the cities of Seoul, Taejon, Tongdaegu, Pusan, and Kyongju, there are special ticketing counters for English-speaking visitors.

Buses connect more destinations than do trains (particularly on the east coast). And while buses are not quite as comfortable, they are generally just as fast as the super-express trains, and less expensive. Each city, too, has its own local bus system. In Seoul and Pusan, however, the subway is easier to use.

Several ferry routes connect coastal ports to Korea's outlying islands. The most heavily traveled are those from P'ohang to Ullungdo, and from Pusan or Mokp'o to Chejudo. Also, a coastal hydrofoil operates along the southern coast between Pusan and Yosu via the Hallyo Waterway.

Many travelers take the ferry between Korea and Japan, but the most commonly travelled route is between Shimonoseki and Pusan, on the Pukwan ferry. Departing at 5 P.M. from either port, the ferry arrives at 8:30 A.M. the following day. Fares run from US$90 for 1st class A (double bed) to US$55 for 2nd class B (deck passage).

"Coming from Japan, where the people are quite self-consciously reserved, I was surprised to see how outgoing and open most Koreans are. Young Koreans are most eager to talk and make friends. At the same time, they are not afraid to show their anger. The dedication to political change I witnessed among students there is something not seen here in the U.S. and made a great impression on me."
—Randy Nash, Atlanta, Georgia

Especially for Students and Young People

The Korea International Student Exchange Society (KISES) is South Korea's student travel bureau and issuer of the International Student Identity Card. With headquarters in Seoul (Room 505, YMCA Building, 92-KA, Chongno Gu) KISES has branch offices in Kangnam, Pusan, Daegu, and Daejon. It provides a variety of services to students, including selling plane and ferry tickets, booking accommodations, distributing tourist information, and arranging special tours.

Holders of the International Student Identity Card and the International Youth Card receive a discount on domestic flights in South Korea, as well as reduced air fare on international flights. There is also a discount for cardholders on ferries to Japan. KISES distributes a booklet that lists specific museums, hotels, restaurants, and shops of all kinds that provide discounts to cardholders.

In addition to the large number of inexpensive rooming houses throughout Korea, the Korea Youth Hostels Association (27, Sup'yo-dong, Chung-gu, Seoul) operates some 20 hostels which charge between US$6 and US$10 per night.

Meeting the People

KISES has a homestay program through which short stays with a Korean family can be arranged. The price for one week is approximately $150; for two weeks, the cost is $200.

For Further Information

The best guide for the budget traveler is *Korea: A Travel Survival Kit*, newly updated with a chapter on visiting North Korea. Available from Lonely Planet Publications (Embarcadero West, 112 Linden Street, Oakland, CA 94607) the book costs $11.95 (plus $1.50 book-rate postage; $3 for first-class). *South Korea Handbook* is another very good guide to the country. You can order it for $14.95 from Moon Publications (722 Wall Street, Chico, CA 95928). General tourist information, including a list of hotels, hostels, and Ys, is available from the Korean National Tourism Corporation (460 Park Avenue, Suite 400, New York, NY 10022).

For a review of social, political, and economic events of the last decade, read *Korea Briefing, 1990*, the first volume of an annual series published by the Asia Society. To order, send $14.85 (plus $3 postage and handling) to the Asia Society, 725 Park Avenue, New York, NY 10021. An analysis of the rivalry between North Korea and South Korea can be found in *The Two Koreas*, by Bruce Cumings, available for $4 (plus $1.75 postage and handling) from the Foreign Policy Association, 729 Seventh Avenue, New York, NY 10019.

WORK

U.S. citizens need a work permit in order to hold regular employment in South Korea. To apply, it is necessary to secure a job offer before residing in the country. A letter of support from the prospective employer is necessary. The application process takes about two months. For further information, contact the Embassy of the Republic of Korea, 2370 Massachusetts Avenue NW, Washington, DC 20008.

Internships/Traineeships

Programs offered by members of the Council on International Educational Exchange are listed below.

AIESEC-US. Reciprocal internship program for students in economics, business, finance, marketing, accounting, and computer sciences. See page 18 for more information.

Association for International Practical Training. "IAESTE Trainee Program." On-the-job training for undergraduate and graduate students in technical fields such as engineering, computer science, agriculture, architecture, and mathematics. See page 18 for more information.

Voluntary Service

For persons interested in voluntary-service work, the Year Abroad Program sponsored by the International Christian Youth Exchange offers persons ages 18 to 24 voluntary-service opportunities in health care, education, the environment, construction, and so on. See page 23 for more information.

STUDY

For information on direct enrollment in universities in South Korea, contact the Korean Cultural Service at the Korean Consulate General (460 Park Avenue, New York, NY 10022).

The following educational programs are offered by CIEE-member institutions. Consult Appendix I for the addresses of the colleges and universities listed below. In addition to these programs, Lewis and Clark College and the University of California offer study programs open only to their own students.

Semester and Academic Year

General Studies

Brigham Young University. "Spring Term in Korea." Language, international relations, Asian studies, and selected internships. Sophomores, juniors, and seniors. Apply by February 1.

International Student Exchange Program. Direct reciprocal exchange between U.S. universities and Korea University and Yonsei University. Full curriculum options. Summer, semester, or academic year. Open only to students at ISEP-member institutions.

State University of New York at Stony Brook.
Chonnam. Juniors, seniors, and graduate students with one year of Korean language and 3.0 GPA. Apply by April 1.
"Yonsei University in Seoul." Academic year or semester. Korean studies. Juniors proficient in Korean. Apply by April 1 for fall; November 1 for spring.

University of Oregon. "OSSHE—Yonsei and Ewha Universities Exchange Programs." Seoul. Sophomores, juniors, and seniors with 2.75 GPA. No language prerequisite. Preference given to Oregon State System of Higher Education (OSSHE) students. Apply by March 1.

EXPLORING KOREAN CULTURE

Readings

During the period of the Japanese occupation, the Korean language was formally outlawed and Koreans were forced to adopt Japanese. For this reason, Korean writers continue to attach enormous importance to the free use of their native tongue. The writer Hwang Sun-won's personal story is fairly typical of many Korean intellectuals of his generation growing up under occupation rule, as he spent his university years studying English in Tokyo. An astute social critic, Hwang perceptively describes the ways Koreans of all walks of life communicate in words and signs. Selected works are translated in *Masks and Other Stories*.

A younger writer, Yun Heung-gil, is known for his depictions of the forces of modern warfare and industry and their effects on Koreans. At the same time, he displays a deep knowledge of Korean traditions, most especially shamanism. *The House of Twilight* presents his major stories.

The best new collection of modern Korean writers, both in poetry and prose, is *Modern Korean Literature: An Anthology*, edited by Peter H. Lee. Zong In-sob's collection, *Folk Tales From Korea*, offers more traditional fare, as does Suzanne Crowder Han's *Korean Folk and Fairy Tales*.

TAIWAN (REPUBLIC OF CHINA)

A part of China since 1684, the island of Taiwan became a separate nation in 1949, when Chiang Kaishek's Kuomintang was driven off the mainland by Mao Zedong's Communist forces. Though the Communists controlled the People's Republic of China, the most populous nation on earth, Taiwan's government was recognized for many years as the official representative of China by the Western world. This period came to an end in 1971, when the Kuomintang lost China's U.N. seat. Today, few nations continue to support the Taiwanese government's claim to be the legitimate ruler of mainland China.

Over the last two decades, the Kuomintang has gradually if stubbornly relinquished its dream of regaining control of the mainland and is beginning to adapt its policies to present realities. In 1991, Taiwan officially declared an end to all counter-revolutionary actions, in effect recognizing the legitimacy of the Communist government. Despite what may seem a lack of international political recognition, however, Taiwan has enjoyed booming economic growth and now boasts the highest standard of living in Asia after Japan. Today, Taiwanese corporations are investing heavily in the mainland, pursuing a strategy of increased activity with their Chinese kin that they hope will give them an advantage over the Japanese.

Taiwan represents a model of development in which economic success is achieved through a rigid, authoritarian system. Though the vast majority of Taiwan's citizens are natives of the island, the Kuomintang's historic one-party rule has placed control of politics and industry primarily in the hands of mainland families. Chiang Kaishek and his son, Chiang Chingkuo, governed the island with military discipline. Their successor, President Lee Teng-hui, has begun to liberalize the country, permitting the existence of opposition parties, the chief of which is the Democratic Populist Party. But many of his critics maintain that he still has a long way to go.

Taiwan is also one of the last living repositories of traditional Chinese culture. Buddhism, Taoism, and Confucianism, banished from the mainland, are still practiced here as an intermingling set of beliefs and social customs. But while Taiwanese youths still receive a traditional Confucian education, many are strongly attracted to what they perceive as more liberal Western lifestyles. English teachers are in high demand throughout this country that seeks to consolidate its relationships with Western nations such as the United States. Such relationships seem especially important now, as Hong Kong prepares to be reabsorbed by China and U.S. military forces plan to scale down their own activities in the region. Taiwan has plenty of reasons to feel concern for its future, but as it embarks on a course of skillful diplomacy with China, the country feels an increasing optimism.

—*Howard Beans, Albany, New York*

Official name: Republic of China. **Area:** 13,895 square miles (about twice the size of Hawaii). **Population:** 20,454,000. **Population density:** 1,460 inhabitants per square mile. **Capital and largest city:** Taipei (pop. 2,637,000). **Language:** Mandarin Chinese (official), Taiwan, Hakka dialects. **Religions:** Buddhism, Taoism, Confucianism. **Per capita income:** US$6,200. **Currency:** New Taiwan dollar. **Literacy rate:** 90%. **Average daily high/low*:** Taipei: January, 66°/54°; July, 92°/76°. **Average number of days with precipitation:** Taipei: January, 9; July, 10.

TRAVEL

U.S. citizens need a passport and visa for travel to Taiwan. Visitor visas are good for stays of up to two months and may be renewed twice. There's no charge for a visa but two photos are required. The U.S. does not have official diplomatic relations with the Republic of China but does have friendly semi-official ties. Instead of an embassy or consulate, Taiwan's interests in the United States are represented by the Coordination Council for North American Affairs, 4201 Wisconsin Avenue NW, Washington, DC

---

*All temperatures are Fahrenheit.

20016. Additional offices are located in Atlanta, Boston, Chicago, Honolulu, Houston, Kansas City, Los Angeles, Miami, New York, San Francisco, and Seattle.

Getting Around

Travel in Taiwan is both cheap and efficient. The main rail line runs from Taipei along the western coastal plain to Kaohsiung in the south. A second line runs down the east coast to Taitung. Trains vary from locals to high-speed luxury expresses that travel the length of the island in four hours.

Buses serve all parts of the island, and those which drive along the new Taipei-Kaohsiung freeway are faster than the trains. While it's possible to rent a car and drive it yourself (you'll need an International Driving Permit), few foreigners do so. Unless you can read the Chinese road signs and are willing to battle heavy traffic, you'll be better off taking a taxi, which are quite inexpensive by American standards.

The principle domestic airlines are China Air Lines (CAL) and Far Eastern Airlines Transport (FAT). However, with good ground transportation available, you probably won't need to use either of them.

"Taiwan is often considered a model of development. By going there, I was able to see the benefits and problems of such a rapidly developing country. For example, Taiwan has a huge middle class, yet the environment has suffered due to the expansion of industry. The island's cities are crowded, noisy, and very dirty, but the natural areas of the country remain to this day some of the loveliest I've ever seen."
—Selby Stebbins, Petaluma, California

Especially for Students and Young People

Taiwan's student travel organization is the Kan Wen Culture and Education Foundation (9F-B, 148 Fu Hsing S. Road, Sec 2, Taipei). Holders of the International Student Identity Card in Taiwan benefit from discounts on accommodations, museum and theater admission, and in a variety of shops. A list of establishments offering discounts to cardholders is available from the Kan Wen Culture and Education Foundation.

For Further Information

The best budget guidebook to Taiwan is Lonely Planet's *Taiwan: A Travel Survival Kit*. If you can't find it in a bookstore, you can order it from Lonely Planet Publications (Embarcadero West, 112 Linden Street, Oakland, CA 94607) for $11.95 (plus $1.50 book-rate postage; $3 for first-class).

WORK

Foreigners need a work permit for regular paid employment in Taiwan. For further information on working in Taiwan contact the Coordination Council for North American Affairs (address above).

Teaching English

English teachers are especially in demand in Taiwan, where the economy depends to a large extent on international trade and commerce.

The Overseas Service Corps YMCA sponsors a volunteer teaching program in Taiwan; participants teach conversational English as a Second Language in community-based YMCAs for one year. A bachelor's degree is required; teaching experience and training are desirable. Housing is arranged through the YMCA in the form of a modest apartment or homestay. Transportation from Taiwan back to the U.S. is provided by the YMCA but note that volunteers are responsible for airfare from the U.S. to Taiwan. For more information, contact the International Office of Asia, YMCA of the USA, 909 4th Avenue, Seattle, WA 98104.

Internships/Traineeships

A program sponsored by one of the member organizations of the Council on International Educational Exchange is listed below.

AIESEC-US. Reciprocal internship program for students in economics, business, finance, marketing, accounting, and computer science. See page 18 for more information.

STUDY

For information on study in Taiwan, write to the Cultural Division of the Coordination Council for North American Affairs (address above), indicating your level of study.

The following educational programs are offered by CIEE-member institutions. Consult Appendix I for the addresses of the colleges and universities listed in this section. In addition to the programs below, California State University, Pennsylvania State University, and the University of California offer programs open only to their own students.

Semester and Academic Year

Architecture

Michigan State University. "Landscape Architecture in Taiwan." Taichung. Spring quarter. Study at Tunghai University, with emphasis on analysis of the natural and cultural physical environment in Taiwan. Juniors and seniors with background in landscape architecture. Apply by February 1.

Summer

Chinese Language

Miami University. "Chinese Language and Culture Program." Some travel. Freshmen to graduate students and teachers. Apply by February 28.

University of Massachusetts—Amherst. "Summer at Tunghai." Sophomore to graduate students and recent graduates (for undergraduate credit only). One year of college Mandarin and 3.0 GPA required. Apply by March 1.

University of Pennsylvania. "Penn-in-Taipei." Third and fourth year modern Chinese. Two years of intensive Chinese study required. Apply by March 1.

EXPLORING TAIWANESE CULTURE

Readings

Taiwan, which shares many of the cultural traditions of mainland China, has also become the last refuge for many of the traditions that have been repressed by the Communist government. Modern Taiwanese writers, therefore, have developed attitudes quite different from those of their mainland counterparts.

Pai Hsien-yung, the son of a powerful Kuomintang general, has had the rare opportunity of witnessing the lives of the last Chinese aristocrats as they acclimated themselves to exile. *Wandering in the Garden, Waking from a Dream: Tales of Taipei Characters* (1971) gives an ironic but sympathetic account of his society in a tumultuous time of transition.

On the other side of the coin, Huang Ch'un-ming, a native Taiwanese, was born in a small coastal town and has lived a restless, itinerant life. His humorous tales, which revolve around the lives of the lower classes, have been collected in *The Drowning of an Old Cat and Other Stories*.

Two recent novels to come out of Taiwan reveal that contact with the West has led to new topics and styles of expression. In *Crystal Boys* (1990), the first novel in Chinese to deal with homosexual themes, Pai Hsien-yung describes the gay community in Taiwan. Chang Shi-kuo's *Chess King* (1988) comments on social change in his country using an allegorical science-fiction form.

Stories by seven women writers from Taiwan and Hong Kong have been collected in *Contemporary Women Writers: Hong Kong and Taiwan*, edited by Eva Hung. Two good historical selections of Taiwanese literature are *The Unbroken Chain: An Anthology of Taiwan Fiction Since 1926*, edited by Joseph S. Lau, and *Chinese Stories from Taiwan, 1960–1970*, also edited by Lau with Timothy A. Ross.

Like Japan, Taiwan has become an attractive destination for recent college graduates. *The Ouroboros* (1990), by Howard Coale, tells the story of a young man teaching English in Taipei who ends up becoming involved in military matters and an artificial intelligence program.

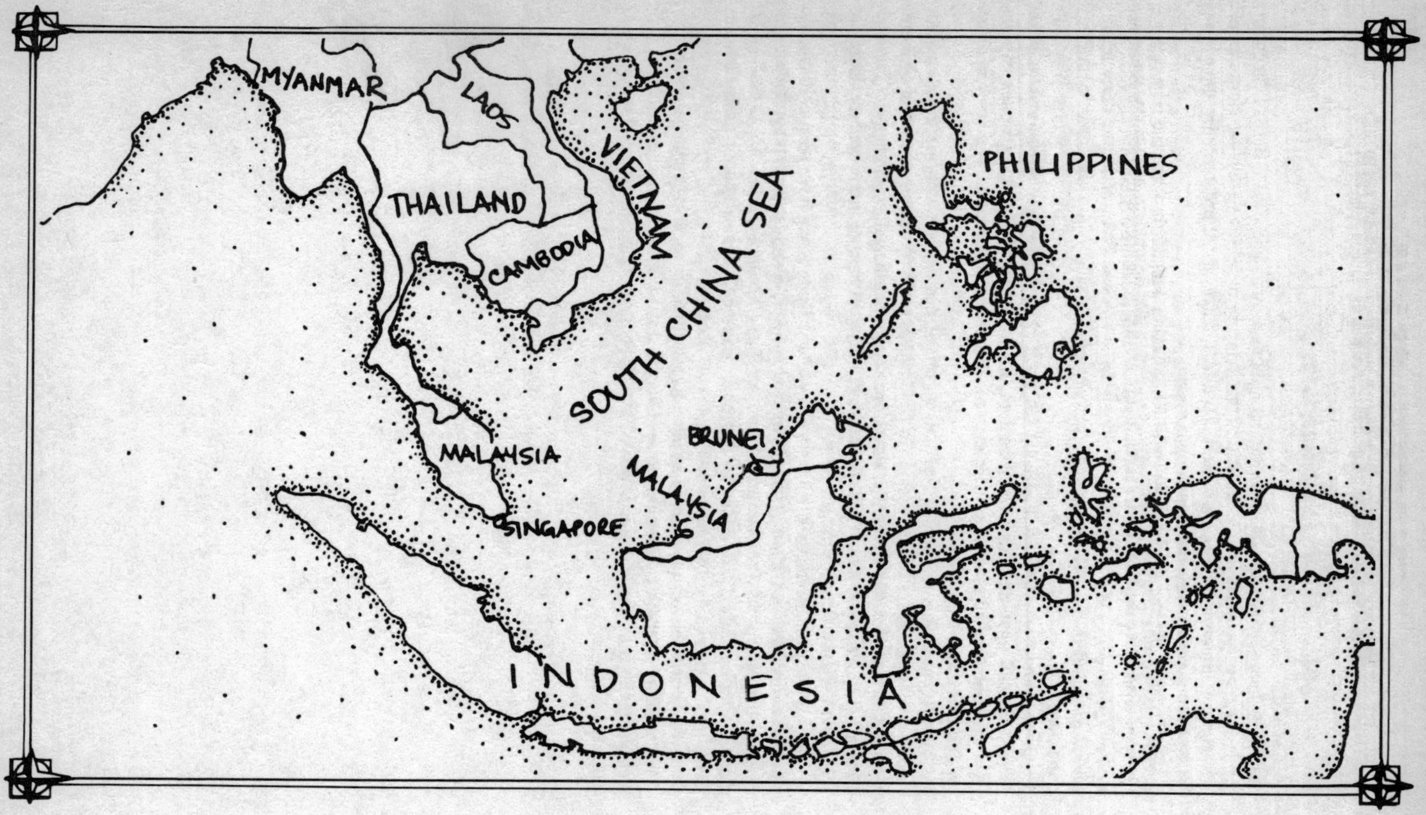
MYANMAR
LAOS
THAILAND
CAMBODIA
VIETNAM
SOUTH CHINA SEA
PHILIPPINES
MALAYSIA
BRUNEI
MALAYSIA
SINGAPORE
INDONESIA

CHAPTER ELEVEN
SOUTHEAST ASIA

Although some countries of Southeast Asia—such as Thailand, Malaysia, and Singapore—are rapidly developing modern industrialized economies, the region also contains some of the world's most traditional cultures and isolated nations. Having emigrated from other parts of Asia, a myriad of racial and religious groups inhabit Southeast Asia. For the most part, their various adherents coexist in peace. But despite the generally tolerant character of these different peoples, many have suffered through years of political strife in their emergence from the period of European colonialism and World War II.

From the conquest of the Philippines in 1898 to the end of the Vietnam War in the mid-1970s, the United States has had a history of direct involvement in Southeast Asia, but gives little attention to the region today. However, the growing importance of Asian economies such as Singapore and Thailand, as well as the largely untapped potential of nations such as Indonesia—the world's fifth most populous country—promise an important future role for these countries. Recent Japanese investment in a number of Southeast Asian countries has stimulated the local economies and created a Japanese-dominated trading bloc. But while many of these countries are becoming increasingly prosperous, they have achieved this through strict social regulation and authoritarian power structures.

For many Americans, Southeast Asia remains one of the most mysterious regions of the world. Americans visiting Southeast Asia today have an excellent opportunity to experience many different ways of life, from the cosmopolitan flavor of some of the world's most modern cities to the easygoing pace of beachside fishing villages. Southeast Asia is known for its lush and mountainous landscapes and for the enchanting ruins of ancient kingdoms. Whether you're looking for exotic cultures, enchanting natural beauty, or just plain adventure, Southeast Asia is sure to be much more than you expect.

Getting There

At press time, many international carriers were offering APEX and/or budget fares from several U.S. cities to Bangkok, Manila, and Singapore. One such bargain was Thai International Airlines' student fares, currently available from a number of U.S. cities to Bangkok. Sample *one-way* fares in effect for the summer of 1991 are listed below. For more up-to-date information on available fares, contact a Council Travel office (see listing on pages xix–xxi).

Seattle–Bangkok	$649
Los Angeles–Bangkok	$649
Dallas–Singapore	$679
New York–Manila	$629

From the East Coast one of the cheapest ways to get to destinations in Southeast Asia is via Europe. Holders of the International Student Identity Card (see page 8) or the International Youth Card (see page 10) may take advantage of special youth/student fares on scheduled flights connecting various European cities with Bangkok, Kuala Lumpur, Singapore, Jakarta, Manila, and Penang. These fares are excellent bargains. Sample *one-way* student fares that were in effect for the summer of 1991 are listed below. Council Travel offices have more information and can also book these flights for you.

London–Bangkok	$705
London–Singapore	$705
Frankfurt–Bangkok	$575
Paris–Jakarta	$759

In the East Asia and South Asia chapters, we've listed sample fares from cities in these regions to destinations in Southeast Asia. For fares between Southeast Asia and Australia, check the chapter on Australia that follows.

Traveling Around Southeast Asia

Bus and train service extends along the length of the Malay peninsula linking Singapore, Malaysia, and Thailand. To get to the islands of the Philippines or Indonesia, the most convenient means of travel is by plane. Airfares within Southeast Asia are generally low. In Bangkok particularly, it's possible to get especially good bargains on flights to other cities in the region, as well as round-the-world tickets. Sample *one-way* student/youth fares that were in effect for the summer of 1991 are listed below; eligibility requirements are the same as for the student/youth fares from Europe described above. Check with a Council Travel representative for more information.

Bangkok–Singapore	$155
Bangkok–Jakarta	$245
Bangkok–Manila	$235

If you're looking for a truly memorable experience, try traveling by ship. In Thailand, Malaysia, Singapore, Indonesia, and the Philippines, you'll find a variety of old steamers, freighters, and modern cruise ships setting sail for points throughout the region. Local ships are a bargain, even for first-class travel. And as very few people take advantage of ocean travel, it's a great way to see a different side of Asia.

Later in this chapter you'll find more detailed information about travel, work, and study opportunities in Indonesia, Malaysia, the Philippines, Singapore, Thailand and Vietnam. For travel to other countries, we've provided basic information below.

Brunei: This tiny independent sultanate is tucked between the Malaysian provinces of Sarawak and Sabah on the island of Borneo. With few people (less than 300,000), and huge reserves of oil and gas, Brunei boasts one of the world's highest per capita incomes and the world's richest man, Sultan Hassanal Bolkiah, as its ruler. Flights link the capital city, Bandar Seri Begawan (population about 60,000) with major Southeast Asian cities as well as with Darwin, Australia. It is also possible to reach the country by boat from neighboring Malaysia. However, a visit to this small nation won't be cheap, with the prices of food and lodging particularly expensive. U.S. citizens need a passport and a visa to enter the country, officially named Negara Brunei Darussalam; contact the Embassy of Brunei (Suite 300, 2600 Virginia Avenue NW, Washington, DC 20037) for more information.

Cambodia: Like Vietnam, Cambodia is only beginning to normalize relations with the United States. This fact, in addition to the hostile stalemate between the Cambodian government and rebel groups dominated by the Khmer Rouge, makes travel to Cambodia somewhat difficult. The only way to see Cambodia at the present time is to go with an organized tour group, which usually costs upwards of $100 per day. Because the U.S. government prohibits U.S. firms from operating such tours to Cambodia, you must make arrangements through a third country. Tourist visas must also be obtained through a Cambodian embassy in a third country, the most popular being Thailand.

Despite the complication and cost, however, Cambodia is well worth visiting. A beautiful and fascinating country, Cambodia was the heart of the Khmer empire which ruled most of Southeast Asia between the 9th and 13th centuries. The magnificence of this empire has been well preserved in the ancient city of Angkor. The present capital of Phnom Penh remains peaceful and the tourist route to Siem Reap (near Angkor) is well protected. Travel arrangements are best made several months in advance. The largest tour operator in Thailand is Diethelm Travel, Kian Gwan Building 11, 140/1 Wireless Road, Bangkok, 10500. A good Australian firm is Orbitours (7th Floor, Dymocks Building,

428 George Street, Sydney NSW 2000). With the latter, travelers may depart from Australia or join the tour in Bangkok.

Laos: The Laotian government doesn't go out of its way to promote tourism but independent travel is possible in this seldom-visited country. U.S. citizens may obtain tourist visas good for one month (apply well in advance). For details write to the Embassy of Laos, 2222 S Street NW, Washington, DC 20008.

It's possible to enter Laos from Thailand by taking a ferry across the Mekong River at Nong Khai. Otherwise, most travelers fly in to the capital, Vientiane, a modern city built by the French. The vast repository of Laos's historic, religious, and cultural treasures is the city of Luang Prabang, usually reached by air from Vientiane. Overland travel is made difficult by the extremely mountainous landscape and poor road conditions that worsen during the summer rainy season. Prices are low in this quiet country, and the lack of tourists adds to the pleasure of traveling here.

Myanmar: Formerly Burma, this country changed its name in 1989 after the military took over the government to put down mounting civil unrest. During the first several years of martial rule, the Myanmar government allowed foreign visitors to enter the country only on group tours. Now that the situation has become more stable, independent travelers are once again permitted as long as they stick to a prearranged itinerary. Tourist visas are valid for a maximum of 15 days, and only air entry (into Yangon or Pagan) is permitted. For information on individual and group travel, contact the Myanmar National Tourist Office, 2514 University Drive, Durham, NC 27707. For further information, contact the Embassy of Myanmar (2300 S Street NW, Washington, DC 20008).

Bordered on three sides by mountains, Myanmar has always been somewhat isolated from its Southeast Asian neighbors, and now that land entry is prohibited, it remains so. The best way to get between Yangon and Mandalay is by train, though you can also travel by boat along the Irrawaddy River. Road conditions are generally poor and buses are crowded. The U.S. State Department warns against travel on Myanmar Airways. For updated information, contact the Citizens Emergency Center (see page 8).

For Further Information

At press time the most up-to-date guidebook to the region is the *Southeast Asia Handbook*, by Carl Parkes. Full of useful information, detailed maps, and thorough historical background, the first edition (1990) costs $16.95 (plus $3.50 postage) and is available from Moon Publications, 722 Wall Street, Chico, CA 95928-5629.

The longtime favorite budget traveler's guide to southeast Asia (known as the "Yellow Book") is Tony Wheeler's *Southeast Asia on a Shoestring*. The sixth edition is available for $14.95 (plus $1.50 book-rate postage; $3 for first-class) from Lonely Planet Publications (Embarcadero West, 112 Linden Street, Oakland, CA 94607). This book will be revised in 1992.

Lonely Planet also publishes a number of other guides to the region. Budget travelers to Myanmar can't do without *Burma: A Travel Survival Kit* ($8.95). The countries of Indochina are well researched in *Vietnam, Cambodia, and Laos: A Travel Survival Kit* ($15.95). Other books from Lonely Planet and Moon are listed in the appropriate country sections later in this chapter.

A good introduction to the many different cultures throughout the region is *A Traveler's Guide to Asian Culture*, by Kevin Chambers (John Muir Publications). For a look at modern Southeast Asia through other travelers' eyes, try *Video Night in Kathmandu*, by Pico Iyer, and *Music in Every Room*, by John Krich. A good source for books on Southeast Asia is the Asia Society, 725 Park Avenue, New York, NY 10021. Write for their catalog.

Study

A number of study programs take place in single countries in Southeast Asia. Below you will find a program that visits several regional destinations.

Semester and Academic Year

General Studies

University of Pittsburgh. "Semester at Sea." Fall or spring semester. Students, based aboard the S.S. *Universe*, attend classes on board and travel to various countries in Europe, the Middle East, Africa, Asia, and South America. Sophomores, juniors, and seniors with 2.75 GPA. Contact: Semester at Sea, Eighth floor, William Pitt Union, University of Pittsburgh, Pittsburgh, PA 15260; (412) 648-7490.

INDONESIA

Tourists in Indonesia frequently remark upon the apparent timelessness of the cultural traditions they encounter. Yet a discerning traveler is likely to be equally taken by the country's dynamism and the rapid changes transforming Indonesian society. In the 40-odd years since it declared its independence from colonial rule, Indonesia has emerged as a major Southeast Asian political force, experienced tremendous economic growth, and managed to foster a palpable—albeit arguably fragile—atmosphere of social unity.

These achievements are particularly striking in a land where hundreds of ethnic groups, speaking more than 250 distinct languages, are scattered over an archipelago comprising nearly 14,000 islands. Subjected to 350 years of colonial rule, Indonesians have only recently come to envision themselves as a unified nation. Five major faiths are recognized within the country and various animist religions and mystical, spiritual sects have their adherents as well. Though approximately 90 percent of the population claims to be Muslim, that figure includes a broad spectrum ranging from the devoutly orthodox to those who are merely Muslims "on paper." "Unity in Diversity," the slogan emblazoned on the national seal of the Republic of Indonesia, is, then, more than a motto. It is a challenge that is continually negotiated by the modern state and its citizenry.

Due partly to increased exports of natural commodities, Indonesia has recently become the focus of much world attention. As in the past, when the islands of Indonesia were known to Europeans as the Spice Islands, foreign commercial interests play an important role in the country's fortunes. Ancient maritime empires based in Java and Sumatra carried on trade with Chinese, Indian, and later Arab merchants. In time, the Portuguese established a niche in the archipelago. Among the most important foreign influences was that of the Dutch, who created an expansive colonial empire known as the Netherlands East Indies. Indonesia's revolution and the eventual capitulation and expulsion of the Dutch remains a major theme in official rhetoric and the "Spirit of '45" still figures importantly in the popular imagination.

Today executive power in Indonesia lies in the hands of the president. The incumbent, Suharto, has run unopposed since being elected acting president in 1967. Prior to assuming office Suharto commanded the armed forces, which continue to play a major role in local and national politics. Opposition to state policies is strongly suppressed.

Though the world's fifth most-populous country, Indonesia is rarely on the itineraries of American travelers. Those who do visit generally go only to the most populated island, Java, or the neighboring island of Bali. But visitors with more time and the inclination to experience the less familiar might also want to venture to such islands as Sumatra, Kalimantan (Indonesian Borneo), or Irian Jaya (New Guinea). Obviously, a longer stay will enable the traveler to make a deeper exploration into the richness of the complex cultures that make up Indonesia.

—*Anne Schiller, Ithaca, New York*

Official name: Republic of Indonesia. **Area:** 735,268 square miles (about three times larger than Texas). **Population:** 191,266,000. **Population density:** 255 inhabitants per square mile. **Capital and largest city:** Jakarta (pop. 8,800,000). **Language:** Bahasa Indonesia (official), Dutch, English, and other regional languages. **Religion:** Islam. **Per capita income:** US$435. **Currency:** Rupiah. **Literacy rate:** 85%. **Average daily high/low*:** Jakarta: January, 84°/74°; July, 87°/73°. **Average number of days with precipitation:** Jakarta: January, 18; July, 5.

TRAVEL

U.S. citizens need a passport (valid six months beyond the date of arrival) for travel to Indonesia, but a visa is not required for stays of less than two months. You must also have an onward or return ticket. Check with the Embassy of the Republic of Indonesia (2020 Massachusetts Avenue NW, Washington, DC 20036) or the Indonesian consulate in New York for further details. Also, be sure that you plan to enter Indonesia through an *approved* gateway city. Most popular gateway cities are approved, but you should check just in case. If you plan to enter through an unapproved city, you must obtain a one-month visa in advance from a consulate.

Getting Around

There are several options for ground transportation in Indonesia. A rail system connects the main cities of Java and there are three unconnected local rail lines on the island of Sumatra; however, in most other parts of this vast nation, rail transport is not an option.

Throughout the country, both express intercity coaches and local buses serving the countryside are a common form of transport. For the most part, rental cars are not available, although cars with a driver can be readily obtained on Bali or in Jakarta. You'll also find motorcycles for rent in a number of locations (an International Driver's Permit is required). Avoid traveling during religious holidays: Prices go up and the crowds are overwhelming.

In the cities, transportation is provided by taxis, buses, and minibuses. In some cities you'll find *becaks*, bicycle rickshaws that can be hired by the hour or according to the distance traveled; you should bargain and decide on a price before you get in, however.

Since Indonesia is a nation of islands, much of its transportation system is comprised of ferries. The national shipping line, PELNI, operates large, air-conditioned passenger ships with regular sailings between the major seaports on either end of the archipelago. In addition, many cargo ships offer passengers cabin or deck space.

A faster mode of transport between the islands is provided by several domestic airlines. Since you'll probably only have two months in the country, doing some flying is almost mandatory if you want to see the islands beyond Java, Sumatra, and Bali. Flights are moderately priced, but be sure to book well in advance. Garuda Indonesia Airways offers a Visit Indonesia Air Pass. Throughout the year, tourists can visit four to twelve destinations that are served by Garuda and its sister airline, Merpati Nusantara. The four-city, 20-day pass costs $350; eight cities in 30 days, $500; and 12 cities in 60 days, $600. The air pass is not available in Indonesia but may be bought through Garuda Indonesia's overseas office at 41 East 42nd Street, 6th floor, New York, NY 10017; (212) 370-0707.

If you're going to spend some time traveling around Indonesia, don't expect to live your life by the clock. A boat scheduled to take you from one Indonesian port to another may be held over a day or two, while you'll be left to fend for yourself during the delay. Your only option in such situations will be patience.

"Indonesian rail travel is not for the impatient or the weak of heart. One- or two-hour stops in the hottest part of the day are not uncommon. Once I sat on an uncushioned,

---

*All temperatures are Fahrenheit.

wooden seat for 54 hours with a goat as one of my fellow passengers! This was in third class. I recommend that others invest the few extra dollars and travel first- or second-class instead. It's worth it."
—Grace Gianinni, Seattle, Washington

"Too many people leave Indonesia without seeing any more than the beaches of Bali. Indonesia has thousands of other islands, and 70 percent of the population lives on Java. Spend some time in Java away from the other foreigners. You won't be disappointed."
—Jennifer Shapiro, Los Angeles, California

Especially for Students and Young People

The organization that issues the International Student Identity Card in Indonesia is STA, a student travel organization that originated in Australia. The two representatives in the country are located at the Kuta Beach Club Hotel in Denpasar (Bali) and in Jakarta at Indo Shangrila Travel, Jalan Gajah Mada No. 219G. At both locations you can get discounted plane tickets, book accommodations, or make arrangements for local tours. Garuda Indonesia Airways offers discounts to students, but your best bet with the International Student Identity Card is just to flash it whenever you book a room, buy a train ticket, and so on. You'll often be pleasantly surprised. The International Youth Card is also good for selected discounts on international flights, accommodations, and retail purchases.

For Further Information

The most comprehensive travel guide to the country is the *Indonesia Handbook*, by Bill Dalton, published by Moon Publications. Containing over a thousand pages of maps, budget traveling tips, and accurate historical reporting, this "gypsy-style" manual costs $17.95 (plus $3.50 postage) from Moon Publications, 722 Wall Street, Chico, CA 95928-5629. Dalton has also written the *Bali Handbook* available from Moon for $12.95. Take note: Because of certain passages critical of the Indonesian government, the *Indonesia Handbook* is banned in the country; hide it in your pack or slap a cover on it if you don't want yours to be confiscated by the police.

Other guidebooks for the budget traveler are *Indonesia: A Travel Survival Kit* ($19.95) and *Bali and Lombok: A Travel Survival Kit* ($13.95), which can be ordered from Lonely Planet Publications, Embarcadero West, 112 Linden Street, Oakland, CA 94607 or by calling (800) 229-0122. Add $1.50 for book-rate postage; $3 for first-class. Lonely Planet also has a useful *Indonesia Phrasebook* ($2.95).

WORK

Foreigners need an employment visa to work in Indonesia. It is necessary to secure a job before going to the country and applying for the visa. Application is made to the Office of Immigration under the Ministry of Justice. Getting a permit for casual work is impossible; for long-term employment, the applicant must have a skill that is not available locally. For more information contact the Embassy of the Republic of Indonesia, 2020 Massachusetts Avenue NW, Washington, DC 20036.

Internships/Traineeships

A program sponsored by a member of the Council on International Educational Exchange is listed below.

AIESEC-US. Reciprocal internship program for students in economics, business, finance, marketing, accounting, and computer science. See page 18 for more information.

STUDY

The following educational programs are offered by CIEE-member institutions. Consult Appendix I for addresses of the colleges and universities listed in this section. In addition to the programs below, Lewis and Clark College and the University of California offer programs open only to their own students.

Semester and Academic Year

General Studies

Experiment in International Living/School for International Training. "College Semester Abroad." Bali. Fall or spring semester. Intensive Indonesian language study, seminar on Indonesian and Balinese culture, field-study methods seminar, village homestay, and independent-study project. Sophomores, juniors, and seniors with 2.5 GPA. Apply by May 15 for fall and October 15 for spring.

Southeast Asian Studies

Council on International Educational Exchange. "Cooperative Southeast Asian Studies Program." Malang, Java. Fall or spring semester. Sophomores to seniors with one Asian studies course and 2.75 GPA. Apply by April 1 for fall and October 1 for spring. Contact University Programs Department.

Summer

Southeast Asian Studies

Lisle Fellowship. "Modernization in Paradise: Encounters of the Human Kind." Exploration of Balinese culture and education, with special focus on interaction between tradition and modernization. Three weeks. Open to recent high-school graduates, college students, and adults. Apply by April 1.

EXPLORING INDONESIAN CULTURE

Readings

The first novels about the Indonesian archipelago were written by Dutch writers during the colonial period. Douwes Dekker's *Max Havelaar*, first published in 1860, depicts the exploitation of the Javanese peasant under the colonial system. *Country of Origin*, by E. du Perron, and Louis Couperus's masterpiece of psychological fiction, *The Hidden Force*, are also excellent portraits of life in colonial Indonesia. Maria Dermout, a Dutch writer born in Java, is the author of *The Ten Thousand Things*, a haunting novel set in Indonesia's Moluccan Islands. First published in 1955, it has lost none of its timeless appeal.

In *The Fugitive*, Pramoedya Ananta Toer portrays the revolution against Dutch colonial rule from an Indonesian point of view. Pramoedya was imprisoned by the Dutch authorities for his involvement in the fight for independence, and his novel was smuggled out of prison by sympathetic Dutch intellectuals. T. B. Simatupang, another Indonesian writer, deals with this period in *Report from Banaran: The Story of the Experiences of a Soldier during the War of Independence*.

Twilight in Djakarta, by Lubis Mochtar, is a disturbing novel about political corruption in post-independence Indonesia. Finished in jail in 1957, Mochtar's book paints a vivid portrait of the seamier side of life in the Indonesian capital. Ismail Marahimin is another contemporary Indonesian author who has received international recognition. In *And the War Is Over*, published in 1977 but set at the end of the Second World War, Marahimin brilliantly portrays three cultures—each alien to the others—in an ironic story of Javanese and Dutch prisoners plotting an escape from their Japanese captors.

Ring of Fire, by Lawrence and Lorne Blair, is the companion volume to an acclaimed BBC television series of the same name. Published in 1988, this nonfiction account of the authors' ten-year journey of exploration and adventure across the Indonesian archipelago captures much of the diversity and excitement of modern Indonesia, especially its most isolated islands and primitive tribal peoples.

MALAYSIA

Malaysia, with an estimated population of approximately 18 million, is a mélange of cultures and peoples: Malays make up 48 percent of the population, Chinese comprise 35 percent, Indians represent 10 percent, and various indigenous ethnic groups make up the rest. The tension among these groups as they vie for political and economic power in this relatively prosperous nation is a constant source of problems—and, at times, factional violence—but also creates a cultural vibrancy not found in more racially uniform countries.

Malaysia's large Chinese population arrived in large numbers in the late 19th century to work on the country's rubber plantations and in its tin mines, many fleeing from the war and famine in China. Today, the Chinese in Malaysia dominate the economy, a position obtained by hard work and perseverance. However, the Malays, who consider themselves to be the indigenous population of Malaysia, hold most of the political power.

Malaysia is divided into two regions. Peninsular Malaysia extends from the southern tip of Thailand to the island nation of Singapore; East, or Insular, Malaysia includes Sabah and Sarawak, the two states that share the tropical island of Borneo with the Indonesian state of Kalimantan. Malaysia's strategic location—smack in the heart of Southeast Asia and alongside the Straits of Molucca—has made it an attractive addition to any imperial power's portfolio. Over the years the country has been dominated by the Portuguese, the Dutch, and, most recently, the British, who granted independence to Malaya in 1957. In 1963, Malaya changed its name to Malaysia after the British colonies of Sabah and Sarawak agreed to join the republic. Today the country is booming economically, thanks to a lucrative combination of plentiful natural resources, a solid infrastructure, and a relatively well-educated labor force.

The state religion is Islam, and everywhere there is evidence of a nationwide surge of Islamic consciousness. On the East Coast, women wear black robes and remain veiled in *purdah*; laws have been passed that forbid conversion attempts to any religion except Islam; and punishments meted out by Islamic courts seem harsh by Western standards (such as the stoning to death of adulterers).

Peninsular Malaysia's East and West Coasts show the traveler two completely different sides of Asian culture. The East Coast has remained rather isolated against the tide of industrialization and remains a bastion of sleepy fishing villages, deserted beaches, and colorful markets filled with exotic fruits and batik sarongs. This is home for many easygoing Malays, who work as farmers or fishermen. The West Coast is populated primarily by Chinese and is more business-oriented as a whole. Filled with excitement and energy, the West Coast boasts historic sights and a vibrant night life. The island of Borneo offers yet another experience for the traveler: rain forests, incredible national parks, and perhaps a visit to a jungle-surrounded longhouse to peer at a collection of dusty skulls. Sarawak has recently attracted international attention, as press coverage has

focused on the struggle of the Penan tribespeople to save their ancestral homelands from indiscriminate logging, a policy that threatens to destroy Malaysia's rain forests forever.
—*Edythe Antal, Baltimore, Maryland*

Official name: Federation of Malaysia. **Area:** 127,316 square miles. **Population:** 17,053,000. **Population density:** 132 inhabitants per square mile. **Capital and largest city:** Kuala Lumpur (pop. 1,000,000). **Language:** Malay, Chinese, Tamil, English. **Religion:** Islam, Buddhism, Hinduism, Christianity. **Per capita income:** US$2,000. **Currency:** Ringgit. **Literacy rate:** 80%. **Average daily high/low*:** Kuala Lumpur: January, 90°/72°; July, 90°/73°.

TRAVEL

A passport (which is valid at least a month beyond the end of your declared stay) is required for U.S. citizens entering Malaysia. A visa is not required for stays of up to three months; a visa is required, however, if you're planning to work, do research, or study at an educational institution in Malaysia. For specific requirements, check with the Embassy of Malaysia (2401 Massachusetts Avenue NW, Washington, DC 20008) or with a Malaysian consulate in New York or Los Angeles. Be aware that Malaysia expressly forbids the entrance of "hippies," a term loosely defined as any traveler who arrives wearing dirty or strange clothes, thongs, or long hair. In the past such visitors have been asked to leave the country after having their passports stamped SH for "suspected hippie." This is true. Nowadays things have calmed down a bit, but it is better to arrive at the border wearing clean clothes and carrying enough money to prove your solvency.

Warning: While in Malaysia, remember that the Malaysian government has strong views on drugs. The penalties for trafficking and possession—even of minuscule amounts—are severe and include death. No distinction is made between hard and soft drugs, nor is culpability taken into account. As recently as 1984, foreigners have been hanged for trafficking.

GETTING AROUND

Malayan Railways (Keretapi Tanjah Melayu or KTM) operates a network of modern trains, many with air-conditioning, sleeping compartments, and dining cars. Peninsular Malaysia has two train lines: West Coast service from Singapore to Thailand, and an East Coast line from Gemas to Kota Baru. (The famous train journey from Singapore to Bangkok takes you through Kuala Lumpur and along the populous west coast of the country.) Malayan Railways has also introduced a rail pass that's available to foreign visitors; a 10-day pass costs approximately $35, and a 30-day pass is approximately $75, not much of a deal because of the limited extent of the railway lines. The passes may be purchased at railway stations in Malaysian cities, at the station in Singapore, or at any student travel office.

The roads in peninsular Malaysia are among the best in Southeast Asia. Buses run on all the main roads, including long-distance express buses between the major cities. This highway network, which provides access to the beautiful beaches and tropical rain forest of the peninsula's east coast, also makes the country good for those who wish to rent a car. Avis, Hertz, and other international rental firms are represented in Malaysia, but you'll get better prices from Malaysian firms like Sintat and Mayflower. Shared taxis are also a travel option, costing about as much as an air-conditioned bus or a second-

---

*All temperatures are Fahrenheit.

class train. Ferries fill in many gaps by providing service between resort islands and mainland towns. However, the roads are not as good in Malaysian Borneo and bus service is often provided by trucks or four-wheel-drive vehicles. The national airline, Malaysian Airlines Systems, has good connections between Malaysian Borneo and the Malaysian mainland as well as Singapore, or you can climb aboard one of the small passenger-cargo ships of the Straits Steamship line for a more leisurely crossing. Hitchhiking is popular and generally fairly easy along the more traveled roads of Malaysia's west coast.

"Malaysia is a multicultural society comprised largely of three racial groups: Malays, Chinese, and Indians. Religious freedom is legally protected, but Islam is the state religion. Dress modestly and behave appropriately. Malay businesses are closed on Friday afternoons for prayer."
—Lawrence Tyler, Kalamazoo, Michigan

Especially for Students and Young People

Malaysia's student travel organization is MSL Travel SDN BHD. You'll find offices in Kuala Lumpur (First floor, Asia Hotel, 69, Jln Hj Hussin, 50300 Kuala Lumpur), on the resort island of Penang (Ming Court Inn Lobby, Macalister Road, 10400 Penang and 340 Chulia Street, 10200 Penang), and in Petaling Jaya (Lot 2, Wisma MCIS Annexe, Jln Barat, 46200 Petaling Jaya). You'll find that these offices provide a full range of services, including providing information, booking accommodations, and selling bus, rail, and plane tickets.

Students with the International Student Identity Card or the International Youth Card get a discount on international airfares from Kuala Lumpur and reduced rates at certain hotels. There is also a discount on tours in Kuala Lumpur and Penang for cardholders. If you are studying in Malaysia, you can get discounts on domestic flights and rail prices. Cardholders also receive a discount on international ferries. Contact MSL Travel for more information. The International Youth Card is also good for discounts on accommodations and tours.

"In Kuala Lumpur, there are a lot of cheap accommodations—mostly hostels and Chinese hotels. However, some of these hotels are really brothels, and might refuse to rent you a room. Although the situation isn't particularly dangerous, women should be aware of it. It's usually pretty easy to tell what's what, though. Signs that say 'RUMAH TUMPANGAN' are good indication of this sort of activity."
—Lara Curran, Las Vegas, Nevada

For Further Information

General tourist information is available from the Malaysian Tourist Information Center in Los Angeles, 818 West Seventh Street, Los Angeles, CA 90017-3432. The best guidebook for the budget traveler is *Malaysia, Singapore, and Brunei: A Travel Survival Kit* available for $18.95 (plus $1.50 Book-rate postage; $3 for first-class) from Lonely Planet Publications, Embarcadero West, 112 Linden Street, Oakland, CA 94607. If you are planning to spend a significant amount of time in Malaysia, it might be worth your while to pick up a copy of *Malaysia: A Foreigners' Guide*, by Lynn Withum. Designed to answer many of the questions asked by tourists, foreign residents, and visiting business people, this book includes information on everything from dog licenses to the local Alcoholics Anonymous contact.

WORK

Foreigners are required to have a work permit in Malaysia. You'll also need a Malaysian who agrees to assure your maintenance and repatriation. For more information contact the Embassy of Malaysia, 2401 Massachusetts Avenue NW, Washington, DC 20008.

Internships/Traineeships

Programs offered by members of the Council on International Educational Exchange are listed below. For further information, consult Appendix I for the appropriate addresses.

AIESEC-US. Reciprocal internship program for students in economics, business, finance, marketing, accounting, and computer science. See page 18 for more information.

Association for International Practical Training. "Hotel and Culinary Exchanges Program." On-the-job training for young people beginning a career in the hotel and food-service industries. Participants must have graduated or be currently enrolled in a university or vocational school, and possess at least six months of training or experience in the chosen field. Training usually runs from 6 to 18 months.

THE PHILIPPINES

About 500 miles off mainland Southeast Asia is an archipelago comprised of 7,100 islands and islets known as the Philippines. Because of the physical characteristics of Philippine geography there are noticeable changes in dialect, language, and even styles of clothing as one moves through the different regions of the archipelago. Despite these differences, however, there has been a concerted effort to develop a national identity and move the country out from under the shadows of its Spanish- and American-influenced past.

The Spanish, who ruled the Philippines from 1521 to 1898, were so successful in introducing Catholicism to the islands of the archipelago that the Philippines today is the only predominantly Roman Catholic country in Asia. (The Muslim south resisted Spanish attempts at Christianization and has maintained an Islamic identity.) Aside from religion, the Spanish introduced Western technology, Western economic and political institutions, and a public education system, all of which aided the spread of nationalism among the Filipinos.

When the archipelago was ceded to the United States in 1898, Filipinos were more than happy to be relieved of their Spanish masters and welcomed the professed commitment of the United States to Philippine independence. However, it took the U.S. government 48 years to make good on its promise. In the interim, the Philippines became acquainted with political democracy and equal economic opportunity. English became the medium of instruction, and still remains the language of education, business, and government transactions. The Philippines became the first Southeast Asian country to have an elective legislative body. And when the Philippine constitution was drawn up in 1935, it closely resembled its American model.

Today, the country is recovering from a period of economic instability and political turmoil that reached its peak with the 1986 coup against Ferdinand Marcos. Despite guarantees, however, the new Philippine government under Corazon Aquino has yet to fulfill its promises of improvement. Nevertheless, Filipinos are filled with hope about their future.

It is the Filipino's basic nature not to dwell on the negative but rather to adapt to new situations. In the past years, there has been a proliferation of restaurants, boutiques, discos, and resorts all over the country. This is characteristic of the Filipino's innate desire to enjoy, to entertain, and to be entertained. It is not uncommon to find a Filipino, whether living in a modest nipa hut in the remote province of Vigan or in a grand home in the bustling city of Manila, celebrating the arrival of a guest. The numerous foreigners who come to the Philippines are always moved by the enthusiastic welcome they receive. It is the immense pride of the Filipinos in their culture and country that compels them to receive guests with open arms, exclaiming "Welcome . . . Mabuhay!"

—*Moyen F. Lagdameo, Franklin Lakes, New Jersey*

Official name: Republic of the Philippines. **Area:** 115,831 square miles (about the size of Arizona). **Population:** 66,647,000. **Population density:** 535 inhabitants per square mile. **Capital and largest city:** Manila (pop. 1,700,000). **Language:** English, Tagalog (and its official form, Pilipino). **Religion:** Roman Catholic, Islam. **Per capita income:** US$667. **Currency:** Philippine peso. **Literacy rate:** 88%. **Average daily high/low*:** Manila: January, 82°/69°; July, 88°/75°. **Average number of days with precipitation:** Manila: January, 6; July, 24.

TRAVEL

U.S. citizens need a passport (valid at least six months beyond the date of your entry) to enter the Philippines. If arriving at the Manila airport, an onward or return ticket is required but a visa is not necessary for stays of up to 21 days. For stays of over 21 days, U.S. citizens need a visa (no charge) as well as onward or return tickets. For requirements at other points of entry, check the Embassy of the Philippines (1617 Massachusetts Avenue NW, Washington, DC 20036) or an office of the Consulate General of the Philippines, located in Chicago, San Francisco, Los Angeles, Seattle, Houston, or New York (556 Fifth Avenue, Third floor, New York, NY 10036).

Getting Around

The natural boundaries of mountains and sea make getting around the islands somewhat slow unless you travel by air. The most common form of land transportation is bus, with dozens of companies providing some of the world's cheapest bus service; the most popular routes out of Manila feature luxury air-conditioned buses. Rail service is virtually nonexistent except on Luzon, the largest island in the Philippines, where there is only one route and the service is slow and unreliable. An expensive alternative is to rent a car from a company such as Hertz and Avis in Manila, Cebu City, or Davao City. In cities throughout the Philippines, however, cars *with* drivers can be hired at rates that may be cheaper than rental cars. The jeepney (usually a U.S. Army-surplus vehicle with added benches) is another popular form of transportation, crowded but cheap.

There are several options for getting around the islands. The national airline, PAL (Philippine Air Lines), provides domestic service to points throughout the archipelago. Most service is from the Manila Domestic Airport, but Cebu's airport is also an important hub. Regularly scheduled ferries provide convenient transportation on some of the more heavily traveled routes. However, getting to many of the less populated islands means making arrangements with one of the many local shipping companies that transport cargo as well as passengers between Manila and ports around the archipelago. Information can be obtained by consulting a commercial phone directory and making some calls or by simply going to the port area (the domestic shipping terminals of the North Harbor area in Tondo, Manila) and making arrangements in person. Standards vary on these ships, and some are dirty and overcrowded. There have also been problems with safety in the past. Never board ferries at night, during bad weather, or when they look overloaded; they can capsize. If you find a good ship, however, interisland travel can be a real pleasure.

"The Philippines is not metro Manila, even though 15 percent of the population lives there. Make sure you get to visit provincial cities like Vigan, Bagio, and Cebu. The people are very friendly and you can usually communicate in English."
—J. J. Brennan, Winter Park, Florida

---

*All temperatures are Fahrenheit.

"Some of the coastal towns served by steamers can hardly have changed since Conrad's day. Arriving in port where the entire local population seems to turn out to greet you is a real travel experience."
—Mark Thompson, Rochester, New York

Especially for Students and Young People

YSTAPHIL is the Philippines' student travel agency. You'll find its office beside the Excelsior Hotel on Roxas Boulevard at 4227 Tomas Claudio Street, Paranaque, Metro Manila. The organization provides information and a range of student/youth travel services, including a number of organized tours. YSTAPHIL is also the secretariat of the local youth hostel association and sells the IYHF Card and the *International Youth Hostel Handbook* (see page 53).

Cardholders can obtain a discount at hotels in Manila and a number of other key cities when the booking is made through YSTAPHIL. The organization also provides a list of shops, restaurants, bars, and clubs that offer discounts to cardholders. There is also a discount for students traveling on Philippine National Railways as well as on some interisland ferries. The International Youth Card is also good for discounts on accommodations, museums, and restaurants.

For Further Information

General travel information is available from the Philippine Ministry of Tourism, which has offices in New York (556 Fifth Avenue, New York, NY 10036) and Los Angeles (3660 Wilshire Boulevard, Suite 216, Los Angeles, CA 90010).

The Philippines: A Travel Survival Kit is one of the better guidebooks for the budget traveler. It's available for $14.95 (plus $1.50 book-rate postage; $3 for first-class) from Lonely Planet Publications (Embarcadero West, 112 Linden Street, Oakland, CA 94607).

WORK

Foreigners are required to have a work permit for regular employment in the Philippines. Application is made by the employer after a job has been offered. Generally speaking, work permits are only granted when the foreigner has a needed skill that is not available locally. For more information contact the Embassy of the Philippines, 1617 Massachusetts Avenue NW, Washington, DC 20036.

Internships/Traineeships

Programs offered by the Council on International Educational Exchange are listed below. For further information, consult Appendix I for the appropriate addresses.

AIESEC-US. Reciprocal internship program for students in economics, business, finance, marketing, accounting, and computer science. See page 18 for more information.

Association for International Practical Training. "IAESTE Trainee Program." On-the-job training for undergraduate and graduate students in technical fields such as engineering, computer science, agriculture, architecture, and mathematics. See page 18 for more information.

Voluntary Service

The Partnership for Service Learning sponsors a study/service program in the Philippines which includes study at an accredited college in the host country and service work in the local community. Generally participants are involved in human-services work, teaching, health care, recreation, and community development. For more information see page 24. Another service program is sponsored by the Overseas Development Network; for more information see page 29.

STUDY

A program offered by a CIEE-member institution is listed below. Consult Appendix I for the address of this institution.

Semester and Academic Year

General Studies

International Student Exchange Program. Direct reciprocal exchange between U.S. universities and institutions in Manila, Iloio City, Miag-ao, and Quezon City. Semester or academic year. Full curriculum options. Open only to students at ISEP-member institutions.

EXPLORING FILIPINO CULTURE

Films

During the American occupation of the Philippines in the first half of this century, most films produced were patterned after boy-meets-girl formats of early Hollywood movies. Even long after the Philippines attained its independence, the American influence prevailed. Love themes camouflaged in vaudeville-type productions have long attracted wide audiences, although none of these films has received much attention outside the country.

Changes in the social norms and shifts in political currents are reflected in many of the films produced in the 1970s and 1980s. As the society became less traditional, filmmakers started experimenting with new ideas that exposed the darker side of life in the Philippines. An array of soft-core pornographic films called "bomba" movies went beyond the boundaries of exploration to the point of exploitation. One such movie which won rave reviews nationally was *Burlesque Queen*. In spite of the fury of the religious sector and the censorship board, the graphic depiction of the life of a female stripper won the approval of the film community, allowing movies with similar themes to dominate the industry in the 1970s. Films such as *Manila by Night*, *Kontrobersyal*, and *Brutal* followed the same lines, each one creating a scandal, only to encourage production of movies more intense and pornographic.

The revolutionary spirit in the 1980s didn't escape the already-unconventional film community. *Sister Stella L.* is a movie about a nun who led a popular protest of blue-collar workers against a powerful corporate magnate. In a similar vein, *Balweg* is a true story of a rebel priest who joined the communist insurgents in the mountains during the Marcos era. *Bulaklak ng City Jail* attacks the legal establishment by showing the violent experiences of an incarcerated woman. Another noteworthy movie, *Gabi na, Kumander*, explores the contrasts of Filipino society and ideology, depicting the conflict between a military man and his radical brother.

SINGAPORE

Singapore—a modern city-state—sits on a small island at the end of the Malay Peninsula. It is also an enclave of Chinese culture sandwiched between two predominantly Muslim nations, Indonesia and Malaysia. This nation has a singular and fixed vision that focuses on productivity and achievement. It seems that Singaporeans are always going somewhere to do something. Indeed, even leisure is performed on a certain schedule and in designated venues set by the government.

The country prides itself on order and effective management. Facilities and services are the best in Southeast Asia. Everything, from housing to eating, is centralized, organized, and properly bureaucratized. What Singapore does not have is space. As a result, the government has managed to relocate most of the population into high-rise housing estates. These estates, with their precisely planned features and government-legislated organization, are symbolic of the Singaporean government and its extensive control of almost every aspect of life.

But in spite of controls and uniformity, Singapore is also a marvelous cultural enigma. Although a majority of the population is Chinese, there are substantial minorities of Malays, Indonesians, and Indians. Diversity is everywhere, continually asserting itself in the face of conformity. In most sections of the city, uniformity of design and purpose is complemented by a flair and originality that reflects the cultural panoply of Southeast Asia. The discordant sounds of Chinese funerals and the vaguely familiar melodies of local bands playing at Malay weddings are continually heard in housing estates. Hawkers in food centers sell everything from Chinese soup to Malay versions of hamburgers, from Indian curries to tropical-fruit shakes. Turbaned Sikhs and businessmen in Western-style dress walk side-by-side with Indian women in saris. The range of food and the diversity of restaurants are nothing short of amazing. In the face of such mind-boggling variety, one entrepreneur has even designed a "food map" of Singapore, which lists the best of everything and where to find it.

Life in Singapore, because of the large number of Europeans and Americans, can appear deceptively Western. But, despite the Western-influenced forms in architecture and government and the Western-style clothes and fast-food restaurants, Singapore is very Asian. A personal understanding of this fact—that the people of Singapore are not Westerners with Asian faces—is well worth the investment of time and energy required. Living in the "crossroads" of Asia, where East truly meets West, is a remarkable experience.

—*Joseph Stimpfl, Lincoln, Nebraska*

Official name: Republic of Singapore. **Area:** 224 square miles (smaller than New York City). **Population:** 2,703,000. **Population density:** 11,910 inhabitants per square mile. **Capital and largest city:** Singapore (pop. 2,703,000). **Language:** Malay, Chinese (Mandarin), Tamil, English (all official). **Religion:** Buddhism, Christianity, Islam, Taoism. **Per capita income:** US$6,200. **Currency:** Singapore dollar. **Literacy rate:** 85%. **Average daily high/low*:** January, 86°/73°; July, 88°/75°. **Average number of days with precipitation:** January, 17; July, 13.

TRAVEL

A passport is required for U.S. citizens traveling to Singapore; however, a visa is not required for tourist stays or social visits of up to 90 days. Visas are required for other

---

*All temperatures are Fahrenheit.

purposes. You'll also need a return or onward ticket. Check with the Embassy of the Republic of Singapore (1824 R Street NW, Washington, DC 20009) for specific requirements.

Getting Around

There are a number of ways to get around this small island-nation, which is comprised chiefly of the city of Singapore. Taxi, bus, or foot are the most popular means. Explorer bus tickets allow you to board any Singapore or Trans-Island Bus and break up your journey as often as you wish. Most road signs are in English, and you'll be able to rent a car without any problem (an International Driving Permit is required); driving is on the left-hand side of the road. Taxis in Singapore are metered, honest, and decently priced. Singapore's brand-new mass transit system has two main lines: the north-south line runs from Yishun to Marina Bay and the east-west line connects Pasir Ris near the airport to Boon Lay. Trishaws (pedicabs) can also be rented. For those who want to travel north, a causeway connects the island with the Malaysian mainland, and there is both bus and train service from Singapore to Kuala Lumpur.

Singapore boasts of being the cleanest city in Asia, and steep fines for littering are enforced. The city authorities also are not tolerant of long hair, beards, or disheveled-looking clothing. If you want to be welcome in Singapore and not be bothered, you will have to conform to their standards and tastes.

"The great masses of Singaporeans live in tremendous housing complexes where Chinese, Indians, Malays, even Europeans intermingle. Singapore is in the process of nation building—that means living together, finding a common language (quite a problem when even the Chinese don't all speak the same language) and creating a common culture."
—Ilse Brunner, Minneapolis, Minnesota

Especially for Students

STA, a student travel organization that originated in Australia, has three offices in Singapore:

- 02-17 Ming Court Road, 1 Tanglin Road, Singapore 1024
- Canteen No. 5, Singapore Polytechnic, 500 Dover Road, Singapore 0513
- Nanyang Technological Institute, Students' Union, Nanyang Avenue

Students with the International Student Identity Card can get reduced airfares on international flights from Singapore here. However, there aren't many other discounts available to cardholders in Singapore.

Accommodations in Singapore are generally the most expensive of any other city in Southeast Asia. Students with the International Student Identity Card can get special rates in several tourist-class hotels, but even then they are not cheap. There are also several Ys in Singapore where relatively inexpensive accommodations can be found. Check at an STA office.

For Further Information

General information on tourism can be obtained from the offices of the Singapore Tourist Promotion Board in Los Angeles (8484 Wilshire Boulevard, Suite 510, Beverly Hills, CA 90211), Chicago (333 North Michigan, Suite 818, Chicago, IL 60601), and New York (590 5th Avenue, 12th floor, New York, NY 10036). The best guidebook for the budget traveler is *Malaysia, Singapore and Brunei: A Travel Survival Kit*. It can be ordered for $18.95 (plus $1.50 book-rate postage; $3 for first-class) from Lonely Planet Publications (Embarcadero West, 112 Linden Street, Oakland, CA 94607).

WORK

Nonresidents must apply for an employment pass. Applicants must be sponsored by an employer, who must prove that the skills necessary for the position are not available among the country's work force. The application is processed by the local sponsor in Singapore. For more information contact the Embassy of Singapore, 1824 R Street NW, Washington, DC 20009.

Internships/Traineeships

A program offered by a member of the Council on International Educational Exchange is listed below.

AIESEC-US. Reciprocal internship program for students in economics, business, finance, marketing, accounting, and computer science. See page 18 for more information.

STUDY

A program offered by a CIEE-member institution is listed below. Consult Appendix I for the address where you can write for more information. In addition to the program below, Indiana University offers a program open only to its own students.

Semester and Academic Year

General Studies

State University of New York at Albany. Academic year. Liberal arts and business administration or intensive study of Mandarin Chinese at the National University of Singapore. Juniors and seniors with 3.0 GPA. Apply by February 15.

THAILAND

Thailand, a land famous for the friendly smiles of its inhabitants, might be excused for grinning a bit more broadly these days. The past few years have seen the Thai economy grow at the world's fastest rate, spurred on by low-cost exports and a booming tourist industry. Economists are already anointing the country as the next "Asian Miracle," and travel magazines are busily touting its tropical beaches, hill-tribe cultures, and historical monuments as "must see" items on travel itineraries. Not even the shock of the bloodless military coup in February 1991 has been able to dampen Thailand's prospects. Some observers are now seeing a silver lining in the coup's cooling effect on Thailand's hot-running economy.

Thailand's current prosperity and stability is even more remarkable given the problems facing other countries in the region. Unlike neighboring Myanmar (Burma), Cambodia, Vietnam, and Laos, Thailand has maintained a relatively stable and functioning government. Since its inception in 1932, Thailand's constitutional monarchy has remained intact despite repeated military coups and attempted coups. Though it suffers from rampant vote-buying and corruption, the Thai political system continues to operate without significant opposition. King Bhumibol Adulyadej, currently the world's longest reigning monarch, receives much of the praise for this accomplishment. His selfless efforts to assist the poorest of the poor contrasts sharply with the often venal and material interests of political and military leaders.

Thailand has also managed to avoid the sort of ethnic and social divisions that plague many of its neighbors. Buddhism, which is the state religion and one of the country's most pervasive institutions, helps to maintain social harmony. One of Thailand's most enduring images is the early morning ritual of monks collecting food from store owners and villagers. Young Thai males still show respect to their parents by ordaining as monks. The Thai live-and-let-live attitude also ensures that minority groups such as Muslims, Hill Tribes, and ethnic Chinese are not left out of the picture.

All this does not mean that Thailand is immune from its share of problems. Environmental degradation, inadequate infrastructure, rural poverty, and a severe AIDS crisis threaten to slow or derail Thailand's future development. Even Thailand's widely successful tourism industry, which is the country's largest foreign currency earner, must eventually ask how much is too much. In the process of chasing tourist dollars, marks, and yen, Thailand runs the risk of turning its vital cultural traditions and art forms into mere tourist commodities. In facing these challenges in the 1990s, Thailand must utilize the same resourcefulness that made the past decade such a success.

—*Andrew Shaw, New York, New York*

Official name: Kingdom of Thailand. **Area:** 198, 456 square miles (about twice the size of Wyoming). **Population:** 54,890,000. **Population density:** 277 inhabitants per square mile. **Capital and largest city:** Bangkok (pop. 4,700,000). **Language:** Thai, Chinese, English. **Religion:** Buddhist. **Per capita income:** US$771. **Currency:** Baht. **Literacy rate:** 89%. **Average daily high/low*:** Bangkok: January, 89°/68°; July, 90°/76°. **Average number of days with precipitation:** Bangkok: January, 1; July, 13.

TRAVEL

U.S. citizens need a passport to enter Thailand; however, a visa is not required for visitors arriving and departing by air, staying 15 days or less, and possessing an onward/return ticket. Transit visas cost $10 and are good for stays of up to 30 days; tourist visas good for stays of up to 60 days are available for $15. Nonimmigrant and business visas are $20 and permit the holder to stay in the country for up to 90 days. A four-month double-entry visa is available for $20. For specific requirements, check with the Royal Thai Embassy (2300 Kalorama Road NW, Washington, DC 20008) or with one of Thailand's consulates in New York, Los Angeles, or Chicago.

Getting Around

An efficient network of trains is run by the State Railways of Thailand, which offers service to most parts of the country. Thai trains are comfortable, punctual (though slow), and inexpensive. You can also get connecting service to Malaysia and Singapore. The "Rail Travel Aids" counter in Bangkok's Hualampong Station has train schedules; you can also ask here about the 20-day Thailand Rail Pass, available in two colors: blue (unlimited second- and third-class travel, supplemental charges not included, around $55) and red (supplemental charges included, around $110). Bus service is crowded but inexpensive and available throughout the country. Buses are fairly comfortable; air-conditioning is available and some buses even show video movies. Thailand is a good country

---

*All temperatures are Fahrenheit.

for renting a car; traffic is manageable (except in Bangkok), highways are in good condition, and most directional signs are also in English. Avis and Hertz are represented, although you might get a better deal with smaller local companies. You can also rent motorcycles and scooters. An International Driver's License is required and insurance is mandatory.

Minibuses or vans that operate between cities and towns, dropping off and picking up people along the way, are another option. An enjoyable alternative to land transport is the passenger boat service from Bangkok north along the Chao Phya River to Ban Pan and Ayutthaya, the ancient capital of the Kingdom of Siam. Thai Airways provides frequent service from Bangkok to the other major cities as well as to Phuket, an island off Thailand's west coast that is rapidly developing as an international tourist destination.

The chief means of getting around Bangkok used to be via the city's many canals. However, while canals are still prevalent in certain parts of the city, more and more they are being filled in to allow the construction of modern roads. Today, Bangkok is a bustling city that seems to contain far more than its share of traffic jams and new construction projects.

Council Travel offers a variety of tour options in Thailand, including trekking in the mountains of the north and visits to important historical, archaeological, and scenic sites. Some tour itineraries also include Burma and other parts of Southeast Asia. Contact a Council Travel office for more information.

Especially for Students and Young People

Thailand's student travel organization is the Educational Travel Centre (ETC), Room 318, Royal Hotel, 2 Rajdamnoen Avenue, Bangkok 10200. Their office provides travel information, books accommodations, and buys plane, bus, and train tickets. STA (Australia's student travel organization) also has an office in Thailand; it's located at the Thai Hotel, 78 Prachatipatal Road, Bangkok 10200.

Holders of the International Student Identity Card get a discount on international airfares from Bangkok as well as discounts at a number of hotels in Bangkok, Chiang Mai, Pattaya, and Phuket. Reduced rates are also available for a wide range of tours, from a half-day boat tour of Bangkok's floating market to a four-day river rafting trip on the River Kwai to a 12-day trekking adventure in northern Thailand. Inquire at ETC and STA offices for details.

"Many are intimidated by the seeming difficulty of the ancient Thai language. However, basic grammar and syntax are fairly easy to master in a short time. The most difficult aspect of the language is pronunciation. Each word can be spoken in five different tones—low, middle, high, rising, or falling—and each tone gives the word a different meaning. Also, be sure you know how to count in Thai, as bargaining is a common practice."

—Howard Rabinovich, Paterson, New Jersey

For Further Information

For general tourist information, contact the Tourism Authority of Thailand in New York (5 World Trade Center, Suite 3443, New York, NY 10048) or Los Angeles (3440 Wilshire Boulevard, Suite 1100, Los Angeles, CA 90010). The best guidebook for budget travelers is *Thailand: A Travel Survival Kit* ($13.95) available from Lonely Planet Publications, Embarcadero West, 112 Linden Street, Oakland, CA 94607 (include $1.50 book-rate postage; $3 for first-class). An interesting book for anyone expecting extensive interaction with the people and culture of Thailand is *A Common Core: Thais and North Americans*, by John Paul Fieg. The book can be obtained for $11.95 (plus $1.50 for shipping) from the publisher, Intercultural Press (PO Box 700, Yarmouth, ME 04096).

WORK

In order to work in Thailand, a nonimmigrant visa (rather than a tourist visa) is necessary. Then, to get a work permit, you will need to apply at the Department of Labor and have an employment contract in which your prospective employer specifically states the terms and length of employment. Foreigners seeking casual employment should not expect to be able to find work or obtain the necessary work permit.

Internships/Traineeships

Programs offered by members of the Council on International Educational Exchange are listed below.

AIESEC-US. Reciprocal internship program for students in economics, business, finance, marketing, accounting, and computer science. See page 18 for more information.

Association for International Practical Training.
"IAESTE Trainee Program." On-the-job training for undergraduate and graduate students in technical fields such as engineering, computer science, agriculture, architecture, and mathematics. See page 18 for more information.
"Hotel & Culinary Exchanges Program." On-the-job training for young people beginning a career in the hotel and food-service industries. Participants must have graduated from a university or vocational school and possess at least six months of training or experience in the chosen field. Training usually runs from 6 to 12 months. Consult Appendix I for the appropriate address.

Voluntary Service

WorldTeach sponsors a volunteer teaching program in Thailand; for more information see page 26.

STUDY

The following programs are offered by CIEE-member institutions. Consult Appendix I for the addresses of the colleges and universities listed in this section. In addition to the programs below, the University of California offers a program open only to its own students.

Semester and Academic Year

General Studies

Council on International Educational Exchange. "Cooperative Southeast Asian Studies Program." Khon Kaen. Thai language and area studies. Fall or spring semester. Sophomores to seniors with 2.75 GPA and one Asian studies course. No language prerequisite. Apply by April 15 for fall; October 15 for spring. Contact University Programs Department.

Experiment in International Living/School for International Training. "College Semester Abroad." Chiang Mai. Fall or spring semester. Intensive language, seminar in Thai life and culture, development study, field-study methods seminar, village excursions and homestay, and independent-study project. Sophomores to seniors with 2.5 GPA. Apply by May 15 for fall and October 15 for spring.

International Student Exchange Program. Direct reciprocal exchange between U.S. universities and Thammasat University in Bangkok. Summer, semester, or academic year. Full curriculum options. Open only to students at ISEP-member institutions.

St. Olaf College. "Term in the Far East." Japan, Taiwan, China, and Thailand. Fall semester plus January. Cross-cultural experience with academic study of the non-Western world, including three-month family stay in Chiang Mai, Thailand. Sophomores, juniors, and seniors. Apply by March 1.

University of Wisconsin—Madison. Chiang Mai. Academic year. Participants normally complete a summer course in Thai language and culture at Madison prior to departure. Sophomores to seniors with 3.0 GPA. Apply by February 1.

Summer

Western Michigan University. "Thailand: An Educational Adventure." Bangkok, Chiang Mai, Hong Kong. Study in education. Open to graduate students and teachers. Apply by May 15.

EXPLORING THAI CULTURE

Readings

As Thailand is unique in the region for having never been under colonial rule, its society and culture make for an interesting comparative study alongside the rest of southeast Asia. For an excellent account of turn-of-the-century Thai society in contrast with China, read *Letters from Thailand*. Translated by Susan Fulop Morrell, these letters from Bangkok were written by a Chinese visitor to his family.

An important writer as well as a leading personality in contemporary Thailand, Kukrit Pramoj has been a movie actor, journalist, and Prime Minister. His historical novel *Si Phaendin* (Four Reigns) follows the life of a woman named Ploi as she comes of age in the Royal Thai court during the turn of the century. This book covers the crucial period of 1892–1946 when "Siam" evolved into the modern state of Thailand.

Pira Sudham is one of the most important chroniclers of rural Thai society. *Monsoon Country* (1987)—written in English while the author was living in England—presents a semi-autobiographical account of a poor farmer boy who by the strength of his intellect gains an education in Bangkok and London only to return to his home. *People of Easarn* (1988) describes life in Thailand's poorest region, detailing the hardships of vast, arid plains while exploring a rich, ancient culture.

A new release, *Behind the Painting and Other Stories*, introduces English readers to Siburapha (Kulap Saipradit). Siburapha began as a writer of popular romances but took a political turn after World War II. Imprisoned from 1952 to 1957, he later found asylum in China. *Behind the Painting and Other Stories* contains one love story and three political tales.

VIETNAM

For Americans, at least, Vietnam is a name freighted with near mythic significance. Now increasingly accessible, travel to Vietnam is perhaps the best way to begin to dispel wartime images and appreciate the country and culture within a broader historical context.

More importantly, visiting Vietnam enables the traveler to view the Vietnamese people on their own terms, rather than through the distorting lenses of the various foreign powers against whom they have struggled.

By any economic measure, Vietnam is currently among the world's poorest nations, having been ravaged by decades of war, socialist experimentation, and isolation from international commerce. The average citizen's annual per capita income hovers around US$200, and severe shortages in the country's basic infrastructure are readily apparent. The recent collapse of its communist benefactors in Eastern Europe and the U.S.S.R. has added to Vietnam's hardships, as has the ongoing U.S. trade embargo. Nevertheless, enormous strides have been taken with market reforms introduced by the socialist government in the last couple of years, and given the nation's large petroleum and mineral resources as well as the dynamism of its educated workforce, there is reason to be hopeful about the future, especially as relations with the U.S. move toward normalization.

Against the scars of war and widespread evidence of poverty, Vietnam's physical beauty is unexpectedly alluring. Lush tropical scenery abounds; the terrain is washed by rivers that flow down from verdant inland mountains through dense jungle forests to the pristine coastlines of the South China Sea.

The Vietnamese people tend to be warm and friendly, eager to renew contacts with the Western world. Despite successive periods of domination by foreign powers—China, France, the U.S.—the Vietnamese are a proud people, with rich artistic, literary, and religious traditions which remain strong today.

Evidence of former north-south divisions linger on in the stark contrast between Hanoi and Ho Chi Minh City. Every inch the stately capital, Hanoi is a city of elegant tree-lined avenues, lakes, and parks. Soviet-inspired edifices dot the city (Workers' Cultural Palace, Ho Chi Minh's Mausoleum). Vestiges of nearly 100 years of colonial rule, graceful French-style villas now in dusty disrepair, line the boulevards of the central city. One of Hanoi's most striking sights is an imposing replica of the Paris Opera House, which sits at the end of a narrow downtown street.

By contrast, Ho Chi Minh City is a bustling commercial hub, which plays the role of New York City to Hanoi's Washington, DC. Ho Chi Minh City functions at both a geographical and an ideological distance from the capital city, experimenting more openly with free-market principles and foreign cultural influences. One of the best ways to see this busy metropolis is to venture into the crowded streets on the back of a motorscooter or in a hired pedicab.

Exploring Vietnam invokes a barrage of intense sensory impressions. Despite the scarcity of automobiles in the cities, you will be struck by the din and the dust raised by the continuous traffic of passing motorscooters and bicycles, with the occasional ox-drawn cart or diesel exhaust-spouting truck or bus. Given the tropical climate, much of life is lived out of doors, and sidewalks are lined with vendors selling everything from quick meals to haircuts, French *baguettes* to farm produce, and dental work to bicycle repairs. Western visitors attract considerable curosity and attention from local citizens, whose recent international contacts have largely been limited to Soviet or Eastern European tourists.

Vietnam is poised to enter a period of rapid social and economic change, during which it seems likely to emerge once again as a significant force within Southeast Asia. Visitors today are in a unique position—able to appreciate Vietnam's recent past, and also to catch a glimpse of its future.

—*Margaret Shiba, New York, New York*

Official name: Socialist Republic of Vietnam. **Area:** 128,401 square miles (the size of New Mexico). **Population:** 68,488,000. **Population density:** 519 inhabitants per square mile. **Capital:** Hanoi (pop. 3,100,000). **Largest city:** Ho Chi Minh City (pop. 3,900,000). **Language:** Vietnamese (official), French. **Religion:** Buddhism, Confucianism, Taoism. **Per capita income:** US$180. **Currency:** Dong. **Literacy rate:** 78%. **Average daily**

high/low*: Hanoi: January, 68°/56°; July, 91°/78°. Ho Chi Minh City: January, 89°/70°; July, 88°/75°. **Average number of days with precipitation:** Hanoi: January, 7; July, 15. Ho Chi Minh City: January, 2; July, 23.

TRAVEL

In the recent past, it was only possible to arrange a tourist visa to Vietnam in neighboring Bangkok, Thailand. But recently these restrictions have been lifted. Now you can obtain a visa through the Vietnamese Mission to the United Nations (20 Waterside Plaza, New York, NY 10010). Contact the Mission for the proper application forms. The process takes at least six weeks and costs US$90. Tourist visa time-limits vary according to individual needs.

Still, it may be easier and less expensive to arrange a visa and onward ticket to Vietnam through a travel agent in Bangkok. The largest such agency is Diethelm Travel (Kian Gwan Building 11, 140/1 Wireless Road, Bangkok 10500). There are, however, many smaller agencies that may offer the service for less.

The U.S. government continues to keep its own restrictions in place, limiting the amount of money U.S. citizens can spend in Vietnam, a well as the value of articles they can bring back into the U.S. For current regulations, contact the Licensing Division, Office of Foreign Assets Control, Department of the Treasury, 1331 G Street NW, Washington, DC 20220.

Getting Around

Air Vietnam makes daily flights between Ho Chi Minh City (Saigon) and Hanoi. It's possible to make stopovers in several cities along the way. Tickets must be bought with American dollars, but the flights are reasonably priced. However, tickets are hard to reserve or purchase outside of Vietnam.

The national rail line, parts of which are very scenic, winds up along the coast from Ho Chi Minh City to Hanoi and points north. Trains come in two classes, hard-seat and hard-sleeper, and are very slow, taking two days to travel the 1,000 miles (1,759 km) from Hanoi to Ho Chi Minh City. As for domestic flights, demand for seats exceeds their number; early booking is therefore advisable. Reservations can only be made for trains originating from the city you're in. Tickets must be paid for in U.S. dollars, and prices are artificially inflated above what locals have to pay, making long trips almost as expensive as flying. You may be able to insist on paying in Vietnamese dong, in which case you will still pay more than the locals, but less than you would in dollars. Generally, airfares are a much better deal, but short trips by train can be fun.

Buses go everywhere. Most cities have several stations that serve as points of departure to different parts of the country; make sure you're in the right terminal. Most Vietnamese buses are very old and suffer frequent breakdowns, though some express buses, which make few stops, run smoothly.

Vietnam's highway system is generally good, especially the southern roads built by U.S. armed forces. Cars with drivers can be rented from government and private concerns, but self-drive cars are nearly impossible to find. In the cities, cyclos or pedicabs are an inexpensive way to get around. Probably the best way to travel between cities and villages is by bicycle, as many Vietnamese do themselves. The terrain is flat and you can stow your bike on both trains and buses. And while it's difficult to rent one, you can buy a cheap bike or bring your own. Hitchers generally have no problem finding rides but, as always, are wise to exercise caution.

---

*All temperatures are Fahrenheit.

Another option for seeing the country is presented by the numerous passenger boats and ferries that operate out of the Red River and Mekong River deltas.

For Further Information

One of the best guidebooks to Vietnam is Lonely Planet's *Vietnam, Cambodia and Laos: A Travel Survival Kit*. Brand-new in 1991, this carefully researched book is full of detailed advice for the budget traveler to this seldom-visited country (the visa section, however, is already out of date). You can order the book for $15.95 (plus $1.50 book-rate postage; $3 for first-class) from Lonely Planet Publications, Emabarcadero West, 112 Linden Street, Oakland, CA 94607. Also good is *The Vietnam Guidebook*, by Barbara Cohen, available for $18.95 from Eurasia Press, 168 State Street, Teaneck, NJ 07666-3516.

WORK

Voluntary Service

Volunteers in Asia sponsors a volunteer teaching program in Vietnam for graduates with a B.A. degree and teaching experience. It is strongly recommended that the applicant have ESL or TOEFL training and language skills, or experience living and working in Asia. Volunteers serve for one year. For more information contact Volunteers in Asia, Vietnam Program, PO Box 4543, Stanford, CA 94309.

STUDY

The following educational programs are offered by CIEE-member institutions. Consult Appendix I for the addresses of the colleges and universities listed below.

Semester and Academic Year

General Studies

Experiment in International Living/School for International Training.
"College Semester Abroad." Hanoi. Intensive language, seminar on Vietnamese life and culture, field-study methods seminar, homestays, independent-study project, and excursions. No language prerequisite. Sophomores to seniors with 2.5 GPA. Apply by October 31 for spring; May 31 for fall.
"College Semester Abroad." Ho Chi Minh City. Intensive language, seminar on Vietnamese life and culture, field-study methods seminar, homestays, independent-study project, and excursions. No language prerequisite. Sophomores to seniors with 2.5 GPA. Apply by October 31 for spring; May 31 for fall.

Council on International Educational Exchange.
"Cooperative Southeast Asian Studies Program." Hanoi. Fall or spring semester. Vietnamese language, history, and society. Sophomores to seniors with 2.75 GPA and one Asian studies course. No language prerequisite. Apply by April 15 for fall; October 15 for spring. Contact University Programs Department.

CHAPTER TWELVE
AUSTRALIA AND THE SOUTH PACIFIC

Spread over the vastness of the South Pacific is an array of small islands that can be loosely grouped into Polynesia, which stretches from New Zealand to Hawaii, and Melanesia, which extends from Fiji to New Guinea. Most Americans know little about these islands, except for images of white beaches, turquoise lagoons, and deep green vegetation. These images are not unfounded, but the region also has a varied cultural and political life that is also worth exploring. Formerly colonies of Britain or France, a number of newly independent nations—with unfamiliar names like Kiribati, Vanuatu, Tuvalu—have emerged in the South Pacific in the last two decades.

Australia, on the other hand, occupies a larger portion of the American psyche. A number of popular films, ranging from *Gallipoli* to *Crocodile Dundee*, have provided a fresh perspective on this rugged, vast land and the uniquely wry character of its people. As airfares to the region decrease, Australia and its surrounding islands are seeing a sharp rise in visitors from the U.S.—succumbing, perhaps, to promises of "another shrimp on the barbie" with their name on it. Many see Australia and its kiwi-growing neighbor, New Zealand, as one of the last real frontiers left. Both Australia and New Zealand are virtual havens for nature enthusiasts, with unparalleled opportunities for all types of outdoor activities including bushwalking, scuba diving, mountain climbing, and surfing. This is not to mention the collection of indigenous flora and fauna—the kangaroo, the platypus, the Tasmanian devil, and the kookaburra are only part of the exotic menagerie. There are also clean, modern cities, such as Auckland, Sydney, and Melbourne, that provide the artistic and cultural enticements associated with large metropolises: museums, nightclubs, opera, and a great pub music scene.

Romantic images of the South Pacific, as depicted in the paintings of Gauguin, persist. Indeed, many of the less inhabited islands may seem to be paradise on earth. Equally enticing are images of Australia's Outback as one of the planet's last great open areas where humans have not yet had much effect on nature. Part of the interest in this portion of the world is that it is one of the last to be industrially developed. In the South Pacific islands, and even in the modern nations of Australia and New Zealand, the feeling of an unspoiled vastness remains.

Getting There

APEX and promotional fares are offered by most carriers flying between the U.S. and Australia. Some fares even include stopovers in Honolulu, Tahiti, Fiji, or other South Pacific islands. Sample *one-way* fares from the U.S. to the South Pacific region in effect during the summer of 1991 are listed below. For more up-to-date information, contact any Council Travel office (see listing on pages xix—xxi).

San Francisco–Sydney	$995
Los Angeles–Auckland	$995
Los Angeles–Nandi	$575
Honolulu–Sydney	$660

Holders of the International Student Identity Card (see page 8) or the International Youth Card (see page 10) are eligible for reduced airfares from several major European cities to points in Australia and the South Pacific. And with some student/youth fares,

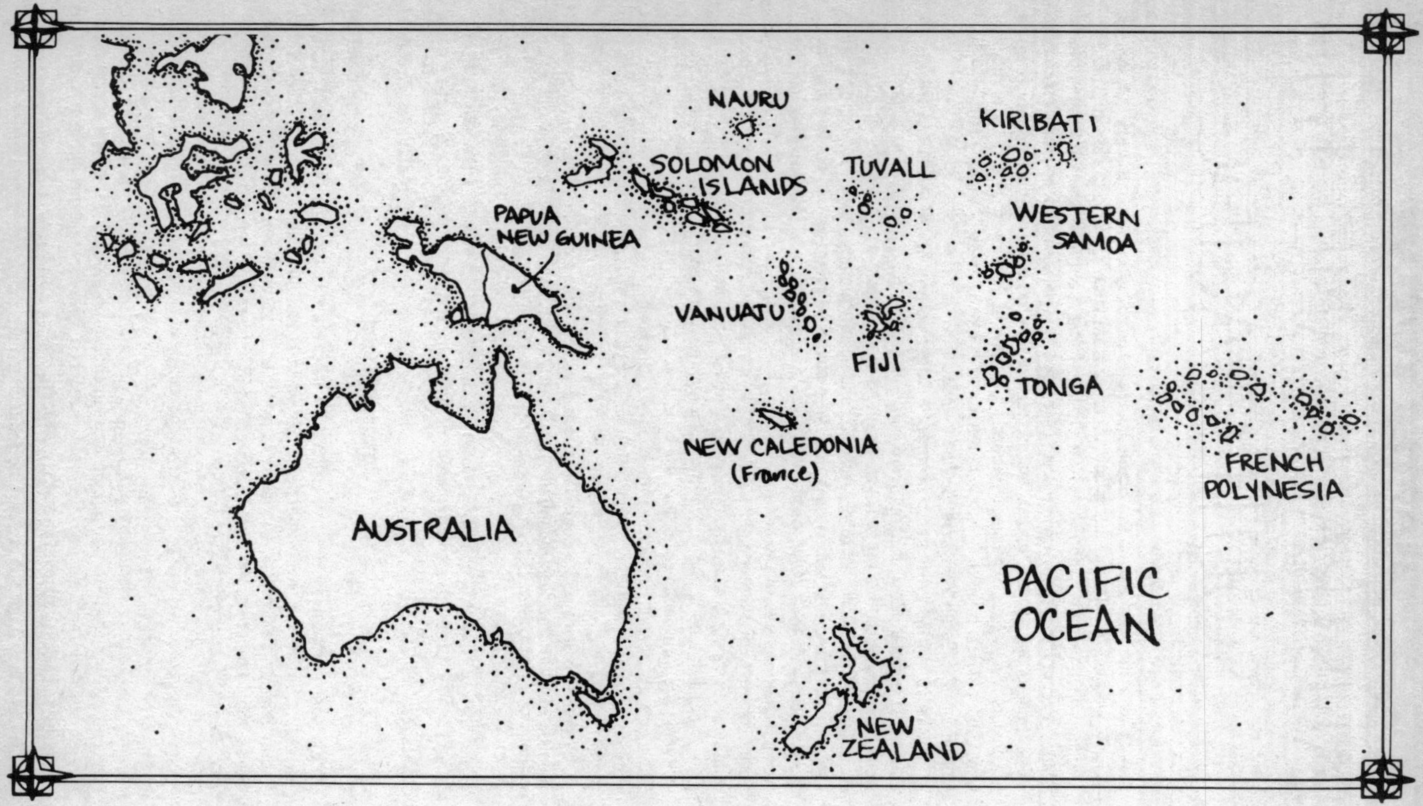
NAURU
KIRIBATI
SOLOMON ISLANDS
TUVALL
PAPUA NEW GUINEA
WESTERN SAMOA
VANUATU
FIJI
TONGA
NEW CALEDONIA (France)
FRENCH POLYNESIA
AUSTRALIA
PACIFIC OCEAN
NEW ZEALAND

stopovers in Asian cities along the route are permitted. For example, in 1991, Thai Air's one-way student/youth fare from London to Sydney was $905 and one way from Athens to Perth was $785; both permitted a free stopover in Bangkok. Council Travel offices have up-to-date information.

If you're departing from an Asian city, you can also take advantage of student/youth fares to Sydney. To be eligible, you must meet the same requirements as those described above for youth/student fares from Europe. These fares can be booked through any Council Travel office. Sample fares in effect during the summer of 1991 are listed below:

Bangkok–Sydney	$455
Singapore–Sydney	$369
Hong Kong–Sydney	$575

Getting Around

The island-nations of the South Pacific are connected by regular air service, provided mostly by Air Pacific and Polynesian Airlines. Routes from Australia or New Zealand to the smaller islands are also served by larger carriers. Because the territory of the South Pacific is so far-flung, travel between the archipelagos can be an expensive matter. Within each country's island chain, however, domestic air service is generally quite cheap. Some sample *round-trip* regional airfares in effect during the summer of 1991 are listed below:

Sydney–Auckland	$ 449
Auckland–Fiji	$ 587
Sydney–Tahiti	$1,150

A number of regional air passes or special multiflight fares make Pacific travel a little more affordable. Polynesian Airways' Polypass ($999) is valid for 30 days of unlimited travel over the airline's South Pacific routes. In addition, it includes one round-trip each from Western Samoa to Australia and New Zealand. The Polypass cannot be used for travel beginning in the months of December or January. It can be purchased in the U.S., Australia, or Fiji.

Air Pacific offers several less expensive Pacific Air Passes which include neither New Zealand or Australia. For $449 you can travel between Western Samoa, Tonga, and Vanuatu; $499 adds Fiji to this itinerary; $549 includes the Solomon Islands. The Pacific Air Pass is good for 30 days. It can be purchased in the U.S. through Qantas Airlines (800-227-4500).

The best deal in Pacific air travel, at $383, is Polynesian Airlines' Pacific Triangle Fare. Good for a full year, this fare allows one trip each, in a continuous direction, between Western Samoa, Fiji, and Tonga.

While travel by plane is certainly the most effortless and direct way to get around the islands, it isn't the only way. Once you're in the South Pacific, it isn't too difficult to find a boat going where you want, assuming you're headed for one of the larger ports. Cruise ships, of course, are costly. But it's possible to work your passage on some freighters. Perhaps the greatest boon to island-hopping travelers are private yachts in need of extra crew. Crew members usually work for free and share the cost of food and other necessities. It helps to have some knowledge of sailing, but even the inexperienced should be able to find a ride (except during hurricane season, November through March). You can try your luck at marinas and boating clubs, or look for notices in newspapers and boating magazines. Essentially, this method of travelling is a form of hitching; the same precautions that apply to hitchhiking on land should be used at sea. If you accept a ride on a boat, you can't get off until you've reached your destination. Women should be especially careful, or travel in pairs with men.

For Further Information

The comprehensive *South Pacific Handbook*, by David Stanley, is the best general guide to this little-known but vast expanse of islands. It's available for $15.95 (plus $3.50 postage) from Moon Publications, 722 Wall Street, Chico, CA 95928. David Stanley has spent many years wandering the Pacific and knows the region well. His books show you how to get around (especially helpful if you want to crew on yachts) and give a good account of South Pacific history and culture. Among his other guides (also available from Moon Publications) are the *Tahiti-Polynesia Handbook* and the *Micronesia Handbook*, both $9.95.

Lonely Planet publishes a plethora of detailed travel guides to the South Pacific's many island groups. There are *Travel Survival Kit*s for Micronesia, New Caledonia, Papua New Guinea, Rarotonga and the Cook Islands, Western and American Samoa, Solomon Islands, Tahiti and French Polynesia, Tonga, and Vanuatu. Write for a catalog to Lonely Planet Publications, Embarcadero West, 112 Linden Street, Oakland, CA 94607.

Listed below are addresses where you can write for general information as well as details on visa requirements on some of the smaller nations not covered in separate country sections later in this chapter:

- Nauru Consul, Davies Pacific Center, 841 Bishop Street, Suite 506, Honolulu, Hawaii 96813
- Embassy of Solomon Islands, 910 17th Street NW, Suite 331, Washington, DC 20008
- Mission of Western Samoa to the United Nations, 820 Second Avenue, New York, NY 10017
- Tonga Consulate General, 2900 Vallejo Street, San Francisco, CA 94123

AUSTRALIA

Australia, the only continent occupied by a single country, is a young nation in which egalitarianism runs deep amid increasing ethnic diversity. Its indigenous population is the Aborigines who migrated to Australia at least 30,000 years ago and invented, among other things, the boomerang and an amazingly sophisticated sign language. Great Britain claimed the continent in 1770, but did little with it until the American Revolution, when it decided to use the region to house its convicts. The prisoners were followed by thousands of European (mostly British) settlers, who were soon joined by American miners in search of gold discovered in 1853. Today, four in 10 Australians are either immigrants or the children of immigrants—active people looking to build a new life. Originally from European nations, but now increasingly from elsewhere, immigrants have helped push the nation towards the adoption of multiculturalism as national policy.

A member of the British Commonwealth, Australia recognizes Queen Elizabeth II as its official head of state, but is governed by a prime minister and parliament seated in Canberra, a planned city created to serve as the nation's capital.

Sixty percent of Australia's 17 million people live in the five largest cities, all with populations exceeding one million and all located on the coast. This leaves much of Australia's 7.6 million square kilometers very sparsely populated. And with good reason: 50 percent of Australia has less than 12 inches of rainfall a year. This aridity has not limited the development of Australia's flora and fauna. Indeed, it may have even favored the marsupials, animals like kangaroos with pouches for the young. Australia is the only continent where this fauna grouping has become so prevalent, evolving for millions of years in almost complete isolation. Australia boasts intriguing indigenous animals like the koala, the Tasmanian devil, the platypus, and the kookaburra, as well as imported (now wild) buffalos, rabbits, and camels.

While an Asian or African visitor probably would see Australia as a Western nation, Australia is taking advantage of its Pacific Rim location, and enthusiasm for expanding Asian trade and communications is rising. Americans or Europeans might see many cultural similarities between their nations and Australia, but the differences are substantial. Australian society is neither European nor North American—nor is it merely a mixture of the two. A unique history, cultural makeup, and topography have all had a hand in the construction of the sardonic, egalitarian Australian character.

Australians have a heritage of antiauthoritarianism, directness, and a self-mocking brand of humor. For example, in restaurants, service is usually friendly but never servile. The implicit assumption is of equality and tipping is usually not expected. Today, there is an increased confidence in being Australian and an increasing examination of just what that means.

—Simon Avenell, Perth, Australia

Official name: Commonwealth of Australia. **Area:** 2,966,200 square miles (about ¾ the size of the U.S.). **Population:** 16,460,000. **Population density:** 5.4 inhabitants per square mile. **Capital:** Canberra (pop. 273,300). **Largest city:** Sydney (pop. 3,500,000). **Language:** English. **Religion:** Protestant, Roman Catholic. **Per capita income:** US$14,458. **Currency:** Australian dollar. **Literacy rate:** 99%. **Average daily high/low*:** Melbourne: January, 78°/57°; July, 56°/42°. Perth: January, 85°/63°; July, 64°/48°; Sydney: January, 78°/65°; July: 60°/46°. **Average number of days with precipitation:** Melbourne: January, 9; July, 17. Perth: January, 3; July, 19. Sydney: January, 14; July, 12.

TRAVEL

U.S. citizens will need a passport and visa to enter Australia. A visitor visa is valid for an unlimited number of visits over a three-year period. Proof of onward or return transportation is required for each entry, however. For specific details check with the Australian Embassy (1601 Massachusetts Avenue NW, Washington, DC 20036) or with an Australian consulate in Los Angeles, San Francisco, Honolulu, Chicago, Houston, and New York.

Getting Around

Keep in mind that Australia is a very large country, with much of it sparsely populated. Most of the nation's population is concentrated in five state capitals—Sydney, Melbourne, Brisbane, Adelaide, and Perth. The traveler will have to cross long distances between these population centers.

"If time in Australia is short, plan the holiday carefully so as to include at least some of the outback areas of the country. The cities are exciting, but the outback is extraordinary."

—Thomas Lundberg, Syracuse, New York

Due to the great distances involved, Australians (or Aussies as they generally call themselves) often travel by air. Several Australian airlines offer discounts on internal flights for international visitors. QANTAS, for example, offer discounts of up to 50 percent to overseas visitors. Two domestic carriers, Ansett and Australia Air, offer "See Australia" airfares to non-Australian residents equivalent to 25 percent off regular economy fares. They must be purchased in conjunction with journeys begun outside Australia on international round-trip excursion or promotional airfares, however, and all travel must

---

*All temperatures are Fahrenheit.

be completed within 60 days of your arrival in Australia. Eastwest Airlines, a domestic carrier affiliated with Ansett, offers eight combinations of Eastwest Airpasses, each restricting the pass holder to a specific direction or travel itinerary and valid for a specified number of days (usually either 14 or 60). For example, the Sun Airpass costs AUS$769 (US$600) and permits travel up to 60 days in a circular route; the Coastal Airpass is good for one-way directional travel on Eastwest's services from Cairns to Hobart or vice versa. It is valid for 60 days of travel and can be purchased in the U.S. for US$525.

Australia's rail system is both a slower and cheaper alternative for getting around the country. The rail network links the five state capitals and serves Alice Springs in the Northern Territory as well. The famous trans-Australian run from Adelaide to Perth covers some 1,316 miles and takes two days and two nights. Going all the way across the continent from Sydney to Perth takes even longer. A good bargain for anyone planning to travel around Australia by train is the Austrain Budget Pass, which entitles you to unlimited rail travel for 14 days (US$344), 21 days (US$444), one month (US$540), two months (US$772), or three months (US$888). However, the pass must be purchased before entering Australia. A "Kangaroo Road 'n' Rail Pass" is also available; it provides unlimited travel on government-owned railways plus Greyhound coaches throughout Australia within a 28-day period.

Bus travel is generally faster and almost as cheap as the train. There are four major bus companies: Pioneer Express, Deluxe, Bus Australia, and Greyhound Australia. Pioneer offers the Aussiepass and Greyhound has the Bus Pass, both of which entitle you to unlimited bus travel anywhere in Australia served by that particular line. The Greyhound Bus Pass is sold in seven-, 10-, 15-, 21-, 30-, 60-, 90-, and 120-day versions; at press time the 7-day pass cost US$241.60, the 15-day pass is US$388.80, the 30-day pass is US$651.20, and the 60-day pass runs US$1,069. With Bus Australia's FlexiPass, youth hostel association members receive a 10-percent discount.

Renting a car in Australia costs about the same as renting one in the United States. Aussies drive on the left-hand side of the road—which, in the outback, might be poorly paved or full of wild buffalo. The biggest car rental companies in Australia are Hertz, Avis, Budget, and Thrifty, and you can get rates and make reservations by calling their toll-free numbers in the U.S. Campervans and mobile homes can also be rented for longer journeys. Ferries operate between the mainland and Tasmania; contact the Tasmanian Travel Centre at 256 Collins Street, Melbourne (03-635-7999), for information.

Hitchhiking is common. As long as the hitchhiker stands off the road, it is legal in all states of Australia except Queensland.

"Women shouldn't hitchhike alone, and hitchhiking in Queensland should be avoided altogether, since it is illegal there and carries a hefty fine. I hitched with another girl from Sydney to Melbourne, and we made it there in 13 hours, met some terrific people, and saw some interesting countryside."
—Julie Clawson, St. Louis, Missouri

Especially for Students and Young People

Student Travel Australia (STA) has offices in Sydney (1A Lee Street, Sydney, New South Wales 2000), as well as in Adelaide, Brisbane, Canberra, Darwin, Melbourne, and Perth. STA, affiliated with SSA (Student Services Australia), provides a wide range of services for student travelers, including plane or bus tickets, accommodation bookings, local tour sign-ups, and travel information. A number of unique adventure tours are also offered by STA, including "Reef Exploring" (11 days) and tours through the outback.

The International Student Identity Card is good for a number of discounts in Australia, including reduced fares on international flights from Australia (Australian Air and Eastwest) as well as discounts with certain companies on bus transportation and hotels. Contact STA for further information and ask for their free brochure listing student discounts in

Australia. The International Youth Card is good for discounts on international flights from Melbourne and Sydney to Bangkok.

Eating and Sleeping

There are a number of options for travelers seeking inexpensive accommodations in Australia. Possibilities include:

- Hostels: For $7, the American Youth Hostels Association will send you a copy of the *Australian Handbook*, which lists the many hostels throughout the country. Write to AYH, PO Box 37613, Washington, DC 20013-7613, or call (880) 673-2733. The Australian Youth Hostel Association (PO Box 61, Strawberry Hills, Sydney, 2012, New South Wales) also has a brochure that lists hostels and includes a map that shows how to get to them.
- YMCAs and YWCAs: For a *YWCA of Australia Accommodation Directory*, write to National Headquarters, YWCA of Australia, PO Box 171, Clifton Hills, Victoria 3068. YMCAs and YWCAs are also listed in Frommer's *Australia '91–'92 on $40 a Day* (see "For Further Information" below).
- University dormitories: The Australian Tourist Commission can provide you with a booklet entitled *Campus Accommodation*, which lists university accommodations available during vacation periods—December through February, May, and August through September. These accommodations are open to all—not just students. With an International Student Identity Card you also can get access to cafeterias and student union facilities—gyms, libraries, and so on.

If you are planning on staying in one place for a while, another possibility is to go to the nearest university housing office or youth hostel bulletin board and check listings to see who is seeking a roommate to share a flat.

There are a number of commercial campgrounds around the country—one of the cheapest accommodation alternatives. Most of these, however, lie far from the center of towns and therefore are not very practical unless you have a vehicle. Campgrounds generally cater to "caravaners" (persons with house trailers or campers) rather than tent campers. But you can still pitch a tent and take advantage of the hot showers, laundry facilities, drinking water, and more. Most tourist offices in Australia have a list of campgounds.

"Outside the major cities, Australia is one big campout. It is a good country to travel in with a sleeping bag, as there is always a place to throw it in relative safety."
—Nick Ragsdale, Mobile, Alabama

Meeting the People

Friends Overseas: Australia (FOA) offers a meet-the-people plan that informally brings American visitors together with residents, matching people with similar interests. FOA provides you with names and addresses of Australian members that you then contact on your own. The membership fee is $25. For more information, contact Friends Overseas: Australia, 68–01 Dartmouth Street, Forest Hills, NY 11375, or call (718) 261-0534.

"Much of the social life in Australia revolves around the local pubs—they are some of the best places to meet the Aussies."
—Victoria Schwartz, Columbia, South Carolina

For Further Information

For general tourist information, contact the Australian Tourist Commission (489 Fifth Avenue, 31st floor, New York, NY 10017). Ask for a copy of their 128-page booklet *Destination: Australia*. There are several guides designed especially for the budget traveler in Australia, and *Australia: A Travel Survival Kit* is one of the best. You can order it for $19.95 (plus $1.50 book-rate postage; $3 for first-class) from Lonely Planet Publications (Embarcadero West, 112 Linden Street, Oakland, CA 94607). Another such guide is Frommer's *Australia on $40 a Day*, which can be picked up at most bookstores for $13.95. In both books you'll find information on getting around and cheap places to stay and eat, as well as historical and sightseeing information. A good guide for those interested in hiking in various regions of Australia is Lonely Planet's *Bushwalking in Australia*, by John and Monica Chapman, available for $8.95. Lonely Planet also publishes *Islands of Australia's Great Barrier Reef—A Travel Survival Kit* ($16.95).

WORK

To obtain employment in Australia, it is necessary to find an employer who is prepared to file temporary residence sponsorship papers with the Department of Immigration, Local Government, and Ethnic Affairs. The employer sponsors a particular position for a specified period of time and the Immigration Department decides whether or not that sponsorship can be approved, taking into account such factors as the need for the skills the applicant has to offer, and whether or not the position being offered can be filled through local labor sources.

If you are a teacher of Japanese or Chinese language, mathematics, or science, your skills are in demand in the public schools. Australia is currently experiencing a shortage of teachers in these disciplines. To find out about openings in these areas, write to the Education Department of the state in which you are interested in working; for specific addresses, contact the Embassy of Australia, 1601 Massachusetts Avenue NW, Washington, DC 20036.

Internships/Traineeships

Listed below are the programs offered by institutions and organizations that are members of the Council on International Educational Exchange. Consult Appendix I for the addresses where you can write for more information. In addition to the programs below, Moorhead State University offers a program open only to its own students.

AIESEC-US. Reciprocal internship program for students in economics, business, finance, marketing, accounting, and computer science. See page 18 for more information.

Association for International Practical Training.
"IAESTE Trainee Program." On-the-job training for undergraduate and graduate students in technical fields such as engineering, computer science, agriculture, architecture, and mathematics. See page 18 for more information.
"Hotel & Culinary Exchanges Program." On-the-job training for young people beginning a career in the hotel and food-service industries. Participants must have graduated or be currently enrolled in a university or vocational school and possess at least six months of training or experience in the chosen field. Training usually runs from 6 to 18 months.

Curtin University. Internships (up to 12 months) in Perth for majors in liberal arts, business, agriculture, engineering, and the health sciences, with or without credit. The Public Affairs Office at the university assists North American students in locating a suitable position. For more information, contact Curtin University, North American Office, 2 Appletree Square, Suite 144, 8011 34th Avenue South, Minneapolis, MN 55425.

Voluntary Service

The Australian Trust for Conservation Volunteers sponsors service opportunities for six-week terms that involve tree planting, erosion-control work, and fence construction. Participants stay in trailers, tents, farm houses, or shearer's quarters; no special skills are required. For more information, contact the Australian Trust for Conservation Volunteers, PO Box 423, Ballarat, Victoria, Australia 3350.

"The opportunity, not only to visit Australia, but to actually to work there provided me with a far better understanding of the culture. As a worker, I was viewed differently than a tourist and accepted with more enthusiasm by the locals."
—Kristina MaLean, Tampa, Florida

STUDY

Persons considering applying to an Australian institution of higher education should write an Australian consulate to get a copy of their information packet *Study in Australia*, which provides basic information on visas, fees, application procedures, exchange programs, and so on. Another good publication is *Australian Study Opportunities*, which provides annually updated information about studying in Australia as well as information about the various programs of specific schools. Most Australian consulates can supply you with these publications.

Students considering direct enrollment should be aware that Australian students entering a university are generally at a higher educational level than their American counterparts. The sophomore or junior year of an American university is considered the equivalent of the first year at an Australian university.

The school year in Australia extends from early March to late November. In general, student life in Australia is lived with zest. You will be welcomed warmly and should have no trouble being accepted. Regulations allow full-time students with a student visa to work up to 20 hours a week on a casual basis during their course of study, and during vacations overseas students can work full time.

The following academic programs are offered by CIEE-member institutions. Consult Appendix I for the addresses of the colleges and universities listed below. In addition, California State University, Colorado State University, Cornell University, Lewis and Clark College, Pennsylvania State University, the University of California, and the University of Oregon offer programs open to their own students only.

Semester and Academic Year

Australian Studies

Gustavus Adolphus College. "Gustavus at Melbourne." Semester or academic year. Full curriculum options at the University of Melbourne. Juniors and seniors with 2.75 GPA. Apply by October 1 for spring semester; March 1 for fall.

Michigan State University. "Australia: Its People, Government, Justice System, and Public Policies." Sydney and Canberra. Winter quarter. Sophomores to seniors. Apply by November 20.

Engineering

University of Illinois at Urbana-Champaign. "International Programs in Engineering." Sydney. Semester or academic year. Priority given to engineering students. Freshman to graduate students. Apply by March 1 for fall and December 1 for spring.

General Studies

Council on International Educational Exchange.
"Cooperative Studies Program." Perth. Fall or spring semesters. Sophomores to seniors with 2.75 GPA. Apply by April 15 for fall; November 15 for spring. Contact University Programs Department.

Experiment in International Living/School for International Training. "College Semester Abroad." Spring or fall semester. Melbourne, with excursion to Queensland and Sydney. Interdisciplinary seminars, field-study methods seminar, homestay, and independent-study project. Sophomores to seniors with 2.5 GPA. Apply by May 15 for fall and October 15 for spring.

International Student Exchange Program. Direct reciprocal exchange between U.S. universities and institutions in Perth, Geelong (Victoria), Toowoomba (Queensland), and North Ryde (New South Wales). Semester. Full curriculum options. Open only to students at ISEP-member institutions.

Rollins College.
"Rollins Academic Year in Melbourne." Sophomores, juniors, and seniors with 2.8 GPA. Apply by March 1.
"Rollins Fall Term in Sydney." Sophomores, juniors, and seniors with 2.8 GPA. Apply by March 1.

State University of New York at Plattsburgh. Bond University, Gold Coast. Fall, spring, or summer. Sophomores to seniors with 3.0 GPA. Apply by June 1 for fall; October 1 for spring; February 1 for summer.

University of North Carolina—Chapel Hill. "Australia, Wollongong." Semester or academic year. Sophomores, juniors, seniors, and graduate students with 2.7 GPA. Apply by November 1 for spring; April 1 for fall.

University of Oregon.
Curtin University in Perth. Freshman to graduate students with 3.0 GPA. Apply by October 15 for spring and year; March 1 for fall.
La Trobe University in Melbourne. Academic year. Freshmen to graduate students with 3.0 GPA. Apply by October 15.

Natural and Human Environment

Experiment in International Living/School for International Training. "College Semester Abroad." Spring or fall semester. Cairns, Queensland, and field trips to ecologically important sites. Ecology and field-study method seminars, independent-study project, and homestay. Sophomores to seniors with 2.5 GPA. Apply by May 15 for fall and October 15 for spring.

Teacher Education

State University of New York College at Buffalo. Adelaide. Fall semester. Teacher education and liberal-arts courses. One-for-one exchange with the South Australian College of Advanced Education. Sophomores, juniors, and seniors with 3.0 GPA. Apply by January 15.

AUSTRALIA AND THE SOUTH PACIFIC: AUSTRALIA   **389**

EXPLORING AUSTRALIAN CULTURE

Readings

Contemporary Australian literature is marked by a strong interest in the past. Peter Carey's *Oscar and Lucinda* (1988), a novel set in the mid-19th century, illustrates the strange turns that love, religion, commerce, and colonialism took in the Victorian Age. Patrick White's *Voss* (1957), an account of a German explorer leading an expedition deep into the hostile continent, also looks backward into Australian history.

A number of Australian books deal with the current and historical situation of the Aborigines. Randolph Stowe's *To the Islands*, for example, is the surreal saga of a disillusioned missionary who embarks on a voyage of self-discovery through the desert to the Aboriginal islands of the dead. Thomas Keneally, a Catholic writer, deals with the problems that arise when a half-caste Aborigine tries to integrate into mainstream Australian society in *The Chant of Jimmy Blacksmith* (1972). (This book was made into a film, produced by Fred Schepisi in 1978.) For an historically accurate novel of the Aborigines, read Colin Johnson's *Dr. Wooreddy* (1989). Set in the nineteenth century, this book deals with the relationships the Aborigines had with the convicts, the pioneers, and other groups they encountered. *The Songlines* (1990), by Bruce Chatwin, explores aboriginal conceptions of Australia's vast geography.

If you're looking for Australian classics, you may want to read *Such Is Life* (1944), by Joseph Furphy (alias Tom Collins), and *My Brilliant Career*, by Miles Franklin. *Such Is Life* is an affirmation of the country lifestyle in Australia. *My Brilliant Career*, originally published decades ahead of its time in 1901, deals with the terrible conflicts of a young girl coming of age in a man's world. The main character, Sybylla Melvyn, has ambitions that stretch far beyond her place and time—a small-town village in the Australian outback in 1895.

A woman's view of life in Australia is provided by several contemporary Australian writers. Jessica Anderson's romantic novel, *Tirra Lirra by the River* (1978), focuses on an old woman's reflections on her life in Australia during the 1920s, 1930s, and 1940s. Jill Conway's *The Road from Coorain* (1989) is an autobiographical account of her youth, and *My Place* (1988), by Sally Morgan, presents the story of her Aboriginal family history. The struggle of growing up in Australia from a male point of view is the focus of *Johnno* (1975), by David Malouf.

To get a flavor of some of the varied social groups in Australia, *Hunting the Wild Pineapple*, by Thea Astley, presents a compilation of short stories that involve hippies, cane cutters, and pioneer families, among others. For an insight into contemporary life in Sydney, be sure to read Kate Grenville's book of short stories, *Bearded Ladies* (1985). In another collection of short stories, *The Fat Man in History*, Peter Carey offers a relentless critique of modern Australian society.

Films

Beginning in the 1970s, a flurry of Australian filmmaking activity has produced a variety of films. Perhaps dominant among these, at least in terms of popularity and visibility outside Australia, are the "ocker" movies. An "ocker" is slang for the archetypal uncultivated Australian working man: boorish, uncouth, and chauvinistic, but always a good mate with a wonderful sense of humor. Bruce Beresford's *The Adventures of Barry McKensie* (1972) is a classic example of this type of film; more recent examples are the *Crocodile Dundee* films (1986, 1988) and Yahoo Serious's *Young Einstein* (1988).

Nationalism is a prime topic of Australian film and can often be found hand-in-hand with the concept of Australian "mateship." Peter Weir's *Gallipoli* (1981) is a historical drama about the World War I massacre of Australian soldiers by the Turks (and the British). Bruce Beresford's *Breaker Morant* (1979) is an anti-imperialist film about the

British using three Australian soldiers as scapegoats during the Boer War. Both of these films frame an attitude toward the British colonial period through its effects on Australia's young men.

Australia's "Aboriginal question" is detailed in a number of films including *The Last Wave* (1977), by Peter Weir, which represents the distance between the Aborigine and white worlds, evidenced by a group of Aborigines living in caves below Sydney. Nicholas Roeg's *Walkabout* (1971) formulates a comparison and contrast of the two cultures through the interaction of a young Aboriginal male and two suburban, white children.

Praised for its aesthetics, *Picnic at Hanging Rock* (1986) presents the Australian landscape brilliantly. This film (which is also a book) takes place in 1900, when a group of girls from an elite private school decide to go on a picnic at Hanging Rock, and disappear.

"Australia is much influenced by American culture, and you will find the people quite knowledgeable about U.S. politics and policies. But beware of assuming that Australians are 'just like Americans.' Part of the fun of getting to know Australia is learning to appreciate the differences between its culture and that of the U.S."
—Patricia Lancaster, Winter Park, Florida

FIJI

"The Crossroads of the Pacific," Fiji is situated about halfway along the main air route between the U.S. and Australia. Its largest island, Viti Levu, is the major communications and transportation hub of the South Pacific. Its capital city, Suva, is home to the University of the South Pacific, jointly operated by 11 island-nations. Comprised of over 300 scattered islands—of which 100 are inhabited—Fiji encompasses a myriad of peoples and cultures, including Melanesians, Polynesians, Micronesians, Indians, Chinese, and Europeans.

The earliest Fijians were themselves a hybrid race of Melanesian and Polynesian descent whose society is formed by patriarchal tribes. These seagoing people were long feared by European sailors as fierce warriors and cannibals. European and American traders, supported by their various governments, battled over control of the islands' valuable resources until 1874, when the Fijian ruler ceded the islands to Great Britain.

British colonial rule created the political conditions which persist to this day. In a move to preserve the Fijian tribal structure, the British decreed early on that their communal land could never be sold to nonindigenous Fijians, only leased. At the same time, thousands of Indian laborers migrated to Fiji to work the sugarcane fields. The result of this colonial practice is a system in which Fijians own the vast majority of the land while Indians and part-Fijians dominate the business world.

Since independence in 1970, Fijian politics have centered on issues of race. In the weeks following the 1987 victory of Dr. Timoci Bavadra's Fiji Labour Party in national elections, Fijian landowners began a series of violent protests against what they claimed to be Indian domination. In the ensuing unrest, Lieutenant Colonel Stivendi Rabuka ousted Bavadra and took over the government in a military coup. Although Rabuka handed over rule to a nominally civilian government at the end of 1987, many Indians—who previously formed the majority of the population—have departed, seeing no future for themselves in the closed political system. In fact, many of Rabuka's policies, such as the return of power to the old aristocracy and the institution of a fundamentalist style of Christianity as the state religion, have alienated indigenous Fijians as well. Fiji's greatest struggle will be to create a political system that equitably accommodates all groups.

Although tourism dropped off in the wake of the 1987 coup, recently it has begun to pick up again—and for good reason. Fiji's beautiful beaches, unspoiled rain forests, and fascinating ocean reefs make it one of the South Pacific's natural treasures. And the coexistence of traditional Fijian and Indian peoples makes for a unique blend of cultures.

Despite past political unrest, most Fijians and Indians are at peace with one another and are extraordinarily hospitable to visitors. It's more than likely that you will be invited on several occasions to stay in local homes or asked to participate in village activities. Travelers are accepted with greater respect in Fiji than perhaps in any other country, as long as they respect the local culture in turn.

—Alice Tabor, Cheyenne, Wyoming

Area: 7,056 square miles (about the size of New Jersey). **Population:** 772,000. **Population density:** 107 inhabitants per square mile. **Capital and largest city:** Suva (pop. 69,000). **Language:** English (official), Fijian, Hindustani. **Religion:** Christian, Hindu, Islam. **Per capita income:** US$1,680. **Currency:** Fijian dollar. **Literacy rate:** 80%. **Average daily high/low*:** Suva: January, 86°/74°; July, 79°/68°. **Average number of days with precipitation:** Suva: January, 18; July, 14.

TRAVEL

A passport and onward or return ticket are required for U.S. citizens traveling to Fiji. For holders of U.S. passports, a visa is issued upon arrival and is good for a stay of up to 30 days; visas can be extended to a maximum of six months. Proof of financial support (a bank statement, traveler's checks, or the like) for the length of stay in Fiji is necessary. For specific requirements, check with the Embassy of Fiji, 2233 Wisconsin Avenue NW, #240, Washington, DC 20007.

Getting Around

While the international airport at Nandi is the hub of South Pacific air lanes, Suva, the nation's capital on the other side of the island of Viti Levu, is Fiji's domestic transportation center. The main domestic carrier is Fiji Air, with flights departing Suva several times a week to many surrounding islands. In general, airfares within the Fiji islands are extraordinarily low.

A variety of small shipping companies provides freight and passenger service between the inhabited islands. While traveling by boat takes longer than going by plane, the price is lower and the trip more interesting.

Ground transportation on the two major islands—Viti Levu and Vanua Levu—is by bus, truck, or taxi. Bus service, fast and reliable, is the best way to go. Car rental is easy, with all the familiar U.S. companies, but costs much more than it does in the U.S. You can also hitch, but chances are you will end up having to pay.

One of the delights of traveling in Fiji is staying in Fijian villages. Villages are communal property, so it is polite to ask permission of a resident before passing through. If you would like to stay overnight, you must personally ask the village chief (*turangani-koro*). It is customary to pay your hosts a small fee for their trouble and to present a small gift.

"Yanggona, or kava, is a mild drink made from the dried root (waka) of the pepper plant, which plays a central role in indigenous social ceremonies. You can't associate with Fijians and not drink kava at some time. With this in mind, it's a good idea to carry around a bag of waka wherever you go. A bundle of waka is a customary gift as thanks in exchange for hospitality. You can buy it in many places, and it isn't expensive."

—Brad Meir, New York, New York

---

*All temperatures are Fahrenheit.

Especially for Students and Young People

There is no student travel organization on Fiji, and no special discounts have been developed for holders of the International Student Identity Card.

For Further Information

A comprehensive guidebook for the traveler who really wants to get to know the islands is David Stanley's *Fiji Islands Handbook*, available for $8.95 (plus $3.50 postage) from Moon Publications, 722 Wall Street, Chico, CA 95928-5629. *Fiji: A Travel Survival Kit* is also very good. It's available for $11.95 (plus $1.50 book-rate postage, $3 for first-class) from Lonely Planet Publications, Embarcadero West, 112 Linden Street, Oakland, CA 94607.

WORK

It is necessary to obtain a work permit to work in Fiji. The prospective employer and employee apply jointly for the permit to the Permanent Secretary. Foreigners are hired only when there are no Fiji nationals available possessing the required skills for the position. For more information, contact the Embassy of Fiji, 2233 Wisconsin Avenue NW, Washington, DC 20007.

STUDY

A program offered by a CIEE-member institution is listed below. Consult Appendix I for the addresses where you can write for more information.

Semester and Academic Year

General Studies

International Student Exchange Program. Direct reciprocal exchange between U.S. universities and the University of the South Pacific. Semester or academic year. Full curriculum options. Open only to students at ISEP-member institutions.

NEW ZEALAND

You could rent a car at the north tip of the North Island, drive without a break, sleep while crossing the channel at Wellington, and continue driving as far south as the South Island extends. You could then boast that you'd "covered New Zealand" in 36 hours. What a loss!

You'd miss the miles of golden beaches outside Auckland, the largest and most modern of New Zealand's cities. At the volcanic plateau of Rotorua, with its bubbling mud pools and roaring geysers, you'd miss the cultural center of the Maoris, descendants of the Polynesian canoe navigators who first settled New Zealand. At Christchurch you'd miss Cathedral Square, where citizens daily "soapbox" their opinions on everything from Lady Di to the greenhouse effect against the backdrop of street musicians and food vendors. You'd miss Queenstown, with its white-water rafting and infamous bunji jumping. And you'd miss the diverse and dramatic scenery—the mountains, lakes, harbors, and capes, and the rolling hillsides smothered in sheep—that has been called paradise by Rudyard Kipling, Robert Louis Stevenson, and James Michener.

New Zealand is a country where Americans are genuinely welcome and hikers, or "trampers," are admired. Although hitchhiking is common, to do it is to miss bus drivers who will go out of their way to deliver you to your hostel door, stop at roadside fruit and vegetable stands, and pull over for particularly spectacular views of the Tasman Sea. The country also has a first-rate train system; it follows the coast down to Dunedin, a little bit of Scotland in New Zealand, and crosses the Southern Alps to the ultimate hiking experience at Milford Track or to mountain climbing at Mount Cook.

While New Zealand has just over three million people it has more than 70 million sheep and eight million cattle; it remains heavily dependent on agricultural exports such as wool, mutton, and dairy products. After Great Britain joined the Common Market and eliminated itself as New Zealand's number one importer of animal products, the nation has tried to achieve greater economic diversification. Increasingly the country's economic future is tied to Australia and Japan rather than Europe.

New Zealanders were the first people in the world to grant suffrage to women and the first U.S. ally to deny nuclear-armed and powered vessels port rights. Dominated for decades by the National Party, whose focus was on industrialization, social activism, and environmental awareness, New Zealand is currently led by the Prime Minister of the Labor Party, whose focus is on the economic stability of its three million citizens.

You'll want to spend some time getting to know the people of New Zealand, a mixture of the British, Scottish, Maori, and Pacific Islanders, who are all referred to, along with the fruit and the bird, as Kiwis. Although certain aspects of Kiwi culture appear very British, the clothing styles, the Big Band mania, the vintage cars, the radio dramas, and the popularity of James Dean and Marilyn Monroe are clearly reminiscent of the U.S. in the 1940s and 1950s. So is the pace. So take your time and move slowly.

—*Nancy Taylor, Holland, Michigan*

Area: 103,736 square miles (about the size of Colorado). **Population:** 3,397,000. **Population density:** 32 inhabitants per square mile. **Capital:** Wellington. **Largest city:** Auckland (population 806,000). **Language:** English. **Religion:** Protestant, Roman Catholic. **Per capita income:** US$11,040. **Currency:** New Zealand dollar. **Literacy rate:** 99%. **Average daily high/low*:** Wellington: January, 69°/56°; July, 53°/42°. **Average number of days with precipitation:** Wellington: January, 10; July, 18.

TRAVEL

U.S. citizens will need a passport (valid for three months beyond your entry date) and an onward or return ticket; for stays of less than three months, a visa is not required. Proof of sufficient funds may also be required. For specific requirements, check with the New Zealand Embassy (37 Observatory Circle NW, Washington, DC 20008) or with a New Zealand consulate in New York, Los Angeles, or San Francisco.

Getting Around

The main air carriers in New Zealand are Air New Zealand and Ansett New Zealand. Ansett's New Zealand Airpass coupons permit a number of flights at discount prices. For

---

*All temperatures are Fahrenheit.

example, a coupon good for three flights costs NZ$399 (US$250). Ansett's "See New Zealand" fare offers a 20-percent discount on regular flights to foreign travelers. Both plans must be purchased in the U.S. before departure. Mt. Cook, another airline, flies mainly to tourist destinations such as Mount Cook and Rotorua. The Kiwi Air Pass, good for 30 days, allows one trip in each direction on each flight on Mt. Cook Airline for US$525.

Unless you're in a hurry, it's best to use ground transportation. Going by train and bus is inexpensive and gives you a chance to take in New Zealand's beauty.

InterCity operates New Zealand's rail network, as well as the Wellington-Picton ferry across the Cook Strait. Express trains link Auckland and Wellington on North Island, and Christchurch, Dunedin, and Invercargill on South Island. The trains are fast and reliable, but buses travel to far more destinations. Most budget travelers take advantage of both. A good way to do this is to purchase a New Zealand Travelpass, which provides transportation on InterCity trains, buses, and ferries on a number of days within a set period of time. For example, you can travel on any 22 days within a 31-day period for NZ$599 (US$378). While the Travelpass may be purchased in New Zealand, it's a bit cheaper in the U.S. (contact Swain Tours, 800-227-9246). If you plan to fly to New Zealand via Air New Zealand, you can obtain a Travelpass at a special discount price.

The Kiwi Coach Pass provides bus service on Mt. Cook Landline for varying numbers of days, ranging from 7 days within an 11-day period for US$176 to 33 days within a 45-day period for US$396. Those planning to take in Australia as well as New Zealand should look into the Downunder Coach Pass, good for passage on Greyhound lines in Australia in addition to Mount Cook Landline; Downunder passes range from US$219 for 9 days to US$716 for 45 days.

"The beauty and diversity of the land is probably unmatched anywhere in the world. In a country the size of Colorado you will find beaches, farmlands, volcanoes, geysers, snowcapped mountains, fjords, forests, lakes, and glaciers. New Zealand preserves the characteristic traditions of both its British and Polynesian peoples and remains one of the last unspoiled frontiers of the world."
—Jennifer Borth, Wilmington, Delaware

New Zealand's road system is exceptionally well maintained, except in a few very mountainous areas. Driving around on your own will be no problem, since traffic is generally light and roads are well marked. But remember, driving is on the left-hand side of the road. Gasoline prices are high but controlled by the government so that the price is the same at every station in the country. While all the major car-rental firms are represented in New Zealand, you'll probably be better off with less expensive local agencies. Most rental contracts include unlimited mileage.

Bicycling is becoming an increasingly popular way to see New Zealand. The terrain is hilly, but the country is compact and the climate is mild. Bicycles may be rented by the hour or the day in most cities, or you can bring yours with you (contact the airlines for more information). An informative guide for the cyclist is *Cycle Touring in New Zealand*, available for $14.95 (plus $2 shipping) from Mountaineers Books, 1011 S.W. Klickitat Way, Suite 107, Seattle, WA 98134.

Hitchhiking is popular with students in New Zealand (helpful New Zealanders often give young people rides). Another way to see parts of New Zealand, and one that's popular among young people, is hiking, or "tramping" as New Zealanders call it.

"New Zealand has some of the world's best backpacking. The most famous trails are the Milford Track (open November to March only), which has to be booked through the chief ranger at Fiordland National Park; the Routeburn Track, summer only unless you're experienced; and the Heaphy Track near Waikaremoana. All these require good boots, cooking gear, sleeping bags, and waterproof and woolen clothing."
—Paula Mills, Sacramento, California

AUSTRALIA AND THE SOUTH PACIFIC: NEW ZEALAND

Especially for Students

Student Travel Services (NZ) is the country's student travel organization and issuing agency for the International Student Identity Card. The main office is located in Auckland at 10 High Steet, but they also have offices in Christchurch, Dunedin, Hamilton, Palmerston North, and Wellington, as well as two others in Auckland. These offices can provide general information, book local tours, arrange accommodations, and sell plane and bus tickets.

Students with the International Student Identity Card can get a 50-percent discount on standby fares on domestic airlines as well as discounts on international flights from New Zealand. There are also special fares available to International Student Identity Card holders on certain bus lines and discounts at a number of shops and movie theaters. Further information is available from student association offices at universities around the country.

Eating and Sleeping

The Youth Hostels Association of New Zealand (YHANZ) administers a network of large and small hostels scattered throughout the country. Hostels are situated in most urban centers as well as near beaches, ski areas, and national parks. The YHANZ National Reservations Centre can arrange bookings for all hostels as long as they have 14 days' notice; November to March is the busiest time. YHANZ also offers a series of "go it alone" tours combining public transportation and accommodations in YHA hostels. For further information, write to YHANZ, PO Box 436, Christchurch 1, New Zealand.

Students visiting New Zealand during summer vacations (December to March) can usually take advantage of available space at university dormitories. These kind of accommodations are inexpensive and often near the center of town. Travel information offices can direct you to local dormitory accommodations.

For Further Information

For general tourist information, contact the New Zealand Tourist Office, 502 Santa Monica Boulevard, Suite 300, Santa Monica, CA 90401. Probably the most comprehensive guidebook for the budget traveler is *New Zealand: A Travel Survival Kit*, which includes information on how to get around, where to go, and where to stay as well as special sections on tramping and skiing. It's available for $15.95 (plus $1.50 book-rate postage; $3 for first-class) from Lonely Planet Publications (Embarcadero West, 112 Linden Street, Oakland, CA 94607). Also good is the *New Zealand Handbook*, by Jane King. It can be ordered for $14.95 (plus $3.50 postage) from Moon Publications (722 Wall Street, Chico, CA 95928).

WORK

Getting a Job

To get a full-time job in New Zealand, it is necessary to obtain a written offer of employment from the prospective employer. A list of occupations with openings is available from the Embassy of New Zealand. After securing a job offer, a work visa is necessary. For more information, contact the Embassy of New Zealand, 37 Observatory Circle NW, Washington, DC 20008.

For American students seeking temporary work in New Zealand, however, the process is much simpler. CIEE's Work in New Zealand program gives college and university students the opportunity to seek temporary employment for up to six months between April 1 and October 31. The program is conducted through an agreement with the Immigration Division of the Department of Labour of New Zealand and the Student Travel Services (NZ). To qualify, an individual must be at least 18 years of age, a college or university student, and a U.S. citizen or permanent resident. The cost of the program is $125. Since the work exchange program began in 1979, more than 1,600 U.S. students have participated, most doing unskilled outdoor work such as shearing sheep, picking fruit, or working at a ski resort. For more information, contact CIEE's Work Exchanges Department.

"I traveled and worked in New Zealand more than I actually stayed in one place and worked. This meant finding jobs en route on farms and homesteads, which proved to be an enriching experience. Jobs weren't difficult to come by, generally speaking, but you have to be willing to try anything for a week or two."
—William P. Huxley III, New York, New York

Internships/Traineeships

A program offered by the Council on International Educational Exchange is listed below.

AIESEC-US places students in internships in fields such as economics, business, finance, marketing, accounting, and computer science. See page 18 for more information.

Voluntary Service

For persons interested in voluntary-service work, the Year Abroad Program sponsored by the International Christian Youth Exchange offers persons ages 18 to 24 voluntary-service opportunities in the fields of health care, education, the environment, construction, et cetera. See page 23 for more information.

STUDY

The school year in New Zealand extends from early March to late November. According to the New Zealand consulate in New York, the admission of overseas students to New Zealand educational institutions is limited due to the heavy domestic demand for available spots.

A program offered by a CIEE-member institution is described below. Consult Appendix I for the address to write for more information. In addition to those listed here, the University of California and California State University both have programs open only to their own students.

Summer

University of Alabama. "Study Tour of New Zealand." South Island and Christchurch. Sociology and resource development. Freshmen to graduate students.

EXPLORING THE CULTURE OF NEW ZEALAND

Readings

Maurice Shadbolt's *The New Zealanders* (1972) is a collection of enjoyable short stories. Janet Frame's life growing up in a poverty-stricken New Zealand family is recounted in *An Angel at My Table* (1984) and *Owls Do Cry* (1982). (Both of these books have been made into films.) As New Zealand's most famous Maori writer, Patricia Grace gives voice to a culture living amidst an alien society. Her short stories have been collected in *Waiariki* and *The Dream Sleepers and Other Stories*.

Films

The last ten years have seen a burgeoning production of full-length fiction and documentary films in New Zealand. These films focus on many of the same themes that currently garner attention in films throughout the world; however, many also deal with questions of race, national identity, and cultural colonialism that are specific to New Zealand.

Two films, *Skin Deep*, by Geoff Steven, and *Came a Hot Friday*, by Ian Mune, provide perspectives on small-town New Zealand. *Skin Deep* exposes the inner workings of a local community through a satire on civic pride. *Came a Hot Friday* steps back to 1949 to give a stylized impression of a small town which combines two con men with guns, fast cars, fast women, liquor, and a dash of cultural colonialism.

As with Native Americans and Australian Aborigines, the societal status of New Zealand's Maori is an important and sometimes volatile topic. *Utu*, by Geoff Murphy, is a historical fiction about a Maori warrior rebellion in connection with the Anglo-Maori wars of the 1870s. The documentary *Patu*, by Merata Mita, on the other hand, takes a more contemporary stance by documenting the South African rugby team Springbok's 1981 tour of New Zealand and the opposition, attitudes, and violence it provoked.

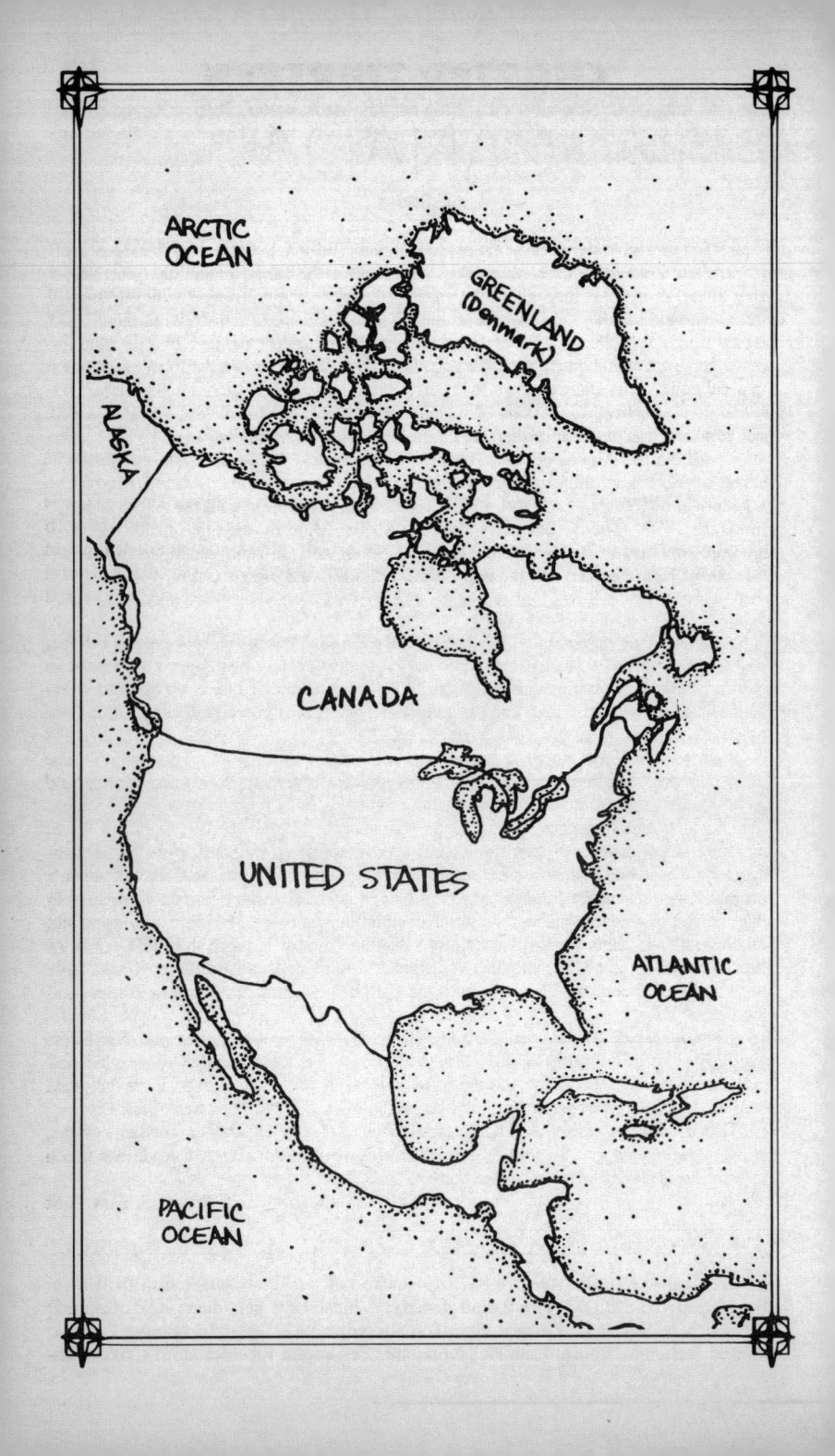

ARCTIC OCEAN
GREENLAND (Denmark)
ALASKA
CANADA
UNITED STATES
ATLANTIC OCEAN
PACIFIC OCEAN

CHAPTER THIRTEEN
CANADA

Although Canada is sometimes regarded as little more than America's 51st state, visitors soon become aware of the distinct, refreshing qualities of this beautiful and diverse country. True, the United States and Canada have a lot in common, including many of the same natural features: the fjords of the Pacific coast, Rocky Mountain peaks, craggy Atlantic Ocean inlets, as well as the wheat fields, forests, and lakes in between. But when asked to define their national identity, most Canadians will launch into an explanation of how they differ from Americans. Whether this is symptomatic of an ingrained sense of inferiority or superiority is debatable, but it usually reflects Canadians' sheer practicality more than it does any overt anti-Americanism; while Canada shares much with the U.S., an awareness of the differences between the two countries will help us to understand Canada's unique qualities.

Larger than the U.S. in total area but only a tenth its size in population, Canada is one of the world's largest but least densely populated nations. This fact, combined with a European sense of social responsibility, is reflected in its high standard of living and its clean, uncrowded, well-organized cities. The latter boast heavily subsidized cultural offerings, excellent public transportation, and little of the homelessness and poverty that plague many large American cities.

Someone once quipped that while Canada could have benefited from French culture, British government, and American know-how, it unfortunately was shaped by American culture, French government, and British know-how. Although this is an obvious oversimplification, it is true that Canada's close ties with all three countries are still very much apparent.

In fact, one of the most striking aspects of Canadian society is its diversity. While the American "melting pot" tends to blur cultural differences, Canadian society and governmental legislation have encouraged the country's many immigrant groups to nurture their customs and languages. Established by colonists loyal to the British Empire, Canada has long since dispensed with its political accountability to England, even as English-speaking Canadians maintain great respect for this heritage. At the same time, Canada's official bilingual French-English status has helped keep the French joie de vivre alive in the French province of Quebec, the Acadian communities of the Maritime provinces, and other smaller pockets across the country. But the country is more than just a mix of French, British, and U.S. influences; different communities across the continent have become cultural centers for peoples from the Caribbean, Central and Eastern Europe, and the Pacific Rim.

Geography has also shaped Canada's diversity. The remote Yukon and Northwest Territories have a frontier atmosphere to this day. French Canada's geographic and political center, Quebec City, has the pulse and personality of a European capital. And Toronto, Canada's fast-paced financial center, is often compared to New York City.

This diversity means that whether your objective is to experience another culture, enjoy stunning scenery, or join in the excitement of a dynamic city, Canada has much to offer. And it's all just across the border.

—*Sarah Wood, Brooklyn, New York*

Official name: Canada. **Area:** 3,852,019 square miles (slightly larger than the U.S.). **Population:** 26,527,000. **Population density:** 7 inhabitants per square mile. **Capital:** Ottawa (pop. 819,263). **Largest city:** Toronto (pop. 3,427,168). **Language:** English, French. **Religion:** Roman Catholic, Protestant. **Per capita income:** US$13,700. **Currency: Canadian dollar. **Literacy rate:** 99%. **Average daily high/low*:** Montreal: January, 21°/6°; July, 78°/61°. Vancouver: January, 41°/32°; July, 74°/54°. Winnipeg: January, 7°/−13°; July, 79°/55°. **Average number of days with precipitation:** Montreal: January, 15; July, 12. Vancouver: January, 20; July, 7. Winnipeg: January, 12; July, 10.

TRAVEL

Entering Canada is easy enough for a U.S. citizen. As long as you don't intend to stay longer than three months (which may be extended to six months), you won't need either a passport or a visa. But the U.S. government recommends that you carry personal identification of some type such as a birth or naturalization certificate or a valid passport. U.S. citizens entering Canada from a third country are required to have a valid passport. Student authorization is required for persons seeking to enter Canada to attend an educational institution (more information is provided under "Study" later in this chapter). Check with the Canadian Embassy (1746 Massachusetts Avenue NW, Washington, DC 20036) or a consulate for specific details. Canadian consulates are located in Atlanta, Boston, Buffalo, Chicago, Dallas, Detroit, Los Angeles, Minneapolis, New York, Philadelphia, Pittsburgh, San Francisco, Seattle, and Washington, DC.

Getting There

Most major U.S. airlines as well as several Canadian airlines provide service between the two countries. As with domestic travel within the two countries, airfares are constantly changing—you'll have to shop around a little to get the lowest fare. Council Travel offices can provide more information and make arrangements for you. Sample fares in effect during the summer of 1991 are listed below:

	One-way	Round-trip
San Francisco–Vancouver	$256	$390
New York–Montreal	$137	$244
Chicago–Toronto	$141	$305

Most visitors from the U.S. arrive by automobile; crossing the border usually involves few formalities and is done in minutes. It's a good idea to pick up a Nonresident Interprovincial Motor Vehicle Liability Insurance Card from your insurance agent before you go, however. Although it is not required by law, it's helpful if you run into any problems while you're in the country.

For persons wishing to travel by train, Amtrak provides service from the Eastern seaboard to Montreal and Toronto, where connections can be made to Via Rail, Canada's national railroad system. International bus service is also provided by Greyhound. Call Amtrak or Greyhound for schedules and fares, or check with a travel agent.

"Most Americans just don't realize that a wonderful travel opportunity exists right under their own noses. Canada is just across the border, but it's really another world. You'll be greatly surprised to see how different much of this country is from the U.S."
—Marjorie Pease, Buffalo, New York

Getting Around

Canada's airline industry experienced the same deregulation that the American industry did early in the 1980s. Thus the fare structure, including travel restrictions on discounted

---

*All temperatures are Fahrenheit.

tickets, is similar to that in the United States. While none of the major airlines offers domestic air passes, you can arrange low-cost excursion fares with a number of stopovers across the country. Book in advance to obtain the cheapest fares. For the up-to-date information, contact Air Canada (800-776-3000) or Canadian Airlines International (800-426-7000).

One of the most exciting ways to see Canada is by train. The 3,000-mile trip from Montreal to Vancouver takes four days and three nights. Other interesting rail trips can be made across the vast wilderness areas of Canada's northern frontier; one such trip is from Winnipeg to Churchill (famous for its polar bears) on the icy shores of Hudson's Bay. Service is also available to New Brunswick and Nova Scotia. If you plan to travel extensively in Canada by train, you should look into Via Rail's Canrail pass. Valid for 30 consecutive days, it costs US$300 for young people under 24 traveling in the high season (June 1 to September 30) and US$197 for the remainder of the year (excluding Christmas). Those over 24 pay US$343 and US$231 respectively. These prices provide for coach seating only. An upper berth in a sleeper from Montreal to Vancouver, for example, will cost an extra US$156. Contact Via Rail for further information at (800) 361-3677.

Road travel in Canada is another pleasant experience. Because Canada's population remains small in proportion to its land mass, roads and highways are less crowded than they are in the U.S. And the roadsides are not so developed, which makes for more scenic drives. Bus routes are plentiful, and prices are comparable to those in the U.S. Driving your own car will allow you the most freedom. The largest car-rental firm in Canada is Tilden Rent-A-Car; for information, call its U.S. affiliate, National Car Rental. Avis, Budget, and Hertz are other major car-rental companies in Canada. In Canada, most cars rent for a per-day (sometimes a per-week) fixed fee that includes a limited number of free kilometers. However, because unlimited mileage rates are generally not available in Canada, renting a car can be an expensive proposition if you plan to cover a lot of miles. A cheaper alternative might be to rent one in the U.S., where a number of companies still offer unlimited mileage options, and then cross into Canada (make sure the rental contract allows you to take the car across the border).

"A couple of friends and I decided to take a road trip across Canada, and it was one of the best months of my life. The roads were a joy to drive, and everyone was very helpful whenever we got lost or needed a place to stay. If you have a bike, bring it: It's a beautiful country for cycling and a lot of fun to explore."
—Natasha Wittig, Corpus Christi, Texas

Canada is a cyclist's dream, though just as in the U.S., you should try to avoid major roads and use secondary routes. The best source of information is the Canadian Cycling Association (1600 James Naismith Drive, Gloucester, Ontario K1B 5N4). This organization's free brochure lists the titles and prices of its own publications as well as those of the various provincial bicycle clubs. Publications available include *The Complete Guide to Bicycling in Canada* ($12.95), *The Canadian Rockies Bicycling Guide* ($18.95), *The Great Canadian Bicycle Trail* ($15.95), and *Newfoundland by Bicycle* (free); add 15 percent of the price for postage.

For those who like the great outdoors, another option is hiking or backpacking in Canada's spectacular national parks and vast wilderness areas. Organizations that offer backpacking or camping trips include the Sierra Club of Western Canada (Room 314, 620 View Street, Victoria, BC V8W 1J6) and the Alpine Club of Canada (PO Box 1026, Banff, Alberta T0L 0M0).

A number of hiking, bicycling, and canoe trips in Canada are also offered by CIEE-member institutions. American Youth Hostels offers three summer packages: Canada's Great Divide, a 16-day hiking tour in the Rockies; Bay of Fundy Loop, a three-week bicycle tour through New Brunswick, Nova Scotia, and Prince Edward Island; and French Canadian Adventure, a 15-day bicycle tour from Montreal to Quebec City. Canada's

Association of Student Councils, through its student travel subsidiary Travel CUTS, sponsors several summer wilderness trips in Ontario, including an Algonquin Park Canoe Trip and Killarney Park Wilderness Tours. Consult Appendix I for the addresses of these two organizations.

Eating and Sleeping

You'll find a listing of Canadian hostels in *The International Youth Hostel Handbook, Volume 1* (see page 53). For information on the activities of the Canadian Hosteling Association, contact them at 1600 James Naismith Drive, Suite 608, Gloucester, Ontario K1B 5N4. Inexpensive lodging can also be found at most YMCAs and YWCAs across Canada. A directory listing their facilities is available from the YWCA of Canada (80 Woodlawn Avenue East, Toronto, M40 1C1 Ontario) or the National Council of YMCAs of Canada (2160 Yonge Street, Toronto, M4S 2A9 Ontario). In addition, most Canadian universities have residence halls open to travelers from mid-May to mid-August; you can get information on these from Travel CUTS offices or from provincial government tourist offices (addresses below).

There are virtually unlimited opportunities for camping in Canada. You can get specific information on sites and facilities from the various national and provincial government tourist offices in the United States. These offices can also give you information on affordable bed-and-breakfasts.

Especially for Students and Young People

The Association of Student Councils/Canadian Federation of Students—Services is the issuer of the International Identity Student Card and the major student travel organization in Canada. At the organization's Travel CUTS (Canadian Universities Travel Service) offices you can get information about student/youth discounts, cheap accommodations, and budget air fares (as well as the canoe trips mentioned above). You can contact Travel CUTS at 187 College Street, Toronto, Ontario M5T 1P7; Travel CUTS offices are also located in Burnaby, Calgary, Edmonton, Guelph, Halifax, Montreal, Ottawa, Quebec City, Saskatoon, Sudbury, Vancouver, Victoria, Waterloo, and Winnipeg.

By flying on a standby basis, holders of the International Student Identity Card are eligible for a discount of up to 45 percent on domestic airfares. Cardholders also get discounts on air travel from Canada to destinations around the world. In addition, over 6,000 retail establishments, museums, and theaters give discounts of 10 to 20 percent; a directory of these establishments and institutions is available free upon presentation of an International Student Identity Card at any Travel CUTS office.

For Further Information

There are branches of the Canadian government's Office of Tourism in 14 U.S. cities—the same cities in which there are Canadian consulates (see listing above). These offices have a number of useful brochures covering all aspects of travel in Canada. For specific information on any particular province, you can contact the provincial tourist office in Canada.

- Travel Alberta, (800) 661-8888
- Tourism British Columbia, (800) 663-6000
- Travel Manitoba, (800) 665-0040
- Newfoundland and Labrador Tourism, (800) 563-6353
- Arctic Territories Travel, (800) 661-0788
- Nova Scotia Tourist Information Office, (800) 341-6096
- Ontario Travel, (800) 668-2746
- Department of Tourism and Parks of Prince Edward Island, (800) 565-0267

- Tourisme Quebec, (800) 363-7777 (eastern U.S. only)
- Tourism Saskatchewan, (800) 667-7191
- Tourism Yukon, (403) 667-5340

The best general guide to the country is *Canada: A Travel Survival Kit*, available for $18.95 (plus $1.50 book-rate postage; $3 for first-class) from Lonely Planet Publications, Embarcadero West, 112 Linden Street, Oakland, CA 94607.

Those planning to explore Canada west of the Rockies will find lots of useful information in the *British Columbia Handbook* and the *Alaska-Yukon Handbook*, both available for $11.95 (plus $3.50 postage) from Moon Publications, 722 Wall Street, Chico, CA 95928-5629. Also helpful is *Let's Go: Pacific Northwest, Western Canada, and Alaska* ($14.95), published by Harvard Student Agencies.

WORK

Getting a Job

A work permit is required for regular full-time employment in Canada; application for the permit must be made from outside the country. The permit will not be granted unless it is determined that no permanent resident of Canada is qualified for the job. For the specific requirements and procedures, contact the Canadian embassy or any Canadian consulate.

The process is much easier, however, for college and university students seeking summer employment in Canada. CIEE, in cooperation with the Canadian Federation of Students, can obtain permission for you to work in Canada for a period of up to six months (May 1 to October 31). In addition to work authorization, CIEE gives participants information on living and working in Canada and details on the best way to find work. Past participants have worked in hotels, done hospitality work, housekeeping, conservation work, and reforestation, among other things. You can expect to make enough money to cover your daily living expenses and usually save something toward the cost of travel once you finish your job. To be eligible, you must be a U.S. citizen at least 18 years of age, enrolled as a full-time student in an accredited U.S. college or university, and reside in the U.S. at the time of application. There is a $125 fee for the service; applications are available from CIEE's Work Exchanges Department.

Internships/Traineeships

Programs offered by members of the Council on International Educational Exchange are listed below.

AIESEC-US. Reciprocal internship program for students in economics, business, finance, marketing, accounting, and computer science. See page 18 for more information.

Association for International Practical Training. "IAESTE Trainee Program." On-the-job training for undergraduate and graduate students in technical fields such as engineering, computer science, agriculture, architecture, and mathematics. See page 18 for more information.

Voluntary Service

CIEE places young people in voluntary service workcamps in Canada organized by the Canadian Bureau for International Education (CBIE), 85 Albert Street, Suite 1400, Ottawa, Ontario K1P 6A4. At these workcamps, volunteers from various countries work together on projects such as helping disabled children, providing social services, or helping with the maintenance and construction of recreational facilities. Volunteers receive room and board in return for their labor and must be 18 years of age or older. The applications of U.S. residents are processed by CIEE. For more information, contact the Voluntary-Service Department at CIEE.

Frontiers Foundation/Operation Beaver (2615 Danforth Avenue, Suite 203, Toronto, Ontario M4C 1L6) sponsors voluntary-service projects throughout the year. The projects, which last from 3 to 18 months, usually involve renovation/construction (low-cost housing, community centers, schools) or recreation programs. Participants from all countries are eligible, but you must be at least 18 years old. Room, board, and transportation (within Canada) to and from the project site are provided.

In addition, the Fourth World Movement sponsors work/information camps in Canada. For more information see Chapter Three.

STUDY

Many U.S. students enroll in Canadian universities and colleges each year. If you're planning on becoming one of them, you'll need special student authorization. You can get this from the Immigration Division of any Canadian consulate, but first you must present proof of funds and a letter of acceptance from the Canadian school that you will be attending. If you are going to study in the province of Quebec, a certificate of acceptance from the Quebec Immigration Service also is required.

General information on Canada's higher-education system, including admission costs and immigration requirements, can be found in Reference Paper #36, *University Study in Canada*, published by Canada's Department of External Affairs and available at Canadian consulates abroad. Most consulates can also supply you with the addresses of Canadian universities, a list of French language programs, and other materials.

The Canadian Bureau for International Education (CBIE) also provides information for foreign students in Canada. Its *International Students Handbook* includes information on everything from Canadian political history to how to obtain housing in Canada. It can be ordered for CAN$8 (about US$7) from CBIE, 85 Albert Street, Suite 1400, Ottawa, Ontario K1P 6A4.

The Canadian Embassy has established a Canadian Studies Graduate Student Fellowship that enables doctoral candidates to complete their dissertation in Canada. Details are available from the Academic Relations Section, Canadian Embassy, 1771 N Street NW, Washington, DC 20036.

Following are the study programs offered by CIEE-member institutions. Consult Appendix I for the addresses where you can write for further information. In addition to those listed below, California State University, the University of California, and the University of Rhode Island all offer programs open only to their own students.

Semester and Academic Year

English Language Institute at the University of British Columbia. Vancouver. Wide variety of English language courses. Academic year, semester, or summer. Open to students 18 years and over.

International Student Exchange Program. Direct reciprocal exchange between U.S. universities and institutions in Calgary, St. Catharines (Ontario), and Sudbury (Ontario). Semester or academic year. Full curriculum options. Open only to students at ISEP-member institutions.

State University of New York at Plattsburgh.
"Study in Toronto." University of Toronto. Academic year or semester. Sophomores to seniors with 3.0 GPA. Apply by April 1 for fall or academic year; October 20 for spring.
"Study in Quebec City." Université Laval. Academic year or semester. Sophomores to seniors with 2.5 GPA. Apply by April 1 for fall or academic year; October 15 for spring.

"Study in Montreal." McGill University. Academic year or semester. Sophomores to seniors with 3.0 GPA. Apply by April 1 for fall or academic year; October 15 for spring. "Study in Ottawa." Carleton University. Academic year or semester. Sophomores to seniors with 3.0 GPA. Apply by April 1 for fall or academic year; October 15 for spring. Contact: Study in Canada Programs, Center for the Study of Canada. SUNY Plattsburgh, Plattsburgh, NY 12901; (518) 564-2086.

Summer

French Language

State University of New York at Plattsburgh.
"French Immersion in the Summer." Montreal, Quebec City, or Chicoutimi. Six-week sessions. High-school graduates entering college, undergraduates, and graduates in good academic standing. Apply by April 1. Contact: Center for the Study of Canada, SUNY Plattsburgh, Plattsburgh, NY 12901; (518) 564-2086.

University System of Georgia/Georgia College.
Quebec. Special French language program for speakers of other languages at Laval University. All students with minimum 2.5 GPA. Apply by March 15.

University of Iowa. "CIC Summer French Program in Quebec." Sophomores to graduate students with one year of college French and 3.0 GPA. Apply by March 1.

General Studies

Michigan State University. Toronto, Ottawa, Montreal, and Quebec City. "Multiculturalism in Canada: Issues of Global Diversity." An examination of social, political, and economic issues in Canada. Freshman to seniors. Apply by April 20.

Health Services

State University of New York at Brockport. "Comparative Health Systems Overseas Study Program." Toronto. Open to graduate students in health administration with 2.5 GPA. Apply by May 1.

Natural Science

Michigan State University. Branff, Jasper, Kootenay, and Yoho National Parks. Day trips from base camps and backpacking trips to observe geology and ecology of the region. Freshman to seniors. Apply by April 20.

Physical Education

State University of New York at Brockport. "Dalhousie University Physical Education Exchange." Halifax, Nova Scotia. Fall or spring semester. Junior and senior physical-education majors with 2.5 GPA. Apply by November 1 for spring; February 15 for fall.

EXPLORING CANADIAN CULTURE

Readings

Canadian writing often seems marked by a search for a literary identity outside that of British or American styles. It is sometimes characterized by solitude and images of a vast, cold land peopled with introspective souls. Classic Canadian novels include *Settlers of the Marsh* (1925) by F. W. Grove; *The Two Solitudes* (1945), Hugh McLennan's famous novel about French and English Canada; Sinclair Ross's *As for Me and My House* (1941), the best prairie novel around; and Margaret Lawrence's *The Stone Angel* (1964).

Margaret Atwood is probably Canada's best-known contemporary writer. Her latest novel, *Cat's Eye* (1989), focuses upon a woman artist as she relives her Toronto childhood. In *The Handmaid's Tale* (1986), Atwood projects a futuristic North America dominated by patriarchial religious fundamentalists. Alice Munro, by contrast, writes about life in small rural Ontario towns in books such as *Lives of Girls and Women* (1971) or *Who Do You Think You Are?* (1978). Her collection *The Moons of Jupiter* consists of short stories set in rural and urban Canada. Another contemporary Canadian writer, Robertson Davies, uses Canada and the character of its people in such novels as *Fifth Business* (1970), *The Rebel Angels* (1982), and *What's Bred in the Bone* (1985) as metaphors for the modern world and its more bizarre and disturbing aspects.

Canada's multiculturalism is echoed in the mosaic of its literature. *Diamond Jubilee*, by John Chalmers and others, is a set of three anthologies of Alberta writers that includes works from many of the 50 identifiable ethnic groups in Alberta. Mordecai Richler, a popular Jewish writer from Montreal, is another important Canadian literary figure. His latest novel, *Solomon Gursky Was Here* (1990), is a hilarious parody of an established Jewish Montreal family; *Home Sweet Home: My Canadian Album* (1984) is a lighthearted collection of his personal reminiscences.

In Quebec, the license plates read *Je me souviens* ("I remember"), harkening back to the happier days when France ruled much of North America. The current movement in Quebec to gain independence has borne a revolutionary literature, full of vitality and linguistic tensions. This distinct genre is notable for its political humor and satire and its linguistic play on the mixture of French, English, and *Joual* (the Quebec dialect). Two prolific authors in this vein are Marie-Claire Blais (*A Season in the Life of Emmanuel*, 1966) and Roche Carrier (*The Boxing Match*, 1990). Anne Herbert is generally regarded as Canada's most important French poet of the 20th century (*Selected Poems*, 1987).

For a view of Canada from the eyes of an outsider, read *Maple Leaf Rag* (1988), by Stephen Brook. Brook is an Englishman who travels across Canada noting his perceptions humourously in this tongue-in-cheek travelogue.

Films

The bright lights of Hollywood have long drawn Canadian directors and actors southward, integrating them into the U.S. film industry. However, Canada's film community recently has been given a shot in the arm by a new crop of young filmmakers working north of the border. Toronto and Vancouver are new production centers for North American film. *Jesus of Montreal* (1989) is the most recent film by Canada's premier director, Denys Arcand. Combining weighty religious imagery, striking cinematography, and a complex play-within-a-play format, the story surrounds a group of Canadian actors and actresses who decide to perform a passion play and meet with resistance from various Canadian religious and social groups. Arcand's earlier film, *The Decline of the American Empire* (1986), is a lighter sexual comedy.

Another top Canadian director is Patricia Rozema. Her film *I've Heard the Mermaids Singing* (1987) is a whimsical comedy about an awkward "temp" worker in Montreal with a penchant for photography. Jacques Benoit's *How to Make Love to a Negro without Getting Tired*, also set in Montreal, is a satire about interracial relationships. The top avant-garde director in Canada is Atom Egoyan; *Speaking Parts* is a bizarre, well-made film. Yves Simoneau's *Perfectly Normal* (1990) is another recent Canadian release. For a glimpse into life in rural Alberta in the 1940s, see *Bye Bye Blues* (1990), directed by Anne Wheeler. The film revolves around a middle-aged woman and the survival tactics she embraces when her husband becomes a POW in the Second World War.

CHAPTER FOURTEEN
THE CARIBBEAN

Each island of the Caribbean offers its own blend of African, native American, Asian, and European cultures. Each island also has a unique past, although they all share a common history of hundreds of years of European rule. In fact, there are still islands in the region under British, French, and Dutch (as well as U.S.) control. In recent years, however, more of the islands of the Caribbean have become independent states; there are now 13 independent island-nations in the region. The newest Caribbean nations are Antigua and Barbuda, St. Kitts and Nevis, St. Lucia, and St. Vincent and the Grenadines.

Once this part of the world brought great wealth to the colonial masters whose slave labor produced tropical agricultural products, such as sugar, for consumption in Europe. Today, agriculture has been supplanted by tourism as the number-one source of income on the islands. One exception is Cuba, where frigid diplomatic relations still keep Cuban products out of the U.S. and U.S. tourists out of Cuba.

In contrast to the popularity of the islands as a vacation destination, relatively few Americans head to the Caribbean to study or work. Nevertheless, a variety of study and work options exist in the Caribbean, and electing to take advantage of them will be rewarded by a greater understanding of the nations in this beautiful and culturally fascinating region.

Getting There

It's easy to get a flight to the Caribbean from the United States; a variety of U.S. and Caribbean airlines provide nonstop service to a number of the larger islands. Miami and New York are the main gateways, but nonstop flights are also available from a number of other U.S. cities. However, to get to some of the smaller, less-visited islands, you may have to fly to a major international hub such as San Juan, Puerto Rico, and make a connection. APEX fares are one of the cheapest ways to go (see Chapter Five for a general explanation of airfares), but be sure to check the ads in the Sunday travel section of a large newspaper for special promotional fares. Sample *one-way* fares in effect during the summer of 1991 are listed below. More up-to-date information is available at Council Travel offices (see listing on pages xix–xxi).

Miami–San Juan	$145
Miami–Nassau	$125
New York–Santo Domingo	$185
New Orleans–Kingston	$225

For persons planning a short-term stay (one week or less) at a tourist destination in the Caribbean, the cheapest way of traveling is to buy a package that includes airfare, transfers, and hotel. Most airlines serving the Caribbean offer a wide variety of packages; some even include low-cost car rentals. Most packages give you a choice of accommodations from budget to luxury categories. Since tour operators can make discount volume purchases, packages generally are cheaper than making your own arrangements. In fact, Council Travel arranges special low-cost spring vacation packages geared toward students and teachers interested in making their spring-break getaway an international experience. Check at a Council Travel office or look in the Sunday travel section of any metropolitan newspaper for more information on a wide range of Caribbean packages. Also, keep in mind the fact that airfares and room rates fluctuate widely with the changing of the seasons; July, August, and the pre-Christmas season have the lowest rates.

Another way of getting to the Caribbean is by ship. A number of cruise ships depart

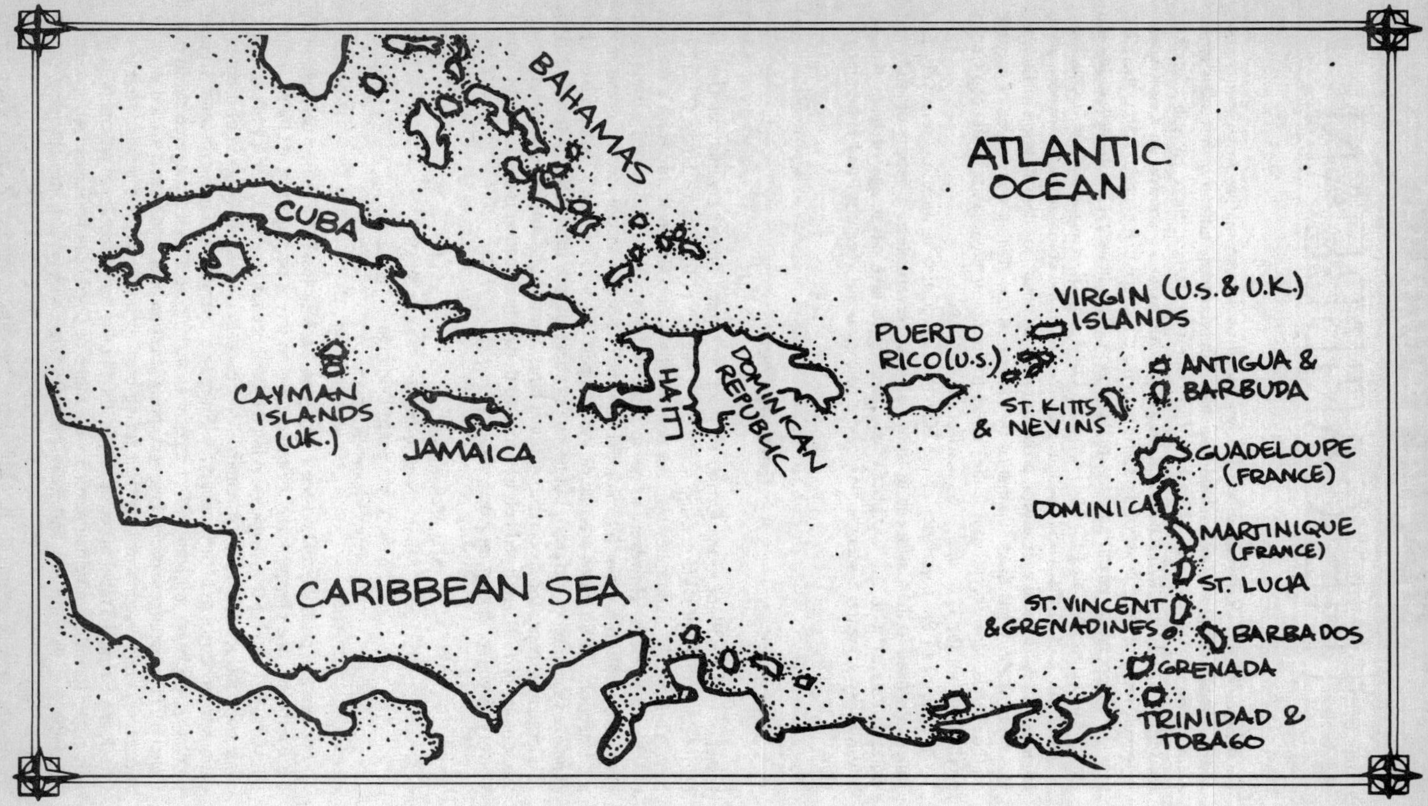
BAHAMAS
ATLANTIC OCEAN
CUBA
VIRGIN ISLANDS (U.S. & U.K.)
PUERTO RICO (U.S.)
ANTIGUA & BARBUDA
CAYMAN ISLANDS (U.K.)
JAMAICA
HAITI
DOMINICAN REPUBLIC
ST. KITTS & NEVINS
GUADELOUPE (FRANCE)
DOMINICA
MARTINIQUE (FRANCE)
ST. LUCIA
CARIBBEAN SEA
ST. VINCENT & GRENADINES
BARBADOS
GRENADA
TRINIDAD & TOBAGO

for Caribbean destinations from Miami, Fort Lauderdale (Port Everglades), and other U.S. ports. Although cruise ships no longer cater only to the retired and wealthy, they are definitely not for those who want maximum contact with local cultures.

Getting Around

Island-hopping in the Caribbean can be done either by airplane or boat. A number of airlines serve the larger islands and the major tourist destinations, and smaller airlines provide scheduled service even to the smaller and more remote islands. Among the major regional airlines that serve the region are Liat and BWIA, both of whom offer passes that can be bought in the West Indies.

While more than 300 cruise ships ply the Caribbean, passenger boats providing simple transportation (rather than the "total vacation" of cruise ships) are harder to find. However, some islands are connected to nearby islands by regular local boat service. For example, from Tortola (British Virgin Islands) you can get frequent boats to other islands in both the U.S. and British Virgin Islands, and from St. Maarten (Netherlands Antilles) you can get boats to nearby French, Dutch, and British islands. Another option is to ask around the port area for information about passenger services on cargo boats or crewing on a yacht.

Arrangements can be easily made to visit any country of the region except Cuba. Americans are not barred from traveling to Cuba, but Treasury Department restrictions on U.S. travel agents, airlines, and individual citizens have made travel to Cuba difficult, unless one enters through a third country, such as Mexico or Jamaica. Journalists, some researchers, and graduate-degree candidates, as well as people with family on the island, are exempt from these restrictions and can make arrangements through Marazul Tours (250 West 57th Street, Suite 1311, New York, NY 10107), the only travel agency in the U.S. authorized to arrange travel to Cuba. Others will need to make their travel arrangements through a travel agency or airline in a third country such as Canada or Mexico. To obtain a visa to visit Cuba, U.S. citizens must apply to the Cuban Interests Section of the Embassy of Switzerland (2630 16th Street NW, Washington, DC 20009). *Getting to Know Cuba*, a travel guidebook by Jane McManus, an official with the Cuban government, was recently published by St. Martin's Press ($14.95).

For Further Information

The most comprehensive guidebook to the region is the *Caribbean Islands Handbook* ($16.95), published by Prentice-Hall and available in most bookstores. Another good guide for the budget traveler is Frommer's *Caribbean* ($14.95). In addition, a number of travel guidebooks not specifically geared to the budget traveler are readily available at bookstores, including Fodor's *Caribbean* ($15.95) and Birnbaum's *Caribbean, Bermuda, and the Bahamas 1991* ($14.95). *Best Places to Stay in the Caribbean* ($13.95), by Bill and Cheryl Alters Jameson, gives descriptions of over 150 hotels and inns, ranging from places with names like "Hedonism II" to natural havens such as the Papillote Wilderness Retreat.

Many islands of the Caribbean have tourist offices in the United States. We've listed these offices in the individual country sections later in this chapter. For those not dealt with in a separate country section, we've listed the addresses where you can write for general tourist information below.

- Aruba Tourist Authority, 521 Fifth Avenue, 12th floor, New York, NY 10175
- Barbados Tourist Board, 800 Second Avenue, New York, NY 10017
- Curaçao Tourist Board, 400 Madison Avenue, Suite 311, New York, NY 10017
- French West Indies Tourist Board, 610 Fifth Avenue, New York, NY 10020
- Haiti Tourist Office, 18 East 41st Street, New York 10017
- Trinidad and Tobago Tourist Board, 25 West 43rd Street, New York, NY 10036

Few nations of the Caribbean region require visas for U.S. citizens visiting as tourists for less than a month or two. However, study, work, or a longer stay on one of the islands may require a visa or residence permit. We've provided more information in the individual country sections that follow. For other countries, contact the embassies and/or consulates listed below for more information.

- Embassy of Antigua and Barbuda, Intelsat Building, 3400 International Drive NW (#4M), Washington, DC 20008
- Embassy of Barbados, 2144 Wyoming Avenue NW, Washington, DC 20008
- Embassy of Grenada, 1701 New Hampshire Avenue NW, Washington, DC 20009
- Embassy of Haiti, 2311 Massachusetts Avenue NW, Washington, DC 20008
- Embassy of St. Kitts and Nevis, 2500 M Street NW, Suite 608, Washington, DC 20037
- Embassy of St. Lucia, 2100 M Street NW, Suite 309, Washington, DC 20037
- Consulate of St. Vincent and the Grenadines, 801 Second Avenue, 21st floor, New York, NY 10017
- Embassy of Trinidad and Tobago, 1708 Massachusetts Avenue NW, Washington, DC 20036

Study in the Caribbean Region

In the individual country sections that follow, you'll find additional study programs listed. In this section we've listed only the study programs of CIEE-member institutions that take place in more than one country of the region. Consult Appendix I for the addresses where you can write for further information.

Semester and Academic Year

General Studies

University of Arkansas at Little Rock. "Latin America and Caribbean Exchange Program." Academic year or semester. Juniors and seniors at Arkansas Consortium for International Education schools only. Rolling admissions.

Science

Michigan State University. "Natural Science in the Caribbean." British and U.S. Virgin Islands. Environmental field studies by direct observation in the field and from text and lectures. Winter break (mid-December to first week of January). Freshmen to seniors. Apply by November 10.

Summer

International Relations

Michigan State University. "Summer School in the Caribbean." Barbados, Trinidad, Tobago, and Guyana. Political science, sociology, and international relations. Sophomores, juniors, and seniors. Apply by April 20.

Science

Portland State University. "Natural History of the Virgin Islands." U.S. and British Virgin Islands. Various facets of reef and shore biology and dynamics. Four quarters of biology or geography. High school seniors to university graduates. Apply by May 9.

BAHAMAS

Beginning just 50 miles off the coast of Florida, the 700 islands of the Commonwealth of the Bahamas are the vacation destination of three million tourists a year. Tourists are so important to the economy of the Bahamas that they provide nearly 70 percent of the country's gross national product. This has produced a standard of living well above most Third World countries. Unfortunately, tourism is not a stable industry, and the Bahamas' reliance on it makes its economy extremely vulnerable to volatile market conditions; a warm winter or a recession in North America can keep tourists away and instantly affect every Bahamian pocketbook. The government has attempted to diversify the economy, but a scarcity of natural resources—the sun, sea, and beautiful beaches excepted—makes it unlikely that other industries will soon replace tourism as the economic engine of the Bahamas.

Bahamian coral sand beaches may be the best known part of the islands, but they are certainly not the most interesting part. Foreign visitors with a keen eye for cultural nuances will detect in Bahamian culture a rich mosaic of elements from Africa, England, the United States, and the rest of the Caribbean. Junkanoo music from the slave era and colorful parades mix with British-derived government and legal systems—complete with judges in traditional wigs—that in turn blend with American-style business practices. West Indian calypso and reggae music share the airwaves with Miami television and radio stations.

Politics in the Bahamas is worthy of special attention. The Bahamas has one of the oldest parliaments in the Western Hemisphere; its House of Assembly has governed the islands for over 300 years. Visitors are welcome to listen to the parliamentary debate in the historic House of Assembly building in downtown Nassau. The current Prime Minister, Lynden O. Pindling, brought political independence to the Bahamas in 1973, though the Bahamas remains a member of the British Commonwealth of Nations.

Although the congested city of Nassau, with its mixture of British colonial and American modern architecture, is the center of Bahamian society and home to 65 percent of the 250,000 Bahamian citizens, foreign visitors can learn much about the cultural roots of the Bahamas by visiting some of the small settlements on Abaco, Andros, Eleuthera, and other islands. Inexpensive mail boats (passengers welcomed) regularly ply the aquamarine sea between the 20 or so inhabited islands. It was on one of these islands, probably San Salvador, that Columbus first stepped ashore in the Western Hemisphere. And it is in such places that the subsequent history of colonization, slavery, and emancipation can best be appreciated. A visit to a small settlement church or a boat-building shop will introduce visitors to two more important features of Bahamian life: religion and the sea. Down-home religion and the isolation imposed by the surrounding ocean have produced a society which, though modern, retains many of the close-knit qualities of human relationships that people usually ascribe only to the good old days. In the Bahamas, the old and the new live side by side.

—*Dean W. Collinwood, Bountiful, Utah*

Official name: Commonwealth of the Bahamas. **Area:** 5,380 square miles (about the size of Connecticut). **Population:** 251,000. **Population density:** 45 inhabitants per square mile. **Capital and largest city:** Nassau (pop. 139,000). **Language:** English. **Religion:**

Protestant, Roman Catholic. **Per capita income:** US$7,598. **Currency:** Bahamian dollar. **Literacy rate:** 95%. **Average daily high/low*:** Nassau: January, 77°/65°; July, 88°/75°. **Average number of days with precipitation:** Nassau: January, 6; July, 14.

TRAVEL

U.S. citizens do not need a passport or a visa for stays of up to eight months. However, proof of citizenship (a birth or baptismal certificate, or a passport) is required, as is an onward or return ticket. With the baptismal or birth certificate, two additional forms of ID are necessary, one with a photo. A passport and a residence/work permit are required for residence, business, or missionary work. For specific details, contact the Embassy of the Bahamas (600 New Hampshire Avenue NW, Washington, DC 20037) or a Bahamian consulate in New York or Miami.

Getting Around

The Bahamas is probably the most accessible country to travelers from the United States after Canada and Mexico. Grand Bahama, for example, is only 60 miles from the east coast of Florida, and numerous flights and boats (ranging from hydrofoils to cruise ships) link Florida to the islands. In fact, from some islands it's easier to get to Florida than to Nassau, the nation's capital and largest city.

Getting around the Bahamas, on the other hand, is not easy except by air. Even by air, however, service to some of the less-visited islands is infrequent and often means going through either Nassau or Miami. A number of small private companies—Bahamas Air, Mackey, Chalk's, Helda Air, and Shawnee—operate scheduled flights between various islands. In addition, inexpensive ferry service (which takes 15 to 16 hours) connects Nassau (New Providence Island) and Freeport (Grand Bahama), the nation's two main cities and tourist centers. A slow but interesting way of getting to other islands is via the mail boats, which carry passengers, mail, and merchandise. The Bahamas Family Islands Association has a helpful brochure that lists fares and schedules. Another travel option is chartering a yacht and mapping your own course around the islands.

Cars can be rented in the main tourist resorts, as can bicycles, mopeds, and motorcycles. Bicycles are especially well suited for the islands, since most are small and the terrain is flat. Driving is on the left-hand side of the road.

For persons considering making a vacation trip to the Bahamas an educational experience as well, there's a one-week December study-tour offered by Ohio University. "Marine and Tropical Field Studies" on Andros Island is open to college students and secondary-school teachers; apply by November 1. Additional information is available from Dr. Weldon Witters, 427 Irvine Hall, Ohio University, Athens, OH 45701.

Especially for Students and Young People

There is no student travel organization in the Bahamas, and no special discounts have been developed for holders of the International Student Identity Card.

For Further Information

General tourist information is available from the Bahamas Tourist Office (150 East 52nd Street, New York, NY 10022). Some, but not all, guidebooks to the Caribbean include information about the Bahamas, which (as noted above) is technically not located in the

---

*All temperatures are Fahrenheit.

Caribbean. One of the better ones is Fodor's *The Bahamas*, which comes in both a pocket-sized and regular edition ($10.95). Birnbaum's *Caribbean, Bermuda & Bahamas 1991* ($14.95) includes a comprehensive guide to the region and maps. The *Caribbean Islands Handbook* ($16.95), published by Prentice-Hall, also has a lengthy section on the Bahamas.

WORK

Getting a Job

It is necessary to obtain a work permit to work in the Bahamas. The prospective employer applies for the permit prior to the applicant entering the country. Positions are only granted to foreigners if there are no qualified Bahamians available. For more information contact the Ministry of Employment & Immigration, PO Box N-3002, Nassau, Bahamas.

STUDY

Programs offered by CIEE-member institutions are listed below. Consult Appendix I for the addresses of the colleges and universities in this section.

Semester and Academic Year

Ecology

Miami University. "Tropical Flora of the Bahamas." Ecology and botany of the Andros Islands. Two-week program in May. Sophomores to graduate students with six hours of biology coursework.

Oceanography

State University of New York at Brockport. San Salvador. January. Designed for biology, earth-science, and geology majors. Juniors, seniors, and graduate students. Apply by September 15.

DOMINICAN REPUBLIC

According to its tourism bureau, the Dominican Republic, which occupies the eastern two-thirds of the island of Hispaniola, is "the best-kept secret in the Caribbean." In fact, in comparison to other Caribbean islands, the Dominican Republic is a relative latecomer to the tourist industry. As a result, it retains much of its intrinsic character and charm. But things are changing. Sugar, once its principle export, has been surpassed by tourism as the country's primary income generator, and a growing number of assembly plants, built by multinational companies attracted by low labor costs, are transforming the nation's economic base. There are now nine duty-free industrial parks in the Dominican Republic, many housed in former sugar refineries.

A relatively stable democratic system has been in place since the American Marines ended their occupation of the country in 1966. Despite a long history of U.S. intervention, however, anti-American sentiment is not pronounced. Dominicans have a comfortable, Puerto Rico–like relationship with the U.S.; in fact, after Santo Domingo, New York

City could be considered the country's second-largest city, thanks to its large Dominican population.

Discovered by Columbus in 1492, the Dominican Republic boasts the first Spanish settlement in the New World, the first cathedral, and the oldest university. For three hundred years the island was controlled by Spain, and for briefer periods after that was controlled by France and Haiti, which occupies the western part of the island. It nearly came under U.S. control in 1904 when a shaky Dominican government requested American statehood, a motion that was narrowly defeated in the U.S. Senate. Still, the U.S. has not hesitated to exert its political influence and the Marines have occupied the country twice in this century. In 1966, after the most recent U.S. intervention, Joaquin Balaguer was elected president. Power has since alternated between his rule (he has been re-elected three times) and parties of the center-left.

The Dominican people are primarily of African and Spanish descent (the native population was virtually exterminated in the 16th century), and baseball (not soccer) and merengue dancing are their passions. The population is fairly evenly divided between urban and rural areas, with Santo Domingo the political capital and Santiago, the second-largest city, the center of the nation's agricultural production.

In spite of a recent economic downturn, the last decade has been one of healthy economic growth. The booming tourist industry and foreign investment in new clothing and textile industries are signs that the Dominican Republic in the 1990s is a nation in transition.

—*Nancy Robinson, Santiago, Dominican Republic*

Official name: Dominican Republic. **Area:** 18,816 square miles (about twice the size of Vermont). **Population:** 7,253,000. **Population density:** 388 inhabitants per square mile. **Capital and largest city:** Santo Domingo (pop. 1,700,000). **Language:** Spanish. **Religion:** Roman Catholic. **Per capita income:** US$800. **Currency:** Peso. **Literacy rate:** 68%. **Average daily high/low*:** Santo Domingo: January, 84°/66°; July, 88°/72°. **Average number of days with precipitation:** Santo Domingo: January, 7; July, 11.

TRAVEL

U.S. citizens need a passport or proof of U.S. citizenship and a tourist card or visa to enter the Dominican Republic. The tourist card costs $10 (available from a consulate or the airlines serving the Dominican Republic) and is valid for 60 days. Visas are issued by a consulate for no charge and are valid for a year. Check with the Embassy of the Dominican Republic (1715 22nd Street NW, Washington, DC 20008) for specific details.

Getting Around

Several companies offer long-distance bus service between the country's cities and resorts, including Autobuses Metro, Terrabus, and Caribe Tours. Local buses, called *guaguas*, provide slow but very inexpensive service to virtually every village in the country. In addition, public transport is provided by cars called *publicos*, which travel on major highways picking people up and dropping them off along a specified route. Rail transport is virtually nonexistent.

Renting a car is another option for getting around the country. Main roads are generally well maintained, driving is on the right-hand side of the road, and a U.S. driver's license is valid. Budget and Hertz are among the firms with operations in the Dominican; you can check rates and minimum-age requirements by calling their toll-free numbers in the

---

*All temperatures are Fahrenheit.

THE CARIBBEAN: DOMINICAN REPUBLIC **415**

U.S. A number of local companies also operate in Santo Domingo and resort areas such as Puerto Plata.

Especially for Students and Young People

ODTE is the main student travel organization in the Dominican Republic. In addition to its main office at General Luperon Street #51 (corner of Hostos Street), Zona Colonial, Santo Domingo (mailing address: PO Box 25135, Santo Domingo), there are also offices in Santiago and La Vega. The organization arranges city and beach tours in Santo Domingo, and offers one-week packages (including accommodations and meals) at various beach resorts. Students with the International Student Identity Card get a discount on international airfares from Santo Domingo as well as discounts at some shops. Contact ODTE for more information.

For Further Information

General tourist information is available from the Dominican Republic Tourist Information Center (1 Times Square, New York, NY 10036). In addition, guidebooks to the Caribbean region (see page 409) invariably include a section on the Dominican Republic.

WORK

It is very difficult for foreigners to obtain work in the Dominican Republic. For more information contact the Embassy of the Dominican Republic, 1712 22nd Street NW, Washington, DC 20008. For another type of work experience, see the internship and voluntary-service sections below.

Internships/Traineeships

A program offered by a member of the Council on International Educational Exchange is described below.

AIESEC-US places students in internship positions in fields such as economics, business, finance, marketing, accounting, and computer science. See page 18 for details.

Voluntary Service

Amigos de las Americas sponsors a volunteer program in the Dominican Republic; see page 21 for more information.

STUDY

The following programs are offered by CIEE-member institutions. Consult Appendix I for the addresses of the colleges and universities listed in this section.

Semester and Academic Year

Spanish Language and Caribbean Area Studies

Council on International Educational Exchange. "Spanish Language and Caribbean Area Studies Programs." Santiago. Academic year or semester. Sophomores, juniors, and seniors with four semesters of college Spanish for fall semester or academic year and five for spring semester. Apply by May 1 for fall semester or academic year and October 15 for spring. Contact University Programs Department.

Experiment in International Living/School for International Training. "College Semester Abroad." Santo Domingo. Fall or spring semester. Spanish language, development studies, field-methods seminar, Caribbean studies seminar, independent-study project, one-week village homestay, and ten-week Santo Domingo homestay. Sophomores to seniors with 2.5 GPA and three semesters of college Spanish. Apply by May 15 for fall semester; and October 15 for spring.

International Student Exchange Program. Direct reciprocal exchange between U.S. universities and the Universidad Católica Madre y Maestra and the Instituto Tecnologico de Santo Domingo. Semester or academic year. Full curriculum options. Open only to students at ISEP-member institutions.

Michigan State University. "Spanish Language, Literature, and Culture in the Dominican Republic." Santiago. Winter quarter. Sophomores, juniors, and seniors with two years of college Spanish. Apply by November 20.

University of Arkansas at Little Rock. "Latin America and Caribbean Exchange Program." Academic year or semester. Juniors and seniors at Arkansas Consortium for International Education schools only. Rolling admissions.

Summer

Agriculture

Ohio State University. "Summer Program in Dominican Agriculture." Sophomores, juniors, and seniors with one quarter of Spanish. Instituto Superior de Agricultura (ISA), Santiago. Apply by April 1.

JAMAICA

Jamaica, the third largest of the Caribbean islands, is 90 miles away from its closest neighbor, Cuba, and 340 miles from the U.S. mainland. At the time of Christopher Columbus's arrival on the island during his second trip to the new world in 1494, the inhabitants were the now-extinct Arawak Indians, who gave the island its name. Briefly a Spanish colony, the island retains a few traces of Spanish culture in the names of some of the island's more exotic destinations such as the tourist center of Ocho Rios and the well-known rafting spot of the Rio Grande, as well as in the architecture of its oldest towns. It is the period as a British colony, however, that has most clearly defined the population, politics, and culture of modern Jamaica.

The descendants of African slaves brought from West Africa as labor for the sugar plantations now form 96 percent of the island's population. Indentured labor from India, China, and Europe, and the descendants of former British colonial rulers compose the remainder of the population. Jamaicans have mixed freely over the centuries, resulting in an interesting variety of facial features and skin tones.

The period of British rule has strongly influenced Jamaica's political institutions. By 1962 when the island attained its political independence, a two-party parliamentary democracy had been installed. Headed by a Prime Minister, the island is ruled by a bicameral

Parliament with legislative and executive powers. The nominal head of state remains the Queen of England, represented locally by a Jamaican-born Governor General. Official business and conversation on the island is conducted in English, the official language. The educational system is also patterned after that of the United Kingdom.

However, the traditions carried over and retained by the African slaves and their descendants have the strongest influence on Jamaican culture. The local dialect most closely resembles broken English, but its African syntax plays tricks on the ear of those new to the island. Reggae, made popular and internationalized by its most famous star, Bob Marley, is a hypnotic combination of bass rhythm, reminiscent of African drums, combined with lyrics of social significance. This music is heard everywhere on the streets of the island. "Reggae Sunsplash," the annual summer festival, attracts participants and audiences from all over the world. Other, less well-known African traditions live on among the population in its dances, religious practices, and superstitions.

Kingston, the political and economic capital, is the center of Jamaica's modern development. The island, however, suffers from an unemployment rate of 22 to 30 percent. Traditionally a colonial, agricultural economy heavily dependent on sugar production, the island has since introduced light industry, crop diversification, tourism, and bauxite mining. The United States is the island's major trading partner. This, along with its proximity, has introduced a high level of knowledge about and interest in the United States.

The island has a tropical, maritime climate, which makes it a popular tourist destination for North Americans. At the same time, its mountainous interior provides alternatives for those seeking cooler, less crowded destinations. Jamaicans are hospitable, and enjoy sharing their island with visitors.

—Andrea Ewart Simon, Brattleboro, Vermont

Official name: Jamaica. **Area:** 4,232 square miles (about the size of Connecticut). **Population:** 2,513,000. **Population density:** 556 inhabitants per square mile. **Capital and largest city:** Kingston (pop. 635,000). **Language:** English. **Religion:** Protestant. **Per capita income:** US$1,160. **Currency:** Jamaican dollar. **Literacy rate:** 82%. **Average daily high/low*:** Kingston: January, 86°/67°; July, 90°/73°. **Average number of days with precipitation:** Kingston: January, 3; July, 4.

TRAVEL

For visits of up to six months, U.S. tourists do not need a passport or a visa if they are arriving directly from the United States, Puerto Rico, or the U.S. Virgin Islands. However, tourists must have a return or onward ticket and proof of citizenship, along with a photo ID and sufficient funds. A tourist card is issued on arrival and is returned to immigration authorities on departure. Visas *are* required for Americans going to the island for business or study. For specific requirements, check with the Embassy of Jamaica (1850 K Street NW, Suite 355, Washington, DC 20006) or at a Jamaican consulate in New York, Miami, Chicago, or Los Angeles.

Getting Around

One of the most interesting and least expensive ways of seeing more of Jamaica than its beaches is to take the train between Kingston and Montego Bay. The six-hour trip across the heart of the island provides beautiful scenery as well as a glimpse into the everyday life of Jamaicans. Another cheap way of getting around are the local buses that serve

---

*All temperatures are Fahrenheit.

most areas of the island. (Travel by bus after dark, however, is not recommended.) In addition, there are minibuses that serve the most popular routes between the island's cities and resorts; these operate as *colectivos*, leaving only when full and picking up and discharging passengers anywhere along the route. Although inexpensive, these are often overcrowded and chaotic.

Most international flights arrive at the Montego Bay airport. From there many tourists, especially those who have no desire to see little more than their resort hotel, take air shuttles to tourist resorts such as Ocho Rios and Negril. In these resort areas, as well as at the international airport in Kingston, you'll find a variety of car-rental companies. Due to the slow and unreliable nature of public transportation in Jamaica, many visitors elect to rent a car; your U.S. driver's license is valid (most agencies insist on a minimum age of 25), but remember that driving is on the left-hand side of the road. The largest car rental firms operating in Jamaica are Avis, Budget, and Hertz; you can call their toll-free numbers in the U.S. to compare rates or find out about minimum-age requirements. Bicycle, moped, and motorcycle rentals are also available in tourist areas.

"It can be hard for an outsider to envision how the huge phenomenon of reggae music came out of a country only 144 by 49 miles in size. Reggae is the root of Jamaican culture and in many ways the people epitomize their music, which is vibrant, rhythmic, and colorful."

—Sara Hirsch, Sunnyside, New York

Especially for Students and Young People

Jamaica's student travel organization and issuer of the International Student Identity Card is JOYST (Jamaica Organization of Youth and Student Tourists). Their office is located at 9 Eureka Crescent, Kingston 5. With the International Student Identity Card, students can get a 50-percent discount on ALM Airlines to all destinations, a 15-percent discount on Copa Airlines, as well as reduced rates at some hotels, museums, cinemas, and theaters. The card also provides free entry to all national parks. Contact JOYST for more information.

For Further Information

General tourist information is available from the Jamaican Tourist Board, 866 Second Avenue, New York, NY 10017. Other Jamaica Tourist Board offices are located in Chicago, Miami, Los Angeles, and Dallas. You'll find information about Jamaica in guidebooks to the Caribbean. An especially complete section on Jamaica can be found in the *Caribbean Islands Handbook* ($16.95), published by Prentice-Hall.

WORK

Getting a Job

To work in Jamaica it is necessary to obtain a work permit; the prospective employer applies for it on behalf of the applicant. Jamaica encourages skilled and professional workers from abroad. For more information contact the Embassy of Jamaica, 1850 K Street NW, Washington, DC 20006.

CIEE's Work in Jamaica program gives college or university students the opportunity to seek employment in Jamaica during the summer vacation period (June 1 to October 1). The program is conducted with the cooperation of JOYST, which meets participants upon arrival, provides an orientation on working in Jamaica, and assists with any problems that may arise. Students are responsible for finding their own jobs; however, JOYST uses local contacts and listings from previous Work in Jamaica participants to locate potential employers. Participants should realize that the summer job market in Jamaica is quite different from that of the United States. Unemployment in Jamaica is generally higher while wages are lower. Furthermore, summer is the off-season for the Jamaican tourist trade. While you should not expect to find employment related to your field of study, still jobs will be available in the tourist and service industries. To qualify, an individual must be at least 18 years of age, a college or university student, and a U.S. citizen or permanent resident. The cost of the program is $125. For more information, contact the Work Exchanges Department at CIEE.

"Jamaica has a lot more to offer than sunny Caribbean beaches for winter or spring break. Living and working in Jamaica will give you a glimpse of the Caribbean lifestyle that cannot be seen by the ordinary tourist."
—Linda Samuels, Cleveland, Ohio

Internships/Traineeships

Two programs offered by members of the Council on International Educational Exchange are described below.

Association for International Practical Training. "IAESTE Trainee Program." On-the-job training for undergraduate and graduate students in technical fields such as engineering, computer science, agriculture, architecture, and mathematics. See page 18 for more information.

University of Minnesota. "Minnesota Studies in International Development." Academic year. Predeparture coursework at the University of Minnesota in the fall quarter; an internship in development-related research or an action project in the winter and spring quarters. Juniors to graduates and adults with an interest in development. A 2.5 GPA is required; apply by May 15. See Appendix I for address.

Voluntary Service

The Partnership for Service Learning sponsors a study/service program in Jamaica; for more information see page 24.

STUDY

Programs offered by CIEE-member institutions are listed below. Consult Appendix I for the addresses of the colleges and universities in this section.

Semester and Academic Year

Performing Arts

State University of New York at Brockport. "Jamaica Performing Arts Exchange Program." Spring semester. Study Jamaican art and culture at the Cultural Training Centre in Kingston. Homestay. Juniors and seniors with 2.5 GPA. Apply by November 1.

Summer

Cultural Studies

Lisle Fellowship. "Jamaica: A Country of Cultural Diversity and Development." Four weeks. Open to individuals 18 years and older. Apply by April 1.

General Studies

State University of New York at Brockport. "Summer Program in Jamaica." University of the West Indies in Kingston. On-campus housing. Juniors and seniors with 2.5 GPA. Apply by May 1.

EXPLORING JAMAICAN CULTURE

Readings and Films

The novels of Roger Mais, especially *Brother Man* (1974) and *The Hills Were Joyful Together* (1981), are concerned with the victims of the oppressive cultural and economic legacy of colonialism. He brings the Jamaican slums alive, particularly the huge Kingston shantytowns, and through his portrayal indicts the ruling upper class. His book *Black Lightning* (1983) is a more heavily symbolic work employing a pastoral setting. The protagonist, Jake, is a blacksmith trying to confront human imperfection by creating a statue of Samson, whose tragic story mirrors Jake's own.

Another portrait of the Jamaican lower class is Michael Thelwell's sociological work, *The Harder They Come* (1980), and Perry Henzell's 1973 film from which the book took its name. The film, something of a cult classic in the U.S., is about a country boy who wants to be a reggae singer in Kingston but can't get his record played until he becomes an outlaw. The more infamous he becomes, the more records he sells.

Edgar White's plays, *The Nine Night* and *Ritual by Water* (1984) concern the conflict in consciousness among modern Jamaicans and West Indian expatriates. In *The Nine Night*, the protagonist returns to Jamaica from England to try to undo England's effect upon his family. *Ritual by Water* looks at a worker in a youth center wrestling with ideals and despair.

For a historical perspective on Jamaica read V. S. Reid's *New Day* (1949), which chronicles Jamaica from the 1865 rebellion to 1944, or Claude McKay's *Banana Bottom* (1933), about a young girl adopted by English missionaries and sent to England for her education.

CHAPTER FIFTEEN
MEXICO AND CENTRAL AMERICA

Many people travel to Mexico and Central America for no other reason than its warm weather and beautiful beach resorts like Acapulco and Cancún. Others, however, become more deeply involved. Many North Americans are traveling to the region as volunteers to help fight poverty, as scientists to help preserve the rain forest, as students to understand the region's language and culture, as businesspeople to help develop industry and commerce, and as archaeologists to explore the mysteries of ancient cities, which still rise as testimony to the great empires that flourished long before Columbus's arrival in the Americas. Whatever the reason for their trip, few travelers are disappointed.

For nearly 300 years, Mexico and the republics of Central America were all part of the Spanish empire. Because of this, these nations share a common heritage and many common characteristics. But making sweeping generalizations would be a serious error. For example, while the official language of most of these nations is Spanish, in Belize it is English. The largest population group in the region is the mestizo, a mixture of Spanish and Indian ancestry, but Guatemala remains predominantly Indian. Most of these countries maintain a fairly low standard of living, but Costa Rica is surprisingly affluent. And while you can expect tropical weather in coastal areas, most cities of the region— including Mexico City, Guatemala City, and San José—lie inland far above sea level and enjoy surprisingly temperate climates.

Mexico and Central America are closely linked to their powerful neighbor to the north. As home of the Panama Canal, market for U.S. products, supplier of food and raw materials (including petroleum), and a major source of immigration (both legal and illegal), the region has long played a major role in the economy and society of the U.S. But in spite of their proximity and importance to the U.S., these nations remain little understood by most North Americans.

Today, merely mentioning Central America brings to the minds of most North Americans images of violence and strife. Although it is true that political, social, and economic problems plague the region, the image of political instability and violence is not entirely accurate. Mexico, Costa Rica, and Belize have enjoyed decades of political stability and social peace. Now even such countries as Nicaragua and El Salvador may be following suit as opposing factions begin laying down their arms. At press time, however, the State Department continues to warn against travel in Panama and parts of El Salvador. Situations can change quickly, so before going anywhere in the region, check with the Citizens Emergency Center at the U.S. State Department (see page 8) for any travel advisories that may be in effect.

The Essentials

A tourist card, issued by the authorities when you enter the country, is enough to allow U.S. citizens to enter Mexico and most Central American countries. To get a tourist card you will need proof of U.S. citizenship; a passport, birth certificate, or voter's registration card is acceptable. Many countries of the region also have an onward transportation requirement that may be enforced somewhat arbitrarily. Especially when confronted with young travelers, officials may ask for proof of a ticket out of the country or sometimes just sufficient funds to buy such a ticket. Check with the embassy or consulate for further information.

You'll find entry requirements and embassy addresses given in the individual country

GULF OF MEXICO
MEXICO
BELIZE
HONDURAS
PACIFIC OCEAN
GUATEMALA
EL SALVADOR
NICARAGUA
PANAMA
COSTA RICA

sections that follow. Addresses for the embassies of countries not covered in a separate section of this chapter are listed below.

- Embassy of Belize, 1575 I Street NW, Suite 695, Washington, DC 20005
- Embassy of El Salvador, 2308 California Street NW, Washington, DC 20008
- Embassy of Nicaragua, 1627 New Hampshire Avenue NW, Washington, DC 20009
- Embassy of Panama, 2862 McGill Terrace NW, Washington, DC 20008

Getting There by Air

The cheapest fares from the U.S. to Mexico and Central America are generally APEX fares (see Chapter Five for a general explanation of airfares). Below are some examples of *one-way* fares in effect during the summer of 1991. More up-to-date information is available at Council Travel offices (see listing on pages xix–xxi).

New York–Mexico City	$195
Los Angeles–Mexico City	$185
Houston–Mexico City	$229
New York–Guatemala City	$195
Miami–San José	$135

For persons planning a short-term stay (anywhere from four days to a couple of weeks), the cheapest way of traveling may be to buy a vacation package that includes airfare, transfers, and hotel. Generally speaking, packages are available to Mexico City, Guadalajara, Mérida, and beach resorts such as Cancún, Acapulco, Puerto Vallarta, Mazatlán, and Ixtapa. Packages range from budget to luxury, and can be booked through travel agents in the U.S. or through airlines flying to Mexico from the U.S. (including the Mexican carriers Mexicana and Aeroméxico). Packages are generally cheaper than making your own arrangements, since tour operators can mass-book hotels and make volume purchases. Council Travel arranges special low-cost spring vacation packages geared toward students and teachers interested in making their spring-break getaway an international experience. Options generally include Cancún among other destinations. Contact a Council Travel office for more information.

Other Means of Travel

Millions of Americans cross the border by car into Mexico each year. Until recently, however, civil war in El Salvador and Nicaragua discouraged most people from venturing beyond Mexico into Central America by car. As the region becomes more stable, Americans are again beginning to take to the Pan American Highway, which extends as far as eastern Panama, where it is interrupted by an expanse of marshland, resuming again in Colombia. Road conditions, while generally good, are inconsistent. Lack of maintenance and shortages of gasoline make passage through some parts of the road a real adventure.

If traveling by train or bus to Mexico, you will have to stop at a U.S. border town (such as El Paso and Brownsville, Texas, or San Diego, California) and walk across the border, where you can arrange connecting service to your destination. While the Mexican railway network is well developed and expanding, most other Central American countries have fairly minimal systems, usually connecting capital cities to ports and little else. Though they can be fun, trains generally travel less frequently, more slowly, and to fewer places than buses. As a result, the bus is the favorite mode of overland transportation in Central America. You'll find more specific information about traveling around Costa Rica, Guatemala, Honduras, and Mexico in the country sections that follow.

Organized Tours

Various nonprofit groups in the U.S. sponsor educational tours of Central American nations designed to increase public awareness of the region and its problems. The Center for Global Education at Augsburg College (731 21st Avenue South, Minneapolis, MN 55454) offers a variety of regional "travel seminars" to the general public. It can also create special tours for student, professional, or community groups. Another nonprofit organization, the Network of Educators on Central America (1118 22nd Street NW, Washington, DC 20037), conducts organized tours primarily to El Salvador. Its tours, geared toward teachers, administrators, and education majors, involve visits to schools and meetings with representatives of various organizations and government agencies concerned with education in the country. A good source of information on public-awareness tours sponsored by various groups across the U.S. is the publication, *Travel Programs in Central America* (see "For Further Information" below).

Work

Except for Costa Rica, where CIEE's Work Abroad Program makes summer employment a possibility for U.S. students, stringent labor regulations and high unemployment rates make it almost impossible for foreigners to obtain employment in Mexico or Central America. Nevertheless, resourceful persons fluent in Spanish can find informal employment (mostly as English tutors) once they've arrived in the region. Persons with a degree in TESOL should check Chapter Three for teaching opportunities in Latin America.

You'll find internship possibilities for Mexico, Guatemala, and Costa Rica listed in the individual country sections later in this chapter. In addition, AIESEC offers internship possibilities in Panama; see page 18 for additional information about this program.

Study

Persons considering study in Latin America might want to take a look at *Funding for Research, Study, and Travel: Latin America and the Caribbean*, edited by Karen Cantrell and Denise Wallen (Phoenix: Oryx Press, 1987), even though most of the grants and scholarships listed in this 300-page reference work are for graduate study. The book is expensive ($37.50), so look for it in your college library.

The following study program is offered by a CIEE-member institution. Consult Appendix I for the address of the university listed.

Summer

Latin American Studies

University of Pittsburgh. "Latin American Studies Field Seminar." Country in which seminar takes place varies each year. Open only to students in Pittsburgh area schools. Juniors and seniors. Proficiency in Spanish required.

For Further Information

There are very few guidebooks to Central American countries other than Mexico and Guatemala; if you are considering a broader intinerary, it may be useful to consult the *Mexico & Central America Handbook* ($29.95), published in Britain and distributed in the United States by Prentice-Hall. Also, a brand-new guidebook, *Central America on a Shoestring*, is available for $15.95 (plus $1.50 book-rate postage; $3 first-class) from Lonely Planet Publications, Embarcadero West, 112 Linden Street, Oakland, CA 94607.

Persons considering a trip to Central America in order to become more actively involved in its internal struggles will be interested in *Travel Programs in Central America*. This 60-page publication contains information on 300 organizations sponsoring study programs, delegations, work brigades, and short- and long-term voluntary-service projects in a number of fields. Put out by the Interfaith Task Force on Central America (PO Box 3843, La Mesa, CA 91944-3843), this booklet costs $6 and includes a trip calendar updated on a quarterly basis.

BELIZE

Ancient Maya heartland, pirate settlement, logger outpost, crown colony, and in 1981, independent nation—Belize (formerly British Honduras) has a remarkable heritage. It remains virtually unspoiled, untarnished by time, and somewhat of a last frontier for the unassuming and adventurous traveler.

With a land mass no larger than the state of Massachusetts, Belize is a country of immense cultural and geographic diversity. Lush tropical rain forests, barren savannas, pine forested mountains, tangled mangrove swamps, impressive limestone caves, and the world's second-longest coral reef all contribute to a bountiful legacy of ecological heterogeneity. Furthermore, its wide variety of fascinating flora and fauna, and its more than 300 picturesque offshore islands make Belize a naturalist's paradise of breathtaking beauty and a haven for the outdoor enthusiast.

While the country is nestled between Mexico and Guatemala, it displays a distinctly Caribbean island atmosphere. This is immediately evident in its music, food, and way of life. With schools in every tiny village and compulsory education until grade eight, the country boasts a 90-percent literacy rate. Indeed, along with its democratically elected bipartisan government, its less apparent social class divisions, and sociopolitical stability, Belize can truly be considered the anomaly of Central America.

The population (175,000) is composed of a colorful medley of cultures. The Afro-European Creoles, who live in Belize City and along the coast, are the largest ethnic group. The mestizos, of Spanish colonist and Amerindian ancestry, migrated to the region from the Yucatan in the 19th century. The Garifuna, descendants of African slaves and Carib Indians, live along the Southern coast and practice a maritime way of life. Inland, the native Maya, with a cultural heritage spanning two millennia, still live in thatched wattle-and-daub houses within the vicinity of the hundreds of archaeological sites scattered across the countryside. During the 20th century, immigrants to Belize have included Lebanese, Chinese, East Indians, German-speaking Mennonites, and more recently, refugees from El Salvador and Guatemala.

Each of the six major towns—Corozal, Orange Walk, Dangriga, Punta Gorda, San Ignacio, and Belmopan, the new "planned" capital carved out of the jungle—has its own distinct ambience. In every community, there is a high level of cultural integration readily expressed by the sharing of the creole language. This linguistically interesting version of "broken English" has evolved as the lingua franca of its people. Although English is the national language, most people also speak Spanish.

Approximately one third of the country's populations reside in Belize City, the old colonial capital built at sea level. It is the commercial and, to a large extent, cultural center of Belize. The city is renowned for its "swing bridge" and especially for its vibrant local market set alongside the wharf. Fishermen can be seen almost any time unloading their daily catches of lobster, fish, and conch. Huge rainwater vats, and a mixture of shabby, unpainted structures and colonial houses line the narrow crowded streets. Vendors pedalling bicycles are relentlessly hawking everything from pumpkin seeds to mahogany carvings, while Rastafarians "hang out" in their favorite alleyways. There is a constant bustle of activity, and everywhere you hear the musical, rhythmic sound of the creole language.

The economy is based on agriculture rather than industrial production; in fact, the entire country can be considered rural by North American standards. Each community retains a rustic flavor and the people thrive on a way of life that is rich in its own simplicity. Whitewashed wooden houses built on stilts display rusty red tin roofs that glisten in the brilliant sun. In the neighborhood, the graceful fronds of the coconut palms rustle, as the morning laundry flaps in the gentle breeze. This laid-back atmosphere is occasionally shattered by the roar of the supersonic jets above, a frequent reminder of the British commitment to protect this fledgling nation.

Travelers expecting an exquisite holiday in the sun complete with fancy nightclubs, casinos, posh five-star hotels and international cuisine, will be lost in the "jungles" and rural setting of Belize. There are no highrise buildings, few luxury accommodations, and a four-wheel drive vehicle is essential for access to the more remote spots. And yet, the intoxicating sound of punta music, the gracious gentility of the Belizean people, and the unspoiled beauty of the land are so contagious that once you've visited this tranquil nation, it's sure to lure you back.

—*Cynthia Bennett Awe, Peterborough, Ontario*

Official name: Belize. **Area:** 8,867 square miles (about the size of New Hampshire). Population: 180,400. **Population density:** 20 inhabitants per square mile. **Capital:** Belmopan (pop. 5,000). **Largest city:** Belize City (pop. 48,000). **Language:** English and Spanish. **Religion:** Roman Catholic, Protestant. **Per capita income:** US$1,250. **Currency:** Belize dollar. **Literacy rate:** 93%. **Average high/low:** Belize City: January, 83°/72°; July, 92°/73°. **Average number of days with precipitation:** Belize City: January, 8; July, 20.

TRAVEL

A passport is required for U.S. citizens, but visas are not required for tourist stays of up to six months if in possession of return/round-trip ticket beginning in and returning to the United States. Check with the Embassy of Belize, 1575 Eye Street NW, Suite 695, Washington, DC 20005 (202-289-1416/7), for specific requirements.

Getting Around

For many years, rivers were the only means of inland travel. Likewise, coastal towns were connected by boat. Today, small boats continue to navigate the waterways, especially in the sugar-producing north, but are no longer the primary mode of transport. One of the nicest trips is to travel by boat from Punta Gorda to Guatemala or Honduras (make sure you have the proper visas). You can also explore the offshore cays by boat.

A good highway network with regular bus and truck service connects the country's few towns, as well as with Chetumal on the Mexican border and Melchor de Mencos on the Guatemalan border. A number of smaller unpaved roads are not as dependable, especially during rainy times, making four-wheel drive vehicles a necessity in many parts.

The country's main airport is ten miles outside of Belize City. Most towns, however, are equipped with some form of landing strip, making regular air travel possible within the country. Maya Airways has daily flights to several towns and a number of other companies offer charter service to more out-of-the-way destinations.

---

*All temperatures are Fahrenheit.

Organized Tours

Ohio University offers a study tour of Belize, one of Central America's least-visited countries. This two-week winter tour, open to the general public, also includes a trip to Flores, Guatemala. Contact the Sociology Department at (614) 593-1383. The application deadline is October 15.

For Further Information

An excellent guide to seldom-explored parts of Belize is *La Ruta Maya: Yucutan, Guatemala and Belize—a Travel Survival Kit*, which traces a 1,500-mile long route connecting the region's ancient Maya sites. It's available for $16.95 (plus $1.50 book-rate postage; $3 for first-class) from the publisher, Lonely Planet Publications, Embarcadero West, 112 Linden Street, Oakland, CA 94607.

WORK

To work in Belize it is necessary to obtain a temporary employment permit which is issued by the Principal Immigration Officer. Permits are granted only after securing a job offer. For further information contact the Immigration and Nationality Service, Belmopan, Belize.

Voluntary Service

The Sisters of Charity of Nazareth sponsors a volunteer program for those interested in health care, social service, education, or ministry. Participants serve from two weeks to three months; room and board are provided. For service periods of three months or more, at least nine months' prior notification is required. For more information, contact the Sisters of Charity of Nazareth, SCNA Center, Nazareth, KY 40048. Other voluntary-service opportunities are available through Overseas Development Network; see page 29 for more information.

COSTA RICA

Costa Ricans see their Central American nation as a rose among thorns. The country offers democracy, social stability, and relative economic prosperity in a region where all three are generally lacking.

The people of Costa Rica value their two-party democracy, tradition of nonviolence, and educational system. They also prize the traditional family structure that remains the central focus of their lives. A strong sense of history has helped keep these attitudes alive in the "Ticos" (the name by which the Costa Ricans are often called), and they will point with pride to the establishment of free and mandatory education for all citizens in 1869, the abolition of the death penalty in 1882, and the disbanding of a standing army in 1949.

But Costa Rica is not entirely immune to the maladies that plague the region. Rapid population growth, deforestation, and external debt (the highest per capita debt of any Third World nation) are among the problems confronting the country. And some people question whether Costa Rica can continue to avoid the political strife and economic ills experienced by many of its Central American neighbors.

Although the country is officially neutral, Costa Ricans are strongly pro-American and view the United States as a friend and ally. Much economic support is gained by this relationship both through the public and private sectors. An increasing number of

U.S. firms are locating their Latin American headquarters or branch offices in Costa Rica because of the nation's political and economic stability as well as the availability of an educated and hardworking labor force. Also visible are a growing number of retired Americans who have settled here to enjoy the good quality of life and pleasant climate at an economical price. Americans—whether businesspeople, retirees, students, or travelers—generally find Costa Rica safer, more comfortable, and less "foreign" than other Latin American nations.

—G. Bernard Yevin, Rockford, Illinois

Official name: Republic of Costa Rica. **Area:** 19,575 square miles (about twice the size of Maryland). **Population:** 3,032,000. **Population density:** 149 inhabitants per square mile. **Capital and largest city:** San José (pop. 278,500). **Language:** Spanish. **Religion:** Roman Catholic. **Per capita income:** US$1,584. **Currency:** Colón. **Literacy rate:** 93%. **Average daily high/low*:** San José: January, 75°/58°; July, 77°/62°. **Average number of days with precipitation:** San José: January, 3; July, 23.

TRAVEL

U.S. citizens need a passport to enter Costa Rica (although immigration officials will sometimes accept other proof of U.S. citizenship such as a birth certificate and driver's license). Upon your arrival, you will be issued a tourist card valid for 30 days. The tourist card may be extended an additional 90 days by permission of Costa Rican immigration authorities. Longer stays require a visa. An onward or return ticket is also necessary. For specific details, check with the Embassy of Costa Rica (2112 S Street NW, Washington, DC 20008) or with the Costa Rican consulate in New York.

Getting Around

Traveling around Costa Rica is fairly easy, both because the country is compact and because it has one of the region's best transportation systems. Roads and rail lines link the capital with Puerto Limón on the Caribbean and Puerto Arenas and Puerto Caldera on the Gulf of Nicoya. In addition, the Pan American Highway extends the length of the country, and express highways radiate from San José, connecting the capital to the other major cities of the central plateau as well as to Pacific ports and beaches. There are numerous companies in San José offering car and jeep rentals, including major U.S. companies such as Hertz, Avis, Budget, National, and Dollar as well as local firms. Costa Rica is also great for biking, with relatively light traffic and good asphalt roads.

Especially for Students and Young People

The student travel organization and issuer of the International Student Identity Card in Costa Rica is OTEC (Organización Turística Estudiantil y Juvenil). Its main office is in San José (Av. 3 calle 3, Edificio Ferencz, 275 Norte del Teatro, Nacional). At OTEC offices you can get information, buy international air tickets, book accommodations, and sign up for tours. Tours offered by OTEC include a one-day Pacific island cruise, a one-day white-water rafting trip on the Reventazón River, and a three-day "jungle tour" in Tortuguero National Park.

In Costa Rica, students with the International Student Identity Card are entitled to reduced airfares on international routes from San José, discounts at some hotels, and free or reduced admissions to several museums and theaters. OTEC will supply a list of restaurants and shops that provide discounts to International Student Identity Card holders.

---

*All temperatures are Fahrenheit.

For Further Information

An excellent guide to the country is *Costa Rica—a Travel Survival Kit*, available for $11.95 (plus $1.50 book-rate postage; $3 for first-class) from Lonely Planet Publications, Embarcadero West, 112 Linden Street, Oakland, CA 94607. General tourist information is available from the Costa Rica Tourist Board, 1101 Brickell Avenue, BIV Tower, Suite 801, Miami, FL 33131.

WORK

Getting a Job

It is very difficult for foreigners to obtain regular, salaried employment in Costa Rica. For more information, contact the Direccion General de Migracion Extranjera San José, Costa Rica. If you are a student, or you're interested in voluntary-service work, see the programs below.

CIEE's Work in Costa Rica program allows U.S. college students to receive authorization to accept temporary employment in Costa Rica for up to four months during their summer vacation (June 1 to October 1). Participants are responsible for finding their own jobs; the most likely categories of employment include unskilled work in the service industries (especially tourism) as well as language institutes. The program is conducted with the cooperation of OTEC, which meets participants upon arrival, provides an orientation, and assists with problems that may arise. Participants should realize that the summer job market in a Third World country like Costa Rica will be quite different from that of the United States. Salaries may be low compared to the U.S., but should cover the cost of daily expenses. To qualify, an individual must be at least 18 years of age, a college or university student, and a U.S. citizen or permanent resident. The cost of the program is $125. For more information, contact the Work Exchanges Department at CIEE.

Internships/Traineeships

Two programs sponsored by members of the Council on International Educational Exchange are described below.

AIESEC-US. Reciprocal internship program for students in economics, business, finance, marketing, accounting, and computer science. For more information see page 18.

University of Illinois at Urbana-Champaign. "Semester Internships in Costa Rica." San José. Fall or spring semester. Internships in community service or government agencies, along with enrollment in regular courses at the University of Costa Rica. Juniors, seniors, and graduate students with a minimum of five semesters of college Spanish; 3.0 GPA. Apply by March 1 for fall; October 1 for spring. See Appendix I for address to write for more information.

Voluntary Service

The Year Abroad Program sponsored by the International Christian Youth Exchange offers persons ages 18 to 24 voluntary-service opportunities in the fields of health care, education, the environment, construction, and so on. See page 23 for more information. Volunteer teaching positions are available through WorldTeach; for more information, see page 26. In addition, Goshen College offers a study-service term in Costa Rica that is open primarily to Goshen students; sometimes a limited number of spaces are available to students at other colleges and universities.

STUDY

The following academic programs are offered by CIEE-member institutions. Consult Appendix I for the addresses of the colleges and universities listed in this section. In addition, the University of California offers a study program that is open only to its own students.

Semester and Academic Year

General Studies

Associated Colleges of the Midwest. "Tropical Field Research: Natural and Social Sciences." San José. Spring semester only. May be combined with "Latin American Culture and Society" for full year of study. Sophomores, juniors, and seniors with social-science and natural science courses and one year of college Spanish. Apply by March 15 for early response; final deadline is November 1.

Friends World College. "Latin American Studies." San José, with trip to Nicaragua. Academic year or semester. Latin American studies, Spanish, and individualized program combining independent study with fieldwork or internships. Sophomores, juniors, and seniors; others may participate but will not receive credits. Apply by May 15 for fall; November 15 for spring.

International Student Exchange Program. Direct reciprocal exchange between U.S. universities and the Universidad Nacional de Heredia. Academic year or semester. Full curriculum options. Open only to students at ISEP-member institutions.

State University of New York at Albany. San José. Juniors, seniors, and graduate students with more than two years of college Spanish and 2.8 GPA. Apply by April 1 for fall; November 15 for spring.

University of Arkansas at Little Rock. "Latin American and Caribbean Exchange Program." Academic year or semester. Juniors and seniors at Arkansas Consortium for International Education schools only. Rolling admissions.

University of Illinois. "Semester Internships in Costa Rica." Internships working in community service and parliament, classes at the University of Costa Rica, San José. Juniors, seniors, and graduate students with 5 semesters of Spanish course work in Latin American studies and 3.0 GPA. Apply by March 1 for fall semester; October 1 for spring.

University of Kansas. "Academic Year Abroad at the University of Costa Rica." San José. Sophomores with four semesters of college Spanish and 3.0 GPA. Apply by October 1 for spring or year (August 1 for early decision); March 15 for fall.

Latin American Studies

Associated Colleges of the Midwest. San José. "Latin American Culture and Society." Fall semester only. May be combined with "Tropical Field Research" program for full year of study. Sophomores, juniors, and seniors with at least one year of college Spanish. For early response, apply by November 1; final deadline is March 15.

Summer

Biology

Council on International Educational Exchange. "Ecology of the Rain Forest: Tropical Biology and Conservation." Monteverde. Sophomores, juniors, and seniors with two semesters of college biology and 2.75 GPA. Apply by March 15. Contact University Programs Department.

General Studies

University of Alabama. San Pedro and San José. Freshmen to graduate students. Apply by April 1.

Ecological Studies

Lisle Fellowship. "Costa Rica: Integrating Cultural, Environmental, and Spiritual Ecology." Five weeks. Open to individuals 18 years and older. Apply by April 1.

GUATEMALA

Guatemala, like its Central American neighbors, has an intriguing past, a troubled present, and an uncertain future. Its Mayan roots are still strongly felt throughout the country in its ancient ruins, its textiles and customs, and its languages. Eighty percent of Guatemala's population consists of indigenous people who are descended from the Maya and in many ways spend their days much as their ancestors did: tilling small plots of land, weaving, forming almost self-supporting communities in the western highlands and Alta Verapaz. Over forty *indigena* languages are spoken in Guatemala, in addition to Spanish. The beautiful mountainous land and the low costs of Guatemalan transport add to the appeal for travelers exploring the region.

The Spanish language is only one of a number of legacies left by the Spaniards during their many years of rule, which began in 1523 when they arrived from Mexico City looking for precious metals. Many of the Spaniards who stayed in Guatemala intermarried with the indigenous people, forming the basis for the Mestizo population, which now accounts for about 20 percent of the total. However, those of primarily European descent, the *ladinos*, wield much of the country's economic and political power, making their money from coffee, sugarcane, and banana plantations in the countryside.

After it gained independence from Spain in 1821, Guatemala endured numerous military and civilian dictators, as well as extreme labor unrest and U.S. involvement. The country maintains an army consisting of indigenas who are, for the most part, untrained and unwilling participants. Rebels join the guerilla bands that roam the countryside. Between these two groups, thousands have been killed over the last ten years. In the mid-1980s, the country experienced a period of extreme political violence and terror. This period has shaped much of the American impression of the country but, while the traveler should still use caution, Guatemala is currently undergoing a period of relative political stability under civilian president Vinicio Cerezo Arévalo.

—*Pearl Douglas, Charleston, West Virginia*

Official name: Republic of Guatemala. **Area:** 42,042 square miles (the size of Tennessee). **Population:** 9,340,000. **Population density:** 233 inhabitants per square mile. **Capital and largest city:** Guatemala City (pop. 1,800,000). **Language:** Spanish. **Religion:** Roman Catholic. **Per capita income:** US$810. **Currency:** Quetzal. **Literacy rate:** 48%.

high/low*: Guatemala City: January, 73°/53°; July, 78°/60°. **Average number of days with precipitation:** Guatemala City: January, 4; July, 21.

TRAVEL

U.S. citizens need a tourist card or a visa to enter Guatemala. Tourist cards are available for $5 from the airlines and are good for one visit of up to 30 days. To get a tourist card, you'll need proof of U.S. citizenship, such as a passport, birth or naturalization certificate, driver's license, or voter registration card. Visas are issued free and are good for one year with multiple entries of 30 days each. Although not officially required, some airlines may not allow you to board a flight to Guatemala without an outward ticket. Contact the Embassy of Guatemala (2220 R Street NW, Washington, DC 20008) or a Guatemalan consulate.

Getting Around

In Guatemala, the bus is king. Fast buses traverse the Pan-American highway every half hour or so, and slower ones cover the countryside, serving even the tiniest of villages. Only the wealthy own cars while the rest of the population relies entirely on buses for transportation. For the most part, buses are very cheap and easy to use, usually operating out of bus terminals located on the edge of town. Between towns you can hail buses and they'll usually stop for you. There are two classes: first class means you buy a ticket in advance and get a seat on an old Greyhound, while in second class you buy the ticket on the bus (usually an old U.S. school bus). Buses, usually packed to the bursting point, are a great way to meet people.

Other travel options are trains, planes, and automobiles. There's twice-weekly train service between Tecun Uman on the Mexican border and Puerto Barrios on the Caribbean coast, but there's talk that this might be discontinued. At any rate, the trains are in poor shape. Four companies vie for the flights between Guatemala City to Flores (the gateway to the spectacular ruins at Tikal), which takes 45 minutes as opposed to 18 hours on the bus. Renting a car is quite expensive (about $50 a day), and it won't allow you much contact with the country's populace. Most of the main routes are paved, but gas stations are few and far between (as are spare parts). Car theft and vandalism continue to be major problems. Taxis are available for intercity travel, but most don't have meters so be sure to set a price before getting in. Biking is very popular in Guatemala, and in Antigua mountain bikes can be rented by the day, week, or month. Motorbikes can be rented in Guatemala City and Antigua. Hitchhiking is common, but it's polite to offer a small fee.

For Further Information

An excellent guide to Guatemala's Mayan sites is *La Ruta Maya: Yucatan, Guatemala and Belize—A Travel Survival Kit*, available for $16.95 (plus $1.50 book-rate postage; $3 for first-class) from Lonely Planet Publications, Embarcadero West, 112 Linden Street, Oakland, CA 94607. There's also a chapter on Guatemala in *Let's Go: Mexico* ($13.95) available in most bookstores and Council Travel offices. General tourist information is available from the Guatemalan Tourist Bureau, Consulate of Guatemala, 57 Park Avenue, New York, NY 10016.

---

*All temperatures are Fahrenheit.

WORK

It is necessary to obtain a labor permit in order to be employed in Guatemala. You must secure a job before the permit will be issued. For further information, contact the Ministerio de Trabajo, Y Prebision Social, Palacio Nacional, 1er Nivel Zone 1, Guatemala, Guatemala.

Internships/Traineeships

A program offered by one of the member institutions of the Council on International Educational Exchange is listed below.

AIESEC-US. Reciprocal internship program for students in economics, business, finance, marketing, accounting, and computer science. See page 18 for more information.

EXPLORING GUATEMALAN CULTURE

Readings

Guatemala's most famous author is Miguel Angel Asturias. The history and culture of Guatemala are recurrent themes in his work. *Men of Maize* (1949), considered his masterpiece, deals with the complexity of Indian culture in magical realist style. *El Señor Presidente* (1946) offers a glimpse into social chaos and dictatorial rule, based on the dictatorship of Guatemalan president Cabrera. In *Weekend en Guatemala* (1956) he describes the downfall of the Arbenz government, and *El Papa Verde* (1954) delves into the shady world of the United Fruit Company. Rigoberta Menchu provides an insider's perspective on life in the highlands in *Rigoberta Menchu: An Indian Woman in Guatemala* (1985), an account of the abuse of the Indian population and of the complexity of Indian culture.

Authors from other countries have also written about Guatemala. In Henry J. Frundt's *Refreshing Pauses: Coca-Cola and Human Rights in Guatemala* (1987), we encounter a tale of foreign greed and the Guatemalan effort to organize a union. *The Volcano Above Us*, by Norman Lewis, is a depressing and gripping novel that includes banana companies, trigger-happy troops, political instability, and racism. Paul Bowles recounts his experiences in Guatemala in *Up Above the World* (1982).

HONDURAS

Flat land is at a premium in Honduras, especially in the nation's capital, Tegucigalpa, which is built on the slopes of the mountain El Picacho. Tegucigalpa was the site of some early Spanish gold mines; however, the Spanish soon realized there was little easily convertible wealth (gold, silver, copper) to be found in Honduras and moved on. Honduras was subsequently largely ignored by Spain as a colony and later as a trading partner, and remained fairly isolated until the United Fruit Company, with the support of the U.S. government, started to cultivate large cash-crop (chiefly banana) plantations in the arable Northwest. A succession of military and civilian rulers, internal rebellions, civil wars, and changes of government since independence in 1821 indicate a political instability that has scared away most foreign investment. The banana companies, which have used the lack of a stable Honduran government to their advantage, are the exception; Honduras was the original "Banana Republic."

Economically, Honduras shot itself in the foot by withdrawing from the Central American Common Market during the aftermath of the 1969 "Soccer War" with El

Salvador. Only considerable U.S. aid has kept the Honduran economy from complete disaster. Honduras traditionally has been the poorest nation in Central America; at present, however, Nicaragua's drawn out civil war has given Nicaragua that distinction. The result of Honduras's dependence on U.S. aid and U.S. companies for investment is the country's military alliance with the U.S., which has made it a base for U.S. military operations in Central America. The American influence is strong, from the *supermercados* and shopping malls that exist in defiance of the poverty of most Hondurans to the U.S. pop music that can be heard all over Tegucigalpa.

During the 1980s, Honduras was the base for Contra activity against the Sandinista government in Nicaragua. Though Contra-Sandinista activity has ceased, the Contras remain a force along the Honduras-Nicaragua border and according to some, the entire country is a powderkeg waiting to explode. However, in 1986, as a result of U.S. pressure, the first peaceful transfer of political power in 30 years occurred. So far the political peace has continued, although a military coup is always a possibility.

Most of Honduras is mountainous except the low swamplands (Paul Theroux's "Mosquito Coast") in the Northeast. Partly because of its inhospitable topography, Honduras is one of the least populous Central American republics although it is the largest in area. In contrast to the Spanish-speaking South, in many areas of the North Coast both Spanish and English are commonly spoken, a result of West Indian laborers migrating to Honduras for work on coastal railways and banana and coffee plantations in the late 19th and early 20th centuries. There are no well-known tourist resorts, except for the Bay Islands off the Caribbean Coast, which attract a mix of people seeking cheap beach life off the beaten path.

—*Fraser Brown, New York, New York*

Official name: Republic of Honduras. **Area:** 43,277 square miles (about the size of Tennessee). **Population:** 5,261,000. **Population density:** 117 inhabitants per square mile. **Capital and largest city:** Tegucigalpa (pop. 571,400). **Language:** Spanish. **Religion:** Roman Catholic. **Per capita income:** US$1,000. **Currency:** Lempira. **Literacy rate:** 56%. **Average daily high/low*:** Tegucigalpa: January, 77°/56°; July, 83°/63°. **Average number of days with precipitation:** Tegucigalpa: January, 1; July, 8.

TRAVEL

For U.S. citizens planning on traveling to Honduras, a passport (valid for at least six months after the date of entry), a visa, and an onward or return ticket are required. Visas are issued for stays of up to 90 days. For specific regulations, check with the Embassy of Honduras, 4301 Connecticut Avenue NW, Washington, DC 20008.

Getting Around

As a result of an aggressive road-building program, roads now link most parts of the country, and getting around by car or bus is much easier than it used to be. Frequent buses travel the country's main route, which connects the nation's commercial center of San Pedro Sula with Tegucigalpa, the capital. Buses serve most of the rest of the country as well, except for parts of the Mosquito Coast, which are still not accesible by road. Cars can be rented in San Pedro Sula or Tegucigalpa. The country's limited railroad network is confined to the banana-producing areas of the coast and transports a lot of bananas but not many people. There are several small airlines—SAHSA, Aero Servicios, Islena—which offer daily flights between Tegucigalpa, San Pedro Sula, La Ceiba, and the Caribbean costal towns and islands. In the most isolated areas, travel is still by mule and foot.

---

*All temperatures are Fahrenheit.

For Further Information

Good travel information about Honduras can be found in *Central America on a Shoestring*, available for $15.95 (plus $1.50 book-rate postage; $3 for first-class) from Lonely Planet Publications, Embarcadero West, 112 Linden Street, Oakland, CA 94607. General tourist information is available from the Honduras Information Service, Box 673, Murray Hill Station, New York, NY 10156. Please include a large, self-addressed stamped envelope with your request.

WORK

It is very difficult for foreigners to obtain employment in Honduras. For more information, contact the Embassy of Honduras, 4301 Connecticut Avenue NW, Washington, DC 20008.

Voluntary Service

For persons interested in voluntary-service work, the Year-Abroad Program sponsored by the International Christian Youth Exchange offers persons ages 18 to 24 voluntary-service opportunities in the fields of health care, education, the environment, construction, and so on. See page 23 for more information.

STUDY

The following programs are offered by CIEE-member institutions. Consult Appendix I for the addresses of the colleges and universities listed in this section.

Semester and Academic Year

General Studies

University of Arkansas at Little Rock. "Latin American and Caribbean Exchange Program." Academic year and semester. Juniors and seniors at Arkansas Consortium or International Education schools only. Rolling admissions.

International Student Exchange Program. Direct reciprocal exchange between U.S. universities and the Universidad José Cecilio del Valle. Full curriculum options. Only open to students at ISEP-member organizations.

MEXICO

A 2,000-mile border—sometimes a shallow river but more often just an imaginary line in the desert—separates Mexico and the United States. While the border itself is crossed legally and illegally by thousands of people every day, the real division is a linguistic, economic, historic, and cultural one that is not so easily crossed. Nowhere else does the Third World rub shoulders so closely with one of the world's wealthiest nations. And while the two nations coexist peacefully but uncomfortably, each tries as much as possible to ignore the other. Yet as much as Americans and Mexicans might each like to be rid of their backyard neighbor, the futures of the two countries are inextricably linked.

In the 16th century the Spanish defeated the Aztecs, took their land and silver, and enslaved or killed much of the native population. In the 19th century, Mexico gained its independence from Spain, but little changed for the average Mexican. Early in this century the Mexican Revolution brought far-reaching changes, including land redistribution and an end to the power of the traditional elite: the landed aristocracy, the church, and the military. But its promise of power to Mexican workers and *campesinos* was never realized; Mexico remains split by stark class differences.

Since 1982, Mexico has been in the throes of a financial crisis that has left the country demoralized and with a standard of living lower than that of ten years earlier. This crisis was brought about by a drop in the price of petroleum on world markets and Mexico's resultant inability to make the required payments on its foreign debt. One result of the crisis has been increased emigration—legal and illegal—across the U.S. border. Another has been challenges from both the left and right to the PRI, the political party that has controlled Mexico since the end of the Revolution. President Carlos Salinas de Gortari has promised to give a greater role to the opposition and enforce fair elections. But the political stability of Mexico, like its economic future, is uncertain.

Nowhere is this uncertainty more evident than in Mexico City, the economic, political, and cultural heart of the country. With nearly 20 million people, the metropolitan area is by most counts the world's largest city. Not surprisingly, rapid population growth has strained the infrastructure of the city, producing overcrowding, pollution, and sprawling slums. But in spite of its problems, Mexico City—once the capital of New Spain and before that of the Aztec empire—remains one of the world's most lively and interesting cities. And rising on the northern edge of the city are the ruins of Teotihuacán, once the center of a great empire that reached its zenith a millenium before the arrival of the Aztecs. Even now, Teotihuacán's Pyramids of the Sun and Moon are among the world's most impressive sights.

Although power radiates from Mexico City, the spiritual heart of the country beats in the villages of Mexico. Here the pace of life is slower and traditional ties to the land, the church, and family are strong. Visitors to the highlands of central Mexico will encounter picturesque villages and a way of life that is attractive because it seems unaffected by the ills of modernity. But a closer examination will also reveal that these villages are not lost in time; like all Mexican society today, they are products of the dynamic interplay between ancient Indian ways, the legacy of Spanish colonialism, and the contemporary cultural, political, and economic influence of Mexico's powerful northern neighbor.

Whether you come for unsurpassed beach resorts such as Acapulco or Cancún, the ruins of ancient Indian civilizations, or the natural beauty of its mountains, jungles, and deserts, strike out on your own to explore Mexico's cities, villages, and countryside. Your efforts will be richly rewarded as you develop a new perspective on the U.S.-Mexican relationship and encounter a very different way of life that's just across the border.

—*Del Franz, New York, New York*

Official name: United Mexican States. **Area:** 761,604 square miles (almost three times the size of Texas). **Population:** 88,335,000. **Population density:** 115 inhabitants per square mile. **Capital and largest city:** Mexico City (pop. 20,000,000). **Language:** Spanish. **Religion:** Roman Catholic. **Per capita income:** US$2,082. **Currency:** Mexican peso. **Literacy rate:** 88%. **Average daily high/low*:** Acapulco: January, 85°/70°; July, 89°/75°; Mérida: January, 83°/62°; July, 82°/73°; Mexico City: January, 66°/42°; July, 73°/53°. **Average number of days with precipitation:** Acapulco: January, 0; July, 11; Mérida: January, 8; July, 20; Mexico City: January, 4; July, 27.

---

*All temperatures are Fahrenheit.

TRAVEL

U.S. citizens do not need a passport or a visa to enter Mexico for tourist/transit stays of up to 90 days. Tourist cards, which are required, are issued free of charge upon presentation of proof of citizenship (a birth certificate, passport, or naturalization papers). They can be obtained at immigration offices at points of entry along the border, at Mexican consulates and tourist offices, or from airlines serving Mexico. The tourist card is valid three months for single entry up to 180 days, and requires proof of U.S. citizenship, photo ID, and sufficient funds. Minors traveling alone, or without both parents must have notarized consent from the absent parent or copies of divorce papers or a death certificate in either eventuality. For entry for purposes other than tourism, check with the Embassy of Mexico (2829 16th Street NW, Washington DC 20036) or with one of the nearly 50 Mexican consulates in the U.S.

Getting Around

Mexico's hundreds of bus companies lend credence to the saying that in Mexico where there's a road, there's a bus. Buses range from comfortable air-conditioned intercity buses to trucks with wooden benches, and half the excitement of visiting a remote village may be the bus trip there. Traveling by bus is cheap and immerses you in Mexican culture in a way that is not possible if you drive or fly.

Mexico also has a well-developed rail network, although it's not nearly as comprehensive as the bus system. Generally speaking, trains are slower and subject to more frequent delays than buses. On the other hand, they are usually more comfortable and even cheaper than the buses. Trains with sleeping cars provide overnight service between Mexico City and the other major cities of central Mexico, while long-distance trains link Mexico City to cities along the U.S. border—a journey that can take a couple of days, depending on the route selected.

Air service is provided by several domestic airlines, the best known of which are Aeroméxico and Mexicana. In Mexico, travel by plane is safe and convenient and a popular alternative for travelers covering long distances.

In this mountainous country of few navigable rivers, travel by boat is generally not an option. An exception are the car ferries that cross between the Baja Peninsula and various cities on the Mexican mainland.

Mexico will accept a U.S. driver's license without any further documentation. However, persons planning to drive in Mexico should be aware that Mexican roads are characterized by unpredictable hazards most U.S drivers are not accustomed to, including animals, slow-moving carts, people, and potholes. Mexican driving habits are also quite different; for example, passing is done with less margin of safety and little attention is paid to the concept of traffic lanes (which are seldom marked on the wider roads). Unleaded gasoline, used only by tourists with U.S. vehicles, can be found only in large towns and resorts. Remember, too that U.S. auto insurance generally is not valid in Mexico; Americans driving their own cars will have to buy Mexican auto insurance to protect themselves while they are south of the border. If you bring in your own car, you will need a free Tourist Permit, which is good for 180 days. Don't overstay: After five days the fine rises to half the value of the car! In spite of these obstacles, thousands of Americans drive in Mexico. A car provides comfort and independence and can be an enjoyable means of getting around, especially in northern Mexico, where traffic is light. Cars can also be rented in cities and tourist centers throughout Mexico. In addition, hitchhiking is socially acceptable and done by both Mexicans and foreigners.

"The main difference surrounds the concept of time. When you go to a Latin American country, relax. Take your time. I found it difficult to adjust my sense of time once I returned to the States."
—Gloria Abeja, Bridgeview, Illinois

Eating and Sleeping

If you avoid the most touristy places, Mexico can be one of the world's most inexpensive countries. There's an abundance of budget hotels in every Mexican city, but be aware that new establishments resembling places you might see in the U.S. are generally on the more expensive side. Older-looking hotels are usually more economical, spacious, and comfortable. There is also a host of inexpensive youth hostels. For a nationwide listing of these, contact the Asociacion Mexicana de la Juventud, Avenida Francisco 1, Madero No. 6, Despacho 314, Delegacion Cuauhtemoc, 06000 Mexico D.F.

Dining in Mexico can also be quite cheap, and those who are used to American versions of Mexican food are in for a tasty surprise. Real Mexican cuisine is much more varied than the tacos and burritos familar to Americans. The staples of any Mexican meal are rice, beans, and tortillas, which are commonly served with a main dish of meat, chicken, or fish. The major meal of the day is eaten in the afternoon, usually between 2 and 5 P.M. Most restaurants serve a fixed-price *comida corrida*, or meal of the day.

Especially for Students and Young People

SETEJ Mexico (Hamburgo No. 301, Colonia Juarez, 06600 Mexico D.F.) is Mexico's student travel organization and issuer of the International Student Identity Card. There are branch offices in five other cities: Cuernavaca, Guadalajara, Guanajuato, Oaxaca, and Monterrey. At most SETEJ Mexico offices you can get travel information, book accommodations, and buy international train and plane tickets. SETEJ Mexico also operates youth hostels in Acapulco and Mexico City, and conducts tours for students and young people. Contact SETEJ Mexico for more information.

In Mexico, holders of the International Student Identity Card receive discounts on international airfares from Mexico City. Some museums, theaters, shops, and hotels also offer discounts to students with the International Student Identity Card. A listing of participating establishments is available at SETEJ Mexico offices throughout the country.

Meeting the People

SETEJ Mexico can help arrange a homestay with a Mexican family. Homestays are generally several weeks in length. Contact SETEJ Mexico's main office in Mexico City for more information.

For Further Information

General tourist information is available from the Mexican Government Office of Tourism (405 Park Avenue, New York, NY 10022). The Mexican government also has tourist offices in a number of other U.S. cities.

There are a good number of guidebooks to Mexico. One of the favorites for students traveling on a budget is *Let's Go: Mexico* ($13.95), which also includes information on Guatemala and Belize. For good, detailed descriptions of Mexican culture and history in relation to the sights, try *The Real Guide: Mexico* ($11.95). Those who want to go off the beaten path might turn to *Mexico: A Travel Survival Kit* ($17.95) or *La Ruta Maya —Yucatan, Guatemala, and Belize: A Travel Survival Kit* ($15.95), both published by Lonely Planet Publications, Embarcadero West, 112 Linden Street, Oakland, CA 94607 (include $1.50 book-rate postage; $3 for first-class).

An extremely useful resource, Carl Franz's *The People's Guide to Mexico* ($17.95) is not a guidebook in the traditional sense, in that it does not describe hotels or the most interesting towns to visit; what it does is provide, through a series of anecdotes, one of the best pictures of what travel in Mexico is all about. While most informative for the first-time visitor, the book also makes for interesting and enjoyable reading for the seasoned traveler. If you can't find it in bookstores, you can order it from John Muir Publications, PO Box 613, Sante Fe, NM 87504.

The uneasy relationship between Mexico and the United States is sure to enter into discussions you have with Mexicans. A recent book, *Limits to Friendship: The United States and Mexico* ($10.95) by Jorge G. Castañeda, provides a Mexican perspective on the political, economic, and cultural issues that divide the two countries. If you can't find it in bookstores, you can order it from Random House (400 Hahn Road, Westminister, MD 21157; add $1.50 for postage). A good, concise analysis of foreign policy options from a U.S. point of view is provided by Peter H. Smith in *Mexico: Neighbor in Transition* ($4, plus $1.50 for postage), published by the Foreign Policy Association, 729 Seventh Avenue, New York, NY 10019. Another look at the relationship from a U.S. perspective can be found in *Distant Neighbors* (Viking, $8.95) by *New York Times* correspondent Alan Riding. Finally, *Good Neighbors: Communicating with the Mexicans*, by John C. Condon, takes a look at Mexicans' and Americans' misperceptions of each other and suggests ways to overcome these prejudices. Available from Intercultural Press (PO Box 700, Yarmouth, ME 04096), the book costs $10.95.

WORK

Obtaining regular salaried employment in Mexico is nearly impossible for foreigners; it's not permitted unless specifically requested by a Mexican company. The employer then must apply for the requisite work permit, on the applicant's behalf, to the Mexican immigration authorities. For more information contact the Embassy of Mexico, Consular Section, 1019 19th Street NW, Suite 810, Washington, DC 20036.

Internships/Traineeships

Internship programs offered by member institutions and organizations of the Council on International Educational Exchange are described below.

AIESEC-US. Reciprocal internship program for students in economics, business, finance, marketing, accounting, and computer science. For more information see page 18.

Association for International Practical Training. "IAESTE Trainee Program." On-the-job training for undergraduate and graduate students in technical fields such as engineering, computer science, agriculture, architecture, and mathematics. See page 18 for more information.

Brigham Young University. "Spring Term Internship in Mexico." Internships in pre-med, dietetics, nutrition, home economics, and health-related fields. Six weeks in May and June; fluency in Spanish required. Students live with Mexican families and work in hospitals and other health-related facilities. Apply by February 1. Consult Appendix I for the address you can write to for more information.

Voluntary Service

The Year Abroad Program sponsored by the International Christian Youth Exchange offers persons ages 18 to 24 voluntary-service opportunities in the fields of health care, education, the environment, construction, and so on. See page 23 for more information.

The Lisle Fellowship sponsors a short-term study/service program, "Art and Culture in Mexico: Artisans and Community Development." This programs is open to recent high-school graduates, college students, and adults. Apply by October 15. See Appendix I for the address you can write for more information.

In addition, Los Ninos—Helping Children at the Border works with and helps support orphanages in the Mexican border cities of Mexicali, Tecate, and Tijuana. Short- and long-term voluntary-service opportunities are available in the orphanages. No special skills are required, but participants must be at least 18 years old. For more information, contact Los Ninos, 1330 Continental Street, San Ysidro, CA 92073.

Other voluntary-service opportunities are available through The Partnership for Service Learning, Overseas Development Network, and Amigos de las Americas. For more information on these programs see Chapter Three.

"Living in a materialistic society such as the United States, one sometimes forgets how important human relationships are to a full life. Mexicans have not neglected this important area of life. Mexico taught me the importance of living a simpler life, one unhampered by an excess of material possessions and monetarily motivated career goals."
—Shannan Mattiace, Cedar Rapids, Iowa

STUDY

The Embassy of Mexico (address above) can provide information on language schools for foreign students as well as on independent postgraduate study.

The Universidad Autónoma de Guadalajara, a CIEE-member institution in Mexico, hosts a number of exchange students on programs sponsored by certain U.S. colleges and universities. It also accepts students enrolling independently from the U.S. Contact the study-abroad office at your school for further information about this university.

The following study programs are offered by CIEE-member institutions. Consult Appendix I for the addresses of colleges and universities listed in this section. In addition to these programs, the American Graduate School of International Management, California State University, the University of Oregon, the University of Pittsburgh, and Valparaiso University offer study programs open only to their own students.

Semester and Academic Year

Ecology

University of La Verne. "Natural History of Baja California." January. Juniors to graduate students with 2.5 GPA. Apply by October 31.

Education

University of Iowa. "Iowa/Yucatán Semester Study Abroad." Spring semester. Spanish, anthropology, and education aimed at undergraduates preparing to teach. Sophomores to graduate students with 2.5 GPA. Apply by October 10. Contact: Associate Dean, College of Education, N459E Lindquist Center, University of Iowa, Iowa City, IA 52242.

General Studies

Alma College. "Program of Studies in Mexico." Mexico City. Academic year and semester. Homestays and excursions. Courses offered through Universidad Iberoamericana. Sophomores, juniors, and seniors with three semesters of Spanish and 2.5 GPA.

Central University of Iowa. "Central College in Yucatán." Mérida. Fall, winter, or spring quarter. Freshmen to seniors with 2.5 GPA. Apply two months prior to beginning of term.

Central Washington University. Morelia. Liberal arts curriculum, including history, literature, and intensive language. Homestay. Undergraduates and teachers. 2.5 GPA, two quarters of college coursework, and one Spanish course required.

Experiment in International Living/School for International Training. "College Semester Abroad." Oaxaca and Guanajuato. Fall or spring semester. Intensive language, Mexican life and culture seminar, field-study seminar, independent-study project, educational travel, and homestays. Sophomores to seniors with 2.5 GPA. Apply by May 15 for fall and October 15 for spring.

International Student Exchange Program. Direct reciprocal exchange between U.S. universities and institutions in Guadalajara, Mexico City, Monterrey, and Puebla. Summer, semester, or academic year. Full curriculum options. Open only to students at ISEP-member institutions.

Northern Illinois University. "Mexican and Latin American Studies." Mexico City. Semester or academic year. Courses, offered through the Universidad Autónoma de México, are taught in Spanish by Mexican faculty. Apply by June 1 for fall; and November 1 for spring.

Rollins College. "Rollins Spring Term in Mérida." Sophomores, juniors, and seniors with 2.8 GPA. Apply by November 1.

Rutgers University. "Junior Year in Mexico." University of the Yucatan, Mérida. Juniors with two years of college Spanish, Spanish literature, and 3.0 GPA. Apply by March 1.

University of Arkansas at Little Rock. "Mexican Exchange Program." Guadalajara. Open to students at schools in the state of Arkansas. Sophomores, juniors, and seniors. Rolling admission.

University of North Carolina—Chapel Hill. "UNC Program to Mexico City." Semester or academic year. Study at Universidad Autónoma de México. Juniors and seniors. Rolling admissions.

University of Notre Dame. "International Study Program in Mexico City." Semester or academic year. Spanish language, Spanish and Latin American literature, and Latin American civilization. Sophomores and juniors with two years of college Spanish and 2.5 overall GPA (3.0 in Spanish). Apply by December 1 for fall and October 15 for spring.

University of Wisconsin—Platteville. "Mexico Study Center." Puebla. Academic year or semester at Universidad de las Americas. Sophomores, juniors, and seniors with two years of college Spanish and 3.0 GPA. Apply by April 15 for fall and academic year; October 20 for spring.

Human Ecology

Lisle Fellowship. "Art and Culture in Mexico: Artisans and Community Development." Three and a half weeks over Christmas break. Learning of community development efforts by indigenous artisans. Open to individuals 18 years and older. Apply by September 15.

Latin American and Mexican Studies

Colorado State University. "Latin American Studies in Mexico." Puebla. Academic year or semester at Universidad de las Americas. Sophomores, juniors, and seniors.

Guilford College. "Semester in Guadalajara." Fall. Sophomores, juniors, and seniors with one year of college Spanish. Apply by October 31.

Spanish Language and Mexican Culture

Brigham Young University. "Spring Term in Mexico." Includes study tour. Sophomores, juniors, and seniors with some knowledge of Spanish. Apply by February 1.

Davidson College. "Summer in Mexico." Guadalajara. Summer in even-numbered years only. Sophomores and juniors with intermediate Spanish and 2.75 GPA. Apply by February 1.

Northern Arizona University. "Study Abroad in Mexico." Cuernavaca. Fall or spring semester. Sophomores to graduate students. One semester of Spanish recommended. Apply by May 1 for fall; October 15 for spring.

Ohio State University. "The Cuernavaca Program." Winter, spring, summer, and fall quarters. Elementary Spanish language study. Sophomores to graduate students with 2.7 GPA. Apply by July 10, October 15, January 15, or April 10.

State University of New York at Brockport. "Cuernavaca Program." Language instruction and homestay. Fall or spring semester. No language prerequisite. Juniors and seniors 2.5 GPA. Apply by November 1 for spring; March 1 for fall.

University of Colorado at Boulder. "Semester in Guadalajara." Centro de Estudios para Extranjeros at the University of Guadalajara. Fall or spring semester. Freshmen to seniors with 2.75 GPA. Apply October 15 for spring; March 1 for fall.

University of La Verne.
"Study in Cuernavaca." Cuauhnahuac Institute. Academic year, semester, or summer. Juniors to graduate students with 2.5 GPA. Apply by September 31 for spring; March 1 for summer or fall.
"Semester/Year in Mexico." Universidad Iberoamericana in Mexico City. Most work done in Spanish. Juniors to graduate students with knowledge of Spanish and 2.5 GPA. Apply by September 31 for spring; March 1 for fall.

University of Minnesota.
"Spanish in Cuernavaca." Fall, winter, or spring quarter. Beginning and intermediate Spanish language. Undergraduates and adults. Apply by June 15 for fall, October 15 for winter, December 15 for spring. University of Utah.
"Cuernavaca Spanish Language Program." Nine weeks (end of March to end of May). Freshmen to graduate students and others. Minimum of one or two quarters of college Spanish is required. Apply by January 1.

Western Washington University. "Study in Mexico." Morelia. Semester or quarter options. Open to high school students with 15 hours of college classes, high-school graduates, and college undergraduate and graduate students with 2.5 GPA. Apply one month prior to beginning of the program.

World College West. "World Study in Mexico." Morelia, Michoacán, and nearby villages. Academic year or semester. Intensive cultural immersion. Language and culture studies, field-study methods, independent-study project, urban and village homestays, potential internships. Juniors and seniors with one year of Spanish and one cultural-studies class. Apply by March 15.

Latin American and Mexican Studies

University of Alabama. "Alabama in Yucatan." Merida. Three week program in May. Undergraduates and graduates.

Summer

Art History

Syracuse University. "The Mural Painting of Los Tres Grandes." Mexico City and Guadalajara. Study of Orozco, Siquieros, Rivera. Graduate students.

General Studies

Alma College. "Program of Studies in Mexico." Mexico City. Study at Universidad Iberoamericana. Homestays, excursions. Sophomores, juniors, and seniors with 2.5 GPA. Apply by March 15.

Central Washington University. Morelia. Liberal arts curriculum including history, literature, and intensive language. Homestay. Undergraduates and teachers. 2.5 GPA, two quarters of college coursework, and one Spanish course required.

Social Science

Michigan State University. "Social Science in Mexico." Queréntaro, Mexico City, Guanajuato, Morelia, and Pátzcuaro. Impact of change on Mexico. Freshmen to graduate students. Apply by April 20.

Spanish Language and Mexican Culture

Eastern Michigan University. "Intensive Spanish Language Program." Cuernavaca. Freshmen to seniors. Apply by May 15.

Indiana University. "Overseas Study in Mexico." Mexico City. Freshmen to seniors with one year of college Spanish and 2.8 GPA. Apply by early March.

Miami University. Language workshops in Puebla. Students with four semesters of Spanish. Apply by February 15.

New York University. "NYU in Mexico." Mexico City. One-week graduate seminar on culture and society in contemporary Mexico. All lectures in Spanish. Contact Department of Spanish and Portuguese, Faculty of Arts and Science, 19 University Place, Room 400, New York, NY 10003; (212) 998-8770.

North Carolina State University/Raleigh. "Mexico Summer Program." Cuernavaca. Freshman to graduate students, and elementary and secondary teachers. One semester of high-school Spanish and 2.0 GPA is required. Apply by January 15.

State University of New York at Brockport. "Intensive Spanish in Mexico Program." Homestay. No language prerequisite. Juniors and seniors with 2.5 GPA. Apply by May 1.

State University of New York at Oswego. "Oswego-Mexico City Program." High school seniors, college freshmen to graduate students. Apply by April 1.

Texas Tech University. "Mexico Field Course." San Luis Potosi. Freshmen to graduate students with two years of college Spanish. Apply by February 1.

University of Alabama. "Alabama in Yucatán." Freshmen to graduate students. Interim. Apply by April 1.

University of Arkansas at Little Rock. "Summer in Mexico." Guadalajara. Freshmen to seniors. Students must register for three-week seminar offered prior to departure. Apply by February 28.

University of Colorado at Boulder. "Summer in Guadalajara." Centro de Estudios para Extranjeros at the University of Guadalajara. Freshmen to seniors with 2.75 GPA and 15 hours of college Spanish. Apply by March 1.

University of Kansas. "Summer Language Institute in Guadalajara, Mexico." Eight-week program focusing on language skills, Mexican culture, and Hispanic literature. Undergraduates with four semesters of college Spanish. Apply by April 15.

University System of Georgia/Augusta College.
"Spanish Language and Mexican Culture in Guadalajara." Undergraduates with 2.5 GPA. Apply by March 15.

Western Washington University. "Study in Mexico." Morelia. Open to high-school graduates with 15 hours of college classes, and college undergraduate and graduate students with 2.5 GPA. Apply one month prior to beginning of the program.

Wichita State University. "Summer Program in Puebla." Freshmen to graduate students with two years of high-school Spanish or two semesters college Spanish. Apply by May 15.

University of Wisconsin-Madison. "Mexico Summer Program." Oaxaca. Open to sophomores, juniors, and seniors with three semesters of college Spanish and 3.0 GPA. Apply by March 15.

EXPLORING MEXICAN CULTURE

Readings

It has been said of Octavio Paz that his literary roles as a poet and a cultural critic are just two sides of a single soulful outlook on Mexico, a subject he never tires of writing about. *The Labyrinth of Solitude* (1950), an analysis of the Mexican psyche from the Spanish Conquest to the 20th century, is perhaps his best-known book and a wonderful example of his prose style.

Carlos Fuentes, the son of a Mexican diplomat assigned to Washington, spent his early years in the United States. As a result, when he returned to Mexico, he had to rediscover his homeland and his identity as a Mexican. The novels of the mature Fuentes reflect this preoccupation with what it means to be Mexican, part of the larger preoccupation with history and identity that often surfaces in recent Latin American writing. *The Death of Artemio Cruz* (1962), Fuentes's first and perhaps most popular novel, is the story of a man's life remembered as he is about to die. In his most recent work, *Christopher Unborn*, Fuentes presents an insightful yet humorous picture of his country in a story narrated by a fetus and set in 1992, the 500th anniversary of Christopher Columbus's famous voyage. Some of his other works include *The Old Gringo*, *Terra Nostra*, and *Distant Relations*.

The late Juan Rulfo wrote about Jalisco, the state in western Mexico from which he hailed. In *The Burning Plains and Other Stories* (1953), Rulfo explored the poverty and forlorn lives led by many of the people of his home state in lean, vivid prose. *Pedro Páramo* (1955), probably his most popular work internationally, is a surrealistic view of life and death in rural Mexico.

Mariano Azuela explores Mexican culture and society at the time of the Mexican Revolution. Novels by Mariano Azuela include *The Trials of a Respectable Family* (1918), *The Firefly* (1932), and his classic work, *The Underdogs* (1915), which presents the revolution from the viewpoint of peasants and includes characters such as Zapata and Pancho Villa. Two other novels by Azuela, *The Flies* and *The Bosses* (1918), are satiric and somber writings about the Mexican Revolution.

From an anthropological point of view, Oscar Lewis provides oral histories of a working-class family in Mexico City in *The Children of Sanchez* (1979). His works also include *A Death in the Sanchez Family* (1969), *Pedro Martinez* (1966), and *Five Families* (1959). In *The Alamo Tree* (1984), Ernest Brawley writes about the effects of political, economic, and social changes on two Mexican families. Most Mexicans have some relative living and working in the United States; *Coyotes*, by Ted Conover, explores the secret world of illegal aliens in the U.S.

The experiences of foreigners in Mexico are the subject of a number of books. Some of them are Harry LaTourette Foster's *A Gringo in Mañana Land* (1976), Kenneth's Gangemi's *The Volcanoes from Puebla* (1979), and John Lincoln's *One Man's Mexico* (1966). Mary Morris, a young American writer, recounts her experiences in *Nothing to Declare: Memoirs of a Woman Traveling Alone*.

Films

Although the typical image of Mexico to emerge from American films is of a world of poverty plagued by corruption and violence, the long Mexican film tradition is characterized by infinitely more insightful explorations of the intricate mix of Mexican community and family relations.

Originally known for popular melodramas (such as *Maria Candelaria*, 1943, by Emilio Fernandez) that dominated the Latin American market, the Mexican film industry also harbored Luis Buñuel for much of the second half of his career. During his years in Mexico, Buñuel made several classics including *The Young and the Damned* (1950), an extremely brutal look at life in the slums of Mexico City. Some of his other movies include *El Bruto, Los Olvidados*, and *Exterminating Angel*.

In recent years Paul Leduc has made several innovative films based on historical and cultural themes. *Reed: Insurgent Mexico* provides a twist on the leftist journalist's account of the Mexican Revolution and also serves as a larger metaphor for Mexican-American relations. Leduc's most recent film, *Frida*, is a beautiful biography of the life and work of Mexican painter Frida Kahlo. Presentations of her paintings are interspersed with fictionalized accounts of her relationships with her husband Diego Rivera, Leon Trotsky, Mexican communism, and her own vibrant approach to life.

Jaime Humberto Hermosillo presents some of the contradictions of a modern Mexican society in *Dona Herlinda and Her Son* (1986). Dona Herlinda's son marries a feminist woman and his homosexual lover moves in with the family.

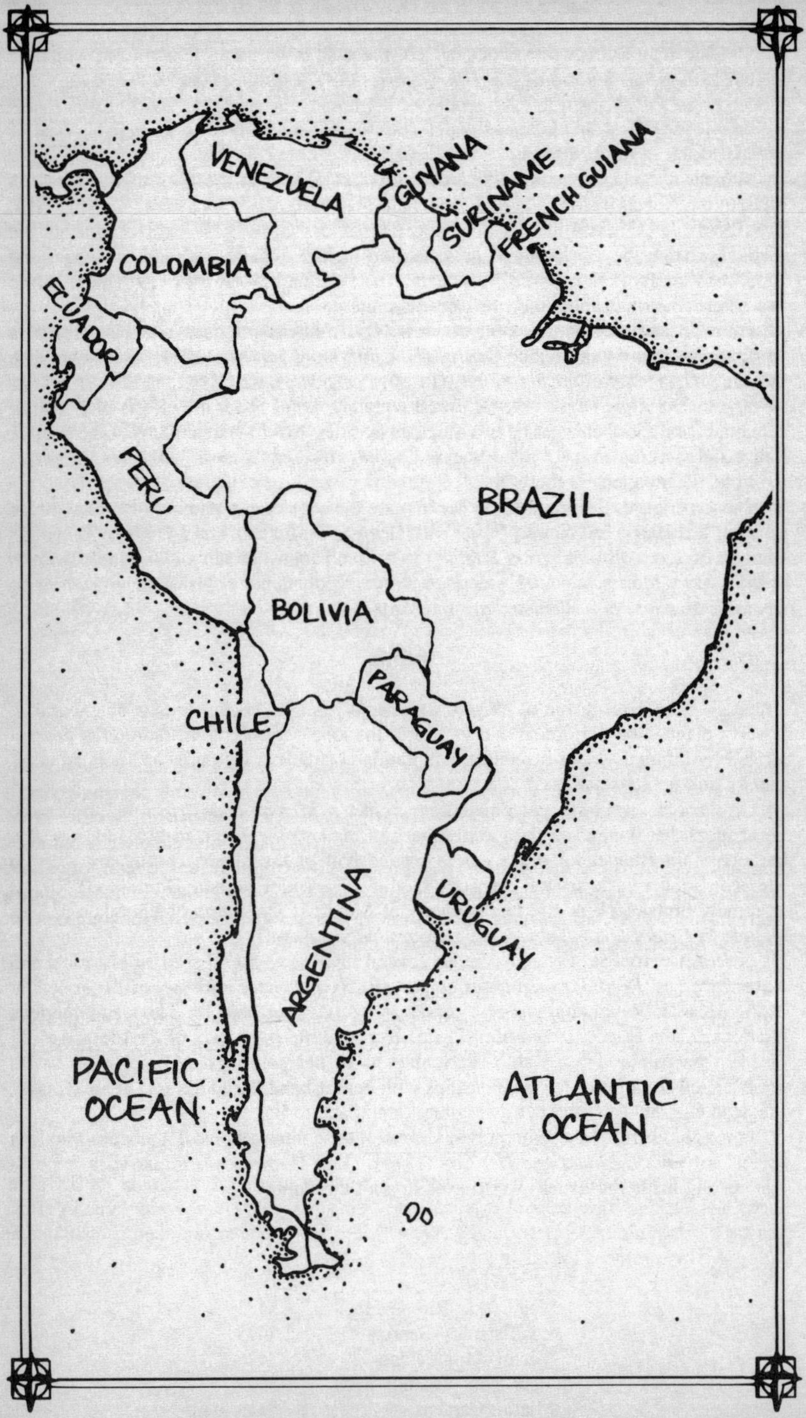
VENEZUELA
GUYANA
SURINAME
FRENCH GUIANA
COLOMBIA
ECUADOR
PERU
BRAZIL
BOLIVIA
PARAGUAY
CHILE
ARGENTINA
URUGUAY
PACIFIC OCEAN
ATLANTIC OCEAN

CHAPTER SIXTEEN
SOUTH AMERICA

In spite of widespread economic problems—most conspicuous of which are debt, inflation, and poverty—democracy is currently on the rise in much of South America. While little more than a decade ago military dictatorships were the rule, today virtually all the countries of the region have popularly elected governments of some sort. This move toward democracy, especially in Argentina, Brazil, and Chile, has fostered a new climate of social and political freedom that enlivens everyday discussions, invigorates educational institutions, and nourishes the arts. As a result, young people from the United States interested in becoming exposed to South American life can expect an especially rewarding experience. Interested North Americans will soon become drawn into discussions of the economic, political, and environmental issues that affect the continent. And as fellow inhabitants of the double continent 16th-century explorers called the New World, North and South Americans generally will find a surprising amount of common ground.

South America offers the visitor enormous physical and cultural variety, from the tropical rain forest of the Amazon Basin to the cold, windy desert of Patagonia, and the ancient Indian way of life that still flourishes in the high valleys of the Andes to the modern European atmosphere of Buenos Aires. While the continent traditionally has been overlooked as a destination by U.S. students going abroad, a growing number of young people are now taking advantage of the possibilities available for studying, working, or simply traveling in the countries of South America.

The Essentials

Usually a passport and a tourist card, which is obtained at the border or at the airport, are enough to gain you entry to most South American countries; some, including Brazil and Argentina, require visas as well. Most South American countries also require proof of onward transportation such as a return plane ticket, although this rule often is enforced somewhat arbitrarily. Check with the specific embassy or consulate for further information. You'll find entrance requirements and embassy addresses given in the individual country sections that follow. To get more information on entrance requirements for countries not covered in a separate section of this chapter, contact:

- Embassy of Guyana, 2490 Tracy Place NW, Washington, DC 20008
- Embassy of Paraguay, 2400 Massachusetts Avenue NW, Washington, DC 20008
- Embassy of Suriname, 4301 Connecticut Avenue NW, Washington, DC 20008

Getting There

The cheapest fares from the United States to South America are generally APEX fares (see Chapter Five for a general explanation of airfares). Sample *one-way* fares in effect during the summer of 1991 are listed below. More up-to-date information is available at Council Travel offices (see listing on pages xix–xxi).

New York–Rio de Janeiro	$435
Los Angeles–Santiago	$425
Miami–Montevideo	$425
New York–Buenos Aires	$509
Miami–Caracas	$139

Getting Around South America

The ease—or difficulty—in getting around South America varies by country. In Argentina, Chile, or southern Brazil, traveling by car or bus is as easy and convenient as it is in the U.S., once you are accustomed to slightly different customs and procedures of each individual country. On the other hand, in the Andean countries (Colombia, Ecuador, Peru, and Bolivia) natural boundaries and poorly developed road and rail systems make traveling by train or bus time-consuming and often uncomfortable. But the rewards, in the form of spectacular scenery and contact with native American cultures, generally make the effort well worthwhile.

Traveling by train is one of the most interesting ways to see South America. However, with the exception of Argentina, you won't find much in the way of integrated national railway systems; most countries have only one or two lines with passenger service, and Venezuela and Uruguay have none. Throughout the continent, equipment is antiquated and travel is slow. Although not known for speed and efficiency, South American trains allow you to slow down, enjoy the scenery, and come into contact with workers and *campesinos*.

Buses are the most popular form of transportation in South America, and they range from luxury air-conditioned intercity express buses to trucks with wooden benches. No matter where you might want to go—if there's a road, there's a bus that travels it. For anyone interested in traveling around the continent by bus, the Amerbuspass is a single ticket good for up to 10,000 kilometers of travel on the routes of 17 cooperating Latin American bus companies over a 99-day period. For price and other information, contact Autobuses Sudamericanos, S.R.L., Bernardo de Irigoyen 1370, 1138 Buenos Aires, Argentina.

Hitchhiking is fairly easy and safe in most parts of Latin America. Of course, females should not hitchhike alone, and everyone will find it easier to get rides if they look neat and clean. Don't be surprised if the driver who gives you a ride asks for a fee. As in other areas of the world, it's best to get your information on hitchhiking from someone who has done or is doing it.

In most countries, it's also quite easy to rent a car; while there are certain advantages to this mode of transportation, it is an expensive alternative and tends to remove the traveler from contact with the people. If you do plan to drive in South America, you'll need a driving permit. All South American countries recognize the Inter-American Driving Permit; Argentina, Chile, Ecuador, Paraguay, and Venezuela also recognize the International Driving Permit. You can get either of these permits at an office of the American Automobile Association in the United States; however, you must be 18 years of age, have a valid U.S. driver's license, and pay a fee of $10 (see page 52).

Air travel is certainly the fastest and most convenient way of covering long distances in South America. Nearly all the countries of the continent have air passes of some sort that allow foreigners unlimited travel in that country over a specified period of time. Generally speaking, these passes are good—even exceptional—bargains for anyone planning to visit several regions of a country. You'll find more information on these passes in the individual country sections that follow.

There are also two passes that allow international air travel throughout the continent:

- AeroPeru offers the Visit South America pass, which is valid for 45 days. The pass consists of six coupons, each good for one international flight. One coupon can be used for the flight from Miami to Lima, and the others for the flight to any city AeroPeru serves, including Bogotá, Buenos Aires, Caracas, Guayaquil, La Paz, Lima, Rio de Janeiro, Santiago, and São Paulo. The only problem with the Visit South America pass is that you'll have to do a lot of backtracking; for example, flying between Rio and Buenos Aires requires a connection through Lima. The pass costs $813 during the low season, but jumps to $963 during the high season.

- Lineas Aereas Paraguayas (LAP) also offers a special fare called the Visit South America pass. Like AeroPeru's pass, it consists of six coupons, each good for one international flight. It is valid for only 30 days. LAP serves Asunción, Buenos Aires, Lima, Montevideo, Rio, Santa Cruz (Bolivia), Santiago, and São Paulo. You must use Asunción as a travel hub but you'll have to do less backtracking, since Asunción is fairly centrally located. The price of the pass, including the flight from Miami, the only U.S. city served by LAP, is $899.

Eating and Sleeping

You'll find an abundance of inexpensive hotels in South American cities. The student travel offices listed under the individual country sections later in this chapter can often help you find inexpensive places to stay. In addition, volume two of the *International Youth Hostel Handbook* lists a limited number of hostels in Argentina, Chile, and Uruguay. For a listing of hostels in Brazil, write to the Fundação Casa do Estudante do Brasil (Praça Ana Amelia, 9, 22220 Rio de Janeiro).

For Further Information

An excellent guidebook for independent travelers, especially those trying to keep costs to a minimum, is *South America on a Shoestring* ($19.95), by Geoff Crowther. Published by Lonely Planet Publications (Embarcadero West, 112 Linden Street, Oakland, CA 94607), the book is available in most bookstores or can be ordered directly from the publisher (add $1.50 for book-rate postage; $3 for first-class).

Another comprehensive guidebook to Latin America is the *South American Handbook*, which is updated annually and distributed in the U.S. by Prentice-Hall. Designed especially for travelers who want to get off the beaten tourist path and explore South America on their own, this 1,152-page manual isn't cheap—$29.95—but it's worth the price, especially if you're planning to visit several countries in the region.

Work

Stringent labor regulations and high unemployment rates make it difficult for foreigners to obtain employment in South America. Nevertheless, resourceful persons with some knowledge of Spanish or Portuguese often find informal employment, mostly as English tutors or translators.

The internship and voluntary service opportunities offered by members of the Council on International Educational Exchange are listed in the individual country sections later in this chapter. In addition, the Association for International Practical Training offers the IAESTE Trainee Program in Paraguay; see page 18 for more information about this program.

Study

Persons seeking scholarships or grants for study in South America might want to take a look at *Funding for Research, Study, and Travel: Latin America and the Caribbean* (see page 424).

You'll find the study programs offered by CIEE-member institutions listed in the country sections that follow. Here we've included only those programs that take place in more than one country of the region. Consult Appendix I for the addresses of the colleges and universities listed in this section.

Semester and Academic Year

Business

University of La Verne "Analysis of Latin American Business." Rio de Janeiro, Brazil; Buenos Aires, Argentina; and Santiago, Chile. Six-week program (three weeks abroad) in January or August. Juniors to graduate students with 2.5 GPA. Apply in September for January; April for August.

General Studies

University of Pittsburgh. "Semester at Sea." Fall or spring semester. Students, based abroad the S.S. *Universe*, attend classes on board and travel to various countries in Europe, the Middle East, Africa, Asia, and South America. Sophomores, juniors, and seniors with 2.75 GPA. Contact: Semester at Sea, Eighth Floor, William Pitt Union, University of Pittsburgh, Pittsburgh, PA 15260; (412) 648-7490.

Summer

Latin American Studies

University of Pittsburgh. "Latin American Studies Field Seminar." Country in which seminar takes place varies each year. Open only to students in Pittsburgh area schools. Juniors and seniors. Proficiency in Spanish required.

ARGENTINA

The history of Argentina has been as hot and cold, as thrilling and melancholy as the strains of its national music, the tango. Once the envy of the developing world, and only 50 years ago as wealthy as France or Austria, this proud nation has suffered more than its share of political and economic reversals. Argentines have battled debilitating rates of inflation and brutal military dictatorships, but stubbornly, their morale remains high. They have now enjoyed a decade of relatively unimpeded democracy, and they live alongside some of the greatest natural resources and boldest natural beauty to be found in the hemisphere.

This sprawling nation—eighth largest in the world—has long drawn floods of immigrants, and in the early part of this century, Argentina served, like the U.S., as a "land of opportunity," attracting newcomers from all over Europe, and, in smaller numbers, from the Middle East and Asia. Expecting the usual Spanish-Indian and Afro-Caribbean blends that characterize most of Latin America, visitors are often surprised at the "European" features and Italian, English, or Slavic surnames of many Argentines. While some ethnic groups formed isolated communities in rural areas—Welsh farmers and Jewish cowboys set up shop in Patagonia—the great majority laid roots in the capital of Buenos Aires, which was transformed from a muddy pirate port into today's cosmopolitan metropolis of more than 11 million. *Porteños*, as the people of Buenos Aires call themselves, are intensely proud of their city and rarely venture outside it. The wide boulevards, busy pedestrian malls, outdoor cafes, and wonderfully detailed churches and public buildings of Buenos Aires are indeed, as *porteños* proudly assert, reminiscent of Europe. But one need only take a ramshackle, colorfully painted bus into the neighborhoods of San Telmo or La Boca and watch an elderly couple dance a sensual, romantic tango on the street to be reminded that this is, in fact, a land apart.

SOUTH AMERICA: ARGENTINA

As one ventures away from the capital, the wonders and contradictions of the country become clearer. To the west of the city, stretching out from the shore of the Rio Plata, lie Argentina's famous pampas, a land of incredibly rich topsoil. The vast herds of cattle grazing here, descended from the few hundred left behind by the first explorers, are the backbone of the Argentine economy and supplier of the innumerable *parrilladas*, or meat grills, found throughout the country. The pampas are also the ancestral home of the most famed of Argentine figures, the gaucho. Star of song and literature, this flamboyant cousin to the American cowboy can still be found, in greatly reduced numbers, on many Argentine cattle ranches.

Nestled amongst the Andes near the Chilean border, Argentina's surprisingly large wine industry flourishes, and many tours are available to friendly local bodegas, or vineyards. As the Andes stretch down into Patagonia, the stark southern cone of the country, they become the site of a spectacular lake district, dotted with vivid blue glacial pools. Local ski resorts like Bariloche are favorite vacation spots for Argentines and foreigners alike. With the exception of the lake district, Patagonia is almost entirely flat and dry, and its limitless horizons and unique culture and wildlife have enchanted poets and explorers since Darwin. In striking contrast, the northeastern part of the country is largely lush, sub-equatorial jungle, broken up here and there by tremendous waterfalls, the most spectacular of which is the famed Iguazú Falls.

Argentines are justifiably proud of their magnificent land, and eager to share it with outsiders. While much is made of the way in which the national character is split between its Germanic and Latin elements, even a short time here reveals the inadequacy of such categories. Argentina has distinguished itself both from its neighbors and ancestors, and despite past and present political and economic hardships, the land and its people remain rich in possibility.

—*Michael Kovnat, Brooklyn, New York*

Official name: Argentine Republic. **Area:** 1,065,189 square miles (about ⅓ the size of the U.S.). **Population:** 32,291,000. **Population density:** 30 inhabitants per square mile. **Capital and largest city:** Buenos Aires (pop. 10,000,000). **Language:** Spanish. **Religion:** Roman Catholic. **Per capita income:** US$2,360. **Currency:** Austral. **Literacy rate:** 94%. **Average daily high/low*:** Buenos Aires: January, 85°/63°; July, 57°/42°. **Average number of days with precipitation:** Buenos Aires: January, 7; July, 8.

TRAVEL

U.S. citizens will need a passport to enter Argentina, though a visa is not required for stays of up to three months. For specific regulations, check with the Embassy of the Argentine Republic (1600 New Hampshire Avenue NW, Washington, DC 20009) or with an Argentine consulate in Chicago, Honolulu, Houston, Los Angeles, New York, or San Francisco.

Getting Around

Because of the great distances involved, most tourists interested in seeing different parts of the country end up doing some flying. Foreigners can purchase Visit Argentina air passes that entitle them to a number of discounted coupons for flights within the country. Coupons are valid for 30 days and are honored by Aerolineas Argentinas and Austral Airlines. Four coupons cost $359; six cost $409; and eight cost $459. Visit Argentina passes can be purchased from a travel agent or directly from the airlines before your arrival in Argentina.

---

*All temperatures are Fahrenheit.

Argentina has an extensive network of paved highways. A variety of bus lines serve all parts of the country, providing comfortable and reliable service. But remember that distances are great: express buses from Buenos Aires to Iguazú Falls take 24 hours; Buenos Aires to Bariloche is a 22-hour trip. Hitchhiking is popular and fairly easy throughout the entire country, except in the south, where traffic is light. All Argentine cities have rental car agencies. Avis, Hertz, and National are among the car rental companies operating in Argentina; you can get more information on rates and age requirements by calling their toll-free numbers in the United States. U.S. motorists should obtain either the Inter-American Driving Permit or the International Driving Permit (see page 52), both of which are recognized in Argentina.

Argentina has the best and most comprehensive rail network of any country of South America; however, it does not extend to the Brazilian frontier and Iguazú Falls in the northeast or cover much of the sparsely populated southern region of the country. The system, built with British investment in the late 19th and early 20th centuries, fans out across the pampas to Bariloche and Mendoza in the west and into Bolivia and Paraguay in the north. Travel by train is inexpensive and comfortable. However, trains are slower than buses; the trip from Buenos Aires to Bariloche, for example, takes 30 hours.

Especially for Students and Young People

Argentina has three student/youth travel organizations, all of which issue the International Student Identity Card.

- ATESA has offices in Buenos Aires (Tucuman 1584, 2-A, 1050) as well as in Córdoba, Rosario, Salta, Mar del Plata, Tucumán, Mendoza, and Ushuaia.
- AAAJ (Asociación Argentina de Albergues de la Juventud) also has a Buenos Aires office (Talcahuano 214, 2 Piso, Oficina 6, 1013) as well as offices in La Plata, Mar del Plata, and Rosario.
- ASATEJ has its office in Buenos Aires at Florida 833, Piso 1°, Oficina 104, (1005). Its mailing address, however, is CC307, (1000) Buenos Aires.

All of them issue air, rail, and bus tickets and also provide accommodation booking services. In addition, ATESA offers Buenos Aires city tours, a ten-day excursion to Bariloche, and a six-day tour to Iguazú Falls.

Holders of the International Student Identity Card are entitled to reduced airfares to various destinations in Latin America, the U.S., and Europe. Students up to 20 years of age are eligible for discounts on domestic flights to the southern part of the country. Student discounts are also available for train and bus travel. Information regarding these discounts and those available at a number of individual shops, theaters, museums, and youth hostels can be obtained at AAAJ and ATESA offices.

"Spend time in the parks and squares, where it's easy to meet Argentines. Americans and Argentines have a lot in common; most obviously, they are both descendants of immigrants from Europe."
—Jill Strauss, New York, New York

For Further Information

One of the few guidebooks to focus on Argentina is *Argentina: A Travel Survival Kit*, available for $10.95 from Lonely Planet Publications, Embarcadero West, 112 Linden Street, Oakland, CA 94607. General tourist information is available from the Argentine National Tourist Information Office (12 West 56th Street, New York, NY 10019).

WORK

To work in Argentina, a foreigner must obtain a work permit. Getting regular, salaried employment in some fields can be challenging. For more information, contact the Ministerio de Trabajo, Avenida Julio a Roca 609, Buenos Aires 1067 Argentina.

Internships/Traineeships

Three programs sponsored by members of the Council on International Educational Exchange are described below.

AIESEC-US. Reciprocal internship program for students in economics, business, finance, marketing, accounting, and computer science. See page 18 for more information.

Association for International Practical Training. "IAESTE Trainee Program." On-the-job training for undergraduate and graduate students in technical fields such as engineering, computer science, agriculture, architecture, and mathematics. See page 18 for more information.

University of Illinois at Urbana-Champaign. "Summer in Argentina." Engineering internship and advanced study of Spanish and history or literature. Juniors, seniors, graduate students at any institution; 3.0 GPA. Four semesters of college-level Spanish required. See Appendix 1 for the address to write for more information.

STUDY

"Studying in Argentina, I gained an understanding of a people who, although they live in Latin America, have a very European mentality. And living in this economically troubled country gave me a better understanding of economics from a Latin American perspective."
—Alvin Realuyo, Jersey City, New Jersey

The following academic programs are offered by CIEE-member institutions. Consult Appendix I for the addresses of the colleges and universities listed in this section. In addition to the programs below, Lewis and Clark College offers a program open only to its own students.

Semester and Academic Year

General Studies

International Student Exchange Program. Direct reciprocal exchange between U.S. universities and institutions in Buenos Aires. Semester or academic year. Full curriculum options. Open only to students at ISEP-member institutions.

State University of New York at Plattsburgh. "Study Program in Argentina." Universidad del Salvador, Buenos Aires. Fall or spring semester. All instruction in Spanish. Undergraduates with strong Spanish skills and 2.5 GPA. Apply by March 15 for fall; October 15 for spring.

University of Arkansas at Little Rock. Academic year or semester. Juniors and seniors at Arkansas Consortium for International Education schools only. Rolling admissions.

University of North Carolina—Chapel Hill. "UNC Program to Belgrano." Semester or academic year. Juniors and seniors fluent in Spanish with 3.0 GPA. Apply by February 12 for fall; November 1 for spring.

Social Science

American University. "Buenos Aires Semester." Fall semester. Focus on Argentine politics, economics, and culture. Internships with multinational agencies. Juniors and seniors with two years of college Spanish and 2.75 GPA. Apply six months prior to start of program.

Council on International Educational Exchange. "Advanced Social Science Program." Buenos Aires. Fall or spring semester. Advanced undergraduate or graduate students with five semesters of college Spanish and coursework in social sciences. Apply by March 15 for fall semester and October 15 for spring. Contact University Programs Department.

Summer

Engineering

University of Illinois. "International Program in Engineering." Buenos Aires. Junior to graduate engineering students with four semesters of college Spanish and 3.0 GPA. Internships with engineering firms. Apply by March 1.

General Studies

University of Illinois at Urbana-Champaign. "Summer Program in Argentina." Buenos Aires. Juniors to graduate students with four semesters of college Spanish and 3.0 GPA. Internships available. Apply by March 1.

University of Massachusetts at Amherst. Buenos Aires. Sophomores, juniors, and seniors with proficiency in Spanish. Apply by March 1.

EXPLORING ARGENTINE CULTURE

Readings and Films

Argentina's best-known literary figure in this century was Jorge Luis Borges. In books such as *Labyrinths* (1941) and *Fictions* (1949), Borges created unusual existential situations characterized by their erudite verbal pyrotechnics. His *Six Problems for Don Isidro Parodi* (1942) is a collection of six detective stories that Borges wrote "as a challenge to the frenetic action of American detective stories" and the "cold intellectualism of the British school."

Julio Cortazar also plays with the reader's perception of reality. His novel *Hopscotch* (1963), for instance, is divided into chapters that can be read in different orders, each arrangement suggesting a different meaning.

Manuel Puig, the author of *Heartbreak Tango* (1969) and *Betrayed by Rita Hayworth* (1968) among other novels, is a younger writer whose surreal visions of modern life reveal the influence of Hollywood and American cartoons. *Heartbreak Tango* presents the life of a working-class woman who longs to become involved with a Don Juan. *Betrayed by Rita Hayworth* is the story of a boy growing up in a drab Argentine town and his escape from his reality by going to the movies. *Kiss of the Spiderwoman* (1985), Puig's most famous work (thanks to the success of the movie version), is the story of two prisoners, one a political dissident and the other a homosexual window dresser; it provides a vividly realistic picture of the mechanisms of political repression that were employed by the military government during its "Dirty War" against the Argentine left in the 1970s.

Diary of the War of the Pig, Adolfo Bioy Casares's 1969 novel, is eerily prophetic of the "Dirty War." It details the war of extermination between the young (the killers) and the old (the willing victims). In a nonfiction vein, Jacobo Timerman's *Prisoner without a Name, Cell without a Number* (1985) is based on the well-known newspaper editor's imprisonment during the 1970s when the military dictatorship used imprisonment and torture as a routine political tool. Compare it to Lawrence Thornton's *Imagining Argentina* (1987), a novel about the redemptive imagination of a man whose wife has become one of the *desaparecidos* in the 1970s. The disappeared and the question of what became of their children is a subject poignantly explored in Luís Puenzo's *The Official Story* (1985). In this movie, the wife of an Argentine businessman wonders if her adopted daughter might have come to her by less-than-honorable means.

Another novel of Argentine life during the mid 1970s is Humberto Constantini's *The Gods, the Little Guys, and the Police* (1979), at once a whimsical fantasy and a frightening picture of political terror. The plot deals with Greek gods who concern themselves with the members of an apolitical group of poets suspected by the police of subversive activities; a hilarious but bitter allegory of the torture and disappearance of liberals in Argentina in the seventies. Ernesto Sabato's *On Heroes and Tombs* (1961) is a novel that presents a history of Argentina as represented by the obsessions of a well-to-do family.

While few tourists visit the remote region of Argentina known as Patagonia, as one of the world's last frontier regions it has captured the interest of a number of writers from around the world. The late Bruce Chatwin's *In Patagonia* is a classic account of the author's travels through that harsh landscape. In the same vein, be sure to check out Paul Theroux's *Patagonia Revisited*.

BOLIVIA

Few nations can equal the geographical diversity found in Bolivia, a country that encompasses both dry barren plains and verdant mountain valleys, snowcapped mountain peaks and tropical rain forests. And although it is landlocked, Bolivia still campaigns quixotically through diplomatic channels to reclaim the corridor to the sea, which it lost to Chile in a military campaign more than a century ago.

On a dry, windswept plain 12,000 feet above sea level, La Paz, the nation's modern capital, coexists with indigenous villages where ancient Indian languages and customs still prevail. Although bleak, cold, and treeless, the altiplano ("high plateau"), which comprises about 30 percent of the nation's land area, contains about 62 percent of the nation's people. Studded with white-capped peaks rising above 20,000 feet, the altiplano is a hostile environment of rare beauty. The altiplano is also one of the most mineral-rich regions on earth; large quantities of silver, gold, tin, copper, tungsten, lead, and zinc have been dug up and exported to satisfy the needs of the world's more industrial nations. The colonial splendor of San Luis Potosí (altitude 13,340), which sent more than two billion dollars worth of gold and silver to Spain, is still very much in evidence.

Ironically, the nation that produced so much of the world's gold and silver now has South America's lowest standard of living. First the deposits of gold, then silver, and now its tin have been largely depleted, forcing the nation to look elsewhere for economic viability. As a result, agriculture (chiefly cotton, sugar, and cattle) is becoming increasingly important as a contributor to GNP and producer of exports.

The tropical lowlands that sweep from the foothills of the Andes toward Brazil, Paraguay, and Argentina, are said to be Bolivia's future. Here are few people but about half of the nation's land area. The area around Santa Cruz, center of the nation's agricultural and petroleum exports, has developed rapidly over the last 20 years. Santa Cruz, now Bolivia's second-largest city, is challenging La Paz as the nation's economic center.

Historically, Bolivia, perhaps more than any other Latin American nation, has been plagued by political and economic instability. Recently, however, the country has enjoyed unusual stability. For the first time in memory, power has been transferred peacefully from one elected leader to another. And the inflation rate, which hit an astronomical 24,000 percent a few years ago, has declined to manageable levels.

—*Chad Isaaks, Jacksonville, Florida*

Official name: Republic of Bolivia. **Area:** 424,165 square miles (the size of Texas and California combined). **Population:** 6,730,000. **Population density:** 16 inhabitants per square mile. **Capitals:** Sucre (legal, pop. 63,000) and La Paz (de facto). **Largest city:** La Paz (pop. 955,000). **Language:** Spanish, Quechua, Aymara. **Religion:** Roman Catholic. **Per capita income:** US$570. **Currency:** Peso. **Literacy rate:** 63%. **Average daily high/low*:** La Paz: January, 63°/43°; July, 64°/33°. **Average number of days with precipitation:** La Paz: January, 21; July, 2.

TRAVEL

U.S. citizens need a passport to enter Bolivia; for tourist stays of less than 90 days, a visa is not required. For specific requirements, check with the Embassy of Bolivia, 3014 Massachusetts Avenue NW, Washington, DC 20008.

Getting Around

Mountainous terrain and poorly developed road and railway systems make air travel an attractive alternative in Bolivia. Lloyd Aereo Boliviano, the national airline, serves most Bolivian cities. Its Visit Bolivia ("Vi Bol") air pass is good for unlimited travel within the country for a period of 28 days and costs $150. It is sold only in the U.S. to travelers flying to Bolivia on Lloyd Aereo Boliviano (from Miami) and should be purchased in conjunction with your international ticket to Bolivia.

A surprising number of rail lines cross Bolivia; however, equipment is antiquated, and service is slow and infrequent. Trains are even less expensive than the bus and offer views of interesting scenery as well as contact with the rural population of the country. Rail lines connect most highland cities and link Bolivia to Chile, Peru, Argentina, and Brazil, but fail to connect Bolivia's two main cities, Santa Cruz and La Paz.

Buses are the most frequently used form of transportation in Bolivia, and service between the major cities is generally good. During the rainy season, however, buses providing service on unpaved roads are subject to frequent delays. Rental cars are not available, although taxis can be rented by the hour or day; four-wheel drive vehicles can be rented in La Paz.

For Further Information

Bolivia: A Travel Survival Kit ($10.95) is the best guidebook for the independent traveler on a budget who really wants to get to know the country. If you can't find it in bookstores, it can be ordered from the publisher, Lonely Planet Publications, Embarcadero West, 112 Linden Street, Oakland, CA 94607 (add $1.50 for book-rate postage; $3 for first-class).

---

*All temperatures are Fahrenheit.

WORK

It is difficult for foreigners to obtain work in Bolivia. For information contact the Embassy of Bolivia, 3014 Massachusetts Avenue NW, Washington, DC 20008.

Voluntary Service

The Year Abroad Program sponsored by the International Christian Youth Exchange offers persons ages 18 to 24 voluntary service opportunities in the fields of health care, education, the environment, construction, et cetera. See page 23 for more information. In addition, the Overseas Development Network sponsors volunteer opportunities in Bolivia; see page 29 for more information.

STUDY

The following programs are offered by CIEE-member institutions. Consult Appendix I for the addresses of the colleges and universities listed below.

Semester and Academic Year

General Studies

Experiment in International Living/School for International Training. "College Semester Abroad." Cochabamba and La Paz. Intensive language study, interdisciplinary seminars on Bolivian life and culture and development issues, field-study methods seminar, homestay, educational excursions, and independent-study project. Sophomores to seniors with 2.5 GPA and three semesters of college Spanish. Apply by October 31 for spring; May 31 for fall.

State University of New York at Stony Brook. "Stony Brook in Bolivia." Social sciences and humanities. Juniors with two years of college Spanish. Apply by April 1 for fall; November 1 for spring.

EXPLORING BOLIVIAN CULTURE

Readings

Few Bolivian authors have been translated into English. Arturo Von Vacano's *Biting Silence* (1987) is dedicated "to liberty, although it may last 15 minutes," a reference to the political turmoil of a country where there have been more than 250 governments in the last century or so. It delves into the corruption of the political machinery and into the daily lives of the Bolivian populace.

Writers from other countries have also contributed to the available reading list on Bolivia. *Bolivia: Gate of the Sun* (1970) is a travelogue by Margaret J. Anstee that conveys the geographical diversity and the atmosphere of everyday life in Bolivia. Eric Lawlor's *In Bolivia* (1989) is another travelogue which searches out the essence of the country. His travels take him from La Paz through the forbidding countryside.

BRAZIL

A few images of this enormous country shape most people's impressions of it. Prospectors and ranchers slash and burn their way through the ecologically delicate Amazon forest. Gold miners clamber over one another in an open pit mine. The Girl from Ipanema strolls seductively along a Rio beach. Clusters of futuristic buildings form a brave new capital in Brasília. These images are accurate but incomplete, for Brazil is much more.

Brazil was a premier colony of Portugal. It was part of the Latin American independence movement, securing its freedom not with battles but with a single word from its new Emperor, Pedro I. It was a hotbed of logical positivist philosophy, an influence still noted today in Brazilians named for Socrates, Newton, and Edison. In World War II, it harbored Nazi sympathizers but its countrymen fought alongside the U.S. in Italy. Beginning in the 1960s, Brazil endured a quarter century of military dictatorship during which thousands of Brazilians were tortured, and many detainees "disappeared" or were killed. During this time, Brazil amassed the highest national debt in the Third World to build factories, power plants, and transportation networks—a debt its economy still struggles under the effects of today.

Except for the United States, Brazil is the largest country in the world to have essentially one language. In its forests, just 100,000 or so indigenous inhabitants remain. In spite of Brazil's European, African, and native heritage, there is no clear notion of racial difference. However, to be black or Indian there is to be considered socially inferior, official proclamations to the contrary, though there is little agreement as to exactly who fits into each category.

Scholars have long felt that there are "two Brazils." One is modern, urban and cosmopolitan, a Brazil of large and growing cities where all the material comforts are available to those who can afford to acquire them. The other is rural and backward, a land of primitive agriculture, illiteracy, and disease. Little connects these two worlds except the buses that bring people full of hope to the cities and that take many of them back again when their dreams die.

Brazilians are often intensely interested in Europe and the United States, and many middle- and upper-class Brazilians have traveled more extensively in Europe and the U.S. than they have within their own country or elsewhere in Latin America. Brazilians tend to be informal and hospitable. Visitors invariably find a warm welcome, particularly when they try to speak Portuguese, no matter how well.

—*James Buschman, Alma, Michigan*

Official name: Federative Republic of Brazil. **Area:** 3,286,470 square miles (about the same size as the U.S.). **Population:** 153,771,000. **Population density:** 47 inhabitants per square mile. **Capital:** Brasilia (pop. 1,576,657). **Largest city:** São Paulo (pop. 10,100,000). **Language:** Portuguese. **Religion:** Roman Catholic. **Per capita income:** US$2,020. **Currency:** New Cruzado. **Literacy rate:** 76%. **Average daily high/low*:** Rio de Janeiro: January, 84°/73°; July, 75°/63°. Manaus: January, 88°/75°; July, 89°/75°. São Paulo: January, 81°/63°; July, 71°/49°. **Average number of days with precipitation:** Rio de Janeiro: January, 7; July, 8. Manaus: January, 20; July, 8. São Paulo: January, 19; July, 6.

TRAVEL

Both a passport and a visa (multiple-entry, valid up to 90 days) are required for U.S. citizens traveling to Brazil. In addition, tourists must have an onward/return ticket or

---

*All temperatures are Fahrenheit.

notarized bank letter as proof of sufficient funds. For specific regulations, check with the Embassy of Brazil (3006 Massachusetts Avenue NW, Washington, DC 20008) or a Brazilian consulate in New York, Miami, Atlanta, New Orleans, San Francisco, or Los Angeles.

The U.S. State Department warns that all tourists are at risk of robbery at all times of the day or night, especially on buses or at beaches and sightseeing locations. Travelers checks, a cheap camera, and no jewelry are the best policy, especially in Rio.

Getting Around

Since Brazil is larger than the continental United States or the whole of Europe, and long-distance travel via road and rail is slow, most travelers intent on visiting different regions of the country generally resort to air transport for at least part of their journey. Fortunately, Brazil's domestic air-transport network is among the world's best, providing comfortable and reliable service to even the most-remote areas of the country. The Brazil Air Pass, valid on Brazil's three major domestic carriers, Varig, Transbrasil, and VASP (though you cannot mix carriers), is good for five stopovers in 21 days. The pass costs $440 and must be purchased before departure from the United States. Passes to be used on Varig must be bought in conjunction with an international ticket on Varig. Because airfares in Brazil are already quite cheap, you ought to do some research to see if the pass will save you money.

"Most Americans never get beyond Rio and miss most of the other equally interesting attractions of this country. For example, Salvador, a city full of color, activity, and rhythm, is the center of Afro-Brazilian culture and one of the most interesting cities of Brazil. It was the first capital of Portuguese Brazil and still has beautiful, if somewhat rundown, historical neighborhoods dating from colonial times."
—Sandra A. White, Hartford, Connecticut

Brazil's railroads were built to transport raw materials from the interior to the coast. As a result, while there are thousands of miles of track, most of it is not integrated into a national system; in fact, there are five different track gauges in use in Brazil. And even where rail lines do exist, there is not always passenger service. The relatively few passenger trains in operation are used mainly for local transportation in the more densely populated areas. However, there is good intercity rail service between Rio and São Paulo, Belo Horizonte, and Brasília. But remember that distances are great; even the "short" trip between Rio and São Paulo will take about 10 hours, and traveling from São Paulo to Brasília by train takes about 24 hours.

Most overland travel is by bus. Brazil has a rapidly expanding highway network which is especially well developed in the south. In other regions of the country, roads are not as good and travel is slower, but even in the Amazon region, travel by road is now a realistic option, with paved roads extending as far as Manaus in the heart of the Amazon basin. Numerous bus companies provide comfortable and frequent service between the major cities of Brazil. Special luxury buses (called *leitos*) with fully reclining seats, curtained partitions, and attendants, make overnight trips. Less-comfortable buses service even the most remote towns, although bus service on the unpaved roads of the Amazon basin is subject to frequent delays in the best of conditions, and is especially unreliable in the rainy season.

It is also possible to rent a car in most Brazilian cities. Both Hertz and Avis have extensive operations in the country. There are also several large Brazilian rental firms, such as Nobre. However, you will most likely get a better deal through smaller local agencies. U.S. drivers' licences are valid in Brazil but many local rental companies require the International Driving Permit (see page 52). Hitching is possible for short local trips, but is generally discouraged for long-distance travel.

The best way to see the Amazon region is by boat. Riverboats still provide most of the transportation in this vast area, allowing you to travel the 2,000 miles up the Amazon to Iquitos, Peru, or simply make a short hop between neighboring towns. The trip between Manaus and Belém, the two metropolises of the Amazon basin, takes five or six days, with stops at cities and towns along the way. There are also a number of ferry services in other rivers and along the coast.

"Be prepared to ease up on many different levels. Time is often less constraining and regimented. Relationships among friendly acquaintances are warmer—kisses, handshakes, and abraços are part of the greeting routine. Yet the insecurities caused by the tremendous social disparities in wealth are apt to make one tighten up. For example, due to high crime rates in the cities, you'll have to keep any valuables you have to carry with you in a travel safe sack at all times."
—Miguel Carter, Minneapolis, Minnesota

Especially for Students and Young People

Brazil's student travel organization and issuer of the International Student Identity Card is CONTEJ (Rua do Catete 311, sala 408, 22220 Rio de Janeiro). At its main office in Rio and its branch office in São Paulo (Rua Goias 108, 01244 São Paulo), you can get travel information, buy international air tickets, book accommodations, and sign up for tours.

Students receive a discount on travel insurance as well as domestic and international plane tickets. In addition, holders of the International Student Identity Card get reduced admission to many museums, theaters, and cultural events.

"Don't miss a Brazilian soccer game. Soccer is an unquestioned basic value of Brazilian society, much like wine is to the French. Boys begin kicking soccer balls around as soon as they can walk. Go to any park or any beach and you'll find a soccer game going on; if you stop and watch for a few minutes, you'll probably be invited to join in. In Rio go to Maracanã, the world's largest soccer stadium, where the generally good-natured but passionate crowd is one of the most exciting spectacles in the world of sport."
—Mark Falango, New York, New York

For Further Information

One of the most up-to-date guidebooks to Brazil is *The Real Guide: Brazil* ($13.95), full of budget travel information, as well as essays on history and culture. Also good is *Brazil: A Travel Survival Kit*, available for $13.95 (plus $1.50 book-rate postage; $3 for first-class) from Lonely Planet Publications, Embarcadero West, 112 Linden Street, Oakland, CA 94607. General tourist information is available from the Brazilian Tourist Information Office—EMBRATUR (551 Fifth Avenue, Suite 421, New York, NY 10176).

WORK

Getting regular salaried employment in Brazil is difficult for foreigners; work visas are only issued upon presentation of a work contract certified by the Brazilian Ministry of Labor. For more information, contact the Consular Section of the Brazilian Embassy, 3006 Massachusetts Avenue NW, Washington, DC 20008.

Internships/Traineeships

Three programs sponsored by members of the Council on International Educational Exchange are described below.

AIESEC-US. Reciprocal internship program for students in economics, business, finance, marketing, accounting, and computer science. See page 18 for more information.

Association for International Practical Training. "IAESTE Trainee Program." On-the-job training for undergraduate and graduate students in technical fields such as engineering, computer science, agriculture, architecture, and mathematics. See page 18 for more information.

Brigham Young University. "Internship in Brazil." Spring term (May 1 to June 22). Eight credit-hours of Portuguese language, with internships in business, education, health services, and other fields. Sophomores, juniors, and seniors with two semesters of college Portuguese. Apply by February 1.

Voluntary Service

For persons interested in voluntary service work, the Year Abroad Program sponsored by the International Christian Youth Exchange offers persons ages 18 to 24 voluntary service opportunities in the fields of health care, education, the environment, construction, et cetera. See page 23 for more information. In addition, Amigos de las Americas sponsors voluntary service opportunities in Brazil; see page 21 for more information.

STUDY

"Studying in Rio de Janeiro was more about facing the crude realities of the Third World than living the life of a happy tourist. There is so much more to Rio than carnival and Copacabana. I saw firsthand the explosive effects that can arise in a society of boiling social contradictions. The day bus fares were raised (to keep up with an annual inflation rate of 900 percent), office workers and laborers rioted in downtown Rio and set fire to 40 buses. Living through the madness and hallucinations of a society in deep crisis was something I could have only experienced by being there—the best books and lectures would never have conveyed the same message. And my studies at Rio's Catholic University helped me develop a more coherent and critical perspective upon which to pursue my studies and develop my understanding of Latin American politics and society. The overall experience strengthened my belief in and appreciation for the importance of social and political activism."

—Miguel Carter, Minneapolis, Minnesota

The following educational programs are offered by CIEE-member institutions. Consult Appendix I for the addresses of the colleges and universities listed below. In addition, California State University, the American Graduate School of International Management, the University of California, and the University of Tennessee offer programs open only to their own students.

Semester and Academic Year

Brazilian Studies

Council on International Educational Exchange. Rio de Janeiro and Campinas, São Paulo. Cooperative Portuguese Language and Brazilian Studies Program. Fall semester. Sophomores to seniors with two semesters of college Portuguese or three semesters of college Spanish. Apply by April 1 for fall; November 1 for spring. Contact University Programs Department.

Ecology

Antioch University. "Environmental Resource Management in Brazil." Paraná State. Mid-August through mid-November. Work opportunities from November to December. Research and environmental conservation. Some Spanish required. Portuguese preferred. Juniors to graduate students majoring in science or environmental studies. Apply by February 1.

Experiment in International Living/School for International Training. "College Semester Abroad." Spring or fall semester. Belém, Santarém, Manaus, and field visits. Language study, seminar on Amazon studies and ecology, field-study methods seminar, homestay, and independent-study project. Sophomores to seniors with 2.5 GPA. Apply by May 15 for fall; October 15 for spring.

Michigan State University. "Social Issues, Environment, and Business." São Paulo. Winter quarter. Sophomores to seniors. Apply by November 20.

General Studies

Council on International Educational Exchange. "Interuniversity Study Program in Brazil." São Paulo. 12-month program. Juniors and seniors with 3.0 GPA and two years of college Portuguese or Spanish (or one year of each language). Apply by March 1. Contact University Programs Department.

Experiment in International Living/School for International Training. "College Semester Abroad." Spring or fall semester. Study in Fortaleza, with excursions to Recife, Ceará, Bahia, and the Amazon Basin. Language study, interdisciplinary seminars, development issues, field-study methods, homestay, and independent-study project. Sophomores to seniors with 2.5 GPA. Apply May 15 for fall; October 15 for spring.

International Student Exchange Program. Direct reciprocal exchange between U.S. universities and the Pontifícia Universidade Católica de Minas Gerais and Pontifícia Universidade Católica do Rio de Janeiro. Semester or academic year. Full curriculum options. Open only to students at ISEP-member institutions.

State University of New York at Albany. Brasília and Campinas. Juniors, seniors, and graduate students with two years of college Portuguese and above-average academic record. Apply by April 15 for fall; November 1 for spring.

University of Maryland. "Study in Brazil." Rio de Janeiro. Fall semester. Sophomores, juniors, and seniors with two semesters of Portuguese. Apply by May 1.

University of North Carolina—Chapel Hill. "UNC Program to Rio de Janeiro." Sophomores to seniors with 2.7 GPA. Previous Spanish or Portuguese required. Apply by February 12.

University of Wisconsin—Madison. São Paulo. Academic year. Sophomores to graduate students with two years of Portuguese and 3.0 GPA. Apply by February.

Summer

Business

University of Louisville. "Marketing in São Paulo and Rio de Janeiro." Freshmen to graduate students. Apply by April 30.

Engineering

University of Illinois at Urbana-Champaign. "International Programs in Engineering." Recife. Priority is given to engineering schools. Internships in engineering firms. Freshmen to graduate students with 3.0 GPA. Apply by March 1.

Portuguese Language

University of Illinois at Urbana-Champaign. "Portuguese Language." Basic through advanced Portuguese. Internships available. Freshmen to graduate students with 3.0 GPA. Apply by March 1.

EXPLORING BRAZILIAN CULTURE

Readings

Most Brazilian authors are closely identified with a particular region of the country, a fact that reflects the strong regional identities found in this vast and diverse country. Jorge Amado, the country's best-known contemporary novelist, writes about the Northeast. His books include *Gabriela, Clove and Cinnamon* (1958), the entertaining story of a young migrant worker whose beauty and cooking skill make her the most sought-after woman in town; *Dona Flor and Her Two Husbands* (1966), a farce about a woman whose dead first husband comes back to visit her after she has remarried; *Showdown*, a multigenerational saga set in the cacao-producing heartland of Amado's home state of Bahia; and *Jubiaba*, an interracial love story set in Bahia. *Dona Flor* and *Jubiaba* have been made into popular movies.

A number of other Brazilian authors are also worth reading for the insights they provide into their country and region. Marcio Souzas writes about the Amazon region in novels such as *The Emperor of the Amazon* (1980) and *Mad Maria* (1985). Inácio de Loyola Brandão offers a dark vision of 21st century São Paulo in *And Still the Earth* (1985). Graciliano Ramos's *Barren Lives* (1938) is considered one of the best modern Brazilian novels. It reveals much about life in the Brazilian *sertão*, the arid northeast interior. In *Of Men and Crabs* (1967), Josue de Castro exposes the miseries, poverty, disease, and hunger of rural Brazil.

Less focused on a particular region, *Celebration* (1976), by Ivan Angelo, deals with Brazil's recent political past, specifically with the censorship imposed by the military government during the 1970s. Gilberto Freyre's writings are credited for the creation of a national identity in Brazil. *The Masters and the Slaves* (1943) is a monumental study of Brazilian civilization in which a first-person account reveals history.

Clarice Lispector, one of the best-known contemporary women writers of Brazil, writes about a woman from the northeast who finds herself in the big city in *Hour of the Star* (1977). Rachel de Querioz's *The Three Marias* (1985) deals with the problems faced by women and men in a country where *machismo* is still very much a part of everyday life; it is the story of three girls growing up, each with a different view of reality. In *Dora, Doralina* (1984), she presents a woman's gradual achievement of independence and dignity in modern Brazil. Daphne Patai's *Brazilian Women Speak: Contemporary*

Life Stories (1988) allows ordinary women from the Northeast and Rio to speak about the struggles, constraints, and hopes of their lives.

Joao Trevisan's *Perverts in Paradise* (1986) is a fascinating survey of Brazilian gay life ranging from the papal inquisition to pop idols, transvestite macumba priests, and guerrilla idols. This contemporary account should be compared to Adolpho Caminha's *Bom Crioulo: The Black Man and the Cabin Boy*, Latin America's first novel of homosexual relations.

The experiences of North Americans in Brazil have also made their way into print. In Gay Courter's *River of Dreams* (1985), a young woman from New Orleans sets off to join her parents in a saga that captures the atmosphere and spirit of Brazil in its post–civil war period. The life of a New England woman on a Brazilian *fazenda* (plantation) in Mato Grosso is the theme of Ellen B. Geld's *The Garlic Tree* (1970).

Films

Closely linked to the country's music, dance, and carnival traditions, Brazilian film is often vibrant, witty, and entertaining, while simultaneously satirical and politically aggressive.

In the 1960s, a group of young filmmakers began producing a series of low-budget independent films that initiated Cinema Nôvo (literally, "New Cinema"), Brazil's best-known film movement. In its initial stage, film topics revolved around the lives, trials, and tribulations of rural people and their communities. Glauber Rocha's *Barravento* (1961), for example, is a rhythmic but jolting presentation of the hardships, religion, and myths of a rural fishing village. Rocha's *Black God—White Devil* (1964) also looks at the mythic traditions of rural regions. Other films within this vein include *Vidas Secas* (1962), by Nelson Pereira dos Santos, and *Ganga Zumba*, by Carlos Diegues's.

Among more recent Brazilian films is *Pixote* (1981), by Hector Babenco (who also directed the film adaption of Manuel Puig's *Kiss of the Spider Woman*), the story of an orphan growing up in the streets of Rio. *Dona Flor and Her Two Husbands* (1978), by Bruno Barreto, is the movie version of Jorge Amado's novel about a woman torn between her irresponsible dead husband who keeps returning to earth and her considerate but dull second husband. Carlos Diegues's *Bye Bye Brazil* (1980) is a comedy-drama about a group of traveling entertainers touring Brazil's small towns. Diegues's *Subway to the Stars* (1988) is set in contemporary Rio de Janeiro, where a young musician searches for his missing girlfriend and encounters the colorful citizens of the underworld. Also noteworthy are two films by Pereira dos Santos: *Tent of Miracles*, an interesting look at Brazilian racial problems and religions in the state of Bahia, and *How Tasty Was My Little Frenchman*, a critique of the Brazilian government.

Perhaps the best-known film about Brazil, however, is *Black Orpheus* (1959), by the French director Marcel Camus, a hauntingly beautiful and witty combination of Brazilian carnival and Greek mythology.

CHILE

Geographic diversity is the most obvious feature of Chile, which stretches some 1,800 miles from the tropics to Punta Arenas, the world's southernmost city. Squeezed between the Pacific Ocean to the west and the Andes mountains to the east, Chile occupies a thin strip of land that encompasses deserts and rain forests, farmlands and fjords, mountain peaks and grassy plains. Nearly half the country's inhabitants reside in Santiago, the capital city, which—not surprisingly—dominates the political, economic, and cultural life of the country. The majority of other Chileans live in central Chile between Santiago and Puerto Montt, leaving the southern forest and copper- and nitrate-rich northern desert sparsely populated.

Chile is now in the process of transition, establishing democratic rule after 16 years of military dictatorship under General Augusto Pinochet Ugarte. In 1973, Pinochet seized power from Marxist President Salvador Allende and instated a brutally repressive regime; during the 16 years of military dictatorship, thousands of Chileans were imprisoned, tortured, murdered, or forced into exile. In 1988, Pinochet relented to widespread demands for free elections and was swiftly ousted. Centrist Patricio Alwyn now heads a broad but tenuous coalition and is attempting to lead the country toward democracy and limit the role of the army in the political life of the country. Some exiles have quietly returned and an exhilarating, albeit cautious, sense of optimism can be felt throughout the country.

Some, however, fear that democracy, considering Chile's wide spectrum of political parties and divided electorate, will be difficult. Others point to the 46 years of uninterrupted constitutional democracy before Pinochet's violent coup as an indication of Chile's potential for peace. Regardless, observers agree that Chile, the last major country of South America to reject military government, is entering a crucial stage of its history.

Chile is in many ways a traveler's paradise: Genuine hospitality and a relative lack of theft against tourists make it one of the more relaxing Latin American countries to explore. At the same time, the country's unique geography and political situation make it one of the most interesting.

—*Mercedes Gaylord-Garcia, Venice, California*

Official name: Republic of Chile. **Area:** 292,257 square miles (slightly larger than Texas). **Population:** 13,000,000. **Population density:** 44 inhabitants per square mile. **Capital and largest city:** Santiago (pop. 4,858,000). **Language:** Spanish. **Religion:** Roman Catholic. **Per capita income:** US$1,520. **Currency:** Peso. **Literacy rate:** 92%. **Average daily high/low*:** Santiago: January, 85°/53°; July, 59°/37°. **Average number of days with precipitation:** Santiago: January, 0; July, 6.

TRAVEL

U.S. citizens need a passport to enter Chile; however, a visa is not required for stays of up to three months (this may be extended to six months). For specific regulations, check with the Embassy of Chile, 1732 Massachusetts Avenue NW, Washington, DC 20036.

Getting Around

Chile's eastern border runs along the crest of the Andes. Between this and the coastal range runs a long valley, through which the Pan American Highway is the main travel artery. Paved all the way from the Peruvian border, it links the main cities of Chile as far south as Puerto Montt. The region below Puerto Montt, where the ocean has flooded into the valley, is a wild coastline of rocky fjords and islands. Intermittent road access south of Puerto Montt is provided by the Carretra Austral Presidente Pinochet. Otherwise, passenger boat service is available to Punta Arenas on the Strait of Magellan and several points along the way. Intercity bus service along the Pan American Highway is inexpensive and frequent, and several bus services link Chile and Argentina. It is also possible to rent cars in major Chilean cities, with Hertz, Budget, and Avis among the major car rental companies operating in the country. Chile's main rail line extends from Iquique in the desert north to Puerto Montt. However, there is no passenger service north of Santiago.

Traveling is easiest in central Chile, where most of the country's population is concentrated in and around Santiago. For tourists wishing to venture far from Santiago the most popular way of travel is by plane. Chile's two domestic carriers, LanChile and

---

*All temperatures are Fahrenheit.

LADECO, both offer "Visit Chile" fares. Valid for 21 days, these fares for northern or southern routes cost $250; for the entire continental loop the fare is $450. Ladeco covers 16 cities, however, whereas LanChile only covers 11. Visit Chile fares that include a round trip to Easter Island are considerably more expensive. They must be purchased before your arrival in Chile.

Especially for Students and Young People

The student travel organization in Chile is Fundación de Desarrollo para la Juventud (Providencia 2594, Officina 421, Santiago). Discounts available to holders of the International Student Identity Card include a 25-percent discount on state railways and up to a 50-percent discount on some ferries. Students also get free entrance to museums and a discount at a number of theaters and tourist attractions.

For Further Information

Chile and Easter Island: A Travel Survival Kit ($11.95) is a comprehensive guide for budget travelers interested in getting to know Chile. If you can't find it in your local bookstore, it can be ordered from Lonely Planet Publications, Embarcadero West, 112 Linden Street, Oakland, CA 94607 (include $1.50 book-rate postage; $3 for first-class). General tourist information is available from the Chilean National Tourist Board, 510 West Sixth Street, Suite 1210, Los Angeles, CA 90014.

WORK

To work in Chile it is necessary to obtain a temporary-resident permit which is valid for one year and renewable in the country. Applications may be initiated by mail or in person, but a personal appearance at the Chilean embassy is required for completion of the visa. For more information, contact the Embassy of Chile, 1732 Massachusetts Avenue NW, Washington, DC 20036.

Internships/Traineeships

Two programs sponsored by members of the Council on International Educational Exchange are described below.

AIESEC-US. Reciprocal internship program for students in economics, business, finance, marketing, accounting, and computer science. See page 18 for more information.

University of Illinois at Urbana-Champaign. "Political Internships in Chile." Internships in the National Congress in Valparaiso. Courses in Chilean society, politics, and international relations. Sophomores, juniors, seniors, and graduate students with advanced Spanish; fall and spring semesters. See Appendix I for the address to write for more information.

Voluntary Service

Overseas Development Network sponsors voluntary-service opportunities in Chile; see page 29 for more information.

STUDY

Programs sponsored by CIEE-member institutions are described below. Consult Appendix I for the addresses to write for more information.

Semester and Academic Year

General Studies

American University. "Santiago Semester." Spring. Politics, economics, and society. Internships available. Homestays. Two years of college Spanish required. Juniors and seniors with 2.75 GPA. Apply 6 months prior to start of program.

Experiment in International Living/School for International Training. "College Semester Abroad." Santiago with excursions to Temuco and other sites. Intensive language study, interdisciplinary seminars on Chilean life and culture, field-study methods seminar, homestay, and independent-study project. No language prerequisite. Sophomores to seniors with 2.5 GPA. Apply by October 31 for spring; May 31 for fall.

State University of New York at Plattsburgh. "Study Program in Chile." Universidad Católica de Valparaiso, Universidad de Chile, or Pontificia Universidad Católica de Chile. Fall or spring semester. Undergraduates with ability to participate in a Spanish language classroom and 2.5 GPA. Apply by March 15 for fall; October 30 for spring.

Latin American Studies

Council on International Educational Exchange. "Comparative Latin American Studies Program." Santiago. Semester or academic year. Juniors and seniors with five semesters of college Spanish. Apply by March 15 for fall or academic year; October 15 for spring. Contact University Programs Department.

Spanish Language and Culture

State University of New York at Plattsburgh. "Intensive Spanish Immersion Course." Instituto Chileno Norteamericano de Cultura, Santiago. Fall or spring semester. Undergraduates with 2.5 GPA. Apply by March 15 for fall; October 30 for spring.

Summer

University of Illinois at Urbana-Champaign. "Summer Program in Chile." Universidad Católica de Valparaiso. Language study and social science. Juniors to graduate students with three semesters of college Spanish, two courses in history, social sciences, or Latin American Studies, and a 3.0 GPA. Apply by April 1.

EXPLORING CHILEAN CULTURE

Readings

Much of modern Chilean literature deals with the 1973 coup and the subsequent military dictatorship. Isabel Allende, niece of the late President Salvador Allende, has become one of the most popular contemporary Chilean writers. Although she has lived in exile since the coup, her novels are set in Chile. Magical realism provides the style for Allende's novels, but the fantastic aspects of each story are securely fastened to real events in Chile. Her works include *The House of the Spirits* (1982), *Of Love and Shadows* (1984), and *Eva Luna* (1987). Another Chilean writer that presents recent Chilean history in his works is Ariel Dorfman. In *Widows* he focuses on the women who continue looking year after year for loved ones who have "disappeared" (and are probably dead) under the military regime.

Mercedes Valdivieso's *Breakthrough* (1961), regarded as the first feminist novel of Latin America, is a novel of a rebellious woman who struggles to assert her individuality and freedom among the patriarchal Chilean bourgeoisie.

Two Chilean authors who should also be mentioned are Gabriela Mistral and Pablo Neruda. Both of them are winners of the Nobel prize and their poetry is considered some of the best to come out of Latin America. Mistral's works are identified by a number of themes that disclose the troubled human being, the consummate teacher, the passionate crusader, and the innovative artist in her. Her books include *Desolation* (1922), *Tenderness* (1924), *Telling* (1938), and *Wine* (1954). Neruda's poetry changed over the years to reflect personal changes, from his vision of a troubled world, to a world of loneliness and solitude, to a down-to-earth and simple outlook on life. His books include *Residence on Earth and Other Poems* (1925), *Five Decades: Poems 1925–1970*, *New Poems: 1968–1970*, and *The Heights of Macchu Picchu*.

Films

Cinema in Chile moved to the cultural and political forefront during Salvador Allende's Unidad Popular government of the early 1970s. The unexpected election of Allende's socialist government lent credibility to a group of young political filmmakers who took as their main focus the recent changes in Chilean society, and who attempted to create a style of narrative that reflected the leftist political attitudes of the period. *The Promised Land* and *The Jackal of Nahueltoro*, by Miguel Littin, both explore the trials and tribulations of landless peasants, workers, and rural communities as they contend with the country's governing bodies, industry, and the military.

Perhaps the most symbolic film of this period is Patricio Guzman's epic documentary, *Battle of Chile*, which attempts in no uncertain terms to investigate the political, cultural, and economic forces that eventually resulted in the military overthrow of Salvador Allende's government and the assassination of Allende himself. Filmed under remarkable circumstances, the footage had to be smuggled bit by bit out of Chile and was not completely edited until several years after the coup. Costa-Gavras's *Missing* provides a non-Chilean view of the overthrow of Allende's government, focusing on the families desperately looking for *desaparecidos* and hoping to find them still alive. In this story a North American father seeks his son, who has disappeared in Chile during the military clampdown after the coup.

Since the fall of Allende, a number of Chilean exiles have been working actively in Europe and elsewhere in Latin America. Most prolific of these filmmakers is Raoul Ruiz, who has produced more than 70 films in 15 years. Ruiz's films are informed by an intricate mix of subjective fantasy and historical episodes, cultural references, and political critique. Best known are *Tres Tigres Tristes*, *Three Crowns of a Sailor*, *Hypothesis of a Stolen Painting*, and *Of Great Events and Ordinary People*.

COLOMBIA

One of the striking themes of novelist Gabriel García Márquez's *One Hundred Years of Solitude*, a mystical chronicle of one hundred years in the life of a Colombian family, is the role that nature plays in the fabric of family life. Certainly, the unusually diverse geography of Colombia has contributed to the shaping of the nation. Bordered by both the Atlantic and the Pacific and intersected on a north-south axis by three ranges of the Andes Mountains, Colombia encompasses everything from tropical swamps to snow-dusted volcanoes. Regionalism, the result of mountain barriers, has discouraged unity throughout Colombia's history and even today the country revolves around numerous regional centers such as Medellín, Cali, and Barranquilla, in addition to the national capital of Bogotá. Close proximity to the equator means that the climate in each city is roughly the same year-round, although cities at different altitudes experience radically different climates. Always a land of contradictions, this climactic predictability is unsettled all too often by earthquakes and volcanic eruptions.

Colombia's 16th-century settlers came in search of gold. A visit to the Gold Museum (Museo de Oro) in Bogotá—an awesome vault of pre-Columbian artifacts—is proof that those pioneers found what they were looking for. Today, the country still owes its relative prosperity to its abundant natural resources. Exports of agricultural products, textiles, coal, oil, and precious stones, as well as illicit drugs, are responsible for providing the hard currency that has made Colombia one of the few countries of Latin America to keep pace with the payments on its foreign debt.

Despite the image that Colombia is out of control, an impression strengthened several years ago by a wave of political assassinations and bombings and more recently by the war between the government and the drug lords, Colombia is in fact one of South America's oldest democracies. Colombians have learned to deal creatively with recurring and violent power struggles. Some 30 years ago, for example, several years of bloodshed between members of the Liberal and Conservative parties ended with a power-sharing agreement that provided for alternating Liberal and Conservative governments from 1958 to 1974. Recently the government and opposition groups have negotiated agreements whereby insurgent groups have laid down their weapons and entered the political arena as legitimate parties. Likewise, violence between the government and drug cartels is waning. The intense national pride shared by all disparate factions in Colombia seems to be saving the nation from the total breakdown of law and order that seemed possible a couple of years ago.

In fact, Colombians have much to be proud of, and the visitor who is willing to avoid involvement in the country's political conflicts will find much to enjoy. The nation's spectacular mountains, forests, and coastline are obvious attractions. So, too, are its people and culture. And everywhere the visitor travels, exuberant Latin American hospitality and Colombian pride will welcome them.

—*Sarah Wood, Brooklyn, New York*

Official name: Republic of Colombia. **Area:** 439,735 square miles (almost three times the size of California). **Population:** 32,598,000. **Population density:** 72 inhabitants per square mile. **Capital and largest city:** Bogotá (pop. 4,208,000). **Language:** Spanish. **Religion:** Roman Catholic. **Per capita income:** US$1,140. **Currency:** Peso. **Literacy rate:** 80%. **Average daily high/low*:** Bogota: January, 67°/48°; July, 64°/50°. **Average number of days with precipitation:** Bogotá: January, 6; July, 18.

TRAVEL

U.S. citizens need a passport to enter Colombia for stays of up to 90 days. An onward or return ticket is also required. Tourist cards are issued at the airport upon arrival. For specific regulations, check with the Embassy of Colombia (2118 Leroy Place NW, Washington, DC 20008).

At press time, the U.S. State Department was warning against travel to certain remote regions of Colombia. Bogotá, the Caribbean resorts, and all other cities and resort areas are among the areas considered safe for foreign visitors. However, due to a high incidence of theft, travelers in all parts of the country are cautioned against walking alone at night and should not wear jewelry or carry valuables in the street. Current information is available from the Citizens Emergency Center at the U.S. State Department (see page 8).

---

*All temperatures are Fahrenheit.

Getting Around

Four mountain ranges running north to south create formidable natural barriers to travel in Colombia. As a result, the country has developed one of the best domestic air systems in South America. Avianca, a privately owned international carrier, also operates the most domestic flights. Its Discover Colombia ticket allows ten stopovers within a 30-day period and costs $325; if the purchaser is willing to forego visits to Leticia, Colombia's Amazon port, as well as to the Island of San Andrés in the Caribbean, the price drops to $224. Avianca's Discover Colombia 8 ticket, good for five stopovers in eight days, costs $190 (or $112 if visits to Leticia and San Andrés are not included). The Discover Colombia 8 ticket is not valid for travel in June, July, August, or December. Both tickets must be purchased before your arrival in Colombia.

Ground transportation has greatly improved in recent years. Highways link the cities of the interior with each other as well as with coastal ports, and the new Trans-Caribbean Highway greatly improves connections between the cities along Colombia's northern coast. Highways also connect the country to Venezuela and Ecuador, but no roads cross Colombia's borders with Panama or Brazil. Within Colombia, buses are the principle means of transportation. Bus service between the major cities is good, while in more remote areas local buses provide interesting but usually slow and uncomfortable transportation. Alternatives to the buses include *busetas* (minibuses) and *colectivos* (shared taxis). Car rental agencies can be found in the major cities; more information can be obtained by calling the toll-free numbers in the United States for Avis, Hertz, National, General, Budget, or Dollar—all of which have operations in Colombia. U.S. drivers' licenses are valid.

Colombia has only a few rail lines, and passenger service is dwindling. Mountain passage makes journeys by rail almost painfully slow. Few Colombians take the train, preferring faster buses. Trains, however, are extremely inexpensive and afford a fascinating view of Colombia's mountainous interior.

While the Magdalena River continues to be a main transportation artery, scheduled ferry service on the river has been discontinued. However, it is possible to travel by riverboat from Colombia's Amazon port of Leticia to either Peru or Brazil.

For Further Information

Colombia: A Travel Survival Kit ($11.95) is the best guidebook for the independent traveler on a budget. If you can't find it in bookstores, it can be ordered from Lonely Planet Publications, Embarcadero West, 112 Linden Street, Oakland, CA 94607 (include $1.50 book-rate postage; $3 for first-class). Anyone planning on spending time in the country might be interested in *Living in Colombia*, by William Hutchison and Cynthia Poznanski. First published in 1987, the book is available for $16.95 from Intercultural Press (PO Box 768, Yarmouth, ME 04096). In addition, general tourist information is available from the Colombia Government Tourist Office, 140 East 57th Street, New York, NY 10022.

WORK

Persons wishing to hold regular salaried employment in Colombia need a work visa. However, work visas are only granted for jobs for which no citizen of Colombia has the required training or skills. For more information contact the Embassy of Colombia, 1825 Connecticut Avenue NW, Suite 218, Washington, DC 20009.

Internships/Traineeships

Two programs sponsored by members of the Council on International Educational Exchange are described below.

AIESEC-US. Reciprocal internship program for students in economics, business, finance, marketing, accounting, and computer science. See page 18 for more information.

Association for International Practical Training. "IAESTE Trainee Program." On-the-job training for undergraduate and graduate students in technical fields such as engineering, computer science, agriculture, architecture, and mathematics. See page 18 for more information.

Voluntary Service

For persons interested in voluntary-service work, the Year Abroad Program sponsored by the International Christian Youth Exchange offers persons ages 18 to 24 voluntary-service opportunities in the fields of health care, education, the environment, construction, and so on. See page 23 for more information.

STUDY

The following educational programs are offered by CIEE-member institutions. Consult Appendix I for the addresses you can write to for further information.

Semester and Academic Year

General Studies

International Student Exchange Program. Semester or academic year. Direct reciprocal exchange between U.S. universities and institutions in Bogotá, Cali, and Baranquilla. Full curriculum options. Open only to students at ISEP-member institutions.

University of Arkansas at Little Rock. "Latin American and Caribbean Exchange Program." Semester or academic year. Juniors and seniors at Arkansas Consortium for International Education schools only. Rolling admissions.

EXPLORING COLOMBIAN CULTURE

Readings

In *One Hundred Years of Solitude*, Gabriel García Márquez presents his image of a Latin American world of myth, sensuality, violence, and conspiracy. Since this novel was published in 1967, it has given birth to a movement in Latin American literature known as "magical realism" and made García Márquez the preeminent novelist of Latin America. This book traces several generations of the Buendia family in the mythical town of Macundo. Less famous but perhaps equally fascinating are his more recent works, including *The Autumn of the Patriarch* (1975), in which he reveals the thoughts of a dying Latin American dictator who has ruled for two centuries; *Chronicle of a Death Foretold* (1983), the story of a man whose imminent murder is known to everyone in town except himself; and *Love in the Time of Cholera* (1988), a love story set at the turn of the century in Cartagena, on Colombia's Caribbean coast.

Another well-known Colombian writer is José Eustasio Rivera. *The Vortex* (1924), the story of a couple that flees to the jungle only to be transformed and eventually destroyed there, is a powerful denunciation of exploitation in the upper Amazon during the rubber boom of the early 1900s.

ECUADOR

Ecuador derives its name from the equator, which bisects the nation; but in spite of its tropical location, the nation encompasses a wide variety of climates. Hot, humid rain forest characterizes the northwest coast and the Amazon basin that makes up the eastern half of the country. However, equally characteristic of Ecuador are snowcapped mountains and cool plateaus. The Andes Mountains, whose peaks rise to more than 20,000 feet, run on a north-south axis through the country. In Ecuador, climate depends on altitude.

The country's geographic diversity is mirrored by its cultural diversity: The country's population includes a large number of Indian tribes, each of which retains its own clothing, way of life, and, in some cases, language. Another interesting cultural influence comes from the many mestizos, descendants of both Indians and the Spaniards who conquered the region in the 16th century. Less than 10 percent of the population is of European descent and about an equal number are blacks whose ancestors were brought as slaves by the Spanish.

Spain, during nearly 300 years of colonial domination, left a strong imprint on Ecuador. Spanish is the official language of the country and the one most commonly spoken. Similarly, Catholicism is the religion of nearly all Ecuadorians. Churches from the colonial period are centerpieces of large cities and small villages alike. But perhaps the most interesting evidence of the Spanish conquest can be found in Ecuadorian art—a mixture of Spanish and Indian motifs, techniques, and styles. Such art continues to flourish in the handicrafts sold in busy markets in cities, towns, and villages.

The Spanish domination generated a sharp division between the upper and lower classes that continues to exist today. Richly blessed by nature, Ecuador has been at different times one of the world's leading exporters of cacao, bananas, rice, and, currently, shrimp. However, the country's wealth—and power—have traditionally been concentrated in the hands of a few leading families. In recent years, the development of petroleum resources in the Amazon basin has enabled the government to carry out programs beneficial to the population at large—one reason Ecuador has not suffered the bloody social upheavals and political violence that have affected many other countries of the region.

For centuries Ecuador has also been divided by the conflict between its two major cities, Guayaquil and Quito, each of which represents different economic interests, social groups, and regional ties. Guayaquil dominates the coastal region and is the country's leading port, largest city, and economic center. Quito—more isolated and more traditional—is the hub of the Andean region and the nation's capital.

No introduction to Ecuador can be complete without mentioning the Galapagos Islands. Like Darwin, current visitors to the Galapagos are amazed by the plants and animals found in these remote and sparsely populated islands.

—*Hector Correa, Pittsburgh, Pennsylvania*

Official name: Republic of Ecuador. **Area:** 109,483 square miles (the size of Colorado). **Population:** 10,506,000. **Population density:** 95 inhabitants per square mile. **Capital:** Quito (pop. 1,200,000). **Largest city:** Guayaquil (pop. 1,600,000). **Language:** Spanish, Quechua, Jibaro. **Religion:** Roman Catholic. **Per capita income:** US$1,040. **Currency:** Sucre. **Literacy rate:** 90%. **Average daily high/low*:** Guayaquil: January, 88°/70°; July, 84°/67°. Quito: January, 72°/46°; July, 72°/44°. **Average number of days with precipitation:** Guayaquil: January, 20; July, 2. Quito: January, 16; July, 7.

---

*All temperatures are Fahrenheit.

TRAVEL

For stays of less than three months, U.S. citizens need a passport and a return or onward ticket. Visas are necessary for stays of three to six months. An AIDS test is required for stays of over three months; the U.S. test is acceptable. For specific regulations, check with the Embassy of Ecuador (2535 15th Street NW, Washington, DC 20009).

Getting Around

Frequent air service links the Pacific port of Guayaquil with Quito, which is located high in the Andes nearly 10,000 feet above sea level; the flight takes about 40 minutes (compared to a day-long bus journey). Flights are also available from Quito and Guayaquil to other major cities in Educador, as well as to several outposts in the Oriente, the eastern half of the country located in the Amazon basin.

Passenger and freight service remains suspended on most of the rail line between Guayaquil and Quito as a result of heavy rains and flooding in 1982–83. The government, however, is in the process of reconstructing Ecuador's lone rail route—and one of the world's most spectacular—and it is expected to reopen shortly.

Most transportation is provided by buses, which provide frequent service throughout the country except in the Oriente, where transportation by small boat is the rule. Ecuador's road system provides easy access to the cities and points of interest in the Andean and coastal regions of the country. The road network also extends from the Andes eastward to river towns, where people and goods are transferred to boats going to points farther east. Car rentals can be readily arranged in Quito and Guayaquil. Hertz, Avis, Dollar, and Budget are among the car rental agencies with operations in Ecuador; call their toll-free numbers in the U.S. for more information.

For anyone with an interest in nature, one of the world's most fascinating destinations is the Galapagos Islands. Most visitors arrive by plane, although a dual pricing system makes the flight expensive for foreigners. A daily flight connects Guayaquil with a landing strip on the uninhabited island of Baltra, where passengers are then picked up by boats. However, you can't simply fly to the islands on your own and look around. The Ecuadorian government restricts the number of visitors and requires that they be accompanied by a guide. Arrangements must be made through a tour operator authorized to conduct tours to the islands. Metropolitan Touring (C.P.O. Box 2542, Quito) is the largest; you can also contact their U.S. representative, Adventure Associates, at (800) 527-2500.

Especially for Students and Young People

Ecuador's student and youth travel organization is IDAL; the central office is located in Quito at Venezuela 1459 y Oriente. Holders of the International Student Identity Card can get discounts on domestic and international flights and on food and accommodations. Discounts on the entrance fee to national museums in Quito, Guayaquil, and other cities are also available.

For Further Information

Probably the best guidebook for the independent traveler on a budget is *Ecuador and the Galapagos Islands: A Travel Survival Kit* ($10.95). It's available in most bookstores or can be ordered from the publisher, Lonely Planet Publications, Embarcadero West, 112 Linden Street, Oakland, CA 94607 (include $1.50 book-rate postage; $3 for first-class). General tourist information is available from the government tourism office, FEPROTUR (7270 Northwest 12th Street, Suite 400, Miami, FL 33126).

WORK

Regular salaried employment in Ecuador is possible only if you are being brought in by an Ecuadorean company for professional reasons; a work permit and a visa are required. A contract must be in place before going to Ecuador. For more information, contact the Embassy of Ecuador, Information Services, 2535 15th Street NW, Washington, DC 20009.

Internships/Traineeships

Two programs sponsored by members of the Council on International Educational Exchange are described below.

AIESEC-US. Reciprocal internship program for students in economics, business, finance, marketing, accounting, and computer science. See page 18 for more information.

University of Minnesota. "Minnesota Studies in International Development." Academic year. Predeparture coursework at the U of M in the fall quarter; internship with development-related research or action project in winter and spring quarters. Juniors to graduates and adults with an interest in development; 2.5 GPA and two years of Spanish required. Apply by May 15. See Appendix I for address.

Voluntary Service

The Partnership for Service Learning and Amigos de las Americas sponsor voluntary-service opportunities in Ecuador; see pages 24 and 21 for more information.

STUDY

The following educational programs are offered by CIEE-member institutions. Consult Appendix I for the addresses of the colleges and universities listed in this section. In addition, Lewis and Clark College and the University of California offer programs open only to their own students.

Semester and Academic Year

Ecology

Experiment in International Living/School for International Training. "College Semester Abroad—Comparative Ecology." Fall or spring semester. Intensive language, comparative ecology and field-study methods seminars, homestays, and independent project. Sophomores to seniors with 2.5 GPA and one year of college Spanish. Apply by May 15 for fall, October 15 for spring.

General Studies

Beloit College. "Ecuador Seminar." Quito. Fall semester. Sophomores to graduate students with intermediate Spanish and 2.5 GPA. Apply by April 1.

Brethren Colleges Abroad. University of Azuay in Cuenca. Full range of academic programs, including social work. Excursions including study tour to the Galapagos Islands.

English teaching work can be arranged. Intermediate Spanish required. Sophomores to seniors with 2.8 GPA. Apply by April 15 for fall and academic year; November 1 for spring.

Experiment in International Living/School for International Training. "College Semester Abroad." Quito and Cayambe. Fall or spring semester. Intensive language, seminar in Ecuadorian life and culture, field-study methods seminar, homestays, and independent project. Sophomores to seniors with 2.5 GPA and one year of college Spanish. Apply by May 15 for fall; October 15 for spring.

Kalamazoo College. "Kalamazoo in Quito." University of San Francisco in Quito. Two tracks: intermediate and advanced. Fall or academic year. Juniors and seniors with 15 quarter-hours of Spanish and 2.75 GPA. Apply by May 1.

Scripps College. "Scripps Program in Quito." Academic year or semester at the Ponificia Universidad Católica. Sophomores to seniors with B average and four semesters of college Spanish. Apply by March 1 for fall or academic year; October 15 for spring.

University of Arkansas at Little Rock. Academic year or semester. Juniors and seniors at Arkansas Consortium for International Education schools only. Rolling admission.

University of Illinois at Urbana-Champaign.
"Semester in Ecuador." San Francisco University of Quito. Academic year or semester. Sophomores to seniors with five semesters of college Spanish and 3.0 GPA. Apply by April 1 for fall; October 1 for spring.

University of La Verne. "Semester/Year in Ecuador." See listing under Brethren Colleges Abroad.

University of Wisconsin—Madison. Quito. Academic year. Juniors and seniors with five semesters of Spanish and 3.0 GPA. Apply by November 15.

Latin American Culture and Civilization

University of Oregon. "OSSHE Ecuador Exchange." Fall term or academic year. Sophomores, juniors, and seniors with two years of college Spanish and 2.75 GPA. Apply by March 1.

Summer

Ecology

Experiment in International Living/School for International Training. "Summer Academic Study Abroad—Comparative Ecology." Andes and Galapagos. Intensive language and ecology seminars, including field trips and homestays. Freshmen to seniors. Apply by March 15.

Science

Eastern Michigan University. "Galapagos Islands Adventure." Quito, Galapagos Islands, and Amazon rain forest. Freshmen to graduate students. Apply by May 1.

EXPLORING ECUADORIAN CULTURE

Readings

Some of the best Ecuadorian writers have dealt with the lives of the lower class of the country. Jorge Icaza paints a brutal confrontation of Indians and whites in *The Villagers (Huasipungo)* (1934), one of the most moving novels of Latin American literature. Adalberto Ortiz's *Juyungo* (1942), the story of a black person's search for identity in a society plagued by racial injustice, depicts the tough challenges of daily survival for the inhabitants of Ecuador's Esmerelda coast.

PERU

For a thousand years before Columbus came to America, advanced empires were rising and falling in Peru. It is here that the Spanish conquerors found cities of fabulous wealth, temples whose walls were splashed with gold and studded with precious stones, and splendid palaces where even today the air still smells of plaster and varnish. Quintessentially, Peru represents the history of the South American continent. This can be seen best in the way different elements like man, culture, region, and language interact with each other.

Peru has three distinctive physical regions, generating contrasting social and economic features. The coast, a dry but relatively well-off region, is home of most industry and urban centers including Lima, the nation's rapidly growing capital that already contains about a fourth of Peru's people. The sierra is composed of the Andean mountain range, a world of snowcapped peaks and chilly valleys that contain such ancient provincial cities such as Cuzco and Ayacucho. The Quechua-speaking Indian inhabitants of this region have been largely excluded from the political and economic life of modern Peru; here is the base for the rebel guerrilla movement, the Sendera Luminosa ("Shining Path"). The jungle region, with its tropical forests, comprises the eastern half of the country. Until recently this region, which extends over the upper regions of the Amazon River, has experienced little settlement because of its inaccessibility. Today, however, colonization is making it a dynamic and growing region.

Cuzco, at 11,480 feet above sea level, was once the capital of the empire of the Incas stretching over 12,000,000 square miles. The Incas, who rose in the sierra eight or nine centuries ago, have been called the first and most successful urban planners in history. Cuzco is one of their masterpieces. It lies on a small river, which the Incas tamed, running its clear water in stone culverts throught the paved streets of the city for household use. The essential lines were preserved in the Spanish-colonial town, because Inca stone masonry proved too difficult to change. The central square remains with Inca foundations intact, but the palaces have been replaced by churches and public buildings.

About 70 miles north of Cuzco are the ruins of Machu Picchu, one of the most awesome and mysterious sights in the world. Getting to Machu Picchu is in itself an unforgettable journey. In order to get there, one must travel by train, bus, and foot. A deep valley, a sacred river, and precipitous mountains characterize this trail. However, the trip is only a prelude to what lies ahead in the "lost city of the Incas," which was discovered only in 1911.

Another highlight of any trip to Peru is Iquitos, Peru's river port with access to the Atlantic Ocean via the Amazon River. Bearing little resemblance to Lima, Iquitos exists in a world of its own. Iquitos was built by Europeans during the rubber boom at the turn of the 20th century and a traveler can still see a few architectural reminders of its former glory.

Today, Peru is slowly trying to recuperate from a decade of economic depression and internal civil strife. Austerity measures adopted by a newly elected administration have

caused hardship but have yet to control inflation. Nonetheless, contemporary problems can do little to dim the beauty of Peru's dramatic landscape or the glory of its history.
—*Gerardo D. Berthin, Washington, DC*

Official name: Republic of Peru. **Area:** 496,222 square miles (about four times the size of Arizona). **Population:** 21,904,000. **Population density:** 43 inhabitants per square mile. **Capital and largest city:** Lima (pop. 5,493,000). **Language:** Spanish, Quechua (both official). **Religion:** Roman Catholic. **Per capita income:** US$940. **Currency:** Intl. **Literacy rate:** 79%. **Average daily high/low*:** Lima: January, 82°/66°; July, 67°/57°. **Average number of days with precipitation:** Lima: January, less than 1; July, 1.

TRAVEL

U.S. citizens will need a passport and an onward/return ticket; a visa is not required for stays of up to 90 days (extendable after arrival). For specific regulations, check with the Embassy of Peru, 1700 Massachusetts Avenue NW, Washington, DC 20036.

At press time, the U.S. State Department was warning against travel in many parts of Peru due to attacks by the Shining Path guerrillas. Cuzco and Lima are still considered relatively safe, although because of both street crime and terrorist activity, visitors are warned against traveling after dark in Lima or on the roads around Lima. Current information is available from the Citizens Emergency Center at the U.S. State Department (see page 8).

Getting Around

Two airlines, AeroPeru (state owned) and Faucett (privately owned), provide service to most of Peru's provincial cities from Lima. AeroPeru (800-255-7378) offers "Peru Passes," which consist of three coupons, each good for one domestic flight. All travel must be done within 45 days. The pass costs $120; additional coupons can be purchased for $40 each.

In general, intercity highways are paved in the coastal region of Peru, are gravel in the the Andes, and are virtually nonexistent in the Amazon region (which comprises about half the country). The best road in Peru is the Pan American Highway, which stretches the entire length of the coast; a paved road also runs from the coast to Cuzco, the ancient capital of the Incan empire, which is situated in a valley more than 11,000 feet above sea level. Roads also connect Peru with Bolivia, Chile, and Ecuador, but none cross the border to Brazil or Colombia. Buses of various types provide the most common means of transportation for Peruvians. Shared taxis, called *colectivos*, serve the same routes, and although they are faster and more comfortable, they are also more expensive. It is also possible to rent a car in Lima and a few other cities, though not recommended due to the cost and danger involved. An Inter-American driving permit is required (see page 52).

Peru has a handful of rail lines that connect a few cities of the interior to port cities on the Pacific. In addition, a railroad from Cuzco provides access to Machu Picchu, the spectacular mountaintop city of the Incas and one of the leading tourist attractions in South America. Another of the world's most interesting railway journeys is the trip from Lima to Huancayo, which takes the traveler more than 16,000 feet above sea level; however, service has been suspended due to terrorist activity. Peruvian trains are said to be comfortable and cheap, but are also known for a high incidence of petty theft.

In the eastern half of Peru, transport is mainly by small boat. In fact, Iquitos, the

---

*All temperatures are Fahrenheit.

biggest city in Peru's Amazon region, can be reached only by plane or by boat. From Iquitos boats provide frequent passenger service down the Amazon into Brazil, stopping at towns along the way.

Especially for Students and Young People

INTEJ (Av. San Martin 240, Barranco, Lima) is Peru's student/youth travel bureau and issuer of the International Student Identity Card. Students with an International Student Identity Card receive a discount on some domestic and international flights and buses in Peru. In addition, they are eligible for discounts on student tours and at a limited number of hotels, hostels, restaurants, and discos.

For Further Information

Peru: A Travel Survival Kit ($14.95), a guidebook designed for the independent traveler interested in really getting to know the country, is probably the best one on the market. If you can't find it in bookstores, it can be ordered from the publisher, Lonely Planet Publications, Embarcadero West, 112 Linden Street, Oakland, CA 94607 (include $1.50 book rate postage; $3 for first-class). In addition, general tourist information is available from the Peru Tourist Office, 1000 Brickell Avenue, Suite 600, Miami, FL 33131.

WORK

It is difficult for foreigners to obtain regular employment in Peru. For more information, contact the Embassy of Peru, 1700 Massachusetts Avenue NW, Washington, DC 20036.

Internships/Traineeships

A program sponsored by a member of the Council on International Educational Exchange is described below.

AIESEC-US. Reciprocal internship program for students in economics, business, finance, marketing, accounting, and computer science. For more information see page 18.

STUDY

The Embassy of Peru's Cultural Department (1700 Massachusetts Avenue NW, Washington, DC 20036) has a packet of information sheets titled "Universities in Peru." The packet includes general information and lists Peruvian institutions that teach English, English schools in Lima, and Peruvian institutions of higher learning and their fields.

Following are the educational programs offered by CIEE-member institutions. Consult Appendix I for the addresses of the colleges and universities listed below. In addition, the University of California offers a program open only to its own students.

Semester and Academic Year

General Studies

State University of New York at Stony Brook. Lima. Fall semester or academic year. Study at Universidad de Lima and Universidad Católica del Perú; internships available. Juniors, seniors, and graduate students with 2.5 GPA and two years of college Spanish. Apply by April 1.

University of Arkansas at Little Rock. Academic year or semester. Juniors and seniors at Arkansas Consortium for International Education schools only. Rolling admissions.

EXPLORING PERUVIAN CULTURE

Readings

The leading contemporary Peruvian writer is Mario Vargas Llosa, who became even better known as a presidential candidate in Peru's most recent elections. *Aunt Julia and the Scriptwriter* (1982) is a comic novel centered on a Bolivian scriptwriter who arrives to work in Peru and falls in love with his older aunt (by marriage). In *Conversation in the Cathedral* (1969), two men from different social classes discuss Peruvian life, violence, and social decay in a bar called the Cathedral. *The Real Life of Alejandro Mayta* (1984) is based on the assassination of a revolutionary figure and deals with violence in Peru. Peruvian society's outdated social system is explored through life in a military academy in Llosa's *The Time of the Hero* (1962).

Ciro Alegria provides a view of Indian civilization and life in Peru in *Broad and Alien is the World* (1941), and in *The Golden Serpent* (1935), while José Maria Arguedas explores a white boy's relationship with the Indians in *Deep Rivers* (1958). Peru's contemporary poet Cesar Vallejo denounces the brutal treatment of Andean mine workers in *Tungsten*. A novel dealing with the miners' struggle in the sierra is *Drums for Runcas* (1977), by Manuel Scorza.

A foreigner's perspective on Peru is provided by Ronald Wright in *Cut Stones and Crossroads: A Journey in Peru* (1986). He travels from the Ecuadorian border across Peru to Bolivia, providing a fascinating account of the Peruvians he meets.

URUGUAY

Uruguay, one of South America's smallest nations, is often overshadowed by its two neighboring giants—Brazil and Argentina. In fact, Uruguay owes its existence to the stalemate between its two neighbors over which one should control the area. And for centuries before Uruguay's independence in 1828, Spain and Portugal had vied for control of the region as well.

Today, more than half the population of Uruguay lives in a single city, Montevideo, which dominates the political, economic, and cultural life of the country. But 90 percent of the country is still devoted to raising livestock, chiefly cattle. This has led to the description of Uruguay as "a big city with a large ranch." Of course, this oversimplification doesn't justly describe the country. Other interesting spots include the world famous beach resort of Punta del Este and the city of Colonia, which is known for its well-preserved Portuguese colonial architecture.

The European immigrants who settled in Uruguay created an agricultural economy that generated one of the world's highest standards of living early in this century. However, with the country unable to make the transition to a successful industrial economy, the standard of living steadily eroded. Gradually one of the world's most egalitarian and progressive countries increasingly resembled the other countries of Latin America as class divisions mounted and the role of the military heightened. In the 1970s and early 1980s, hundreds of thousands of Uruguayans emigrated to Argentina, Brazil, and Spain in order to escape economic hardship and political repression. Since 1985, when the military government turned power over to a popularly elected civilian government, attempts to revitalize the country's economy and political system have met with limited success.

—*Charles Sattler, Washington, DC*

Official name: Oriental Republic of Uruguay. **Area:** 68,037 square miles (about the size of Minnesota). **Population:** 3,002,000. **Population density:** 43 inhabitants per square mile. **Capital and largest city:** Montevideo (pop. 1,246,000). **Language:** Spanish. **Religion:** Roman Catholic. **Per capita income:** US$1,701. **Currency:** Peso. **Literacy rate:** 96%. **Average daily high/low*:** Montevideo: January, 83°/62°; July, 58°/43°. **Average number of days with precipitation:** Montevideo: January, 6; July, 7.

TRAVEL

U.S. citizens will need a passport to enter Uruguay; a visa is not required for stays of up to three months. For specific regulations, check with the Embassy of Uruguay, 1918 F Street NW, Washington, DC 20006.

Getting Around

The rail system, built by the British in the late 19th century, had slowly decayed, providing increasingly inadequate service, until the economically hard-pressed government abandoned it entirely in 1988. Persons wishing to travel within the country are now limited to planes, automobiles, or buses. Several bus companies provide comfortable service throughout the country—Onda is the largest, but smaller companies might be cheaper. Cars can be rented in Montevideo or Punta del Este. Domestic flights are offered by PLUNA, which provides service from Montevideo to a limited number of other Uruguayan cities. Tamu, the military airline, offers considerably reduced fares on many internal flights. In addition, a variety of boats (including hydrofoils) link Colonia, about three hours west of Montevideo, with Buenos Aires across the Rio de la Plata.

Especially for Students and Young People

AUTE (Associación Uruguaya de Turismo Estudiantil, Andes 1358, Of. 405, Montevideo) is Uruguay's student travel bureau and issuer of the International Student Identity Card. Their office provides tourist information, sells international air tickets, and books accommodations. Holders of the International Student Identity Card are entitled to reduced airfares on certain international flights; discounts with some bus, hydrofoil, and ferry companies; and reduced rates at several hotels and hostels in Montevideo. AUTE distributes a list of shops that offer discounts to International Student identity Card holders.

WORK

It is difficult for foreigners to obtain regular employment in Uruguay. For more information contact the Embassy of Uruguay, 1919 F Street NW, Washington, DC 20006.

Internships/Traineeships

Two programs sponsored by the Council on International Educational Exchange are described below.

AIESEC-US. Reciprocal internship program for students in economics, business, finance, marketing, accounting, and computer science. See page 18 for more information.

---

*All temperatures are Fahrenheit.

Association for International Practical Training. "IAESTE Trainee Program." On-the-job training for undergraduate and graduate students in technical fields such as engineering, computer science, agriculture, architecture, and mathematics. See page 18 for more information.

STUDY

A program sponsored by a member institution of the Council on International Educational Exchange is described below. Consult Appendix I for the address to write for more information.

Semester and Academic Year

General Studies

International Student Exchange Program. Direct reciprocal exchange between U.S. universities and the Universidad Católica del Uruguay in Montevideo. Semester or academic year. Full curriculum options. Open only to students at ISEP-member institutions.

VENEZUELA

The discovery of oil early in this century transformed Venezuela from a poor, agrarian nation into the country with the highest standard of living in South America. Oil revenues, which once made up almost 80 percent of the GNP, made possible grandiose industrial, development, transportation, mining, and agricultural projects. Oil prosperity produced an affluent middle class and helped this country become what is today South America's longest standing and most stable democratic system. During the last decade, Venezuela has tried to reduce its dependence on petroleum production; however, about 50 percent of the GNP still comes from oil. Falling petroleum prices in the 1980s dealt a serious blow to the nation's economy, causing massive cutbacks in government spending, inflation, and debt repayment problems, as well as political demonstrations and riots.

Venezuela, along with Colombia and Ecuador, achieved independence from Spain under the leadership of South American hero Simón Bolívar in the 1820s. Bolivar envisioned a single state stretching from Venezuela to Ecuador to be called "Gran Colombia." Local loyalties quickly fragmented Gran Colombia, even before Bolivar's death in 1830; still, he is venerated all over the continent. Nowhere is this more prevalent than in Venezuela, where the bolivar is the main currency unit and everywhere there are statues, squares, shopping centers, museums—and even a city—named after him.

Travelers to Venezuela will find a modern nation with glass-and-concrete office blocks, shopping malls, traffic jams, and urban air pollution. More than any other South American country, Venezuela is urbanized and industrialized. Some 80 to 85 percent of its people now live in cities. Caracas, the nation's capital and home of one out of every six Venezuelans, lies 3,000 feet above sea level, enjoying a surprisingly temperate climate. Due to an influx of immigrants in the last 30 years, one out of four *Caraquenos* are foreign-born. Immigrants from countries like Colombia and Haiti have come for economic opportunity, while others have come to escape oppression under military regimes in countries such as Argentina, Chile, and Spain.

But tourists come mainly to enjoy Venezuela's natural splendors. Margarita Island, Venezuela's leading Caribbean beach resort, is especially popular. A sharp contrast is provided by the Andes mountains, which run eastward from Colombia across northern

Venezuela. The center of the Venezuelan Andes is Mérida, a colonial city surrounded by snowcapped peaks reaching above the 16,000-foot level. Here the world's longest and highest cable car makes scaling the Andes a popular tourist attraction.

In the extreme south of the country is the Amazonas Federal Territory, a region of unexplored "cloud" forests, stone-age tribes, unmapped mesas, and remote waterfalls. The headwaters of the Orinoco are here, as well as a northern section of the Amazon basin. Here also is Angel Falls, the world's highest waterfall. Venezuela has taken steps to preserve its southern wilderness; a national park the size of Belgium stretches to the borders of Brazil and Guyana.

Tropical beaches, snowcapped peaks, modern cities, unmapped wilderness—whatever your preference, Venezuela has something special to offer.

—*João Castaneda, San Francisco, California*

Official name: Republic of Venezuela. **Area:** 352,143 square miles (about three times the size of Arizona). **Population:** 19,753,000. **Population density:** 54 inhabitants per square mile. **Capital and largest city:** Caracas (pop. 3,508,000). **Language:** Spanish. **Religion:** Roman Catholic. **Per capita income:** US$2,629. **Currency:** Bolivar. **Literacy rate:** 88%. **Average daily high/low*:** Caracas: January, 75°/56°; July, 79°/61°. **Average number of days with precipitation:** January, 6; July, 15.

TRAVEL

U.S. citizens will need a passport and a tourist card to enter Venezuela. Tourist cards, valid for 60 days (and nonextendable), are issued at the border or by the airlines serving Venezuela, provided the traveler has purchased a return or onward ticket. For a multiple-entry visa good for one year, proof of sufficient funds and certification of employment are also necessary. For specific requirements, check with the Embassy of Venezuela (2445 Massachusetts Avenue NW, Washington, DC 20008) or a Venezuelan consulate.

Getting Around

Avensa, the country's main domestic air carrier, offers a pass that provides unlimited travel in Venezuela. The 14-day pass is $333 and can be purchased through any of the international airlines serving Venezuela or at any Avensa counter.

There is an excellent road system extending to all areas of the country except the south. Roads also connect Venezuela with Colombia, but there are no roads across the border to either Brazil or Guyana. Buses form the backbone of the nation's transportation system. Other alternatives are *por puesto* cars (shared taxis that leave when full) or car rentals (Avis, Budget, Hertz, and National are among those agencies operating in the country). Passenger train service is virtually nonexistent.

Venezuela has become a popular destination for travelers who want to explore remote rain forests, see "lost" mesas, or climb Andean peaks. Angel Falls, located in a remote wilderness in the southern part of the country, always tops the lists of destinations for travelers seeking an "adventure" experience in the country, and there are a number of companies operating adventure tours—camping, backpacking, canoeing, mountain climbing, horseback riding, and so on. Tours can be booked through travel agents in Venezuela; arrangements can also be made through many travel agents in the United States.

---

*All temperatures are Fahrenheit.

Especially for Students and Young People

ONTEJ (Parque Central, Avenida Lecuna, Edificio Catuche, Nivel Bolívar, Oficina 37, PO Box 17696, Caracas 1015-A) is the student travel organization in Venezuela. Holders of the International Student Identity Card can obtain reduced air fares to numerous international destinations from Venezuela. For travel within the country, they receive discounts on Aeropostal flights as well as long-distance public buses. Students also receive free admission to some museums and reduced admission to several theaters in Caracas. ONTEJ distributes a full list of the 800 establishments that offer discounts to holders of the International Student Identity Card.

For Further Information

General tourist information is available from the Venezuela Government Tourist Center, 7 East 51st Street, New York, NY 10022.

WORK

A work visa is required for regular salaried employment in Venezuela; application is made by the Venezuela company seeking permission to hire a foreigner, to the Ministry of Interior Relations in Caracas. Work visas can be issued for 60 days, 120 days, or a year.

Internships/Traineeships

A program sponsored by a member of the Council on International Educational Exchange is described below.

AIESEC-US. Reciprocal internship program for students in economics, business, finance, marketing, accounting, and computer science. See page 18 for more information.

STUDY

The following program is offered by a CIEE-member institution. Consult Appendix I for the address to write for more information.

Semester and Academic Year

University of Arkansas at Little Rock. Academic year or semester. Juniors and seniors at Arkansas Consortium for International Education schools only. Rolling admissions.

APPENDIX I

MEMBERS OF THE COUNCIL ON INTERNATIONAL EDUCATIONAL EXCHANGE

Adelphi University
International Student Services
Levermore Hall, Room 317
Garden City, NY 11530
(516) 877-4990

Adventist Colleges Abroad
Board of Higher Education
General Conference of SDA
12501 Old Columbia Pike
Silver Spring, MD 20904-1608
(301) 680-6444

AFS International/Intercultural Programs
313 East 43rd Street
New York, NY 10017
(212) 949-4242, ext. 400

AIESEC/US
841 Broadway, Suite 608
New York, NY 10003
(212) 979-7400

Alma College
International Office
614 E. Superior Street
Alma, MI 48801
(517) 463-7247

American Center for Students and Artists
29 rue de la Sourdiere
75001 Paris
France

American Council on the Teaching of Foreign Languages (ACTFL)
6 Executive Boulevard
Yonkers, NY 10701
(914) 963-8830

American Graduate School of International Management
Thunderbird Campus
Glendale, AZ 85306
(602) 978-7688

American Heritage Association
PO Box 147
Flavia Hall
Marylhurst, OR 97036
(503) 635-3702

American University
4400 Massachusetts Ave. NW
Washington, DC 20016
(202) 885-2398

American University in Cairo
866 United Nations Plaza
Suite 517
New York, NY 10017-1889
(212) 421-6320

American Youth Hostels, Inc.
724 9th Street NW
Suite 700
Washington, DC 20001
(202) 783-6161

COUNCIL ON INTERNATIONAL EDUCATIONAL EXCHANGE

Antioch University
Antioch Education Abroad
Yellow Springs, OH 45387
(513) 767-1031

Associated Colleges of the Midwest
International Programs Associate
18 South Michigan Avenue, Suite 1010
Chicago, IL 60603
(312) 263-5000

Association for International Practical
 Training
10 Corporate Center
10400 Little Patuxent Parkway, Suite 250
Columbia, MD 21044-3510
(301) 997-2200

Association of College Unions—
 International
400 East Seventh Street
Bloomington, IN 47405
(812) 332-8017

Association of Student Councils
171 College Street, Second floor
Toronto, Ontario M5T 1P7
Canada
(416) 977-5228

Bates College
Lane Hall
Lewiston, ME 04240
(207) 786-6223

Beaver College
Center for Education Abroad
Glenside, PA 19038
(215) 572-2901

Beloit College
700 College Street
Beloit, WI 53511
(608) 365-3391

Boston College
Chestnut Hill, MA 02167
(617) 552-8000, ext. 3830

Boston University
232 Bay State Road
Boston, MA 02215
(617) 353-2963

Brandeis University
Kutz Hall/215
Waltham, MA 02254-9110
(617) 736-3480

Brethren Colleges Abroad
International Studies
Box 184, Manchester College
North Manchester, IN 46962
(219) 982-2141, ext. 238

Brigham Young University
International Programs
204 HRCB
Provo, UT 84602
(801) 378-3308

Brown University
OIP
Box 1973
Providence, RI 02912
(401) 863-3555

Bucknell University
623 St. George Street
Lewisburg, PA 17837
(717) 524-3796

Canadian Bureau for International
 Education
85 Albert Street, Suite 1400
Ottawa
Ontario K1P 5A4
Canada
(613) 237-4820

California State University
Office of International Programs
400 Golden Shore, Suite 300
Long Beach, CA 90802-4275
(213) 499-6092

California State University/Long Beach
Center for International Studies
1250 Bellflower Boulevard
Long Beach, CA 90840
(213) 985-8432

California State University/Sacramento
Overseas Study/Programs
6000 J Street
Sacramento, CA 95819-2694
(916) 278-6686

Carleton College
Director, Off-Campus Studies
One North College Street
Northfield, MN 55057
(507) 663-4332

Carroll College
100 North East Avenue
Waukesha, WI 53186
(414) 547-1211

Central University of Iowa
International Studies Office
812 University
Pella, IA 50219
(515) 628-5287

Central Michigan University
Mt. Pleasant, MI 48859
(517) 774-4308

Central Washington University
Office of International Programs
Barge Hall 308
Ellensburg, WA 98926
(509) 963-3612

Chapman College
Office of International Programs
333 N. Glassell Street
Orange, CA 92666
(714) 997-6829

College of Charleston
International Programs
66 George Street
Charleston, SC 29424
(803) 792-5660

Colorado State University
315 Aylesworth Hall
Fort Collins, CO 80523
(303) 491-7977

Cornell University
Center for International Studies
474 Uris Hall
Ithaca, NY 14853-7601
(607) 255-6224

Council on International Educational
   Exchange
University Programs Department
205 East 42nd Street
New York, NY 10017
(212) 661-1414

Curtin University
North American Office
Two Appletree Square
8011 34th Avenue South, Suite 144
Minneapolis, MN 55425
(612) 854-5800

Dartmouth College
Hanover, NH 03755
(603) 646-3753

Davidson College
Office for Study Abroad
PO Box 1719
Davidson, NC 28036
(704) 892-2000

Depauw University
307 E. Seminary
International Center
Greencastle, IN 46135-0037
(317) 658-4373

Drake University
Center for International
   Programs & Services
Des Moines, IA 50311
(515) 271-2084

Earlham College
International Programs
National Road West
Richmond, IN 47374
(317) 983-1200

Eastern Michigan University
International Studies
333 Goodison Hall
Ypsilanti, MI 48197
(313) 487-2424

Ecole Centrale de Paris (Ecole
   Centrale des Arts et Manufactures)
Grande Voie des Vignes
92295 Chatenay-Malabry Cedex
France
(46) 836246

Elmira College
Park Place
Elmira, NY 14901
(607) 734-3911

Empire State College
Office of International Programs

1 Union Avenue
Saratoga Springs, NY 12866
(518) 587-2100, ext. 231

European Association for
 International Education
Van Diemenstraat 344
NL-1013 CR Amsterdam
(31) 20-625-27-27

Experiment in International Living
Academic Studies Abroad
101 Kipling Road
Brattleboro, VT 05301
(802) 257-7751

Faith Evangelical Lutheran Seminary
3504 N. Pearl
PO Box 7186
Tacoma, WA 98407
(206) 752-2020

Fontainebleau Fine Arts and Music
 Schools Association
c/o Davis, Brody, and Associates
315 Hudson Street
New York, NY 10013
(212) 633-4790

Friends World College
Student Services
Plover Lane
Huntington, NY 11743
(516) 549-5000

Fudan University
220 Handan Road
Shangai 200433
China
(86-021) 5484906, ext. 2644

Georgetown University
Office of International Programs
37th and O Streets NW
Washington, DC 20057
(202) 687-5867

Gonzaga University
Office of Studies Abroad
502 East Boone Avenue
Spokane, WA 99258-0001
(509) 328-4220

Goshen College
International Education
1700 South Main Street
Goshen, IN 46526
(219) 535-7346

Great Lakes Colleges Association
2929 Plymouth Road, Suite 207
Ann Arbor, MI 48105-3206
(313) 761-4833

Grinnell College
Nollen House
Grinnell, IA 50112
(515) 269-3460

Guilford College
Off-Campus Education
5800 West Friendly Avenue
Greensboro, NC 27410
(919) 292-5511

Gustavus Adolphus College
Office of International Education
St. Peter, MN 56082
(507) 931-7545

Hampshire College
International Studies
West Street
Amherst, MA 01002
(413) 549-4600, ext. 542

Hartwick College
Off-Campus Programs
Oneonta, NY 13820
(607) 431-4423

Harvard College
Career Services
54 Dunster Street
Cambridge, MA 02138
(617) 495-2595

Hebrew University of Jerusalem
Office of Academic Affairs
11 East 69th Street
New York, NY 10021
(212) 472-2288

Heidelberg College
310 East Market Street
Tiffin, OH 44883
(419) 448-2216

Hiram College
Director, Extra Mural Studies

Hiram, OH 44234
(216) 569-5160

Hollins College
Hollins Abroad Programs
PO Box 9706
Roanoke, VA 24020
(703) 362-6331

Hope College
International Education Office
Holland, MI 49423
(616) 394-7605

Illinois State University
Office of International Studies and
  Programs
105 McCormick Hall
Normal, IL 61761
(309) 438-5365

Indiana University
Office of Overseas Study
Franklin Hall 303
Bloomington, IN 47405-2801
(812) 855-9304

Institute of International Education
809 United Nations Plaza
New York, NY 10017
(212) 984-5425

International Christian University
International Affairs
3-10-2, Osawa
Mitaka, Tokyo, 181
Japan
(422) 33-3043

International Christian Youth Exchange
134 West 26th Street
New York, NY 10001
(212) 206-7307

International Student Exchange Program
1242 35th Street NW
Washington, DC 20057
(202) 687-6956

Iowa State University
Study Abroad Center
E.O. Building
Ames, IA 50011
(515) 294-1120

James Madison University
South Main Street
Harrisonburg, VA 22807
(703) 568-6119

Kalamazoo College
Study Abroad Office
1200 Academy Street
Kalamazoo, MI 49007
(616) 383-8470

Kent State University
Center for International & Comparative
  Programs
Kent, OH 44242-0001
(216) 672-7980

Lake Erie College
391 West Washington Street
Painesville, OH 44077
(216) 352-3361, ext. 314

Lancaster University
University House
Bailrigg
Lancaster LA1 4YW
England
(52) 465201

LaSalle University
LaSalle-in-Europe
20th & Olney Streets
Philadelphia, PA 19141
(215) 951-1200

Lewis & Clark College
Office of Overseas and Off-Campus
  Programs
615 SW Palatine Hill Road
Campus Box 11
Portland, OR 97219
(503) 293-2697

Lisle Fellowship, Inc.
433 West Sterns Road
Temperance, MI 48182
(313) 847-7126

Louisiana State University
Academic Programs Abroad
Baton Rouge, LA 70803
(504) 388-6801

Macalester College
International Center
1600 Grand Avenue
Saint Paul, MN 55105
(612) 696-6310

Marquette University
Milwaukee, WI 53233
(414) 288-7059

Mary Baldwin College
International Studies Program
Staunton, VI 24401
(703) 887-7050

Miami University
Office of International Programs
Langstroth Cottage
Oxford, OH 45056
(513) 529-7383

Michigan State University
International Studies & Programs
211 Center for International Programs
East Lansing, MI 48824-1035
(517) 355-2350

Middlebury College
Middlebury, VT 05753
(802) 388-3711, ext. 5508

Millersville University of Pennsylvania
International Affairs
Millersville, PA 17551
(717) 872-3526

Monterey Institute of International
  Studies
Dean's Office, Language Studies
425 Van Buren Avenue
Monterey, CA 93940
(408) 647-4185

Moorehead State University
Box 336
Moorhead, MN 56563
(218) 236-3287

NAFSA: Association of International
  Educators
1875 Connecticut Avenue NW
Suite 1000
Washington, DC 20009-5728
(202) 462-4811

National Association of Secondary
  School Principals
1904 Association Drive
Reston, VA 22091
(703) 860-0200

New York University
Office of Academic Affairs
Elmer Holmes Bobst Library, Rm 1104
70 Washington Square South
New York, NY 10012
(212) 998-2300

Northeastern University
400 Meserve Hall
360 Huntington Ave.
Boston, MA 02115
(617) 437-5172

Northern Arizona University
Office of International Studies
PO Box 5598
Flagstaff, AZ 86011
(602) 523-2409

Northern Illinois University
International and Special Programs
Lowden Hall 203
DeKalb, IL 60115-2854
(815) 753-1989

Northern Michigan University
Office of International Education
Marquette, MI 49855
(906) 227-1220

Northfield Mount Hermon School
International Programs Office
Northfield, MA 01360
(413) 498-5311, ext. 251

Oberlin College
Oberlin, OH 44074
(216) 775-8654

Obirin University
3758 Tokiwa-machi, Machida
Tokyo 194-02
Japan
427-97-2661, ext. 353

Ohio University
Center for International Studies
56 East Union Street

Athens, OH 45701-2987
(614) 593-1840

Ohio State University
Office of International Affairs
308 Dulles Hall
230 West 17th Avenue
Columbus, OH 43210
(614) 292-9660

Open Door Student Exchange
250 Fulton Avenue
PO Box 71
Hempstead, NY 11551
(516) 486-7330

Pace University
International Education
Pace Plaza
New York, NY 10038
(212) 346-1368

Pennsylvania State University
Office of International Programs
222 Boucke Building
University Park, PA 16802
(814) 865-7681

Pitzer College
External Studies
1040 North Mills Ave.
Claremont, CA 91711
(714) 621-8104

Pomona College
International Education
Oldenberg Center
Claremont, CA 91711
(714) 621-8154

Portland State University
International Programs
PO Box 751
Portland, OR 97207
(503) 725-4011

Purdue University
Programs for Study Abroad
1100 Schleman Hall, Room 223
West Lafayette, IN 47907-1104
(317) 494-2383

Ramapo College of New Jersey
International Programs
505 Ramapo Valley Road
Mahwah, NJ 07430-1680
(201) 529-7463

Reed College
Office of International Programs
3203 SE Woodstock Boulevard
Portland, OR 97202
(503) 777-7290

Rhode Island School of Design
2 College Street
Providence, RI 02903
(401) 331-3511

Rochester Institute of Technology
External Programs
One Lomb Memorial Drive
Rochester, NY 14623
(716) 475-2293

Rollins College
International Programs
Box 2759
Winter Park, FL 32789
(407) 646-2466

Rosary College
International Studies
7900 West Division Street
River Forest, IL 60305
(708) 366-2490

Rutgers University
International Programs Office
165 College Avenue
The Parker House
New Brunswick, NJ 08903
(908) 932-7263

St. John Fisher College
Foreign Study
3690 East Avenue
Rochester, NY 14618
(716) 385-8000

St. Lawrence University
Office of International Education
Carnegie 108
Canton, NY 13617
(315) 379-5991

St. Olaf College
Office of International Studies
Northfield, MN 55057
(507) 663-3069

COUNCIL ON INTERNATIONAL EDUCATIONAL EXCHANGE

St. Peter's College
Foreign Study Programs
2641 Kennedy Boulevard
Jersey City, NJ 07306
(201) 915-9170

Scandinavian Seminar, Inc.
24 Dickinson Street
Amherst, MA 01002
(413) 253-9736

School Year Abroad
Phillips Academy
Andover, MA 01810
(508) 749-4420

Scripps College
Office of Off-Campus Study
1030 Columbia
Claremont, CA 91711
(714) 621-8306

Skidmore College
Junior Programs Abroad
North Broadway
Saratoga Springs, NY 12866
(518) 584-5000, ext. 2383

Southern Illinois University
  at Carbondale
International Programs and
  Services
Carbondale, IL 62901
(618) 453-7670

Southern Methodist University
105 Fondren Library West
International Programs Office
Dallas, TX 75275
(214) 692-2295

Southwest Texas State University
Center for International Education
San Marcos, TX 78666
(512) 245-2339

Spelman College
Study Abroad Office
350 Spelman Lane SW
Atlanta, GA 30314
(404) 223-7550

Springfield College
International Center
263 Alden Street
Springfield, MA 01109
(413) 788-3216

Stanford University
Overseas Studies Program
Sweet Hall, 1st floor
Stanford, CA 94305-3089
(415) 725-0235

State University of New York
International Programs
State University Plaza
Room T801
Albany, NY 12246
(518) 443-5124

Stephens College
Off-Campus Studies
PO Box 2053
Columbia, MO 65215
(314) 876-7153

Stetson University
Office of International Exchange
Box 8412
DeLand, FL 32720
(904) 822-8165

Syracuse University
Division of International
  Programs Abroad
119 Euclid Avenue
Syracuse, NY 13244-4170
(315) 443-3471

Texas A & M University
Study Abroad Office
161 Bizzell West
College Station, TX 77843
(409) 845-0544

Texas Tech University
Office of International Programs
PO Box 4248
242 West Hall
Lubbock, TX 79409
(806) 742-3667

Trinity College
Educational Services
300 Summit Street
Hartford, CT 06106
(203) 297-2437

Tufts University
Tufts Programs Abroad
Ballou Hall
Medford, MA 02155
(617) 381-3152

Tulane University
1229 Broadway
New Orleans, LA 70118
(504) 865-5339

United Negro College Fund
Programs and Public Policy
500 East 62nd Street
New York, NY 10021
(212) 326-1100

Universidad Autónoma de Guadalajara
Av. Patria 1201 Lomas del Valle,
  Apdo.
  Postal 1-440
Guadalajara 44100
Jalisco
Mexico
(36) 41-3829

Universidad de Belgrano
International Exchange Department
Federico Lacroze 1959 piso 1
1426 Buenos Aires
Argentina
(1) 772-4014

Universite de Bordeaux III
Domaine Universitaire
Talence Cedex 33405
France
(56) 84-50-50

University College London
Gower Street
London WCIE 6BT
England
(01) 380-7007

University of Alabama
Capstone International Program Center
PO Box 870254
Tuscaloosa, AL 35487
(205) 348-5312

University of Alabama at Birmingham
Center for International Programs
336 Ullman
Birmingham, AL 35294
(205) 934-5643

University of Arkansas at Little Rock
33rd and University
Little Rock, AR 72207
(501) 569-3374

University of British Columbia
Language Institute
5997 Iona Drive
Vancouver V6T 2A4
Canada
(604) 228-2181

University of California
Education Abroad Program
Santa Barbara, CA 93106
(805) 893-2918

University of Colorado at Boulder
Office of International Education
Campus Box 123
Boulder, CO 80309-0123
(303) 492-7741

University of Connecticut
Study Abroad Programs
U-207
843 Bolton Road
Storrs, CT 06269-1207
(203) 486-5022

University of Copenhagen (DIS Study)
Vestergade 7
DK-1458 Copenhagen K
Denmark
(31) 11-01-44

University of Essex
International Programs
Wivenhoe Park, Colchester
Essex CO4 3SQ
England
(0206) 873333

University of Evansville
Harlaxton Coordinator
1800 Lincoln Avenue
Evansville, IN 47722
(812) 479-2146

University of Hartford
200 Bloomfield Avenue
West Hartford, CT
06117

University of Illinois
306 Coble Hall

801 South Wright Street
Champaign, Il 61820
(217) 333-7741

University of International Business
 and Economics
An Ding Men Wai
He Ping Li
Beijing 100013
China
(861) 421-2022

University of Iowa
International Education and Services
Iowa City, IA 52242
(319) 335-0336

University of Kansas
Office of Study Abroad
203 Lippincott Hall
Lawrence, KS 66045-1731
(913) 864-3742

University of La Verne
1950 Third Street
La Verne, CA 91750
(714) 593-3511 ext. 4240

University of Louisville
International Center
2301 South Third Street
Louisville, KY 40292-0001
(502) 588-6602

University of Maine
International Programs
Clapp Greenhouse
Orono, ME 04469
(207) 581-2073

University of Maryland
Study Abroad Office
2109 Skinner
College Park, MD 20742
(301) 314-7746

University of Massachusetts
International Programs
William S. Clark International Center
Amherst, MA 01003
(413) 545-2710

University of Michigan
International Center
603 East Madison Street
Ann Arbor, MI 48109-1270
(313) 747-2256

University of Minnesota
ISTC
102 Nicholson Hall
216 Pillsbury Drive, SE
Minneapolis, MN 55455
(612) 626-9000

University of New Hampshire
Center for International Perspectives
Hood House
Durham, NH 03824
(603) 862-2398

University of North Carolina at Chapel
 Hill
Office of International Programs
207 Caldwell Hall
Chapel Hill, NC 27514-3130
(919) 962-7001

University of North Texas
Study Abroad Center
Box 13795
Denton, TX 76203-3795
(817) 565-2207

University of Notre Dame
Foreign Study Programs
420 Administration Building
Notre Dame, IN 46556
(219) 239-5882

University of Oklahoma
Office of International Progams
601 Elm Room 142
Norman, OK 73019
(405) 325-1607

University of Oregon
Office of International Services
330 Oregon Hall
Eugene, OR 97403-5209
(503) 346-3206

University of the Pacific
Office of International Programs
Bechtel International Center
Stockton, CA 95211
(209) 946-2591

University of Pennsylvania
Office of International Programs

133 Bennett Hall
Philadelphia, PA 19104-6275
(215) 898-4665

University of Pittsburgh
Study Abroad Office
4G-32 Forbes Quadrangle/UCIS
6200 Fifth Avenue
Pittsburgh, PA 15260

University of Rhode Island
Study Abroad
Taft Hall
Kingston, RI 02882
(401) 792-5546

University of St. Thomas
International Education Center
PO Box 4036
2115 Summit Avenue
St. Paul, MI 55105
(612) 647-5693

University of South Carolina
702 Byrnes Building
Columbia, SC 29208
(803) 777-7810

University of Southern California
Overseas Studies, FIG-109
Los Angeles, CA 90089-1261
(213) 740-3636

University of Sussex
North American Programmes
Falmer, Brighton
East Sussex BN1 9QN
England
(0273) 678373

University of Tennessee
Center for International Education
201 Alumni Hall
Knoxville, TN 37996-0620
(615) 974-3177

University of Texas at Austin
100 West 26th Street
University Station
Austin, TX 78713-7206
(512) 471-1211

University of Toledo
Center for International Studies and Programs
2801 West Bancroft
Toledo, OH 43606-3390
(419) 537-4313

University of Utah
International Center
Salt Lake City, UT 84112
(801) 581-8876

University of Vermont
Living/Learning Center, Box #8
Burlington, VT 05405
(802) 656-4296

University of Virginia
109 Cabell Hall
Charlottesville, VA 22903-3196
(804) 924-3548

University of Washington
Foreign Study Office
572 Schmitz Hall, PA-10
Seatle, WA 98195
(206) 543-9272

University of Wisconsin at Madison
International Studies and Programs
1410 Van Hise Hall
1220 Linden Drive
Madison, WI 53706
(608) 262-2851

University of Wisconsin at Platteville
Institute for Study Abroad Programs
1 University Plaza
Platteville, WI 53818
(608) 342-1726

University of Wisconsin at River Falls
Semester Abroad Program
River Falls, WI 54022
(715) 425-3992

University of Wisconsin—Green Bay
2420 Nicolet Drive
Green Bay, WI 54311
(414) 465-2484

University of Wollogong
Development & International Affairs
P.O. Box 1144
Wollogong, NSW 2500
Australia
(42) 268800

University of Wyoming
International Programs
PO Box 3707
University Station
Laramie, Wyoming 82071
(307) 766-5193

University System of Georgia
International Intercultural Studies
  Programs
1 Park Place South, Suite 817
Atlanta, GA 30303
(404) 651-2450

Valparaiso University
International Studies
Valparaiso, IN 46383
(219) 464-5333

Volunteers in Asia
Box 4543
Stanford University
Stanford, CA 94309
(415) 723-3228

Wake Forest University
International Studies
PO Box 7385
Winston-Salem, NC 27109
(919) 759-5938

Washington State University
Office of International Education
Bryan Hall 108
Pullman, WA 99164-5110
(509) 335-4508

Wayne State University
Junior Year in Germany
401 Manoogian Hall
Detroit, MI 48202
(313) 577-4605

Wesleyan University
North College
Middletown, CT 06457
(203) 344-8544, ext. 2243

Western Michigan University
Office of International Affairs
2090 Friedman Hall
Kalamazoo, MI 49008-5011
(616) 387-3951

Western Washington University
Foreign Study Office
Old Main 530
Bellingham, WA 98225
(206) 676-3298

Westminster College
Old Main 102
Market Street
New Wilmington, PA 16172-0001
(412) 946-7123

Whitman College
345 Boyer
Walla Walla, WA 99362
(509) 527-5132

Whitworth College
Center for International &
  Multicultural Education
Spokane, WA 99251
(509) 466-3733

Wichita State University
Office of International Programs
Wichita, KA 67208
(316) 689-3730

Wilmington College
Director, International Education
Wilmington, OH 45177
(513) 382-6661, ext. 212

Wittenberg University
International Education
PO Box 720
Springfield, OH 45501
(513) 327-6185

Wofford College
429 North Church Street
Spartanburg, SC 29303
(803) 597-4510

World College West
101 South Antonio Road
Petaluma, CA 94952
(707) 765-4500

YMCA of the USA
International Program Services
356 West 34th Street
New York, NY 10001
(212) 563-3471

Youth for Understanding International
  Exchange
3501 Newark Street NW
Washington, DC 20016
(202) 966-6808

APPENDIX II
HIGH SCHOOL PROGRAMS

If you're a high school student considering a trip abroad, you'll have some special things to think about as you begin to plan. Although the travel opportunities and student discounts described in this book are open to you, most of the programs are not. This book focuses on programs for college students. But don't be discouraged—although many of these programs are not for you (at least not yet), many others are.

Most high school students choose to join a tour, study program, or voluntary-service project. What you choose will depend on a careful evaluation not only of the program but also of your own interests and maturity. Traveling abroad is a wonderful experience when done at the right time and under the right conditions, but it can be a grave disappointment if it's not carefully planned.

To help in planning your trip to another country, you might want to pick up a copy of the Council's *The Teenager's Guide to Study, Travel, and Adventure Abroad*, published by St. Martin's Press. An updated edition of this book is produced every two years. Written specifically for those between the ages of 12 and 18, *The Teenager's Guide* anticipates and addresses potential questions and concerns about an international experience. The book's early chapters cover preparation—practical, emotional, and intellectual—including such information as how to write your first letter to the sponsors of the program, how to get academic credit, how to understand different concepts of time, and how to confront cultures vastly different from your own. It also provides responsible guidelines and self-evaluation instruments, plus interviews with past participants, to help teenagers decide what's best for them. Nearly 200 organizations that sponsor international programs for teenagers are listed and described in the book. You can order *The Teenager's Guide* from CIEE for $11.95 (plus appropriate state sales tax and $1.50 for book-rate postage or $3 for first-class postage). It's also available in bookstores and at Council Travel offices.

Below you'll find brief descriptions of programs abroad that are designed for high school students and sponsored by organizations or institutions that are members of the Council on International Educational Exchange. Only a brief outline of programs are provided here; if a travel, study, or service program sounds interesting, be sure to write or call for more information well before the application deadline.

AFS Intercultural Programs.
"Year Program." High school students live with a family and attend a local high school. Programs in 55 countries. High school students ages 15 to 18 with 2.6 GPA. Departure in January, February, or March for study in countries of the southern hemisphere and July or August for countries in the northern hemisphere.

"Semester Program." Same as above but only a semester. Options in nine countries. February and August departures.

"Summer Program." Options include family homestay, language study, outdoor adventure, cultural studies, and a Soviet youth camp. Programs in more than 40 countries. High school sophomores, juniors, or seniors; for outdoor adventure, applicants must be in excellent physical condition. Apply by April 1. Address: 313 East 43rd Street, New York, NY 10017; (212) 949-4242 or (800) AFS-INFO.

American Heritage Association. Programs custom-designed to suit group needs. Options can include homestays, study, and travel. Most groups travel in summer or during spring

HIGH SCHOOL PROGRAMS

break. Programs arranged for junior high and high school groups. Address: Marylhurst College Campus, PO Box 147, Marylhurst, OR 97036; (503) 635-3702 or (800) 654-2051.

American Youth Hostels. International bicycling and hiking tours in Canada, Europe, and the United States. Two to six weeks. Most tours operate in summer. Youth tours open to persons ages 15 to 18; young adult tours open to ages 17 to 25. Address: PO Box 37613, Washington, DC 20013.

Council on International Educational Exchange.
"School Partners Abroad." Reciprocal exchange of student groups for three- to four-week program of school attendance and homestay. Partner schools in eight countries. Selection of participants by home school.
"Youth in China." Summer program in which U.S. students study Chinese language, history, and culture while living with Chinese roommates studying English. Students ages 15 to 18 with one semester of Chinese language and area studies. Apply by April 15. Address: Professional and Secondary Education Programs, CIEE, 205 East 42nd Street, New York, NY 10017.

Experiment in International Living. Summer programs range from four to six weeks and include orientation, homestay, and sightseeing. Six weeks of language courses and academic seminars for advance college credit included in some programs. Other programs include special interest activities such as bike touring or mountaineering. Programs in 28 countries. Ages 14 to 22. Apply by April 1. Address: Kipling Road, Brattleboro, VT 05301.

International Christian Youth Exchange. High school participants live with families and attend high school in the host country. Choice of 26 countries. Ages 16 to 24. The experience abroad begins in July and lasts for one year. Apply by March 15, or as soon as possible thereafter. Address: 134 West 26th Street New York, NY 10001; (212) 206-7307.

Michigan State University. "High School Honors Program in French." College de Riviere du Loup, Quebec. Summer language program. Students must be 15 years old with two years of high school French and a B-plus average. Apply by April 20.

Northfield Mount Hermon. "Summer Abroad." Homestay, study, and travel included in six-week summer program. Choice of China, France, and Spain. For France and Spain, two years of appropriate language study required; one year of Chinese required for China. Sixteen- and 17-year-olds with good academic records. Apply by March 15. Address: Northfield Mount Hermon School, International Programs Office, East Northfield, MA 01360.

Open Door Student Exchange.
"Semester Abroad." Participants stay with families and attend high school. Programs in 13 countries. Fall semester only. Ages 15 to 18. Two years of language study required for programs in French-, Spanish-, Russian-, and German-speaking countries. Apply by April 1; early application recommended.
"Academic Year Abroad." Same as above except for entire academic year (September to May). Programs in seven countries.
"Summer Homestay Experience" and "Summer Homestay/School Program." Four to six weeks living with a family. Summer homestay programs in 12 countries of the northern hemisphere; homestay with school attendance programs available in eight countries of the southern hemisphere. Special programs include teacher assistant programs in Hungary

and Poland and a journalism program in Latin America. Ages 15 to 18. Apply by April 1; early application recommended.
Address: 250 Fulton Avenue, PO Box 71, Hempstead, NY 11551; (516) 486-7330.

School Year Abroad. Homestay with rigorous academic program. High school credit and college preparation. Options in Barcelona, Spain, or Rennes, France. Fall semester or full academic year. High school students entering eleventh or twelfth grade with two years of Spanish or French. Apply by March 1.
Address: School Year Abroad, Department WWH, Phillips Academy, Andover, MA 01810; (508) 749-4420; fax: (508) 749-4425.

Youth For Understanding International Exchange.
"YFU Academic Year." Homestays and high school attendance. Programs in 21 countries. Ages 14 to 19 with 3.0 GPA. Apply by April 1; early applicants are more likely to receive their country choice.
"YFU Semester." Same as above except for a semester. Programs in seven countries. Apply by April 1 for fall; October 15 for spring.
"Summer Program." Homestays of six to eight weeks. Programs in 22 countries. Ages 14 to 19 with 2.0 GPA. Apply by April 1.
"Sport for Understanding." Adult coach and 12 to 16 U.S. students are hosted by a sports club and its coaches in another country. Options include 27 different sports. Ages 14 to 19 with average or better sports abilities and 2.0 GPA. Programs generally take place in summer and last up to a month.
Address: 3501 Newark Street NW, Washington, DC 20016; (800) 424-3691 or (202) 966-6800.

INDEX

Adventist Colleges Abroad, 77, 109, 186
AFS, 26, 326, 496
AIESEC—U.S., 18, 75, 81, 84, 89, 94, 100, 107, 123, 134, 138, 142, 146, 152, 163, 166, 171, 174, 178, 182, 193, 197, 204, 226, 232, 243, 249, 255, 258, 261, 271, 273, 276, 279, 282, 285, 287, 290, 295, 299, 308, 331, 340, 348, 352, 360, 365, 367, 371, 374, 386, 396, 403, 415, 424, 429, 433, 439, 453, 461, 466, 471, 474, 478, 480, 483
ALGERIA, 240
Alma College, 76, 111, 117, 128, 129, 183, 187, 440, 443
American Council on the Teaching of Foreign Languages (ACTFL), 108
American Farm School, 134
American Friends Service Committee, 21
American Heritage Association, 76, 78, 90, 111, 115, 124, 153, 156, 176, 185, 207, 214, 217, 496–497
American Heritage Progam, 326
American Institute of Indian Studies (AIIS), 308
American Medical Student Association, 30
American Nurses Association, 30
American Scandinavian Foundation, 94, 95, 100, 142, 143, 165, 170, 171, 193
American University, 76, 82, 90, 139, 153, 175, 186, 208, 213, 326, 454, 467
American University in Cairo, 243–244
American Youth Hostels (AYH), 17, 53, 66, 497
American Zionist Youth Foundation, 248, 249
Amigos de las Americas, 21–22
Antioch University, 69, 128, 244, 309
Archaeological Institute of America (AIA), 22
ARGENTINA, 450–455
Armstrong State College, 214
Asia Society, 304, 308, 318
Associated Colleges of the Midwest, 68, 153, 227, 299, 309, 341, 430
Association for International Practical Training, 18, 75, 81, 86, 89, 94, 100, 107, 123, 134, 138, 142, 146, 152, 161, 163, 166, 171, 174, 178, 182, 193, 197, 204, 226, 232, 243, 249, 258, 261, 276, 287, 290, 304, 340, 348, 365, 367, 374, 386, 403, 418, 439, 449, 453, 461, 471, 481
Atlantis—Norwegian Foundation for Youth Exchange, 170
Augusta College, 187, 444
AUSTRALIA, 382–390
Australian Trust for Conservation Volunteers, 387
AUSTRIA, 72–79
Austrian Cultural Institute, 75

BAHAMAS, 411–413
Beaver College, 76, 77, 135, 146, 147, 204, 206, 207, 208, 212, 213, 214, 218
BELGIUM, 79–82
BELIZE, 425–427
Beloit College, 111, 124, 139, 324, 474
BOLIVIA, 455–457
Boston University, 71, 86, 107, 109, 114, 115, 153, 156, 157, 186, 188, 204, 212, 217, 250, 274
BRAZIL, 458–464
Brethren Colleges Abroad, 111, 124, 134, 183, 209, 324, 340, 474
Brethren Volunteer Service, 23
Brigham Young University, 70, 77, 155, 186, 209, 217, 326, 343, 349, 439, 442, 461
British Universities North America Club (BUNAC), 203

Brown University, 111
BRUNEI, 356
BULGARIA, 82–84

CAMBODIA, 356–357
CAMEROON, 270–272
Camping, 67
CANADA, 17, 21, 399–406
Canadian Bureau for International Education, 21, 404
Canadian Cycling Association, 401
Canadian Federation of Students—Services, 17
Carl Duisberg Sprachcolleg München, 123
CS International, 122
Central University of Iowa, 77, 109, 128, 167, 186, 209, 324, 440
Central Washington University, 111, 125, 188, 209, 441, 443
CHILE, 464–468
CHINA, 319–328
Citizen Exchange Council, 224–225
Club du Vieux Manoir, 108
COLOMBIA, 468–471
Colorado State University, 209, 441
Columbus College, 111
Community Service Volunteers (CSV), 205
Cornell University, 125, 198, 324
COSTA RICA, 427–431
COTE D'IVOIRE, 272–274
Council for British Archaeology, 205
Council on International Educational Exchange (CIEE), Council Charter, 44–47
  Encounter Ireland program, 146
  International Student Identity Card, 8–9
  International Student Identity Card Travel Grant Fund, 39
  International Teacher Identity Card, 9–10
  International Youth Card, 10
  Work Exchanges, 16–17, 89, 105–106, 122, 145–146, 182, 203, 395–396, 403, 418–419, 429
  International Voluntary Services, 20–21, 81, 84, 89, 95, 107–108, 123–124, 166, 175, 178, 182, 204, 226, 232–233, 241, 255, 258, 261, 276, 403–404
  Professional and Secondary Education Programs Department, 321–322, 497
  University Programs, 90, 107, 109, 112, 116, 129, 139, 175, 182, 186, 188, 227, 228, 324–325, 326, 341, 343, 361, 374, 378, 388, 415–416, 431, 454, 461, 462, 467
Couriers, 48–49
CUBA, 409
Curtin University, 386
CYPRUS, 84–86
CZECHOSLOVAKIA, 87–91

Dalton College, 71
Davidson College, 112, 125, 186, 309, 442
DENMARK, 91–97
DIS, 96
Disabled travelers, 14–15
DOMINICAN REPUBLIC, 413–416
Drake University, 153, 155–156

Earlham College, 339
Earthwatch, 22
Eastern Michigan University, 68, 71, 78, 228, 443, 475
ECUADOR, 472–476
EGYPT, 241

INDEX

Elderhostel, 43
Empire State College, 86, 96, 251
Episcopal Church's Volunteers for Mission, 23
Eurail passes, 61–62
Eurocentres, 42–43
Experiment in International Living/School for International Training, 17, 20, 69, 109, 112, 116, 125, 135, 139, 148, 153, 183, 186, 188, 198, 227, 256, 271, 279, 280, 283, 294, 299, 304, 309, 314, 325, 341, 361, 374, 378, 388, 416, 441, 457, 462, 467, 474, 475, 497

Faculty Exchange Center (FEC), 27
Faith Evangelical Lutheran Seminary, 117
Fellowships, 39–40
FIJI, 390–392
FINLAND, 97–101
Foundation Center, 39
Foundation for Field Research, 22
Fourth World Movement, 21, 81, 197, 204, 404
FRANCE, 101–119
Friends Overseas, 94, 192
Friends Overseas: Australia (FOA), 385
Friends World College, 69, 250, 279, 309, 326, 342, 430
Frontiers Foundation/Operation Beaver, 404
Fulbright Teacher Exchange Branch, 27

Georgia College, 117, 405
Georgia Southern University, 71
Georgia State University, 130, 405
German Academic Exchange Service, 124
GERMANY, 119–132
GHANA, 274–277
Global Social Venture Network, 225
Global Volunteers, 293
Gonzaga University, 153
Goshen College, 124
Great Lakes Colleges Association, 69, 209, 340
Grinnell College, 209
GREECE, 132–136
GUATEMALA, 431–433
Guilford College, 112, 125, 442
Gustavus Adolphus College, 387

Health, 6–7
Hebrew University of Jerusalem, 250, 252
Heidelberg College, 125, 186
Hiram College, 128, 153, 156, 209, 214
Hitchhiking, 65
Hollins College, 112, 209
HONDURAS, 433–435
HONG KONG, 328–332
Hope College, 78
HUNGARY, 136–140

ICELAND, 140–143
Illinois State University, 116, 129, 228
INDIA, 305–311
Indiana University, 78, 112, 116, 125, 153, 156, 167, 184, 188, 229, 443
INDONESIA, 358–362
Insurance, 8
International Association for the Exchange of Students for Technical Experience (IAESTE), see Association for International Practical Training
Institute of International Education (IIE), 39, 40, 122
International Christian University, 342, 343
International Christian Youth Exchange (ICYE), 23, 75, 81, 101, 124, 143, 152, 171, 175, 197, 282, 287–288, 323, 340, 348, 396, 429, 435, 439, 457, 461, 471, 472
International Liaison of Lay Volunteers in Mission, 23
International School's Internship Program (ISIP), 26

International Schools Services (ISS), 27
International Student Exchange Program, 77, 82, 86, 101, 112, 125, 139, 153, 163, 167, 184, 198, 210, 274, 279, 283, 293, 295, 297, 332, 349, 368, 375, 388, 392, 404, 416, 430, 435, 441, 453, 462, 471, 481
International Student Identity Card, see CIEE
International Student Travel Confederation (ISTC), 9
International Teacher Identity Card, see CIEE
International Voluntary Services, 23–24
International Youth Card, see CIEE
Intourist, 223, 226
IRELAND, 143–149
ISRAEL, 245–252
ITALY, 149–159

JAMAICA, 416–420
JAPAN, 332–345

Kalamazoo College, 112, 125, 128, 186, 279, 285, 288, 475
Kent State University, 153, 198
KENYA, 277–281
Kibbutz Aliya, 249

Lake Erie College, 112, 125, 154, 167, 184, 210, 217
Lancaster University, 210
LAOS, 357
La Salle University, 198
Lewis and Clark College, 125, 128
Lisle Fellowship, 309, 361, 420, 431, 439, 441
Loans, 39–40
Los Ninos, 440
Louisiana State University, 117, 156, 217
LUXEMBOURG, 159–161

Macalester College, 69, 110
MALAYSIA, 362–365
MALTA, 161–163
Marquette University, 112, 116, 129, 184
Mary Baldwin College, 116, 156, 216, 217, 218
Mennonite Central Committee (MCC), 24
Medical College of Georgia, 213
MEXICO, 435–445
Miami University, 70, 115, 116, 129, 161, 228, 352, 413, 443
Michigan State University, 70, 71, 72, 82, 110, 116, 126, 128, 129, 147, 155, 156, 157, 166, 176, 186, 188, 194, 199, 207, 210, 214, 215, 216, 217, 218, 219, 220, 233, 251, 299, 319, 326, 342, 343, 352, 387, 405, 410, 416, 443, 462, 497
Middlebury College, 110, 128, 154, 186, 227
Millersville University, 126, 210
Mir Initiative, 226
Mobility International USA (MIUSA), 14
Moorhead State University, 69, 325
MOROCCO, 252–256
MYANMAR, 357

NAFSA—Association of International Educators, 39
NEPAL, 311–314
NETHERLANDS, 163–168
New York University, 90, 96, 112, 115, 116, 117, 155, 157, 184, 187, 214, 216, 217, 218, 220, 229, 251, 310, 319, 443
NEW ZEALAND, 392–397
NIGERIA, 281–283
North Carolina State University, 78, 186, 217
Raleigh, 295, 443
Northeastern University, 68, 69, 147, 227
Northern Arizona University, 113, 126, 167, 210, 442

INDEX

Northern Illinois University, 76, 78, 82, 110, 126, 184, 210, 441
NORTHERN IRELAND, see UNITED KINGDOM
Northfield Mount Hermon School, 497
NORWAY, 168–172
Notre Dame Law School, 213, 218

Ohio State University, 115, 184, 188, 218, 227, 416, 442
Ohio University, 77
Open Door Student Exchange, 497–498
Overseas Development Network (ODN), 18, 29

Partnership for Service-Learning, 24
Passports, 4–5
People to People International, 18
PERU, 476–479
PHILIPPINES, 365–368
Pitzer College, 299, 314
POLAND, 172
Portland State University, 113, 126, 128, 135, 154, 157, 184, 187, 210, 325, 327, 344, 411
PORTUGAL, 176–179
Presbyterian Church's Mission Volunteers/International, 24
Purdue University, 113, 126, 184

Quaker International Social Projects, 205

R.E.M.P. ART, 108
Rollins College, 147, 187, 388, 441
Rosary College, 113, 157, 210
Royal Society for Mentally Handicapped Children and Adults (MENCAP), 205
Rutgers University, 113, 116, 126, 147, 154, 184, 188, 210, 218, 250, 441

St. Lawrence University, 77, 113, 184, 210, 280
St. Olaf College, 239, 304, 318, 375
Scandinavian Seminar, 95, 96, 101, 172, 193, 194
Scholarships, 39–40
School Year Abroad, 498
Scripps College, 110, 126, 475
SENEGAL, 284–286
SIERRA LEONE, 286–288
SINGAPORE, 369, 371
Sisters of Charity of Nazareth, 308, 313, 427
Skidmore College, 113, 117, 184
SOUTH AFRICA, 288–291
Southern College of Technology, 215
Southern Illinois University at Carbondale, 70, 135, 215, 319, 342, 343
Southern Methodist University, 78, 113, 116, 155, 184, 215, 217, 342
SOUTH KOREA, 346
SPAIN, 179
SPUTNIK, 223, 224
Stanford University, 153, 343
State University of New York (SUNY): 86, 95, 96, 207, 251
  Albany, 115, 126, 129, 140, 167, 187, 210, 227, 251, 325, 342, 371, 430, 462
  Binghamton, 77, 110, 211, 256
  Brockport, 110, 136, 155, 207, 213, 214, 216, 219, 276, 405, 413, 419, 420, 442, 443
  Buffalo, 110, 154, 176, 188, 211, 343
  College at Buffalo, 154, 211, 342, 388
  Cortland, 114, 124, 126, 129, 148, 185, 198, 211, 326
  Fredonia, 76
  Oneonta, 71, 129
  Oswego, 110, 116, 126, 185, 187, 188, 211, 215, 218, 325, 443
  Plattsburgh, 388, 404, 405, 453, 467

Stony Brook, 110, 113, 116, 126, 147, 154, 157, 175, 349, 457, 478
Stetson University, 110, 126, 187, 211, 227
Study Abroad, 32–43. See each country's section for listings.
SWEDEN, 190–194
SWITZERLAND, 194–199
Syracuse University, 70, 71, 113, 117, 126, 152, 154, 155, 156, 157, 185, 187, 188, 197, 198, 204, 211, 215, 219, 251, 331, 443

TAIWAN, 349–353
TANZANIA, 292–294
Teaching Abroad, 25–28
Teaching of English as a Foreign Language (TOEFL), 25–26
Teaching of English as a Second or Other Language (TESOL), 25–26
Texas Tech University, 211, 444
THAILAND, 371–375
TOGO, 294–295
TransCentury, 30
Trinity College, 154, 156
Trip Safe Insurance, 8
Tufts University, 113, 126, 185, 211
TUNISIA, 256–258
TURKEY, 258–261

UNION OF SOVIET SOCIALIST REPUBLICS, 221–230
UNITED KINGDOM, 199–221
Universidad Autónoma de Guadalajara, 440
University of Alabama, 116, 130, 188, 216, 227, 325, 396, 431, 443, 444
University of Arkansas, 77
  Little Rock, 78, 116, 188, 410, 416, 430, 435, 441, 444, 453, 471, 475, 479, 483
University of British Columbia, English Language Institute, 404
University of California; Berkeley, 22
University of Colorado, 71; Boulder, 113, 127, 130, 155, 211, 215, 442, 444
University of Connecticut, 71, 109, 113, 154, 167, 175, 185
University of Essex, 211
University of Evansville, 211
University of Georgia, 70, 72, 157
University of Hartford, 109, 154, 207, 214, 217
University of Illinois, 206; Urbana-Champaign, 228, 387, 429, 430, 453, 454, 463, 466, 467, 475
University of Iowa, 117, 148, 211, 405, 440
University of Kansas, 110, 113, 115, 116, 130, 157, 188, 211, 216, 218, 344, 430, 444
University of La Verne, 111, 127, 135, 185, 211, 228, 280, 285, 318, 325, 332, 342, 440, 442, 450, 475
University of Louisville, 107, 115, 129, 130, 156, 188, 215, 216, 219, 228, 239, 276, 463
University of Maine, 77
University of Maryland, 114, 130, 189, 212, 276, 462
University of Massachusetts: Amherst, 11, 127, 139, 140, 154, 175, 176, 187, 189, 199, 216, 228, 251, 280, 325, 352, 454
University of Minnesota, 70, 77, 111, 185, 189, 207, 255, 279, 285, 308, 326, 419, 442, 474
University of New Hampshire, 114, 212, 217
University of North Carolina, 135: Chapel Hill, 111, 114, 127, 154, 155, 185, 198, 207, 212, 214, 216, 251, 252, 325, 342, 388, 441, 454, 462
University of North Texas, 70, 212
University of Notre Dame, 77, 111, 251, 441
University of Oregon, 96, 114, 127, 128, 139, 154, 155, 157, 167, 172, 185, 194, 212, 251, 325, 341, 342, 349, 388, 475
University of Pennsylvania, 82, 96, 115, 117, 130, 140, 157, 176, 179, 189, 216, 283, 352

INDEX

University of Pittsburgh, 68, 239, 269, 304, 318, 342, 358, 424, 450
University of South Carolina, 325
University of Toledo, 187, 199, 213, 327
University of Utah, 130, 157, 189, 198, 217, 344
University of Virginia, 185
University of Washington, 127
University of Wisconsin, 117
    Madison, 96, 114, 127, 140, 154, 156, 167, 172, 185, 212, 251, 288, 309, 314, 343, 375, 444, 462
    Platteville, 185, 194, 212, 218, 252, 441, 475
University of Wyoming, 212
University System of Georgia, 70, 71, 72, 111, 117, 130, 157, 187, 189, 213, 214, 215, 405, 444
URUGUAY, 479–481
U.S. Government: Agency for International Development, 29
    Department of Agriculture, 29
    Department of Defense, 26
    Department of State, 29
    Department of Veterans Affairs, 40
    Peace Corps, 29
    United States Information Agency, 26, 27
Usit, 145, 146

Valparaiso University, 325
VENEZUELA, 481–483
VIETNAM, 375–378
Visas, 5
Voluntary Service, 20–25. See each country's section for listings.
Volunteers for Peace, 21
Volunteers in Asia, 378

Washington State University, 327
Wayne State University, 127
Wesleyan University, 114, 128, 251
Western Michigan University, 70, 117, 218
Western Washington University, 114, 128, 135, 154, 157, 212, 214, 323, 327, 375, 442, 444
West Georgia College, 70, 117, 189
Wichita State University, 444
Wilmington College, 77
Wittenberg University, 72
Work Abroad, 16–20. See ach country's section for listings.
World College West, 228, 314, 442
World Council of Churches, 21
WorldTeach, 26
Wynant-Clayton Volunteers, 205

Young Men's Christian Association (YMCA), 19, 24, 53
Youth for Understanding International Exchange, 498
Youth Hostels Association of New Zealand, 395
YUGOSLAVIA, 230–233

ZAMBIA, 296–297
ZIMBABWE, 297–300